COUNSELOR
SUPERVISION

COUNSELOR SUPERVISION

Principles, Process, and Practice

Third Edition

Edited by
Loretta J. Bradley, Ph.D.
Texas Tech University
Lubbock, Texas

Nicholas Ladany, Ph.D.
Lehigh University
Bethlehem, Pennsylvania

BRUNNER-ROUTLEDGE
ALERE FLAMMAM
Taylor & Francis Group

USA	Publishing Office:	BRUNNER-ROUTLEDGE
		A member of the Taylor & Francis Group
		325 Chestnut Street
		Philadelphia, PA 19106
		Tel: (215) 625-8900
		Fax: (215) 625-2940
	Distribution Center:	BRUNNER-ROUTLEDGE
		A member of the Taylor & Francis Group
		7625 Empire Drive
		Florence, KY 41042
		Tel: 1-800-634-7064
		Fax: 1-800-248-4724
UK		BRUNNER-ROUTLEDGE
		A member of the Taylor & Francis Group
		27 Church Road
		Hove
		E. Sussex, BN3 2FA
		Tel: +44 (0) 1273 207411
		Fax: +44 (0) 1273 205612

COUNSELOR SUPERVISION: Principles, Process, and Practice

1 2 3 4 5 6 7 8 9 0

Printed by Braun-Brumfield, Ann Arbor, MI, 2000.
Cover design by Nancy Abbott.

A CIP catalog record for this book is available from the British Library.
(∞) The paper in this publication meets the requirements of the ANSI Standard Z39.48-1984 (Permanence of Paper)

Library of Congress Cataloging-in-Publication Data

Bradley, Loretta J.
    Counselor supervision : principles, process, and practice / Loretta J. Bradley, Nicholas Ladany.—3rd ed.
        p. cm.
    Includes bibliographical references and index.
    ISBN 1-56032-873-8 (alk. paper)

    1. Counselors—Supervision of. I. Ladany, Nicholas. II. Title.
BF637.C6 B65 2000
361'.06'0683—dc21   00-030469
                                                                          CIP
ISBN 1-56032-873-8 (case)

CONTENTS

3

A Multicultural Framework for Counselor Supervision

PART II
THEORETICAL APPROACHES
TO COUNSELOR SUPERVISION

Supervision-Based Integrative Models of Counselor Supervision

5 Supervision-Based Developmental Models of Counselor Supervision

Peggy P. Whiting, Loretta J. Bradley, and Kristen J. Planny

6 **Psychotherapy-Based Models of Counselor Supervision**

Loretta J. Bradley and L. J. Gould   **147**

PART III
SPECIALIZED MODELS OF COUNSELOR SUPERVISION

PART IV
PROFESSIONAL ISSUES IN COUNSELOR SUPERVISION

14 Ethical Issues in Supervision

*Loretta J. Bradley, Jeffrey A. Kottler, and
Deborah Lehrman-Waterman*

15 Supervision Training: A Model

Loretta J. Bradley and Peggy P. Whiting

ABOUT THE EDITORS AND CONTRIBUTING AUTHORS

Loretta J. Bradley, Ph.D., is professor of counselor education and chair of the Division of Educational Psychology and Leadership. Prior to her affiliation with Texas Tech University in Lubbock, TX, she was an associate professor of human development counseling at Peabody College of Vanderbilt University and an assistant dean at the College of Education at Temple University. Dr. Bradley earned her Ph.D. at Purdue University. She is a past-president of the American Counseling Association (ACA) (1998–1999) and a past-president of the Association for Counselor Education and Supervision (ACES) (1995–1996). Dr. Bradley has been the recipient of the following awards/honors: 1998 Fellow of the Salzburg Institute, 1996 President's Excellence in Teaching Award, 1995 COE Nominee for Barney Rushing, Jr. Research Award, 1994 Texas Tech University nominee for Leadership Texas, 1993 COE Nominee for President's Achievement Award, 1992 and 1991 COE Nominee for the Barney E. Rushing, Jr. Research Award. In 1990, Dr. Bradley received the ACES Publication Award for her book, *Counselor Supervision: Principles, Process, and Practice*, 2nd ed., and in 1987, she was the co-recipient of the American Counseling Association's Research Award, an award representing an organization with more than 59,000 members. In 1986, Dr. Bradley received the SACES Individual Achievement Award and the 1985 ACES Research Award. Dr. Bradley is a licensed professional counselor (LPC, Texas) and approved LPC supervisor, a licensed marriage and family therapist (LMFT, Texas) and approved LMFT supervisor, a national certified counselor (NCC), and a nationally certified career counselor and a nationally certified supervisor by the National Board for Certified Counselors. Dr. Bradley holds certification as school counselor (K–12) and secondary teacher. Additionally, Dr. Bradley has served as consultant to business and industry, schools and universities, and maintains a small private practice. Dr. Bradley has served as a member of the editorial boards of the *American Counselor* (Chair), *Counselor Education and Supervision Journal, Journal of Counseling and Development, Journal of Humanistic Education and Development,* and *Counseling and Human Development.* She has authored or coauthored 5 books and more than 70 manuscripts and book chapters. Additionally, she has given more than 100 presentations at professional meetings.

Nicholas Ladany, Ph.D., is Associate Professor, Program Coordinator, and Director of Doctoral Training for the Counseling Psychology Program, Department of Education and Human Services, Lehigh University in Bethlehem, Pennsylvania. Prior to his affiliation with Lehigh University, he was an assistant professor at Temple University and a visiting faculty member at the University of Maryland. He received his Ph.D. at the University at Albany, State University of New York in 1992. He has published numerous articles and presented nationally and internationally in the area of counselor supervision and training. Additionally, his primary research interests and activities include counseling and supervision process and outcome issues, such as the working alliance, self-disclosures and nondisclosures, multicultural training, and ethics. He currently is a member of the editorial boards of the *Journal of Counseling Psychology* and *Counselor Education and Supervision*. He is a licensed psychologist in the states of Pennsylvania and Maryland and is a nationally certified counselor.

Julie R. Ancis, Ph.D., is an assistant professor in the Department of Counseling and Psychological Services at Georgia State University. She received her doctorate in counseling psychology at the University at Albany, State University of New York. She has published in the area of racial and gender attitudes, cultural competency training, and the educational experiences of women and students of color and is a frequent presenter at national conferences. She currently serves on the editorial board of the *Journal of Counseling and Development.*

Lorie S. Blackman is currently a doctoral candidate in Counseling Psychology at the University of Georgia. She received her B.A. in psychology and her M.Ed. in counseling, both from Vanderbilt University. Ms. Blackman's research interests include human development and multicultural issues in counseling.

Carolyn Brennan is currently a doctoral candidate in counseling psychology at the University of Georgia.

M. Kristine Bronson, Ph.D., is a licensed psychologist in private practice at The Brandywine Center, LLC in Wilmington and Newark, DE, where she provides individual and group career counseling, psychotherapy, and consultation to businesses and organizations. Dr. Bronson also supervises, trains, and teaches counselors both in her practice and as an instructor at West Chester University, West Chester, PA.

James R. Cheek is a doctoral student in the Counselor Education Program at Texas Tech University in Lubbock, TX, where he holds a Chancellor's Fellowship. His research interests include advocacy, brain-based learning techniques, HIV/AIDS issues, and school counseling.

Mary D. Deck, Ph.D., is a professor in the Counseling Programs in the Department of Human Services at Western Carolina University, Cullowhee, North Carolina. She is currently the director of the Counseling Programs and the School Counseling Program Leader. She received her initial training in supervision during her doctoral program in counselor education at the University of Virginia. She wishes to thank the counseling students over the years who have helped her learn about the significance of the supervisory relationship at its deepest level.

L. J. Gould, Ed.D., received her training in counselor education at Texas Tech University. Her previous publications include coauthoring five book chapters and four journal articles. She has served as Association for Counselor Education and Supervision program committee student chair and has presented programs at national American Counseling Association and ACES conferences. Dr. Gould's major research interests include gender and sexuality issues, stereotyping, and multicultural counseling.

Richard L. Hayes, Ed.D., is a professor and chair in the Department of Counseling and Human Development Services, College of Education, University of Georgia, Athens, GA. A Harvard College graduate, Dr. Hayes received his doctorate in counseling psychology from Boston University. He is a past-president of the Association for Specialists in Group Work (ASGW) and a former editor of the *Journal of Humanistic Education and Development.* His research interests include the application of human development theory to counseling practice, especially in group settings.

C. Bret Hendricks is a doctoral candidate in the Counselor Education Program at Texas Tech University in Lubbock, Texas. He is a frequent presenter at national conferences. His research interests include music therapy techniques utilized with depressed adolescents, counselor supervision, and advocacy awareness for counselors. He has served on several national committees including the International Association of Marriage and Family Counselors Media Committee. He currently is the graduate student coordinator for the American Counseling Association.

Marcia Kaufman, Ph.D., is a licensed psychologist in private practice in Allentown, PA, where she provides individual and family therapy to children, adolescents, and adults. She is also an adjunct assistant professor at Lehigh University in Bethlehem, PA. Her research interests include psychotherapy training and the psychotherapy process, and she has published articles in these areas.

Jeffrey A. Kottler, Ph.D., is professor of Counselor Education at Texas Tech University. He is the author of more than 30 books in counseling, psychology, and education, including *On Being a Therapist, Introduction to Therapeutic Counseling, What You Never Learned in Graduate School, Advanced Group Leadership,* and *Living in the Material World: Exploring and Treating Acquisitive Desire.*

Deborah Lehrman-Waterman, Ph.D., received a master's degree in education from the University of Delaware in 1995 and her doctorate in counseling psychology from Lehigh University in 2000. She has published two journal articles that investigated counseling supervision phenomena. She focused her graduate training upon counseling and psychotherapy and has had numerous experiences working with children, adolescents, and adults in various therapeutic milieus.

Judith A. Lewis, Ph.D., is a professor in the College of Health Professions at Governor's State University, University Park, Illinois. She has published numerous books and articles related to adolescence, family, substance abuse, community, and employee assistance counseling. Her major scholarly interests relate to community empowerment, advocacy, and social action. She has served as president of the International Association of Marriage and Family Counselors and is currently president of the American Counseling Association (2000–2001).

Sandy Magnuson, Ed.D., is an assistant professor of Counselor Education and coordinator of the School Counseling Program at Texas Tech University in Lubbock, TX. The primary focus of her research is supervision of counselors after they graduate from preparation programs.

Keith J. Morgen is a doctoral student in the Counseling Psychology Program at Lehigh University. He has published and presented research on the social-psychological aspects of HIV/AIDS prevention, drug abuse treatment, and teenage pregnancy.

Janet L. Muse-Burke, M.Ed., is a doctoral candidate in the Counseling Psychology Program at Lehigh University in Bethlehem, PA. She earned a master's degree in Counseling and Human Services in 1997 from Lehigh University. She is a frequent presenter at national and international conferences. Her research interests include counselor education, counseling and supervision process and outcome, and religion and spirituality.

Ken Norem, Ph.D., is a visiting associate professor of Counselor Education at Texas Tech University in Lubbock, TX. Dr. Norem's interests in counselor supervision include clinical experiences of counselors-in-training as well as professional and ethical standards. His research extends to supervision of counselors across the professional lifespan.

Gerald D. Parr, Ph.D., is professor and chair of the Division of Educational Psychology and Leadership in the College of Education at Texas Tech University. His teaching and research interests are in the areas of integrative counseling approaches and small group work.

Kristen J. Planny is enrolled in the Counseling and Development Program of Winthrop University in Rock Hill, SC. She will graduate in December 2000 with a master's degree in school counseling. Currently, she is an intern at a middle school in Charlotte, NC and plans to receive K–12 certification in North Carolina.

Peggy P. Whiting, Ed.D., is an associate professor in the Counseling and Development Program of Winthrop University in Rock Hill, SC. She was on the faculty of the Human Development Counseling Program, George Peabody College of Vanderbilt University from 1986 to 1994. In addition to counselor supervision, her professional interests include grief counseling and education, crisis response in schools, posttraumatic stress symptomatology, and lifespan development. She was awarded the 1998 South Carolina Counseling Association's Distinguished Professional Service Award for her work with loss prevention, intervention, and post-vention efforts in the schools.

PREFACE

Counselor Supervision: Principles, Process, and Practice (3rd edition) is intended for counselor educators and counselor supervisor practitioners who work in a variety of educational and mental health settings. Primary supervision theories are reviewed and critiqued with the intent of informing supervisor practitioners, counselor educators, and supervisor trainees. Additionally, cutting-edge topic areas are covered that include (a) multicultural issues in counselor supervision (e.g., how to balance and manage multiple identities such as gender, race, sexual orientation, age, and disability in the context of influencing trainees' multicultural competences), (b) the supervisory relationship (an essential but sometimes forgotten component of supervision) and its influence on supervision process and outcome, (c) supervision of career counselor trainees (e.g., supervision challenges unique to career counseling trainees such as integrating personal and career development), (d) supervision of school counselors (e.g., supervision challenges unique to school counselors such as confidentiality and balancing multiple roles), (e) supervision of family and group counselors, (f) group supervision, (g) understanding and conducting research in counselor supervision and training, (h) ethical and advocacy issues in supervision, and (i) supervisor training. Case examples are used throughout the book to illustrate the application of theory to practical issues that counselor supervisors encounter.

☐ Overview of the Book

The book's 15 chapters are divided into four major parts consisting of Part I: "Counselor Supervision: Essentials for Training"; Part II: "Theoretical Approaches to Counselor Supervision"; Part III: "Specialized Models of Counselor Supervision"; and Part IV: "Professional Issues in Counselor Supervision."

Chapter 1 of Part I gives an overview of the basic principles, roles, and functions involved in effective supervisory practice for clinical and administrative supervisors. Chapter 2 describes how the supervisory relationship provides a foundation for the implementation of supervisory interventions and is also the key to understanding effective and ineffective supervision. Although we infuse multicultural issues throughout the book, Chapter 3 provides a framework for understanding supervision from a multicultural perspective. It is hoped that this multicultural framework will provide the reader with a template for appraising supervision models and interventions.

Part II provides an overview of the primary theoretical models of supervision. We divide the types of supervision models into two categories: those that were devised specifically for the supervision context (Chapter 4, on supervision-based integrative models, and Chapter 5, on supervision-based developmental models) and those that were derived from, or are extensions of, psychotherapy models (Chapter 6). These three chapters present the reviewed models in similar formats to assist the reader in understanding and evaluating the salient tenets of the models. The format in which the models are reviewed consists of the following sections: overall framework, primary concepts and theoretical assumptions, integration of the supervisory relationship, focus and goals, methodology and techniques, a case example, and critique of strengths and weaknesses.

Part III contains four chapters devoted to specialized models of counselor supervision. Even while the field of supervision has embraced expanded general models of supervision, it has been recognized that certain settings and supervisory enterprises would benefit from supervision models geared specifically toward them. To this end, Part III attends to specialized supervision models that include group supervision (Chapter 7), supervision of school counselors (Chapter 8), supervision of career counselors (Chapter 9), and supervision of family counselors (Chapter 10).

Part IV consists of five chapters pertaining to professional issues in counselor supervision. In particular, the necessary process of trainee evaluation is reviewed in Chapter 11. Chapter 12 is intended to help professional counselors interested in supervision research, as well as students conducting supervision research for theses or dissertations, to understand and conduct supervision research. Chapter 13 focuses specifically on how supervisors can integrate advocacy into their supervision practice. The most recent and primary ethical principles and guidelines for supervisors are presented in Chapter 14, and Chapter 15 provides a model for training supervisors.

☐ What's New in This Edition?

Portions of many of the chapters were originally included in *Counselor Supervision* (Boyd, 1978) and, later, in *Counselor Supervision: Principles Process and Practice* (Bradley, 1989). However, these chapters have been modified to bring them up-to-date with current information and references. In particular, the chapters were completely updated to reflect current theory, research, and practice in counselor supervision. Furthermore, we added chapters to reflect innovations in counselor supervision theory, research, and practice that include chapters on multicultural issues in supervision; the supervision of school, career, and family counselors; advocacy in supervision;

trainee evaluation; and understanding and conducting supervision research. This edition also expands upon and highlights how the supervisory relationship is central to supervision as well as its influence on supervision process and outcome.

☐ Audience

This book is intended for both clinical and administrative supervisors. This book should be beneficial to supervisors-in-training, whether enrolled in university graduate training programs or seeking professional development or licensure as a counselor supervisor, as well as to supervisors seeking additional supervisory information. For clinical supervisors enrolled in graduate supervision classes, this book is intended as a primary text. For the clinical and administrative supervisor employed in an agency, the book is intended as a primary tool for in-service training and professional development. For the practicing supervisor regardless of setting, we envision the book as a guide for implementing the supervisory process. Finally, the professional counselor seeking licensure as a Licensed Professional Counselor or Licensed Supervisor should find this book to be a useful and relevant resource.

Although the title *Counselor Supervision* might suggest that the book is only intended for counselors, in reality the book is written for a variety of human service providers. In addition to counselors and counseling psychologists, the book should prove beneficial to clinical psychologists, directors of human resource providers in business and industry, employee assistance coordinators, directors of pupil personnel services, career and vocational counselors and supervisors, family therapy supervisors, psychiatrists, and social workers.

Ultimately, it is our hope that you will find this book useful and relevant to your supervisory purposes.

☐ References

Boyd, J. D. (1978). *Counselor supervision: Approaches, preparation and practices.* Muncie, IN: Accelerated Development.

Bradley, L. J. (1989). *Counselor supervision: Principles, process, and practice.* Muncie, IN: Accelerated Development.

ACKNOWLEDGMENTS

We are extremely grateful for the feedback, insight, and guidance provided to us by people who read selected chapters or all of the book: Susan Allstetter Neufeldt, Karen O'Brien, Lia Pate, L. J. Gould, Susan Rarick, and Jessica Walker. We further thank Brandi Gilmore for her citation assistance. We also extend our appreciation to Tim Julet and Jill Osowa for their laudable editorial assistance throughout the process of putting this book together.

I (Loretta Bradley) want to express my sincere appreciation to Dr. John Boyd, who wrote one of the early books on counselor supervision. I am grateful for Dr. Boyd's advice and encouragement. His work on the supervision process and models of supervision remain an important part of this book. I am grateful to the late Dr. Roger Aubrey for his encouragement and support, which provided the original impetus for writing about counselor supervision. To Dr. Joseph Hollis, I offer thanks for timely advice, support, and encouragement to revise this book. Many of my ideas about supervision were acquired as I supervised students at Peabody College of Vanderbilt University (1978–1987) and Texas Tech University (1987–present). To the many students that I have supervised, I express special thanks. I also thank my former colleagues at Peabody College of Vanderbilt University (Drs. Roger Aubrey, Michael Berger, Brenda Dew, Judy Lewis, Richard Percy, Julius Seeman, and Peggy Whiting) and my colleagues at Texas Tech University (Drs. Camille DeBell, Jeffrey Kottler, Kenneth Norem, Sandra Magnuson, Aretha Marbley, Gerald Parr, and Arlin Peterson) for encouraging me to continue to develop and expand my ideas on supervision. To Dr. Mary Tallent-Runnels, I express thanks for your encouragement. Thanks to Bret Hendricks for all of your help with the library research and to James Cheek for your suggestions. To Margaret Graham goes a special thank you for your help with the typing and formatting. As many of you know, I worked on the revisions of this book when I was President of the American Counseling Association (ACA;1998–1999), and I began thinking about the revisions when I was President of the Association for Counselor Education and Supervision (ACES; 1995–1996). I want to thank my professional colleagues in ACA and ACES who encouraged this work. Finally and most importantly, I want to express my appreciation to my family. To my husband, Dr. Charles Bradley, and my sons, Brian and Brett: Thank you for your support, patience and understanding. Without my family's cooperation, this book would not have become a reality.

I (Nicholas Ladany) want to offer my heartfelt appreciation to the people who have enriched my professional and personal life. To Kris, for her gifts of partnership, encouragement, and support. My accomplishments are in no small part a function of your belief in me. I am also personally indebted to my colleagues and mentors who have fostered the development of my abilities, provided the foundation for my ideas, and inspired me. Thank you Julie Ancis, David Blustein, Madonna Constantine, Susan Drumheller, Mike Ellis, Jane Folk, Anna Maria Francis, Micki Friedlander, Charlie Gelso, Dick Haase, Clara Hill, Bob Kaufman, Marcia Kaufman, Maxine Krengel, Sylvia Marotta, Kathy Miller, Karen O'Brien, Debbie Schult, Jim Smith, Arnie Spokane, Marilyn Stern, and Barbara Thompson. Last, but certainly not least, I am truly grateful to the students with whom I have worked, and from whom I have learned a great deal about supervision. In particular, thanks to you Chris Brittan-Powell, Maureen Corbett, Laurie Gray, Arpana Inman, Sue Kim, Mara Latts, Debbie Lehrman-Waterman, Debbie Melincoff, Max Molinaro, Janet Muse-Burke, Libby Nutt Williams, Lia Pate, Raji Pannu, Manju Pradhan, Susan Rarick, Tim Silvestri, Katja Spradlin, Amanda Tyson, Jay Walker, and Brad Wolgast.

I

COUNSELOR SUPERVISION: ESSENTIALS FOR TRAINING

CHAPTER 1

Loretta J. Bradley
Jeffrey A. Kottler

Overview of Counselor Supervision

A client is being resistant and obstinate. He fails to show up for counseling sessions consistently, and when he does make an appearance, he is surly and uncooperative. His counselor has been struggling with this case for several weeks, finally electing to seek supervision not only for alternative treatment options, but also to deal with her feelings of confusion and frustration.

As is not uncommon in such situations, before consulting with a supervisor, this counselor has talked to others about her strong reactions (without revealing confidential information). She has consulted with her peer counselors about her "difficult" client. She has even spoken to her advisor about the frustrations she has been feeling about her work, questioning whether she is well suited to continue within the field.

The supervisor who has been sought out by this counselor has recently been promoted in her job. She feels her own pressure from within, and from peers, to live up to new expectations as a master practitioner, a holder of "super-vision." As she listens to the counselor recite the details of the case, she feels herself becoming discouraged directly by the counselor's sense of helplessness and indirectly by the client's own despair. She helps the counselor sort out the crucial dimensions of the case and reframes the situation according to an alternative perspective. She then helps the counselor generate alternative ways to proceed in the future.

Feeling new resolve, the counselor introduces these novel ideas to the client. Sure enough, the client responds to the new strategy, but in some surprising ways. In fact, there is a ripple effect that impacts not only the client's behavior but that of everyone else in his family and support system.

The client and counselor, their friends and family, are not the only ones who have been affected by and, in turn, influenced the behavior of everyone else. The supervisor has also been reflecting on this case, her interactions with the counselor, and her roles and responsibilities. She has consulted with her peers about what she has been doing and reflected on the strategies she has employed.

This complex series of interactions among counselor, client, and supervisor is not at all unusual. Parallel processes, or the reenactment of dynamics in one relationship in the context of another one, are quite common in supervision (Ekstein & Wallerstein, 1972; Lombardo, Greer, Estadt, & Cheston, 1997; Stoltenberg, McNeill, & Delworth, 1998). Beyond the dynamics of unconscious reenactment, there are also many reciprocal effects that take place among the primary participants: client, counselor, and supervisor. Each of the individuals directly and indirectly influences the perceptions and behaviors of the others, for better or worse. It is this phenomenon that makes the process of supervision so rich, rewarding, complex, and challenging.

☐ Some Working Definitions

Counselor supervision is a term that can be found throughout counseling literature (Bernard & Goodyear, 1998; Blocher, 1983; Borders & Leddick, 1987; Carroll, 1996; Falvey, 1987; Haber, 1996; G. Hart, 1982; Hess, 1986; Neufeldt, 1999; Stoltenberg, McNeill & Crethar, 1994). The term *supervision* can be divided into two words, "super" and "vision." These two terms imply that supervision is a process in which an experienced person (supervisor) with appropriate training and experience mentors and teaches a subordinate (supervisee). It is a process of professional and personal development in which the supervisor challenges, stimulates, and encourages a counselor to reach higher levels of competence. Implicit in this definition is the ongoing relationship between supervisor and supervisee, the professional role identity to be acquired, and the focus on the behavior to be acquired by the supervisee. In addition to its function of fostering educational and professional development of counselors, any definition of supervision must also include its critical role as an evaluative tool in assessing fitness for the profession (Holloway & Neufeldt, 1995; Temple & Bowers, 1998).

Clinical Versus Administrative Supervision

In a report of the Committee on Counselor Effectiveness conducted over three decades ago (Association of Counselor Education and Supervision, 1969), a three-part definition delineated who a supervisor is, what supervision seeks to achieve, and the activities that constitute this professional activity. Accordingly, counselor supervision was defined as (a) being performed by experienced, successful counselors (supervisors) who have been prepared in the methodology of supervision; (b) facilitating the counselor's personal and professional development, promoting counselor competencies, and promoting accountable counseling and guidance services and programs; and (c) providing the purposeful function of overseeing the work of counselor trainees or practicing counselors (supervisees) through a set of supervisory activities that include consultation, counseling training and instruction, and evaluation.

Since this preliminary formulation, distinctions have been made between administrative (Copeland, 1998; Falvey, 1987; W. Lewis, 1988) and clinical supervision (Bernard & Goodyear, 1998; Borders & Leddick, 1987; Ellis, 1991; Powell, 1993), as well as hierarchical versus peer supervision (Benshoff & Paisley, 1996; Kottler & Hazler, 1997; G. J. Lewis, Greenburg, & Hatch, 1988). The distinctions between these modes have been centered around the tasks performed by the supervisor as well as the roles adopted. In describing administrative supervision, researchers (Abels & Murphy, 1981; Austin, 1981; Black, 1975; Bradley, 1989; Copeland, 1998; G. Hart, 1982; Kadushin, 1992; Simon, 1985; Slavin, 1985; Wiles & Bondi, 1997) have typically described administrative supervision as occurring in bureaucratic organizations (e.g., universities, human service organizations). In administrative supervision, the supervisor helps the supervisee function effectively as a part of the organization with the overall intent to help the organization run smoothly and efficiently. The administrative supervisor usually stresses organizational accountability, case records, referrals, and performance evaluations.

In contrast, clinical supervision focuses on the work of the supervisee in relation to the services received by the client. In clinical supervision, the supervisor focuses on such areas as client welfare, counseling relationship, assessment, diagnosis, clinical intervention, prognosis, and appropriate referral techniques (Ellis, 1991; Hart, 1982; Tarvydas, 1995; Watkins, 1997). The focus of administrative supervision, therefore, is on tasks that directly affect the organization, whereas in clinical supervision the focus is on the supervisee's clinical interventions that directly affect the client, as well as those behaviors related to the supervisee's personal and professional functioning. You will note that throughout this book the focus will be directed towards both administrative and clinical supervision, since they are so closely linked in daily practice.

☐ Roles of the Supervisor

Every profession includes master practitioners who can guide and direct less experienced colleagues and preservice trainees. Master practitioners function within apprenticeships and internships by promoting a transfer of learning from instructional settings to the actual environment where the profession is practiced. Moreover, these individuals are crucial in continued personal and professional development, which extends throughout a professional's career.

In the helping services, and specifically in counseling, master practitioners are called *supervisors*. In other cultures, and in other fields, they might just as legitimately be referred to as mentors, chiefs, captains, leaders, or guides.

They also are known by other labels, such as administrative supervisor, clinical supervisor, human resource supervisor, director of guidance, head counselor, chief psychologist, and/or pupil personnel services director. Whatever the official title, the main role of a supervisor is to perform the function of counselor supervision. Supervisors are responsible for supervising the work of student-counselors and/or a staff of practicing counselors.

Supervisor Qualifications

The necessary academic preparation and background experiences of counselor supervisors have been investigated by Borders et al. (1991), Ellis and Douce (1994), and Richardson and Bradley (1986), and previously by Riccio (1961, 1966) and the Association for Counselor Education and Supervision (ACES) survey (1969). Additionally, ACES has developed standards for supervisors (ACES, 1993). Results from these studies indicate that nearly all supervisors in colleges and universities have attained doctoral degrees, and the majority of supervisors in field settings (i.e., agencies, state departments, and schools) have gained a significant level of education beyond the master's degree. Despite these high levels of educational attainment, the alarming fact remains that only a token number of supervisors, regardless of work setting, have received specific preparation for supervision.

A reasonable assumption is that counselor supervisors in general achieved their supervisory positions on the basis of educational level, tenure, and successful counseling experiences. It would also be realistic to expect that such professionals are well connected politically within their organizations to attain positions of authority and power. However, counseling experience and an accumulation of academic credits must be viewed as insufficient qualifications, by themselves, for supervisors of counselors. This is especially the case with supervisors who attained their positions because they were well connected with the dominant power structure within the organization.

Preparation in supervision methodology must become an entrance criterion if supervision practice is to be validated (Holloway & Neufeldt, 1995). Undergraduate preparation of supervisors is usually in the fields of education and psychology, while graduate preparation and advanced academic work are in counselor education, counseling psychology, or other helping and service disciplines. Supervisors tend to be situation oriented; they gain counseling experience in a particular setting and are likely to remain there for supervisory practice.

Skills and Attributes

The literature on supervision and supervisory job functions generates some information about the necessary personality attributes of a supervisor. The supervisor must be a serious, committed professional who has chosen counseling and supervision as a long-term career (G. Hart, 1982; Hess, 1986). This assumption implies that the supervisor is energetic and ambitious, but not in an egotistical or opportunistic manner. Instead, the supervisor is committed to and ambitious about developing and maintaining accountable helping services.

The supervisor must possess the core conditions of empathy, respect, and concreteness as well as the action-oriented conditions of genuineness, confrontation, and immediacy (Blocher, 1983; Patterson, 1983). In addition to the core conditions, other descriptions of the good supervisor include concern for the growth and well-being of the supervisee (Bernard, 1992; Borders & Fong, 1994; Hess, 1986; Mueller & Kell, 1972) as well as the welfare of the client (Bernard, 1987; Corey, Corey, & Callanan, 1998; Cormier & Bernard, 1982). Other positive supervisor characteristics include integrity, courage, sense of humor, capacity for intimacy, sense of timing, openness to self-inspection (Ellis & Robbins, 1993; Stein & Lambert, 1995), responsibleness (Holloway & Neufeldt, 1995; Leddick & Dye, 1987; Masters, 1992) and a nonthreatening, nonauthoritarian approach to supervision (Allen, Szollos, & Williams, 1986; Bordin, 1983; Dodge, 1982; Ottens, Shank, & Long, 1995); as well as the capacity to be flexible, tolerant, and open to various styles and levels of learning (Borders, 1992; Cross & Brown, 1983; Grater, 1985; Schneider, 1992; Stoltenberg, Solomon, & Ogden, 1986; E. L. Worthington, 1984).

In short, supervisors should be able to model what they ask of their supervisees; they should be able to demonstrate in their own lives everything that they expect of their protégés. This means that they become living examples of all those qualities, skills, and behaviors that they consider so important for others (Kottler, 1999).

Competence and success with a broad range of helping activities are essential criteria for the selection of supervisors, although realistically the supervisor cannot be expected to be omnipotent; thus skills and expertise may be unevenly distributed. In addition to such professionally demonstrable qualities, a supervisor must possess confidence and professional assurance. A hesitant, unsure supervisor cannot offer the kind of leadership that is needed in supervisory positions. In a profession where nurturance is sometimes more prevalent than ego strength, those in leadership roles must be self-assured. This is particularly true in agencies and schools where counselors are subordinate to other administrators. The supervisor must be confident and strong when working with those who have administrative power over counselors, as well as when grappling with the difficult decisions that arise in supervision.

A supervisor should command both the professional and the personal respect of colleagues and associates in the work environment. Professional respect is founded in competence and ability, first as a good counselor and then as a capable supervisor. Personal respect relates to whether the supervisor is totally accepted as a person by his or her associates and is based upon values, attitudes, ethics, and other moral indices that are reflected through professional behavior.

Finally, the supervisor must be highly committed to protecting the welfare of others, including the ability and willingness to serve as an advocate for counselors and their clients. All individuals need support, and counselors as a group suffer from a lack of professional affirmation. Supervisees need to feel that the supervisor believes in their ability or potential to be more effective practitioners.

To summarize, the supervisor is a well-prepared individual who has entered the supervisory position after attaining a high degree of training, experience, and wisdom as a practitioner. The supervisor is regarded as a mentor from whom other counselors can learn and is respected as a person of exemplary character. The supervisor is an advocate for counselors and is dedicated to their personal and professional development.

☐ Purposes of Counselor Supervision

What are the purposes of supervision? There are obvious functions, to be sure, but also subtle ones as well. Statements of purpose are often overlapping, but these documents are extremely important because they register intent and set direction.

Counselor supervision has three main purposes:

1. facilitation of the counselor's professional and personal development,
2. promotion of counselor competencies, and
3. promotion of accountable counseling services and programs.

Singularly and collectively, these purposes provide a rationale for the work of supervisors (Bradley, 1989).

Personal and Professional Development

The first purpose of supervision is a dual one: to facilitate the personal and professional development of counselors. The supervisor acts in the role of mentor and advocate, as well as teacher and consultant.

Assuming agreement that facilitation of counselors' personal development should be a purpose of supervision, the next questions we need to ask are how much and what kind of emphasis should be placed on personal development. Answers to these questions are a matter for debate, but the following guidelines may be helpful in arriving at a partial resolution.

1. Generally, counselor supervision should not attempt to intrude on the personal development of counselors. Supervision should offer the counselor an optimal opportunity for self-initiated personal development and encourage the counselor to take advantage of the opportunity.

2. Supervisory intervention into the counselor's personal development should be undertaken only when psychological distress is obviously and deleteriously affecting the counselor's performance. "Facilitation" of personal development is, however, a continuing supervisory effort.
3. The counselor's personal and professional development are interrelated. Damage to, or facilitation of, one of these concepts has a reciprocal effect on the other. Furthermore, facilitating personal development can be construed as contributing indirectly to all purposes of supervision.
4. The foremost purposes of counselor supervision are facilitating professional development, increasing competencies, and promoting accountability in guidance and counseling. An assumption is that selection and preparation have produced well-adjusted counselors, thus allowing the facilitation of personal development to become a second-priority purpose of supervision.

Since the concept of personal development is inherently vague, the supervisor must be able to put the concept into concrete terms so that supervisory techniques and strategies can be applied. No attempt is made here to give tangibility to the concept, because personal development is being treated as a general purpose. This concept will be treated more concretely in subsequent chapters.

Professional development, an interrelated part of the dual purpose of supervision, is a concept that must be clearly defined if the supervisor is to functionalize its intent. In a broad sense, professional development encompasses all that makes the counselor a professional, including increasing and improving competencies. In the context of this presentation, however, a more narrow definition is used, since competency improvement is designated as a separate supervisory purpose. Professional development, as here defined, refers to four tasks that have been adapted from concepts of Becker and Carper (1956), D. H. Hart and Prince (1970), Zerface and Cox (1971), and Steffire (1964).

1. The counselor must accept the name and image of the profession as part of his or her self-concept. This task causes problems for counselors because their preparation may lead to a wide variety of positions, each with a different job or professional title (e.g., child/adult development specialist, counseling psychologist, guidance counselor, group facilitator, human development counselor, mental health counselor, family therapist, human resource specialist, or school counselor).
2. One must have a commitment to, and a clear perception of, the professional role and function. Counselors do not typically enter positions where their role and function have already been established. In fact, establishing this operational base is one of the most important and difficult functions of the newly employed counselor. Occasionally, situational conditions can be so restrictive that the environment is unfit for good professional practice.

A frequently slighted facet of the counselor's role and function is support of the profession and contribution to its growth and strength. Counselors are in dire need of professional affirmation however; ironically, the only way to receive this affirmation is to produce it! Participation in local, state, and national professional associations is a start.

3. The counselor must be committed to the goals of the institution in which counseling services are performed. This commitment does not preclude the counselor's influence on establishment or alteration of institutional goals.

4. The counselor will recognize and appreciate the significance of the profession for individuals, groups, institutions, and society as a whole. A true profession exists to meet the needs of society, and professional accountability begins with recognition of these needs, an understanding of how the profession meets them, and an assessment of the profession's impact.

An integral component in the supervisory purpose to facilitate personal and professional development is the assumption of responsibility by both the counselor and the supervisor for achieving this development. As Ekstein and Wallerstein (1972) noted, counselor preparation should help counselors separate themselves from formal preparation and carry on a continuous process of independent learning. Similarly, responsible self-development (Arnold, 1962; Bernard, 1997; Blocher, 1983; Goodyear & Bernard, 1998; Hess, 1986; Ward & House, 1998) permeates the purposes of supervision.

Competency Development

The second purpose of supervision, to increase counselor competencies, incorporates helping the counselor acquire, improve, and refine the skills required by the counselor's role and function. Unfortunately, the purpose has become associated more with counselor education programs than with in-service supervision because field supervisors often are reluctant to accept responsibility for colleagues' competency development. Before entering the position of supervisor, the master counselor was responsible only for self-improvement, and to monitor a colleague's skill level would have been presumptuous. Upon entering the supervisory role, however, the responsibility for supervisee competency development must be accepted, and here the personal characteristics discussed earlier in the chapter become crucial. Does the supervisor feel confident enough to help others with his or her skills? Is the supervisor respected as a capable counselor who has something to offer?

Another reason for field supervisors to be uncomfortable with responsibility for supervisee competency development is that many of them have not been prepared in the methodology of supervision. Although supervisors in counselor education programs may lack formal supervisory preparation, they have the advantages of modeling the supervisory behavior of colleagues, being encouraged by eager students to assume a supervisory role, and the controlled conditions of a laboratory setting or a counseling center.

Still another reason why competency development has been almost exclusively associated with formal preparation programs is the assumed existence of a competency ceiling—a point at which the counselor has "learned it all." Such a terminal point is often perceived to be a graduate degree or state certification. A different perspective is needed by both supervisor and supervisee if competency is to be seen as something to be upgraded throughout one's professional career. After all, the development of counselor competency can be conceptualized as a continual process with several distinguishable levels along a continuum.

The first level represents the skills that are reached through a master's degree counselor education program. Although such programs strive for the ideal of producing a fully functioning counselor, more realistically the first level may be described as the acquisition of a repertoire of fundamental skills and a basic foundation of knowledge that extends beyond entry skill boundaries. The repertoire of entry skills are those that the profession and the preparing institution have identified as necessary for competent counselor performance. Attainment and demonstration of these skills should be criteria for awarding a professional degree in counseling. The basic foundation of knowledge at level 1 provides a background of understanding that enables the counselor to broaden the repertoire of entry skills via experience and supervision. Progress leads to the level-2 goal of a "fully functioning counselor."

Level 3 on the continuum is devoted to refinement of the fully functioning repertoire of skills. At level 2 the competency dimension of quantity (i.e., the number of skills) was the target, but at level 3, the focus is on quality. The counselor achieves level 3 by improving existing competencies and moving toward the goal of a repertoire of refined and polished skills.

Advanced skills are the goal at level 4 of the competency continuum. This level is achieved, after several years of experience, advanced preparation, and supervision by a small percentage of counselors who may be called "master practitioners." The work of "master practitioners" is outstanding in all respects. These individuals possess and perform advanced skills that would be unethical for the neophyte to attempt. Other professionals use such persons as models and depend on them for guidance and leadership because of their demonstrated effectiveness. One of the competencies that may be gained at this level is counselor supervision.

Beyond level 4 is a continual process of competency development. The neophyte at level 1 may think that the supervisor, who always seems to know what to do, has reached the ceiling of competency development. However, this is a misconception, and perhaps the supervisor should share the truth that despite advanced preparation, successful performance, and the professional prestige of being a master counselor, there is always more to be learned, for the process of competency development never ends.

Promotion of Accountability

To say that the helping professions, and particularly counseling, are presently in an "age of accountability" would be an understatement. Accountability is being demanded by the public and managed care organizations that fund these enterprises. The consequence of not being able to satisfy public expectations could be disastrous for helping professionals. More than ever before, counselors and their supervisors are called upon to articulate clear treatment plans and specific, realistic goals that can be reached within relatively brief periods of time. Furthermore, pressure is increasing to demonstrate results.

To ignore the realities of jeopardized funding would be irresponsible, but these forces should not be the motivation for helping services and programs to respond to the need for demonstrating accountability. Such forces from outside the profession may serve as cues to raise serious questions about effectiveness, but the motivation for demonstrating accountability must come from within.

A profession emerges in response to the needs of society and exists for the purpose of meeting those needs. Accountability is the profession's index of validity and evidence that the profession is meeting society's needs. The profession's obligation, not society's, is to establish accountability.

As a term, *accountability* has been given many definitions (Corey, Corey, & Callanan, 1998; Holahan & Gallassi, 1986; Koerin & Miller, 1995; Sexton, 1998; Upchurch, 1985). The core concept relates to accomplishment of purposes and goals that a person or institution has contracted or promised to accomplish. Glass (1972) compared this core element of meaning to "the simple economic relationship of vendor and buyer" (p. 636). The public is the buyer of helping services, and counselors are the vendors. An accountable relationship between these two parties would involve

1. complete disclosure concerning the service being sold,
2. testing of the effectiveness of the service, and
3. redress if the service is found by the public to be ineffective or falsely advertised.

According to this vendor–buyer paradigm, counselors are accountable to their employers: the public. Counselors must openly and honestly explain their functions and what their services can do. Counselors must test and evaluate their services and share the findings with the public. Lastly, counselors must be responsible for the consequences (good and bad) of their work and make adjustments when their work is ineffective.

Counselor supervision is a means for promoting accountability in services, programs, and relationships between helping services and the public. Supervised assistance to an individual counselor improves that person's accountability, while supervision applied to a staff of counselors involved in program development, management, and evaluation is a route to program accountability. In both cases, a special set of skills—a technical expertise—is needed by the supervisor if accountability is to be achieved.

☐ Activities of Counselor Supervision

Thus far, two aspects of counselor supervision have been reviewed. The person who performs supervision has been described and the purposes of supervision have been discussed. The third part of the definition states that counselor supervision is the purposeful function of overseeing the work of counselor trainees or less experienced counselors through a set of supervisory activities, which include

1. support,
2. consultation,
3. counseling,
4. training and instruction, and
5. evaluation.

In terms of our definition, supervision as a function is the characteristic action or activity involved in implementing a purpose. The term that best describes the characteristic actions and activities of supervision is *overseeing* —the act of "watching over." Whatever diverse activities comprise the work of counselor supervision, they are subsumed under the principal supervisory function of being aware of and monitoring the work (and development) of less experienced practitioners.

Support

Counseling, especially for beginners, is a stressful business. Neophytes are often confused, frustrated, disoriented, anxious, and obsessed with their imperfections and failures. Even experts, as well, are known to struggle with these doubts and insecurities (Kottler & Blau, 1989).

In the same sense that a counselor provides a type of "holding environment" for clients, supervisors often do the same for beginning practitioners. Supervisees are offered a safe environment in which to disclose their fears and concerns, to explore difficult issues, and to work through areas of weakness, confusion, and conflict. Apart from any of the other consultation, educational, and administrative activities that take place, supervisees are offered the support they need to take constructive risks, increase their confidence, and develop personally and professionally.

Consultation

Counselors are known to take on different roles for their clients, depending on chosen theoretical orientation, as well as particular needs in a given session (Bernard, 1979). Thus, the roles of parent figure, coach, teacher, guru, manager, and consultant are but a few of the options often used. Likewise, supervisors perform various functions for individual supervisees in the context of particular roles.

Consultation is one of the most frequent activities that occur in both hierarchical supervision between a supervisor and subordinate and in relationships between peers of equal status who share responsibility for the client's welfare. There is little doubt that consultation activities are distinctly different from those that involve administrative or evaluative functions. It is essentially a problem-solving process in which the two participants in the process identify the relevant difficulties, collaborate on some intervention, and then assess the results, making adjustments as needed. This model of supervision is frequently employed within a solution-focused counseling approach in which the supervisor functions as a consultant to coax higher levels of expertise from the counselor (Thomas, 1994). Many other approaches, as well, take on the consultant's role during times when it is appropriate to help the supervisee develop treatment options through a collaborative process.

We envision supervisory consultation as including the following components:

1. The consulting supervisor is most often an expert—a master counselor, rather than a peer—who has wide training and experience in various areas.
2. If consultees are practicing or postdegree counselors, they are accepted as capable professionals by the consulting supervisor. Presumably a selection process has been applied before employment and counselors have been judged competent. If counselors are still in a counselor preparation program, they are accepted as potentially capable counselors. In either case, if the supervisor cannot accept the consultee in the manner described, supervision will be compromised.
3. A compatible and complementary relationship must exist between the roles of supervisor and counselor if consultation is to succeed. The role of the consulting supervisor is to help the counselor with personal and professional development, competency development, and establishment and maintenance of accountable services and programs. The role of the counselor is to seek and capitalize upon the supervisor's assistance in the achievement of responsible self-development. Development through supervision is a joint responsibility, but the central obligation is on the counselor, since self-development is the goal.
4. Supervisory consultation leads to objectives that are mutually agreed upon by supervisor and counselor. Objectives tend to fall into the four following categories:

(a) personal problems that are interfering with the counselor's work,
(b) concerns about professional development,
(c) acquisition of new skills or improvement of existing competencies, and
(d) program development, maintenance, and evaluation.

To determine which supervisory consultation objectives are pertinent to a given situation, some type of preliminary assessment is needed. Both self-assessment by the counselor and cooperative assessment by counselor and supervisor are encouraged.

5. To accomplish objectives in supervisory consultation, effective strategies must be applied. Some strategies allow the supervisor to remain in the consulting role. In other strategies the supervisor may need to conduct training sessions and other forms of instruction or render appropriate conditions to shift into counseling. Strategies that lead the supervisor out of the consultation activity and into other supervisory activities should be regarded as acceptable but temporary aberrations. A return to consultation should later be accomplished, thus reaffirming consultation as the dominant activity of supervision.

6. Evaluation has been designated as a supervisory activity separate from consultation, and evaluation will be discussed in that context at a later time. These two aspects of supervision are frequently considered antithetical, with consultation being viewed as threat free and the latter role involving critical assessment (Bernard, 1997; Brown, Pryzwansky, & Schulte, 1987; Galhessich, 1982; Richman, Aitken, & Prather, 1990; J. A. Lewis, Lewis, & Souflee, 1991; Stenack & Dye, 1982; Thomas, 1994; Turner, 1982). As employed within supervision, the consulting activity is rarely completely nonevaluative. Supervision, as previously stated, is the function of overseeing the counselor's work. Evaluation is implied in the overseeing function and is obviously a necessity for accomplishment of the purposes of supervision. Evaluation can and should be used in conjunction with supervisory consultation without raising the counselor's anxiety level enough to hamper supervision. The main problem seems to occur when the respective roles and expectations for the relationship are not clearly defined and negotiated (Olk & Friedlander, 1992; Temple & Bowers, 1998).

Whether or not the supervisor should evaluate the counselor's performance is a practical rather than just a theoretical question. How can the supervisor nurture counselor self-development while concurrently assuring that supervisory purposes are being achieved? If an autocratic or directive stance that excludes counselor input is adopted, the objective of self-development is sacrificed. If the supervisor is totally nonevaluative in the relationship with a counselor, the situation may be too benign to be effective. An imperfect but realistic compromise is for the consulting supervisor to encourage counselor self-evaluation, to generate cooperative evaluation wherever efficacious, and to judiciously apply some evaluatory procedures on a unilateral basis.

Counseling

One area of considerable debate and disagreement is the extent to which the supervisory relationship addresses personal issues in the counselor's life. Whereas some supervisors believe this constitutes an inappropriate dual relationship, others believe that it is virtually impossible to deal with professional conflicts and struggles without also examining the impact on one's personal life. We believe that the question is not *whether* a supervisor should ever listen to counseling issues, but rather *how* the supervisor chooses to manage these issues when they inevitably arise.

The issue of whether supervisory consultation should be permitted to revert to counseling may be dealt with in the context of two related questions. Question 1 is, "Does the supervisee ever need counseling, and/or could the supervisee profit from counseling?" Clearly, the rationale upon which counseling is founded gives an affirmative answer to this question. Counseling exists to help individuals with the developmental tasks, stages, and personal adjustment concerns that beset everyone (Blocher, 1966; Gibson & Mitchell, 1995; Goodyear & Bernard, 1998; Hansen, Stevic, & Warner, 1986; Kell & Burow, 1970; Shertzer & Stone, 1980; Sprinthall, 1971; Ward & House, 1998). The professional counselor (supervisee) may at times be facing quite stressful events in his or her life that affect job performance, and at these particular times, the supervisee can profit from counseling.

Question 2 is, "Who should provide counseling to the supervisee and in what situation?" With few exceptions, the supervisor (a master counselor), although qualified to do counseling, should refer the supervisee for counseling. However, before the counselor is referred, it is important that the supervisor have enough information to assess and make a competent referral.

Typically, the supervisor will be engaged in the consulting activity with the supervisee when cues emerge from the supervisee indicating that he or she wishes to discuss a particular concern. When such cues become apparent, the supervisor can follow the counselor's lead with the intent of determining whether the concern interferes with the counselor's ability to counsel. If extensive counseling is needed, the supervisor should make a referral to another agency or counselor. Assuming that extensive treatment is not usually needed, focus on these issues will be short term, and the transition back into consultation can be achieved through the supervisor's adept management of the interaction.

During those intervals when supervisory time is devoted to addressing a counselor's personal issues, two main questions should be addressed:

1. To what extent is this personal material relevant to the professional management of the case? If there is a direct relationship, such as evidence

of strong countertransference reactions, then the issues must be worked through. If, on the other hand, the counselor's issues are part of some ongoing personal struggle that are not directly related to the supervisory work, it is usually best to refer the individual for counseling with another professional.

2. To what extent is there role confusion and ambiguity that pollutes the supervisory relationship? There is little doubt that a supervisory relationship is a complex and multifaceted encounter in which the participants slip seamlessly into various roles and different functions many times throughout a session. This can be the best part of what supervision has to offer, or it can present a number of problems in which the supervisee feels manipulated. The main issues are related to trust in the relationship, as well as the ways that power and authority are managed (Kaiser, 1992). Many ethical conflicts can be prevented if the supervisor is clear about expectations and deals with issues related to inequitable power in the relationship.

Training and Instruction

There are few established approaches for training and instruction in counselor supervision, and yet training and instructional activities are two of the more common supervisory procedures.

Developmental models (Blocher, 1983; Borders, 1989; Grater, 1985; Heppner & Roehlke, 1984; Hess, 1986; Meredith & Bradley, 1989; Sansbury, 1982; Stoltenberg, 1981; Stoltenberg & Delworth, 1987; Stoltenberg, McNeill, & Crethar, 1994; Stoltenberg, McNeill, & Delworth, 1998; Skovholt & Ronnestad, 1992; Wiley & Ray, 1986; Williams, 1994) suggest that training and instruction should vary according to the developmental level of the counselor. For example, inexperienced counselors prefer that the supervisor give them specific information about how to do counseling. Beginning counselors prefer teaching approaches that emphasize direct (structured) instruction such as didactic presentations, direct observations of the supervisor demonstrating effective counseling, and written materials describing counseling interventions (Borders & Leddick, 1987; Leddick & Dye, 1987).

In contrast, more experienced counselors want less emphasis on the mechanics and tasks of supervision and more emphasis on sharing ideas and thoughts (Bernard & Goodyear, 1998; Borders & Leddick, 1987; Ward & House, 1998; E. L. Worthington, 1984; W. Worthington & Stem, 1985). As counselors gain experience and confidence in their counseling skills, their behavior becomes more autonomous, and they take more responsibility for and direct involvement in the supervisory process. They begin to view the supervisor as a consultant or collaborator for a specific case or problem and soon realize the supervisor also learns from the supervisory experience. Additionally, experienced counselors prefer discussions of theoretical issues, more responsibility for case conceptualization, and collaborative supervisory sessions than do inexperienced counselors (Bernard & Goodyear, 1998; Borders & Leddick, 1987; Hanna & Smith, 1998; Leddick & Dye, 1987; Stoltenberg, McNeill, & Crethar, 1994).

While researchers (Bradley & Richardson, 1987; Holloway & Neufeldt, 1995; Robyak, Goodyear, Prange, & Donham, 1986) have reported that supervision techniques differ, some interventions emerge more frequently than others. For example, in teaching basic helping skills, support has been reported for microtraining (Baker, Scofield, Munson, & Clayton, 1983; Forsyth & Ivey, 1980; Greenwald & Young, 1998; Ivey, 1987; Richardson & Bradley, 1984), modeling and reinforcement (Akamatsu, 1980; Froehle, Robinson, & Kurpius, 1983; Knoff, 1988; Martin & McBride, 1987), role playing and simulation (Gladstein & Feldstein, 1983; Holloway & Neufeldt, 1995; Scott, Cormier, & Cormier, 1980), video- and audiotaping (Bernard & Goodyear, 1998; Kagan, Krathwohl, & Miller, 1963; Smith, 1984; Stewart & Johnson, 1986), direct observation (Bernard, 1981; Constantine, 1984; Myrick & Sabella, 1995; Walker, 1985; West, 1984), and case conceptualization (Greenwald & Young, 1998; Hulse & Jennings, 1984; Kaiser, 1992; Loganbill & Stoltenburg, 1983; Seem & Johnson, 1998; Stoltenburg & Delworth, 1987). In addition to learning basic techniques, counselors value support, encouragement, and understanding (Bordin, 1983; Jacobs, 1991; E. L. Worthington, 1984; Young & Borders, 1998) as well as honest, constructive feedback (Allen, Szollos, & Williams, 1986; Bernard & Goodyear, 1998) from their supervisors describing counseling interventions (Borders & Leddick, 1987; Leddick & Dye, 1987) that are multiculturally sensitive (Haber, 1996; Hoffman, 1996; Leach, Stoltenberg, McNeill, & Eichenfield, 1997; Nelson, 1997; O'Bryne & Rosenberg, 1998; Seem & Johnson, 1998).

A rationale for effective use of training and instructional activities in the context of supervision should begin with the setting of objectives for these activities within the total framework of supervisory consultation. Strategies would then be selected or constructed to reach the objectives, and they would be of two types:

1. self-managed learning programs, and
2. programs involving the supervisor as an active trainer.

In a self-managed training program the supervisor remains in a consultative stance and assists the counselor (supervisee) in progressing through the program, whereas strategies of active instruction and training put the supervisor outside the consultation activity. The differentiating criterion between the consultative stance and that of active trainer is counselor input. A shared responsibility for learning, with maximal input from the counselor, characterizes consultation. Conversely, the supervisor, when functioning as an active trainer, carries most of the responsibility, with the flow of information and direction being principally from supervisor to counselor, and with counselor input at a minimum.

When engaged in consultation, the supervisor can digress to engage temporarily in active training and then return to consultation, just as was done with the counseling activity. One can also feasibly be engaged in the consulting activity with a number of individual counselors (supervisees) while concurrently conducting an in-service training program for the group. Determining when and how to use instruction and training versus consultation is a matter of professional judgment. As an alternative to choosing one or the other, the supervisor can alter the character of an instructional program and incorporate some of the advantages of consultation. Counselors' input can be solicited by letting them select instructional goals, by including counselors as peer trainers, and by using counselors' own tapes and cases as instructional material.

More recently, the internet has been employed as another means by which to monitor ongoing development, as well as to answer questions that emerge between scheduled supervision sessions (Myrick & Sabella, 1995). This should not be used as a substitute for face-to-face supervisory interactions, but rather as an adjunct to deepen the relationship and provide more frequent contact and rapid responses to immediate concerns.

Evaluation

Evaluative functions in supervision represent the very best and worst of the experience for participants. First, evaluation allows the counselor to receive direct, honest, and constructive feedback about behaviors that are most effective and ineffective. It may be one of the few places in which it is possible to hear the "truth" about how one comes across to others. Counselors receive specific input about their nonverbal and verbal actions, examining their impact on others. They hear an expert's assessment of their functioning levels in relation to desired goals. In addition, such evaluation is unfortunately necessary to protect the public from trainees who might be unscrupulous or dangerous.

If such evaluative functions are useful to help the counselor, as well as to protect consumers, many participants also report their greatest levels of stress and confusion related to the dual characteristics of supervision as both benevolent and critical. How are counselors supposed to trust the supervisor with their vulnerabilities, weaknesses, and most troubled areas if these disclosures may be used against them at some future time? Is this conflict of roles not a setup for possible betrayal of trust? This is certainly the case when these often conflicting functions are not discussed openly.

Evaluation is clearly essential for accountable supervision and for accountable counseling in both administrative (Beck & Hillmar, 1986; Bernard & Goodyear, 1998; Copeland, 1998; Falvey, 1987; Gilbert, 1982; J. A. Lewis, Lewis, & Souflee, 1991) and clinical supervision (G. Hart, 1982; Holloway, 1984; Knoff, 1988; Stoltenburg, Solomon, & Ogden, 1986; Stoltenberg &

Delworth, 1987; Tyler & Weaver, 1981). Potential roadblocks in the path of evaluation include lack of skills in performing evaluation (Carney, Cobia & Shannon, 1996; Falvey, 1987; Goodyear & Bradley, 1983; J. L. Lewis, Lewis, & Souflee, 1991; Wiles & Bondi, 1997), confusion about the compatibility of supervision and evaluation, and anxiety-evoking qualities attributed to evaluation (Tracey, Ellickson, & Sherry, 1989; Yager & Beck, 1985). The first two roadblocks mentioned are easier to overcome than the third. Skills can be acquired through training; a conceptualization of the appropriate relationship between supervisory consultation and evaluation can be clarified. But the debilitating fear associated with evaluation is the most pervasive roadblock. This fear has led to an anti-evaluation attitude among those who think that more learning and performance can take place if evaluation and its accompanying threat are removed from learning and performance situations. An oversight in anti-evaluation reasoning, however, is that evaluation itself need not be anxiety evoking. Rather, the real antecedents of fear are misperceptions about evaluation.

Evaluation was never intended to be a fearful activity, although in many cases it is difficult to escape such feelings when being judged whether one is "good enough" to remain in the field. To the contrary, evaluation was meant to be an eagerly sought activity that answers the basic accountability question that should be asked by every professional, "Am I accomplishing my objectives?" The challenge in supervision is to manage the evaluation so that it creates positive motivation rather than anxiety.

Several conditions prerequisite for low-threat evaluation are inherent in the consulting guidelines that were proposed previously. The foremost condition is that the goals for evaluation are known to both supervisor and counselor (supervisee), and the counselor has input into selection of these goals. This condition does more to relieve anxiety than any other. Another condition is that the counselor is aware of the evaluative procedures being conducted and performs some of them (self-evaluations). In a nutshell, evaluation in conjunction with consultation by the supervisor should be performed cooperatively whenever possible (Drapela, 1983; Harvey & Schramske, 1984; Tracey et al., 1989). Finally, the goal of evaluation should be perceived as documentation of success in obtaining objectives and the identification of areas for improvement. Evaluation should be proactive rather than being aimed at punishing counselors whose work is not matching objectives.

Whatever evaluative methods the supervisor employs, three things need to be evaluated: the work of each supervisee, helping service programs, and supervision itself. The scope of this task is beyond the capability of any one supervisor, a condition that provides another reason for sharing evaluation with counselors.

Evaluation of each counselor's progress toward objectives is completed most ethically in individual sessions; program evaluation is performed most efficiently by a division of labor among a counseling staff, and evaluation of supervision can be done by the supervisor with feedback from supervisees and superiors. In each of these areas, evaluation is incorporated into the general planning operation. The supervisor and counseling staff plan a program of services geared toward criterion-referenced objectives, and the supervisor prepares a planned program of supervisory activities. Evaluation thus permeates most of the supervisor's work.

☐ Summary

In spite of the differences in opinion among practitioners about the nature, roles, and functions of supervision, there are several broad activities that most supervisors would endorse: support, consultation, counseling, training and instruction, and evaluation.

Consultation includes establishment of the objectives and strategies of supervision and is the supervisor's predominant activity. Strategies for consultation may allow the supervisor to remain consistently in the consulting activity, or they may involve the activities of counseling and training and instruction, during which the supervisor digresses temporarily from the consultant stance. Evaluation is another major activity of supervision that is often a companion to consulting and training and instruction.

Counselor supervision has been presented as a professional specialty with a methodology requiring highly developed skills. Successful counseling experience is a necessary but insufficient prerequisite for supervision and should be supplemented with advanced preparation in supervisory methods.

The importance of supervision to the future of help-giving services should again be stressed. Counselor supervision is an indispensable component of counselor preparation programs. Coupled with the counselor's self-development process, counselor supervision is a key to accountable helping services and attainment of a counselor's professional potential.

Saying that counselor supervision can be one of the most instrumental factors affecting future development of the helping professions is not an exaggeration. Furthermore, counselor supervision can have a similarly facilitative effect on counselor-offered services in other disciplines.

☐ References

Abels, P., & Murphy, M. (1981). *Administration in human services. A normative systems approach.* Englewood Cliffs, NJ: Prentice-Hall.

Akamatsu, T. J. (1980). The use of role-play and simulation techniques in the training of psychotherapy. In A.K Hess (Ed.), *Psychotherapy supervision: Theory, research and practice* (pp. 209–225). New York: Wiley.

Allen, G., Szollos, S., & Williams, B. (1986). Doctoral students' comparative evaluations of best and worst psychotherapy supervision. *Professional Psychology: Research and Practice, 17,* 91–99.

Arnold, D. L. (1962). Counselor education as responsible self development. *Counselor Education and Supervision, 1,* 185–192.

Association for Counselor Education and Supervision, Committee on Counselor Effectiveness. (1969). *Commitment to action in supervision: Report of a national survey of counselor supervision.* Alexandria, VA: Author.

Association for Counselor Education and Supervision. (1993). *Ethical guidelines for clinical supervisors.* Alexandria, VA: Author.

Austin, M. (1981). *Supervisory management for the human services.* Englewood Cliffs, NJ: Prentice-Hall.

Baker, S., Scofield, M., Munson, W., & Clayton, L. (1983). Comparative effects of training basic counseling competencies through brief microskills practice versus mental practice. *Counselor Education and Supervision, 23,* 71–83.

Beck, A. C., & Hillmar, E. D. (1986). *Positive management practices.* San Francisco: Jossey-Bass.

Becker, H. S., & Carper, J. W. (1956). Development of identification with an occupation. *American Journal of Sociology, 41,* 289–298.

Benshoff, J. M., & Paisley, P. O. (1996). The structured peer consultation model for school counselors. *Journal of Counseling and Development, 74,* 314–318.

Bernard, J. M. (1979). Supervisory training: A discrimination model. *Counselor Education and Supervision, 19,* 60–68.

Bernard, J. M. (1981). In service training for clinical supervisors. *Professional Psychology, 12,* 740–748.

Bernard, J. M. (1987). Ethical and legal considerations for supervisors. In L. D. Borders and G. R. Leddick (Eds.), *Handbook of counseling supervision* (pp. 52–57). Washington, DC: Association for Counselor Education and Supervision.

Bernard, J. M. (1992). The challenge of psychotherapy-based supervision: Making the pieces fit. *Counselor Education and Supervision, 31,* 232–237.

Bernard, J. M. (1997). The discrimination model. In C. E. Watkins (Ed.), *Handbook of psychotherapy supervision* (pp. 310–327). New York: Wiley.

Bernard, J. M., & Goodyear, R. K. (1998). *Fundamentals of clinical supervision* (2nd ed.). Boston: Allyn & Bacon.

Black, J. (1975). *The basics of supervisory management. Mastering the art of effective supervision.* New York: McGraw-Hill.

Blocher, D. H. (1966). *Developmental counseling.* New York: Ronald Press.

Blocher, D. H. (1983). Toward a cognitive developmental approach to counseling supervision. *The Counseling Psychologist, 11,* 27–34.

Borders, L. D. (1989). A pragmatic agenda for developmental supervision research. *Counselor Education and Supervision, 29,* 16–24.

Borders, L. D. (1992). Learning to think like a supervisor. *Clinical Supervisor, 10,* 135–148.

Borders, L. D., Bernard, J. M., Dye, H. A., Fong, M. L., Henderson, P., & Nance, D. W. (1991). Curriculum guide for training counseling supervisors: Rationale, development, and implementation. *Counselor Education and Supervision, 31,* 58–82.

Borders, L. D., & Fong, M. L. (1994). Cognitions of supervisors-in-training: An exploratory study. *Counselor Education and Supervision, 29,* 71–83.

Borders, L., & Leddick, G. (1987). *Handbook of Counseling Supervision.* Alexandria. VA: Association for Counselor Education and Supervision.

Bordin, E. S. (1983). A working alliance-based model of supervision. *The Counseling Psychologists, 11,* 35–42.

Bradley, L. J. (1989). *Counselor supervision: Principles, process and practice.* Muncie, IN: Accelerated Development.

Bradley, L., & Richardson, B. (1987). Trends in practicum and internship requirements: A national study. *The Clinical Supervisor, 5,* 97–105.

Brown, D., Pryzwansky, W., & Schulte, A. (1987). *Psychological Consultation.* Boston: Allyn & Bacon.

Carney, J. S., Cobia, D. C., & Shannon, D. M. (1996). The use of portfolios in the clinical and comprehensive evaluation of counselors-in-training. *Counselor Education and Supervision, 36,* 122–133.

Carroll, M. (1996). *Counseling supervision: Theory, skills, and practice.* London: Cassell.

Constantine, S. (1984). Live supervision of supervision in family therapy. *Journal of Marital and Family Therapy, 10,* 95–97.

Copeland, S. (1998). Counseling supervision in organization contents: New challenges and perspectives. *British Journal of Guidance & Counseling, 26,* 377–386.

Corey, G., Corey, M., & Callanan. P. (1998). *Issues and ethics in the helping professions* (5th ed.). Pacific Grove, CA: Brooks/Cole.

Cormier, L., & Bernard, J. (1982). Ethical and legal responsibilities of clinical supervisors. *Personnel and Guidance Journal, 60,* 486–490.

Cross, D. G., & Brown, D. (1983). Counselor supervision as a function of trainee experience: Analysis of specific behaviors. *Counselor Education and Supervision, 22,* 333–341.

Dodge, J. (1982). Reducing supervisee anxiety: A cognitive-behavioral approach. *Counselor Education and Supervision, 22,* 55–60.

Drapela, V. (1983). Counseling consultation and supervision: A visual clarification of their relationship. *Personnel and Guidance Journal, 62,* 158–162.

Ekstein, R., & Wallerstein, R. S. (1972). *The teaching and learning of psychotherapy.* New York: Basic Books.

Ellis, M. V. (1991). Critical incidents in clinical supervision and in supervisor supervision: Assessing supervisory issues. *Journal of Counseling Psychology, 38,* 342–349.

Ellis, M. V., & Douce, L. A. (1994). Group supervision of novice clinical supervisors: Eight recurring issues. *Journal of Counseling and Development, 72,* 520–525.

Ellis, M. V., & Robbins, E. S. (1993). Voices of care and justice in clinical supervision: Issues and interventions. *Counselor Education and Supervision, 32,* 203–212.

Falvey, J. (1987). *Handbook of administrative supervision.* Alexandria, VA: Association for Counselor Education and Supervision.

Forsyth, D., & Ivey, A. (1980). Microtraining: An approach to differential supervision. In A. F. Hess (Ed.), *Psychotherapy supervision: Theory, research and practice* (pp. 242–261). New York: Wiley.

Froehle, T., Robinson, S., & Kurpius, D. (1983). Enhancing the effects of modeling through role-play practice. *Counselor Education and Supervision, 22,* 197–207.

Galhessich, J. (1982). *The profession and practice of consultation.* San Francisco: Jossey-Bass.

Gibson, R., & Mitchell, M. (1995). *Introduction to counseling and guidance* (3rd ed.). Englewood Cliffs, NJ: Merrill.

Gilbert, T. F. (1982). A question of performance-Part 1: The probe model. *Training and Developmental Journal, 36,* 20–30.

Gladstein, G., & Feldstein, J. C. (1983). Using film to increase counselor empathic experiences. *Counselor Education and Supervision, 23,* 125–132.

Glass, G. V. (1972). The many faces of educational accountability. *Phi Delta Kappan, 10,* 636–639.

Goodyear, R. K., & Bernard, J. M. (1998). Clinical supervision: Lessons from the literature. *Counselor Education and Supervision, 38,* 6–23.

Goodyear, R., & Bradley, F. (1983). Theories of counselor supervision: Points of convergence and divergence. *The Counseling Psychologist, 11,* 59–67.

Grater, H. A. (1985). Stages in psychotherapy supervision: From therapy skills to skilled therapist. *Professional Psychology, 16,* 605–610.

Greenwald, M., & Young, J. (1998). Schema focused therapy: An integrative approach to psychotherapy supervision. *Journal of Cognitive Therapy: An International Quarterly, 12,* 109–126.

Haber, R. (1996). *Dimensions of psychotherapy supervision: Maps and means.* New York: W.W. Norton.

Hanna, M. A., & Smith, J. (1998). Using rubrics for documentation of clinical work supervision. *Counselor Education and Supervision, 37,* 269–279.

Hansen, J., Stevic, R., & Warner, R. (1986). *Counseling theory and process* (2nd ed.). Boston: Allyn & Bacon.

Hart, D. H., & Prince, D. J. (1970). Role conflict for school counselors: Training versus job demands. *Personnel and Guidance Journal, 48,* 374–380.

Hart, G. (1982). *The process of clinical supervision.* Baltimore, MD: University Park Press.

Harvey, D., & Schramske, T. (1984). Effective supervision and consultation; A model for the development of functional supervision and consultation programs. *Counselor Education and Supervision, 23,* 197–204.

Heppner, P., & Roehlke, H. (1984). Differences among supervisees at different levels of training: Implications for a developmental model of supervision. *Journal of Counseling Psychology, 31,* 76–90.

Hess, A. K. (1986). Growth in supervision: Stages of supervisee and supervisor development. *Clinical Supervisor, 4,* 51–67.

Hoffman, R. M. (1996). Gender: Issues of power and equity in counselor education programs. *Counselor Education and Supervision, 36,* 104–113.

Holahan, W., & Galassi, J. P. (1986). Toward accountability in supervision: A single case illustration. *Counselor Education and Supervision, 25,* 166–173.

Holloway, E. (1984). Outcome evaluation in supervision research. *The Counseling Psychologist, 12,* 167–174.

Holloway, E. L., & Neufeldt, S. A. (1995). Supervision: Its contributions to treatment efficacy. *Journal of Consulting & Clinical Psychology, 63,* 207–213.

Hulse, D., & Jennings, M. L. (1984). Toward comprehensive case conceptualizations in counseling: A visual integrative technique. *Professional Psychology, 15,* 251–259.

Ivey, A. E. (1987). *Counseling and psychotherapy: Integrating skills, theories and practice* (2nd ed.). Englewood Cliffs, NJ: Prentice-Hall.

Jacobs, C. (1991). *Violations of the supervisory relationship. An ethical and educational blind spot.* Washington, DC: National Association of Social Workers.

Kadushin, A. (1992). *Supervision in social work* (3rd ed.). New York: Columbia University Press.

Kagan, N., Krathwohl, D., & Miller, R (1963). Simulated recall in therapy using videotape: A case study. *Journal of Counseling Psychology, 10,* 237–43.

Kaiser, T. L. (1992). The supervisory relationship: An identification of the primary elements in the relationship and an application of two theories of ethical relationships. *Journal of Marital and Family Therapy, 18,* 283–296.

Kell, B. L., & Burow, J. M. (1970). *Developmental counseling and therapy.* Boston, MA: Houghton Mifflin.

Knoff, H. M. (1988). Clinical supervision, consultation, and counseling: A comparative analysis for supervisors and other educational leaders. *Journal of Curriculum and Supervision, 3,* 240–252.

Koerin, B., & Miller, J. (1995). Gate-keeping policies: Terminating students for nonacademic reasons. *Journal of Social Work Education, 31,* 247–260.

Kottler, J. A. (1999). *The therapist's workbook: Self-assessment, self-care, and self-improvement exercises for mental health professionals.* San Francisco: Jossey-Bass.

Kottler, J. A., & Blau, D. (1989). *The imperfect therapist: Learning from failures in therapeutic practice.* San Francisco: Jossey-Bass.

Kottler, J. A., & Hazler, R. (1997). *What you never learned in graduate school.* New York: W. W. Norton.

Leach, M. M., Stoltenberg, C. D., McNeill, B. W., & Eichenfield, G. A. (1997). Self-efficacy and counselor development: Testing the integrated developmental model. *Counselor Education and Supervision, 37,* 115–125.

Leddick, G., & Dye, H. A. (1987). Effective supervision as portrayed by trainee expectations and preferences. *Counselor Education and Supervision, 27,* 139–155.

Lewis, G. J., Greenburg, S. L., & Hatch, D. B. (1988). Peer consultation groups for psychologists in private practice: A national survey. *Professional Psychology: Research and Practice, 9,* 81–86.

Lewis, J. A., Lewis, M. D., & Souflee, F. (1991). *Management of human service programs* (2nd ed.). Pacific Grove, CA: Brooks/Cole.

Lewis, W. (1988). A supervision model for public agencies. *Clinical Supervisor, 6,* 85–91.

Loganbill, C., & Stoltenberg, C. (1983). The case conceptualization format: A training device for practicum. *Counselor Education and Supervision, 22,* 235–241.

Lombardo, L. T., Greer, J., Estadt, B., & Cheston, S. (1997). Empowerment behaviors in clinical training: An empirical study of parallel processes. *The Clinical Supervisor, 16,* 33–47.

Martin, G. E., & McBride, M. (1987). The results of the implementation of a professional supervision model on counselor trainee behavior. *Counselor Education and Supervision, 27,* 155–167.

Masters, M. A. (1992). The use of positive reframing in the context of supervision. *Journal of Counseling and Development, 70,* 387–390.

Meredith, R., & Bradley, L. J. (1989). Differential supervison. In L. J. Bradley (Ed.), *Counselor supervision: Principles, process and practice* (pp. 301–375). Muncie, IN: Accelerated Development.

Mueller, W. J., & Kell, B. L. (1972). *Coping with conflict: Supervising counselors and psychotherapists.* New York: Appleton-Century-Crofts.

Myrick, R. D., & Sabella, R. A. (1995). Cyberspace: New place for counselor supervision. *Elementary School Guidance and Counseling, 30,* 35–44.

Nelson, M. L. (1997). An interactional model for empowering women in supervision. *Counselor Education and Supervision, 37,* 125–139.

Neufeldt, S. A. (1999). *Supervision strategies for the first practicum* (2nd ed.). Alexandria, VA: American Counseling Association.

O'Bryne, K. O., & Rosenberg, J. I. (1998). The practice of supervision: A sociocultural perspective. *Counselor Education and Supervision, 38,* 43–52.

Olk, M., & Friedlander, M. L. (1992). Trainees' experiences of role conflict and role ambiguity in supervisory relationships. *Journal of Counseling Psychology, 39,* 389–397.

Ottens, A. J., Shank, G. D., & Long, R. J. (1995). The role of abductive logic in understanding and using advanced empathy. *Counselor Education and Supervision, 34,* 199–211.

Patterson, C. H. (1983). A client-centered approach to supervision. *The Counseling Psychologist, 11,* 21–25.

Powell, D. J. (1993). *Clinical supervision in alcohol and drug abuse counseling: Principles, models and methods.* New York: Lexington Books.

Riccio, A. C. (1961). The counselor educator and the guidance supervisor: Graduate training and occupational mobility. *Counselor Education and Supervision, 1,* 10–17.

Riccio, A. C. (1966). Counselor educators and guidance supervisors: A second look at graduate training. *Counselor Education and Supervision, 5,* 73–79.

Richardson, B. K., & Bradley, L. J. (1984). Microsupervision: A skill development model for training clinical supervisors. *The Clinical Supervisor, 2,* 43–54.

Richardson, B. K., & Bradley, L. J. (1986). *Community agency counseling: An emerging specialty within counselor preparation programs.* Washington, DC: American Association for Counseling and Development.

Richman, J. M., Aitken, D., & Prather, D. L. (1990). In-therapy consultation: A supervisory and therapeutic experience from practice. *Clinical Supervision, 8,* 81–89.

Robyak, J., Goodyear, R., Prange, M., & Donham, G. (1986). Effects of gender, supervision, and presenting problems on practicum students' preference for interpersonal power bases. *Journal of Counseling Psychology, 33,* 159–163.

Sansbury, D. (1982). Developmental supervision from a skills perspective. *The Counseling Psychologist, 10,* 53–57.

Schneider, S. (1992). Transference, counter-transference, projective identification and role responsiveness in the supervisory process. *Clinical Supervisor, 10,* 71–84.

Scott, A. J, Cormier. W. O., & Cormier, L. S. (1980). Effects of covert modeling and written material on the acquisition of a counseling strategy. *Counselor Education and Supervision, 19,* 259–269.

Seem, S. R., & Johnson, J. (1998). Gender bias among counseling trainees: A study of case conceptualization. *Counselor Education and Supervision, 37,* 257–269.

Sexton, T. L. (1998). Reconstructing counselor education: Supervision, teaching, and clinical training revisited. *Counselor Education and Supervision, 38,* 2–5.

Shertzer, B., & Stone, S. (1980). *Fundamentals of counseling* (3rd ed.). Boston, MA: Houghton Mifflin.

Skovholt, T. M., & Ronnestad, M. H. (1992). *The evolving professional self: Stages and themes in therapist and counselor development.* Chichester, England: Wiley.

Simon, S. (Ed.). (1985). *Managing finances, personnel, and information in human services.* New York: Haworth Press.

Slavin, S. (Ed.). (1985). *Social administration: The management of the social services.* New York: Haworth Press.

Smith, H. D. (1984). Moment to moment counseling process feedback using a dual channel audiotape recording. *Counselor Education and Supervision, 23,* 346–349.

Sprinthall, N. A. (1971). *Guidance for Human Growth.* New York: Van Nostrand Reinhold.

Steffire, B. (1964). What price professionalism? *Personnel and Guidance Journal, 42,* 654–659.

Stein, D. M., & Lambert, M. J. (1995). Graduate training in psychotherapy: Are therapy outcomes enhanced. *Journal of Consulting and Clinical Psychology, 63,* 182–196.

Stenack. R. J., & Dye, H. A. (1982). Behavioral descriptions of counselor supervision roles. *Counselor Education and Supervision, 21,* 295–304.

Stewart, R. M., & Johnson, J. C. (1986). Written versus videotaped precounseling training of clients for counseling. *Counselor Education and Supervision, 25,* 197–210.

Stoltenberg, C. (1981). Approaching supervision from a developmental perspective: The counselor-complexity model. *Journal of Counseling Psychology, 28,* 59–65.

Stoltenberg, C., Solomon, G., & Ogden, L. (1986). Comparing supervisee and supervisor initial perceptions of supervision: Do they agree? *The Clinical Supervisor, 4,* 53–61.

Stoltenberg, C., & Delworth, U. (1987). *Supervising counselors and therapists. A developmental approach.* San Francisco: Jossey-Bass.

Stoltenberg, C. D., McNeill, B. W., & Crethar, H. C. (1994). Changes in supervision as counselors and therapists gain experience: A review. *Professional Psychology: Research and Practice, 25,* 416–449.

Stoltenberg, C. D., McNeill, B. W., & Delworth, U. (1998). *IDM supervision: An integrated developmental model for supervising counselors and therapists.* San Francisco: Jossey-Bass.

Tarvydas, V. (1995). Ethics and the practice of rehabilitation counselor. *Rehabilitation Counseling Bulletin, 38,* 294–306.

Temple, S., & Bowers, W. A. (1998). Supervising cognitive therapists from a diverse field. *Journal of Cognitive Psychotherapy, 12,* 139–151.

Thomas, F. N. (1994). Solution-oriented supervision: The coaxing of expertise. *The Family Journal: Counseling and Therapy for Couples and Families, 2,* 11–18.

Tracey, J. T., Ellickson, J. L., & Sherry, P. (1989). Reactance in relation to different supervisory environments and counselor development. *Journal of Counseling Psychology, 36,* 336–344.

Turner, A. N. (1982). Consulting is more than giving advice. *Harvard Business Review, 60,* 120–129.

Tyler, J., & Weaver, S. (1981). Evaluating the clinical supervisee: A survey of practices in graduate training programs. *Professional Psychology, 12,* 434–437.

Upchurch, D. W. (1985). Ethical standards and the supervisory process. *Counselor Education and Supervision, 75,* 90–98.

Walker, J. H. (1985). Group facilitation supervision through a one-way mirror. *Journal of Counseling and Development, 63,* 578–580.

Ward, C. C., & House, R. M. (1998). Counseling supervision: A reflective model. *Counselor Education and Supervision, 38,* 23–34.

Watkins, C. E., Jr. (Ed.). (1997). *Handbook of psychotherapy supervision.* New York: Wiley.

West, J. D. (1984). Utilizing simulated families and live supervision to demonstrate skill development of family therapists. *Counselor Education and Supervision, 24,* 17–27.

Wiles, J., & Bondi, J. (1997). *Supervision: A guide to practice.* Columbus, OH: Merrill.

Wiley, M., & Ray, P. (1986). Counseling supervision by developmental level. *Journal of Counseling Psychology, 33,* 439–445.

Williams, L. (1994). A tool for training supervisors: Using the supervision feedback form (SFF). *Journal of Marital and Family Therapy, 20,* 311–315.

Worthington, E. L., Jr. (1984). Empirical investigation of supervision of counselors as they gain experience. *Journal of Counseling Psychology, 31,* 63–75.

Worthington, W., & Stem, A. (1985). Effects of supervisor and supervisee level and gender on the supervisory relationship. *Journal of Counseling Psychology, 32,* 252–262.

Yager, G., & Beck, T. D. (1985). Beginning practicum: It only hurt until I laughed! *Counselor Education and Supervision, 25,* 149–157.

Young, S. C., & Borders, L. D. (1998). The impact of metaphor on clinical hypothesis, formation and perceived supervisor characteristics. *Counselor Education and Supervision, 37,* 238–257.

Zerface, J. P., & Cox, W. H. (1971). School counselors, leave home. *Personnel and Guidance Journal, 49,* 371–375.

Janet L. Muse-Burke
Nicholas Ladany
Mary D. Deck

The Supervisory Relationship

Tell me and I will forget. Show me and I will remember. Involve me and I will understand.

—Confucius

At the core, supervision takes place within the context of the supervisory relationship (Holloway, 1997; Watkins, 1997). The interpersonal process between the supervisor and supervisee is the predominant means by which the supervisee becomes involved in supervision and the goals of supervision are achieved (Holloway, 1997). Additionally, the supervisor–supervisee relationship is an essential element to the formation and completion of the process of supervision and mediates what occurs within supervision (Watkins, 1997). In fact, R. Cohen and DeBetz (1977) maintained that the effectiveness of supervision principally relies on the quality of the supervisory relationship. As Hunt (1986) stated, "[i]t seems that whatever approach or method is used, in the end it is the quality of the relationship between supervisor and trainee therapist that determines whether supervision is effective or not" (p. 20). Further, research has demonstrated that the relationship between supervisor and supervisee is a key factor in the professional development of supervisees (Rønnestad & Skovholt, 1993).

The purpose of this chapter is to explore and discuss the supervisory relationship. First, Bordin's (1983) concept of the supervisor working alliance will be offered as a definition of the supervisory relationship. In addition, Holloway's (1997) notions of power and involvement will be provided as meaningful additions to Bordin's definition. Second, the stages of the supervisory relationship (Holloway, 1995), which include the beginning, mature, and terminating phases, will be presented. Third, we will discuss the manner in which strong supervisory relationships are formed. In particular, conditions of effective supervisory relationships will be noted. Fourth, the factors that influence the supervisory relationship, both positively and negatively, will be described. Such factors include the triadic system, supervisee characteristics, supervisor characteristics, and supervisee–supervisor relationship interactions. Finally, we will consider how the supervisory relationship influences supervision process and outcome. This section will include the literature on the games played in supervision, disclosure and nondisclosure, role conflict and ambiguity, and sexual issues.

☐ The Supervisory Relationship Defined

Although the importance of the supervisory relationship to the process of supervision has been well documented in the literature, it appears that a concise definition has not been devised (Watkins, 1997). Various authors (e.g., Bernard & Goodyear, 1998) have defined the supervisory relationship broadly so as to include virtually all interactions between a supervisor and supervisee. We have chosen to use Bordin's (1983) definition of the working alliance, a conception of the supervisory relationship that has been noted in the literature (e.g., Ladany & Friedlander, 1995). Numerous theorists and researchers have affirmed that one must appreciate the role of the supervisor working alliance in order to completely comprehend the process of supervision (Bordin, 1983; Ladany, Brittan-Powell, & Pannu, 1997; Ladany & Friedlander, 1995). The *supervisory working alliance* is defined as a collaboration for change that involves three aspects: (a) mutual agreement and understanding between the supervisor and supervisee of the goals of supervision; (b) mutual agreement and understanding of the tasks of the supervisor and supervisee; and (c) the emotional bond between the supervisor and supervisee (Bordin, 1983).

First, Bordin (1983) outlined what he believed to be the core goals of the supervisory relationship. The goals of supervision for the trainee include: (a) mastering specific skills; (b) enlarging one's understanding of clients; (c) expanding one's awareness of process issues; (d) increasing awareness of one's self and one's impact on the process; (e) overcoming personal and intellectual obstacles toward learning and mastery; (f) deepening one's understanding of concepts and theory; (g) providing a stimulus to research; and (h) maintaining the standards of service. An example of a goal may be the supervisory dyad mutually agreeing to work to improve the trainee's ability to sit in silence with clients. Bordin (1983) suggested that these goals will be emphasized to different degrees depending on the developmental level of the supervisee. Therefore, the neophyte supervisee may be inclined to focus on mastering specific skills of counseling to reduce the confusion and complexity created by a specific client's situation.

Second, the strength of the working alliance depends on the extent to which the supervisor and supervisee comprehend the tasks each of them must fulfill. Further, the more the supervisee understands the connection between the goals and the tasks, the stronger the working alliance. The supervisee must also understand the goodness of fit between the demands of the tasks and her or his ability to complete the task. With regard to the previous example, the trainee and supervisor may agree that reviewing session tapes with specific attention to times at which the trainee did or did not use silence appropriately is a useful task toward achieving their goal. An additional task may be to explore the supervisee's thoughts and feelings regarding silence. Bordin (1983) presented several tasks that may be usefully employed in supervision. One task is for the trainee to prepare an oral or written report of the counseling hours being reviewed. The supervisor can then provide feedback regarding alternative responses to expand the trainee's repertoire. Another task is for the supervisor to participate in objective observation of the therapeutic hour through audio- or videotaped recordings or direct observation. In so doing, the supervisor will not be subject to the selectivity of the trainee. A third task is for the supervisor to allow the trainee to identify the particular questions he or she has and direct the focus of the supervision session. One way this task can be achieved is through asking the trainee at the onset of the supervision session, "What would you like to work on today?"

Third, the emotional bond will arise from carrying out the common process of supervision and spending time together. The emotional bond is described as the feelings of liking, caring, and trusting that the supervisor and supervisee share. Sharing the experience of supervision will strengthen the bond between the supervisor and supervisee, as will mutually agreeing on the goals and tasks of supervision. In his conception of the working alliance, Bordin (1983) alluded to the bonding problem created between the supervisor and supervisee as a result of the evaluative function of supervision. Holloway (1997) extended this discussion and accentuated the importance of power and involvement in defining the supervisory relationship.

According to Holloway (1997), "[s]upervision is a formal relationship in which the supervisor's task includes imparting expert knowledge, making judgments of trainees' performance, and acting as a gatekeeper to the profession" (p. 251). Thus, as expert and evaluator, the supervisor maintains the power in this hierarchical relationship. Although the supervisor holds the formal power in the relationship with the supervisee, he or she does not exercise that power autonomously. The continuous interactions between the supervisor and supervisee and the processes within the relationship permit shared power (Holloway, 1997). The power asserted by the supervisor may also be moderated by the trainee's perceptions of the supervisor's competence, the trainee's peer and senior level support system, and the trainee's age and experience base (Skovholt & Rønnestad, 1992). Additionally, involvement between the supervisor and supervisee influences the exercise and effect of power in the relationship (Holloway, 1997). Involvement is described by Miller and Rogers (1987; as cited in Holloway, 1997) as an intimacy that includes "attachments" (i.e., the degree to which each person in the dyad uses the other for self-confirmation). For example, a supervisor may have considerable power in a relationship with a trainee who has great admiration for the skill level of the supervisor, few peer supports, and limited counseling experience. On the other hand, the power differential will likely be less problematic if both members of the supervisory dyad are equally involved in the relationship. Therefore, both the supervisor and supervisee determine the distribution of power and the degree of involvement in the relationship (Morton, Alexander, & Altman, 1976, as cited in Holloway, 1997).

☐ Phases of the Supervisory Relationship

In her discussion of the systems approach to supervision, Holloway (1995) presented a model of the phases through which the supervisory relationship develops. The three phases of the supervisory relationship are the beginning phase, the mature phase, and the terminating phase. In the beginning stage, the supervisor and supervisee clarify their individual roles and obligations within the relationship. Because they are unfamiliar with each other, the supervisor and supervisee rely on "noninterpersonal" aspects, such as social, cultural, and formal cues, to negotiate the relationship (Holloway, 1995). Further, the supervision contract, which includes a discussion of the evaluative structure of the relationship, the criteria for evaluation, the expectancies and goals of supervision, and the limits of confidentiality, is established (Ekstein & Wallerstein, 1972; Holloway, 1995; Shohet & Wilmot, 1991). The supervisor provides considerable support to the supervisee during this stage, as teaching interventions are implemented and the trainee focuses on developing competencies and treatment plans (Holloway, 1995).

During the mature phase of the supervisory relationship, the nature of the relationship between the supervisor and supervisee becomes more individualized and less role bound. This more developed interpersonal relationship begins to operate according to certain relational rules that were created for that specific, individual relationship. There is an increasing bond between the two in the relationship and there is greater potential for the supervisor to influence the supervisee and vice versa. For instance, the two may determine that it is appropriate and meaningful for the trainee to discuss her or his family of origin in the context of supervision. Moreover, the feelings of trust and sensitivity induced by these discussions may help to strengthen the emotional bond between them. The focus of trainee work in supervision includes expanding case conceptualization skills, improving self-confidence and self-efficacy in counseling, and challenging personal issues as they pertain to professional performance (Holloway, 1995). Providing more of an educational focus, Ekstein and Wallerstein (1972) named this stage of the relationship the "learning phase." They suggested that during this phase the supervisory relationship is used by the trainee to develop increased professional skill, therapeutic sensitivity, and competence.

The terminating phase of the relationship is characterized by the supervisee gaining an increased understanding of the association between counseling theory and practice (Holloway, 1995). Therefore, counseling theory is appropriately applied to work with the trainee's clients. Further, the trainee demonstrates a decreasing need for direction and support from the supervisor. According to Hoffman (1994), the goals of supervision and the progress made should be reviewed during the termination stage of supervision. An examination of the initial expectations of the supervisory relationship held by both the trainee and supervisor and a discussion of the extent to which these expectations were met is also warranted (Hoffman, 1994). Further, it is common that termination of the supervisory relationship corresponds with termination of the trainee's relationships with clients (Bernard & Goodyear, 1998). Moreover, evaluation of both the supervisee and the supervisor typically occurs at the end of the supervisory relationship (Bernard & Goodyear, 1998; Ekstein & Wallerstein, 1972). As such, the termination of the supervisor–supervisee relationship will be made more complex and require special attention.

☐ Formation of Strong Supervisory Relationships

A strong supervisory relationship based on trust and respect is vital to the supervisee's exploration of personal and professional issues that affect supervision and work with clients (Neufeldt, Karno, & Nelson, 1996; Worthen & McNeill, 1996). Additionally, a strong emotional bond with the supervisor leads trainees to judge their own behavior in supervision more positively, to feel more comfortable in supervision, and to perceive their supervisor's personal qualities and performance more positively (Ladany, Ellis, & Friedlander, 1999). Therefore, a key task for supervisors is to create an interpersonal environment in which the trainee feels encouraged to engage in professional self-reflection and to progress through the phases of capable professional functioning (Neufeldt, 1999; Neufeldt, Iverson, & Juntunen, 1995).

Similar to the conditions required to develop a strong relationship between counselor and client, the supervision literature suggests that several elements are necessary to establish an effective supervisory relationship. These conditions include empathic understanding, genuineness, respect, and concreteness (e.g., Blocher, 1983; Carifio & Hess, 1987; Hess, 1986; Ladany & Friedlander, 1995; Moses & Hardin, 1978; Worthen & McNeill, 1996). Moreover, positive supervisory relationships are likely to occur when supervisors offer support, encourage the exploration of behaviors, attitudes and feelings, convey acceptance, and openly discuss and work toward the resolution of conflict. In positive relationships, supervisees' mistakes are not regarded as failures; rather, the supervisor creates an atmosphere of experimentation that allows for trainee risk taking and error (Hutt, Scott, & King, 1983, Worthen & McNeill, 1996). According to Porter (1979 as cited in Gardner, 1980), supervisors also need to use their emotional reactions to supervisees to help the supervisees notice problems in counseling and create an effective supervisory relationship. For instance, a supervisor may experience a supervisee's use of humor as sarcasm, which creates distance within the relationship. The supervisor may note these feelings to the supervisee and add that clients may also sense he or she is being sarcastic and create distance within the relationship. Additionally, Mearns (1991) argued that the supervisor must make a commitment to the supervisee in order to maintain a healthy supervisory relationship. In making a commitment, an understanding is relayed to the trainee that the supervisor is fully involved in the supervisory relationship.

Establishment of these factors provides a foundation of support for confronting the conflict inherent in supervision (Marshall & Confer, 1980). According to Mueller and Kell (1972), if conflict is to be addressed in an active and optimistic manner, the relationship must be characterized by trust, openness, warmth, collaboration, and support. Both the supervisor and the trainee need to be willing to address and work through conflicts and misunderstandings to maintain the health of the supervisory relationship (Mearns, 1991).

Moses and Hardin (1978) categorized and described the aforementioned conditions, as well as others that are necessary to establish an effective supervisory relationship. The two types of conditions are facilitative (i.e., conditions that help ground the relationship in mutual respect and trust) and action oriented (i.e., conditions that aid the supervisee in understanding counseling and acting on this understanding). Facilitative conditions include empathy, respect, and concreteness, whereas action-oriented conditions contain genuineness, confrontation, and immediacy. It is suggested that fulfillment of these conditions will help ensure a strong supervisory relationship and positive supervision experiences (Moses & Hardin, 1978). Although these facilitative and action-oriented conditions are most commonly associated with counseling relationships, they are also applicable to the development of an effective supervisory relationship.

Facilitative Conditions

A supervisor's empathic understanding of the supervisee parallels what Rogers (1957) named the "as if" experience; that is, *empathy* is understanding the supervisee's world "as if" it were the supervisor's without losing the "as if" quality (Moses & Hardin, 1978). The supervisor communicates empathy and understanding to the supervisee through the verbal acknowledgment of the difficult struggles and painful self-reflection in which the supervisee engages to grow and learn (Blocher, 1983). Additionally, Rogers (as cited in Gendlin & Hendricks, 1978) suggested that empathy can be relayed by listening, stating back what was said, and relaying the personal meaning that is being conveyed. An example of demonstrating empathy is when the supervisor remarks to the supervisee how difficult and distressing it can be to reflect on one's current concerns and personal history when examining a countertransference reaction.

Respect conveys the supervisor's acceptance of the supervisee as a person and the belief that the supervisee can work through the anxieties, discomforts, and difficulties of gaining competence in counseling. According to Ivey, Ivey, and Simek-Morgan (1993), respect can be conveyed through individually and culturally appropriate eye contact and body language and by positively identifying strengths. Being aware of the supervisee's style of presentation, attending to the supervisee's life experiences and stage of professional development, and recognizing the care and concern the supervisee feels toward clients are additional ways in which the supervisor can communicate respect (Blocher, 1983). In communicating respect to the trainee, it is likely that the supervisor will strengthen the bond between them. For example, a supervisor can convey the respect he or she feels toward a supervisee by acknowledging strengths, including the supervisee's openness, willingness to be challenged, and commitment to working with clients and the supervisor.

Concreteness has been defined in the counseling literature as the role of the psychologist to clarify and comprehend the vague, ambiguous ideas and problems expressed by the client (Ivey et al., 1993). The use of concreteness during interviewing can enable the counselor to help the client focus on the core concerns and clearly articulate what is needed and wanted from counseling. This concept is also usefully applied to supervision. Concreteness within the supervisory realm refers to the supervisor's specific expression of thoughts, feelings, behaviors, and experiences relative to the supervisee's professional development. Being concrete provides clear, specific information that the supervisee can utilize to gain increased self-awareness, maintain effective behaviors and attitudes, and implement needed professional changes. Providing concrete, direct feedback requires that the supervisor also convey empathy and respect. A supervisor can provide concrete feedback by indicating the times during the counseling session at which the supervisee tended to avoid addressing emotions. Also, the supervisor can share that the supervisee's relaxed posture and steady voice tone seemed to help calm the client.

Expressing empathy, respect, and concreteness helps ground the supervisory relationship in mutual respect and trust. Moreover, these conditions provide the foundation for incorporating genuineness, confrontation, and immediacy into supervision. The action-oriented conditions (i.e., genuineness, confrontation, and immediacy) allow the supervisor to invite the supervisee to develop a deeper understanding of the counseling process and to behave more consistently with this understanding (Moses & Hardin, 1978).

Action-Oriented Conditions

In terms of the counselor–client relationship, to be genuine means that the counselor is freely and deeply herself or himself and experiences in such a way as to be an accurate representation of the self (Rogers, 1957). To be genuine, the practitioner must be true to herself or himself and accurately portray the self in the various moments of the session. Moreover, the counselor must be aware of her or his own feelings and how they may affect the counseling process (Rogers). Similarly, genuineness in supervision requires that the supervisor be herself or himself with the supervisee, model appropriate disclosure, and share the human side of being a counselor. However, it is important to note that genuineness does not mean spontaneously telling all or expressing potentially harmful comments to the supervisee (Moses & Hardin, 1978). In expressing genuine responses, the supervisor should be guided by an understanding of the supervisee and sincere concern for her or his growth. In an example of demonstrating genuineness, the supervisor may share how he or she successfully implemented guided imagery with a client to encourage the supervisee to take a risk and try the intervention in counseling. However, this sharing would not be appropriate if it is a hidden attempt to make a power play or intimidate the supervisee.

In counseling, confrontation is defined as the counselor making the client aware of the particular experiences or behaviors that are being analyzed (Prochaska & Norcross, 1999). Likewise, in supervision, confrontation includes the supervisor sharing perceptions of the supervisee's incongruent feelings, attitudes, or behaviors to assist the supervisee in gaining a deeper awareness as a professional. Confrontation should arise from the supervisor's desire to aid the supervisee in gaining self-understanding and assuming responsibility for change. On the other hand, confrontation is inappropriate when it satisfies the supervisor's need to punish, criticize, or gain power over the supervisee. Research indicates that confrontation of the supervisee's personal issues as they relate to client–counselor interactions do not seem to negatively influence the supervisory relationship as long as the confrontation is conducted in a warm, supportive, and instructional manner (Sumerel & Borders, 1996). An example of a timely confrontation may be a supervisor stopping a videotape at a point where the supervisee is engaging in flirtatious behavior. By viewing the concrete behavior in supervision (i.e., the flirtatious behavior), the supervisor is affording the supervisee the opportunity to consider how her or his behavior may be affecting the client and the therapeutic relationship. This type of confrontation takes advantage of a key teachable moment and allows the supervisee to self-monitor with the supervisor's guidance.

Immediacy concerns focusing on the here-and-now interactions between the supervisor and supervisee. A supervisee may experience difficulties in the client–counselor relationship and recreate similar dynamics when interacting with the supervisor. This "parallel process" (Hart, 1982) offers the astute supervisor an opportunity to employ immediacy to assist the supervisee in resolving difficulties with clients by working through the corresponding supervisory interactions. Immediacy can also be an appropriate focus when the supervisory relationship is stalled or at an impasse (Mueller & Kell, 1972). For example, a supervisee who doubts the supervisor's empathy and trustworthiness may express her or his doubts by questioning the supervisor about the value of empathy. The aware supervisor might hypothesize that this statement has implications for the supervisory relationship. Using immediacy, the supervisor may respond to the supervisee by openly asking whether the supervisee is experiencing doubts about the supervisor's understanding of the supervisee. Immediacy in the supervisory relationship can assist the supervisee in comprehending more fully the power of directly addressing interpersonal dynamics and can encourage the supervisee to use immediacy in the client–counselor relationship.

Role Induction

Bahrick, Russell, and Salmi (1991) concluded that the role induction of trainees helps create effective supervisory relationships and experiences. More specifically, the role-induction program used in their investigation was devised to provide trainees with a conceptual framework from which a comprehension of the roles, expectations, and goals of supervision could be derived. In particular, the procedure involved presenting supervisees with a tape-recorded description of the model of supervision developed by Bernard (1979). The main finding of this investigation suggested that role induction resulted in significant, positive changes in the manner in which supervisees viewed and used supervision. The supervisees stated they had a clearer understanding of supervision, perceived the supervisory relationship as more closely paralleling a counselor–client relationship, and believed the supervisor provided more structure. Preceding the role induction, supervisees reported uncertainty concerning role expectations, a decreased inclination to divulge concerns about counseling, and an increased tendency to evaluate the supervision experience, the supervisor, and themselves negatively. Thus, role induction appears to be another means by which the supervisory relationship can be enriched and more effectively utilized.

☐ Factors That Influence the Supervisory Relationship

Bernard and Goodyear (1998) argued that each person connected with the supervisory relationship (i.e., client, counselor, and supervisor) can affect the other and assert a primary influence on the quality, character, and direction of the alliance. Thus, for the purpose of this discussion, we will address the influence of the triadic system (i.e., client, counselor, and supervisor), supervisee characteristics, supervisor characteristics, and supervisee–supervisor relationship interactions on the supervisory relationship.

The Triadic System

Parallel Process

Parallel process is a significant means by which the supervisory relationship is influenced by the client, counselor, and supervisor. Parallel process is defined as "a phenomena whereby trainees unconsciously present themselves to their supervisors as their clients have presented to them. The process reverses when the trainee adopts attitudes and behaviors of the supervisor in relating to the client" (Friedlander, Siegel, & Brenock, 1989, p. 149). A case study investigation looking at the parallel process among a client, counselor trainee, and supervisor found that supervision and counseling are interconnected processes (Friedlander et al., 1989). First, their data demonstrated that the trainee's reported profile regarding the value of the supervisory sessions was similar to her evaluative profile of the counseling sessions. Additionally, while the client rated the counseling sessions more positively than did the counselor trainee, the counselor trainee viewed the supervision sessions slightly more favorably than did the supervisor. Also, the major pattern of self-presentation made in both the therapeutic and supervisory relationships was complementary. Thus, the supervisor primarily led while the trainee was cooperative, and the counselor trainee mainly led while the client was cooperative. Both relationships were also characterized as primarily friendly and supportive with little conflict, and both were deemed relatively successful in outcome.

In a qualitative investigation of supervisor countertransference, parallel process was found to be relevant (Ladany, Constantine, Miller, Erickson, & Muse-Burke, 2000). Parallel process was typically identified by supervisors in direct relation to their countertransference reactions. For example, one supervisor stated that while he experienced some positive and erotic feelings toward his intern, the intern also felt sexually attracted to one of her clients. In another instance, a supervisor lacked clarity with the intern in terms of how the intern should intercede with the client. Likewise, the intern was unclear in her interactions with the client. Although both of these studies add to the knowledge of parallel process, generalizability is limited due to the small sample sizes. Thus, additional research on this topic is needed.

By resolving the parallel process in supervision, it is anticipated that the pattern in the counseling relationship can also be ameliorated (Ellis & Douce, 1994). Therefore, the supervisor needs to respond to the trainee in supervision in a manner different than that which is prompted by the parallel process. Further, supervisors need to diligently look for and label instances in which parallel process is occurring, so that they may process the interpersonal dynamics with the trainee and help the trainee resolve the impasse in the counseling relationship (Ellis & Douce). Supervisees can also halt the parallel process if they notice and address an atypical thought, feeling, or behavior occurring in supervision (Shohet & Wilmot, 1991). However, for the parallel process to be resolved, there needs to be an open relationship in which discussion of the here-and-now of supervision and the interpersonal interactions between the trainee and supervisor is permitted (Shohet & Wilmot).

Supervisee Characteristics

Supervisee Anxiety

The anxiety experienced by supervisees can greatly affect the supervisory relationship. Supervisees typically experience considerable anxiety in supervision; this reaction appears warranted given the nature of the supervisory relationship. First, the supervisee is continuously being scrutinized and evaluated by both herself or himself and supervisor. Second, the supervisee has to attend to the work conducted in both counseling and supervision (Bernard & Goodyear, 1998). Anxiety is commonly experienced by supervisees who are beginning their practicum, internship, or employment or are moving to a different professional setting (e.g., Ekstein & Wallerstein, 1972; Skovholt & Rønnestad, 1992). Coming into a new professional environment is threatening to most supervisees; subsequently, anxiety is raised. For beginning trainees, anxiety is likely to be intense and pervasive (Rønnestad & Skovholt, 1993; Shohet & Wilmot, 1991). As trainees begin seeing clients, they are anxious about the gap between their theoretical knowledge base and the implementation of therapeutic interventions. Further, Dodge (1982) identified that supervisees maintain some irrational beliefs that underscore their anxiety with regard to performance, competence, approval, and respect. Trainees' anxiety may also stem from being in field placements. Supervisees are typically unfamiliar with the norms, tasks, organizational structures, and social contexts of the work environment (M. L. Nelson, 1997). "Grapevine" information can quickly spread through training and agency networks and create bewildering, frightening, and confusing images for supervisees (L. Cohen, 1980). For example, a trainee's supervisor may state that the trainee must record all counseling sessions. On the other hand, the trainee may understand from others that the training director asserts that all counselors must see the clients assigned to them, regardless of the clients' willingness to be taped. These conflicting messages can create serious worry and turmoil within the trainee.

Evaluation is another area in which supervisees tend to experience considerable anxiety. More specifically, the supervisor's power as the evaluator (Rioch, 1980) has far-reaching and anxiety-producing implications for supervisees. For trainees, anxiety may be focused on the immediate outcomes of the supervisor's evaluation (e.g., a grade). Credentialed supervisees may experience evaluation anxiety in terms of salary increases and promotions. Evaluation, however, is an ethical and essential role of the supervisor in overseeing the welfare of clients, safeguarding the profession, and monitoring the supervisee's growth and development (Association for Counselor Education and Supervision, 1995). Therefore, the supervisor needs to create a supportive environment in which evaluation can be viewed as a mutually agreed upon tool for guiding the professional practice of the supervisee and as a stimulus for ongoing professional development. Recommendations and guidelines have been suggested for learning contracts (Baird, 1999; Costa, 1994) and informed consent agreements (Bernard & Goodyear, 1998; McCarthy et al., 1995) between supervisors and supervisees to establish clear expectations of the purpose of supervision and evaluation procedures. An informed consent for the evaluation process of supervision includes an understanding of the evaluation criteria, methods of evaluation, and ethical responsibilities for evaluation (McCarthy et al., 1995). Using these documents, the supervisor can empower the supervisee by reducing the perception of the hierarchical power structure, clarifying roles and responsibilities in supervision, and inviting the supervisee's participation in the supervisory process.

As counselors work with clients, they need to learn to tolerate ambiguity, be open to the uncertainty of what will occur during the counseling hour, and be comfortable in the presence of unanswered questions and incompleteness (Pietrofesa, Leonard, & Van Hoose, 1978). Should the supervisee's anxiety remain exceedingly high, negative consequences can result. In their review of the literature, Schauer, Seymour, and Geen (1985) concluded that anxiety decreased the accuracy of the counselor's perceptions of the client, reduced the counselor's ability to recollect words and emotions uttered in session, and prompted the practitioner to overelaborate or be argumentative with clients. Friedlander, Keller, Peca-Baker, and Olk (1986) also found that the performance of supervisees was inversely related to their levels of anxiety. Similarly, Dombeck and Brody (1995) noted that during states of high anxiety, a learner's capacity to observe was reduced. Thus, the supervisee's ability to learn from observation decreased when anxiety was high.

Within the context of a strong supervisory relationship, supervisees can feel they have a safe space for learning to cope with and tolerate their anxiety. Supervisors of beginning trainees need to provide supervisees with support, encouragement, and openness. Some beginning trainees want supervisors to help them with skill development by being directive and instructive and providing adequate feedback (Rønnestad & Skovholt, 1993). Supervisors can also help beginning supervisees share personal reactions to clients and the supervisor if they address the value of self-awareness, encourage the expression of fears and doubts, and support the supervisee's continued self-reflection (Baird, 1999; Rønnestad & Skovholt, 1993). In addition, supervisors can reduce performance and approval anxiety by normalizing fears of failure and communicating that mistakes are an expected and accepted part of the process of trying new skills (Costa, 1994; Grater, 1985; Rønnestad & Skovholt, 1993). Having supervisees reflect and list their fears and irrational beliefs in the context of supervision may also help to dispel them (Baird, 1999; Costa, 1994).

Additionally, humor can be used to normalize supervisees' performance and approval anxiety. For example, a beginning supervisee shared a light-hearted story in group supervision. She was counseling a young child who told her he was scared. Imagining the child was going to share a significant experience, the counselor became very serious and asked, "What scares you?" The child responded, "I'm scared my class has already gone to lunch." The entire supervision group laughed. Her disclosure modeled for others that they could be vulnerable and disclose experiences that did not have the outcome they were expecting. Yager and Beck (1985) presented a series of short, humorous vignettes that can be used to reduce a supervisee's performance and approval anxiety. These sketches suggest that supervisors can reduce anxiety by providing an environment in which supervisees can laugh and release tension as they identify with others who are learning through mishaps, miscalculations, and mistakes.

Supervisee Transference

Supervisee transference can also change the dynamics of the supervisory relationship. Transference has traditionally been defined as the emotions and cognitions experienced by a client toward a counselor. Because the counselor presents in a relatively neutral fashion, the client transfers the feelings and thoughts that he or she has toward other people onto the clinician (Ivey et al., 1993). Similarly, the concept of transference has been applied to the supervisor–supervisee relationship (Bernard & Goodyear, 1998; Shohet & Wilmot, 1991). In terms of supervision, transference refers to "feelings that the student experiences in association with a supervisor that are actually displaced—that is, feelings that originate in an earlier significant relationship (often with the primary caretaker) in the student's life" (Jacobs, 1991, p. 131). Similarly, Lane (1986) commented that the supervisee's life history, in particular the relationship with the family of origin, can influence the alliance with the supervisor. Shohet and Wilmot extended this discussion of transference by noting that previous experiences in supervision and relationships with past supervisors can also effect the ways in which trainees behave, think, and feel in the current supervision experience.

It has been noted that supervisee transference can frequently manifest itself in a need to idealize the supervisor (Allphin, 1987). This need on the part of the trainee can lead to two problematic means of responding

(Bernard & Goodyear, 1998). First, the supervisor can simply enjoy the adoration of the trainee without trying to diffuse it. Such a position can cause the supervisor to miss her or his own mistakes as well as disempower the supervisee by preventing her or him from developing a personal sense of competence. Second, the supervisor may not permit the supervisee to use her or him as a model to admire. In so doing, the supervisor may excessively self-disclose or self-efface and deplete the trainee's confidence in the supervisor. Thus, to avoid these problems, it is recommended that the supervisor achieve a meaningful balance between respecting the trainee's need to idealize the supervisor and guiding the supervisee to develop a healthy level of self-efficacy (Bernard & Goodyear, 1998).

Supervisor Characteristics

Borders (1994) summarized the following personal characteristics of the proficient supervisor: (a) being comfortable with authority and evaluation; (b) providing clear and frequent feedback regarding the supervisee's performance; (c) enjoying and engaging in the supervisory process; (d) maintaining a sense of self, including one's strengths and limitations; (e) displaying an openness to self-exploration; and (f) possessing a sense of humor. In addition, Borders mentioned that the professional qualities of good supervisors include being knowledgeable and competent, having a broad base of experiences and professional perspectives, selecting a variety of interventions grounded on awareness and knowledge of the supervisee's needs, and seeking continuous professional development as a supervisor and counselor. Effective supervisors also have skills in assessing and evaluating what the supervisee is learning, setting appropriate learning goals, and collaborating with the supervisee to develop strategies for supervisee and client growth. It is presumed that the aforementioned traits help contribute to a positive and strong supervisory relationship.

Supervisor Anxiety

Like supervisees, supervisors experience anxiety (Shohet & Wilmot, 1991) and this anxiety can alter the supervisory relationship. Supervisors need to be aware of the various factors that may contribute to their anxiety, including performance and competence issues, discomfort with evaluation, unfulfilled personal needs, unresolved former stresses in supervision, and tension between the supervisor and the institution (Alonso, 1983; Hart, 1982; Rønnestad & Skovholt, 1993). Supervisor anxiety prevails in beginning supervisors (Ellis & Douce, 1994; Hess, 1986). The new supervisor may have difficulty responding to supervisee resistance, designing interventions, and understanding client cases (McColley & Baker, 1982). Also, a beginning supervisor often faces abrupt role changes and may experience difficulty shifting gears from counselor to supervisor (Hart, 1982; Hess, 1986; Rønnestad & Skovholt, 1993). Moving from the unconditionally accepting counselor to the evaluative supervisor may contribute to insecurity regarding competence and preparation for the newly acquired responsibilities. Lack of experience and training in supervision may compound issues regarding expectations about the supervisory process, authority roles, and evaluation methods. In this novel position, the new supervisor may find herself or himself closely identifying with the supervisee (Styczynski, 1980). Such identification may result in tendencies to be overly supportive and hesitant to confront (Styczynski, 1980). On the other hand, the supervisor may become rigid and demanding in an effort to separate herself or himself from the supervisee. Therefore, a beginning supervisor may have difficulty setting realistic expectations for herself or himself, the supervisee, or the relationship. It may prove safer for a beginner supervisor to employ concrete techniques and rely more heavily on client–counselor dynamics rather than explore interpersonal concerns involving the counselor's development or the supervisory relationship (Borders, 1994; Hess, 1986; Rønnestad & Skovholt, 1993).

In addition to the anxiety aroused by initiating one's role as a supervisor, supervisors can experience anxiety as a result of other factors. First, a supervisee's level of expertise, advanced knowledge, different life experiences, or high level of personal integration can threaten and arouse anxiety in the supervisor (Hart, 1982). The supervisor may react by raising standards, failing or ceasing to reward performance, and feeling envious. All of these reactions can substantially weaken the supervisory relationship. Anxiety may also revolve around motivations for being a supervisor. A supervisor's need for authority, control, approval, or validation increases the likelihood of a supervisor meeting her or his personal needs within the supervisory relationship (Alonso, 1983; Styczynski, 1980). Furthermore, a supervisor whose experience includes extensive client contact may have difficulty with the third perspective required of the supervisor (Styczynski, 1980). In this instance, the supervisory relationship may initially be less rewarding and fulfilling than the relationship achieved through work with clients.

Hess (1986) proposed a three-stage model of supervisor development that is particularly pertinent to the present discussion of supervisor anxiety. According to this model, the novice supervisor is the most anxious about the supervisory process. As the supervisor becomes more experienced and mature, supervisors become less concerned with power-related issues, such as evaluation and personal validation, and become more committed to the growth of supervisees. At the highest level of development, the supervisor has an integrated supervisor identity and is pursued by supervisees. The supervisor is less concerned about the supervisory relationship and more able to enjoy being in the relationship. Evaluation is provided in a nonthreatening, direct manner. Through a comfortable check and balance system, the focus of the supervisory session is on the supervisee's agenda; this creates greater involvement of and increased professional development for the supervisee. Additionally, this allows for greater equality in the supervisory relationship. At this stage, the supervisor's professional pride and personal integrity are integrated and the supervisor takes pleasure in seeing the supervisee excel and perhaps exceed the supervisor's own ability.

Supervisor Countertransference

The concept of supervisor countertransference has received little attention in the literature (Langs, 1979; Lower, 1972; Strean, 1991; Teitelbaum, 1990), and to date, only one empirical investigation known to us has investigated this phenomenon (Ladany et al., 2000). Despite this fact, supervisor countertransference is pertinent to the supervisory relationship (Bernard & Goodyear, 2000). Based on their empirical inquiry, Ladany and colleagues (2000) defined supervisor countertransference as

> an exaggerated, unrealistic, irrational, or distorted reaction related to a supervisor's work with a trainee. This reaction may include feelings, thoughts, and behaviors that are likely to be in response to both the trainee's interpersonal style and the supervisor's unresolved personal issues, and may also be in response to trainee-supervision environment interactions, problematic client-trainee interactions, trainee-supervisor interactions, or supervisor-supervision environment interactions. (p. 111)

It has been contended that supervisor countertransference can negatively influence trainee and client development. Schlesinger (1981) asserted that supervisor countertransference can inhibit trainee learning and hinder a client's advancement in counseling. Teitelbaum (1990) and Salvendy (1993) similarly noted that supervisor countertransference can be deleterious to trainees. For example, in their eagerness to provide the supervisee with the benefit of their wisdom, supervisors may forgo the vital step of establishing a positive supervisory alliance. Also, Ladany and Lehrman-Waterman (1999) noted that if left unchecked, supervisor countertransference can create emotional distance in the supervisory relationship and constrain the supervisee's learning.

Ladany et al. (2000) found that supervisors identified a wide range of affective, cognitive, and behavioral aspects of their supervisor countertransference experiences. For example, in terms of affect, supervisors typically experienced fear, discomfort, and distress. In the behavioral realm, supervisors occasionally became more avoidant and distant in supervision. Moreover, all of the supervisors believed that the countertransference reaction influenced the supervisory relationship. Specifically, supervisors typically reported that the supervisor countertransference initially weakened but eventually strengthened the supervisory relationship. For instance, one supervisor noted that the supervisor countertransference reaction led to distancing in the relationship. However, in this instance, the supervisor was able to discuss the reaction with the trainee. This discussion positively influenced the relationship by letting the trainee know that she and the supervisor could openly talk about anything that happened within the context of the relationship. Several recommendations were made by the participants regarding the means by which supervisors may manage their supervisor countertransference and prevent their reactions from negatively affecting the supervisory relationship. Supervisors relayed that they might benefit from supervision of supervision, or peer supervision, to uncover and manage supervisor countertransference. Additional suggestions for coping with supervisor countertransference included: (a) consulting with colleagues; (b) discussing the reaction with the trainee when appropriate; (c) increasing supervisor knowledge and skills; (d) expanding self-awareness through self-reflection; and (e) obtaining personal counseling.

Supervisor Adherence to Ethical Guidelines

Counseling supervisors need to refer to the ethical principles of their profession to guide the ethical practice of the trainees they supervise (e.g., American Counseling Association, 1995; American Psychological Association, 1992). However, supervision involves additional roles and responsibilities unique to its triadic nature. Therefore, supervisors need to consult ethical standards and practices for supervision, such as the "Ethical Guidelines for Counseling Supervisors" (Association for Counselor Education and Supervision, 1995) to direct their work with supervisees. Although adherence to the ethical principles of psychology and supervision is vehemently recommended, supervisors do not exclusively maintain the ethical guidelines proposed. In Ladany, Lehrman-Waterman, Molinaro, and Wolgast (1999), supervisees reported that more than half of their supervisors did not adhere to at least one ethical guideline; nevertheless, most of the supervisors maintained most ethical standards. The ethical violations of supervisors reported by trainees were in the following areas: (a) performance evaluation and monitoring of supervisee activities (33%); (b) confidentiality issues in supervision (18%); (c) ability to work with alternative perspectives (18%); (d) session boundaries and respectful treatment (13%); (e) orientation to professional roles and monitoring of site standards (9%); (f) expertise/competency issues (9%); (g) disclosure to clients (8%); (h) crisis coverage and intervention (7%); (i) multicultural sensitivity toward clients (7%); (j) multicultural sensitivity toward supervisee (7%); (k) dual roles (6%); (l) termination and follow-up issues (5%); and (m) sexual issues (1%).

In addition, these researchers examined the influence of adherence to ethical guidelines on the supervisory relationship (Ladany, Lehrman-Waterman, et al., 1999). It was found that trainees who reported their supervisors demonstrated greater adherence to supervisor ethical principles indicated a stronger supervisory working alliance in terms of greater agreement on the goals and tasks and a stronger emotional bond. Alternatively, supervisees who reported that their supervisors exhibited less adherence to the supervisor ethical standards attested to a weaker supervisory working alliance, with less agreement on the goals and tasks and a weaker emotional bond. In fact, more than 47% of the variance in the supervisory working alliance was accounted for by the supervisor's adherence to supervisor ethical guidelines. Therefore, Ladany, Lehrman-Waterman, et al. (1999) argued that supervisors' ethical violations may have a tremendous influence on the strength and effectiveness of the supervisory relationship.

Supervisee–Supervisor Relationship Interactions

Racial Identity Interactions

According to Cook (1993, as cited in Helms & Cook, 1999), it is imperative in supervision that there be a discussion of the supervisor's, supervisee's, and client's racial and cultural socialization as well as the influence of these elements on supervision process and outcome. Further, Helms and Cook (1999) asserted that attention to cultural and racial factors is essential to the promotion of a productive supervisory relationship. As such, Helms's (1994) two racial identity ego status models have been adapted for application to supervision (Helms & Cook, 1999). Both of these models concern one's racial identity development based on how one thinks and feels about one's own race and people of other races. For People of Color, the proceeding statuses have been outlined: (a) conformity (i.e., idealization of the White racial group and a denigration of people from one's own racial group); (b) dissonance (i.e., ambivalence and confusion regarding to which racial group one belongs); (c) immersion (i.e., idealization of one's own group and denigration of the White racial group); (d) emersion (i.e., a sense of group solidarity and euphoria as one is surrounded by one's own group); (e) internalization (i.e., a positive commitment to one's group and the ability to differentially respond to members of one's own and other racial groups); and (f) integrated awareness (i.e., expressing a positive racial self and resisting forces that discourage positive racial self-conceptions).

The following are the statuses of the White Racial Identity model: (a) contact (i.e., no awareness of racism); (b) disintegration (i.e., anxiety provoked by racial moral dilemmas between humanism and White group loyalty); (c) reintegration (i.e., idealization of the White racial-group and denigration of People of Color); (d) pseudoindependence (i.e., an intellectualized understanding of one's racial group); (e) immersion (i.e., a search for understanding about being White and the benefits derived from racism); (f) emersion (i.e., a sense of discovery and group solidarity as one rediscovers what it is to be White); and (g) autonomy (i.e., a positive racial-group commitment without maintaining the privileges of racism). In addition, Helms (1990) and Cook (1994) extended the notion of racial identity and addressed the relationship interactions among people of similar and different racial identities.

These interactions were defined as progressive, regressive, and parallel. Ladany, Brittan-Powell, and Pannu (1997) adapted the discussion of racial identity interactions to fit the supervisory relationship. Moreover, they divided the concept of parallel interactions into two types: parallel-high and parallel-low. Progressive relationships are defined as interactions in which the supervisor has a more advanced racial identity status than the supervisee. Parallel-high interactions are present when both the supervisor and supervisee share high racial identity statuses. A parallel-low interaction occurs when both the supervisor and supervisee share lower racial identity statuses. In a regressive relationship, the supervisee has a more advanced racial identity status than the supervisor.

The empirical literature provides evidence of the important influence that racial identity has on the supervisory relationship. Ladany, Brittan-Powell, and Pannu (1997) concluded that supervisors and supervisees who share higher racial identity statuses (i.e., parallel-high) had the strongest agreement regarding the goals and tasks of supervision and the strongest emotional bond. Progressive relationships shared the next strongest supervisory working alliance, while regressive interactions were found to be connected with the weakest supervisory alliance. In addition, parallel-high and progressive racial identity interactions were associated with trainees perceiving their supervisors as having considerable influence on their multicultural competence. Parallel-low and regressive interactions were determined to be the least influential in terms of the enhancement of trainee multicultural competence.

In their study of 225 Asian, Black, Latino, and Native American supervisees and their experiences in cross-cultural supervision, Cook and Helms (1988) found that supervisees generally reported having a guarded relationship with their supervisors. Further, they found that Asian women supervisees were significantly more satisfied with their supervisory relationships than were Asian men supervisees. Asian, Black, and Latino men were also more satisfied with the supervisory relationship than were Native American men. However, these researchers additionally determined that the supervisees reported greater satisfaction within the supervisory relationship if the supervisor demonstrated conditional interest and liking.

McRoy, Freeman, Logan, and Blackmon (1986), in their investigation of cross-cultural supervisor–supervisee dyads, concluded that both supervisors and trainees cited numerous possible problems in the supervisory relationship. These difficulties included language barriers, lack of knowledge of cultural differences, and student defensiveness. Moreover, although the majority of supervisors reported that they dealt with the problems that arose with trainees, most of the trainees stated they avoided discussing difficulties within the supervisory relationship. This occurred despite the fact that most of the supervisees perceived their supervisors to be sensitive to cultural issues. In contrast, Hilton, Russell, and Salmi (1994) found that the evaluations made by White supervisees of either their White or African

American supervisors did not vary according to the supervisor's race. Rather, high support on the part of the supervisor was found to relate to more positive ratings of the quality of the supervisory relationship and the supervisor's effectiveness.

Gender Identity Interactions

In addition to examining racial identity interactions, both supervisors and supervisees have been advised to examine their gender identities and the manner in which gender influences relationships (Stevens-Smith, 1995). Further, supervisors have been admonished to attend to their own gender biases before and during supervision (Ault-Riche, 1988; T. S. Nelson, 1991). Empirical investigations of the influence of gender identity on the supervisory relationship offer mixed conclusions. Some research has provided evidence suggesting that gender does influence the supervisory relationship. In one examination, Worthington and Stern (1985) found that male trainees reported better relationships with supervisors than female trainees, regardless of the gender of the supervisor. Moreover, the trainees in Worthington and Stern's study rated the supervisory relationship more positively when the supervisor–supervisee dyads were matched by gender than when they were unmatched pairs. Although these determinations were reported by trainees, supervisors reported no distinctions in the supervisory relationship based on gender. Behling, Curtis, and Foster (1988) discovered that supervisory relationships were viewed more positively by supervisees when the instructor and student were placed in same-gender combinations in comparison with being in a female student and male instructor combination. Further, the female trainee and male supervisor relationships were perceived significantly more negatively than all other combinations.

On the other hand, other research studies have proffered indicators to suggest that gender does not mediate the supervisory relationship. Schiavone and Jessell (1988) found that trainee perceptions of supervisor expertness and competence were not influenced by the gender of the supervisor or trainee. The authors proposed that with an increase in the number of women in the field of psychology has come a decrease in the bias against female professionals. Another explanation of this finding suggests that trainee perceptions of supervisor expertness do not vary according to gender because trainees generally view their supervisors as experts. Perhaps the influence of gender is more readily apparent when considered in terms of how the supervisor perceives or interacts with the supervisee. For example, supervisors may be more didactic with female supervisees because they are perceived to be less expert and autonomous than male supervisees. Additional investigations are needed to determine the accuracy of this hypothesis, however.

Other research provides for a more complex understanding of the interaction of gender and the supervisory relationship. For instance, M. L. Nelson and Holloway (1990) discovered that gender did not affect the assumption of power on the part of the supervisor. They determined that both male and female supervisors typically adopt the expert role within the supervisory relationship and the trainee responds by taking the low-power role. However, they also found that both male and female supervisors failed to support their female trainees' attempts to assume some power during the supervision session. Likewise, female trainees were significantly more likely to defer to a powerful authority figure than were male supervisees. Thus, these authors suggested that a female supervisee may decline opportunities to assert herself as an expert within the context of the supervisory relationship. Also, Sells, Goodyear, Lichtenberg, & Polkinghorne (1997) discovered that female supervisors had a greater relational focus and spent more time in supervision concentrated on the trainee than did male supervisors. A greater amount of time was spent on the trainee's clients when the supervisor was male. However, gender did not seem to influence either the evaluation of the impact of supervision by the trainee or the supervisor or the evaluation of the trainee's performance by the supervisor. In sum, understanding of the complex influence of gender on the supervisory relationship is incomplete. Researchers are encouraged to expand this area of the literature so that the impact of gender on supervision can be more readily understood. Additionally, researchers are urged to consider other supervisor–supervisee relationship interaction variables, such as age, sexual orientation, religiousness, and spirituality, when examining the supervisory relationship. In so doing, our understanding of how various personal characteristics influence the alliance will greatly expand.

☐ Influence of the Supervisory Relationship on Supervision Process and Outcome

Games Supervisees and Supervisors Play

In order to minimize the anxiety and interpersonal conflict that emerges within the supervisory relationship, supervisees and supervisors may collude by relying on "games." Kadushin (1968) defined supervisory games as "recurrent interactional incidents between supervisor and supervisee that have a payoff for one of the parties" (p. 23). Payoffs might include gaining power and control or diverting attention from a conflictual situation. Collusion in games can block the authenticity of the supervisory relationship, thereby damaging the alliance as well as the process and outcome of supervision. Games can also diminish potential trainee learning and growth by limiting the material examined in supervision and preventing the necessary reflective process (Bernard & Goodyear, 1998). Kadushin proposed four series of games supervisees play. A brief definition of each game within the four series follows.

Series 1: Manipulating Demand Levels

Two Against the Agency or Seducing the Subversive. A game in which the supervisee attempts to reduce the supervisor's enforcement of agency rules and regulations by focusing attention on the needs of the client population.

Be Nice to Me Because I Am Nice to You. A game of flattery aimed at ingratiating with the supervisor to soften the evaluative focus on the supervisee's client contacts.

Series 2: Redefining the Relationship

Protect the Sick and Infirm; or Treat Me, Don't Beat Me. A game in which the supervisee exposes details regarding her or his personal concerns in lieu of clinical work to appeal to the counselor in the supervisor.

Evaluation Is Not for Friends. A game that redefines the relationship into a more social, informal interaction with the expectation that friends are less accountable.

Maximum Feasible Participation. A game that stresses a peer–peer relationship, granting the supervisee extensive decision-making power to determine what she or he needs to know.

Series 3: Reducing Power Disparity

If You Knew Dostoyevsky Like I Know Dostoyevsky. A game designed to highlight the supervisee's intellectual powers and ability to educate the supervisor.

So What Do You Know About It? A game in which the supervisee alludes to her or his own wealth of information in an area in which the supervisor has little expertise or life experience.

All or Nothing at All. A game that involves the supervisees seeking broader visions and questioning the greater meaning of life, with the intent to make the supervisor feel she or he has abandoned idealism.

Series 4: Controlling the Situation

I Have a Little List. A game in which the supervisee brings in a series of work-related concerns to control and direct the supervisor's attention away from the supervisee.

Heading Them Off at the Pass. A game of supervisee self-flagellation designed to solicit reassurance from the supervisor.

Little Old Me.   A game in which the supervisee gains strength by feigning weakness and seeking a prescription from the supervisor with the question, "What would you do?"

I Did It Like You Told Me.   A hostile, angry game in which the supervisee follows the advice of the supervisor with "spiteful obedience" to put the supervisor on the defensive.

It's All So Confusing.   A game of seeking suggestions and guidance from a number of authorities in an attempt to erode the supervisor's authority.

What You Don't Know Won't Hurt Me.   A game of selective sharing with the supervisor to present a favorable picture and keep distance between the supervisee and supervisor.

   Supervisors, too, can initiate games (Hawthorne, 1975; Kadushin, 1968). Supervisors may rely on games when they feel their positions are threatened, are uncertain or uncomfortable with authority, are hesitant to utilize their authority, or feel hostility toward the supervisee. Like the games initiated by the supervisee, supervisor games can be detrimental to the supervisory relationship. Supervisors' games are categorized into two types, abdication and power (Hawthorne, 1975). Abdication games involve the giving up of responsibility, and power games keep the relationship closed while fostering helplessness in the supervisee. Examples of Hawthorne's (1975) and Kadushin's (1968) supervisor games follow.

Games of Abdication

They Won't Let Me.   A game that indicates a willingness from the supervisor to permit action but is, in reality, an avoidance of decision making through projection of responsibility onto agency or institutional rules or authorities.

Poor Me.   A game in which the supervisor excuses not keeping supervision commitments due to the excessive demands of other tasks, and implies the supervisee should make no additional demands.

I'm Really One of You or I'm Really a Nice Guy.   Approval-seeking games in which the first variation is designed to gain approval by siding with the supervisee's point of view; the second variation is designed to gain approval based on personal qualities.

One Good Question Deserves Another.   A game of answering a question with a question as a ploy to stall for time or to avoid answering, deciding, or disclosing information to the supervisee.

Games of Power

Remember Who's Boss.   A game of explicit reminders of power (e.g., memos and evaluations) and implicit reminders of authority (e.g., "my trainees," "my unit") designed to allow for no contradictions and an omnipotent position.

I'll Tell on You.   A game of threat in which the disciplinary action is carried out by a higher power, allowing both the retention of power and the abdication of responsibility.

Parent (Father or Mother) Knows Best.   A game of validation of the supervisor's experience and wisdom designed to preserve and guide the helpless, dependent supervisee.

I'm Only Trying to Help, or I Know You Can't Really Do It Without Me.   A game of lowered expectations with assumptions of supervisee incompetence or failure disguised in a cloak of help and caring.

I Wonder Why You Really Asked That Question.   A game of redefinition to retain control and imply that the supervisee's question is psychological resistance. Thus, the supervisor is remaining in power while avoiding validation of the supervisee's viewpoint or hypothesis.

According to Kadushin (1968), supervisees frequently play these games due to fear of finding out that they are inadequate with regard to their work or their own self. Therefore, to prevent game playing, supervisors are advised to provide positive feedback to trainees and encourage the development of healthy self-efficacy. Moreover, it is suggested that learning to become a counselor presents a great threat of change as the supervisee's manner of thinking and believing is altered (Kadushin). Empathizing with the supervisee with regard to the ambiguity experienced as a result of training and the confusion which can result from an altering identity may decrease the possibility that a trainee would initiate game playing. Further, to avoid supervisee and supervisor games, the supervisor must be self-aware and willing to risk anger, hostility, and rejection. Supervisors need to be willing to risk being seen as fallible (Kadushin). Supervisors who build open relationships in which direct communication is invited and in which anxiety and conflict are seen as tools for learning reduce the possibility of playing games.

However, should a game occur, steps can be taken by the supervisor to appropriately cope with the problem and amend the supervisory relationship (Kadushin, 1968). First, one can combat the supervisee's games by refusing to play from the onset (Kadushin, 1968). Because some games benefit the supervisor as well as the supervisee, it may prove difficult for the supervisor to abdicate the advantages of game playing. For instance, in the example "protect the sick and infirm; or treat me, don't beat me," the supervisor must remain aware of her or his multiple roles as a supervisor (i.e., lecturer, teacher, case reviewer, collegial, monitor, and counselor; Bordin, 1983). By keeping in mind the many requirements of being a supervisor, the supervisor will more readily dismiss the trainee's urgings to predominantly engage in the counselor role. Similarly, the supervisor will need to recognize the appropriate boundary between supervision and counseling and refer the trainee to personal counseling if necessary. Second, one can manage supervisee game playing using gradual interpretation or confrontation (Kadushin, 1968). Confrontation on the part of the supervisor indicates a refusal on her or his part to tolerate or collude with the game playing of the supervisee. Should confrontation occur, the supervisor is cautioned to consider the timing and dosage and to be compassionate with the supervisee (Kadushin, 1968).

Disclosure and Nondisclosure

Supervisor Disclosure

Self-disclosures refer to personal statements about oneself made to another person (Watkins, 1990). Supervisor self-disclosures can involve the supervisor disclosing personal information to the trainee, including counseling successes and struggles, previous training experiences, or reactions to the trainee or the trainee's clients (Ladany & Lehrman-Waterman, 1999). Norcross and Halgin (1997) asserted that a trusting relationship can be nurtured with trainees when supervisors self-disclose information regarding their own work with clients. Moreover, it has been contended that supervisor self-disclosures produce a supervisory environment in which the trainee is comfortable sharing uncertainties and concerns (Glickauf-Hughes, 1994; Hutt, Scott, & King, 1983; Norcross & Halgin, 1997; Worthen & McNeill, 1996).

In their empirical investigation into supervisor self-disclosures, Ladany and Lehrman-Waterman (1999) found that the most frequently cited supervisor self-disclosures included personal issues, neutral counseling experiences, and counseling struggles. The authors questioned the wisdom of the supervisors who chose to disclose personal issues to their supervisees. They noted that although disclosing personal information could demonstrate trust in the supervisee and deepen the supervisory relationship, such self-disclosures could also reduce the time in supervision focused on the trainee and cause a reversal of roles, whereby the supervisee is supporting the supervisor. On the other hand, self-disclosure of counseling struggles and neutral counseling experiences was mentioned by the authors as a means by which the supervisor may demonstrate vulnerability to the supervisee and strengthen the supervisory relationship. For example, a trainee may note to the supervisor that he or she feels considerable performance anxiety with regard to having counseling sessions taped and evaluated. By admitting to her or his own fears about having been taped as a trainee, the supervisor can demonstrate that she or he, too, is vulnerable, which may help strengthen the alliance.

In addition to the aforementioned self-disclosures, 12% of the trainees said their supervisor made at least one self-disclosure concerning the supervisory relationship. One example was when a supervisor told her supervisee how much she valued their relationship and how much she had learned from her. The authors contended that addressing the supervisory relationship in supervision could strengthen the alliance or aid in the repair of a troubled relationship. Furthermore, focusing on the supervisory relationship may create a type of parallel process and encourage trainees to address the therapeutic relationship in their work with clients (Ladany & Lehrman-Waterman, 1999). Lastly, the results of this study found that the more frequently the supervisor self-disclosed, the stronger was the supervisory working alliance in terms of the goals, tasks, and bond. Subsequently, self-disclosure may be an effectual tool employed by supervisors to help strengthen or repair the supervisory relationship (Ladany & Lehrman-Waterman, 1999). However, these researchers caution supervisors against excessive self-disclosure and encourage supervisors to be aware of occasions in which self-disclosures may be detrimental to the working alliance.

Supervisor Nondisclosure

In a similar study, Ladany and Melincoff (1999) investigated the nature of supervisor nondisclosure. Results of this investigation found that most supervisors (98%) withheld some information from their supervisees. A frequently mentioned nondisclosure concerned supervisors' personal issues. For example, a supervisor decided not to disclose to the trainee that he has a brother who is HIV positive. Not discussing personal information in supervision appears to indicate appropriate boundary setting on the part of the supervisor (Ladany & Melincoff, 1999). The supervisors seemed to recognize the irrelevance of such information to supervision and placed adequate limits on the supervisory relationship. Interestingly, 11% of supervisors stated they did not disclose positive reactions to the trainee's counseling and professional performance. The authors maintained that disclosing positive feedback to supervisees would be an indication of support to the trainee and would likely strengthen the supervisory relationship. Thus, these investigators found this result to be particularly troublesome. Lastly, although a number of reasons were described by the supervisors as to why they chose to nondisclose, two reasons directly related to the supervisory relationship. In particular, supervisors asserted they did not disclose because of concerns that the disclosure would damage the supervisory relationship or that the relationship was insufficiently developed to handle the content of the nondisclosure. Thus, supervisors seem to place relative importance on the supervisory relationship when evaluating the suitability of nondisclosure.

Supervisee Nondisclosure

Most models of counselor supervision suggest that trainees must disclose information regarding clients, the counseling process, the supervisory process, and themselves in order to maximally benefit from supervision (e.g., Blocher, 1983; Bordin, 1983; Littrell, Lee-Borden, & Lorenz, 1979; Loganbill, Hardy, & Delworth, 1982; Stoltenberg, 1981; Stoltenberg & Delworth, 1987). As a result, it can be maintained that supervisee nondisclosure would obstruct the supervisory relationship and ultimately limit trainee learning (Ladany, Hill, Corbett, & Nutt, 1996). The study conducted by Ladany et al. (1996) provides some valuable insight into the issue of trainee nondisclosure in supervision. These researchers found that 97.2% of trainees withheld information from their supervisors. The content of the nondisclosures included the following: negative reactions to the supervisor (90%), personal issues not directly related to supervision (60%), clinical mistakes (44%), evaluation concerns (44%), general client observations (43%), negative reactions to clients (36%), countertransference (22%), client–counselor attraction issues (9%), positive reactions to the supervisor (23%), supervision-setting concerns (18%), supervisor appearance (9%), supervisee–supervisor attraction issues (9%), and positive reactions to clients (5%).

Several reasons were cited by trainees in terms of why they chose to nondisclose, including perceived unimportance, the personal nature of the nondisclosure, negative feelings about the nondisclosure, a poor alliance with the supervisor, the supervisor's agenda, "political suicide," pointlessness, and a belief that the supervisor was not competent. In particular, the reasons related to negative feelings (e.g., "shame" and "embarrassment") and a poor supervisory alliance (e.g., "fear of being hurt" and "mistrust"), speak to the power of the supervisory relationship in mediating trainee nondisclosure. Thus, when the core conditions of the supervisory alliance (i.e., mutual trust, liking, and caring) are not achieved between the supervisor and trainee, the trainee is less likely to disclose information relevant to supervision. Consequently, trainee advancement and client well-being may be jeopardized (Ladany et al., 1996). As a result of these findings, the researchers recommended that supervisors attempt to develop an open, collaborative, and supportive relationship with their trainees to promote appropriate disclosure in supervision.

Role Conflict and Ambiguity

As alluded to earlier, role conflict experienced by the trainee can influence the supervisory relationship as well as the process and outcome of supervision. In terms of supervision, role conflict is defined as an occurrence in which a supervisee is required by the supervisor to either engage in behaviors that are inconsistent with the supervisee's personal convictions or participate in numerous roles that demand conflicting behaviors. More specifically, the empirically derived Role Conflict and Role Ambiguity Inventory (RCRAI) concluded that role conflict tends to concern experiences in which the expectations associated with the role of student oppose the expectations affiliated with the role of counselor (Olk & Friedlander, 1992). Role ambiguity occurs when a trainee is uncertain about the expectations of her or his role, the methods required to fulfill those expectations, and the consequences of positive or negative performance. In particular, the RCRAI discovered that role ambiguity includes: (a) uncertainty about supervisory expectations or how to perform consistently with those expectations and (b) uncertainty about how trainees will be evaluated by their supervisors (Olk & Friedlander, 1992).

Additional research has demonstrated that these two constructs share an important connection with the supervisory relationship. Ladany and Friedlander (1995) discovered that trainees who perceived the supervisory working alliance to be strong tended to experience less role conflict and ambiguity in supervision. Alternatively, trainees who perceived the supervisory alliance to be weak experienced more role conflict and ambiguity. More specifically, these researchers found that trainees who shared a strong emotional bond with their supervisors appeared to be more likely to work through their interpersonal conflicts and experience less role conflict in supervision. On the other hand, Friedlander, Keller, Peca-Baker, and Olk (1986) found that role conflict within the supervisory relationship had no effect on trainee's self-statements, anxiety levels, or performance in counseling. Thus, although role conflict and ambiguity appear to influence the supervisory relationship, their impact on trainee outcome seems less clear.

Sexual Issues

In the context of a close, intense relationship like the supervisory relationship, it is not unusual for a sexual attraction to occur (Bernard & Goodyear, 1998). In fact, issues of sexual attraction between supervisor and trainee have been commonly noted in the literature (e.g., Ellis & Douce, 1994; Ladany et al., 1996; Rodolfa, Rowen, Steier, Nicassio, & Gordon, 1994). Because sexual attraction is a normal occurrence within the supervisory dyad, it appears necessary that supervisors and supervisees be provided with directions regarding how to ethically manage these issues (Ellis & Douce, 1994). This fact remains true despite the discomfort that may be experienced as a result of such discussions (Knapp & Vandecreek, 1997). Supervisors need to remain alert for instances in which sexual attraction may emerge in the supervisory relationship (Ellis & Douce, 1994). Trainees may provide covert clues regarding sexual attraction to their supervisor; therefore, supervisors need to be attentive and willing to explore these issues when they emerge. Finally, it is advised that supervisors create an open, respectful, and sensitive environment in which it is safe for a trainee to mention issues of sexual attraction (Ladany, O'Brien, et al., 1997; Pope, Sonne, & Holroyd, 1993).

Although it may be common for sexual attraction issues to emerge over the course of supervision (Ellis & Douce, 1994), several professional organizations have made strict statements against sexual relationships between a supervisor and supervisee. In the ethical principles devised by both the American Psychological Association (1992) and the Association for Counselor Education and Supervision (1995), it is strongly asserted that supervisors should not participate in any form of sexual contact with supervisees. Despite these concise directions, research has shown that supervisors do in fact engage in sexual relationships with their trainees. In their survey of a group of female members of the American Psychological Association, Glaser and Thorpe (1986) found that 17% of participants reported having had sexual contact with psychology educators during graduate school. Additional research concluded that 25% of women had a sexual relationship with a supervisor (Pope, Levenson, & Schover, 1979). More recently, 1% of trainees reported their supervisors engaged in inappropriate behavior concerning sexual or romantic issues (Ladany et al., 1999). Both the American Psychological Association (1992) and the Association for Counselor Education and Supervision (1995) clearly declared that serious harm can afflict supervisees when they have sexual interactions with their supervisors. In fact, the Association for Counselor Education and Supervision (1995) stated that dual relationships (e.g., sexual contact) may compromise the supervisory relationship and impair the supervisor's objectivity and professional judgment. As a result, supervisors and supervisees should always avoid sexual interactions.

☐ Summary

In sum, it can be asserted that the supervisory relationship is a fundamental component of supervision (Holloway, 1997; Watkins, 1997). Therefore, it is imperative that supervisors and supervisees develop a comprehensive and beneficial understanding of the nature of the supervisory relationship. As such, several aspects of the supervisory relationship were addressed in this chapter. First, Bordin's (1983) supervisor working alliance was presented. This conception of the supervisory relationship contains three primary components: (a) mutual agreement and understanding between the supervisor and supervisee of the goals of supervision; (b) mutual agreement and understanding of the tasks of the supervisor and supervisee; and (c) the emotional bond between the supervisor and supervisee. This definition of the supervisory relationship was augmented by Holloway's (1997) notions of power and involvement. In particular, it was relayed that the supervisor maintains the formal power in the relationship, although the implementation of that power is dependent upon both the supervisor and supervisee. Also, the beginning, mature, and terminating phases (Holloway, 1995) of the supervisory relationship were addressed. It was suggested that the nature of the supervisory relationship changes over time as it becomes more individualized to each particular dyad.

We also discussed the manner in which strong supervisory relationships are formed. Some of the conditions of effective supervisory relationships include empathy, genuineness, and respect. In addition, the elements that influence the supervisory relationship were addressed. First, the triadic system (i.e., client, trainee, supervisor) can influence the relationship through parallel process. Also, the supervisees' experience of anxiety and transference can influence the relationship. Moreover, the supervisor's characteristics, such as anxiety, countertransference, and adherence to ethical guidelines, can impact the working alliance. The effect of such supervisee–supervisor relationship interactions as racial and gender identity were also reviewed. Lastly, we noted how the supervisory relationship influences supervision process and outcome. In particular, game playing, supervisor and supervisee disclosure and nondisclosure, role conflict and role ambiguity, and sexual issues were aspects of the relationship determined to affect the process and outcome of supervision.

Although the supervisory relationship literature reviewed is presently considerable, it would be misleading for the reader to assume that he or she now possesses an exhaustive understanding of the supervisory relationship. In recent years, there have been substantial contributions to the supervision literature; however, more research is needed. For example, examination of the phases of the supervisory relationship (Holloway, 1995) utilizing longitudinal research methods would contribute significantly to our understanding of alliance development. Also, qualitative investigations of the triadic system and parallel process would greatly enrich the field. More research concerning the influence of race, gender, and other characteristics such as age, religiousness, sexual orientation, and spirituality on the supervisory relationship is also warranted. Thus, it is hoped that this chapter provides an impetus to theorists and researchers to extend understanding of this complex and vital topic and that it establishes a foundation on which supervisors and supervisees can develop effective and meaningful supervisory relationships.

References

Allphin, C. (1987). Perplexing or distressing episodes in supervision: How they can help in the teaching and learning of psychotherapy. *Clinical Social Work Journal, 15,* 236–245.

Alonso, A. (1983). A developmental theory of psychodynamic supervision. *The Clinical Supervisor, 1,* 23–36.

American Counseling Association. (1995). *Code of ethics and standards of practice.* Alexandria, VA: Author.

American Psychological Association. (1992). Ethical principles of psychologists and code of conduct. *American Psychologist, 47,* 1597–1611.

Association for Counselor Education and Supervision. (1995). Ethical guidelines for counseling supervisors. *Counselor Education and Supervision, 34,* 270–276.

Ault-Riche, M. (1988). Teaching an integrated model of family therapy: Women as students, women as supervisors. *Journal of Psychotherapy and the Family, 3,* 175–192.

Bahrick, A. S., Russell, R. K., & Salmi, S. W. (1991). The effects of role induction on trainees' perceptions of supervision. *Journal of Counseling and Development, 69,* 434–438.

Baird, B. N. (1999). *The internship, practicum, and field placement handbook: A guide for the helping professions* (2nd ed.). Upper Saddle River, NJ: Prentice-Hall.

Behling, J., Curtis, C., & Foster, S. A. (1988). Impact of sex-role combinations on student performance in field instruction. *Clinical Supervisor, 6,* 161–168.

Bernard, J. (1979). Supervision training: A discrimination model. *Counselor Education and Supervision, 19,* 60–68.

Bernard, J. M., & Goodyear, R. K. (1998). *Fundamentals of clinical supervision* (2nd ed.). Boston: Allyn & Bacon.

Blocher, D. H. (1983). Toward a cognitive-developmental approach to counseling supervision. *The Counseling Psychologist, 11,* 27–34.

Borders, L. D. (1994). *The good supervisor.* Report No. EDO-CG-91-18. Greensboro, NC: ERIC Clearinghouse on Counseling and State Services.

Bordin, E. S. (1983). A working alliance based model of supervision. *The Counseling Psychologist, 11,* 35–41.

Carifio, M. S., & Hess, A. K. (1987). Who is the ideal supervisor? *Professional Psychology: Research and Practice, 18,* 244–250.

Cohen, L. (1980). The new supervisee views supervision. In A. K. Hess (Ed.) *Psychotherapy supervision. Theory, research and practice* (pp. 78–84). New York: Wiley.

Cohen, R., & DeBetz, B. (1977). Responsive supervision of the psychiatric resident and clinical psychology intern. *The American Journal of Psychoanalysis, 37,* 51–64.

Cook, D. A. (1994). Racial identity in supervision. *Counselor Education and Supervision, 34,* 132–139.

Cook, D. A., & Helms, J. E. (1988). Visible racial/ethnic group supervisees' satisfaction with cross-cultural supervision as predicted by relationship characteristics. *Journal of Counseling Psychology, 35,* 268–273.

Costa, L. (1994). Reducing anxiety in live supervision. *Counselor Education and Supervision, 34,* 30–40.

Dodge, J. (1982). Reducing supervisee anxiety: A cognitive-behavioral approach. *Counselor Education and Supervision, 22,* 55–60.

Dombeck, M. T., & Brody, S. L. (1995). Clinical supervision: A three-way mirror. *Archives of Psychiatric Nursing, 9,* 3–10.

Ekstein, R., & Wallerstein, R. S. (1972). *The teaching and learning of psychotherapy* (2nd ed.). New York: Basic Books.

Ellis, M. V., & Douce, L. A. (1994). Group supervision of novice clinical supervisors: Eight recurring issues. *Journal of Counseling & Development, 72,* 520–525.

Friedlander, M. L., Keller, K. E., Peca-Baker, T. A., & Olk, M. E. (1986). Effects of role conflict on counselor trainees' self-statements, anxiety level, and performance. *Journal of Counseling Psychology, 33,* 73–77.

Friedlander, M. L., Siegel, S. M., & Brenock, K. (1989). Parallel process in counseling and supervision: A case study. *Journal of Counseling Psychology, 36,* 149–157.

Gardner, L. M. H. (1980). Racial, ethnic, and social class considerations in psychotherapy supervision. In A. K. Hess (Ed.), *Psychotherapy Supervision: Theory, Research, and Practice* (pp. 474–508). New York: Wiley.

Gendlin, E., & Hendricks, M. (1978). Changes. In E. Gendlin (Ed.), *Focusing* (pp. 118–144). New York: Everest House.

Glaser, R. D., & Thorpe, J. S. (1986). Unethical intimacy: A survey of sexual contact and advances between psychology educators and female graduate students. *American Psychologist, 41,* 43–51.

Glickauf-Hughes, C. (1994). Characterological resistances in psychotherapy supervision. *Psychotherapy, 31,* 58–66.

Grater, H. A. (1985). Stages in psychotherapy supervision: From therapy skills to skilled therapist. *Professional Psychology: Research and Practice, 16,* 605–610.

Hart, G. M. (1982). *The process of clinical supervision.* Baltimore: University Park Press.

Hawthorne, L. (1975). Games supervisors play. *Social Work, 20,* 179–183.

Helms, J. E. (1990). *Black and White racial identity: Theory, research, and practice.* Westport, CT: Greenwood.

Helms, J. E. (1994). Racial identity and other "racial" constructs. In E. J. Trickett, R. Watts, & D. Birman (Eds.), *Human diversity* (pp. 285–311). San Francisco: Jossey-Bass.

Helms, J. E., & Cook, D. A. (1999). *Using race and culture in counseling and psychotherapy: Theory and process.* Boston: Allyn & Bacon.

Hess, A. K. (1986). Growth in supervision: Stages of supervisee and supervisor development. *Clinical Supervisor, 4,* 51–67.

Hilton, D. B., Russell, R. K., & Salmi, S. W. (1994). The effects of supervisor's race and level of support on perceptions of supervision. *Journal of Counseling & Development, 73,* 559–563.

Hoffman, L. W. (1994). The training of psychotherapy supervisors: A barren scape. *Psychotherapy in Private Practice, 13,* 23–42.

Holloway, E. L. (1995). *Clinical supervision: A systems approach.* Thousand Oaks, CA: Sage.

Holloway, E. L. (1997). Structures for the analysis and teaching of supervision. In C. E. Watkins, Jr. (Ed.), *Handbook of psychotherapy supervision* (pp. 249–276). New York: Wiley.

Hunt, P. (1986, Spring). Supervision. *Marriage Guidance,* 15–22.

Hutt, C. H., Scott, J., & King, M. (1983). A phenomenological study of supervisees positive and negative experiences in supervision. *Psychotherapy Theory, Research, and Practice, 20,* 118–123.

Ivey, A. E., Ivey, M. B., & Simek-Morgan, L. (1983). *Counseling and psychotherapy: A multicultural perspective* (3rd ed.). Boston: Allyn & Bacon.

Jacobs, C. (1991). Violations of the supervisory relationship: An ethical and educational blind spot. *Social Work, 36,* 130–135.

Kadushin, A. (1968). Games people play in supervision. *Social Work, 13,* 23–32.

Knapp, S., & Vandecreek, L. (1997). Ethical and legal aspects of clinical supervision. In C. E. Watkins, Jr. (Ed.), *Handbook of psychotherapy supervision* (pp. 589–599). New York: Wiley.

Ladany, N., Brittan-Powell, C. S., Pannu, R. K. (1997). The influence of supervisory racial identity interaction and racial matching on the supervisory working alliance and supervisee multicultural competence. *Counselor Education and Supervision, 36,* 284–304.

Ladany, N., Constantine, M. G., Miller, K., Erickson, C. D., & Muse-Burke, J. L. (2000). Supervisor countertransference: A qualitative investigation into its identification and description. *Journal of Counseling Psychology, 47,* 102–115.

Ladany, N., Ellis, M. V., & Friedlander, M. L. (1999). The supervisory working alliance, trainee self-efficacy, and satisfaction with supervision. *Journal of Counseling & Development, 77,* 447–455.

Ladany, N., & Friedlander, M. L. (1995). The relationship between the supervisory working alliance and trainees' experiences of role conflicts and role ambiguity. *Counseling Education and Supervision, 34,* 220–231.

Ladany, N., Hill, C. E., Corbett, M., & Nutt, L. (1996). Nature, extent, and importance of what therapy trainees do not disclose to their supervisors. *Journal of Counseling Psychology, 43,* 10–24.

Ladany, N., & Lehrman-Waterman, D. E. (1999). The content and frequency of supervisor self-disclosures and their relationship to supervisor style and the supervisory working alliance. *Counselor Education and Supervision, 38,* 143–160.

Ladany, N., Lehrman-Waterman, D. E., Molinaro, M., & Wolgast, B. (1999). Psychotherapy supervisor ethical practices: Adherence to guidelines, the supervisory working alliance, and supervisee satisfaction. *The Counseling Psychologist, 27,* 443–475.

Ladany, N., & Melincoff, D. S. (1999). The nature of counselor supervisor nondisclosure. *Counselor Education and Supervision, 38,* 161–176.

Ladany, N., O'Brien, K., Hill, C. E., Melincoff, D. S., Knox, S., & Petersen, D. (1997). Sexual attraction toward clients, use of supervision, and prior training: A qualitative study of psychology predoctoral interns. *Journal of Counseling Psychology, 44,* 413–424.

Lane, R. C. (1986). The recalcitrant supervisee: The negative supervisory reaction. *Current Issues in Psychoanalytic Practice, 2,* 65–81.

Langs, R. (1979). *The supervisory experience.* New York: Aronson.

Littrell, J. M., Lee-Borden, N., & Lorenz, J. (1979). A developmental framework for counseling supervision. *Counselor Education and Supervision, 19,* 129–136.

Loganbill, C. R., Hardy, E. V., & Delworth, U. (1982). Supervision: A conceptual model. *The Counseling Psychologist, 10,* 3–42.

Lower, R. B. (1972). Countertransference resistances in the supervisory situation. *American Journal of Psychiatry, 129,* 156–160.

Marshall, W. R., & Confer, W. N. (1980). Psychotherapy supervision: Supervisees' perspectives. In A. K. Hess (Ed.), *Psychotherapy supervision: Theory, research, and practice* (pp. 92–100). New York: Wiley.

McCarthy, P., Sugden, S., Koker, M., Lamendola, F., Maurer, S., & Renninger, S. (1995). A practical guide to informed consent in clinical supervision. *Counselor Education and Supervision, 35,* 130–138.

McColley. S. H., & Baker, E. (1982). Training activities and styles of beginning supervisors: A survey. *Professional Psychology, 13,* 283–292.

McRoy, R. G., Freeman, E. M., Logan, S. L., & Blackmon, B. (1986). Cross-cultural field supervision: Implications for social work education. *Journal of Social Work Education, 22,* 50–56.

Mearns, D. (1991). On being a supervisor. In W. Dryden & B. Thorne (Eds.), *Training and supervision for counselling in action* (pp. 116–128). London: Sage.

Moses, H. A., & Hardin, J. T. (1978). A relationship approach to counselor supervision in agency settings. In J. Boyd (Ed.), *Counselor supervision* (pp. 437–480). Muncie, IN: Accelerated Development.

Mueller, W. J., & Kell, B. L. (1972). *Coping with conflict: Supervising counselors and psychotherapists.* New York: Appleton-Century-Crofts.

Nelson, M. L. (1997). An interactive model for empowering women in supervision. *Counselor Education and Supervision, 37,* 125–138.

Nelson, M. L., & Holloway, E. L. (1990). Relation of gender to power and involvement in supervision. *Journal of Counseling Psychology, 37,* 473–481.

Nelson, T. S. (1991). Gender in family therapy supervision. *Contemporary Family Therapy: An International Journal, 13,* 357–369.

Neufeldt, S. A. (1999). *Supervision strategies for the first practicum* (2nd ed.). Alexandria, VA: American Counseling Association.

Neufeldt, S. A., Iverson, J. N., & Juntunen, C. L. (1995). *Supervision strategies for the first practicum.* Alexandria, VA: American Counseling Association.

Neufeldt, S. A., Karno, M. P., & Nelson, M. L. (1996). A qualitative study of experts' conceptualization of supervision reflectivity. *Journal of Counseling Psychology, 43,* 3–9.

Norcross, J. C., & Halgin, R. P. (1997). Integrative approaches to psychotherapy supervision. In C. E. Watkins, Jr. (Ed.), *Handbook of psychotherapy supervision* (pp. 203–222). New York: Wiley.

Olk, M. E., & Friedlander, M. L. (1992). Trainees' experience of role conflict and role ambiguity in supervisory relationships. *Journal of Counseling Psychology, 39,* 389–397.

Pietrofesa, J. J., Leonard, G. E., & Van Hoose, W. (1978). *The authentic counselor* (2nd ed.). Boston: Houghton Mifflin.

Pope, K. S., Keith-Spiegel, P., & Tabachnick, B. (1986). Sexual attraction to clients: The human therapist and the (sometimes) inhuman training system. *American Psychologist, 41,* 147–158.

Pope, K. S., Levenson, H., & Schover, L. R. (1979). Sexual intimacy in psychology training: Results and implications of a national survey. *American Psychologist, 34,* 682–689.

Pope, K. S., Sonne, J., & Holroyd, J. (1993). *Sexual feelings in psychotherapy.* Washington, DC: American Psychological Association.

Prochaska, J. O., & Norcross, J. C. (1999). *Systems of psychotherapy: A transactional analysis* (4th ed.). Pacific Grove: Brooks/Cole.

Rioch, M. J. (1980). The dilemmas of supervision in dynamic psychotherapy. In A. K. Hess (Ed.), *Psychotherapy supervision: Theory, research, and practice* (pp. 68–76). New York: John Wiley.

Rodolfa, E., Rowen, H., Steier, D., Nicassio, T., & Gordon, J. (1994). Sexual dilemmas in internship training: What's a good training director to do? *APPIC Newsletter, 19(2),* 1, 22–24.

Rogers, C. R. (1957). The necessary and sufficient conditions of therapeutic personality change. *Journal of Consulting Psychology, 21,* 95–103.

Rønnestad, M. H., & Skovholt, T. M. (1993). Supervision of beginning and advanced graduate students of counseling and psychotherapy. *Journal of Counseling Development, 71,* 396–405.

Salvendy, J. T. (1993). Control and power in supervision. *International Journal of Group Psychotherapy, 43,* 363–376.

Schauer, A. H., Seymour, W. R., & Geen, R. G. (1985). Effects of observation and evaluation on anxiety in beginning counselors: A social facilitation analysis. *Journal of Counseling and Development, 63,* 279–285.

Schiavone, C. D., & Jessell, J. C. (1988). Influence of attributed expertness and gender in counselor supervision. *Counselor Education and Supervision, 28,* 29–42.

Schlesinger, H. (1981). General principles of psychoanalytic supervision. In R. S. Wallerstein (Ed.), *Becoming a psychoanalyst* (pp. 29–38). New York: International Universities Press.

Sells, J., Goodyear, R., Lichtenberg, J., & Polkinghorne, D. (1997). Relationship of supervisor and trainee gender to in-session verbal behavior and ratings of trainee skills. *Journal of Counseling Psychology, 44,* 1–7.

Shohet, R., & Wilmot, J. (1991). The key issue in the supervision of counsellors: The supervisory relationship. In W. Dryden & B. Thorne (Eds.), *Training and supervision for counselling in action* (pp. 87–98). London: Sage.

Skovholt, T. M., & Rønnestad, M. H. (1992). *The evolving professional self: Stages and themes in therapist and counselor development.* Chichester, England: Wiley.

Stevens-Smith, P. (1995). Gender issues in counselor education: Current status and challenges. *Counselor Education and Supervision, 34,* 283–293.

Stoltenberg, C. D. (1981). Approaching supervision from a developmental perspective: The counselor complexity model. *Journal of Counseling Psychology, 28,* 59–65.

Stoltenberg, C. D., & Delworth, U. (1987). *Supervising counselors and therapists: A developmental perspective.* San Francisco: Jossey-Bass.

Strean, H. S. (1991). Colluding illusions among analytic candidates, their supervisors, and their patients: A major factor in some treatment impasses. *Psychoanalytic Psychology, 8,* 415–438.

Styczynski, L. E. (1980). The transition from supervisee to supervisor. In A. K. Hess (Ed.), *Psychotherapy supervision: Theory, research and practice* (pp. 29–39). New York: Wiley.

Sumerel, M. B., & Borders, L. D. (1996). Addressing personal issues in supervision: Impact of counselors' experience level on various aspects of the supervising relationship. *Counselor Education and Supervision, 35,* 268–286.

Teitelbaum, S. H. (1990). Supertransference: The role of the supervisor's blind spots. *Psychoanalytic Psychology, 7,* 243–258.

Watkins, C. E., Jr. (1990). The effects of counselor self-disclosure: A research review. *The Counseling Psychologist, 18,* 477–500.

Watkins, C. E., Jr. (Ed.). (1997). *Handbook of psychotherapy supervision.* New York: Wiley.

Worthen, V., & McNeill, B. W. (1996). A phenomenological investigation of "good" supervision events. *Journal of Counseling Psychology, 43,* 25–34.

Worthington, E., & Stern, A. (1985). Effects of supervisor and supervisory relationship. *Journal of Counseling Psychology, 32,* 252–262.

Yager, G. G., & Beck, T. D. (1985). Beginning practicum: It only hurt until I laughed! *Counselor Education and Supervision, 25,* 149–157.

Julie R. Ancis
Nicholas Ladany

A Multicultural Framework for Counselor Supervision

The demographic composition of the United States has become increasingly diverse. It is estimated that visible racial/ethnic minority groups will constitute a numerical majority between the years 2030 and 2050 (Sue & Sue, 1999; U.S. Bureau of the Census, 1992, 1996). Also, there have been significant demographic shifts in professional roles and positions, including a greater number of women entering the workforce and in supervisory positions (Gilbert & Rossman, 1992; Munson, 1997). These transformations have implications for both counseling and supervision, as the potential for multicultural interactions among supervisors, supervisees, and clients increases.

Attention to multicultural issues within supervision is essential to training clinicians who are able to conduct ethical and effective practice with diverse clientele, as well as ensuring that supervisors are attending to the needs of diverse supervisees and clients. Research suggests that counselor trainees often possess racial and gender biases, limited self-awareness, and a lack of knowledge regarding multicultural counseling (Ancis & Sanchez-Hucles, 2000; Ancis & Szymanski, 1999; Johnson, Searight, Handal, & Gibbons, 1993; Ponterotto, 1988). Moreover, research has demonstrated that supervisees may perceive their supervisors as lacking in multicultural sensitivity toward clients, as well as toward supervisees (Fukuyama, 1994; Ladany, Lehrman-Waterman, Molinaro, & Wolgast, 1999). Perhaps not coincidentally, many current supervisors likely did not receive multicultural counseling training (or even training in supervision). Thus, supervisees may be more knowledgeable about multicultural counseling than their supervisors (Constantine, 1997; D'Andrea & Daniels, 1997). Overall, although the relevance of multicultural issues within supervision is rather clear, these issues have generally not been addressed in the supervision literature (Brown & Landrum-Brown, 1995; Leong & Wagner, 1994).

☐ Current Models of Supervision

Traditional models of supervision include psychotherapy-theory-based supervision (e.g., Bradley, 1989; Ekstein & Wallerstein, 1972; Rice, 1980; Watkins, 1997), social role supervision models (e.g., Bernard, 1997; Holloway, 1997), and developmental approaches to supervision (e.g., Chagon & Russell, 1995; Skovholt & Rønnestad, 1992; Stoltenberg, 1981).

Psychotherapy theory-based supervision includes approaches from many theoretical perspectives, such as psychodynamic, person-centered, cognitive-behavioral, and systemic, among others. The approach to supervision is influenced by the particular theoretical perspective. For example, consistent with behavioral theory, behavioral supervision focuses on teaching appropriate therapist behaviors and extinguishing inappropriate behaviors (Boyd, 1978; Levine & Tilker, 1974). Psychotherapy-theory-based supervision, like contemporary models of counseling and psychotherapy, has paid little or no attention to multicultural factors in supervision.

Social role supervision models focus on the supervisor's role as related to the supervisee's professional development. The supervisor acts as teacher, counselor, and consultant depending upon the supervisee's learning needs. Two of the most influential models of social role supervision are Holloway's (1997) systems approach to supervision (SAS) and Bernard's (1997) discrimination model. Holloway describes seven interrelated dimensions/factors of the SAS model: four contextual factors (the institution, the supervisor, the client, and the trainee), supervision functions, supervision tasks, and the supervision relationship (the core factor). Multicultural factors are mentioned within the descriptions of two contextual factors, that is, supervisor factors and trainee factors. However, this is done in a cursory fashion and with no specificity with regard to handling multicultural issues within a supervisory framework. Rather, cultural characteristics are generally noted as relevant to the supervisor's performance and to the trainees' attitudes and actions toward their clients and supervisors. Bernard's discrimination model focuses on encouraging the supervisor to consider a range of responses and to discriminate among them for the trainee's maximum development. Bernard (1997) admits that the discrimination model is largely inattentive to cultural variables within supervision.

Developmental approaches to supervision focus on how supervisees change as they gain training and supervised experience (Bernard & Goodyear, 1998). Several developmental models of supervision exist (e.g., Hogan, 1964; Littrell, Lee-Borden, & Lorenz, 1979; Loganbill, Hardy, & Delworth, 1982; Skovholt & Rønnestad, 1992; Stoltenberg, 1981). The trainee is typically conceptualized as moving from a level of dependency and limited personal and professional awareness to increased autonomy, awareness, and skill. Developmental models attempt to match supervisor behavior to the trainees' developmental needs. Several authors (e.g., Loganbill, Hardy, & Delworth, 1982; Stoltenberg & Delworth, 1987) do attend to individual differences as one domain of clinical training and practice. These authors describe the trainee as progressing from stereotypic thinking and a limited awareness of personal prejudices to increased awareness, a view of the client as an individual and a person-in-context, and ongoing self-examination as he or she moves through the various levels of development. While these authors describe appropriate supervisory approaches for trainees at various stages of development, specific strategies for increasing trainees' cultural counseling competence are not addressed.

Several authors have described developmental approaches to training that specifically attend to multicultural counseling competence (e.g., Carney & Kahn, 1984; Sabnani, Ponterotto, & Borodovsky, 1991). Carney and Kahn's (1984) counselor development model, influenced by the work of several authors including Stoltenberg (1981), consists of five stages of trainee development related to the acquisition of cross-cultural counseling competencies and appropriate learning environments. Each stage attends to the trainees' knowledge of cultural groups, attitudinal awareness and cross-cultural sensitivity, and specific cross-cultural counseling skills. Sabnani, Ponterotto, and Borodovsky (1991) also present a multicultural training model for White, middle-class counselors which focuses on White racial identity development. However, these models do not address the implications of each developmental stage in terms of the trainee's clinical interventions. Additionally, these models focus exclusively on the trainee's development of multicultural counseling competence and do not address the supervisor's identity, the supervisor's multicultural competence, or the supervision relationship.

One of the only supervision models that directly addresses the supervisor, supervisee, and client triad is the worldview congruence model (Brown & Landrum-Brown, 1995). This model was influenced by the work of several researchers (Myers, 1991; Nichols, 1976; Nobles, 1972). Brown & Landrum-Brown (1995) describe eight worldview dimensions: (a) psychobehavioral modality, (b) axiology (values), (c) ethos (guiding beliefs), (d) epistemology (how one knows), (e) logic (reasoning process), (f) ontology (nature of reality), (g) concept of time, and (h) concept of self. In addition, they present five patterns of conflict and/or complements relevant to the supervisory triad and assert that worldview conflicts may result in distrust and hostility within the triadic relationship. The authors do not describe specific issues that may arise within the triadic relationship for each of the eight worldview dimensions in each potential worldview situation or related supervisor interventions. Nonetheless, Brown and Landrum-Brown (1995) provide a useful framework that begins to address the multicultural complexities within the supervision relationship.

Overall, the literature focusing on multicultural counseling supervision can be characterized as both general and fragmented. Several authors have discussed various approaches to multicultural counseling supervision, including encouraging the supervisee to examine her or his own sociocultural background, beliefs, and biases (Morgan, 1984; Remington & DaCosta,

1989), recruiting diverse faculty and students (Morgan, 1984), and providing cultural training and courses throughout the curriculum (Remington & DaCosta, 1989). In addition, several authors (e.g., Ault-Riche, 1988; Brodsky, 1980; Cook, 1994; Fong & Lease, 1996; Gardner, 1980; Lopez, 1997; Priest, 1994; Remington & DaCosta, 1989; Vargas, 1989) have written about problems in cross-cultural supervision, including unintentional racism, supervisor gender bias, miscommunication, undiscussed racial-ethnic issues that distort the supervisory relationship, overemphasis on cultural explanations for psychological difficulties, and overdependence on supervisor's knowledge.

While this literature has been helpful in identifying multiple aspects of multicultural supervision and providing suggestions for fostering multicultural counseling practice, there are several limitations to this body of work. Specifically, extant models of multicultural supervision (a) tend to focus on the supervisee's multicultural competence without attending to the supervisor's competence; (b) tend to focus exclusively on race-ethnicity while disregarding other aspects of identity (e.g., gender, sexual orientation); (c) do not provide a comprehensive framework for approaching multicultural issues within a supervisory context (Leong & Wagner, 1994), and (d) lack empirical research support. Moreover, the multicultural supervision literature tends to present global issues and difficulties that may arise and relatively global suggestions for overcoming such difficulties. A model that describes the multiplicity of supervisor and supervisee identities, the relationships between supervisor and supervisee when both possess varied perspectives, and the relationship's influence on supervision and client outcome would contribute to the literature (Brown & Landrum-Brown, 1995). Second, a comprehensive framework of multicultural supervision competencies would help to articulate the salient dimensions of supervisor multicultural competence, thereby rectifying a diffuse and fragmented approach to supervisor multicultural competence.

The purpose of this chapter is to present two comprehensive models, each focusing on two areas of multicultural supervision. The first model, the heuristic model of nonoppressive interpersonal development, attends to the multiple and interrelated dimensions of supervisor's and supervisee's identity. It is designed to offer supervisors a heuristic framework for understanding patterns of thoughts, feelings, and behaviors about themselves, their trainees, and clients across specific demographic variables (i.e., race, ethnicity, gender, sexual orientation, disability, socioeconomic status). Next, we will discuss the multicultural supervision competencies. This framework delineates the multiple dimensions of multicultural competence within the context of supervision. Finally, we will present a case study that highlights the relationships between both models; that is, the multiple identities of both supervisor and supervisee; related thoughts, feelings, and behaviors within supervision; and how these identity interactions influence multicultural supervision competence.

☐ Heuristic Model of Nonoppressive Interpersonal Development

Over the past two decades, there has been a recognition that one's identity can play a key role in understanding clients' as well as counselors' psychological makeup. Moreover, it is presumed that general models of identity development (e.g., Marcia, 1966) as well as the simple knowledge of a particular nominal or demographic variable (e.g., biological sex) insufficiently predicts a person's beliefs and behaviors. Identity models have been created to reflect a variety of specific personal demographic variables, including race (Cross, 1971, 1995; Hardiman, 1982; Helms, 1990, 1995; Helms & Cook, 1999; Sue & Sue, 1999), ethnicity (Phinney, 1989; Sodowsky, Kwan, & Pannu, 1995), gender (Downing & Roush, 1985; McNamara & Rickard, 1989; Ossana, Helms, & Leonard, 1992), and sexual orientation (Cass, 1979; Chan, 1989; Fassinger, 1991; Rust, 1993; Troiden, 1989). To some extent, these models, specifically racial identity and gender identity, have been applied to the supervision context (Carney & Kahn, 1984; Cook, 1994; Helms & Cook, 1999; Ladany, Brittan-Powell, & Pannu, 1997; Porter, 1995; Vasquez & McKinley, 1982). However, levels of identity with respect to multiple demographic characteristics have not been considered within the supervision context. Furthermore, these models have primarily focused on psychological identity, with limited attention being paid to behavioral manifestations of identity. To this end, the purpose of our model of nonoppressive interpersonal development is to offer supervisors a heuristic model for understanding patterns of thoughts, feelings, and behaviors about themselves, their trainees, and clients across specific demographic variables (i.e., race, ethnicity, sexual orientation, gender, disability, socioeconomic status). It is important to begin this discourse by noting that this model is not intended to wholly replace the specific identity models. Instead our intention is to offer supervisors a way of managing the multiple models without diluting their value. In fact, it is our contention that supervisors should learn about the specific identity models across demographic variables as a way of supplementing the tenets of our model. With this caveat in mind, we present our model.

We believe that for any given demographic variable, people can belong to one of two groups: (1) a socially oppressed group (SOG) (female, person of color, gay/lesbian/bisexual, disabled, working class) or (2) a socially privileged group (SPG) (male, White, heterosexual, European American, physically abled, middle to upper class). For example, in terms of the demographic variable sex, women belong to the socially oppressed group and men belong to the socially privileged group. Furthermore, based on this conceptualization, people could reasonably belong to both a SOG and a SPG when considering their multiple personal demographic variables (e.g., female, White).

We also believe that for each demographic variable, people progress through phases of what we call means of interpersonal functioning (MIF): thoughts and feelings about oneself, as well as behaviors based on one's identification with a particular demographic variable (e.g., the psychological and behavioral manifestations of being a person who is disabled). Our position, similar to that of the identity theorists, is that the demographic variable itself does not account for one's thoughts, feelings, and behaviors. Rather, how one perceives oneself and interacts with others is largely due to an environmental press that exerts its influence on individuals based on their demographic characteristics. We also argue that regardless of the group to which one belongs, people progress through similar phases of MIF with respect to each identified group, albeit there are common and unique features depending upon the identified group. As an example, both women and men are capable of progress in terms of their MIF. The developmental stages of MIF for both women and men will have common features (e.g., both will exhibit complacency regarding societal change in the less advanced stages) as well as unique features (e.g., generally, women will feel less empowered and men will perceive greater entitlement). Similar schemes can be produced for race, sexual orientation, ethnicity, disability, and socioeconomic status.

We should note three additional assumptions to our model. First, we believe that people can be more advanced in terms of their MIF for one demographic variable (e.g., sex) than for another (e.g., race). For example, a White woman may have an understanding of sexism and the limiting effects of sex role socialization, but lack an awareness of White privilege. Second, this model restrictively applies to people who live in the United States, the country from which the social context of the model is derived. Third, the work in supervision and counseling can be characterized and predicted by the knowledge of each dyadic member's MIF for each demographic variable.

It is believed that people have the ability to developmentally progress through four phases or stages of MIF (i.e., adaptation, incongruence, exploration, and integration). These stages represent a progression from complacency and limited awareness regarding cultural differences and oppression to increased awareness of multicultural issues, cognitive complexity, and commitment to cultural competence. We will define each stage and include examples of feelings, thoughts, and behaviors that are characteristic of people for each stage across different demographic variables.

Adaptation

The first stage of MIF is adaptation. Adaptation features that are common to both SOG and SPG members involve complacency and apathy regarding, and conformity to, the socially oppressive environment (e.g., "there will always be poor people"), a superficial understanding of differences among people (e.g., "we all are from the same melting pot"), stereotypic attitudes toward particular cultural groups (e.g., "Hispanics are lazy and unmotivated"), minimal conscious awareness of oppressive state of affairs (e.g., unaware of public transportation that is inaccessible to persons who are disabled), and limited emotional awareness (e.g., anger without insight). Although people in this stage are adaptive in the social context in which they live, their intrapersonal and interpersonal functioning is maladaptive and results in the perpetuation of the oppressive status quo (Thompson & Neville, 1999). The primary defense mechanisms include denial and resistance. Behaviors range on a continuum from passive acceptance of oppression of others (e.g., looking the other way) to active endorsement of oppressive contingencies (e.g., endorsement of political figures who advocate oppression of SOGs) to active participation in oppressing members of SOGs (e.g., directed violence against members of SOGs). Unique features of people in a SOG is an idealization of and identification with people in the SPG (e.g., to be healthy is to be wealthy), limited awareness of oppressive events that they personally experience (e.g., a woman who believes she has never been the recipient of an oppressive act), limited motivation to change one's own circumstance, and abandonment of SOG features (e.g., active efforts to hide or deny one's Jewish ethnicity). Unique to SPG members is an obliviousness to differences (e.g., a color-blind perspective on race, such as "we all belong to the human race"), a belief that all people are the same and have similar interpersonal experiences (e.g., women have no obstacles to career advancement), denigration of members of SOGs (e.g., homosexuality is a sin; gay people deserve the diseases that afflict them), and unawareness of privilege associated with being a member of a SPG (e.g., any poor person who works as hard as me has the same opportunities).

Based on an understanding of one's MIF stage, predictions about supervisors' and trainees' thoughts, feelings, and behaviors relevant to supervision and counseling can be made. For a given demographic variable, both SOG and SPG supervisors in the adaptation stage are more likely to (a) minimize and dismiss trainees' expression of multicultural competence, (b) refer to clients based on inaccurate stereotypes, (c) become anxious if oppression issues emerge in supervision, (d) inaccurately perceive oneself as quite multiculturally competent, (e) exhibit oppressive beliefs in the presence of SPG trainees, and (f) demonstrate limited integrative complexity when it comes to conceptualizing trainees and clients within a multicultural framework. Integrative complexity is defined as the ability to differentiate (identify multiple multicultural factors) and integrate (link these factors) when conceptualizing clients (Constantine & Ladany, 2000; Ladany, Inman, Constantine, & Hofheinz, 1997) and can also be extended to conceptualizing trainees. Supervisors in the adaptation stage are less likely to (a) address multicultural issues between the supervisor and trainee (i.e., negative parallel process) and between the trainee and her or his clients, (b) accurately empathize with SOG trainees who are at higher MIF, (c) facilitate

MIF development in SPG trainees, and (d) admit lack of comfort with multi-cultural issues (less likely to attend to areas of less expertise). Adaptation-stage supervisors will not explore either their own or supervisees' biases, background, and worldview and how these are related to supervision. They will be unaware of the limitations of traditional counseling approaches with diverse clients and will foster a limited range of interventions with their trainees. Moreover, they will be unable to identify trainees' personal and professional strengths and weaknesses in the area of multicultural counseling. Supervisors who find themselves in the adaptation stage should ethically seek supervision of supervision or personal counseling to assist them in working through their oppressive beliefs; however, they are unlikely to do so unless they encounter an experience that facilitates their development to the next stage of MIF.

For a given demographic variable, both SOG and SPG trainees in the adaptation stage are less likely to (a) attend to multicultural issues in supervision or with their clients (e.g., not likely to address multicultural issues in case conceptualization reports and presentations, not likely to address multicultural issues with clients) or to (b) consider demographic variables beyond the mere mention of them in case conceptualizations (verbal and written). Trainees are also more likely to (a) blame clients and ignore environmental influences on clients' functioning and (b) miss salient multicultural issues that emerge for the client and between themselves and their clients (e.g., may mistake a client's culturally consistent deference as dependence).

Incongruence

The second stage of MIF is incongruence. People from both SOGs and SPGs in this stage are likely to experience conscious incongruence, whereby their previous beliefs about oppression and privilege seem incongruent, dissonant, or inconsistent with events of which they become aware. For example, a widely publicized news event that describes a violent attack on a person of color due solely to the person's race may conflict with one's beliefs that the world is just and people are treated equally. Additional common features include conflict, confusion, dissonance, and some awareness, yet no real commitment to advocacy. During incongruence, denial is no longer as effective a defense mechanism as it was during adaptation. Rather, minimization and rationalization are the more predominant defense mechanisms. Even though awareness is raised, behaviors are still often congruent with the more passive oppressive interactions (e.g., passive acceptance of gender stereotypes).

Although members of both SOGs and SPGs may experience an event that leads them to question their previously held beliefs, the event itself may be different or will likely involve different personal consequences. For people in SOGs, the event may be a personal discrimination experience that leads to an awareness of oppression (e.g., a White friend tells an African American person that she never thought of her as African American since she is so articulate). A SPG member may experience indirect discrimination through association with a member of a SOG or may witness a discriminatory event (Ancis & Szymanski, 1999). Also, this transition from the adaptation to incongruence stage could be the result of one significant event or the culmination of a series of events such that the person can no longer ignore the reality of oppression. People in SOGs may have some awareness of oppression but are conflicted about their identification with either the SOG or the SPG. For people in SPGs, an event may help them recognize that oppression exists (e.g., salary differences between women and men) but change is still believed to be the responsibility of members of SOGs, and there is little recognition of SPG privilege (e.g., "Affirmative action is not fair!").

Supervisors in the incongruence stage are unlikely to attend to multicultural issues in supervision, or at best, they give it minimal attention. They may attempt to have the trainee collude with their rationalizations regarding SOG members. For example, knowing that trainees will likely feel compelled to agree with them, supervisors may actively try to dismiss multicultural issues as being irrelevant (e.g., supervisor may say to the trainee "I think women deserve equal rights but these feminists take it too far sometimes"), rather than to ignore multicultural issues completely, as they did in the adaptation stage. Supervisors may begin to explore their own background and worldview but find an examination of personal biases too threatening.

Trainees in the incongruence stage are likely to be somewhat aware of multicultural issues but are unlikely to bring them up in supervision, in particular if they believe the supervisor does not consider multicultural issues important and if they are influenced by the supervisory power differential. They may bring it up in supervision in an indirect fashion (e.g., note a particular demographic) but they are likely to take the supervisors' lead on whether to explore the multicultural issue further. They are likely to include demographic information in case conceptualizations, but the information is not well differentiated or integrated. Furthermore, trainees are likely to approach multicultural issues in supervision in an approach/avoidance fashion.

Exploration

The third stage of MIF is exploration. Common features for both SOG and SPG members include active exploration of what it means to be a member of their respective SOG or SPG. Additionally, anger may be a prominent emotion, some of which is founded on current recognition of oppressive situations but also fueled by guilt or shame for not having recognized the oppressive state of affairs previously. Unlike the anger when one is in the adaptation stage, anger in the exploration stage is insightful (i.e., linked to the recognition of the oppressive status quo). Individuals may consider their own role in perpetuating oppressive environments and will likely seek out "encounter-like events" (e.g., reach out to the gay and lesbian community). Furthermore, individuals in the exploration stage are more likely to seek counseling to help them understand and process these experiences. SOG members are likely to immerse themselves in the particular culture (e.g., may wear Asian American clothing, participate in a gay pride event) and affiliate with other members of their SOG (e.g., associate with other people who are disabled). SPG members are likely to explore what it means to be a member of a SPG and consider the resulting privileges (e.g., advantages associated with White privilege; Ancis & Szymanski, 1999; Bulhan, 1985; Fine, Weis, Powell, & Mun Wong, 1997). Finally, what begins as an awareness of oppressive events may lead to a hypervigilance or hyperawareness.

For a particular demographic variable, both SOG and SPG supervisors will likely attend to multicultural issues in supervision and actively engage trainees to facilitate their multicultural awareness. However, their eagerness and enthusiasm to "create insight" may paradoxically result in greater resistance on the part of the trainee, especially if the trainee is in the adaptation or incongruence stage. Supervisors will likely initiate self-exploration among themselves and their trainees. They will be relatively open to exploring alternative conceptualizations and interventions with trainees (e.g., feminist theoretical approaches). A potential danger in terms of process and outcome of supervision is an overemphasis on multicultural issues to explain concerns or difficulties that are not well connected with additional and related unresolved conflicts. Furthermore, supervisors may begin to initiate trainees' personal exploration of biases but then be at a loss as to how to follow through or intervene.

Both SOG and SPG trainees will likely look to their supervisors for guidance and be open to exploring multicultural issues. However, they may overemphasize multicultural issues at the expense of other relevant counseling issues and may have difficulty integrating both personal and multicultural issues in conceptualizing clients. Also, trainees will begin to generalize their exploration stage beliefs for a given demographic characteristic to another demographic characteristic in which they are in the adaptation or incongruence stage. For example, a White trainee who was raised in an upper socioeconomic class home and who is exploring what it means to have White privilege may begin to become aware of socioeconomic advantages as well.

Integration

The fourth stage of MIF is integration. Common features for both SOGs and SPGs include multicultural integrity, integrative awareness, proficiency in associating with multiple SOG groups, recognition of oppressive occurrences, insight into oppressive interactions, and accurate feelings. Behaviorally, there is a committed pursuit of nonoppression in the environment (e.g., engage in advocacy for oppressed groups) and an ability to accurately empathize with members of multiple groups (SPG and SOG). Defense mechanisms are primarily fantasy, imagining what things could be like rather than become overwhelmed from focusing on the multiple components of everyday oppression. The SOG members are likely to reach out to members of their own SOG in order to offer mentoring. Members of SPGs will capitalize on opportunities to counter misguided reasoning presented to them by fellow SPG members who are at less advanced MIF stages (e.g., present counterarguments to misinformed stereotyping). They will likely utilize their privileges toward promoting equality and will work toward changing infrastructures within which they work.

For a given demographic variable, supervisors who are members of either a SOG or a SPG are likely to be adept at facilitating trainee development in their MIF. Supervisors are also able to discuss and process differences and similarities between themselves and their trainees, which in turn models for trainees how to interact with their clients (i.e., positive parallel process). Supervisors can also address multicultural issues in supervision effectively and competently. Supervisors have spent time on their own MIF and strive toward changing the training environment in which they work. Supervisors are able to assist trainees in developing client advocacy skills, use power constructively in supervision, and facilitate discussions of diversity with trainees at different MIF stages.

Trainees in the integration stage are likely to be able to conceptualize clients in an integratively complex fashion across multiple demographic variables. They are also able to (a) accurately empathize with SOG and SPG clients across clients' MIF for a given demographic variable, (b) continue to challenge their own socialized biases in supervision and understand how their internalized biases may influence their work with clients, and (c) be able to distinguish between countertransference-based biases and client transference. Furthermore, trainees in this stage become more adept at generalizing their integrative beliefs across other demographic characteristics and use supervision as one method of accomplishing this process.

☐ Supervision Relationship Types

How can knowledge about stages of interpersonal functioning be used to understand the supervision relationship? Depending on the stage in which the supervisor and trainee belong, relationship dynamics could be hypothesized. These stages are similar to the interpersonal interactions proposed by Helms (1990), Cook (1994), and Helms and Cook (1999) for racial identity interactions. There are two primary extensions: (a) we have extended the conceptualization to multiple demographic groups, and (b) we offer specific supervisory interventions across developmental stages.

In regard to the heuristic model of nonoppressive interpersonal development, there are four possible supervisor–trainee interpersonal interaction dynamics that could be exhibited, depending on the respective stages of the supervisor and trainee. For the purposes of this model, supervisors and trainees are considered in a delayed phase of MIF if they are in the adaptation or incongruence stage and are considered in an advanced phase of MIF if they are in the exploration or integration stage. The four supervisor–trainee interpersonal interaction dynamics are (a) progressive, where the supervisor is at a more advanced stage than the trainee (e.g., supervisor, integration; trainee, adaptation), (b) parallel-advanced, where the supervisor and trainee are at comparable advanced MIF stages (i.e., supervisor, exploration or integration; trainee, exploration or integration), (c) parallel-delayed, where the supervisor and trainee are at comparable delayed MIF stages (i.e., supervisor, adaptation or incongruence; trainee, adaptation or incongruence), and (d) regressive, where the trainee is at a more advanced stage than the supervisor (e.g., trainee, integration; supervisor, adaptation). Types of interpersonal interactions have implications for trainee outcome and client outcome. Specifically, it can be predicted that a variety of supervision processes (e.g., the supervisory working alliance) and outcomes (e.g., trainee multicultural competence) would be enhanced from most to least in the following types of interactions: parallel-advanced, progressive, parallel-delayed, and regressive.

Parallel-advanced interactions would likely involve a mutual collaboration between the supervisor and trainee regarding the importance of facilitating multicultural competence in the trainee. Hence, the supervisory alliance would be enhanced, as would trainee multicultural competence. Progressive interactions would also likely enhance trainee multicultural competence, but there would likely be some resistance on the part of the trainee that would result in a less-than-optimal working alliance. Parallel-delayed and regressive relationships would likely result in weak supervisory alliances and possibly negatively influence trainee multicultural competence. In these instances, both the supervisor's and trainee's less-than-functional defense mechanisms (e.g., resistance and denial) would likely interfere with healthy relationship development. Moreover, because multicultural client issues are not likely to be discussed, or, when discussed, likely to be done in a negative fashion, the trainee's multicultural competence will be stilted and negatively influenced.

In terms of client outcome, a different pattern would likely emerge. Specifically, as with trainee outcome, parallel-advanced supervisory interactions would result in the greatest client outcome (e.g., counseling alliance, client engagement, client satisfaction and participation in counseling). Contrary to trainee outcome, regressive relationships would likely result in the next greatest client outcome. This prediction is due to the supposed buffering effect that a more advanced trainee would provide between the client and the supervisor. However, the trainee risks negative consequences such as receiving a negative supervisor evaluation because the supervisor doesn't believe the trainee is conducting the type of counseling the supervisor wants. Clearly, this is not an ideal supervisory situation, but it will likely offer better client outcomes than in the case of progressive and parallel-delayed interactions, where the trainee is less adept at handling multicultural issues. In these instances either the supervisor is attempting to facilitate the trainee to become more multiculturally adept or the supervisor is doing nothing in terms of working with the trainee on multicultural issues, respectively. A regressive supervisory relationship may also be quite common given that current supervisors in the field were unlikely to have received multicultural training whereas current trainees are very likely to have received multicultural training (Constantine, 1997; Priest, 1994).

☐ Supervisor Interventions

As can be seen in the possible outcomes based on the interaction types, supervisors can play a crucial role in facilitating trainee development. In fact, it is argued that it is the supervisor's ethical and professional responsibility to facilitate trainee nonoppressive interpersonal development (Ladany et al., 1999). Hence, specific supervisor interventions could be effective in moving trainees to an advanced stage of nonoppressive development. It should be noted that movement through stages is not an easy process and will likely involve some resistance from trainees. The supervisor will also likely have to fight an environmental press that tends to push people toward less advanced stages of development. Most importantly, there must be a reasonably strong supervisory working alliance between the trainee and supervisor for interventions to be effective. The primary means by which such a relationship is founded is through empathic understanding of the trainee and her or his level of development.

Across developmental stages, there are a number of effective and appropriate supervisory interventions. Many of these interventions have been identified in the preceding section on behaviors of supervisors in the integration stage (e.g., discuss multicultural issues between the supervisor and trainee). First, for trainees in the adaptation stage, the supervisor's task is to create dissonance and move the trainee to the incongruence stage (e.g., offer readings, focus on the knowledge dimension of multicultural competency, challenge the trainee's oppressive belief system). For trainees in the incongruence stage, supervisors can intervene by facilitating multiple encounter-like events in order to move the trainee to the exploration stage (e.g., give homework to attend a social function of an oppressed group, focus on the knowledge dimension of multicultural competency, challenge the trainee's oppressive belief system). For trainees in the exploration stage, supervisors can intervene by providing emotional support and teach strategies to move beyond guilt (e.g., facilitate trainee movement to integration stage, focus on skills and self-awareness dimensions of multicultural competency). Supervisors can also teach trainees to understand intrapsychic and environmental explanations of events. Furthermore, with the emergence of intense emotions, supervisors could recommend that trainees seek personal counseling to process their intense emotional experiences and help uncover additional unconscious oppressive beliefs. Finally, for trainees in the integration stage, supervisor interventions can include helping trainees integrate multiple experiences (e.g., process trainee experiences in supervision, focus on skills and self-awareness dimensions of competency, use a trainee's integrative status for one demographic variable to help her or him develop along another demographic variable on which she or he is less developed). Also, supervisors can help trainees deal with clients who are at various stages of MIF. Overall, while the optimal effectiveness of these supervisor interventions are presumed to be stage specific, in all likelihood they can be used effectively across all stages.

We also believe it is important to expand upon one assumption that underlies our proposed model. Specifically, we believe that moving through the MIF stages is an ethical imperative for supervisors and trainees. Furthermore, we do not ascribe to the belief that counselors must recognize their multicultural limitations and, as a result, believe they can choose not to work with certain groups of clients who fall outside their desired expertise (e.g., gay or women clients). In most settings in which counselors work (e.g., community mental health centers, schools), they will not be able to decide whether to work with someone who is a member of one of the demographic groups we identified. They will also not have the option of referring clients with whom they would prefer not to work (e.g., gay or women clients). As such, supervisors and counselors must consider whether they can work through their oppressive beliefs, and supervisors should recognize that they are accountable for ensuring that counselors adhere to this responsibility. Moreover, supervisors should assist counselors in recognizing from where oppressive beliefs are derived and should not be distracted by religious overtones of some oppressive beliefs (e.g., homosexuality is a sin, women should be subservient to men). In the end, supervisors should assist counselors in evaluating the extent to which oppressive beliefs can be remediated and whether the counseling profession is an appropriate choice for them.

Research into this model is clearly warranted. For example, additional research is needed to determine if the interventions are indeed optimized in a stage-specific fashion. Furthermore, scales need to be developed that operationalize the stage constructs. Moreover, specific issues across stages for each demographic variable could be further delineated and examined. It is through these investigations and refined conceptualizations that this model can be refined and retested.

The heuristic model of nonoppressive interpersonal development high-lights the multiple and interrelated identities of both supervisors and super-visees. We propose that this model has significant implications for the affect, cognitions, and behaviors of supervisors and supervisees; the super-visory relationship; the supervisee's professional development; and client outcome. The multiple and interrelated dimensions of identity within the supervisor–supervisee–client triad related to multiple demographic variables present challenges to providing culturally competent supervision. In the next section, we provide a framework of multicultural supervision compe-tencies that attends to the supervisory triad.

☐ Multicultural Supervision Competencies as Ethical Practice

Much of the counseling literature that addresses multicultural competence has focused on competencies within the area of assessment and psycho-therapy (e.g., Atkinson, Morten, & Sue, 1993; Ridley, Mendoza, Kanitz, Angermeier, & Zenk, 1994; Sue, Arredondo, & McDavis, 1992; Sue & Sue, 1999). The Division 17 cross-cultural counseling competencies (Sue et al., 1982) and subsequent refinement and operationalization by the Associa-tion of Multicultural Counseling and Development (Arredondo et al., 1996; Sue et al., 1992) describe the characteristics of a culturally competent counselor. Culturally competent counselors strive towards (a) self-awareness of their assumptions about human behavior, values, and biases, (b) an understand-ing of the worldview of culturally different clients, and (c) the develop-ment of culturally appropriate intervention strategies.

However, multicultural competencies have scarcely been addressed within the supervision literature (Leong & Wagner, 1994; Munson, 1997). Super-visors play a significant role in developing trainees' conceptual, diagnostic, and intervention skills. If the counseling profession is truly committed to the promotion of culturally competent practice, supervisors must possess the competencies necessary to foster culturally competent trainees. We propose that competent multicultural supervision is an ethical imperative given the demographic diversity of clients, supervisees, and supervisors. As such, we reviewed American Counseling Association (ACA) and American Psycho-logical Association (APA) documents pertaining to ethical principles and standards to examine the extent to which attention is paid to multicultural issues within supervision.

Traditionally, ethical guidelines for counseling supervisors were embed-ded within, or deemed translatable from, the guidelines for practitioners. The ACA's (1995) *Code of Ethics and Standards of Practice* (1995) includes a section on "Teaching, Training, and Supervision" (Section F). The only areas within Section F that directly attend to diversity are sections F.1.a: "Counselor educators should make an effort to infuse material related to human diversity into all courses and/or workshops that are designed to promote the development of professional counselors" and F.2.i: "Counselors are responsive to their institution's and program's recruitment and retention needs for training program administrators, faculty, and students with diverse backgrounds and special needs." No mention is made of exploring trainees' personal and professional biases or ensuring that trainees are culturally competent. While issues of counselor nondiscrimination and cultural sensitivity are mentioned in other sections of the ACA *Code of Ethics and Standards of Practice*, multicultural issues are given only limited attention in the section on teaching, training, and supervision.

Only recently did the Association for Counselor Education and Supervision (ACES), a division of ACA, develop and publish ethical guidelines specifically for supervisors (ACES, 1990, 1995). Two documents are directly relevant to ethical principles and guidelines for counseling supervision: (a) the "Standards for Counseling Supervisors" developed by the Supervision Interest Network of ACES (1990), and (2) "Ethical Guidelines for Counseling Supervisors" (ACES, 1995).

The "Standards for Counseling Supervisors" (ACES, 1990), adopted by the American Association for Counseling and Development (AACD) Governing Council in 1989, consists of 11 core areas of knowledge, competencies, and personal traits characterizing effective supervisors. The standards do acknowledge that effective counseling supervisors are sensitive and knowledgeable about individual differences and understand the impact of these differences in supervisory relationships. However, the standards provide only a superficial acknowledgment of multicultural issues, and thus supervisors lack a guiding framework from which to provide culturally competent supervision. Interestingly, the ACES's (1995) "Ethical Guidelines for Counseling Supervisors" provide no mention of multicultural competence. Even though this document was first published 3 years after the "Standards for Counseling Supervisors" (see Hart, Borders, Nance, & Paradise, 1993), standards related to multicultural issues were not transferred into the ethical guidelines.

The lack of significant attention to multicultural supervision and training in documents that serve as guiding principles of the counseling profession is a major limitation within a diverse society. A comprehensive framework of multicultural supervision competencies would provide supervisors with a more complete definition of multicultural supervision that would serve as a guide in the education and training of counselors. First, this framework would delineate how multicultural competencies are manifested in supervision. Second, a comprehensive framework would go beyond an exclusive focus on race and ethnicity and attend to the multiple and interrelated dimensions of identity. Third, a comprehensive framework of multicultural supervision competencies would hold supervisors accountable in providing effective, ethical, and appropriate supervision. Fourth, such a framework would facilitate systematic empirical research by providing specific and relevant dimensions of multicultural supervision. As such, the purpose of this chapter is to provide a multicultural framework for counselor supervision.

Background of Multicultural Supervision Competencies

The present multicultural supervision competencies were influenced by several documents in the fields of counseling and psychology: the "Guidelines for Culturally Competent Practice, and Education and Training" endorsed by Divisions 17, 35, and 45 of the APA (Ivey, Fouad, Arredondo, & D'Andrea, 1999); Porter's (1995) description of integrating antiracist, feminist, and multicultural perspectives in supervision, ACA and APA codes of ethics for supervision and training; Sue et al.'s (1992) cross-cultural counseling competencies; and the extant multicultural supervision literature described above (e.g., Lopez, 1997).

Our multicultural supervision guidelines are divided into five domains: personal development (supervisor-focused and supervisee-focused), conceptualization, interventions, process, and evaluation. These areas have been most consistently identified in the literature as relevant to the supervisor's and supervisee's personal and professional development, as well as activities most frequently related to counseling/clinical situations. The guidelines also include supervisor activities that are consistent with the role of social activist. The role of the counselor as social activist is becomingly increasingly recognized as essential to eradicating oppression and promoting psychological, physical, and spiritual growth. In fact, the new organizational affiliate of ACA, Counselors for Social Justice, endorses confronting societal oppression and privilege as part of its mission (Guerra, 1999).

The domain of personal development has two components, supervisor focused and trainee focused. Supervisor-focused personal development refers to supervisor self-exploration regarding her or his own values, biases, and personal limitations. This dimension also refers to being knowledgeable about cultural differences. Moreover, personal development refers to participation in educational, consultative, and training experiences that promote one's self-exploration and knowledge. For example, a White supervisor in the exploration stage recognizes and actively challenges her tendency to evaluate African American supervisees as less competent than White supervisees by attending antiracism training. Supervisee-focused personal development refers to fostering the self-exploration, awareness, and knowledge of supervisees. For example, an integration-stage supervisor might engage an incongruence-stage supervisee who is counseling a gay couple considering adopting a child to explore the supervisee's attitudes toward gay parenting.

The conceptualization dimension refers to promoting an understanding of the impact of individual and contextual factors on clients' lives, an understanding of the impact of stereotyping and oppression on presenting concerns, and an encouragement of alternative explanations for events. For example, an integration-stage supervisor might assist an integration-stage supervisee who is counseling a recently laid-off and depressed Asian American client to identify the potential relationships among the client's situational stressors, experiences of racism and ethnic identity development, and psychological difficulties.

The skills dimension refers to encouraging flexibility with regard to counseling interventions and practicing relevant and sensitive interventions when working with diverse clientele. For example, the integration-stage supervisor and exploration-stage supervisee could role-play a gender role analysis for use with a female client who has expressed feeling restricted by sex-role stereotypic behaviors.

The process dimension refers to a relationship between the supervisor and the supervisee characterized by respect and open communication. This dimension attends to the use of power in supervision and the development of a supervisory climate where diversity issues can be addressed. For example, the exploration-stage supervisor might openly process an incongruence-stage Asian supervisee's expressions of anxiety with regard to feeling misunderstood by White clients. This dimension also refers to demonstrating flexible approaches to supervision when working with diverse supervisees.

The outcome/evaluation dimension is consistent with the notion that the primary goal of supervision is helping the client of the counselor (ACES, 1990). Moreover, the evaluation dimension is consistent with Guideline 2.12 of the ACES's (1995) "Ethical Guidelines for Counseling Supervisors":

> Supervisors, through ongoing supervisee assessment and evaluation, should be aware of any personal or professional limitations of supervisees which are likely to impede future professional performance. Supervisors have the responsibility of recommending remedial assistance to the supervisee and of screening from the training program, applied counseling setting, or state licensure those supervisors who are unable to provide competent professional services.

The ACA's (1995) *Code of Ethics* reiterates these responsibilities. An example of this dimension is an integration-stage supervisor who diligently listens to the audiotapes of an exploration-stage supervisee's counseling sessions with diverse clients and evaluates the supervisee's multicultural competence. It should be noted that, given the multiple and interrelated nature of supervisors' roles and responsibilities, there is some overlap among the multicultural supervision competencies across the dimensions identified in the subsequent sections.

Multicultural Supervision Competencies

Domain A1: Supervisor-Focused Personal Development

- Supervisors actively explore and challenge their own biases, values, and worldview and how these relate to conducting supervision.

- Supervisors actively explore and challenge their attitudes and biases toward diverse supervisees.
- Supervisors are knowledgeable about their own cultural background and its influence on their attitudes, values, and behaviors.
- Supervisors possess knowledge about the background, experiences, worldview, and history of culturally diverse groups.
- Supervisors are knowledgeable about alternative helping approaches other than those based in a North American and Northern European context.
- Supervisors possess knowledge and keep informed of the theoretical and empirical literature on multicultural counseling and multicultural supervision, e.g., impact of race on trainees' expectations of supervisor.
- Supervisors are knowledgeable about the limitations of traditional therapies with diverse clientele, such as women, racial/ethnic minorities, and gay and lesbian clients. Supervisors are aware of the cultural values inherent in traditional counseling theories and how these values may be inconsistent with the worldview of culturally different clients (e.g., focus on individualism, emotional/behavioral expressiveness, mind/body dichotomy, self-disclosure, intrapsychic causes).
- Supervisors maintain an ongoing network of feedback regarding personal and professional cultural competence (e.g., a diverse group of supervisors meet regularly to discuss issues related to supervision and diversity).

Domain A2: Supervisee-Focused Personal Development

- Supervisors facilitate the exploration of supervisees' identity development (e.g., race, ethnicity, gender, sexual orientation).
- Supervisors facilitate supervisees' exploration of their values, attitudes, and behaviors and their relationship to working with diverse clients.
- Supervisors facilitate supervisees' exploration of biases which may impede effective and competent practice.
- Supervisors help supervisees understand the impact of social structures on supervisee and client behavior, including how class, gender, and racial privilege may have benefited the counselor.
- Supervisors encourage supervisees' participation in professional groups that attend to multicultural counseling (e.g., ACA's Association of Multicultural Counseling and Development).
- Supervisors encourage supervisees to participate in activities that foster multicultural competence; e.g., support groups, reading groups, attendance at conferences.
- Supervisors emphasize that counselor self-exploration is an ongoing process.

Domain B: Conceptualization

- Supervisors facilitate supervisees' understanding of the impact of oppression, racism, and discrimination on client's lives and presenting concerns to minimize victim blaming and pathologizing.

- Supervisors facilitate supervisees' understanding of both individual and contextual factors in clients' lives.
- Supervisors facilitate supervisees' understanding of culture-specific norms, as well as heterogeneity within groups.
- Supervisors facilitate supervisees' understanding of the intersections of multiple dimensions of diversity, or socio-identities, in clients' lives.
- Supervisors encourage supervisees to examine clients' individual, group, and universal identities in case conceptualization.
- Supervisor promotes supervisees' understanding of how stereotyping influences case conceptualizations, treatment objectives, and choice of interventions.
- Supervisors discuss with supervisees the implications of an overreliance or underreliance on cultural explanations for psychological difficulties.
- Supervisors helps supervisees explore alternative explanations to traditional theoretical perspectives.
- Supervisors explore with supervisees the limitations and cultural biases of traditional psychological assessment and testing.

Domain C: Skills/Interventions

- Supervisors model and train supervisees in a variety of verbal and non-verbal helping responses.
- Supervisors encourage supervisee flexibility with regard to traditional interventions and the use of alternative therapeutic interventions, such as those emphasizing group participation and collective action.
- Supervisors encourage supervisees to gain knowledge of community resources that may benefit clients.
- Supervisors encourage an appreciation of multiple sources of support, including indigenous helping networks.
- Supervisors encourage supervisees to collaborate with the client in the development of goals and objectives.
- Supervisors assists supervisees in developing client advocacy skills.
- Supervisors encourage supervisees to interact in the language requested by the client. Referral to an outside resource may be necessary.
- Supervisors train supervisees in multiple methods of assessment and evaluation.
- Supervisors ensure that supervisees do not enter into counseling situations where their biases or prejudices would adversely impact the supervisees' ability to effectively work with clients.

Domain D: Process

- Supervisors are honest about their biases and struggles to achieve cultural competence.

- Supervisors are able to competently and effectively work with diverse supervisees.
- Supervisors foster a climate that will facilitate discussion of diversity issues.
- Supervisors model respect for diversity and equality with supervisees and clients.
- Supervisors use power constructively in supervision, including jointly establishing objectives and criteria for performance, developing mechanisms for feedback pertaining to both the performance of supervisees and the supervisor, and handling supervisees' self-disclosures with respect and sensitivity.
- Supervisors attend to and process issues related to power dynamics between supervisor and supervisee and supervisee and client.
- Supervisors facilitate discussions of diversity, including the supervisees' diversity attitudes and their relationship to counseling clients.

Domain E: Outcome/Evaluation

- Supervisors are able to identify supervisees' personal and professional strengths and weaknesses in the area of multicultural counseling.
- Supervisors provide ongoing evaluation of supervisees to ensure multicultural competence.
- Supervisors are familiar with instruments that assess multicultural competence (e.g., Ancis & Ladany, 1999; D'Andrea, Daniels, & Heck, 1991; Ponterotto et al., 1996; Sodowsky, Taffe, Gutkin, & Wise, 1994).
- Supervisors are able to recommend appropriate remedial training to supervisees who do not demonstrate multicultural competence.
- Supervisors recognize their responsibility to recommend remedial assistance and screen from the training program, applied counseling setting, or state licensure those supervisees who do not demonstrate multicultural competence.
- Supervisors recognize their responsibility for ensuring that their supervisees provide multiculturally competent counseling.

It follows that supervisors who are in the integration stage in terms of their MIF are most likely to demonstrate multicultural supervision competencies. Similarly, integration-stage supervisees are most likely to demonstrate multicultural counseling competencies with clients, as well as in supervision. Such supervisees will exhibit opennesss to (a) exploring their attitudes, worldview, and biases; (b) alternative conceptualizations of client concerns; (c) engaging in varied counseling approaches; and (d) processing multicultural issues within supervision. In the following section, we present a case example highlighting how the heuristic model of nonoppressive interpersonal development and the framework of multicultural supervision competencies may manifest in a supervision context.

☐ **Case Example**

Mary, the supervisee, is a 22-year-old, Chinese American female complet-ing her doctoral practicum in a Veteran's Administration (VA) Hospital. For the past 5 months, Mary has been assigned to the rehabilitation medicine division of the hospital. Mary has developed positive professional relation-ships with both patients and staff and has consistently received favorable evaluations from her two supervisors. One of Mary's supervisors, Tom, is a 45-year-old White male psychologist who has worked in the VA Hospital for the past 12 years, having completed his doctoral internship at the same site. One of Mary's patients, Juan, is a 42-year-old Nicaraguan male who has been working in construction for most of his life. He injured his back after falling off a ladder 2 months ago and is receiving disability payments. In order to supplement the family income, Juan's wife has pursued several part-time jobs cleaning houses. During the first several sessions, Juan indi-cated that he was having a difficult time adjusting to his physical condition and related financial burdens. He indicated that he felt as though he was not really contributing to the family and that he thus felt worthless. At the fourth session, Juan began to sexually harass Mary. He described explicit fantasies involving Mary and stated that since she was "so cute" he could not control himself. For the next several sessions, Mary waivered between ignoring these comments and asking Juan to explain why he verbalized these fantasies to her. Although Mary was feeling very anxious and un-comfortable with Juan, she was reluctant to discuss this situation with her supervisor. Despite receiving consistently positive evaluations, she felt as though this experience was somehow reflective of her counseling abilities. However, to some extent Mary also understood that she was not to blame for the sexual harassment. Moreover, Mary empathized with Juan's eco-nomic, physical, and vocational stressors and wanted to be of assistance to him. After much thought and feeling at a loss as to how to handle the situation, Mary discussed the situation with her supervisor, Tom. Initially, Tom expressed empathy and stated that this must be an uncomfortable experience. However, Tom indicated that since this was a VA Hospital with primarily male patients, Mary needed to become accustomed to "this sort of thing." He did not discuss any strategies for handling the situation and indicated that continuing to counsel Juan would be good practice; i.e., it would help her to tolerate this behavior in the future. In addition, Tom suggested that Juan's behavior as a Hispanic male was culturally consistent and to be expected, and that Mary should become more aware of any seductive behavior on her part.

Mary left supervision feeling confused and frustrated. She respected her supervisor and had heard many glowing comments about his abilities from her professors. Nonetheless, Mary did not agree with her supervisor's as-sessment of Juan's behavior as culturally consistent and continued to doubt that she was somehow responsible for Juan's behavior. She began to feel angry at her supervisor's statements and lack of help. Mary had heard prejudicial and stereotypic statements about Asians throughout her life and understood their irrational basis. Moreover, Mary was currently enrolled in a multicultural counseling course that explored issues of gender, and she was knowledgeable about the prevalence of sexual harassment. Mary began to feel uncomfortable in her supervision sessions and became increasingly reluctant to discuss any personal issues with her supervisor. Feeling increasingly anxious with Juan's behavior, Mary decided to discuss the situation with one of her female professors. The professor validated Mary's anxiety and frustration and offered her suggestions for confronting the situation.

For purposes of this example, the supervisor, Tom, may be characterized as a SPG member in terms of his gender and race. The supervisee may be characterized as a SOG member in terms of her gender and ethnicity. In regards to MIF, Tom is in the adaptation stage in the area of ethnicity and gender issues. He demonstrates stereotypic attitudes toward Hispanics and a lack of awareness with regard to gender issues. Mary is in the exploration stage in the area of gender issues and in the integration stage in the area of ethnic issues. With regard to gender issues, Mary has begun to develop an understanding of the significance of being female and related power dynamics in counseling. She is struggling with issues of self-blame and feelings of powerlessness. She has sought guidance from her supervisor and professor. Mary empathizes with the ethnic stereotypes and social stressors experienced by Juan, but does not overidentify to the point of dismissing the sexual harassment. In the area of ethnic and gender issues, the supervisee–trainee interpersonal interaction may be characterized as regressive. The supervisor's MIF have significant implications for the degree to which he engages in multiculturally competent supervision. For example, in the area of personal development, it is clear that Tom has neither explored nor challenged his own biases and values and how these relate to conducting supervision. Moreover, as a function of his lack of awareness and understanding of gender issues, he is unable to facilitate an exploration of Mary's ethnic or gender identity. It is quite likely that Tom would not appreciate the benefit of such an exploration. Since Tom possesses ethnic stereotypes, he promotes a stereotyped understanding of Juan's behavior. He does not provide Mary with training in ways of approaching and/or confronting Juan's inappropriate behavior. Issues related to power imbalances between Mary and Juan and between Mary and Tom are unattended to and, in fact, encouraged. As such, there is a poor supervisory working alliance characterized by supervisee anxiety and limited communication. However, Mary's advanced MIF in the areas of ethnicity and gender may still result in a meaningful counseling relationship. Mary may choose to demonstrate empathy with Juan's condition and foster his coping skills. In addition, she may confront Juan's inappropriate behavior, assert her rights to be treated fairly and with respect within the counseling relationship, and continue to counsel Juan under the conditions that the sexual harassment ceases. If Juan decides to continue in counseling within the established boundaries, counselor and client may develop a relationship based on mutual respect and open communication. Discussions of how power dynamics within the larger society have impacted Juan's life and that of his family may ensue.

☐ Summary

The potential for diversity within the supervisor–supervisee–client triad is enormous given demographic trends. Models for both a better understanding of the complexity of multicultural supervision and to effective intervention are needed. In the present chapter, we have presented both a model to aid supervisors in understanding the multicultural supervision process and a framework to provide multiculturally competent supervision. Further theoretical and empirically based work in this area is imperative to furthering an understanding of the personal and professional development of supervisors and supervisees and, relatedly, facilitating clients' psychological health and well-being.

☐ References

American Counseling Association. (1995). *Code of ethics and standards of practice.* Alexandria, VA: Author.

Ancis, J., & Ladany, N. (1999, August). Development and Validation of the Counseling Women Competencies Scale. In J. Ancis (Chair), *New and innovative instruments for understanding and counseling diverse women.* Paper presented at the meeting of the American Psychological Association, Boston, MA.

Ancis, J. R., & Sanchez-Hucles, J. V. (2000). A preliminary analysis of counseling students' attitudes toward counseling women and women of color: Implications for cultural competency training. *Journal of Multicultural Counseling and Development, 28,* 16–31.

Ancis, J. R., & Szymanski, D. (1999, April). *Counseling students' multi-leveled reactions to White privilege.* Paper presented at the meeting of the American Counseling Association, San Diego, CA.

Arredondo, P., Toporek, R., Brown, S. P., Jones, J., Locke, D. C., Sanchez, J., & Stadler, H. (1996). Operationalization of the multicultural counseling competencies. *Journal of Multicultural Counseling and Development, 24,* 42–78.

Association for Counselor Education and Supervision. (1990). Standards for counseling supervisors. *Journal of Counseling and Development, 69,* 30–32.

Association for Counselor Education and Supervision. (1995). Ethical guidelines for counseling supervisors. *Counselor Education and Supervision, 34,* 270–276.

Atkinson, D. R., Morten, G., & Sue, D. W. (1993). *Counseling American minorities: A cross-cultural perspective* (3rd ed.). Madison, WI: Brown & Benchmark.

Ault-Riche, M. (1988). Teaching an integrated model of family therapy: Women as students, women as supervisors. *Journal of Psychotherapy and the Family, 3,* 175–192.

Bernard, J. M. (1997). The discrimination model. In C. E. Watkins (Ed.), *Handbook of psychotherapy supervision* (pp. 310–327). New York: Wiley.

Bernard, J. M., & Goodyear, R. K. (1998). *Fundamentals of clinical supervision* (2nd ed.). Needham Heights, MA: Allyn & Bacon.

Boyd, J. (1978). *Counselor supervision: Approaches, preparation, practices.* Muncie, IN: Accelerated Development.

Bradley, L. J. (1989). *Counselor supervision: Principles, process, practice.* Muncie, IN: Accelerated Press.

Brodsky, A. M. (1980). Sex role issues in the supervision of therapy. In A. K. Hess (Ed.), *Psychotherapy supervision: Theory, research, and practice* (pp. 474–508). New York: Wiley.

Brown, M. T., & Landrum-Brown, J. (1995). Counselor supervision: Cross-cultural perspectives. In J. G. Ponterotto, J. M. Casas, L. A. Suzuki, & C. M. Alexander (Eds.), *Handbook of multicultural counseling* (pp. 263–286). Thousand Oaks, CA: Sage.

Bulhan, H. A. (1985). *Frantz Fanon and the psychology of oppression.* New York: Plenum.

Carney, C. G., & Kahn, K. B. (1984). Building competencies for effective cross-cultural counseling: A developmental view. *The Counseling Psychologist, 12,* 111–119.

Cass, V. C. (1979). Homosexual identity formation: A theoretical model. *Journal of Homosexuality, 4,* 219–235.

Chagon, J., & Russell, R. K. (1995). Assessment of supervisee developmental level and supervision environment across supervisor experience. *Journal of Counseling and Development, 73,* 553–558.

Chan, C. S. (1989). Issues of identity development among Asian-American lesbians and gay men. *Journal of Counseling & Development, 68,* 16–20.

Constantine, M. G. (1997). Facilitating multicultural competency in counseling supervision. In D. B. Pope-Davis & H. L. K. Coleman (Eds.), *Multicultural counseling competencies: Assessment, education and training, and supervision* (pp. 310–324). Thousand Oaks, CA: Sage.

Constantine, M. G., & Ladany, N. (2000). Self-report multicultural counseling competence instruments and their relation to multicultural case conceptualization ability and social desirability. *Journal of Counseling Psychology, 46,* 155–164.

Cook, D. A. (1994). Racial identity in supervision. *Counselor Education and Supervision, 34,* 132–141.

Cross, W. E., Jr. (1971). The Negro-to-Black conversion experience. *Black World, 20,* 13–27.

Cross, W. E., Jr. (1995). The psychology of nigrescence: Revising the Cross model. In J. G. Ponterotto, J. M. Casas, L. A. Suzuki, & C. M. Alexander (Eds.), *Handbook of multicultural counseling* (pp. 93–122). Thousand Oaks, CA: Sage.

D'Andrea, M., Daniels, J., & Heck, R. (1991). Evaluating the impact of multicultural counseling training. *Journal of Counseling and Development, 70,* 143–150.

D'Andrea, M., & Daniels, J. (1997). Multicultural counseling supervision: Central issues, theoretical considerations, and practical strategies. In D. B. Pope-Davis & H. L. K. Coleman (Eds.), *Multicultural counseling competencies: Assessment, education and training, and supervision* (pp. 290–309). Thousand Oaks, CA: Sage.

Downing, N. E., & Roush, K. L. (1985). From passive-acceptance to active commitment: A model of feminist identity development for women. *The Counseling Psychologist, 13* (4), 695–709.

Ekstein, R., & Wallerstein, R. S. (1972). *The teaching and learning of psychotherapy* (2nd ed.). New York: International Universities Press.

Fassinger, R. E. (1991). The hidden minority: Issues and challenges in working with lesbian women and gay men. *The Counseling Psychologist, 19,* 157–176.

Fine, M., Weis, L., Powell, L. C., & Mun Wong, L. (Eds.). (1997). *Off-White: Readings on race, power, and society.* London: Routledge.

Fong, M. L., & Lease, S. H. (1996). *Cross-cultural supervision: Issues for the White supervisor.* Newbury Park, CA: Sage.

Fukuyama, M. A. (1994). Critical incidents in multicultural counseling supervision: A phenomenological approach to supervision research. *Counselor Education and Supervision, 34,* 142–151.

Gardner, L. M. H. (1980). Racial, ethnic, and social class considerations in psychotherapy supervision. In A. K. Hess (Ed.), *Psychotherapy supervision: Theory, research, and practice* (pp. 474–508). New York: Wiley.

Gilbert, L. A., & Rossman, K. M. (1992). Gender and the mentoring process for women: Implications for professional development. *Professional Psychology: Research and Practice, 23,* 233–238.

Guerra, P. (1999, May). Counselors for Social Justice becomes organizational affiliate. *Counseling Today,* pp. 1, 25.

Hardiman, R. (1982). White identity development: A process-oriented model for describing the racial consciousness of White Americans. *Dissertation Abstracts International, 43,* 104A. (University Microfilms No. 82–10330)

Hart, G., Borders, L. D., Nance, D., & Paradise, L. (1993). Ethical guidelines for counseling supervisors. *ACES Spectrum, 53,* 5–8.

Helms, J. E. (1990). *Black and White racial identity: Theory, research, and practice.* Greenwood: New York.

Helms, J. E. (1995). An update of Helms' White and people of color racial identity models. In J. G. Ponterotto, J. M. Casas, L. A. Suzuki, & C. M. Alexander (Eds.), *Handbook of multicultural counseling* (pp. 181–198). Thousand Oaks, CA: Sage.

Helms, J. E., & Cook, D. A. (1999). *Using race and culture in counseling and psychotherapy: Theory and process.* Boston, MA: Allyn & Bacon.

Hogan, R. A. (1964). Issues and approaches in supervision. *Psychotherapy: Theory, Research, and Practice, 1,* 1739–1741.

Holloway, E. L. (1995). *Clinical supervision: A systems approach.* Thousand Oaks, CA: Sage.

Holloway, E. L. (1997). Structures for the analysis and teaching of supervision. In C. E. Watkins (Ed.), *Handbook of psychotherapy supervision* (pp. 249–276). New York: Wiley.

Ivey, A. E., Fouad, N. A., Arredondo, P., & D'Andrea, M. (1999). *Guidelines for multicultural counseling competencies: Implications for practice, training, and research.* Unpublished manuscript.

Johnson, M. K., Searight, H. R., Handal, P. J., & Gibbons, J. L. (1993). Survey of clinical psychology graduate students' gender attitudes and knowledge: Toward gender-sensitive psychotherapy training. *Journal of Contemporary Psychotherapy, 23,* 233–249.

Ladany, N., Brittan-Powell, C. S., & Pannu, R. K. (1997). The influence of supervisory racial identity interaction and racial matching on the supervisory working alliance and supervisee multicultural competence. *Counselor Education and Supervision, 36,* 284–304.

Ladany, N., Inman, A. G., Constantine, M. G., & Hofheinz, E. (1997). Supervisee multicultural case conceptualization ability and self-reported multicultural competence as functions of supervisee racial identity and supervisor focus. *Journal of Counseling Psychology, 44,* 284–293.

Ladany, N., Lehrman-Waterman, D., Molinaro, M., & Wolgast, B. (1999). Psychotherapy supervisor ethical practices: Adherence to guidelines, the supervisory working alliance, and supervisee satisfaction. *The Counseling Psychologist, 27,* 443–475.

Leong, F. T. L., & Wagner, N. S. (1994). Cross-cultural counseling supervision: What do we know? What do we need to know? *Counselor Education and Supervision, 34,* 117–131.

Levine, F. M., & Tilker, H. A. (1974). A behavior modification approach to supervision and psychotherapy. *Psychotherapy: Theory, Research, and Practice, 11,* 182–188.

Littrell, J. M., Lee-Borden, N., & Lorenz, J. A. (1979). A developmental framework for counseling supervision. *Counselor Education and Supervision, 19,* 119–136.

Loganbill, C., Hardy, E., & Delworth, U. (1982). Supervision: A conceptual model. *Counseling Psychologist, 10,* 3–42.

Lopez, S. R. (1997). Cultural competence in psychotherapy: A guide for clinicians and their supervisors. In C. E. Watkins, Jr. (Ed.), *Handbook of psychotherapy supervision* (pp. 570–588). New York: Wiley.

Marcia, J. E. (1966). Development and validation of ego identity status. *Journal of Personality and Social Psychology, 3,* 551–558.

McNamara, K., & Rickard, K. M. (1989). Feminist identity development: Implications for feminist therapy with women. *Journal of Counseling and Development, 68,* 184–189.

Morgan, D. W. (1984). Cross-cultural factors in the supervision of psychotherapy. *The Psychiatric Forum, 12*(2), 61–64.

Munson, C. E. (1997). Gender and psychotherapy supervision: The partnership model. In C. E. Watkins, Jr. (Ed.), *Handbook of psychotherapy supervision* (pp. 549–569). New York: Wiley.

Myers, L. J. (1991). Expanding the psychology of knowledge optimally: The importance of worldview revisited. In R. L. Jones (Ed.), *Black psychology* (3rd ed., pp. 15–28). Berkeley, CA: Cobb & Henry.

Nichols, E. (1976, November). *The philosophical aspects of cultural differences*. Paper presented at the conference of the World Psychiatric Association, Ibadan, Nigeria.

Nobles, W. (1972). African philosophy: Foundation for Black psychology. In R. L. Jones (Ed.), *Black psychology* (1st ed., pp. 18–32). New York: Harper & Row.

Ossana, S. M., Helms, J. E., & Leonard, M. M. (1992). Do "womanist" identity attitudes influence college women's self-esteem and perceptions of environmental bias? *Journal of Counseling & Development, 70,* 402–408.

Phinney, J. S. (1989). Stages of ethnic identity development in minority group adolescents. *Journal of Early Adolescence, 6,* 34–49.

Ponterotto, J. G. (1988). Racial consciousness development among White counselor trainees: A stage model. *Journal of Multicultural Counseling and Development, 16,* 146–156.

Ponterotto, J. G., Rieger, B. P., Barrett, A., Sparks, R., Sanchez, C. M., & Magids, D. (1996). Development and initial validation of the Multicultural Counseling Awareness Scale. In G. R. Sodowsky & J. C. Impara (Eds.), *Multicultural assessment in counseling and clinical psychology* (pp. 247–282). Lincoln, NE: Buros Institute of Mental Measurements.

Porter, N. (1995). Supervision of psychotherapists: Integrating anti-racist, feminist, and multicultural perspectives. In H. Landrine (Ed.), *Bringing cultural diversity to feminist psychology* (pp. 163–175). Washington, DC: American Psychological Association.

Priest, R. (1994). Minority supervisor and majority supervisor: Another perspective on clinical reality. *Counselor Education and Supervision, 34,* 152–158.

Remington, G., & DaCosta, G. (1989). Ethnocultural factors in resident supervision: Black supervisor and White supervisees. *American Journal of Psychotherapy, 43*(3), 398–404.

Rice, L. N. (1980). A client-centered approach to the supervision of psychotherapy. In A. K. Hess (Ed.), *Psychotherapy supervision: Theory, research, and practice* (pp. 136–147). New York: Wiley.

Ridley, C. R., Mendoza, D. W., Kanitz, B. E., Angermeier, L., & Zenk, R. (1994). Cultural sensitivity in multicultural counseling: A perceptual schema model. *Journal of Counseling Psychology, 41,* 125–136.

Rust, P. C. (1993). "Coming out" in the age of social constructionism: Sexual identity formation among lesbian and bisexual women. *Gender & Society, 7,* 50–77.

Sabnani, H. B., Ponterotto, J. G., & Borodovsky, L. G. (1991). White racial identity development and cross-cultural counselor training: A stage model. *The Counseling Psychologist, 19,* 76–102.

Skovholt, T. M., & Rønnestad, M. H. (1992). Themes in therapist and counselor development. *Journal of Counseling and Development, 70,* 505–515.

Sodowsky, G. R., Kwan, K. L. K., & Pannu, R. (1995). Ethnic identity of Asians in the United States: Conceptualization and illustrations. In J. G. Ponterotto, J. M. Casas, L. A. Suzuki, & C. M. Alexander (Eds.), *Handbook of multicultural counseling* (pp. 123–154). Newbury Park, CA: Sage.

Sodowsky, G. R., Taffe, R. C., Gutkin, T. B., & Wise, S. L. (1994). Development of the Multicultural Counseling Inventory: A self-report measure of multicultural competencies. *Journal of Counseling Psychology, 41,* 137–148.

Stoltenberg, C. (1981). Approaching supervision from a developmental perspective: The counselor-complexity model. *Journal of Counseling Psychologists, 28,* 59–65.

Stoltenberg, C., & Delworth, U. (1987*). Supervising counselors and therapists*. San Francisco: Jossey-Bass.

Sue, D. W., Arredondo, P., & McDavis, R. J. (1992). Multicultural counseling competencies and standards: A call to the profession. *Journal of Counseling and Development, 70,* 477–486.

Sue, D. W., Bernier, J. B., Durran, M., Feinberg, L., Pedersen, P., Smith, E., & Vasquez-Nuttal, E. (1982). Position paper: Cross-cultural counseling competencies, *The Counseling Psychologist, 10,* 45–52.

Sue, D. W., & Sue, D. (1999). *Counseling the culturally different: Theory and practice* (3rd ed.). New York: Wiley.

Thompson, C. E., & Neville, H. A. (1999). Racism, mental health, and mental health practice. *The Counseling Psychologist, 27,* 155–223.

Troiden, R. R. (1989). The formation of homosexual identities. *Journal of Homosexuality, 17,* 43–73.

U.S. Bureau of the Census. (1992). *Statistical abstract of the United States: The national data book* (112th ed.). Washington, DC: U.S. Government Printing Office.

U.S. Bureau of the Census. (1996). *Population projections of the United States by age, sex, race, and Hispanic origin: 1995–2000.* United States Department of Commerce. Washington, DC: U.S. Government Printing Office.

Vargas, L. A. (1989, August). *Training psychologists to be culturally responsive: Issues in supervision.* Paper presented at a symposium at the 97th Annual Convention of the American Psychological Association, New Orleans.

Vasquez, M. J., & McKinley, D. L. (1982). Supervision: A conceptual model: Reactions and an extension. *The Counseling Psychologist, 10,* 59–63.

Watkins, C. E., Jr. (Ed.). (1997). *Handbook of psychotherapy supervision.* New York: Wiley.

PART

II

THEORETICAL APPROACHES TO COUNSELOR SUPERVISION

4

CHAPTER

Loretta J. Bradley
L. J. Gould
Gerald D. Parr

Supervision-Based Integrative Models of Counselor Supervision

The integrative model is one of the most, if not the most, frequently used model for counselor supervision. Integrative approaches to counselor supervision may be theoretically based (supervision theory, theoretical integration) or they may be a combination of methodology from two or more supervisory approaches (technical eclecticism). Moreover, integrative models of supervision typically operate from the assumption that counselor trainees will be working from the perspective of integrative models of counseling. As such, many different kinds of integrative approaches can be formed by creating various combinations of theory and techniques. While there are many reasons to explain the popularity of the integrative model, perhaps one of the best explanations is that supervisors seek new and varied techniques to improve their supervision effectiveness and the effectiveness of their trainees. Unlike the models discussed in the chapter on psychotherapy-based models of supervision, the models in this chapter were derived specifically for supervision.

Many supervisors advocate Lazarus's (1995, 1996) principle of technical eclecticism. Lazarus argued that technical eclecticism in counseling is the most useful of the integrative models because it permits the selection of techniques from any discipline without necessarily endorsing the theories from which the techniques are derived. Supervisors attempt to buttress themselves with a host of supervision techniques originating from various approaches to counseling and supervision and construct integrative methodological approaches. The rationale for this approach is that an integrative set of techniques prepares one to be more effective across the infinite variety of supervision and counseling situations than does a single approach with a narrow range of techniques.

Three integrative models—the discrimination model, the interpersonal process recall, and the systems approach to supervision—are discussed in this chapter. Each model will be examined according to its framework (concepts/assumptions and supervisory relationship, focus and goals, methodology and techniques); a case example and critique will complete each discussion. Then, the use of an integrative model in supervision is described. Finally, three additional and recent integrative models are briefly presented.

☐ Discrimination Model of Supervision

Bernard's (1997) discrimination model was conceived as a teaching model for use with novice supervisors in introducing them to the process of supervision. It is designed to reduce counseling supervision to its simplest components by first helping the supervisor determine what to address in supervision and then identifying the most functional style. The discrimination model is atheoretical and based on technical eclecticism. This model, therefore, allows the supervisor great flexibility in responding to supervisee dilemmas (Bernard, 1979, 1997).

Framework of the Discrimination Model of Supervision

Primary Concepts and Theoretical Assumptions

The discrimination model of supervision is atheoretical. The primary concepts of the model—supervisory focus and roles—deal with supervisee issues found in virtually all counseling theories: conceptual understanding, mastery of intervention skills, and the inter- and intrapersonal dynamics which occur in both the counseling and supervision dyads. Bernard (1997) stated that the discrimination model differs from therapy-based models, which rely on the same principles for both counseling and supervision, by operating parallel to theory rather than within it. Additionally, the model provides a language for supervision that is different from the one used in counseling, thereby decreasing the likelihood that the two will be confused causing the supervisee to perceive herself or himself as a client.

  The central assumption of the discrimination model is that the focus of supervision should be on the supervisee in the action of counseling rather than on the supervisee's internal reality. With the action of counseling as the primary focus, it is necessary that supervision relate directly to that activity by identifying the component factors that describe the salient features of counseling. Thus, the discrimination model uses focus and roles to organize the supervisory process around the activity of counseling. Three focus areas of supervision—intervention skills, conceptualization skills, and personalization skills—and three supervisory roles—teacher, counselor, and consultant—are identified.

Supervisory Relationship

Bernard (1997) does not directly address the supervisory relationship in the discrimination model. However, some inferences can be made from other areas within the model. Since supervision is considered to be a dynamic activity that attends to the inter- and intrapersonal issues of counseling, the supervisor and supervisee must form a relationship that allows communication to occur; thus, it may be assumed that the facilitative conditions of empathy, genuiness, warmth, trust, and positive regard are present. The supervisee's individual personality (cultural background, sensitivity to others, sense of humor, etc.) is considered an aspect of the personalization skills focus area. By recognizing the importance of the individual in counseling, the individual must be recognized as equally important in supervision. Additionally, in the role of consultant, the supervisor encourages the supervisee to share in the responsibility for her or his learning. Finally, Bernard (1997) acknowledged the importance of considering the developmental level of supervisees (beginning, intermediate, advanced) in using the discrimination model. Thus, it may be assumed that the supervisory relationship is one in which communication, collaboration, and individual differences are respected and encouraged.

Focus and Goals of the Discrimination Model of Supervision

Focus

The primary focus of supervision is supervisee action; therefore, the supervisor must attend to that action by using the three focus areas (intervention skills, conceptualization skills, and personalization skills) and the three supervisor roles (teacher, counselor, and consultant). Other foci are considered within each of the focus areas and supervisor roles.

Focus Areas. *Intervention (or process) skills* are the essence of the supervisee's observable activity. These skills, ranging from simple to complex, include all the behaviors that distinguish counseling as a purposeful therapeutic interpersonal activity, from greeting the client at the beginning of a session to using empathy, confrontation, interpretation, pacing, salience, or other counseling skills. The focus of this area is the supervisee's ability to skillfully deliver interventions. *Conceptualization skills*, the second focus area, are more subtle, requiring the supervisor to interview the supervisee in order to determine her or his level of competence. This area includes the supervisee's ability to conceptualize client information, identify themes, and discriminate essential client information from the nonessential or inconsequential. In addition to assessment, the supervisee must be able to select an appropriate response to client information, although the delivery of that response is an intervention skill. The final focus, *personalization skills*, addresses the supervisee's unique individual contribution to counseling, that is, the effects of such individual elements of the supervisee's persona as her or his personality, cultural background, sensitivity to others, and sense of humor on the counseling process. It is often difficult for the supervisor to define and identify these elements; therefore, misinterpretation is common. Thus, the supervisor must be willing to discuss her or his perceptions about the supervisee's personalization skills in order to avoid misinterpretation. Because they are so important to client interactions, at least initially, personalization skills must be addressed in supervision.

Although the three foci are discrete areas to be addressed as necessary in supervision, Bernard (1997) notes that they do overlap. When this overlap of skills is recognized and appreciated, supervision becomes a dynamic process. However, for every counseling skill, a potential skill deficit exists. Therefore, when a skill deficit is identified, the supervisor must determine if it occurred because the supervisee (a) did not know what to do (conceptualization); (b) did not know how to deliver the skill (intervention); or (c) was uncomfortable with either the client or using the skill (personalization). Identification of the focus area containing the skill deficit allows the supervisor to use an appropriate supervisory intervention to rectify it.

Supervisor Roles.   Within the supervisory process, the supervisor plays three roles: teacher, counselor, and consultant. In the *teacher role*, the supervisor takes the responsibility for determining the action necessary for the supervisee's acquisition of counseling competence. The teacher role is evaluative in the areas of skill deficit, skill learning, and skill delivery. The second role, *counselor*, addresses the interpersonal and intrapersonal reality of the supervisee. As counselor, the supervisor asks the supervisee to reflect on the meaning of events occurring in counseling relationships. Through reflection of meaning, the supervisee experiences insight—those moments when her or his thoughts, behaviors, and personal reality merge—which enhances professional development. The final supervisory role is *consultant*. As consultant, the supervisor allows the supervisee to share the responsibility for her or his learning. The consultant-supervisor serves as a resource while encouraging the supervisee to trust her or his own thoughts, insights, and feelings about working with clients. The consultant role is at times difficult because it requires supervisee autonomy, which can be difficult for both supervisor and supervisee. Additionally, it is "far easier to tell someone how to do something than to create a context for learning" (Bernard, 1997, p. 312).

Goals

As with the supervisory relationship, goals are not specifically addressed in the discrimination model but may be deduced by examining the focus areas and supervisory roles. From the focus areas, it may be inferred that the goal of supervision is the supervisee's mastery of the skills required to be effective in the craft of counseling. From the supervisory roles, it may be concluded that the supervisor's goal is to facilitate the supervisee's development as a professional counselor by teaching, exploring, encouraging, and evaluating the learning process.

Methodology and Techniques of the Discrimination Model of Supervision

Several issues should be considered by supervisors selecting the discrimination model for use in the supervisory process. The first issue is the supervisor's use the focus areas and roles. Bernard (1997) stated that many supervisors tend to pair one role with one focus area (teacher/intervention, consultant/conceptualization, counselor/personalization) which, while logical, limits the supervisor's repertoire and impact. Rarely does a problem fit into a single focus area; and it is the supervisor's responsibility to help the supervisee determine the primary focus. Additionally, the supervisor must be sensitive to the overuse of any one role or focus area. The supervisor should periodically review her or his notes on supervisee/client sessions and supervisory sessions to check her or his use of focus areas and roles. If the same focus or role area is used consistently with either a single supervisee or several supervisees, the supervisor needs to reconsider her or his supervisory style. A second issue involves evaluating the supervisee's counseling skills. Effective use of the discrimination model requires a reliable picture of the supervisee in counseling, one difficult to obtain from supervisee self-report. Therefore, the supervisor must observe the supervisee's counseling either directly or through audio- or videotapes. Not only does observation allow the supervisor to help the supervisee select and learn to use appropriate interventions, but it is also necessary for the evaluation of conceptualization and personalization skills.

Supervisees, especially those in their first supervised experience, spend a great deal of time and energy in attempting to determine what the supervisor wants. By using the discrimination model, with its attention to the three focus areas, the supervisor can direct supervisees in the action of counseling. The focus areas allow the supervisee to receive feedback with more discrimination as supervision progresses. Evaluation criteria are constant and firmly based in the model. Descriptions of the supervisory roles encourage dialogue on how supervisees learn to be counselors. Additionally, this model allows the supervisee to request the supervisory role that he or she believes to be most helpful to her or him. Working collaboratively within the context of the model communicates respect for the supervisee as a partner in the learning process.

Researchers have taken the discrimination model and built on its basic concepts in order to expand its effectiveness. Stenack and Dye (1982) determined that clear distinctions existed between the supervision roles in the discrimination model and identified five supervisor activities specific to each role. Neufeldt, Iversen, and Juntunen (1995) used Stenack and Dye's outline, which they referred to as "beginning strategies," in developing a manual for supervisor training. They proposed 11 "advanced strategies," each with specific behaviors, which combine two or more of the supervisory roles. Bernard (1997) suggested that supervisors can benefit from the analysis of advanced strategies in learning to skillfully combine roles to accomplish complex learning. Finally, Bernard's discrimination model has received some support from empirical research (Ellis & Dell, 1986; Ellis, Dell, & Good, 1988; Putney, Worthington, & McCullough, 1992).

Case Example in Using the Discrimination Model of Supervision

Chris, a practicum student enrolled in his first supervised practice, is working at a university counseling center. One of his clients, Lucy, a sophomore, is having trouble acclimating to school following the death of her father. Chris, who has never lost anyone close to him, is having difficulty responding to her grief. After viewing a videotape of a session between Chris and Lucy, the supervisor realizes that Chris needs help in designing interventions to aid Lucy in her grief process and therefore decides to use the role of teacher in the supervisory session. The supervisor begins by using the intervention focus and modeling a more empathic and caring response to Lucy's admission of overwhelming grief, and suggests some interventions designed to help survivors express their grief. In the conceptualization focus, the supervisor reviews the stages of grief with Chris and discusses the implications of Lucy's stage. In the personalization focus, the supervisor suggests that Chris search the counseling literature for relevant information on the loss of a parent. The supervisor is cognizant of the fact that the roles of counselor and consultant would also offer Chris necessary information on Lucy's problem and his reactions to it, but does not wish to confuse him by using other roles without giving him time to process the information from each. For example, in the counselor role, the supervisor might explore Chris's response to Lucy's grief and discuss his personal reactions. In the consultant role, the supervisor might encourage Chris to brainstorm useful techniques for grief processing and explore Lucy's possible reactions to them.

Critique of the Discrimination Model of Supervision

Strengths

A major strength of the discrimination model is its atheoretical basis, which allows it to be used effectively with different theories and models. Because it is atheoretical, the discrimination model does not emphasize one focus area over another, which, according to Bernard (1997), can balance the emphasis placed on a specific area by other theories. Additionally, the model is relatively easy to apply to the supervision process, which makes it useful to inexperienced supervisors.

Although designed to be acultural, the discrimination model encourages the infusion of multicultural awareness (Bernard, 1997). Supervisors are urged to be aware, especially in the evaluation of personalization skills, that many aspects of personality are actually cultural expressions. Additionally, supervisors are warned that they must consider the context of behaviors, especially the multicultural reality in the client–supervisee and supervisor–supervisee dyads.

Finally, although not extensive, some research supports and expands the concepts of the discrimination model. However, more empirical research in the model would enhance its usefulness to supervisors.

Weaknesses

A major weakness of the discrimination model is its lack of specific information in two areas: the supervisory relationship and supervision goals. Although it is evident that both are important to the model, specific information is lacking, which causes the user to distill information from other concepts. This could lead to problems for novice supervisors attempting to use the model. Additionally, although examples are helpful, the model does not provide enough specific techniques and interventions for use in the supervision process.

Although the model is relatively easy to use, inexperienced supervisors may have difficulty in using the supervisor roles effectively, which in turn can compromise the model's use (Bernard, 1997). Supervisors should be cautioned to think about what they wish to accomplish before selecting a supervisory role.

☐ Interpersonal Process Recall

Interpersonal Process Recall (IPR) was developed by N. I. Kagan, Krathwohl, and Miller (N. I. Kagan, 1980; N. I. Kagan & Krathwohl, 1967; N. I. Kagan, Krathwohl, & Miller, 1963). Kagan et al. observed that when a counselor and client were shown a videotape immediately following the counseling session, each was able to recall her or his thoughts and feelings in both detail and depth and with some self-evaluation. If a third person, trained in encouraging verbalization and elaboration, was present, the recalled information was more reliable. Research and further development of IPR has resulted in an impressive body of literature (Bernard, 1989; Borders & Leddick, 1987; Cashwell, 1994; Clark, 1997; Dendy, 1971; H. Kagan & N. I. Kagan, 1997; N. I. Kagan, 1980; N.I. Kagan & Kagan, 1990, 1991).

Framework of the IPR Model

Primary Concept and Theoretical Assumptions

A primary concept of the IPR model is related to basic human nature: people need other people (N. I. Kagan, 1980; N. I. Kagan, Holmes, & Kagan, 1995). People provide stimulation for one another and thus become a source of pain and fear which, in turn, teaches people to fear one another early in life. The most common fears are disapproval, punishment, abandonment, rejection, and being hurt, or of hurting someone else, either physically or emotionally. These fears contribute to an individual's sense of vulnerability and are usually vague and irrational. One's fears often cannot be referred to a reasonable source and are usually unlabeled, unseated, and unrecognized. Thus, many of the "gut-level" feelings reported in IPR sessions appear to be infantile (N. I. Kagan, 1980). This need for and fear of others manifests in a variety of approach/avoidance behaviors that characterize most human interactions. Each individual appears to establish a unique "safe" distance between herself or himself and others in an attempt to balance the pain of boredom with the potential danger of interaction. One's fears are typically translated into interpersonal expectations whereby the anticipated reactions create a self-fulfilling prophecy (H. Kagan & Kagan, 1997).

IPR allows these levels of interpersonal communication to be acknowledged through viewing and commenting on videotaped sessions (Aveline, 1997; Clark, 1997; Dowrick, 1991; N. I. Kagan & Kagan, 1990, 1991). Recall sessions, in which the counselor (supervisee), client, or both are encouraged to remember thoughts and feelings, are the method used to facilitate interpersonal communication. The inquirer (supervisor) is trained in soliciting and encouraging response.

Supervisory Relationship

The supervisory relationship is not addressed in IPR. It may be inferred, since the recall inquirer is trained in soliciting and encouraging response, that the supervisor has the facilitative conditions of empathy, genuiness, warmth, trust, and positive regard. However, the supervisory relationship is not collaborative in developing either goals or methods, as both are specified by the use of IPR. The IPR method is insight oriented, and therefore does not involve technique acquisition and performance in a learning alliance. The personal relationship that characterizes most supervisory relationships and involvement between supervisor and supervisee appears to be missing.

Focus and Goals in the IPR Method

Focus

Several focus areas exist in the IPR method. The focus for the supervisee (counselor) is on becoming a better counseling practitioner by learning how to listen carefully and fully understand the client's communication. The supervisor's (inquirer's) focus is on training the supervisee to be a better counselor by using IPR methods to recognize the meaning in the client's and supervisee's interpersonal communication. The focus for the client is awareness of and sensitivity to her or his own feelings.

Goals

Although not always easily achieved, the goal of the IPR method is straightforward and simply stated. The major goal is the improvement of the supervisee's interpersonal communication skills, which, in turn, will result in her or him becoming a more successful and effective counselor. A secondary goal is for the supervisee to learn how to use recall to help clients in their interpersonal relationships.

Methodology and Techniques of the IPR Method

In examining the methodology of the IPR, it is necessary, first, to understand the inquirer's (supervisor's) role in recall, second, to consider what occurs in a recall session, and third, to consider the three specific types of recall sessions: counselor recall, client recall, and mutual recall.

The Inquirer's Role

N. I. Kagan and Kagan (1991) stated that the most fundamental and unique characteristic of IPR is the inquirer role and function. The inquirer (supervisor) expects that participants have an encyclopedic knowledge of interactions that can be brought to awareness by her or his facilitative behaviors in the recall sessions. The supervisor augments the playback exposure to the videotape by using inductive questions directing the supervisee's (and/or client's) attention to the intrapersonal and interpersonal dynamics of the interaction, thus encouraging the identification and recall of her or his own feelings and thoughts that interfered with effective communication in the counseling situation. The following questions, adapted from several articles, illustrate those a supervisor might use when conducting a recall session (Borders & Leddick, 1987; Dendy, 1971; H. Kagan & Kagan, 1997; N. I. Kagan, 1980):

- What do you think he or she was trying to say?
- What do you think he or she was feeling at this point?
- What does her or his nonverbal behavior tell you?
- What were you thinking when he or she said that?
- What were you feeling at that time?
- Did anything prevent you from sharing your feelings at that time?
- What do you wish you had said to her or him?

- How do you think he or she would have reacted?
- If you had another chance, would you have said something different?
- What would have been the risk of saying what you really wanted to say?
- How do you want the client to perceive you?
- What do you think her or his perceptions of you are?

The methodology of IPR requires a supervisor with advanced skills who is thoroughly trained in the process. Training begins with learning the rationale, function, and technique of recall. Although the supervisor-trainee must be nonjudgmental, he or she must learn to be assertive and confrontational although not hostile nor aggressive. He or she is taught to identify cues that indicate questions to be asked. Cues include: abrupt changes of ideas/themes in the session; changes in body posture, voice level, or visual focus; description indicating intense affect; clear misinterpretation by either supervisee or client; and inappropriate affect (N. I. Kagan & Krathwohl, 1967). Cues may indicate heightened underlying emotion and are potential insight points.

The Recall Session

Ideally, the recall session occurs immediately following the counseling session. The supervisor (inquirer) and supervisee (counselor) and/or client watch the videotape of the previous session. The supervisee or client (in client recall) is given control of the videoplayer remote control so that he or she can start and stop the videotape as any thoughts, feelings, impressions, conflicts, images, or other covert processes are recalled. When the tape is stopped, the supervisee and/or client recalls thoughts and feelings. Questions, such as the samples listed above, are used to encourage the participants in recalling thoughts and feelings.

Counselor Recall

The counselor (supervisee) recall session is designed to aid the supervisee in learning to identify, organize, and use information that he or she has previously acquired about the client by becoming aware of messages he or she denied or ignored (N. I. Kagan & Kagan, 1991). Counselor recall gives the supervisee a chance to see herself or himself in action and overcome dynamics interfering with her or his ability to understand the client and communicate that understanding to the client. Two dynamics that interfere with counselor effectiveness are feigning clinical naiveté and tuning out. In feigning clinical naiveté, the supervisee acts as if he or she did not perceive or understand the meanings behind client statements, although recall indicates that he or she did understand the meanings but was unable to act on that perception. Tuning out occurs when the supervisee actually does not see or hear the client for periods of time during the session. Tuning out usually occurs either when the supervisee is trying to determine what to do next or when he or she is concerned about the impression he or she is making on the client. From recall, the supervisee can learn to recognize when and how he or she failed to hear or deal with the client's messages and become more sensitive to her or his own feelings in the counseling interaction.

Client Recall

The purpose of client recall is to expand the supervisee's knowledge of the client's wants, needs, perceptions, and aspirations. The supervisee asks the client if he or she is willing to review the videotape with the supervisor (inquirer) but without the supervisee being present. The supervisee may also ask if the recall session can be videotaped or if he or she can observe through a one-way mirror. During the session, the client is encouraged to be open about her or his aspirations, satisfactions, and dissatisfactions about the counseling process and the supervisee.

Mutual Recall

Both the supervisee and the client view the videotape together with the supervisor (inquirer). Each is asked to share her or his thoughts and feelings, with particular attention being focused on how they perceived each other and what meanings were ascribed to the other's behaviors. The purpose of mutual recall is to aid the supervisee in learning to use the here-and-now, to act overtly on client behavior as it occurs, and to make covert communication overt.

Case Example in the IPR Method

Geoffrey is a student in his first practicum. In counseling, he quickly established rapport and was off to a great start with his first client. However, after reviewing videotapes of his counseling sessions, the supervisor noticed that Geoffrey was being manipulated by his client, which in turn was detrimental to the counseling progress. Crucial topics were being avoided by the client, who placed responsibility for solving his problems on Geoffrey. The supervisor conducted IPR with the client and counselor so that their thoughts and feelings during counseling could be recalled and examined. Through IPR, Geoffrey became aware of his feelings of inadequacy, his desire to have the client like him, and how these dynamics were affecting his interpersonal counseling behaviors. Client recall revealed disappointment in Geoffrey's lack of assertiveness, with this disappointment being masked effectively by the client's controlling behavior, a response to his fear of "being told I'm maladjusted." After IPR, Geoffrey's behavior was more congruent and effective. Insight into himself and the client enabled him to act out of professional intent, rather than solely from personal needs.

Critique of the IPR Method
Strengths

The IPR method has an impressive body of research supporting its effectiveness in enhancing interpersonal communication between counselor and client (Bernard, 1989; Clark, 1997; H. Kagan & Kagan, 1997; N. I. Kagan, 1980; N. I. Kagan & Kagan, 1990, 1991). Research has also demonstrated that IPR has multiple applications for professionals and paraprofessionals to learn and improve their abilities to interview, communicate with, and help others (N. I. Kagan & Kagan, 1990, 1991). Additionally, research in IPR has produced an effective program and film series for training new practitioners (N. I. Kagan, Holmes, & Kagan, 1995).

Successful IPR sessions increase a supervisee's communication skills and confidence in working with clients. Results from client and/or mutual recall sessions give the supervisee insight into the client's wants and needs as well as satisfactions and dissatisfactions with counseling and the supervisee. Additionally, IPR is atheoretical and can be used with any theory that places an emphasis on interpersonal communications in counseling.

Weaknesses

Neither the supervisory relationship nor multicultural issues are specifically addressed in IPR. The supervisory role is limited to that of a facilitator. He or she does not interpret information or insights for the supervisee, nor does the supervisor aid the supervisee in skill acquisition and use beyond the insights gained from IPR. The limitations of supervisor role and function along with the lack of working/learning alliance leads to the question of whether IPR is a model of supervision or an extremely successful method to be used in supervision.

☐ Systems Approach to Supervision

Early models of supervision relied on existing conceptual structures—counseling theories, social role theories, or developmental theories—for supervision contexts. Holloway (1995) developed the systems approach to supervision (SAS) to provide a framework and language designed specifically to guide the teaching and practice of supervision; she based this approach on empirical, conceptual, and practice knowledge in the field of supervision. The SAS model was conceived to raise questions about what the supervisor does rather than to tell her or him what to think or do in supervision.

Framework of the SAS Model

Primary Concepts and Theoretical Assumptions

The factors consistently identified as important to the process and outcome of supervision were used to build a dynamic model capable of assisting supervisors in a systematic assessment of supervisee learning needs and supervision teaching interventions (Holloway & Neufeldt, 1995). Therefore, the SAS model is applicable to both conducting supervision as well as teaching others how to conduct supervision. The model attempts to expand understanding of supervision by offering a common language relevant to supervisors without regard to theoretical points of view.

Holloway (1995) identifies four components of support in supervision: a descriptive base, guidelines stating common goals and imperatives, ways to discover meaning as it relates to the participants and the profession, and a systematic mode of inquiry to determine the objectives and strategies for interaction used in supervision. The SAS model meets these needs. Seven dimensions of supervision were identified from empirical, practical, and conceptual knowledge to serve as the bases of supervision: the supervisory relationship (the core factor); supervision tasks; supervision functions; and contextual factors of the supervisor, supervisee, client, and institution (Holloway, 1995, 1997). The model components are part of a dynamic process, and are, therefore, mutually influential and highly interrelated. For example, the functions and task of a supervisor in a mental health agency (contextual factor: institution) will affect the supervisory relationship differently than those of a supervisor in a university setting; the different purposes and responsibilities of the settings will be reflected in how the roles and functions are structured in importance.

Supervisory Relationship

According to Holloway (1995, 1997), the supervisory relationship is a dynamic process in which the supervisor and supervisee negotiate a personal interaction within the structure of power and involvement surrounding the supervisee's learning and training. The supervisory relationship is composed of three essential elements: interpersonal structure, relationship phases, and the supervision contract. The relationship is the basis for empowerment of the supervisee by aiding her or him in the acquisition of counseling knowledge and skills. Both the supervisor and supervisee are responsible for establishing a relational structure flexible enough to accommodate the supervisee's unique needs in a collaborative learning alliance. The other factors in the SAS model are embodied in and influenced by the supervisory relationship.

Interpersonal Structure. Supervision is a formal relationship in which the supervisor's tasks include imparting expert knowledge, evaluating supervisee performance, and acting as gatekeeper for the profession. The formal power of the relationship lies with the supervisory role. In the SAS model, power through involvement is the interpersonal structure of the relationship. Involvement, or intimacy, influences the exercise and effects of power and is crucial to the creation of an individualized (versus role-bound) relationship. The supervisor and supervisee determine the distribution of power which, in turn, influences the degree of social bonding and persuasiveness of the relationship. As the relationship develops, relevant interpersonal, psychological, and differential information needed to make predictions of the other's behavior become available, thus reducing interpersonal uncertainty.

Relationship Phases.   Holloway (1995) proposed three phases of the supervisory relationship: beginning (or developing), advanced (or mature), and termination. In the beginning relationship phase, supervisees are discovering the role expectations in supervision, and they generally seek a reduction in ambiguity and an increase in support and assurance from the supervisor. In the advanced phase, supervisees, while still seeking reduced ambiguity and increased support, show an increase in self-confidence and skill application in counseling. They seek personal challenge and confrontation of interpersonal behaviors from supervision. In the termination phase, supervisees have developed an understanding of the connections between theory and practice in relation to specific clients; these supervisees demonstrate a decreasing need for direction from the supervisor. The supervision process develops as the relationship becomes more focused on the idiosyncratic (i.e., individualized) rules surrounding the learning style and needs of the supervisee and the teaching styles of the supervisor. However, the phase of supervision alone does not determine the level of involvement in the relationship; other factors (providing personal information, presentation style, urgency of client problems) also contribute.

Supervision Contract.   Supervision is composed of idiosyncratic (individualized) rules surrounding the learning style and needs of the supervisee and the teaching styles of the supervisor. For example, some supervisees learn best by reading about a subject rather than in the lecture format, whereas some supervisors teach better by lecture than by demonstration. Role expectations and functions in the supervision process are an aspect of the idiosyncratic rules of the supervisory relationship. The supervision contract allows these role expectations and functions to be clearly stated and specific learning goals established. The contract also specifies evaluation structures and criteria. Both the supervisor and supervisee take part in establishing the contract, and this collaboration increases the likelihood that the contract expectations will be met. The supervision contract should be reevaluated periodically to address the changing needs and goals of the supervisee.

Focus and Goals in the SAS Model

Focus

The primary focus of the SAS model is the supervisory relationship; all other factors revolve around and interact with it. The supervisory relationship provides the context for supervision. A secondary focus is on the tasks in and functions of supervision, which make up the process of supervision.

Goals

The primary goal of supervision is the enhancement of the supervisee's effective professional functioning, that is, her or his ability to perform according to the profession's guidelines and expectations for an individual acting as a counselor. A secondary goal is to provide an opportunity for the supervisee to learn a broad spectrum of professional attitudes, knowledge, and skills in an effective and supportive manner.

Methodology and Techniques in the SAS Model

The seven dimensions of the SAS model define the methodology and techniques of the SAS model. The supervisory relationship—the core dimension—was described above. The remaining six dimensions are described below.

Tasks of Supervision

The tasks of supervision are defined by the professional knowledge required by the counselor role. The supervisee and supervisor select specific learning goals determined by the needs of the supervisee. The tasks of supervision, or teaching objectives, originate from five categories: counseling skills, case conceptualization, professional role, emotional awareness, and self-evaluation. *Counseling skills* focus on actions or specific skills fundamental to counseling. *Case conceptualization* involves understanding the client's history and presenting problem within a framework of human development and change. *Professional role* involves the principles and ethics of professional counseling practice. *Emotional awareness* refers to the supervisee's self-awareness of intra- and interpersonal dynamics in working with clients and the supervisor. *Self-evaluation* is the supervisee's willingness and skill in recognizing her or his own limits of competence and effectiveness relating to client treatment and participation in supervision.

Functions of Supervision

The functions of supervision in the SAS method are the dynamic interactions between supervisor and supervisee. Each function is characterized by behaviors typical of its social role and relational power. The five functions of supervision are: monitoring/evaluating, instructing/advising, modeling, consulting, and supporting/sharing. The *monitoring/evaluating* function is limited to instances when judgments and evaluation of supervisee skills are communicated. The evaluation may be formal and standardized or informal and unique, but the power is the supervisor's, and it is exercised in unidirectional communication. The *instructing/advising* function is an example of teacher–student communication in which information, opinions, and suggestions based on professional knowledge are provided. The power is the supervisor's, and communication is unidirectional. The *modeling* function may be implicit (supervisor as mentor and role model) or explicit (role-playing as a teaching method). Communication is bidirectional, and power is shared in a collaborative process. The *consulting* function involves facilitating problem solving in collaboration with the supervisee. Power is shared, and communication is bidirectional and interactive. The *supporting/sharing* function involves empathic attention, encouragement, and constructive confrontation. Supervisors support supervisees at an interpersonal level by sharing actions, emotions, and attitudes. Communication is bidirectional and interactive.

Task + Function = Process

The combination of task and function describes the action of the supervisory process. The task is the "what" of supervision and involves an examination of the objectives and strategies used in teaching and learning. The function is "how" the task is accomplished. In theory, any task can be combined with any function; however, in reality several specific task/function combinations are more likely to occur (emotional awareness/support, counseling skills/advising). Combinations are influenced by the supervisee's experience, the client's situation, and the supervisory relationship. The method of combining task and function allows for analysis of a prior session's effectiveness and planning of strategies for use in subsequent sessions.

Contextual Factors of Supervision

Contextual factors are conditions related to the choice of task and function and the formation of a relationship, with the supervisor, supervisee, client, or institution. Contextual factors are often difficult to differentiate from the actual interactional process. Participants engaged in conversation perceive, intend, and understand both their own and the other's messages. Factors that influence information processing and decision making in supervision must be inferred by the observer of the conversation.

Supervisor Factor.   The ideal supervisor is empathic, understanding, flexible, concerned, attentive, invested, curious, and open and has unconditional positive regard for her or his supervisee (Carifio & Hess, 1987). These qualities are valuable but focused on the supervisor's inter- and intrapersonal characteristics. The supervisor can enhance her or his unique interpersonal style by the way in which he or she uses her or his repertoire of interpersonal skills and clinical knowledge. Five factors are relevant to supervisor performance in the SAS method: professional experience, roles, theoretical orientation, cultural elements, and self-presentation. *Professional experience* in counseling and supervision appears to be related to the types of judgments regarding self-disclosure, supervisee performance, and instructional approach. *Roles* are the behavior of the supervisor within the supervisory relationship; the most common roles are teacher, counselor, and consultant. *Theoretical orientation* is explicitly and implicitly relied upon in determining what and how to teach. *Cultural elements* are evident in the way one views human behavior, interpersonal relationships, and social institutions and are, therefore, salient to the supervisor's attitudes and actions in supervision. The SAS model encourages the recognition of the importance of cultural factors in supervision and attention to the interaction of these issues with the other factors in the model. *Self-presentation* refers to one's interpersonal presentation of self and includes the affective, verbal, and nonverbal behaviors that convey a desired impression to another. Behaviors may be habitual or regulated, and they characterize the individual and her or his manner of enacting her or his role.

Supervisee Factors.   The characteristics of the supervisee that influence the supervisory relationship are experience in counseling, theoretical orientation, learning style and needs, cultural characteristics, and self-presentation. *Experience in counseling* is related to supervisor expectations of supervisee competence and the need for support and structure in supervision. *Theoretical orientation* affects the supervisee's views on human behavior and change. *Learning style and needs* refer to the developmental factors relevant to the supervisee's approach to and perception of the supervision experience in acquiring, assimilating, and using knowledge. *Cultural characteristics* include gender, ethnicity, sexual orientation, religious beliefs, and personal values central to an individual's group identity. In the SAS method, cultural values are salient to the supervisee's attitudes and actions in interpersonal situations. *Self-presentation* is the same for the supervisee as for the supervisor.

Client Factors.   The client is always a part of supervision and may, in fact, be the reason for its existence, since supervision is designed to ensure that the supervisee can effectively serve the client's needs. Three factors are identified for clients: client characteristics, client-identified problem and diagnosis, and counseling relationship. *Client characteristics* and variables have been studied in relation to the process and outcome of psychotherapy, but the relevance of these characteristics has not been studied in the context of supervision or training (Holloway & Neufeldt, 1995). Supervisors should recognize that client characteristics may play an important role in effectiveness of counseling. *Identified problem and diagnosis* play a role in the assignment of clients to supervisees because the supervisor is responsible for assuring that the client receives adequate treatment. This requires an assessment of the match between the supervisee's level of competence and the client's needs. The *counseling relationship* is a dynamic interpersonal interaction that allows the supervisee to understand the impact of different treatment strategies and the effectiveness of creating a therapeutic relationship (Holloway & Neufeldt). To insure the learning process, the supervisor must identify and confront inappropriate dynamics in the counseling relationship.

Institutional Factors.   All supervision takes place in the context of institutional organizations, whether university counseling centers, hospitals, community agencies, schools, or other service providers. The demands of the organization must be considered in establishing supervision goals and functions. Institutional characteristics consist of organizational clientele, organizational structure and climate, and professional ethics and standards. The *organizational clientele* is relevant to the type of training that the supervisee needs and receives. Agencies may require specific training or supervisory techniques related to client age, developmental stage, or diagnosis. *Organizational structure and climate* effect the supervisory relationship by the demands placed on both supervisor and supervisee. Organizational norms and politics may intrude on the relationship by prescribing roles and functions that differ from roles and functions outside the organization. *Professional ethics and standards* guide the supervisor in her or his work with a supervisee. An agency or organization may have specific rules, standards, and obligations to clients that comply with or differ from professional ethics and standards. Supervisors may find themselves balancing the standards of the profession with the needs of an agency.

Case Example in SAS Method of Supervision

Kelly is completing her practicum at a community agency that offers brief therapy to low-income clients. From tapes of her sessions with Brenda, one of her clients, the supervisor determines that Kelly is not addressing Brenda's presenting problem of coping with her rebellious teenager. The sessions involve friendly conversation and advice-giving on parenting. The supervisor realizes that she needs to confront Kelly's inappropriate behaviors and chooses to combine the task of counseling skills with the functions of monitoring/evaluating followed by instructing/advising. Confronting Kelly's inappropriate behaviors involves evaluating her professional role as counselor, which is being compromised by her overly friendly relationship with Brenda. Instructing/advising involves providing suggestions for and instruction in more appropriate techniques to help Brenda with her presenting problem.

Critique

Strengths

The primary strength of the SAS model is in its approach to the supervisory relationship as the core aspect of supervision. Supervision is focused on the relationship, which is dynamic, with change expected and encouraged. Cultural influences and interpersonal characteristics are recognized in the supervisor, supervisee, and client, and their influences are embodied in the supervisory relationship.

The SAS method provides a framework specifically designed to guide supervision based on empirical, conceptual, and practice knowledge from the field of counseling and supervision. The nature of SAS allows its application by supervisors from different theoretical orientations. It is designed to provoke questions about supervision rather than to offer a "cookbook" approach.

Weaknesses

Since the SAS method is very complex and involved, an inexperienced supervisor might find some of the concepts difficult to use effectively. Additionally, its lack of specific techniques and methods may discourage some supervisors who feel the need for a more directive approach to supervision.

Supervisors who are not convinced of the importance of dynamic interaction and interpersonal communication may feel that there is too much emphasis on interpersonal relationships. Although the SAS method is based on concepts found in empirical research, its concepts and methods have not been subjected to systematic research to determine their effectiveness in supervision.

☐ Using Integrative Approaches in Supervision

As stated at the beginning of this chapter, the "technique-mixing" process, although unscientific, reflects the actual practice of supervision more accurately than any one theoretical approach. Supervisors, like counselors, tend to use techniques that they are comfortable with and that are effective with their supervisees without regard for theoretical origin. Freeman and McHenry (1996) reported in their study of counselor educators that only 19.5% of the respondents specifically mentioned research, models, or the names of researchers in the field of counselor supervision. Thus, we suspect that few supervisors consider formalizing their methods of supervision into an integrative model of supervision.

Bradley, Parr, and Gould (1999) described the development of an integrative approach to counseling as requiring the following considerations: (a) recognition of the diversity of ideas in the various theories and an understanding of their philosophies, constructs, and goals; (b) knowledge of one's personal values, beliefs, perceptions, and philosophy; (c) the types of clients that will be seen and where they will be working with clients; and (d) the realization that some theories cannot be realistically combined into an effective approach. Applying these considerations to the development of an integrative model of supervision requires that the supervisor first understand the philosophy, constructs, and goals of the various theories of supervision by studying them, along with their techniques and strengths and weaknesses. Second, the supervisor must consider her or his own values, beliefs, and perceptions about supervision, because a supervision theory cannot be used effectively when a basic philosophical conflict exists. However, the supervisor should note that techniques do not necessarily reflect the theory, and therefore may be used without endorsing the theory from which they are drawn. Next, the supervisor must consider the supervisees that he or she will supervise and the roles required of her or him in the supervision process. Rønnestad and Skovholt (1993) note the difference between beginning and advanced supervisees: beginning supervisees often exhibit a large "theory–practice" gulf and are eager to learn specific skills, while advanced supervisees are more concerned with autonomy and professional growth. Thus, the beginning supervisee requires a supervisor comfortable with skill training, whereas the advanced supervisee requires a supervisor comfortable in the role of consultant. Finally, the supervisor must recognize that combining some supervision theories may prove problematic.

Norcross and Halgin (1997) describe supervision as a complex and demanding undertaking. The integrative perspective does not relieve the pressure inherent in supervision and may, in fact, require more of the supervisor and supervisee than single theory systems. Along with the conventional problems involved in producing competent counselors, the integrative supervisor must help the supervisee acquire competence in multiple treatment combinations and adjusting her or his therapeutic approach to fit the needs of the client. Norcross and Halgin call integrative supervision a formidable challenge and a promising opportunity.

Competence in a single system includes not only the effective use of that system but also the ability and ethical responsibility to know how and when to refer a client and her or his problems to a more suitable system. Norcross and Halgin (1997) note that competence in a single theory is a necessary prerequisite for integrative training because "one cannot integrate what one does not know" (p. 206). Competence in integrative practice is a broader and more ambitious task than competence in a single theory system, and therefore, it requires more time and effort to learn. Of critical importance to integrative practice is the assumption that the supervisee can learn and apply several models competently (Beutler & Consoli, 1992; Lazarus, 1992; Prochaska & DiClemente, 1992).

Andrews, Norcross, and Halgin (1992) reported that the general consensus among supervisors and educators is that training in integration should follow training in specific systems and techniques. Training in a specific single theory's systems and techniques and systematic referral should begin early in a student's graduate program, with students being exposed to all therapeutic systems without judgment on their effectiveness. Integration can be introduced but should not be stressed as a possible choice until the student is advanced in her or his training program. Schacht (1991) stated that integration may take one of two broad forms differentially accessible to novice versus expert. The form accessible to novices emphasizes conceptual products entering the curriculum as content additions. The second form emphasizes a special mode of thinking that comes from accumulated and supervised experiences promoting effective performance and metacognitive skills and is available primarily to advanced students.

Defining Psychotherapy Integration

The three most common approaches to integrative supervision are common factors, technical eclecticism, and theoretical integration. Each goes beyond the confines of a single theory and its associated techniques, but differ in the manner and level of integration (Norcross & Newman, 1992).

Common Factors

The common factors approach searches for the basic elements shared by various theories and attempts to create effective treatments based on commonalities. This approach is based on the belief that the commonalities within theories are more important in counseling outcome than the unique elements discrete theories possess (Lambert, 1992; Lambert & Ogles, 1997). Norcross and Halgin (1997) note that supervision is seldom conducted from the common factors perspective. However, supervisors often urge supervisees to seek out commonalities in counseling alliances, behavior acquisition, and practice, and then select what works best (Grencavage & Norcross, 1990; Norcross & Halgin, 1997; Weinberger, 1995). Integrative supervision should emphasize common factors and capitalize on their contributions of specific techniques in counseling.

Technical Eclecticism

The premise of technical eclecticism is finding the best treatment for the client and her or his problem on the basis of experience and research. Lazarus (1989, 1992) stated that it is possible to use methods and techniques from various sources without subscribing to the contributing theories. Technical eclecticism, also called prescriptive eclecticism, attempts to customize interventions and relationship stances to the unique needs of the individual in both the counseling and supervision processes. Norcross and Halgin (1997) note that the supervisor using technical eclecticism is involved in an intentional parallel process of tailoring supervision to the unique needs of the supervisee, and thereby enhancing the supervisee's ability to tailor counseling to the unique needs of the client.

Theoretical Integration

Theoretical integration is the process by which two or more discrete theories are synthesized in an attempt to form a more effective theory leading in new directions. Theoretical integration is more than the pragmatic blending of procedures; it involves a commitment to a new theoretical creation. In supervision, the distinctions between technical eclecticism and theoretical integration are often difficult to discern; they are not mutually exclusive because neither can ignore the influence of the other (Norcross & Arkowitz, 1992).

Principles of Integrative Supervision

The emphasis of integrative supervision should be on "how to think" rather than on "what to think." To aid supervisors implement this emphasis into their own integrative system, Norcross and Halgin (1997) suggested that the following essential elements be considered by supervisors considering the use of integrative supervision.

Customize Supervision to the Individual Student

As integrative counseling is tailored to the needs of the client, so integrative supervision should be tailored to the unique needs of the supervisee. This is the most important principle in integrative supervision.

Conduct a Needs Assessment

Supervisees approach supervision with a multitude of expectations and needs, both conscious and unconscious. A needs assessment allows the supervisor to discover what the supervisee wants to accomplish in supervision (personal growth, validation of theoretical stance, improve skills) which allows her or him to design unique supervision objectives for the supervisee. Discovery of supervisee needs is the beginning of the process of supervision; however, supervisee needs and expectations change during the supervision process, so it is necessary to periodically reevaluate and modify supervision objectives. Conflict between what the supervisee wants from supervision and what the supervisor believes is in her or his best interest may occur. The supervisor should elicit the supervisee's opinion and consider her or his wants; but as supervision is the responsibility of the supervisor, he or she should not be guided solely by the supervisee's agenda (Norcross & Halgin, 1997)

Construct Explicit Contracts

Along with assessing needs and expectations, perceptions about supervision relationships should be shared. At the initial supervision session, a contract with explicit goals and objectives related to interpersonal roles, learning and skill acquisition, attendance, evaluation methods, and provisions for revision should be constructed. Acquisition of objectives should be periodically reviewed in collaboration with the supervisee rather than merely critiqued by the supervisor.

Blend Supervision Methods

Because integrative supervision is eclectic in counseling content and teaching methods, the supervisor's interventions are guided by the needs of both the client being discussed and the supervisee. Therefore, if the supervisee requires instruction and practice in specific techniques, supervision should be directive and educational; but if the supervisee needs to examine the historical context of a client's problem or her or his own interpersonal difficulties, an exploratory approach may be used (Halgin & Murphy, 1995). It is the supervisor's responsibility to select the methodology most appropriate to the supervisee's needs. The methods used in supervision are drawn from a variety of techniques associated with a multitude of theoretical systems and are dictated by needs and specific situations; they include didactic presentations, reading assignments, discussions, modeling, experiential activities, and case examples.

Address "Relationships of Choice"

Integrative supervision has long been associated with systematic selection of clinical interventions and techniques (technical eclecticism), but the importance of the therapeutic relationship has never been questioned. Relationship stances or styles should be differentially customized for the particular needs of the supervisee.

Operate From a Coherent Framework

The use of a coherent framework or schema is responsible for integrative supervision being perceived by the supervisee as either understandable or confusing. A guiding perspective that specifies the reason behind treatment selection helps the supervisee learn to apply interventions more effectively in specific client circumstances. Examples of systematic frameworks are: Lazarus's (1992) multimodal therapy, Prochaska and DiClementi's (1992) transtheoretical therapy, and Wachtel's (1991) integrative psychodynamic and behavioral approach (Bradley et al., 1999).

Match Supervision to Supervisee Variables

Because it is impossible to create a style of supervision that guarantees an identical supervisory experience for every supervisee, supervisors must consider supervisee variables when systematically blending methods from diverse theories. Norcross et al. (1990) suggested that, although it is impossible to determine which variables will be important in a supervisory relationship, three—therapy approach, clinical experience, and cognitive style—appear to be most commonly indicated from experience and research.

Therapy Approach.   As much as possible, the methods and content of supervision should parallel the treatment approach being used by the supervisee in counseling. If the supervisee is using an insight-oriented, verbal approach with clients, then supervision should explore countertransference reactions; conversely, a behavioral or action-oriented approach indicates a supervision strategy of instruction and role play.

Clinical Experience.   Developmental needs of supervisees change over the course of training, which indicates that supervisory styles are differentially effective according to the supervisee's level of experience (Baird, 1998; Brack, Brack, & McCarthy, 1997; Braver, Graffin, & Holahan, 1990; Duryee, Brymer, & Gold, 1996; Freeman & McHenry, 1996; McLeod, 1998; Rønnestad & Skovholt, 1993; Stoltenberg & McNeill, 1997; Stoltenberg, McNeill, & Crethar, 1994). Beginning supervisees are usually interested in learning techniques, whereas advanced supervisees are more interested in alternative methods and concepts or the dynamics of counseling. The goals of supervision should reflect the developmental level of the supervisee and progress from support and training to the integration of theory into a unique personal style.

Cognitive Style.   The conceptual level of the supervisee is an important aspect of consideration in creating a unique supervision experience that, depending on supervisee needs, stresses self-direction or external control. Another important aspect is interpersonal reactance, which refers to the supervisee's reaction to supervisory style and directiveness.

Attending to Supervisees' Personal Idioms

Each supervisee manifests a unique blend of personality and method that forms her or his personal idiom (Hogan, 1964). The supervisor must recognize the supervisee's personal approach in order to avoid problems resulting from imposing her or his own style on the supervisee. Integrative supervision allows for a generalized approach to clients that capitalizes on the supervisee's unique style, interests, and experiences.

Assess Therapeutic Skills

Criteria-based rating scales for assessing skills can enhance their acquisition. Although rating scales for integrative therapies have not been developed, the scales created for various diverse theories can be used together to define procedures and describe behaviors of effective use. Additionally, the use of rating scales allows exploration of the differences and similarities of the various approaches (Norcross et al., 1990).

Nurture the Supervisory Relationship

As the counseling relationship is a primary curative factor in counseling, so the supervisory relationship is an important aspect of successful supervision. The integrative supervisor has the ability to blend a variety of methods and techniques (supportive, directive, exploratory, interpersonal) in the supervisory relationship that enhances supervisee experience. Although the supervisor should not deny differences in knowledge and power or abdicate her or his responsibilities, he or she should attempt to create an empathic and collaborative relationship with an environment that encourages the expression of insecurities, respectful disagreements, and alternatives.

Share Our Work With Supervisees

Modeling, although particularly effective for teaching complex behaviors, is seldom used in supervision (Norcross & Halgin, 1997). Most supervisors use consulting techniques to teach methods in counseling. Additionally, supervisors seldom discuss their mistakes or anxieties about clinical practice. However, sharing clinical work can initiate a dialogue that shows the supervisor's willingness to be vulnerable. This vulnerability, in turn, demonstrates the supervisor's commitment to a relationship of trust and openness.

Evaluate the Outcome

The training and supervision of students requires some demonstration of its efficacy. Integrative supervision probably increases the problem of measuring outcomes. Little research has been done on evaluating supervision, either in discrete theories or integrative systems (Beutler, 1988; Greenberg & Goldman, 1988; Strupp, Butler, & Rosser, 1988).

Critiques of Integrative Supervision

Strengths

The use of an integrative approach in supervision is characterized by flexibility, exploration, experimentation, and freedom. It is also more imaginative, spontaneous, changeable, and challenging for both the supervisor and supervisee.

Integrative supervision is tailored to the individual supervisee and her or his needs and variables. The supervisory relationship is collaborative and nurturing without the authoritarian and dogmatic style often found in the supervisory models of individual theories. Expectations and evaluation criteria are clearly explained. Although not specifically addressed, multiculturalism is implied by the attention focused on the individual and his personality variables.

Weaknesses

If integrative supervision is introduced to supervisees who are not ready, it can be confusing and anxiety provoking in its ambiguity and uncertainty. Even advanced supervisees who are competent in single theory usage have difficulties in blending counseling methods and interventions effectively at first. Some supervisees are frustrated by having to learn multiple therapy competencies. Additionally, supervisees may have to use methods and techniques that they do not enjoy using or that make them uncomfortable for the benefit of the client.

Research in the use of integrative supervision is extremely limited. Efficacy reports have predominantly resulted from supervisor experience. Since research is limited, no manuals or criteria-based skill assessment scales are available.

☐ New Models in Integrative Supervision

The following models are presented as examples of current research and development in integrative supervision.

Reflective Learning Model of Supervision

Ward and House (1998) propose a supervision model integrating reflective learning theory with the concurrent development of both the supervisee as a professional and the supervisory relationship. Reflective learning applied to counselor development and supervision may be defined as "the process whereby trainees meaningfully reconstruct counseling experiences using a repertoire of understandings, images, and actions to reframe a troubling situation so that problem solving interventions can be generated" (Ward & House, 1998, p. 25). The quality of the supervisory relationship determines if reflective learning occurs and if the knowledge of how to change behavior develops (Mahon & Altmann, 1991; Sexton & Whiston, 1994). Ward and House's (1998) model links the principles of reflective learning theory to the dynamics of counseling supervision and the phases of supervision development.

The reflective learning methodology is composed of four phases. Phase 1 is contextual orientation, in which supervisors are challenged by supervisees' maladaptive thoughts and feelings (guilt, anxiety, perfectionism, anger, confusion) in their attempt to promote professional development. In phase 2, establishing trust, the supervisee's perception of the supervisor's support is important to both the level of trust in the supervisory relationship and the supervisee's learning and growth. Conceptual development is phase 3. The supervisory relationship must address supervisee conceptual dissonance before it can enhance the understanding of client issues and case planning. Phase 4 is clinical independence, in which supervisees are encouraged and supported in their development of independence in clinical self-assessment and case planning.

Solution-Oriented Model of Supervision

The solution-oriented model of supervision originates in the family therapy literature and is based on solution-focused therapy combined with narrative and competency-based theories (Berg & Miller, 1992; deShazer, 1991; Durrant, 1993; Furman & Ahola, 1992; O'Hanlon & Weiner-Davis, 1989). Thomas (1994) stated that the major focus of solution-oriented supervision is curiosity and respect "in that it seeks to coax and author expertise from the life, experience, education, and training of a supervisee rather than deliver or teach expertise from a hierarchically superior position" (p. 11). Thomas suggested two steps in solution-oriented supervision: (a) the conceptual map, which includes examining what supervisees want from supervision, the supervisory relationship, and assumptions about solution-oriented supervision; and (b) the implementation of solution-oriented supervision, which includes socializing, saliency, setting goals, and future orientation. The conceptual map is a guide to the concepts of solution-oriented supervision. It includes the needs and requirements of the supervisee, the nature of the supervisory relationship, and the basic assumptions of solution-oriented supervision.

Thomas (1994) suggests seven themes relevant to the needs and requirements of supervisees in solution-oriented supervision: there must be mutual respect between supervisor and supervisee; the supervisory relationship should be collegial rather than hierarchical; cooperative evaluation based on the achievement of well-defined goals; the supervisor should assume that the supervisee is basically competent to work with clients, knows her or his strengths and weaknesses, and is willing to work toward increased expertise; the supervisor should affirm and empower the supervisee based on her or his successes and competencies; supervision is a human experience; and a successful supervisory experience is based on the supervisor's consideration of her or his evolving abilities as a consultant and on the supervisee's changing needs.

The supervisory relationship in solution-oriented supervision assumes that the supervisee is the expert on and has the resources to resolve his problems. Thus, the supervisor sets up a cooperative, goal-oriented relationship based on the assumption that the supervisee has the strength, ability, and resourcefulness to resolve problems and achieve her or his supervision goals. The cooperatively defined goals, directions, and options are future oriented with positive expectations building on the unique assets of the therapist.

Schema-Focused Model of Supervision

Greenwald and Young (1998) propose a supervision model based on schema-focused therapy (SFT; Bricker, Young, & Flanagan, 1993; McGinn & Young, 1996; Young, 1994) that incorporates cognitive, behavioral, experiential, and interpersonal interventions. Perris (1994) suggested that cognitive supervision required that the supervisee be encouraged to develop conceptualizations of client problems connecting thinking, emotions, behavior, and underlying meanings; build a secure, collaborative therapeutic relationship with the client; define and adhere to explicit goals; select and apply appropriate strategies and techniques; determine when goals are met; recognize and evaluate interpersonal reactions in herself or himself as well as the client; and understand how to deal with them. SFT supervision incorporates these elements and adds assessment and conceptualization of schema processes and modes, while focusing supervision on the counseling relationship and staging interventions in areas of cognitive, behavioral, experiential, and interpersonal change. The three main components in the supervision process are case conceptualization and treatment planning, role playing to improve skills and techniques, and focus on the supervisee's own schemas and schema process and the therapy process.

Greenwald and Young (1998) described eight supervisory experiences incorporated into SFT training and supervision. The first experience is getting acquainted. Discussions might include previous training and counseling experience, types of clients the supervisee is most and least comfortable with, areas of sensitivities that might arise in counseling, what would be most helpful in supervision, and questions about the supervisor's experience and expectations. After the early sessions, the supervisor and supervisee set agendas for each session. The agenda primarily involves deciding what type of help the supervisee wants and which case or cases he or she wants to focus on. Typically, the SFT supervisor offers help in one of seven areas (supervisory experiences): case conceptualization, case strategy, case implementation, resolving technical case problems, working on counseling relationship issues, providing support and personal help for the supervisee, and discussing general conceptual and treatment issues. In most sessions, the supervisor and supervisee will consider only one or two help areas.

☐ Conclusions

The models presented in this chapter, the discrimination model, interpersonal process recall, and the systems approach to supervision, differ in their focus and design, but some commonalities can be found. First, each method provides for some sort of skill acquisition by the supervisee, although emphasis and methodology differ. Additionally, to a greater or lesser extent, each method provides for evaluation of the supervisee's skills and performance. Finally, each method is concerned with improving the supervisee's professional performance as a counselor

A supervisor who elects to use an integrative supervisory method should consider Norcross and Halgin's (1997) suggestions when either adopting a model or developing her or his own model. For many supervisors, techniques drawn from several different theories may be the extent to which integrative supervision is used. For others, a complete integration of two or more theoretical models may be desired. We suggest that supervisors wishing to use integrative models try several to determine which is the best fit for her or his needs.

☐ References

Andrews, J. D. W., Norcross, J. C., & Halgin, R. P. (1992). Training in psychotherapy integration. In J. C. Norcross & M. R. Goldfried (Eds.), *Handbook of psychotherapy integration* (pp. 563–592). New York: Basic Books.

Aveline, M. (1997). The use of audiotapes in supervision of psychotherapy. In G. Shipton (Ed.), *Supervision of psychotherapy and counseling* (pp. 80–92). Philadelphia: Open University Press.

Baird, B. W. (1998). *The internship, practicum, and the field placement handbook: A guide for the helping professions* (2nd ed.). Upper Saddle River, NJ: Prentice-Hall.

Berg, I. K., & Miller, S. D. (1992). *Working with the problem drinker: A solution-focused approach.* New York: Norton.

Bernard, J. M. (1979). Supervisor training: A discrimination model. *Counselor Education and Supervision, 19,* 60–68.

Bernard, J. M. (1989). Training supervisors to examine relationship issues using IPR. *The Clinical Supervisor, 7,* 103–112.

Bernard, J. M. (1997). The discrimination model. In C. E. Watkins, Jr. (Ed.), *Handbook of psychotherapy supervision* (pp. 310–327). New York: Wiley.

Beutler, L. E. (1988). Introduction: Training to competency in psychotherapy. *Journal of Consulting and Clinical Psychology, 56,* 651–652.

Beutler, L. E., & Consoli, A. J. (1992). Systematic eclectic psychotherapy. In J. C. Norcross &

M. R. Goldfried (Eds.), *Handbook of psychotherapy integration* (pp. 264–297). New York: Basic Books.

Borders, L. D., & Leddick, G. R. (1987). *Handbook of counseling supervision*. Alexandria, VA: American Association for Counseling and Development.

Brack, G., Brack, C. J., & McCarthy, C. (1997). A model for helping novice therapists to integrate their affective reactions and cognitive appraisals in supervision. *Clinical Supervisor, 15*(2), 37–48.

Bradley, L. J., Parr, G., & Gould, L. J. (1999). Counseling and psychotherapy: An integrative perspective. In D. Capuzzi & D. R. Gross (Eds.), *Counseling and psychotherapy: Theories and interventions* (pp. 459–480). Upper Saddle River, NJ: Merrill.

Braver, M., Graffin, N., & Holahan, W. (1990). Supervising the advanced trainee: A multiple therapy training model. *Psychotherapy, 27*(4), 561–567.

Bricker, D. C., Young, J. E., & Flanagan, C. M. (1993). Schema-focused cognitive therapy: A comprehensive approach for characterological problems. In K. T. Kuehlwein & H. Rosen (Eds.), *Cognitive therapies in action* (pp. 88–125). San Francisco: Jossey-Bass.

Carifio, M. S., & Hess, A. K. (1987). Who is the ideal supervisor? *Professional Psychology: Research and Practice, 3*, 244–250.

Cashwell, C. S. (1994). Interpersonal process recall. In L. D. Borders (Ed.), *Supervision: Exploring the effective components* (ERIC/Cass Counseling Digest Series). Greensboro, NC: ERIC/Cass.

Clark, P. (1997). Interpersonal process recall in supervision. In G. Shipton (Ed.), *Supervision of psychotherapy and counselling* (pp. 93–104). Philadelphia: Open University Press.

Dendy, R. F. (1971). *A model for the training of undergraduate residence hall assistants as paraprofessional counselors using videotape playback techniques and interpersonal process recall.* Unpublished doctoral dissertation, Michigan State University, East Lansing, MI.

deShazer, S. (1991). *Putting difference to work*. New York: Norton.

Dowrick, P. W. (1991). *Practical guide to using video in the behavioral sciences*. New York: Wiley.

Durrant, M. (1993). *Residential treatment: A cooperative, competency-based approach to therapy and program design*. New York: Norton.

Duryee, J., Brymer, M., & Gold, K. (1996). The supervisory needs of neophyte psychotherapy trainees. *Journal of Clinical Psychology, 52*(6), 663–671.

Ellis, M. V., & Dell, D. M. (1986). Dimensionality of supervisor roles: Supervisors' perceptions of supervision. *Journal of Counseling Psychology, 33*, 282–291.

Ellis, M. V., Dell, D. M., & Good, G. E. (1988). Counselor trainees' perceptions of supervisor roles: Two studies testing the dimensionality of supervision. *Journal of Counseling Psychology, 35*, 315–324.

Freeman, B., & McHenry, S. (1996). Clinical supervision of counselors-in-training: A nationwide survey of ideal delivery, goals, and theoretical influences. *Counselor Education and Supervision, 36*(2), 144–158.

Furman, B., & Ahola, T. (1992). *Solution talk: Hosting therapeutic conversations*. New York: Norton.

Greenberg, L. S., & Goldman, R. L. (1988). Training in experiential therapy. *Journal of Consulting and Clinical Psychology, 56*, 696–702.

Greenwald, M., & Young, J. (1998). Schema-focused therapy: An integrative approach to psychotherapy supervision. *Journal of Cognitive Psychotherapy: An International Quarterly, 12*(2), 109–126.

Grencavage, L. M., & Norcross, J. C. (1990). Where are the commonalties among the therapeutic common factors? *Professional Psychology: Research and Practice, 21*, 372–378.

Halgin, R. P., & Murphy, R. A. (1995). Issues in the training of psychotherapists. In B. Bongar & L. E. Beutler (Eds.), *Comprehensive textbook of psychotherapy: Theory and practice* (pp. 434–455). New York: Oxford University Press.

Hogan, R. A. (1964). Issues and approaches in supervision. *Psychotherapy: Theory, Research, and Practice, 1*, 139–141.

Holloway, E. L. (1995). *Clinical supervision: A systems approach*. Thousand Oaks, CA: Sage.

Holloway, E. L. (1997). Structures for the analysis and teaching of supervision. In C. E.

Watkins, Jr. (Ed.), *Handbook of psychotherapy supervision* (pp. 249–276). New York: Wiley.

Holloway, E. L., & Neufeldt, S. A. (1995). Supervision: Contributors to treatment efficacy *Journal of Consulting and Clinical Psychology, 65,* 207–213.

Kagan, H., & Kagan, N. I. (1997). Interpersonal process recall: Influencing human interaction. In C. E. Watkins Jr. (Ed.), *Handbook of psychotherapy supervision* (pp. 296–309). New York: Wiley.

Kagan, N. I. (1980). Influencing human interaction—Eighteen years with IPR. In A. K. Hess (Ed.), *Psychotherapy supervision: Theory, research, and practice* (pp. 262–283). New York: Wiley.

Kagan, N. I., Holmes, M., & Kagan, H. (Eds.). (1995). *Interpersonal process recall manual.* Houston, TX: Mason Media.

Kagan, N. I., & Kagan, H. (1990). IPR—A validated model for the 1990s and beyond. *Counseling Psychologist, 18,* 436–440.

Kagan, N. I., & Kagan, H. (1991). Interpersonal process recall. In D. W. Dowrick (Ed.), *Practical guide to using video in the behavioral sciences* (pp. 221–230). New York: Wiley.

Kagan, N. I., & Krathwohl, D. R. (1967). *Studies in human interaction: Interpersonal process recall stimulated by videotape.* East Lansing, MI: Educational Publishing Services.

Kagan, N. I., Krathwohl, D. R., & Miller, R. (1963). Stimulated recall in therapy using videotape—A case study. *Journal of Counseling Psychology, 10,* 237–243.

Lambert, M. J. (1992). Psychotherapy outcome research: Implications for integrative and eclectic therapists. In J. C. Norcross & M. R. Goldfried (Eds.), *Handbook of psychotherapy integration* (pp. 94–129). New York: Basic Books.

Lambert, M. J., & Ogles, B. M. (1997). The effectiveness of psychotherapy supervision. In C. E. Watkins, Jr. (Ed.), *Handbook of psychotherapy supervision* (pp. 421–446). New York: Wiley.

Lazarus, A. A. (1989). *The practice of multimodal therapy.* Baltimore: Johns Hopkins University Press. (Originally published in 1981 by McGraw-Hill.)

Lazarus, A. A. (1992). Multimodal therapy: Technical eclecticism with minimal integration. In J. C. Norcross & M. R. Goldfried (Eds.), *Handbook of psychotherapy integration* (pp. 231–263). New York: Basic Books.

Lazarus, A. A. (1995). Different types of eclecticism and integration: Let's be aware of the danger. *Journal of Psychotherapeutic Integration, 5*(1), 27–39

Lazarus, A. A. (1996). The utility and futility of combining treatments in psychotherapy. *Clinical Psychology: Science and Practice, 3,* 59–68.

Mahon, B. R., & Altmann, H. A. (1991). Skill training: Cautions and recommendations. *Counselor Education and Supervision, 17,* 42–50.

McGinn, L. K., & Young, J. E. (1996). Schema-focused therapy. In P. M. Salkovskis (Ed.), *Frontiers of cognitive therapy* (pp. 182–207). New York: Guilford.

McLeod, S. (1998). Student self-appraisal: Facilitating mutual planning in clinical education. *The Clinical Supervisor, 15*(1), 87–101.

Neufeldt, S. A., Iversen, J. N., & Juntunen, C. L. (1995). *Supervision strategies for the first practicum.* Alexandria, VA: American Counseling Association Press.

Norcross, J. C., & Arkowitz, J. (1992). The evolution and current status of psychotherapy integration. In W. Dryden (Ed.), *Integrative and eclectic psychotherapy: A handbook* (pp. 1–40). London: Open University Press.

Norcross, J. C., & Halgin, R. P. (1997). Integrative approaches to psychotherapy supervision. In C.E. Watkins, Jr. (Ed.), *Handbook of psychotherapy supervision* (pp. 203–222). New York: Wiley.

Norcross, J. C., & Newman, C. F. (1992). Psychotherapy integration: Setting the context. In J. C. Norcross & M. R. Goldfried (Eds.), *Handbook of psychotherapy integration* (pp. 3–45). New York: Basic Books.

O'Hanlon, W. H., & Weiner-Davis, M. (1989). *In search of solutions: A new direction in psychotherapy.* New York: Norton.

Perris, C. (1994). Supervising cognitive psychotherapy and training supervisors. *Journal of Cognitive Psychotherapy: An International Quarterly, 8,* 83–103.

Prochaska, J. O., & DiClemente, C. C. (1992). The transtheoretical approach. In J. C. Norcross & M. R. Goldfried (Eds.), *Handbook of psychotherapy integration* (pp. 300–334). New York: Basic Books.

Putney, M. W., Worthington, E. L., Jr., & McCullough, M. E. (1992). Effects of supervisor and supervisee theoretical orientation and supervisor-supervisee matching on interns' perception of supervision. *Journal of Counseling Psychology, 39,* 258–265.

Rønnestad, M. H., & Skovholt, T. M. (1993). Supervision of beginning and advanced graduate students of counseling and psychotherapy. *Journal of Counseling and Development, 71*(4), 396–405.

Schacht, T. E. (1991). Can psychotherapy education advance psychotherapy integration? *Journal of Psychotherapy Integration, 1,* 305–319.

Sexton, T. L., & Whiston, S. C. (1994). The status of the counseling relationship: An empirical review, theoretical implications and research directions. *The Counseling Psychologist, 22*(1), 7–70.

Stenack, R. J., & Dye, H. A. (1982). Behavioral descriptions of counseling supervision roles. *Counselor Education and Supervision, 22,* 295–304.

Stoltenberg, C. D., & McNeill, B. W. (1997). Clinical supervision from a developmental perspective: Research and practice. In C.E. Watkins, Jr. (Ed.), *Handbook of psychotherapy supervision* (pp. 184–202). New York: Wiley.

Stoltenberg, C. D., McNeill, B. W., & Crethar, H. C. (1994). Changes in supervision as counselors and therapists gain experience: A review. *Professional Psychology: Research and Practice, 25*(4), 416–449.

Strupp, H. H., Butler, S. F., & Rosser, C. L. (1988). Training in psychodynamic psychotherapy. *Journal of Consulting and Clinical Psychology, 56,* 689–695.

Thomas, F. N. (1994). Solution-oriented supervision: The coaxing of expertise. *The Family Journal: Counseling and Therapy for Couples and Families, 2*(1), 11–18.

Wachtel, P. L. (1991). From eclecticism to synthesis: Toward a more seamless psychotherapeutic integration. *Journal of Psychotherapy Integration, 1,* 43–54.

Ward, C. C., & House, R. M. (1998). Counseling supervision: A reflective model. *Counselor Education and Supervision, 38*(1), 23–33.

Weinberger, J. (1995). Common factors aren't so common: The common factors dilemma. *Clinical Psychology: Science and Practice, 2,* 45–69.

Young, J. E. (1994). *Cognitive therapy for personality disorders: A schema-focused approach* (rev. ed.). Sarasota, FL: Professional Resource Press.

5

CHAPTER

Peggy P. Whiting
Loretta J. Bradley
Kristen J. Planny

Supervision-Based Developmental Models of Counselor Supervision

Emerging from the literature are a variety of propositions for a complex model of developmental supervision to assist in explaining the journey of becoming a master clinician. The developmental perspective offers understanding of how the inexperienced supervisee transforms into an accomplished counselor. This viewpoint further illustrates the influence of supervisory behaviors and describes how, when, and why supervisors will assume roles of teacher, model, coach, counselor, and peer. The concept of developmental supervision is presented as a relationship between supervisee and supervisor wherein professional maturity emerges over time. The developmental movement has a desired direction and is distinctive from a mere increase in quantity of clinical skill and knowledge. The desired direction is one of qualitative transformation of the supervisee.

The developmental transformation is movement toward a well-developed clinical identity, an eclectic style sensitive to the impact of factors of diversity, greater introspective and reflective ability, an integration of theory and practice, and an autonomous means of functioning. The supervisory alliance must be considered at all levels of supervision and the supervisory learning environment must be structured to promote development. As the supervisee matures, developmental resources increase and professional complexity emerges in all developmental domains (cognitive, emotional, social, ethical reasoning, interpersonal, etc.). The supervisee can develop into a colleague and seasoned clinician, a movement from supervisee to supervisor.

This chapter focuses primarily upon the recent expansion of the integrated developmental model (IDM) of supervision (Stoltenberg, McNeill, & Delworth, 1998). What follows is a summary of ideas parallel to the theoretical precepts of the IDM. These concepts of supervision are offered by others in the literature and underscore the contribution and significance of the developmental perspective. They are important in understanding the salient underpinnings of developmental supervision.

☐ Developmental Supervision Defined

The developmental perspective of supervision may be viewed through the elaboration of several foundational assumptions. They include, but are not limited to, the concepts of organismic versus mechanistic views of development, cognitive processing and transformation, hierarchical stage sequences, increasing skill and awareness, transformation in identity, motivation theory, variable developmental needs, the learning context, and developmentally appropriate learning activities.

Organismic Versus Mechanistic Views of Development

Development may be viewed in different ways. Two viewpoints of developmental understanding are the organismic and the mechanistic. An organismic understanding of development is akin to Kegan's (1982) concept of meaning-making activity. This perspective sees an individual as changing in how they construct, interpret, and use knowledge. The change occurs as a transformation over time in cognitive complexity, differentiation, and integration. This holistic view of development comprehensively describes how a supervisee internally transforms into a mature professional. This theoretical premise is contrasted with a more mechanistic perspective that views development as the acquisition, through experience, of new skills, techniques, and information. For example, Stoltenberg, McNeill, and Delworth (1998) stated: "We find a general increase in therapist knowledge and skills over time, but qualitative differences in the level of complexity of these and how they are used, which differs from level to level" (p. 12).

Cognitive Processing and Transformation

Theories of cognitive development and processing assist in describing the developmental shift from novice to expert. The issues are how a supervisee structures her or his thought about counselor roles, identity, tasks, accountability, ethical reasoning, etc., how the thinking is transformed over time, and how information is learned and accessed for use. According to cognitive processing theory, initial learning is general in nature and increases in specificity when existing knowledge is challenged and evaluated through experience. The learning environment that provides concrete examples, opportunities for practice, evaluative feedback, and open dialogue will create a context for the development of maturing expertise. The supervisee's trans-formation in thought results from synthesizing and integrating knowledge.

Hierarchical Stage Sequences

Blocher (1983) viewed a goal of supervision to be the development within supervisees of "more complex and more comprehensive schemas for under-standing human interaction" (p. 29). He compares these schemas to stage models of adult development. Shaughnessy & Carey (1996) presented the cognitive-developmental model (CDM) of supervision. This approach as-sumes a sequential, hierarchical stage evolution of understanding that must be measured in a particular learning domain. Assessment of general level of cognitive functioning is insufficient, as discontinuities exist from domain to domain. The CDM views the supervisor's role as being one "to aid the counselor in constructing qualitatively more complex understandings of counseling through probes that are tailored to the trainee's current level of understanding" (Shaughnessy & Carey, 1996, p. 228). Multicultural coun-seling competence is also suggested to occur in a stage sequence (Ivey, Ivey, & Simek-Morgan, 1997) whose progression can be impacted through developmentally appropriate supervisory activities (Leong & Wagner, 1994).

Increasing Skill and Awareness

Borders et al. (1991) presented "The Curriculum Guide for Training Coun-seling Supervisors." The content areas have learning objectives in the areas of self-awareness, theoretical and conceptual knowledge, and skills and techniques. The content areas include models of supervision; counselor de-velopment; supervision methods and techniques; supervisory relationship; ethical, legal, and professional regulatory issues; evaluation; and executive/administrative skills. The authors state: "We . . . suspect that learning to be a supervisor is a spiraling process in which supervisors are recycled through each content area at progressively more sophisticated levels of awareness and understanding" (Borders et al., 1991, p. 78).

Transformation in Identity

Using the sociocultural approach, "the goals of supervision broaden beyond the acquisition of skills or technique; a professional identity is fostered through an apprenticeship with mutual influence, an appreciation for di-versity and the shared cocreation of meaning" (O'Byrne & Rosenberg, 1998, p. 38). In this tradition, learning is a social process within a professional culture. Supervision is process oriented, collaborative, and practice based, and promotes reflective assessment. Transformation in thinking occurs over time as a novice moves toward advancement in skill sophistication, subjective deliberation, and knowledge acquisition.

Motivation Theory

Desire for personal or professional development is highly affected by motivation. Changes in motivation for advancement to a more complex structure of thought will occur. Often, dissonance will fuel the developmental movement, a desire to calm the discomfort in thought and feeling that is experienced within an existing level of development. In developmental supervision, motivation varies more greatly in beginning levels of maturity and tends to stabilize in advancing levels.

Variable Developmental Needs

Gladding (1996) defined supervision as "a facilitative experience that combines didactic and experiential learning in the context of a developmental relationship" (p. 38). Rønnestad and Skovholt (1993) synthesized the literature on beginning supervision and contrasted the findings with those on more advanced supervision. Early supervision is reported to be more effective if oriented toward teaching, feedback, support, directives, and skills and delivered within a trusting supervisory relationship. In comparison, more advanced supervision can be successful if delivered in correcting, clarifying, confronting, reflecting, and consulting ways within a structuring and mediating supervisory relationship. The conclusion is: the needs change as the supervisee matures, and supervision interventions are effective only if they shift to address the changes. Rønnestad and Skovholt (1993) discussed the usefulness of a supervisory contract as a means of structuring the supervision experience. They encouraged the contract to include the developmental needs of the supervisee, the strengths of the supervisor, the opportunities provided by the site, and the goals and methods of supervision (p. 402).

Bernard (1979) offered a discrimination model of supervision that has become a key to understanding the changing role of the supervisor as teacher, counselor, and consultant. Several studies have researched and applied Bernard's model (Ellis & Dell, 1986; Neufeldt, 1994; Neufeldt, Iversen, & Juntunen, 1995; Rønnestad & Skovholt, 1993; Stenack & Dye, 1982). Neufeldt (1994) described a supervision strategy training manual devised to assist beginning supervisors in developing into "reflective practitioners" (p. 328). The manual described 17 basic supervision strategies and 9 advanced strategies within teaching, counseling, consulting, and combined supervisory functions. Table 5.1 depicts the supervision strategies included in the manual, the type of

TABLE 5.1. Supervision strategies

Supervision strategy	Type of supervisory function	Level of strategy
1. Evaluate observed counseling session interactions	Teaching	Basic
2. Ask counselor to provide a hypothesis about the client	Teaching	Basic
3. Identify appropriate interventions	Teaching	Basic
4. Teach, demonstrate, or model intervention	Teaching	Basic
5. Explain the rationale behind specific strategies and/or interventions	Teaching	Basic
6. Interpret significant events in the counseling session	Teaching	Basic
7. Explore trainee feelings during the counseling session	Counseling	Basic
8. Explore trainee feelings during the supervision session	Counseling	Basic
9. Explore trainee feelings concerning specific techniques and/or interventions	Counseling	Basic
10. Facilitate trainee self-explorations of confidence and/or worries in the counseling session	Counseling	Basic
11. Help the trainee define personal competencies and areas for growth	Counseling	Basic
12. Provide opportunities for trainees to process their own affect and/or worries in the counseling session	Counseling	Basic
13. Provide alternative interventions and/or conceptualizing for trainee use	Consulting	Basic
14. Encourage trainee brainstorming of strategies and/or interventions	Consulting	Basic
15. Encourage trainee discussion of client problems, motivations, etc.	Consulting	Basic
16. Solicit and attempt to satisfy trainee needs during the session	Consulting	Basic
17. Allow the trainee to structure the supervision session	Consulting	Basic
18. Assist the trainee in conceptualizing a case	Combined	Advanced

(*Table continued on next page*)

TABLE 5.1. Supervision strategies (*Continued*)

Supervision strategy	Type of supervisory function	Level of strategy
19. Explore the trainee's feelings to facilitate understanding of the client	Combined	Advanced
20. Present a developmental challenge	Combined	Advanced
21. Use parallel process to model appropriate strategies for dealing with clients	Combined	Advanced
22. Explore trainee-client boundary issues	Combined	Advanced
23. Help the trainee to process feelings of distress aroused by the client's experiences	Combined	Advanced
24. Assist the trainee to identify and use cues in the client's and the therapist's behavior	Combined	Advanced
25. Reframe trainee ideas and behaviors in a positive manner and build on them	Combined	Advanced

Note: Adapted from "Use of a Manual to Train Supervisors," by S. A. Neufeldt, 1994, *Counselor Education & Supervision, 33,* pp. 330–331.

supervisory function each requires, and the level of each strategy. The use of the teaching, counseling, and consulting roles of the supervisor changes with the level of developmental functioning of the supervisee.

The Learning Context and the Supervisory Relationship

Furthermore, developmental progression occurs in a context of interaction with a learning environment. The sequence of learning activities, the structure of those lessons, and the role the supervisor assumes will depend upon the supervisee's degree of maturity and the demands of that level of developmental functioning. The developmental process may be more accurately understood as occurring in helix rather than in linear fashion. The process will include periods of advancement, recycling in slightly new ways, and delay. The evolving supervisory relationship, the interpersonal influence of the supervisor, and the motivation of the supervisee impact this cognitive transformation. Supervisees at various levels will change their perceptions of the supervisor's credibility and power, which will allow for differing amounts of interpersonal influence. How one views the self and another will shape the relatedness within any connection (Josselson, 1992).

Additionally, the supervisory relationship is effective only when the supervisor assumes the responsibility to address the issues inherent in individual difference and diversity. The influence of background factors of the supervisee (age, previous training and experience, personal experience) and of a host of diversity factors (ethnicity, gender, multicultural supervisory pairings) should be considered when differentiating supervisory roles, functions, and activities (Leong & Wagner, 1994; Pope-Davis & Coleman, 1997; Rønnestad & Skovholt, 1993).

More attention is being given to the complexities of orchestrating an optimal supervisory learning environment (Bernard & Goodyear, 1998; Skovholt & Rønnestad, 1992; Stoltenberg et al., 1998). The context of the supervisory relationship—the management of the process, boundaries, and dynamics—seems central to the effective delivery of supervision. Holloway (1992) described the "creative moments of an accomplished supervisor with an engaged student" (p. 206). There is an artistry to both counseling and supervision delivery. Rønnestad and Skovholt (1993) described the need for addressing the influence of the supervisor's level of development upon the developmental process of the supervisee. It seems imperative that the supervisor possess a high level of commitment to the ongoing cultivation of professional competence that monitors, polishes, and enhances the repertoire of skills and knowledge the supervisor brings to the supervisory experience.

Ward and House (1998) stated that "the supervisory relationship becomes a container to review counselor's intentionality, belief, and base assumptions surrounding disorienting professional events (p. 25). The interactions within the supervisory relationship, which make up the qualitative dimension of the relationship (Sexton & Whiston, 1994), serve as the context within which to analyze professional dissonance and discomfort. The reflective model incorporates a four-phase process of supervision progressively called contextual orientation, trust establishment, conceptual development, and clinical independence. Reflective dialogue between supervisee and supervisor emphasizes thematic observations and self-assessment.

Separation from supervision is experienced from a developmental perspective. Supervisees at the beginning level of supervision may be reluctant to separate from the security of a guide or mentor and will quickly seek to replace the dependency (Mueller & Kell, 1972). Supervisees at the intermediate level of supervision will resist termination if the supervisory relationship was perceived as positive. Advanced level supervisees accept the separation as inevitable. An advanced supervisee will generate peer supervision options as a means of ongoing mutual reference (Stoltenberg & Delworth, 1987). The supervisee's perception of the supervision experience may very well affect subsequent supervisory alliance formations. Gender does seem to impact termination due to the female emphasis upon affiliation versus the male emphasis upon task completion. The management of the ending of the supervisory relationship should be implemented with knowledge of what is at stake for the supervisee through her or his developmental lens.

A supervisor's conscious attention to closure may assist in teaching and integrating an essential component of clinical work.

Developmentally Appropriate Learning Activities

Stoltenberg (1993) originally entitled the levels of supervisee development "beginning entry level," "trial and tribulation," and "challenge and growth" or "integration." As is characteristic in other developmental models, learning activities that will facilitate maturity change with the developmental level of functioning of the supervisee. For example, beginning entry level trainees require marked amounts of structure, direction, and support from an expert counselor who may help them increase confidence and manage anxiety. Trial and tribulation level trainees respond well to five categories of supervisor interventions proposed by Loganbill, Hardy, and Delworth (1982). They are as follows: facilitative interventions emphasizing support, confrontive interventions emphasizing challenge, conceptual interventions emphasizing praxis, modeling interventions emphasizing alternatives, and catalytic interventions emphasizing process dynamics. Challenge and growth level trainees can participate in collaborative supervisory relationships that focus upon personal-professional integration (Stoltenberg, 1993).

From a developmental perspective, a variety of techniques and approaches may be used at particular phases within the developmental process. Contributions from other theoretical orientations may be useful at different phases. For example, the manner in which the supervisor delivers skill training is a function of supervisee developmental needs, style, and experience level, as well as the theoretical orientation of the supervisor. However, as Rønnestad and Skovholt (1993) stated, "the findings and perspectives converge in a picture of early supervision as having an instructional, didactic, and skill focus" (p. 397). In matching the supervisory teaching role to the developmental needs of the beginning supervisee, methodologies most appropriate are highly structured and contain concrete and immediate means of feedback. The supervisee is "told what to do, is shown what to do, tries out what to do, and receives immediate feedback on performance" (Rønnestad & Skovholt, p. 397).

Teaching methods of this sort include Ivey's (1990) microskill training, Kagan and Kagan's (1990) interpersonal process recall (IPR) method, and the Egan (1998) model. Neufeldt et al. (1995) provide a structured curriculum that teaches discrete skills that are critical to the establishment of a therapeutic relationship, the creation of an empathic relationship, the termination of a counseling context, the response to crisis situations, and the responsiveness to issues of diversity. Constantine (1997) presents a framework for facilitating supervisory discussion about the identification and understanding of "how demographic identities may interact to potentially affect counseling goals, process, and outcome" (p. 320). This framework assists in the development of skill and awareness of the needs of clients in a pluralistic society. Additionally, interventions such as self-reports, live observation modeling, role playing, peer observation and feedback, and live supervision are developmentally appropriate instructional mechanisms for the beginning supervisee.

Several studies have shown appropriate supervisor behaviors for middle level supervision (Neufeldt et al., 1995; Schwitzer, 1996; Stoltenberg et al., 1998). Supervisees highly regard supervisors who display respectful, compassionate confrontation, and who emphasize personal growth over the teaching of technical skills. Activities at this level could focus on improving conceptualizations of client dynamics (Neufeldt et al., 1995; Schwitzer, 1996), expanding competence with new intervention strategies (Stoltenberg et al., 1998), modifying the supervisee's preferred theory base, and exploring the interpersonal processes inherent in both counseling and supervision (Loganbill et al., 1982; Stoltenberg et al., 1998). These activities are developmentally appropriate for the intermediate supervisee who is increasing in self-awareness and professional autonomy although fluctuating in confidence and dependency.

Case conceptualization formats have been used successfully in assisting supervisees to synthesize the cognitive, behavioral, emotional, and interpersonal aspects of the client's issues. Schwitzer (1996) offered the "inverted pyramid heuristic." This conceptualization method gives supervisors "a method of didactic instruction about the systematic organization of client information, a model for demonstrating connections among client concerns, and a reference for discussing selection of treatment focus" (p. 259). Schwitzer's (1996) format includes four steps that are summarized as follows.

Step 1: Supervisees are encouraged to identify the client's salient concerns and current level of functioning. A "wide" listing of these should be generated to ensure a thorough collection of descriptive data about the client and his or her presenting issues.

Step 2: Supervisees are encouraged to group the identified client concerns into meaningful clusters as a way of organizing the wider range of data collected in the first step. An important conceptualization question to consider is how the themes impact the client's life, well-being, worldview, and subjective experience.

Step 3: Supervisees are encouraged to explore implications of the client's concerns from various theoretical perspectives as a way of unifying and explaining the clinical issues to be addressed in treatment. This is a praxis activity enabling the supervisee to translate a theoretical knowledge base into useable practice.

Step 4: Supervisees are encouraged to narrow the clinical issues into specific counseling foci and to apply theory-based methods and techniques in addressing the goals of treatment for that client.

This method is only one of many case conceptualization formats available for use with intermediate supervisees. The supervisor may want to consider a number of other models (Basile, 1996; Neufeldt et al., 1995; Ivey & Ivey, 1999). Case conceptualizations should include the effect of factors of diversity. As the supervisee develops an emerging professional identity and autonomy, he or she can be guided to increase her or his level of awareness of competence with multicultural differences. Supervisees should be encouraged to expand their knowledge base regarding a host of diversity factors in hopes of increasing sensitivity to the influence of these upon the history and present context of the individual's difficulties. A supportive and challenging supervisory environment can provide learning opportunities for the supervisee to better understand the diverse experiences of a particular client, the dynamics of the counseling relationship attributable to difference, and the effectiveness of specific interventions given the diversity factors present (Carney & Kahn, 1984; Leong & Wagner, 1994).

Rønnestad and Skovholt (1993) define the parallel process idea as a perspective that "refers to a phenomenon of correspondence and similarity between the processes occurring in the therapeutic and the supervisory relationships" (p. 402). Parallel process refers to the several levels of conflict within supervision. Supervisees doubt their counseling effectiveness and both want and avoid feedback from the supervisor. Opposing forces of desire for and resistance to change are also experienced by the supervisee in the therapeutic relationship with the client. This mirroring of conflict within both relational contexts is called parallel process and is a basic tool by which the supervisee learns to be an effective clinician (Friedlander, Siegel, & Brenock, 1989).

The supervisory relationship itself is the vehicle for learning within this perspective. Transference, countertransference, and resistance are common to both counseling and supervisory relationships. At the intermediate level of supervision, the supervisee lessens the initial anxiety of the beginning training and is able to employ reflective abilities to gain insight into the dynamics of the client relationship. Insight about the self, the "other," and the process can be emphasized at this juncture of professional maturity. Mueller and Kell (1972) described a similar process called "parallel reenactment" based upon "impasse" in the supervisee–client relationship. Impasse is a disagreement believed to be unsolvable due to client resistance, supervisee retreat from the client, and inappropriate identification with the client. Parallel impasse in the supervisor–supervisee relationship becomes a challenge as the supervisor models how to respond therapeutically to conflict. A greater awareness of the dynamics underlying personal conflict about change sharpens the supervisee's understanding of the client's conflicts.

Particular caution must be used with these perspectives. While the counseling role of the supervisor emerges, it is imperative to distinguish between being a therapist to the supervisee and engaging in a counseling role within the supervisory context. An inability to discern the difference would result in an ethical violation (Bernard, 1987).

Group supervision provides a rich source of interactional learning for group members. The group process within group supervision can facilitate supervisee exploration, openness, responsibility, and risk taking. Supervisees may collaborate, provide peer feedback, discuss ethical judgments, offer support, and case conceptualize together. As with individual supervision, the group context occurs as a series of stages that reflect the issues supervisees confront in their professional development. In light of the necessary and sufficient conditions that promote developmental progression, Stoltenberg and Delworth (1987) advocate a "developmental mix" of supervisee levels in group supervision.

Typically, the advanced supervisee can be more eclectic, selecting interventions because of their effectiveness with a particular client. Usually, they have had experience with a number of intervention strategies and can demonstrate flexibility in adapting style to suit client need. Additionally, advanced supervisees seek to become familiar with the client's culture. Carney and Kahn (1984) described advanced supervisees as engaged in a developmental process of becoming competent as multicultural counselors, establishing identities as advocates and activists for diversity.

Developmental approaches to supervision offer a comprehensive picture of the complex interplay of factors resulting in the emergence of professional identity and maturity (Blocher, 1983; Littrel, Lee-Boden, & Lorenz, 1979; Loganbill et al., 1982; Rigazio-DiGilio, 1998; Shaughnessy & Carey, 1996; Skovholt & Rønnestad, 1992; Stoltenberg et al., 1998). The IDM given by Stoltenberg et al. (1998) illustrates praxis—the application of developmental theory to supervision practice—and represents the prototype of developmental supervision at its best. What follows is a discussion of this approach to supervision. The IDM will be examined through its primary concepts and theoretical assumptions; the supervisory relationship; the focus and goals of the model; and methodology and techniques used in the model. Finally, case examples will be given to illustrate this model and a summary critique will be offered.

☐ Framework of IDM Supervision

Primary Concepts and Theoretical Assumptions

Two models of human development referenced in the IDM are the mechanistic and organismic approaches. As previously stated, the mechanistic approach views development as the acquisition of skills and knowledge over time. The organismic approach views development as an interaction between the organism and the environment. According to Stoltenberg et al. (1998), "one would expect a general continuous development whereby therapists accumulate additional knowledge and skills and achieve qualitatively distinct development that defines changes from various stages" (p. 12). Stoltenberg (1993) perceived training efforts as a desire to "elicit in our trainees new and more complex ways of conceptualizing . . . in addition to acquiring an armamentarium of skills and knowledge" (p. 132).

According to the IDM, "understanding change over time in one's ability to function as a professional is fundamental in the practice of clinical supervision" (Stoltenberg et al., 1998, p. 1). In the IDM, changes in the structures of self-and-other awareness, motivation, and autonomy constitute progression through three developmental levels. The structures and levels are further discussed in the focus and goals section. The direction of the developmental progression in IDM supervision is one of increasing professional identity, competence, and maturity. The process of maturing is identifiable through observing the following shifts in cognitions, emotions, and behaviors:

- increased consistency of performance across domains of clinical activity as evidenced by
  - the ability to effectively demonstrate a repertoire of intervention skills from a variety of theoretical approaches,
  - the ability to accurately assess a client's situation and integrate useful clinical data in case conceptualizing and treatment planning,
  - the ability to include and utilize influences of individual difference in responding to client situations,
  - the ability to deliver and evaluate appropriate means for achieving desired outcomes in clinical work, and
  - the ability to ethically reason the dilemmas of professional practice;
- decreased self-absorption and performance anxiety;
- increased self-confidence and insightfulness;
- increased autonomous functioning;
- consolidation of a professional identity through development of a personal style and preference;
- increased empathy;
- increased clarity of clinical roles and processes; and
- consistency of motivation for the development of continuing expertise.

Stoltenberg et al. (1998) stated that the developmental and maturing process is continually changing and is not illustrated in a linear path. There will be periods of advance and regression in knowledge, skills, and proficiencies. Cognitive research suggests that simply acquiring more facts and skills is not sufficient in explaining how one naturally progresses from a novice to an expert clinician. The increase of knowledge, according to the cognitive model, is limited to storing information for problem solving. However, in the supervisory environment, knowledge, skills, and competencies are integrated to assist the supervisee in responding in a problem-solving manner. Additionally, the supervisory environment utilizes motivation to encourage further understanding, integration, and retention necessary to advance from a novice to an expert clinician. According to Stoltenberg et al. (1998), motivation "can have important implications for the likelihood that one will elaborate on information provided in supervision and therapy contexts, which in turn will affect utilization of relevant schemata and their continued refinement" (p. 10).

Supervisory Relationship

Stoltenberg et al. (1998) stated that "across developmental levels, good supervisory relationships encompass warmth, acceptance, respect, understanding, and trust . . . and create an atmosphere of experimentation and allowance for mistakes" (p. 111). The supervisory relationship provides a primary learning context within which the supervisee matures. Although the function and role of the supervisor will shift according to supervisee need, the core conditions of the supervisory relationship remain the same. Without these conditions of supervision, the supervisee will not feel the safety, nurturance, and "holding" of the environment necessary to ease the discomfort of developmental change.

Stoltenberg et al. (1998) view the supervisory relationship as a place to address issues such as, but not limited to, race, ethnicity, gender, and sexual orientation. Often, supervisees must discuss the impact of discrimination, power differentials, racial and cultural identification, and the feelings accompanying these experiences and struggles. Professional maturation and identity will occur within the powerful influence of factors of diversity unique to the supervisee. "Lack of knowledge of individual differences due to culture, gender, and sexual orientation and lack of understanding of multicultural models and interventions and experience with culturally diverse clients negatively affects the credibility or quality of the message of the supervisor from the perspective of diverse supervisees" (Stoltenberg et al., 1998, p. 125). The supervisory relationship may be viewed as a forum for compassionate conversation on unresolved and unaddressed issues of diversity. The development of a mature identity as a clinical practitioner includes consolidation and integration of all issues of difference specific to an individual supervisee.

Additionally, stage-related supervisory activities may directly support supervisee needs at different levels of supervision. The extent and intensity of the supervisor's role and function at each level is dependent upon the supervisee's maturity and the ability to assume responsibility for and accomplish tasks associated with each level. What follows is a description of the supervisory approach throughout the developmental process as outlined by Stoltenberg et al. (1998).

Level 1 Supervisory Approach

The beginning level supervisee approaches supervision with a marked amount of anxiety undergirded with a high motivation to succeed. Externally, he or she must develop clinical skill and an approach for structuring client interviews that will lead to accomplishment of the client's goals. Concurrently, the demands of internal goals further increase the supervisee's apprehension. The supervisee is taking on a new professional identity and is learning to use the legitimate authority of the supervisor. As with any new situation that threatens esteem and confidence, the supervisee responds anxiously and "prefers more attention to be devoted to the development of intake skills, didactic training in counseling, and more time spent on developing self-awareness" (Stoltenberg et al., 1998, p. 111). A need exists for careful preparation for supervision, clarification of the supervisory expectations, and specificity regarding the content of learning. Much of the anxiety of level 1 supervision can be alleviated through nurturance and encouragement and by outlining realistic expectations.

Level 2 Supervisory Approach

The successful learning experience of the level 1 supervisee should result in "a positive impact on his or her confidence and self-efficacy" regarding the delivery of clinical skill (Stoltenberg, 1993, p. 135). Level 2 supervisees tend to need less directive structure provided by the supervisor and can be encouraged to move toward greater autonomy. However, supervisees at this level struggle to cope with strengths and weaknesses and with the limitations of the counseling experience. An increased awareness of the client's frame of reference can result in an overidentification with the client. Additionally, this submersion within the client's issues may produce an impasse in movement toward the goals of counseling. This feeling of "stuckness" elicits a transference/countertransference situation that is easily superimposed on the supervisory relationship. The supervisee may become so focused on the client as to be ineffective in counseling, and thus doubt the efficacy of therapy itself. The key supervisee issues at this level are disruption, ambivalence, and instability (Stoltenberg et al., 1998).

Level 3 Supervisory Approach

The supervisee at level 3 of development has transcended the fluctuations of level 2. Motivation to the profession is relatively stable and doubts are expressed as concerns about integrating the counselor role with one's professional and personal identity (Stoltenberg & Delworth, 1987). The maturity at this level will enable the supervisee to appreciate the wide diversity of client motivation and the variable strengths and limitations of both self and supervisor. While the level 2 supervisee may become lost in the client's presenting issues, the level 3 supervisee can be empathic with the client while maintaining enough objectivity to process the interaction. This deeper level of awareness also expands the supervisee's heightened sense of the use of self in therapy. The supervisory relationship allows for exploration of the impact of the self upon the client. Supervision at this level emanates from the position of peers who respect the unique contribution each brings to the relationship. Supervisees welcome supervisors who share personal examples of counseling behaviors while allowing the freedom for the supervisee to act on the information as he or she chooses. Typically, the supervisor plays more of a consulting role.

Focus and Goals

Stoltenberg et al. (1998) discussed eight discrete "domains" of clinical activity, three "structures" of supervisee development, and three "levels" of professional development. Collectively, the domains, structures, and levels describe the focus and goals of IDM supervision.

Domains

The domains are representative categories of knowledge central to becoming a professional clinician. The eight domains may be summarized as follows:

1. *Intervention skills competence*: the ability to implement therapeutic interventions with assuredness;
2. *assessment techniques*: the ability to utilize assessment protocols and devices with assuredness;
3. *interpersonal assessment*: the ability to theoretically conceptualize a client's interpersonal dynamics;
4. *client conceptualization*: the ability to organize client data into a meaningful diagnostic understanding upon which to base clinical treatment;
5. *individual differences*: the ability to include the influences of diversity and difference into the understanding of an individual client;
6. *theoretical orientation*: the ability to utilize and integrate different clinical theories and approaches;
7. *treatment plans and goals*: the ability to contract for change with a client and to effectively intervene to achieve therapeutic progress; and
8. *professional ethics*: the ability to coordinate professional and personal ethics with standards of practice.

Structures

The three structures of IDM supervision may be defined as milestones in evaluating developmental maturity. The structures gauge the progression of various levels of professional development across specific domains of clinical activity. The structures used to oversee supervisee development are as follows:

1. *Self and other awareness*: the supervisee's thoughts and feelings about herself or himself and about the client;
2. *Motivation*: the nature and stability of the supervisee's investment in training and practice as seen over time; and
3. *Autonomy*: the supervisee's movement from dependence upon the supervisor's authority toward independent clinical functioning.

Levels

The three levels of clinical development in IDM supervision describe differences in professional functioning along the continuum of the maturing process. These levels are distinguishable as follows:

1. *Level 1 supervisees*: characteristically limited in background in one or more of the domains of supervision, self-consciously concerned with performance, anxious about evaluation, confused about professional behaviors, lacking in confidence, motivated by discomfort, and dependent upon supervisory modeling and directive;
2. *Level 2 supervisees*: characteristically more available to attune to the worldview of the client yet with an increased tendency toward losing objectivity, less preoccupied with performance, more confident about empathetically relating, confused and sometimes overwhelmed by treatment choices, erratically motivated, and conflicted about dependency and autonomy; and
3. *Level 3 supervisees*: characteristically more self-assured, objective, and intentional, aware of interpersonal, intrapersonal, and process dynamics of therapy, more consistently motivated to continue to own and expand upon a professional identity and style, and able to independently and responsibly function.

The maturing supervisee *(Level 3i)* continues to integrate competence across the domains of clinical activity and to associate bases of relevant knowledge. Successful supervision is collaborative in nature with a supervisee at this level.

Methodology and Techniques

The initial session between supervisor and supervisee is singularly important in that it establishes the parameters of supervision and sets the tone for the working relationship. In IDM supervision, the initial session begins the evaluative assessment of the supervisee's level of functioning across domains and structures which will continue throughout the supervisory experience. As the supervisee matures, the goals, objectives, and delivery of supervision will change to meet the new developmental demands. The evaluation of level of developmental functioning is critical to the structure and experience of supervision. "By exposing supervisees to an environment that is too advanced, we run the risk of inducing confusion and anxiety, as well as negatively affecting client welfare. If we expose therapists to an overly structured environment, their growth is frustrated and they become bored, inattentive, and resistant" (Stoltenberg et al., 1998, p.135).

One goal of the initial supervisory session is to establish clear expectations about the structure of supervision and the nature of the supervisory relationship. A high amount of specificity is appropriate for the beginning level supervisee. "Clarifying expectations and slowly establishing trust are the primary initial relationship-building skills" (Stoltenberg et al., 1998, p. 116). In IDM supervision, the high amount of anxiety characteristic of new supervisees must be addressed from the beginning of supervision. As trust increases, willingness to learn will override initial anxiety.

Setting goals is an interactive process within the supervisory relationship. An individual supervisee's goals will naturally change as professional development occurs. A pattern for monitoring goal attainment should be set early in the supervision experience. In selecting goals for beginning supervision, the supervisor and supervisee can successfully identify mutual goals. Levels of professional functioning on domains of clinical activity may be assessed through performance samples such as video- or audiotapes of client sessions, written case conceptualizations, and case notes. Goal setting should occur after formal and informal data give a realistic, holistic, and specific picture of the current developmental level of functioning of the supervisee. Stoltenberg et al. (1998) emphasized that "work samples should not be limited to one modality or another if the goal is an accurate picture of a therapist across domains" (p. 139). A supervisee, for example, might demonstrate greater skill in diagnosing than in implementing a certain therapeutic technique. Performance samples of various types will assist the supervisor in more accurately reading the level of functioning across multiple domains.

Stoltenberg et al. (1998) offer several assessment formats specific to IDM that are helpful in determining goals for supervision. For example, the "Supervisee Information Form" may be completed by the supervisee to give information regarding type and breadth of past experiences, self-perceptions of strength and weakness, and theoretical orientation exposure (p. 193). The "Supervisee Levels Questionnaire–Revised" (SLQ-R) is a measurement of the IDM structures of dependency/autonomy, awareness of self and others, and motivation (p. 197). The SLQ-R includes 47 questions divided into three subscales designed to study the behaviors of supervisees at a certain point in their maturing process. Each question is answered on a 7-point Likert scale, with high scores indicating increased developmental levels. The SLQ-R has been used as a research device and as a method of developmental assessment.

In IDM supervision, direct and specific feedback is given on a continual basis and is based upon the assessment of strengths and weaknesses in levels of performance across specific domains. "IDM places skills and tech-niques in a context of progressive movement toward a desired end state" (Stoltenberg et al., 1998, p. 142). Evaluative feedback is viewed as being a snapshot of the developmental functioning of the supervisee at a given time.

Case Examples

Level 1 Case Example

Leigh is a conscientious new counseling student who has an impressive background of volunteer work related to helping. She has not, however, been employed directly in the field and has had little exposure to the tech-nical or theoretical framework of clinical activity. Leigh hesitates in role-play simulations and seeks reassurance about her level of performance. She reacts to the skills evaluation sheet by stating she feels overwhelmed and nervous, unsure if she can ever master being an effective counselor given that "there is so much to do all at once." She mimics the supervisor when giving responses in the counselor role.

Leigh displays the expected reactions, thoughts, and feelings of a level 1 supervisee. To move toward increased maturity, she will need a nurturing supervisory environment, clear performance criteria, directive assistance, and a strong teaching role played by the supervisor. The supervisor will interact with positive encouragement about the specific strengths demon-strated by the supervisee. The supervisor might tell Leigh, for example, "you are skillful in using reflective and summary skills in this session" or "you seem to pace your interactions with the client in a fluid manner." The supervisor will also provide instructive feedback about specific areas for skill improvement, with statements such as "try using more open-ended statements" or "at this point I might have confronted the contradiction the client stated about her relationship."

Level 2 Case Example

Lewis is providing counseling for a couple experiencing tension after one partner admitted having an affair. The other partner privately discloses to Lewis that she, too, is engaged in an outside sexual relationship but doesn't want Lewis to reveal this fact. Lewis has previously identified with this partner as the one "left" given that this personally happened to him. He is uncertain how to proceed or what the guidelines are for ethical practice in this case. Lewis is not requesting the supervisor's direction.

Lewis displays the confusion, ambivalence, and overidentification char-acteristic of the level 2 supervisee. He needs guidance in separating himself from the partner's issue so that he might more clearly reason his ethical responsibilities and roles with the couple. To move toward increased maturity, Lewis needs assistance in conceptualizing the situation from a more objective standpoint, in reflecting on potential transference/countertransference issues, and in discussing the perceived dilemma of ethics. For example, the supervisor might initiate discussion from a case conceptualization standpoint, requesting that Lewis describe the client's situation objectively and reason the ethical dilemma out loud. The supervisor might ask Lewis, "how is your objectivity clouded by your own personal identification with the partner?" or "What ethical dilemma do you perceive in the request to withhold information from one partner to another when dealing with a couple?"

Level 3 Case Example

Carmen is a maturing clinician who has demonstrated proficiency, competence, and developed ethical reasoning throughout her training. She is a committed professional, self-motivated, skilled, and usually autonomous. Carmen is working with a woman close to her age who is not responding to the approaches used to assist in her grief work related to her terminal illness. Carmen is aware that she may need to confront her fearful identification with her client, as it may be adversely impacting the effectiveness of the therapy. She also wants to utilize other therapeutic approaches as she expands her application of skills and knowledge to grief counseling.

Carmen seeks supervision of a consulting nature. To move toward increased maturity, she needs collaborative dialogue that allows creative conversation about applications of previously mastered techniques and knowledge to grief counseling. Carmen would also be assisted by a supervisor who would converse with her about how she might be a catalyst in the therapeutic relationship despite her fear. For example, the supervisor might open a conversation such as the following. "Carmen, I hear your awareness of how you are identifying so closely with your client. Although this may evoke a high amount of fear as you consider how this would feel to you, it might be useful to consider the vantage point this may give you as you connect with your client in this very anxiety-provoking situation. What might you offer to your client about how to act in an empowered way even when fearful?" Additionally, the supervisor might ask Carmen to "describe three other counseling techniques you feel skilled at using and let's think together about how these might be effective alternative approaches with this client."

Critique

Stoltenberg, McNeill, and Crethar (1994) investigated measurements of developmental approaches and constructs related to the supervision process. They drew a number of conclusions from their investigation, including the following. Research studies need to distinguish the parameters around definitions of the developmental levels of supervisees. More research is needed on techniques and methodologies reflecting the developmental process of transformation from novice to expert counselor. Increased validation is needed on the interplay between supervisee and supervisor traits and the impact of the supervisory environment at the various developmental levels. Additionally, these authors encouraged clinicians to expand their knowledge on issues of gender, ethnicity, and sexual orientation as important, yet neglected, factors in developmental supervision. Stoltenberg et al. (1994) stated: "efforts should be directed at determining which level of supervisor using which supervisory interventions is most effective in supervising which level of trainee at a given point in time working with what types of clients in what contexts" (p. 422).

In their integrative review of research on clinical supervision, Ellis and Ladany (1997) stated that the assumptions and conclusions of supervisee development and the progression in a developmental direction have not been conclusively tested. These authors reported on multiple studies based upon the Stoltenberg model but found numerous methodological problems confounding the data. Adequate testing has not yielded strong empirical evidence for conclusions about cognitive transformation within supervisees, matching environments to developmental levels, or assumptions about distinctions among levels within the IDM. Translation of complex conceptual constructs into conclusions drawn from sound empirical rigor is extremely difficult. Ellis and Ladany strongly endorsed further testing of developmental models like IDM. Based upon their review, the following conclusions are offered with caution: "Supervisees may significantly increase in autonomy as they gain experience, beginning supervisees may prefer more structured supervision, and self-perceived developmental level may not be equivalent to practicum level" (p. 479). Furthermore, the SLQ-R "may become a potentially useful measure if it is more adequately developed and tested psychometrically" (p. 480).

Ellis and Ladany (1997) agreed with Stoltenberg et al. (1998) that clinical supervision is complex and not comprehensively understood through current theories that tend to oversimplify the intersection of factors inherent in this phenomenon. Developmental perspectives, like the IDM, assist the profession in continuing our conceptualizations and conclusions about the process of becoming a mature clinician. The developmental approach attempts to organize and integrate a variety of dimensions of supervision, including the influence of motivation, focus of perspective (self and other), cognitive shifts, learning variability among discrete knowledge and skill groups, interpersonal and instructional pacing, and individual difference.

☐ References

Basile, S. K. (1996). A guide to solution-focused brief therapy. *Counseling and Human Development, 29* (4), 1–10.

Bernard, J. M. (1979). Supervision training: A discrimination model. *Counselor Education & Supervision, 19,* 60–68.

Bernard, J. M. (1987). Ethical and legal considerations for supervisors. In L. D. Borders & G. R. Leddick (Eds.), *Handbook of counseling supervision* (pp. 52–57). Alexandria, VA: American Association for Counseling and Development.

Bernard, J. M., & Goodyear, R. K. (1998). *Fundamentals of clinical supervision* (2nd ed.). Boston, MA: Allyn & Bacon.

Blocher, D. H. (1983). Toward a cognitive developmental approach to supervision. *The Counseling Psychologist, 11,* 27–34.

Borders, L. D., Bernard, J. M., Dye, H. A., Fong, M. L., Henderson, P., & Nance, D. W. (1991). Curriculum guide for training counseling supervisors: Rationale, development, and implementation. *Counselor Education & Supervision, 31,* 58–80.

Carney, C. G., & Kahn, K. B. (1984). Building competencies for effective cross-cultural counseling: A developmental view. *The Counseling Psychologist, 12*(1), 111–119.

Constantine, M. G. (1997). Facilitating multicultural competency in counseling supervision: Operationalizing a practical framework. In D. B. Pope-Davis & H. L. Coleman (Eds.), *Multicultural counseling competencies: Assessment, education and training, and supervision* (Vol. 7, pp. 310–324). Thousand Oaks, CA: Sage.

Egan, G. (1998). *The skilled helper: A problem-management approach to helping, Sixth edition.* Pacific Grove, CA: Brooks-Cole.

Ellis, M. V., & Dell, D. M. (1986). Dimensionality of supervision roles: Supervisees' perceptions of supervision. *Journal of Counseling Psychology, 33,* 282–291.

Ellis, M. V., & Ladany, N. (1997). Inferences concerning supervisees and clients in clinical supervision: An integrative review. In C. E. Watkins (Ed.), *Handbook of Psychotherapy Supervision* (pp. 447–508). New York: Wiley.

Friedlander, M. L., Siegel, S. M., & Brenock, K. (1989). Parallel processes in counseling and supervision: A case study. *Journal of Counseling Psychology, 36,* 149–157.

Gladding, S. T. (1996). *Counseling a comprehensive profession* (3rd ed). Englewood Cliffs, NJ: Prentice-Hall.

Holloway, E. L. (1992). Supervision: A way of teaching and learning. In S. D. Brown & R. W. Lent (Ed.), *Handbook of counseling psychology* (2nd ed., pp. 177–214). Toronto, ON, Canada: Wiley.

Ivey, A. E. (1990). Systematic counselor/therapist training: "Training as treatment" and directions for the future. *The Counseling Psychologist, 18,* 428–435.

Ivey, A. E., & Ivey, M. B. (1999). *Intentional interviewing & counseling* (4th ed.). Pacific Grove, CA: Brooks/Cole.

Ivey, A. E., Ivey, M. B., & Simek-Morgan, L. (1997). *Counseling and psychotherapy: A multicultural perspective* (4th ed.). Needham Heights, MA: Allyn & Bacon.

Josselson, R. (1992). *The space between us—Exploring the dimensions of human relationships.* San Francisco: Jossey-Bass.

Kagan, N., & Kagan, H. (1990). IPR—A validated model for the 1990's and beyond. *The Counseling Psychologist, 18,* 436–440.

Kegan, R. (1982). *The evolving self—Problem and process in human development.* Cambridge, MA: Harvard University Press.

Leong, F. T. L., & Wagner, D. A. (1994). Cross-cultural counseling supervision: What do we know? What do we need to know? *Counselor Education & Supervision, 34*(2), 117–131.

Littrel, J. M., Lee-Boden, N., & Lorenz, J. (1979). A developmental framework for counseling supervision. *Counselor Education & Supervision, 19,* 129–136.

Loganbill, C., Hardy, E., & Delworth, U. (1982). Supervision: A conceptual model. *The Counseling Psychologist, 10*(1), 3–42.

Mueller, W. J., & Kell, B. L. (1972). *Coping with conflict: Supervising counselors and psychotherapists.* New York: Appleton-Century-Croft.

Neufeldt, S. A. (1994). Use of a manual to train supervisors. *Counselor Education & Supervision, 33*(4), 327–336.

Neufeldt, S. A., Iversen, J. N., & Juntunen, C. (1995). *Supervision strategies for the first practicum.* Alexandria, VA: American Counseling Association.

O'Byrne, K., & Rosenberg, J. (1998). The practice of supervision: A sociocultural approach. *Counselor Education & Supervision, 38,* 34–42.

Pope-Davis, D. B., & Coleman, H. L. (Eds.). (1997). *Multicultural counseling competencies: Assessment, education and training, and supervision.* Thousand Oaks, CA: Sage.

Rigazio-DiGilio, S. A. (1998). Toward a reconstructed view of counselor supervision. *Counselor Education & Supervision, 38,* 43–51.

Rønnestad, M. H., & Skovholt, T. M. (1993). Supervision of beginning and advanced graduate students of counseling and psychotherapy. *Journal of Counseling & Development, 71,* 396–405.

Schwitzer, A. M. (1996). Using the inverted pyramid heuristic in counselor education and supervision. *Counselor Education & Supervision, 35,* 258–267.

Sexton, T. L., & Whiston, S. C. (1994). The status of the counseling relationship: An empirical review, theoretical implications and research directions. *The Counseling Psychologist, 22*(1), 7–70.

Shaughnessy, E. A., & Carey, J. C. (1996). Validation of a cognitive-developmental model of clinical supervision. In M. Commons & J. Demick (Eds.), *Clinical approaches to adult development* (pp. 223–238). Norwood, NJ: Ablex.

Skovholt, T. M., & Rønnestad, M. H. (1992). *The evolving professional self: Stages and themes in therapists and counselor development.* New York: Wiley.

Stenack, R. J., & Dye, H. A. (1982). Behavioral descriptions of counseling supervision roles. *Counselor Education & Supervision, 21,* 295–304.

Stoltenberg, C. (1993). Supervising consultants in training: An application of a model of supervision. *Journal of Counseling & Development, 72*(2), 131–138.

Stoltenberg, C., & Delworth, U. (1987). *Supervising counselors and therapists: A developmental approach.* San Francisco: Jossey-Bass.

Stoltenberg, C., McNeill, B., & Crethar, H. (1994). Changes in supervision as counselors and therapists gain experience: A review. *Professional Psychology: Research and Practice, 25,* 416–449.

Stoltenberg, C., McNeill, B., & Delworth, U. (1998). *IDM supervision: An integrated developmental model for supervising counselors and therapists..* San Francisco: Jossey-Bass.

Ward, C. C., & House, R. (1998). Counseling supervision: A reflective model. *Counselor Education & Supervision, 38,* 23–33.

CHAPTER 6

Loretta J. Bradley
L. J. Gould

Psychotherapy-Based Models of Counselor Supervision

Counselor supervisors, like counselors in general, advocate or are influenced by a variety of theories. There is no reason to doubt that the personal theory developed through one's own experiences in education, practicum, internship, and professional practice is carried over into the supervisory role. Leddick (1994) and Freeman and McHenry (1996) noted that most theoretical models of supervision are embedded within the major schools of counseling theory. For example, the psychotherapy-based theories, Rogerian theory, and behavioral theory have long been popular schools of supervision. In the 1980s, other schools, such as developmental, systemic, cognitive, and integrative, gained in popularity. Lochner and Melchert (1997) stated that the (theoretical) orientation of the supervisor was likely to have an impact on both the supervisee's orientation and selection of a supervisor. Unfortunately, few empirical studies of supervisors' theoretical orientation have been conducted (Borders, 1992; M. V. Ellis, 1991; Goodyear & Bernard, 1998; Holloway, 1987; Lockner & Melchert, 1997; Worthington, 1987).

  The purpose of this chapter is to briefly examine supervision from the perspective of three psychotherapy-based supervision-theoretical orientations: psychodynamic, behavioral, and cognitive. Each supervision theory will be examined according to its framework (concepts or assumptions and supervisory relationship, focus and goals, methodology and techniques); a case example and critique will complete each discussion. It should be noted that although each supervision theory may have specific elements unique to its interpretation of the supervisory relationship, there are some elements found in most, if not all, supervision theories and models. Facilitative conditions such as empathy, genuineness, warmth, trust, and positive regard are common to virtually all supervision models. Additionally, the supervisor's primary commitment should be to the supervisee and her or his learning experience (Brack, Brack, & McCarthy, 1997; Gordon, 1995; Pickvance, 1997) while simultaneously monitoring the welfare of the client.

☐ Psychodynamic Model of Supervision

The psychodynamic model of counselor supervision is a synthesis and extension of views conceptualizing supervision as being similar to counseling and psychotherapy (Alpher, 1991; Binder, 1993b; Binder & Strupp, 1997; Boyd, 1978; Edwards, 1997; Gee, 1998; Halgin & Murphy, 1995; D. Jacobs, David, & Meyer, 1995; Thorbeck, 1992). According to this approach, counselor supervision is a therapeutic process focusing on the intrapersonal and interpersonal dynamics in the supervisee's relationship with clients, supervisors, colleagues, and others.

Framework of the Psychodynamic Model of Supervision

In Freud's psychoanalytical process of supervision, termed by Binder and Strupp (1997) as a "master–apprentice" approach, the roles of teacher and analyst and student and analyzed were interchangeable. As training programs in psychotherapy developed, a tripartite model of therapist training composed of a didactic curriculum, supervised analysis of clients, and the supervisee's personal analysis emerged (Dewald, 1997). What began as two roles merged into a model that attempts to integrate the didactic and therapeutic roles (Binder & Strupp, 1997, Teitelbaum, 1990; Thorbeck, 1992; Wolstein, 1994).

Primary Concepts and Theoretical Assumptions

Because dynamic interplay, both interpersonal and intrapersonal, between supervisee and client is instrumental for therapeutic change, a supervisee must be fully aware of these dynamics and use them to the client's benefit. In considering the basic assumptions, it is evident that some writers and practitioners explain how dynamics operate in supervision from a psychoanalytic viewpoint, while others explain dynamics from a phenomenological perspective.

Parallel Process.   Conceptually, supervisors using the psychodynamic model often use parallel process as a context for teaching and learning. At the core of parallel process is the proposition that similar interpersonal dynamics occur concurrently in both the therapy dyad and the supervisory dyad, and this concurrence allows for a unique utility in teaching and learning

(Della Selva, 1996; Goldberg, 1998; M. Jacobs, 1996; Lombardo, Greer, Estadt, & Cheston, 1997; McCue & Lane, 1995; Raichelson, Herron, Primavera, & Ramirez, 1997). Ekstein and Wallerstein (1972), in their seminal work on parallel process, believed that parallel process was most commonly associated with beginning supervisees. Ekstein and Wallerstein stated that while the parallel process might originate in either the counseling or supervisory dyad, it always flows from counseling to supervision. In contrast, Doehrman (1976) believed that the most prevalent movement in parallel process was from supervisory dyad to counseling dyad, with the supervisee acting out supervision conflicts in counseling. Until the supervisory conflict is resolved, counseling is affected by the supervisee behaving toward the client either in the same or exactly opposite manner as the supervisor is behaving toward her or him. According to Binder and Strupp (1997) subsequent research emphasized the direction of influence in parallel process to be from counseling to supervision, which, they noted, may reflect the reluctance of supervisors to admit that interpersonal problems originate in supervision. Some researchers have considered parallel process unavoidable and a valuable teaching aid when worked through in supervision (Berger & Bucholz, 1993; Haesler, 1993; Teitelbaum, 1990).

Internalization. If parallel process is the context in which learning takes place, then internalization is the developmental process by which learning occurs. Beginning supervision is characterized by the formation of a learning alliance and the acquisition of basic counseling skills (Feiner, 1994; Haesler, 1993; Holloway & Neufeldt, 1995; Shechter, 1990). The supervisee depends on the supervisor for explicit and specific guidance in counseling situations, complies with the supervisor's suggestions, and imitates the supervisor's behavior when counseling clients. At the intermediate level of supervision, the supervisee develops a deeper understanding of the counseling process and learns to apply theoretical concepts and techniques to the practice of counseling (Binder & Strupp, 1997). As he or she becomes more proficient in the use of counseling skills and techniques, the supervisee needs less direction from the supervisor. The supervisee's personal counseling style is beginning to develop as specific aspects of supervisor behavior are incorporated. Advanced supervision is characterized by increased autonomy and spontaneity by the supervisee (Casement, 1991; Halgin & Murphy, 1995).

Interpersonal Dynamics. In psychodynamic supervision the interpersonal dynamics occurring between supervisee and client are of primary importance. Communication is both verbal and nonverbal; the supervisee is responsible for being a sensitive and effective communicator, receiving both explicit and implied communication, and sending communication beneficial to the client. Although similar to the supervisee–client interaction, interpersonal dynamics between supervisor and supervisee are of secondary importance. The supervisor teaches the supervisee how to deal with inter-personal dynamics effectively by modeling. The supervisor is therefore re-sponsible for the quality of interpersonal dynamics and psychological con-tact between supervisee and client. Even though the clients being served by neophyte supervisees may receive less than adequate service, the supervisor's primary commitment is to the supervisee and her or his learning experi-ence (Brack et al., 1997; Clarkson, 1995; Duryee, Brymer, & Gold, 1996; Gordon, 1995; Pickvance, 1997).

Intrapersonal Dynamics. Intrapersonal dynamics consist of covert behaviors and sensory processes—feelings, thoughts, perceptions, attitudes, and beliefs—and cognitive routines for attributing meaning to stimuli. In the psychodynamic approach, the nature and amount of supervisory atten-tion given to intrapersonal dynamics varies, depending on the supervisee, the supervisor, and the situation. The supervisor's main task with respect to client–supervisee dynamics is helping the supervisee understand how the client's internalized responses influence her or his overt behavior. The supervisee's intrapersonal dynamics may be very threatening to her or him, and consequently, may be well guarded by resistive defenses that are diffi-cult to penetrate in supervision (Dindia, 1994; Liddle, 1986; Swaney & Stone, 1990; Watson, 1993). Ironically, the supervisee's anxiety surround-ing these dynamics may provide clues as to which dynamics need super-visor attention (Dobbs, 1986; Duryee et al., 1996; Gee, 1998; Mueller & Kell, 1972). The supervisor must address the supervisee's intrapersonal dy-namics because these covert elements are direct and powerful influences on her or his interpersonal behavior. Finally, the supervisor's own intrapersonal dynamics must be considered because her or his overt behavior is also influenced by them. When uncontrolled and unconscious intrapersonal dynamics (such as power needs or a specific interest precipitated by her or his own past experiences) are primary antecedents for the supervisor's conduct, supervision becomes a freewheeling relationship in which both supervisee and supervisor strive to satisfy their own needs. Professional intent guides the supervisor in behaving toward the supervisee in an opti-mally beneficial manner.

Supervisory Relationship

The relationship between supervisor and supervisee in the psychodynamic model of supervision is akin to the therapeutic alliance between counselor and client, except that in supervision the focus is on learning, and there-fore the supervisor is first a teacher. Characteristics of a good psycho-dynamic supervisor include flexibility in theory, techniques, and learning styles; respect for the supervisee; supportive and nonjudgmental attitude; patience; an ability to present concepts concisely and clearly; collaboration on focus and goals; and the ability to model effective counseling strategies and behaviors (Berger & Bucholz, 1993; Clarkson, 1995; Dewald, 1997; Duryee et al., 1996; Feiner, 1994; Freeman & McHenry, 1996; Haesler, 1993; Halgin & Murphy, 1995; Rodenhauscr, 1994; Shanfield, Matthews, & Hetherely, 1993; Shechter, 1990; Snyder & Levy, 1998).

Focus and Goals of the Psychodynamic Model of Supervision

Focus

The psychodynamic approach to supervision is "dynamic" because inter-personal and intrapersonal dynamics are its focus and style. Because the dynamic interplay between supervisee and client is instrumental in thera-peutic change, a supervisee must be fully aware of these dynamics and use them for the client's benefit.

Although the previous discussion treated the dynamic foci of psycho-dynamic supervision as discrete elements, operationally they are expressed in patterns that develop when a number of dynamics have contingencies linking them together. Identification of and intervention in dynamic pat-terns is the essence of therapeutic supervision methodology. Common dy-namic patterns include defensive/resistant clients using counselor insecu-rity to avoid confronting painful issues; client incapability and dependency designed to give responsibility for decisions to the supervisee; an angry, hostile client attacking the supervisee, who responds with a counterattack; and parallel process, in which the supervisee replays significant dynamics of the supervisee–client relationship in supervision (Della Selva, 1996; Jacobs, 1996; McCue & Lane, 1995; Raichelson et al., 1997).

Goals

The goal of psychodynamic supervision is for supervisees to attain aware-ness of and acquire skills in the effective use of dynamics in counseling. Ekstein and Wallerstein (1972) defined the primary goal of supervision as the acquisition of therapeutic skills, regardless of inner conflicts and exter-nal manifestations. Mueller and Kell (1972) suggested a two-part goal, consisting of a process and a product in dynamically oriented supervision. The process goal is for the supervisee to learn what is therapeutic, and the product goal is for the supervisee to behave in a manner that has a therapeutic effect on the client. Goals proposed by other authors (Binder & Strupp, 1997; Dewald, 1997; Goldberg, 1998; Haesler, 1993; D. Jacobs et al., 1995) fit Mueller and Kell's goal framework; the process goal includes skill acquisition in rela-tionships and techniques, while the product goal includes translating ac-quired skills into actual counseling practice. Four sequential subgoals to accomplish are: dynamic awareness, understanding dynamic contingencies, change in dynamics, and therapeutic utilization of dynamics.

Dynamic Awareness. Learning what is therapeutic begins with be-coming aware of interpersonal and intrapersonal dynamics. This subgoal, which acquaints the supervisee with the existence of dynamics, is followed by learning how dynamics influence human relationships. Through this awareness the supervisee recognizes that everyone has a covert world of thoughts, feelings, and attitudes, and that human interaction involves in-terpersonal pathways of communicatory behavior.

Understanding Dynamic Contingencies. After awareness has been achieved, the next step is understanding the operation of dynamics in the supervision relationships. Understanding comes through assessment of dynamics within two contingencies: (a) the influence of intrapersonal dy-namics on interpersonal behavior, and (b) the influence of interpersonal behavior on intrapersonal dynamics. Assessment of the supervisee–client dyad involves asking the following questions: (a) How does the supervisee's in-trapersonal behavior influence her or his interpersonal behavior with the client? (b) How does the interpersonal behavior of the supervisee influence the client's intrapersonal dynamics? (c) How does the client's intrapersonal dynamics influence her or his interpersonal behavior toward the supervisee? The answers to these questions help unravel the dynamic patterns in the supervisee–client relationship. Similarly, questions and answers pertaining to the supervisor–supervisee dyad provide a diagnostic picture of that rela-tionship. Assessment and diagnosis of this kind constitutes a large portion of supervision methodology. The supervisor must comprehend the theoretical rationale underlying the goals and methodology of psychodynamic super-vision if the supervisee is to acquire skill in application of its principles.

Research demonstrates that past learning experiences (interpersonal and intrapersonal dynamics) tend to be reasserted in future situations, particu-larly when similar conditions are perceived (Binder & Strupp, 1997; Gee, 1998; Hosford & Barmann, 1983; Jacoby, 1995; Kurpius, Benjamin, & Morran, 1985; Wallerstein, 1995). When a client shows certain dynamics in the counsel-ing relationship, the supervisee can hypothesize that they indicate the client's dynamic makeup and are, therefore, indicative of the probable dynamics in other relationships. Thus, it is practically impossible for the client to mask dynamic difficulties from a competent supervisee. Correspondingly, dynamic difficulties in the supervisee's counseling efforts can be found in the super-visory relationship. These difficulties will hinder supervision and the super-visee's future counseling performance if they remain unresolved.

Change in Dynamics. Dynamic change is a goal of both dynamically oriented counseling and supervision. In counseling, dynamic change is nec-essary to improve the client's intrapersonal functioning (maladaptive emo-tion, perception, and ideation), as well as her or his interpersonal dynamics (social behavior). Problem aspects of a supervisee's dynamic functioning do exist and can be significant hindrances to counseling, and as such are prime targets for change.

Therapeutic Utilization of Dynamics.   The final goal of supervision is therapeutic utilization of dynamics. Three types of dynamic utility are sought by supervisees: (a) experiencing/control of personal dynamics; (b) planned influence on the dynamics of others; and, (c) management or utilization of dynamics in situations where no direct involvement exists. Because counselors characterize themselves as having high integrity and avoiding the manipulation of others' behavior, the word "control" is unpopular. However, possessing knowledge of dynamic interaction brings a responsibility to use that knowledge for the benefit of clients—thus, the term *dynamic control* is employed. In contrast to spontaneous experiencing, the supervisee's influence on client dynamics is planned and deliberate. Before encountering a client, the supervisee can decide to behave interpersonally in a way that therapeutically affects the client's dynamics. A final application of dynamic utilization is management or control of dynamics not directly involving clients, which occurs in noncounseling situations (composition of discussion groups, consulting with other professionals, altering policies or activities of institutions); the supervisee assesses the dynamics-evoking properties involved and influences them for the dynamic benefit of others. Therapeutic utilization of dynamics, reached through awareness, understanding, and usually some form of change in one's personal dynamics, is the final goal of psychodynamic supervision. By expertly using the dynamics of the supervisory relationship, the supervisor can help the supervisee acquire skill in applying dynamics in the counseling relationship.

Methodology and Techniques of the Psychodynamic Model of Supervision

Didactic knowledge of methodology acquired through the usual modes of reading, lecture, and discussion is often insufficient preparation. The methodology of psychodynamic supervision is particularly susceptible to the barrier between knowledge and performance. Two basic methods exist for implementing the psychodynamic approach to supervision: Kagan's interpersonal process recall (IPR, which is discussed in the next chapter) and unstructured and intensive therapeutic supervision.

Unstructured psychodynamic supervision is the essence of the relationship and intensive interaction between supervisor and supervisee as they examine and explore the supervisee's interactions with clients, consultees, colleagues, and the supervisor (Gordon, 1995; D. Jacobs et al., 1995; Mueller & Kell, 1972; Wallerstein, 1995). The core of the unstructured method of supervision lies in the relationship between the supervisor and supervisee. Facilitative conditions (empathy, genuineness, warmth, trust, positive regard) are of paramount importance, and a relationship characterized by these conditions will be conducive to aiding the supervisee in examining her or his personal dynamics. Unstructured supervision is employed in four areas: dynamic awareness, understanding dynamic contingencies, dynamic change, and therapeutic utilization of dynamics.

Dynamic awareness is achieved through focus and response; the supervisor focuses on the dynamics of an interaction and directs the supervisee's attention to these dynamics. In unstructured supervision, the supervisor depends on cues (supervisee discomfort with clients, therapeutic impass) to indicate where and when to focus and respond. Although focus and response is usually effective, dynamic awareness is difficult to achieve with defensive or affectively blunted individuals. In this technique, the supervisor controls dynamically evocative stimuli to be relatively sure of the consequent dynamics experienced by the supervisee.

In *understanding dynamic contingencies,* random inductive techniques (restatement, reflection, clarification, etc.) may be sufficient for identifying broad dynamic patterns; however, analogy techniques may be needed in order to focus on the dynamics of a single pattern. Other strategies that may be employed are reading case studies or watching films; group supervision; and supervisor modeling, interpretation, and confrontation.

Dynamic change and awareness techniques are effective in altering the supervisee's interpersonal and intrapersonal dynamics (Binder & Strupp, 1997; Gee, 1998; D. Jacobs et al., 1995). Easily attained dynamic change is often taken for granted and attributed to the "natural" experience of learning how to counsel. "Dynamic insight" involves the incorporation into oneself of information previously unknown and often contradictory to one's perceptions of self, others, and the world. Insight experiences are often painful, since confronting a feared piece of knowledge may raise significant anxiety. Unstructured methods (focusing, exploring, interpretation, confrontation) are used by the supervisor to encourage the acquisition of dynamic insight and help the supervisee assume ownership and responsibility for her or his dynamics.

Therapeutic utilization of dynamics requires that the supervisee has achieved the three previous goals and is beginning to function at a fairly sophisticated level in a dynamic sense. The supervisee must be aware of her or his natural emotional reactions, and he or she must assess how best to act appropriately and utilize dynamics therapeutically. Supervisors help supervisees learn to skillfully use dynamics by employing these skills in supervision and by teaching supervisees to use them in counseling. Additionally, the supervisee is assisted in planning dynamic strategies to be used in counseling and other direct interactions.

Case Example in Psychodynamic Supervision

Jill, a student in her first practicum at a community counseling center, was working with a 50-year-old woman recently divorced after 32 years of marriage. After several sessions, Jill reported to her university supervisor that she was having problems coping with the client. The supervisor, after reviewing a videotape of a counseling session between Jill and the client, discovered that the client was resisting Jill's attempts to explore her feelings about the divorce by changing the subject or making comments on Jill's youth and inexperience as a counselor.

The supervisor suggested that she and Jill watch the tape during a supervision session to identify the dynamics of the situation and Jill's reactions to the client. While watching the tape, the supervisor pointed out the change in Jill's body language in response to client comments. Jill admitted that the client made her feel inadequate and angry, so she withdrew and let the client run the session. After acknowledging her reactions and feelings, Jill considered what the client was trying to accomplish by her comments. Jill's insights into her feelings and the client's motivations led to a discussion of options regarding the counseling situation

Critique of the Psychodynamic Model of Supervision

Strengths

The major strength of psychodynamic supervision is its emphasis on recognizing the interpersonal dynamics of both the supervisory and counseling dyads. This emphasis helps the supervisee to identify communication problems in counseling relationships and learn appropriate responses and techniques for working through them. If the supervisor also emphasizes intrapersonal dynamics, the supervisee may learn more about her or his responses to emotional cues occurring in the counseling situation. Insight experienced in supervision can be generalized to other aspects of the supervisee's life.

Another strength of the pyschodynamic approach to supervision is its emphasis on the supervisory relationship. Collaboration on focus and goals strengthens the supervisory relationship, allows for meeting both the learning needs and developmental level of the supervisee, and fosters the growth of autonomy in the supervisee. The process-product goal schema stresses the importance of learning skills and techniques in dynamic interaction and then translating those acquired skills into actual practice.

Finally, the skills and techniques of psychodynamic supervision, including interpersonal communication, focus and response, analogy, and modeling are basic to the practice of counseling. As the supervisee's personal theory develops, he or she will learn other skills and techniques, but the basic skills of interpersonal interaction will always be important to the counseling alliance.

Weaknesses

A major weakness of psychodynamic supervision is its lack of attention to multicultural issues. The literature on psychodynamic theory does not specifically address multiculturalism in either counseling or supervision (Arciniega & Newton, 1999). However, since it is firmly based in the European cultural milieu, it may be inferred that the concepts of psychodynamic theory are not equally valid for all cultural groups. Additionally, when working with clients from diverse cultural groups, there is a danger of errors in interpersonal communication regarding sources of conflict, cognitive orientation, motivations, communication styles, trust, and values (Batten, 1990; Priest, 1994; Ryan & Hendricks, 1989; Remington & DaCosta, 1989; Williams & Halgin, 1995). To be effective, supervisors must be multiculturally aware in the areas of race and ethnicity, gender, and sexual orientation.

A second major weakness of psychodynamic supervision, and most other supervision models as well, is the lack of empirical and evaluative research (Beutler & Kendall, 1995; Binder, 1993a; Holloway & Neufeldt, 1995; Stein & Lambert, 1995). The available research points to another weakness of psychodynamic supervision: the difficulty of teaching interpersonal skills (Beutler & Kendall, 1995; Binder, 1993b; Butler & Strupp, 1993; Stein & Lambert, 1995).

Finally, psychodynamic supervisors must be careful to maintain the boundaries between supervision and counseling. While intrapersonal insight is a goal of supervision, it is not the primary emphasis. If the supervisee's problems are extensive, he or she should be encouraged to seek counseling outside the supervisory relationship.

☐ Behavioral Model of Supervision

Behavioral supervision originated from the theory, goals, skills, and practices of behavioral theory. Behavioral theory, based in learning theory, arose as a reaction to the Freudian emphasis on the unconscious. It has expanded the field of counseling by developing a number of skills and techniques in the areas of classical conditioning (systematic desensitization, flooding, counterconditioning), operant conditioning (reinforcement, extinction, stimulus control), and skills training (modeling, role playing, problem solving). Additionally, behavioral theory is responsible for introducing a rigorous scientific method into research in counseling and therapy (Hayes & Hayes, 1992). Traditional behavior therapy is concerned with changing maladaptive behaviors with little or no emphasis on the causes of those behaviors. In behavioral theory, the counselor's role is comprised of discrete tasks, each of which requires skills that can be behaviorally defined (Craighead, Craighead, & Ilardi, 1995; Day, 1998; Goldfried & Davison, 1994; Moore, 1998).

Framework of the Behavioral Model of Supervision

Primary Concepts and Theoretical Assumptions

According to the point of view of behavioral supervisors, competent counseling performance is a function of learned skills. The purpose of counselor supervision is to teach the supervisee appropriate counseling skills (behaviors) while assisting her or him to extinguish inappropriate counseling behaviors. Although the skill behaviors can be developed through classroom education, the application and refinement of skill behaviors should occur in supervision. The methodology of behavioral supervision is based on learning theory principles.

Supervisory Relationship

Although in behavioral supervision, the supervisory relationship is not considered a primary source of experiential learning or therapeutic growth, it is considered an important and instrumental part of the supervisory process. The supervisory relationship must be conducive to learning and provide a learning atmosphere in which formal learning activities (role play, modeling, reinforcement) can be conducted. Additionally, supervision must attend to the supervisee's covert skill behaviors. A facilitative relationship is necessary for the supervisee's sharing of thoughts and feelings, thus giving the behavioral supervisor needed data for skill assessment and goal setting. Because the supervisory relationship is so important, Follette and Callaghan (1995) recommended taking the time necessary to establish a working alliance before moving on to active methodology. Relationship building requires patience, and rushing the supervision process is a damaging error. An effective supervisor makes the establishment of a working alliance the top priority.

Focus and Goals of the Behavioral Model of Supervision

Focus

Behavioral supervision focuses on the skill behaviors of the supervisee (Mead, 1990; Follette & Callaghan, 1995; Fruzzetti, Waltz, & Linehan, 1997: Fuqua, Johnson, Anderson, & Newman, 1984; Muesser & Liberman, 1995; Rosenbaum & Ronen, 1998). These skill behaviors are broadly conceptualized to include the supervisee's thinking, feeling, and acting behaviors. Skills exist at difficulty levels ranging from fundamental to advanced; some skills may be frequently used (reflection, tacting response) while others are used only when a particular problem or assignment arises (relaxation, thought control, covert sensitization).

Goals

The goal of behavioral supervision is always based upon the person-specific skill needs of the individual supervisee. In general, the minimal broad goal for any supervisee is a level of skill functioning representing the competent performance of the counselor role and function. The "person-specific" nature of behavioral supervision is necessary because each supervisee will be at a different level of skill development. Ideally, supervisees will be proficient in basic skills (reflective responses, open-ended leads, etc.) before entering supervision; however, it is unrealistic to expect that supervisees will be free of skill deficiencies and inappropriate behaviors. Further, skill development is a valid aspect of supervision because the development and refinement of high-level skills (interpretation, confrontation, behavior-change strategies) can and should continue throughout the counselor's career.

The person-specific goal for a supervisee with skill deficiencies and inappropriate behaviors is to help her or him begin to perform the deficient skills at an adequate level and to cease performing the inappropriate behaviors. If skill deficiencies and inappropriate behaviors are too serious for supervision, the supervisee must attain this goal before working with clients, perhaps through repeating practicum preparation courses or special work outside class. The point of following these steps with a low-skill supervisee is the welfare and protection of the client while the supervisee's skills are being promoted through supervision and/or remedial skill training.

Methodology and Techniques of the Behavioral Model of Supervision

The process of behavioral supervision involves a five-step methodological sequence. The first step is the establishment of a relationship between the supervisor and supervisee as discussed above. The second step involves a skill analysis and assessment, which leads to the third step: setting supervision goals. The fourth step is construction and implementation of strategies to accomplish the goal(s). The fifth step is evaluation and generalization of learning, which occurs at the completion of supervision.

Skill Analysis and Assessment

Behavioral supervision is goal directed, and setting goals requires that a skill analysis and assessment be conducted. This step can be performed on a particular supervisee performance, specific skill or task, or the entire skill repertoire. Analysis and assessment of counselor skills necessitates that the behavioral supervisor have an extensive knowledge of the skills required in the supervisee's work. It is to the supervisor's advantage to construct a mental model of a competent supervisee's ideal skill repertoire, according to function or task, to serve as a guide during analysis and assessment. Boylan, Malley, and Scott (1995) provided several forms for self-assessment of basic skills, counseling techniques, and goals to be achieved in supervision.

Skills and Process.   An error can be made in analysis and assessment if the discrete skill behaviors identified are divested of their "process dimension." When this occurs the supervisee loses sight of the purpose of the focal task or function and becomes a mechanical dispenser of skill behaviors. The sequence and flow of skills within a function must be retained, and indeed, performing a set of skills in a smooth process manner is a skill in itself. Nowhere is the process dimension more important than in counseling.

Setting Supervision Goals

After the establishment of a working relationship and analysis/assessment, the next step is defining supervision goals. The supervisee should have increased self-direction in choosing supervision goals, although goals must be acceptable to both the supervisor and the supervisee. Skill behavior goals may be covert or overt. The supervisor may see an inappropriate overt performance of skills and, later in supervision, learn that the supervisee was impaired at the covert rather than overt level. When performing analysis, assessment, and goal setting, the supervisor should keep in mind that overt skill performance usually relies on a combination of knowledge and covert skill behaviors.

Constructing and Implementing Supervisor Strategies

The fourth step in the methodological sequence of behavioral supervision is construction and implementation of strategies (action plans) to accomplish the goals set in the third step. A single strategy may contain numerous learning activities, or it may be simple in structure. In constructing a strategy, the following should be considered: the supervisee's preference for certain learning modes; the effectiveness of the strategy for reaching the goal; and the feasibility of the strategy (facilities, materials, setting). Methodologically, behavioral supervision strategies focus either on the supervisee's self-directedness and personal resources or on output from the supervisor. In the first focus, the supervisor serves as a consultant to the supervisee in constructing and carrying out the strategy, such as self-monitoring or reinforcement. In the second focus, the supervisor acts as a trainer, actively participating in the strategy; microtraining is an example of a supervisor-directed strategy. The two foci are not entirely discrete and each of the supervision techniques to be addressed can vary in the degree to which the supervisor acts as a consultant or active trainer. Consistent with earlier suggestions, we recommend that self-development be promoted as much as possible by the supervisor.

Self-Instructional Modules.   As previously suggested, some supervisees cannot demonstrate requisite skills for competent counseling practice. If these deficiencies are not beyond short-term remediation, a number of training activities may be used by the supervisor (Follette & Callaghan,

1995; Goldfried & Davison, 1994; Muesser & Liberman, 1995). Self-instructional modules contain explicit skill behavior objectives, evaluation procedures for assessing the acquisition and demonstration of skill behaviors, and self-directed learning activities to follow (Cormier & Cormier, 1998). Although modules can be structured packages, such as those used in classroom or laboratory courses, the modules used in supervision should be designed specifically for each supervisee from the supervisor's cache of materials and learning activities. Evaluation procedures stressing demonstration of skill behaviors in role play or other simulations are also appropriate. Skill modules usually result in the supervisee making rapid learning progress.

Self-Appraisal and Skill Monitoring.   Self-appraisal and skill monitoring are self-development strategies. Self-appraisal is a nonthreatening procedure, and one that is perpetual if learned well in supervision. Skill monitoring goes hand-in-hand with self-appraisal. Studies in self-observation indicate that individuals automatically evaluate observed behaviors and attempt to influence these behaviors in a desired direction (Dowrick, 1991; Fuqua et al., 1984; Guidino, 1991; Kurpius et al., 1985; McLeod, 1998). Although not a replacement for supervision, self-appraisal and skill monitoring, using a structure for the supervisee to follow, attend to the important factors necessary for effective performance.

Peer Supervision.   Peer supervision is recognized as a valuable aid to the supervisor (Baird, 1998; Gomersall, 1997; Kottler & Hazler, 1997; Snyder & Levy, 1998). Peers provide a supportive environment as well as reassurance that others are experiencing similar feelings and concerns. Peers acting as raters can be reliable and accurate (Boylan et al., 1995; Carmichael, 1992; Collins, 1990); however, it should be noted that training and structure improve rating performance, and that an untrained rater can give destructive feedback to a peer (supervisee). Therefore, we offer the following suggestions for the use of peer supervisors. First, peer group supervision is not a substitute for a competent supervisor. Second, peer supervision may be helpful or harmful depending on three factors: the attitude of the peer supervisor, the format of peer supervision, and training given in peer supervision. Feedback and sharing should be emphasized while evaluation is deemphasized, and training in format and skill practice are essential. Third, the behavioral supervisor should conduct peer group supervision sessions before allowing peers to supervise each other. Fourth, peer supervision, like self-supervision, has limits: supervisees with serious skill deficiencies and those who are extremely defensive are not candidates for peer supervision. Finally, the expertise of the behavioral supervisor is necessary for supervisees to learn when and where advanced and complex skills are required in counseling.

Modeling and Reinforcement.   Two of the most powerful principles in psychological learning theory are modeling and reinforcement. Research support and clinical application of these principles are well documented (Bandura, 1991, 1996; Chase, 1998; Domjan, 1998; Sternberg, 1997). Application to counselor training and supervision is also documented (Cormier & Cormier, 1998; Rosenbaum & Ronen, 1998; Stewart, 1998). We offer five practical suggestions for using modeling and reinforcement in behavioral supervision. First, modeling and reinforcement can be employed within the immediate supervisor–supervisee interaction (critiquing tapes, role playing) or in activities outside the supervisory dyad (viewing experts on tape, self-managed reinforcement). Second, the supervisor can be a dispenser of modeling and reinforcement, or other experts and activities can be the media. Third, to be most effective, modeling and reinforcement should be focused and concentrated. Fourth, learning complex counseling skills may require complex strategies combining learning principles, discrimination training, and personalization to the supervisee. Fifth, modeling is often sufficient for the acquisition of a skill but not for effective performance.

Role Playing and Simulation.   Role playing and simulation exercises are integral educational methods in counselor training (Cormier, & Cormier, 1998; Itzhaky & Aloni, 1996; Rich & Sampson, 1990). Through role playing, a number of learning situations can be presented to the supervisee. In the role of client, the supervisee attempts to experience the part of the client. Additionally, he or she is in a position to observe and imitatively learn the skills of an effective counselor as shown by the supervisor (as counselor). Simulation is an effective method for facilitating skill generalization beyond the classroom or supervisory session. As in all behavioral methods, the focal skill must be defined and within the supervisee's capability to perform; complex skills should be divided into easily performed components.

Microtraining.   Microtraining is a direct attempt to systematize training. The basic microtraining model (Ivey & Authier, 1978) is a nine-step paradigm that includes selection of a focal skill to attempt; videotaped performance of a focal skill in simulated situations; if the skill involves interpersonal interaction with another person, an evaluation of the performance by that person; reading manuals describing the focal skill followed by discussion and clarification with the supervisor; discrimination training through video models demonstrating (positively or negatively) the focal skill; critique of supervisee's videotaped attempt at focal skill; planning and preparation for another attempt at the focal skill; and feedback and evaluation of supervisee's second videotaped performance. Ivey and Authier offered several reasons for the success of microtraining. First, microtraining focuses on a single skill at a time, allowing the trainee to master it and see herself or himself improve. Second, microtraining affords opportunity for self-observation and confrontation. Third, videotaped models allow for imitative learning. Fourth, microtraining can accommodate any skill that is demonstrable and behaviorally defined. Fifth, actual performance and practice in lifelike situations make microtraining a "real" experience. Daniels, Rigazio-DiGilio, and Ivey (1997) suggested that supervision in combination with microtraining helps the trainee reduce undesirable behavior in addition to increasing the use of focal skills.

Self-Management Techniques.   Self-management is the individual's ability to make behavioral adjustment decisions and actions based on analyses of oneself and one's environment. Thus, in supervision, a self-management technique would be one in which the supervisee changes her or his own skill behavior with only consultative assistance. The supervisor helps the supervisee analyze and assess the skill behaviors required by role and function, he or she then decides what adjustments in skill behavior are needed, and self-direction action plans are constructed to make the adjustment. There are many self-management techniques (J. S. Beck, 1995; Padesky, 1996; Ronen & Rosenbaum, 1998). Two practical applications of self-management techniques used in behavioral supervision are overt-stimulus control and covert-stimulus control

A major part of supervision consists of helping the supervisee adapt to and learn to respond therapeutically to stimuli that elicit unconstructive or nontherapeutic responses. Some applications of overt-stimulus control belong in supervision because response inhibition or stimulus avoidance is an immediate, although temporary, reaction which the counselor can use when cues are overwhelming. The establishment of cues to elicit desired responses is the most useful overt-stimulus control technique of behavioral supervision. If a counselor is responding inappropriately, or at a technique level that is too low, the supervisor can (a) help the counselor learn to perform the desired skill behavior, and (b) help her or him identify the situational cues at which the skill behavior should be directed. When overt stimuli elicit undesirable responses from the counselor, and conditions are such that to control these cues would be unrealistic, then a covert-stimulus control technique may be the answer. Two principle covert-stimulus control techniques are modification of cognitive content and modification of cognitive process. Content addresses ideational content, and process concerns the longitudinal-situational pattern of focal cognitions and their antecedent and consequence contingencies. Although the content emphasis on cognitive modification appears to have more in common with psychodynamic than behavioral supervision, the process emphasis is a more behaviorally oriented self-management technique in which the supervisee learns to control her or his cognitive process, rather than spending a considerable amount of time with the supervisor in a cognitive restructuring dialogue. Promising areas for cognitive process are self-management of counselor anxiety and covert planning and rehearsal to prepare counselor-trainees before an interview.

Follow-Up and Generalization of Learning

The final methodological step in behavioral supervision is to evaluate the strategies and techniques employed. Follow-up evaluation should be conducted during the strategy to determine if it is having the desired effect or if adjustments need to be made. Evaluation of strategy results is relatively easy because skill goals are behaviorally defined and observable; therefore, if the goals have been reached, the strategies are judged effective. When goals have not been reached, an assessment of the reasons for failure should be conducted. Potential reasons for failure include a lack of prerequisite knowledge and/or acquired behavior by the supervisee for successful participation in the strategy or strategies, insufficient supervisee motivation to participate in the strategy and reach the skills goals, a lack of supervisor-offered assistance with the strategy, and/or the supervisee and/or supervisor not fully understanding the strategy and/or goal during strategy implementation. The supervisor should redress failures by whatever methods necessary to achieve the supervisory goals. When follow-up has shown a supervision strategy to be effective, the skills and learning acquired by the supervisee in the context of supervised performance should be generalized to other performance situations that are likely to present themselves. Generalization of behavior change and transfer of training to practical settings are the ultimate success criteria for behavioral supervision. The self-direction of the supervisee is a crucial component in the long-term generalization and transfer of effects in behavioral supervision. Another factor in generalization and transfer is the amount of different situations to which the supervisee has been exposed. Discussing or simulating situations that demand unfamiliar skills help the counselor develop "response ability."

Case Example in Behavioral Supervision

Carlos was enrolled in his second practicum at a facility for juvenile offenders. His counseling skills were adequate, and he was relatively comfortable with his performance as a counselor. However, he had never worked with teenage clients, nor had he worked with any type of incarcerated offenders who were mandated to counseling. Carlos admitted to his supervisor that he felt inadequate in a situation where the primary treatment plan was behavior modification.

The supervisor designed a self-directed module for Carlos that included readings on behavioral modification in juvenile facilities, information on token economies, and videotapes of counseling sessions with juveniles. The supervisor also suggested that Carlos observe more experienced counselors at the facility before seeing clients on his own. Carlos and the supervisor used role playing and simulation exercises to help practice new skills. After several practice sessions, Carlos felt comfortable with the behavioral principles and began seeing clients at the facility.

Critique of the Behavioral Model of Supervision

Strengths

A major strength of behavioral supervision lies in its methodology and techniques adapted for teaching counseling. Behavioral supervisors are realistic in recognizing that skill deficiencies and inappropriate behaviors are not unusual in novice counselors, and they are prepared to train supervisees in the methods and techniques considered necessary for effective behavioral counseling. The techniques used are drawn from the repertoire of behavioral counseling, which has been rigorously researched.

Another strength of behavioral supervision is the person-specific nature of assessment, goal development, and evaluation. Each supervisee is recognized as an individual with different needs, skills, and level of development. Goal setting is collaborative and strengthens the relationship between supervisor and supervisee.

Evaluation and generalization is another strength in behavioral supervision. Evaluation is conceptualized as an ongoing process, first used during strategies to determine if goals are being met and allowing redirection if needed, and then used at termination of supervision to determine if the skills acquired during supervision can be generalized to future situations.

Weaknesses

A major weakness of behavioral supervision is that attention to affect and cognition, except as facets of behavior, is limited. Additionally, motivation for behavior is often ignored. This can lead to treating symptomatic behaviors without addressing the underlying reasons/causes responsible for them.

Another weakness in behavioral supervision is inattention to multicultural components of behavior. Without attention to the cultural background of the supervisee, the supervisor may identify culturally significant behaviors as inappropriate and attempt to impose her or his ideas of appropriate behavior on the supervisee; and, in counseling, the supervisee may mirror the supervisor's behavior with clients.

As with other supervision theories and methods, research specifically directed toward behavioral supervision is limited. However, the methods and techniques used in supervision are drawn from the extensive body of research on behavioral counseling.

Finally, without attention to the process of counseling, behavioral methods and techniques may become mechanical. Supervision must address the process dimension in order to eliminate this possibility. Behavioral supervisors must guard against being so intent on the acquisition of skill behaviors and methods that the person of the supervisee is ignored.

☐ Cognitive Model of Supervision

The cognitive model of supervision is grounded in the cognitive theories of A. Ellis (A. Ellis, 1962; Woods & Ellis, 1996, 1997) and A. T. Beck (1976, 1993, 1997a). Ellis suggested that psychological theories lacked a language aspect of neurosis and believed that the psychological difficulties of most people resulted from an inability to communicate with both others and themselves. In Ellis's rational-emotive behavior therapy (REBT), individuals' irrational thinking is the genesis of psychological disturbance. A. T. Beck (1997b) was dissatisfied with the unconscious view of emotional problems found in psychoanalysis, believing that individuals could be aware of the causes of emotional problems and confused thinking and that behavioral explanations for emotional disturbance were too limited. He suggested that emotional disturbance resulted from faulty learning, incorrect inferences on the basis of inadequate or incorrect information, and the failure to distinguish adequately between imagination and reality.

Framework of the Cognitive Model of Supervision

Hollon and Beck (1994) stated that cognitive therapy has become a dominant force in mental health counseling, a statement that caused Temple and Bowers (1998) to point out that many therapists are drawn to the model with little or no prior background or training, some because they are completing their training as counselors, some from other disciplines (theoretical orientations) who find they must deal with clients exhibiting problems not effectively treated within their orientation, others who want to learn cognitive techniques, and still others who are reacting to the need for a brief therapy model due to job-related or insurance/HMO restrictions. Given this wide range of trainee backgrounds and motivations for learning cognitive therapy, an overarching supervisory framework that is flexible and addresses the needs of a divergent group of supervisees is important (Temple & Bowers, 1998).

Primary Concepts and Theoretical Assumptions

The primary assumption of cognitive therapy is that affect and behavior are determined by one's cognitive structure of the world. Cognitive therapy is a brief, time-limited therapy that is structured and directive. Counselor and client are involved in a supportive and collaborative therapeutic relationship. Cognitive therapy is educational and uses the Socratic (inductive) method to discover distortions in thinking and to implement more adaptive responses. Clients are taught to think of their beliefs as hypotheses requiring testing and verification. Counselors use both behavioral and cognitive techniques to help clients confront their maladaptive behaviors (Hollon & Beck, 1994; Kalodner, 1999).

Cognitive supervision is an interpersonal process that encompasses both education in the techniques and methods of cognitive therapy and recognition of the thoughts and beliefs that contribute to emotional reactions in both the supervisory and counseling process. The supervisor uses the tenets of cognitive therapy within the supervisory relationship to help the supervisee become an effective counselor.

Supervisory Relationship

As in counseling, the supervisory relationship should be empathetic, warm, and genuine. For the relationship to be successful, rapport between the supervisor and supervisee is imperative. The supervisor must address the supervisee's personal issues that are interfering with effective counseling by conceptualizing her or his problems. Once the problem areas have been identified, the supervisor and supervisee work collaboratively to resolve the difficulties. Liese and Beck (1997) stated that problems may be related directly to either the supervisor or supervisee or to an interaction of the two. Supervisee problems may occur for a number of reasons, including lack of experience, inadequate skills, misconceptions or maladaptive beliefs (need to be perfect), or overly emotional reactions (avoidance, defensiveness, aggression). Problems related to the supervisor may include style or approach (overly concerned with hurting the supervisee's feelings, dictatorial), failure to listen to supervisee, or failure to elicit feedback on her or his effectiveness. Supervisors should take the responsibility for problems within the supervisory process because it will contribute to the collaborative nature of supervision, sharpen her or his skills, and help to modify her or his own maladaptive beliefs.

An important aspect of the supervision process is the contract between supervisor and supervisee. The supervisory contract should be clearly negotiated, and it should spell out the objectives and competencies on which supervision will focus (Temple & Bowers, 1998). As in behavioral supervision, the contract is a collaborative effort between the supervisee and supervisor. To facilitate the process of constructing a supervision contract, the supervisor and supervisee should explore the supervisee's motivation for entering supervision, her or his counseling background (training, experience), and her or his assumptions about cognitive therapy.

Focus and Goals in the Cognitive Model of Supervision

Focus

The focus of cognitive supervision is both educational and interpersonal. The educational focus is on teaching cognitive theory and skills to the supervisee. Skills that are particularly important to cognitive therapy (case conceptualization, cognitive restructuring, identifying cognitive distortions, etc.) require practice and homework. Group supervision may be used to supplement individual supervision and as a place to discuss common problems and themes or to see demonstrations about cognitive processes. The interpersonal focus in cognitive supervision is on the supervisee's misconceptions and maladaptive thoughts which contribute to ineffective counseling and problems in supervision.

Goals

There are three major goals in cognitive supervision. The first goal is to become knowledgeable about the skills and methods required in cognitive therapy and capable in performing them in the counseling situation. The second goal is to identify and modify any misconceptions about cognitive therapy that the supervisee may have. Finally, the third goal is to identify the supervisee's personal issues that may be interfering with the effective delivery of therapy and to collaboratively seek solutions to these problems.

Methodology and Techniques of the Cognitive Model of Supervision

Structure of Supervision Sessions

Liese and Beck (1997) maintained that cognitive supervision should be structured, focused, and educational, with both supervisor and supervisee responsible for session structure and content. Individual 1-hour supervision sessions should be scheduled weekly, with supplemental group supervision at least biweekly. Supervisory sessions are structured in a cognitive therapy format. The session opens with an initial greeting and brief friendly conversation. The first supervisory item is agenda setting: the supervisee prepares for sessions by generating and prioritizing items for discussion. Then, concepts and skills from the previous session are reviewed. To facilitate continuity, the supervisor may ask for a brief review of previously discussed cases. The next step is a review of homework assigned in the previous session. The supervisor and supervisee then move on to agenda items, where they may discuss any problems or concerns of the supervisee, or the supervisor may implement strategies or techniques determined helpful in learning needed skills. New homework assignments are made for the coming week. Finally, both the supervisor and supervisee offer feedback, including thoughts and feelings about the session. Throughout the session, the supervisor should offer reflection on and synthesis of the material being discussed to keep supervision focused. Although they stressed the need for structure in the supervision session, Liese and Beck stated that the structure should not compromise the supervisory relationship or cause supervision to become cold and impersonal.

Observation, Monitoring, and Feedback

Supervisees should have the opportunity to observe and model the behaviors of competent, experienced cognitive therapists. This objective can be accomplished in several ways: videotaped or live observation of cognitive counseling sessions conducted by experienced therapists, role playing with the supervisor or an advanced student, and co-therapy of a supervisee's client with the supervisor. After observing the experienced therapist's behavior, the supervisee should be given a chance to practice new behaviors in the supervisory session.

Cognitive-Behavioral Techniques and Interventions

Kurpius and Morran (1988) suggest the use of cognitive-behavioral techniques and interventions to help supervisees improve counseling skills and reduce anxiety in counseling encounters. They propose three techniques (mental practice, covert modeling, and cognitive modeling) and three supervisory interventions (cognitive restructuring, cognitive self-instruction, and cognitive self-management) for use in counselor supervision. Some of these techniques and interventions are behavioral in nature (self-instruction and self-management) and have been previously described. The following techniques and interventions are cognitive in nature, focusing on the supervisee's thoughts and beliefs.

Cognitive-Behavioral Techniques.   The following three techniques (mental practice, covert modeling, and cognitive modeling) are easily applied and can be adapted to brief or extensive supervision periods. They are effective independently or as components of more comprehensive programs. The first technique is *mental practice*. The supervisee is instructed to imagine in detail a counseling session in which he or she did not respond adequately to the client's problem and to practice the required skill by responding in a facilitative manner. The technique is versatile for two reasons: There is a plethora of real or hypothetical counseling situations available that can be mentally constructed to encourage the development of counseling skills, and this type of mental practice allows the supervisee endless trials without needing actual clients. Additionally, mental practice techniques can be used outside the formal supervision session, thus extending supervision time.

Covert modeling, the second technique, is similar to mental practice but requires a more active role by the supervisor. This technique requires detailed instructions from the supervisor aimed at aiding the supervisee imagine a client situation in which a counselor performs a skill or set of skills. It is effective for both learning new skills and enhancing a previously acquired skill. The supervisor maintains control of the learning situation by providing simple or elaborate instructions tailored to the needs of the supervisee. Additionally, the supervisee may be instructed to imagine herself or himself as the counselor (covert self-modeling) or to imagine an expert as the counselor (covert other-modeling).

The third technique, *cognitive modeling*, is a process whereby the supervisor demonstrates effective thinking and conceptual processing as used in counseling sessions. Typically, the supervisee's taped counseling session is used for demonstration with the supervisor sharing her or his thought processes about the client by talking and thinking out loud. By focusing on the supervisor's internal dialogue, supervisees learn to direct their own conceptual skills in an ongoing manner in counseling sessions. This technique is valuable because it can be adapted to almost any training situation.

Cognitive-Behavioral Interventions.   The three interventions (cognitive restructuring, cognitive self-instruction, and cognitive self-management) discussed below have been used widely in counseling and also have been shown to be useful in supervision (Kurpius, 1985; Morran, 1986). Mastery of these intervention programs provides the supervisee with a cognitive set allowing for objectivity, creativity, and anxiety reduction. *Cognitive restructuring* (CR), the first intervention, involves four steps: understanding and accepting that emotional reactions and behaviors are influenced by self-statements, acknowledging the faultiness of some of these statements, seeing how irrational beliefs negatively influence feelings and behaviors, and acknowledging that modifying what is thought and said to oneself changes perceptions. The application of these steps to counseling supervisees learning counseling skills involves five phases: (a) symptom, in which the supervisee experiences feelings of doubt and anxiety; (b) identification, in which the supervisee recalls emotional reactions related to her or his covert internal dialogue (including faulty cognitive labeling, unrealistic expectations, and maladaptive self-statements); (c) irrational challenge, in which the supervisee provides insights challenging the rationality of her or his cognitions, expectations, and self-statements; (d) exploration, in which the supervisee mentally rehearses the situation that is emotionally arousing, thereby enhancing awareness of the relationship between perceived anxiety and the generation of irrational self-statements; and (e) modification, in which the supervisee is taught to stop the production of maladaptive internal dialogues. In each phase, the supervisor provides encouragement and support. CR occurs when the supervisee has learned to recognize her or his anxiety, can accurately identify the source of that anxiety, and takes risks to complement the rational thought.

The second intervention, *cognitive self-instruction* (CSI), is a change strategy that enables supervisees to identify, analyze, and alter unproductive self-statements in an ongoing manner during counseling sessions. CSI enables supervisees to attend more closely to client–counselor communications that, in turn, leads to the improvement of basic counseling skills. The five sequential steps in skill development using CSI are: (a) questions about the nature of the counseling task are developed: (b) the questions are answered through cognitive rehearsal; (c) task performance is guided by internal dialogue concerning what has been and still needs to be done; (d) internal-dialogue coping skills are used to deal with difficulties; and (e) positive self-reinforcement is given throughout the process. The supervisor's role is to aid the supervisee in understanding the meaning of CSI while he or she is molding her or his cognitive processes into an effective personal approach with the expectation that the supervisee will assume more responsibility for interrupting and altering her or his self-talk as a prerequisite for behavior change. Although anxiety may still be present, the shift in focus results in behavioral and emotional changes that allow for greater involvement with the client, increased self-confidence, and reduced anxiety.

The final intervention, *cognitive self-management* (CSM), helps the supervisee assume greater responsibility for changing an unproductive behavior or maintaining a newly acquired one. CSM emphasizes skills to be used in the supervisee's environment and builds differential methods of reacting to different problem situations. The four steps in using CSM as an alternative perspective to reappraise a problem are: (a) monitoring self-talk regarding problem discrimination and definition; (b) learning, experimenting with, rehearsing, and testing new skills aimed at solving the redefined problem; possible solutions may be "brainstormed" with the supervisor or peers as the problem situation is rehearsed; (c) selecting the optimal solution from those experimental behaviors by using a checklist to determine the skill used, frequency of use, consequences of use, and supervisee satisfaction in its use as accurately evaluated by the supervisor; and (d) evaluating performance using self-monitoring, comparison with the desired standard, and self-reinforcement. CSM strategies effectively employed in practice situations should transfer easily to live clients.

The cognitive techniques discussed above may be used with specific and isolated problems of specific supervisees, or they may be integrated into a systematic preparation training program. Kurpius and Morran (1988) stated that cognitive techniques, when combined with traditional behavioral skill training, offer "the potential to aid in the development of counselors who not only possess a set of mechanical performance skills, but who also possess the self-understanding and conceptual abilities necessary to adapt adequately to the real world where spontaneous and unrehearsed interaction is important" (p. 375).

Cognitive Skills Model

Morran, Kurpius, Brack, & Brack (1995) pointed out that traditional approaches to counselor training have emphasized specific behavioral skills with little focus placed on the manner in which such skills could be effectively timed, sequenced, and tailored to engage the client. However, some experts report that the counselor's cognitive processing plays an important role in her or his efforts to effectively formulate and adapt behavioral responses in therapeutic situations and in the generalization of acquired skills to new situations. Cognitive strategies are important aspects of counselor preparation in such areas as empathy, effective communication skills, and application of behavioral skills. Bandura (1996) suggested that systematic training (including instruction, modeling, practice, and feedback) is needed in the use of cognitive skills because individuals left to their own methods in acquiring cognitive skills engage in trial-and-error attempts that may include unnecessary setbacks and failures. Cognitive-skills training can be used to supplement any systematic training program in behavioral skills and can be used with supervisees at any level of training and experience (Morran et al., 1995).

Cognitive Skills.   The cognitive skills presented here focus on supervisee self-talk in three areas: attending to and seeking information about oneself, the client, and the therapeutic relationship; organizing and integrating information into hypotheses and conceptualizations; and planning, guiding, and evaluating therapeutic relationships. The first area is *attending to and seeking information* which involves the following categories of self-talk: reviewing observed client behaviors, forming questions about the client, assessing the counseling relationship, self-monitoring and self-feedback, and awareness of emotional reactions to the client (Morran, Kurpius, & Brack, 1989). The process is both active (relating new data to the ongoing counseling process so that relevant facts may be identified) and creative (associating new data with known information to find new perspectives). The second area is *hypothesis formation and conceptual modeling*. Hypothesis formation involves repeated analysis and synthesis of potential associations and relationships between initially separate pieces of information such as clients' observed or reported behavior (both overt and covert), inferred internal characteristics, and environmental factors. Through consideration of these connections, the supervisee can develop predictive models related to a specific client concern; the models can then be tested by collecting more information. A cycle of developing, testing, refining, and synthesizing hypotheses allows conceptualization of the client's problems and points the supervisee in the direction of purposeful action. The third area is *intervention planning and self-instruction*. Self-instruction is used to assess and organize thoughts and systematically direct responses toward therapeutic goals. The cognitive-skills approach emphasizes the need for supervisees to learn to plan action strategies purposefully rather than using a "cookbook" approach and to monitor and evaluate their counseling performance appropriately. Appropriate instruction can teach supervisees to be systematic in the development and implementation of intervention plans linked to knowledge obtained and hypotheses formulated.

Cognitive Skills Training Approach.   Morran et al. (1995) designed this approach to sensitize the supervisee to the role her or his cognitions play in client–counselor interactions. The supervisee's thinking strategies need to be developed in a way that capitalizes on her or his strengths, experiences, theoretical beliefs, and problem-solving style. The cognitive skills approach includes four phases designed to sensitize supervisees to their own thinking styles, teach cognitive skills and tie them to behavioral skills, encourage critical self-examination of current cognitive strategies, and provide systematic practice in new ways of thinking and responding. *Phase 1* is promoting awareness of cognition with the goal of assisting the supervisee in understanding cognitions in general and the specific link between cognition and behavior. Readings, lectures, and discussions help the supervisee become familiar with research and theory in the field. In *phase 2*, the introduction of cognitive skills, the goal is to introduce the following three cognitive skills previously described: attending to and seeking information, forming hypotheses and conceptual models, and intervention planning and self-instruction. When working with novice supervisees, the introduction of cognitive skills concurrently with behavioral skills (attending behaviors, questioning, reflection, confrontation, etc.) is recommended. *Phase 3* is supervisee cognitive self-assessment. The goal is to aid supervisees in assessing their own internal dialogue patterns and to critically self-analyze the relationship of their cognitions to both effective and ineffective counseling performance. At the beginning of phase 3, the supervisor should closely monitor the supervisee's cognitive assessments, then, as the supervisee gains insight into her or his own cognitive processing styles and becomes more objective in self-assessment of counseling session self-talk, he or she can be encouraged to work more independently. *Phase 4* is cognitive-skill practice, with the goal of encouraging systematic practice and reflection on applying cognitive skills. When possible, cognitive skill practice should be included in all assignments, exercises, and projects. Supervisees learn the skills of good counseling and how to self-critique and self-improve, which ultimately leads to effective self-supervision. Morran et al. (1995) stress the importance of supervisees being encouraged to develop their own unique cognitive strategies. Each supervisee has her or his own unique set of strengths, weaknesses, preferences, and beliefs; thus, the most effective set of cognitive strategies for any supervisee will be reflective of her or his individual personality.

Case Example in Cognitive Supervision

Kesha is completing her internship at a mental health facility that specializes in short-term cognitive therapy. Lacking an extensive background in cognitive therapy, Kesha asked a senior counselor to supervise her. Since her background in techniques is adequate for the performance of cognitive therapy, the supervisor decided to begin with cognitive modeling using tapes from his own counseling sessions to demonstrate the thought processes, internal dialogue, and conceptual skills used in cognitive therapy. Supervision then moved to covert modeling and role playing to enhance

Kesha's skills as a cognitive counselor. Throughout supervision, the supervisor closely monitored Kesha's progress with clients and gave her feedback on her counseling performance. Additionally, Kesha was also encouraged to critique her own performance and identify problem areas needing additional attention. Kesha found that practice, observation, feedback, and a collaborative relationship with the supervisor helped her learn to use cognitive therapy quickly.

Critique of the Cognitive Method of Supervision

Strengths

A major strength of cognitive supervision is its emphasis on a collaborative supervisory relationship in which both supervisor and supervisee set goals and evaluate outcome. The cognitive supervisor uses the techniques of cognitive therapy to help the supervisee discover and address her or his personal issues that are interfering with effective counseling performance, and by doing so, the supervisor models effective cognitive interventions for the supervisee. Another strength of cognitive supervision is the wealth of techniques and methods available to the supervisee.

Supervisors who are relatively inexperienced in supervision methods may find the use of a structured format beneficial in defining the process of a supervision session. With some modification, the structured format can be used with other supervision methods. Another important aspect of cognitive supervision is the emphasis on observation, monitoring, and feedback. Although these methods are not unique to cognitive supervision, in other methods they are often implied rather than specified.

The supervisory contract recommended in cognitive supervision is an important strength of the method. The process for constructing a contract encourages exploration of issues that may have an impact on the counseling performance of the supervisee including counselor training, experience, and motivations for seeking supervision in cognitive therapy.

Weaknesses

As with other discrete theories of supervision, there has been little empirical research into the effectiveness of cognitive supervision. Like behavioral theory, research has been primarily limited to cognitive therapy.

It should be noted that cognitive supervision does not specifically address multicultural issues. However, unlike some other supervision theories, cognitive supervision, with its examination of the thoughts and beliefs of the supervisor and supervisee, can be more open to other cultural influences. The supervisor must be careful not to allow her or his own cultural cognitions to overshadow the equally valid one of other cultural groups.

Although cognitive supervision recognizes that the nature of problems may be affective, there is little attention devoted to feelings or unconscious factors in determining the causes of behavior, nor is attention given to insight. Lack of attention to feelings within problems may allow for intellectualizing the problem rather than understanding and correcting it.

☐ Conclusion

M. V. Ellis (1991) reported that although literature on supervision abounds, literature on supervision theory and supervisor training is sparse. Goodyear and Bernard (1998) suggested three reasons for the absence of efficacy and effectiveness research in supervision: relatively little theory-driven research; the lack of supervision manuals or protocols to follow that ensure that a reasonably accurate version of a specific model is being followed; and the difficulty in designing a research model that would test efficacy and effectiveness while still protecting and ensuring quality treatment for the clients who would be necessarily involved in the research.

In this chapter we have examined three discrete theories of supervision—psychodynamic, behavioral, and cognitive—each with it's own goals, strategies, and perspectives. Although differences are many, all three theories stress the importance of the supervisory alliance and skill acquisition. It should be noted that some researchers believe that supervision is a separate, although closely related, field from counseling with its own processes, skills, and theories (Bernard & Goodyear, 1998; Borders & Leddick, 1987; M. V. Ellis, 1991; Goodyear & Bernard, 1998).

Whatever theory of supervision is used, two considerations must be applied to the overall supervisory process: first, the developmental level of the supervisee, and second, diversity and/or multicultural issues in supervision. Each of these considerations is mentioned briefly, since additional information is available in other chapters of this book. Research has shown that the developmental level of the supervisee in her or his counseling education and/or career has a profound effect on the supervision process and counselor growth (Lombardo, et al., 1997; Neufeldt, Iversen, & Juntunen, 1995; Peace & Sprinthall, 1998; Rønnestad & Skovholt, 1993; Wall, 1994). The supervisor must be attuned to the supervisee's developmental level in order to provide her or him with the type of supervision he or she needs. Diversity and multicultural issues are a focus of research in the counseling field (Arredondo et al., 1996; Helms & Cook, 1999; Ladany, Brittan-Powell, & Pannu, 1997; Ladany, Inman, Constantine, & Hofheinz, 1997; McFadden, 1996; Patterson, 1996; Sue et al., 1998; Weinrach & Thomas, 1996, 1998). However, research in supervision and diversity or multiculturalism has been sparse (Bernard & Goodyear, 1998; Cook & Helms, 1988; Leong & Wagner, 1994; McRoy, Freeman, Logan, & Blackmon, 1986; Priest, 1994; Sells, Goodyear, Lichtenberg, & Polkinghorne, 1997; Stoltenberg, McNeill, & Crethar, 1994).

The supervision models in this chapter stress the importance of viewing each supervisee as an unique individual, and this requires the consideration and understanding of the effects of diversity and/or multiculturalism on the supervisory relationship. Supervisors must recognize their own issues in this area before agreeing to supervise.

☐ References

Alpher, V. S. (1991). Interdependence and parallel process: A case study of structural analysis of social behavior in supervision and short-term dynamic psychotherapy. *Psychotherapy, 28*, 218–231.

Arciniega, G. M., & Newton, B. J. (1999). Counseling and psychotherapy: Multicultural considerations. In D. Capuzzi & D. R. Gross (Eds.), *Counseling and psychotherapy: Theories and interventions* (pp. 435–458). Upper Saddle River, NJ: Merrill.

Arredondo, P., Toporek, R., Brown, S., Jones, J., Locke, D. C., Sanchez, J., & Stadler, H. (1996). *Organization of the multicultural counseling competencies*. Alexandria, VA: American Counseling Association.

Baird, B. W. (1998). *The internship, practicum, and the field placement handbook: A guide for the helping professions* (2nd ed.). Upper Saddle River, NJ: Prentice-Hall.

Bandura, A. (1991). Social cognitive theory of self-regulation. *Organizational Behavior and Human Decision Processes, 50*(2), 248–287.

Bandura, A. (1996). Ontological and epistemological terrains revisited. *Journal of Behavior Therapy and Experimental Psychiatry, 27*(4), 323–345.

Batten, C. (1990). Dilemmas of "crosscultural psychotherapy supervision." *British Journal of Psychotherapy, 7*, 129–140.

Beck, A. T. (1976). *Cognitive therapy and emotional disorders*. New York: International University Press.

Beck, A. T. (1993). Cognitive therapy: Nature and relation to behavior therapy. *Journal of Psychotherapy Practice and Research, 2*(4), 345–356.

Beck, A. T. (1997a). Cognitive therapy: Reflections. In J.K. Zeig (Ed.), *The evolution of psychotherapy: The third conference* (pp. 55–64). New York: Brunner/Mazel.

Beck, A. T. (1997b). The past and future of cognitive therapy. *Journal of Psychotherapy Practice and Research, 6*(4), 276–284.

Beck, J. S. (1995). *Cognitive therapy: Basics and beyond*. New York: Guilford Press.

Berger, S. S., & Bucholz, E. S. (1993). On becoming a supervisee: Preparation for learning in a supervisory relationship. *Psychotherapy, 30*, 86–92.

Bernard, J. M., & Goodyear, R. K. (1998). *Fundamentals of clinical supervision* (2nd ed.) Boston: Allyn & Bacon.

Beutler, L. E., & Kendall, P. C. (1995). Introduction to the special section: The case for training in the provision of psychological therapy. *Journal of Consulting and Clinical Psychology, 63*, 179–181.

Binder, J. L. (1993a). Is it time to improve psychotherapy training? *Clinical Psychology Review, 13*, 301–318.

Binder, J. L. (1993b). Observations on the training of therapists in time-limited dynamic psychotherapy. *Psychotherapy, 30*, 592–598.

Binder, J. L., & Strupp, H. H. (1997). Supervision of psychodynamic psychotherapies. In C. E. Watkins, Jr. (Ed.), *Handbook of psychotherapy supervision* (pp. 44–62). New York: Wiley.

Borders, L. D. (1992). Learning to think like a supervisor. *The Clinical Supervisor, 10*, 135–148.

Borders, L. D., & Leddick, G. R. (1987). *Handbook of counseling supervision*. Alexandria, VA: American Association for Counseling and Development.

Boyd, J. D. (1978). *Counselor supervision: Approaches, preparation, practices.* Muncie, IN: Accelerated Development.

Boylan, J. C., Malley, P. B., & Scott, J. (1995). *Practicum and internship: Textbook for counseling and psychotherapy* (2nd ed.). Washington, DC: Accelerated Development.

Brack, G., Brack, C. J., & McCarthy, C. (1997). A model for helping novice therapists to integrate their affective reactions and cognitive appraisals in supervision. *Clinical Supervisor, 15*(2), 37–48.

Butler, S. F., & Strupp, H. H. (1993). Effects of training experienced dynamic therapists to use a psychotherapy manual. In N. E. Miller, L. Luborsky, J. P. Barber, & J. P. Docherty (Eds.), *Psychodynamic treatment research* (pp. 191–210). New York: Basic Books.

Carmichael, K. (1992). Peer rating form in counselor supervision. *Texas Association of Counseling and Development Journal, 20*(1), 57–61.

Casement, P. J. (1991). *Learning from the patient.* New York: Plenum.

Chase, P. (1998). *First course in applied behavior analysis.* Pacific Grove, CA: Brooks/Cole.

Clarkson, P. (1995). *The therapeutic relationship: In psychoanalysis, counselling psychology, and psychotherapy.* London: Whurr Publishers.

Collins, D. (1990). Identifying dysfunctional counseling skill behaviors. *Clinical Supervisor, 8*(1), 67–79.

Cook, D. A., & Helms, J.E. (1988). Visible racial/ethnic group supervisees' satisfaction with cross-cultural supervision as predicted by relationship characteristics. *Journal of Counseling Psychology, 35*(3), 268–274.

Cormier, S., & Cormier, B. (1998). *Interviewing strategies for helpers: Fundamental skills and behavioral interventions* (4th ed.). Pacific Grove, CA: Brooks/Cole.

Craighead, W. E., Craighead, L. W., & Ilardi, S. S. (1995). Behavior therapies in historical perspective. In B. M. Bongar & L. E. Beutler (Eds.), *Comprehensive textbook of psychotherapy: Theory and practice* (pp. 64–83). New York: Oxford University Press.

Daniels, T. G., Rigazio-DiGilio, S. A., & Ivey, A. E. (1997). Microcounseling: A training and supervision paradigm for the helping professions. In C.E. Watkins Jr. (Ed.), *Handbook of psychotherapy supervision* (pp. 277–295). New York: Wiley.

Day, W. F., Jr. (1998). The historical antecedents of contemporary behaviorism. In R. W. Rieber & K. Salzinger (Eds.), *Psychology: Theoretical-historical perspectives* (2nd ed.; pp. 301–352). Washington, DC: American Psychological Association.

Della Selva, P. C. (1996). *Intensive short-term dynamic psychotherapy: Theory and techniques.* New York: Wiley.

Dewald, P. A. (1997). The process of supervision in psychoanalysis. In C. E. Watkins, Jr. (Ed.), *Handbook of psychotherapy supervision* (pp. 31–43). New York: Wiley.

Dindia, K. (1994). The intrapersonal-interpersonal dialectical process of self-disclosure. In S. Duck (Ed.), *Dynamics of relationships* (pp. 27–57). Thousand Oaks, CA: Sage.

Dobbs, J. B. (1986). Supervision of psychology trainees in field placements. *Professional Psychology, 17,* 296–300.

Doehrman, M. J. (1976). Parallel process in supervision and psychotherapy. *Bulletin of the Menninger Clinic, 40,* 1–104.

Domjan, M. (1998). *The principles of learning and behavior* (4th ed.). Pacific Grove, CA: Brooks/Cole.

Dowrick, P. W. (1991). *Practical guide to using video in the behavioral sciences.* New York: Wiley.

Duryee, J., Brymer, M., & Gold, K. (1996). The supervisory needs of neophyte psychotherapy trainees. *Journal of Clinical Psychology, 52*(6), 663–671.

Edwards, D. (1997). Supervision today: The psychoanalytic legacy. In G. Shipton (Ed.), *Supervision of psychotherapy and counselling: Making a place to think* (pp. 11–23). Buckingham, England: Open University Press.

Ekstein, R., & Wallerstein, R. S. (1972). *The teaching and learning of psychotherapy* (2nd ed.). Madison, WI: International Universities Press.

Ellis, A. (1962). *Reason and emotion in psychotherapy.* New York: Lyle Stuart Press.

Ellis, M. V. (1991). Critical incidents in clinical supervision and in supervisor supervision: Assessing supervisory issues. *Journal of Counseling Psychology, 38*(3), 342–349.

Feiner, A. H. (1994). Comments on contradictions in the supervisory process. *Contemporary Psychoanalysis, 30,* 57–75.

Follette, W. C., & Callaghan, G. M. (1995). Do as I do, not as I say: A behavior-analytic approach to supervision. *Professional Psychology: Research and Practice, 26*(4), 413–421.

Freeman, B., & McHenry, S. (1996). Clinical supervision of counselors-in-training: A nation-wide survey of ideal delivery, goals, and theoretical influences. *Counselor Education and Supervision, 36*(2), 144–158.

Fruzzetti, A. E., Waltz, J. A., & Linehan, M. M. (1997). Supervision in dialectical behavior therapy. In C. E. Watkins Jr. (Ed.), *Handbook of psychotherapy supervision* (pp. 84–100). New York: Wiley.

Fuqua, D. R., Johnson, A. W., Anderson, M. W., & Newman, J. L. (1984). Cognitive methods in counselor training. *Counselor Education and Supervision, 24,* 85–95.

Gee, H. (1998). Developing insight through supervision: Relating, then defining. In P. Clarkson (Ed.), *Supervision: Psychoanalytic and Jungian perspectives* (pp. 9–33). Longon: Whurr Publishers.

Goldberg, D. A. (1998). Structuring training goals for psychodynamic psychotherapy. *Journal of Psychotherapy Practice and Research, 7*(1), 10–22.

Goldfried, M. R., & Davison, G. C. (1994). *Clinical behavior therapy.* New York: Wiley.

Gomersall, J. (1997). Peer group supervision. In G. Shipton (Ed.), *Supervision of psychotherapy and counselling: Making a place to think* (pp. 107–118). Buckingham, England: Open University Press.

Goodyear, R. K., & Bernard, J. M. (1998). Clinical supervision: Lessons from the literature. *Counselor Education and Supervision, 38*(1), 6–22.

Gordon, R. M. (1995). The symbolic nature of the supervisory relationship: Identification and professional growth. *Issues in Psychoanalytic Psychology, 17*(2), 154–162.

Guidino, V. F. (1991). *The self in process: Toward a post-rationalist cognitive therapy.* New York: Guilford.

Haesler, L. (1993). Adequate distance in the relationship between supervisor and supervisee. *International Journal of Psycho-Analysis, 74,* 547–555.

Halgin, R. P., & Murphy, R. A. (1995). Issues in the training of psychotherapists. In B. Boner & L. E. Beutler (Eds.), *Comprehensive textbook of psychotherapy: Theory and practice* (pp. 434–455). New York: Oxford University Press.

Hayes, S. C., & Hayes, L. J. (1992). Some clinical implications of contextual behaviorism: The examples of cognition. *Behavior Therapy, 23,* 225–249.

Helms, J. E., & Cook, D. A. (1999). *Using race and culture in counseling and psychotherapy: Theory and process.* Boston: Allyn & Bacon.

Hollon, S. D., & Beck, A. T. (1994). Cognitive and cognitive-behavioral therapies. In A. E. Bergin & S. L. Garfield (Eds.), *Handbook of psychotherapy and behavior change* (4th ed., pp. 428–466). New York: Wiley.

Holloway, E. L. (1987). Developmental models of supervision: Is it development? *Professional Psychology: Research and Practice, 18,* 209–216.

Holloway, E. L., & Neufeldt, S. A. (1995). Supervision: Its contributions to treatment efficacy. *Journal of Consulting and Clinical Psychology, 63*(2), 207–213.

Hosford, R. E., & Barmann, B. (1983). A social learning approach to counselor supervision. *The Counseling Psychologist, 11*(1), 51–58.

Itzhaky, H., & Aloni, R. (1996). The use of deductive techniques for developing mechanisms of coping with resistance in supervision. *Clinical Supervisor, 14*(1), 65–76.

Ivey, A. E., & Authier, J. (1978). *Microcounseling: Innovations in interviewing, counseling, psychotherapy, and psychoeducation* (2nd ed.). Springfield, IL: Charles C. Thomas.

Jacobs, D., David, P., & Meyer, D. J. (1995). *The supervisory encounter: A guide for teachers of psychodynamic psychotherapy and psychoanalysis.* New Haven, CT: Yale University Press.

Jacobs, M. (1996). Parallel process—Confirmation and critique. *Psychodynamic Counselling, 2,* 55–66.

Jacoby, M. (1995). Supervision and the interactive field. In P. Kugler (Ed.), *Jungian perspectives on clinical supervision* (pp. 78–84). Einsiedeln, Switzerland: Daimon Verlag.

Kalodner, C. R. (1999). Cognitive-behavioral theories. In D. Capuzzi & D. R. Gross (Eds.), *Counseling and psychotherapy: Theories and interventions* (pp. 261–314). Upper Saddle River, NJ: Merrill.

Kottler, J. A., & Hazler, R. (1997). *What you never learned in graduate school.* New York: Norton.

Kurpius, D. J. (1985, April). *Applying cognitive-behavioral theory in a training context.* Paper presented at the American Educational Research Association conference, Chicago, IL.

Kurpius, D. J., Benjamin, D., & Morran, D. K. (1985). Effects of teaching a cognitive strategy on counselor trainee internal dialogue and clinical hypothesis formulation. *Journal of Counseling Psychology, 32,* 263–271.

Kurpius, D. J., & Morran, D. K. (1988). Cognitive-behavioral techniques and interventions for application in counselor supervision. *Counselor Education and Supervision, 27,* 368–376.

Ladany, N., Brittan-Powell, C. S., & Pannu, R. K. (1997). The influence of supervisory racial identity interaction and racial matching on the supervisory working alliance and supervisee multicultural competence. *Counselor Education and Supervision, 36,* 284–304.

Ladany, N., Inman, A. G., Constantine, M. G., & Hofheinz, E. (1997). Supervisee multicultural case conceptualization ability and self-reported multicultural competence as functions of supervisee racial identity and supervisor focus. *Journal of Counseling Psychology, 44,* 284–293.

Leddick, G. R. (1994). Models of clinical supervision. In L. D. Borders (Ed.), *Supervision: Exploring the effective components* (ERIC/Cass Counseling Digest Series, ERIC#:ED372339, pp. 742–760). Greensboro, NC: ERIC/Cass.

Liddle, B. (1986). Resistance in supervision: A response to perceived threat. *Counselor Education and Supervision, 26 (2),* 117–127.

Leong, F. T. L., & Wagner, N. S. (1994). Cross-cultural counseling supervision: What do we know? What do we need to know? *Counselor Education and Supervision, 34*(2), 117–131.

Liese, B. S., & Beck, J. S. (1997). Cognitive therapy supervision. In C. E. Watkins, Jr. (Ed.), *Handbook of psychotherapy supervision* (pp. 114–133). New York: Wiley.

Lochner, B. T., & Melchert, T. P. (1997). Relationship of cognitive style and theoretical orientation to psychology interns' preferences for supervision. *Journal of Counseling Psychology, 44*(2), 256–260.

Lombardo, L. T., Greer, J., Estadt, B., & Cheston, S. (1997). Empowerment behaviors in clinical training: An empirical study of parallel processes. *The Clinical Supervisor, 16*(2), 33–47.

McCue, R. B. II, & Lane, R. C. (1995). Parallel process and perspective: Understanding, detecting, and intervening. *Psychotherapy in Private Practice, 14*(3), 13–32.

McFadden, J. (1996). A transcultural perspective: Reaction to C .H. Patterson's "Multicultural counseling: From diversity to universality." *Journal of Counseling and Development, 74,* 232–235.

McLeod, S. (1998). Student self-appraisal: Facilitating mutual planning in clinical education. *Clinical Supervisor, 15*(1), 87–101.

McRoy, R. G., Freeman, E. M., Logan, S. L., & Blackmon, B. (1986). Cross-cultural field supervision: Implications for social work education. *Journal of Social Work Education, 22,* 50–56.

Mead, D. E. (1990). *Effective supervision: A task-oriented model for the mental health professions.* New York: Brunner/Mazel.

Moore, J. (1998). On behaviorism, theories, and hypothetical constructs. *Journal of Mind and Behavior, 19*(2), 215–242.

Morran, D. K. (1986). Relationship of counselor self-talk and hypothesis formulation to performance level. *Journal of Counseling Psychology, 33*(4), 395–400.

Morran, D. K., Kurpius, D. J., Brack, C. J., & Brack, G. (1995). A cognitive-skills model for counselor training and supervision. *Journal of Counseling and Development, 73,* 384–389.

Morran, D. K., Kurpius, D. J., & Brack, G. (1989). Empirical investigation of counselor self-talk categories. *Journal of Counseling Psychology, 36,* 505–510.

Mueller, W. J., & Kell, B. L. (1972). *Coping with conflict*. New York: Appleton-Century-Crofts.

Muesser, K. T., & Liberman, R. P. (1995). Behavior therapy in practice. In B. M. Bongar & L. E. Beutler (Eds.), *Comprehensive textbook of psychotherapy: Theory and practice* (pp. 84–110). New York: Oxford University Press.

Neufeldt, S. A., Iversen, J. N., & Juntunen, C. L. (1995). *Supervision strategies for the first practicum*. Alexandria, VA: American Counseling Association.

Padesky, C. A. (1996). Developing cognitive therapist competency: Teaching and supervision models. In P. M. Salkovskis (Ed.), *Frontiers of cognitive therapy* (pp. 266–292). New York: Guilford Press.

Patterson, C. H. (1996). Multicultural counseling: From diversity to universality. *Journal of Counseling & Development, 74*, 227–231.

Peace, S. D., & Sprinthall, N. A. (1998). Training school counselors to supervise beginning counselors: Theory, research, and practice. *Professional School Counselor, 1*(5), 2–8.

Pickvance, D. (1997). Becoming a supervisor. In G. Shipton (Ed.), *Supervision of psychotherapy and counselling: Making a place to think* (pp. 131–142). Buckingham, England: Open University Press.

Priest, R. (1994). Minority supervisor and majority supervisee: Another perspective of clinical reality. *Counselor Education and Supervision, 34*(2), 152–158.

Raichelson, S. H., Herron, W. G., Primavera, L. H., & Ramirez, S. M. (1997). Incidence and effects of parallel process in psychotherapy supervision. *Clinical Supervisor, 15*(2), 37–48.

Remington, G., & DaCosta, G. (1989). Ethnocultural factors in resident supervision: Black supervisor and white supervisee. *Journal of Psychotherapy, 43*, 398–404.

Rich, R. O., & Sampson, D. T. (1990). Building intensive simulations in family-therapy training. *Counselor Education and Supervision, 29*(3), 187–196.

Rodenhauser, P. (1994). Toward a multidimensional model for psychotherapy supervision based on developmental stages. *Journal of Psychotherapy Practice and Research, 3*, 1–15.

Ronen, T., & Rosenbaum, M. (1998). Beyond direct verbal instructions in cognitive behavioral supervision. *Cognitive and Behavioral Practice, 5*(1), 7–23.

Rønnestad, M. H., & Skovholt, T. M. (1993). Supervision for beginning and advanced graduate students of counseling and psychotherapy. *Journal of Counseling and Development, 71*(4), 396–405.

Rosenbaum, M., & Ronen, T. (1998). Clinical supervision from the standpoint of cognitive-behavior therapy. *Psychotherapy, 35*(2), 220–230.

Ryan, A. S., & Hendricks, C. O. (1989). Culture and communication: Supervising the Asian and Hispanic social worker. *Clinical Supervisor, 7*(1), 27–40.

Sells, J. N., Goodyear, R. K., Lichtenberg, J. W., & Polkinghorne, D. E. (1997). Relationship of supervisor and trainee gender to in-session verbal behavior and ratings of trainee skills. *Journal of Counseling Psychology, 44*(4), 406–412.

Shanfield, S. B., Matthews, K. L., & Hetherely, V. (1993). What do excellent psychotherapy supervisors do? *American Journal of Psychiatry, 150*, 1081–1084.

Shechter, R. A. (1990). Becoming a supervisor: A phase in professional development. *Psychoanalysis and Psychotherapy, 8*, 23–28.

Snyder, D., & Levy, C. (1998). Supervision. In D. Snyder (Ed.), *Wanting to talk: Counselling case studies in communication disorders* (pp. 256–288). London: Whurr Publishers.

Stein, D. M., & Lambert, M. J. (1995). Graduate training in psychotherapy: Are therapy outcomes enhanced? *Journal of Consulting and Clinical Psychology, 63*, 182–196.

Sternberg, R. J. (1997). Styles of thinking and learning. *Canadian Journal of School Psychology, 13*(2), 15–40.

Stewart, J. B. (1998). Problem-based learning in counsellor education. *Canadian Journal of Counselling, 32*(1), 27–49.

Stoltenberg, C. D., McNeill, B. W., & Crethar, H. C. (1994). Changes in supervision as counselors and therapists gain experience: A review. *Professional Psychology: Research and Practice, 25*(4), 416–449.

Sue, D. W., Carter, R. T., Casas, J. M., Fouad, N. A., Ivey, A. E., Jensen, M., LaFromboise, T., Manese, J. E., Ponterotto, J. G., & Vazquez-Nutall, E. (1998). *Multicultural counseling competencies: Individual and organizational development.* Thousand Oaks, CA: Sage.

Swaney, K. B., & Stone, G. L. (1990). Therapist awareness of covert reactions to client interpersonal behavior. *Journal of Social and Clinical Psychology, 9*(3), 375–389.

Teitelbaum, S. H. (1990). Supertransference: The role of the supervisor's blind spots. *Psychoanalytic Psychology, 7,* 243–258.

Temple, S., & Bowers, W. A. (1998). Supervising cognitive therapists from diverse fields. *Journal of Cognitive Psychotherapy: An International Quarterly, 12*(2), 139–151.

Thorbeck, J. (1992). The development of the psychodynamic psychotherapist in supervision. *Academic Psychiatry, 16,* 72–82.

Wall, J. C. (1994). Teaching termination to trainees through parallel processes in supervision. *The Clinical Supervisor, 12*(2), 27–37.

Wallerstein, R. S. (1995). *The talking cures: The psychoanalyses and the psychotherapies.* New Haven, CT: Yale University Press.

Watson, M. F. (1993). Supervising the person of the therapist: Issues, challenges, and dilemmas. *Contemporary Family Therapy: An International Journal, 15*(1), 21–31.

Weinrach, S. G., & Thomas, K. R. (1996). The counseling profession's commitment to diversity-sensitive counseling: A critical reassessment. *Journal of Counseling and Development, 73,* 472–477.

Weinrach, S. G., & Thomas, K. R. (1998). Diversity-sensitive counseling today: A postmodern clash of values. *Journal of Counseling and Development, 76*(2), 115–122.

Williams, S., & Halgin, R. P. (1995). Issues in psychotherapy supervision between the white supervisor and the black supervisee. *Clinical Supervision, 13*(1), 39–61.

Wolstein, B. (1994). Notes on psychoanalytic supervision (brief commentary). *Contemporary Psychoanalysis, 30,* 182–191.

Woods, P. J., & Ellis, A. (1996). Supervision in rational emotive behavior therapy. *Journal of Rational-Emotive and Cognitive Behavior Therapy, 14*(2), 135–152.

Woods, P. J., & Ellis, A. (1997). Supervision in rational emotive behavior therapy. In C. E. Watkins, Jr. (Ed.), *Handbook of psychotherapy supervision* (pp. 101–113). New York: Wiley.

Worthington, E. L., Jr. (1987). Changes in supervision as counselors and supervisors gain experience: A review. *Professional Psychology: Research and Practice, 18,* 189–208.

PART

III

SPECIALIZED MODELS OF COUNSELOR SUPERVISION

Richard L. Hayes
Lorie S. Blackman
Carolyn Brennan

7

CHAPTER

Group Supervision

In a book devoted entirely to the issue of supervision, some may question the need for a separate chapter on group supervision. Clearly, many of the skills and methods used within a group setting are no different than those used by all counselors and supervisors in whatever setting. The same may be said of the general knowledge and skills that any counselor brings to the tasks of helping. Yet being the supervisor of counselors in a group is not the same as supervising them individually, any more than group counseling is merely the counseling of individuals in a group. Moreover, the supervision of counselors who are learning group facilitation skills provides challenges and opportunities that make special use of the parallel process and group dynamics operating in this form of supervision.

Whatever the model (e.g., psychoanalytic, humanistic-existential, social learning, TA/Gestalt, rational-emotive, eclectic) or setting (e.g., administrative, clinical) of supervision chosen, the supervisor must also choose a modality by which to apply the model. As has been noted in previous chapters in this volume, different modalities have different effects on supervisees and make different demands on the skills of both the supervisees and the supervisor. In general, Hart (1982) has suggested that supervision "begin at the least complex level and proceed gradually to more complex levels. When applied to modality, this rule suggests that supervisors begin with individual supervision and later add group and/or peer supervision" (p. 204). This rule suggests that group supervision represents a median level of supervision that presumes prior experience and demonstrated mastery in individual supervision and that is preparatory to peer supervision. Certainly, any program of supervision might include various patterns of individual, group, and peer supervision that respond to the changing needs of the supervisees and the demand characteristics of the training site (time, staff, availability of space, etc.).

As Savickas, Marquart, and Supinski (1986) suggested, "level of training may be a more important variable in research on effective group supervision than is type of student" (p. 24). In a survey of experienced group psychotherapy supervisors, Dies (1980) found that the preferred sequence of training activities should begin with an academic component and then move progressively through an observational component and an experiential component, and conclude with supervision of actual practice. Notably, these recommendations refer to a sequence of activities that is appropriate from the perspective of the individual supervisee. On the group level, supervisees are not only engaged in a sequence appropriate to their own professional development (as discussed in previous chapters) but are also members of a supervisory group that can be described by its own developmental sequence (as will be discussed in this chapter).

Attempts to integrate these two dimensions (i.e., individual and group development) within supervision have yet to provide a unified group supervision model. Nonetheless, the work of Blocher (1983), Borders and Fong (1989), Rigazio-Digilio and Anderson (1994), and Tennyson and Strom (1986) report attempts to integrate structural developmental interventions into counselor supervision. In addition, the work of a host of researchers suggests that developmental interventions with adults in groups can be an effective stimulant to ego, moral, and ethical development. Particularly noteworthy are Day's (1993) laboratory learning groups, the proposal by Hayes (1991) for promoting ethical development through group work, the "just community" approach of Power, Higgins, and Kohlberg (1989), Swensen's (1980), and D'Andrea's (1988) work investigating the match between counselor and client developmental levels and counselor effectiveness, Weinstein and Alschuler's (1987) research on self-knowledge development, Young-Eisendrath's (1985) analysis of authority issues in counseling, and the success of Amerel (1989), Paisley (1990), and Sprinthall, Reiman, and Thies-Sprinthall (1993) in promoting the development of teachers. Nonetheless, a unified model integrating adult development theory with specific group leadership practices is still unavailable.

Despite these limitations, it is important to note that group supervision is widely practiced in all types of training programs (Riva & Cornish, 1995). Although the use of a group is widely recognized as offering more to supervision than just an efficient method (Bernard & Goodyear, 1998; Holloway & Johnston, 1985; Riva & Cornish, 1995), supervisors are challenged to use the group to its fullest potential. In particular, group supervision encompasses the full range of group work, including attention to group dynamics, individual and group development, and the purposes of the supervision. This dynamic system of relationships becomes complicated even further when one considers that the participants in group supervision are themselves supervising both individuals and groups.

Although studies have reported the application of a developmental framework to group supervision (Cohen, Gross, & Turner, 1976; Cooper & Gustafson,

1985; Getzel & Salmon, 1985; Hillerbrand, 1989; Keith, Connell, & Whitaker, 1992; Leach, Stoltenberg, McNeill, & Eichenfield, 1997; Riva & Cornish, 1995; Sansbury, 1982; Wilbur, Roberts-Wilbur, Morris, Betz, & Hart, 1991; Yogev, 1982), these models are either too linear in accounting for the dynamic relationships among group variables or too simplistic in their selection of variables for consideration. In particular, we are unaware of any report that describes a group supervision model that accounts for the relationship between the levels of mastery of relevant counseling behaviors by both the supervisee and the supervisor, individual and developmental characteristics of the supervisee and the supervisor over the course of training, and the sequence of concerns in group development. The limitations of the present chapter make a complete proposal impossible, but enough is known about group counseling and supervision skills, individual differences, and group development to offer a skeletal hypothesis about what a comprehensive program of group supervision might look like. In response to the challenges these issues present, this chapter outlines a developmental model of group supervision that integrates the dynamic relationships to be found among individuals conducting individual or group counseling within the group supervision context.

☐ Toward a Definition

In defining group supervision, it is important to distinguish between two potential uses of the term: one in which the supervisees constitute the group and one in which the object of the supervision is the leadership of a group. Holloway and Johnston (1985), for example, have defined four distinct forms that supervision in a group might take:

> (a) group supervision of trainees in a practicum setting who are learning individual counseling skills;
> (b) group supervision of trainees learning pre-practicum interviewing skills;
> (c) leaderless groups in which trainees provide peer supervision in a group format; and
> (d) group supervision of trainees in a practicum setting focusing on learning group facilitation skills. (p. 333)

Alternatively, Altfield and Bernard (1997) have delineated the forms that the supervision of group leaders might take, including the supervision of group leaders in a group format. In dyadic supervision, the group leader presents his or her work to the supervisor using a familiar one-to-one model adapted from individual supervision. In dyadic co-therapy supervision, the supervisor co-leads the group with the supervisee followed by supervision of their work together. Triadic supervision combines the two arrangements such that the supervisor works with two supervisees who act as co-leaders for the group. Finally, there is what Altfield and Bernard referred to as group supervision, in which the supervisor utilizes the group setting in which to conduct supervision of persons leading groups themselves. It is their contention that the "collaborative and democratic nature of these groups, in which trainees can share their anxieties and concerns about their work with one another in a safe atmosphere, has proven to be an extremely beneficial experience" (p. 383).

The critical point to be made here is that true group supervision takes place in a group and, as such, "the members see themselves and are seen by others as psychologically interdependent and interactive in pursuit of a shared goal" (Dagley, Gazda, & Pistone, 1986, p. 131). The essential task for the group supervisor, therefore, is to facilitate the development of a productive work group before effective supervision can begin. With this task in mind, the following questions must be addressed by the group supervisor: What should be the shared goals of supervision? What leadership style is most appropriate for the realization of these goals? What balance of approaches is most productive? What role should evaluation play in the various components of group supervision? (See Holloway & Johnston, 1985.)

☐ Benefits of Group Supervision

Group supervision offers many benefits to the supervisor and the supervisee beyond the obvious advantage of reducing supervisory time (Bernard & Goodyear, 1998; Riva & Cornish, 1995; Werstlein & Borders, 1997). The real advantages to be realized in group supervision are from the unique contributions groups have to make to the personal and professional development of supervisees. Bernard and Goodyear (1998), Dagley et al. (1986), and Kaul and Bednar (1978) have enumerated the unique learning opportunities to be found in group as opposed to individual settings. Drawing upon this work, the following advantages can be found for group as opposed to individual supervision:

1. Group supervision offers each supervisee the opportunity to reality-test self-perceptions.
2. Through group interactions, distorted perceptions and false assumptions of self and others may become more apparent and lose their value.
3. Group supervision may provide a sense of psychological safety to support the elimination of self-defeating behaviors.
4. Group supervision provides an opportunity to interact in real-life situations, thus providing supervisees with chances to try out new behaviors in a safe environment.
5. Responses of others, especially one's peers, can help supervisees to appreciate the universality of some personal concerns.
6. Group supervision enables supervisees to increase their abilities to give

and to solicit appropriate self-disclosures and feedback, thus enhancing opportunities to function as both helpers and helpees.

7. Interaction with others in a group can enhance one's empathy and social interest.
8. Group supervision exposes supervisees to alternative modes of helping, which can help supervisees to develop deeper understandings and acceptance of different counseling styles.
9. Consistent feedback from others in group supervision can enhance the supervisee's accuracy of perception and communication.
10. Group supervision provides an arena for the supervisee to learn perspective-taking skills with other group members.
11. Group supervision fosters less dependency on the supervisor than individual supervision.
12. Anxiety of participants in group supervision is lessened as they realize that their peers have similar concerns.
13. Novice counselors find it easier to understand each others' cognitive processes than to understand an expert's cognitive processes (Hillerbrand, 1992). This principle makes the supervision group an excellent place to conceptualize new skills and cases.

☐ Considerations for Group Supervisors

Even though the benefits of group supervision are many, the task of facilitating a supervisory group is complex. The supervisory group leader must consider the multiple issues involved (Bernard & Goodyear, 1998; Ellis & Douce, 1994), or the intended benefits will not be realized. The following list provides considerations for group supervisors:

1. Beginning counselors tend to feel anxious, and that anxiety can be heightened in the group setting. Anxiety can become an issue if it inhibits the learning process of the group participants.
2. Supervisees may begin to compete with each other for the group leader's attention and approval. This competition may appear in the form of monopolizing group time or trying to present oneself as an expert.
3. Multicultural issues can be used to enhance the group experience or, if neglected, can create divisions depending upon the norms that are established.
4. The role of evaluation complicates the position of the group leader. Supervisees may be hesitant to participate fully if the evaluative role is not clearly defined.
5. As in group therapy, supervisees will begin to fill roles in the group (Yalom, 1995). These roles become harmful if scapegoating occurs or if roles are not acknowledged and discussed during supervision sessions.
6. Confidentiality is not as secure in a group as in an individual supervision

setting (Bernard & Goodyear, 1998). The confidentiality of both clients and supervisees is at risk.

Parallel process issues are also relevant in group supervision (Bernard & Goodyear, 1998). For supervisees conducting groups themselves these issues are especially relevant. The dynamics of the group may begin to resemble the dynamics of the supervisees' groups. For example, if supervisees are conducting groups in which the members share little affective content, the supervision group may also exhibit this dynamic. If the supervisor recognizes this pattern, he or she can model how to address the issue in the group. If the issue is not addressed, the supervisees will most likely continue to ignore the issue in their own groups.

A supervisor working with a diverse group must be knowledgeable of between- and within-group cultural differences and how they apply to group process and development. Groups that are designed to intentionally explore issues that are related to cultural identity are more successful in modifying racial attitudes than those that address cultural issues haphazardly (Burke, 1984; Greeley, Garcia, Kessler, & Gilchrest, 1992). In that regard, Gibbs (1985) suggested that group supervision can be effectively employed to elicit different cultural perspectives related to counseling and supervision. Those interested in exploring how characteristics of specific cultures (African Americans, Asian Americans, Hispanic Americans, and Native Americans) can be related to group work are encouraged to refer to Merta (1995). It is important to note, however, that our understanding of how issues of diversity affect all aspects of group work is in its infancy. Recognizing the need to become more "aware, knowledgeable, and skillful in facilitating groups whose memberships represent the diversity of our society," the Association for Specialists in Group Work (ASGW, 1998b) adopted a set of principles for diversity-competent group workers. Although the authors caution that the publication of these principles does not comprise a "how to" document, they have identified a set of attitudes and beliefs, knowledge, and skills related to awareness of self, awareness of group member's worldview, and diversity-appropriate intervention strategies as a starting point for the group supervisor who wants to become more effective in working with supervisees from diverse backgrounds.

More than a decade ago, Holloway and Johnston (1985) observed that "the field of counselor training is at a rudimentary level of explaining and understanding group supervision" (p. 338). Although their observation remains true today (Prieto, 1996), much is known about the specifics of group process and of its potential contributions to the enhancement of interpersonal effectiveness (Gazda, 1989; Yalom, 1995). To understand the nature of group supervision, therefore, one must understand the nature of groups themselves. As will be presented in the pages to follow, group supervision encompasses three dimensions: group type, group dynamics, and group development.

☐ Types of Groups

Groups are commonly classified on the basis of such shared properties as the number of members, duration, function, membership characteristics, setting, level of prevention, leadership style, goals, and so forth. These classifications refer to the focus or content of the group and generally may be said to describe characteristics of the group that are known prior to its first meeting. As such, these dimensions are generally under the control of the supervisor and may be manipulated in the formation of the group.

These characteristics describe separate but interacting elements of the group. The number of supervisees anticipated to be in the group, for instance, will affect the formation of the group along the other dimensions. The greater the number of members, the greater will be the demands on the setting to provide sufficient seating and privacy for the members. Further, increased numbers will change the nature of the supervision if everyone is to be provided an opportunity to speak and to share his or her concerns during the session. In addition, opportunities for each member to give and receive feedback may demand that the group meets longer or that the interactions are held to certain previously agreed upon limits. How one decides whether and to what extent to involve each member depends in part upon the purposes of supervision and its level of prevention.

Member characteristics such as level of experience and expertise or diversity of work or practicum sites, for example, will affect the level and focus of supervision. Experienced supervisees employed in a community agency are more likely to possess wider variability of experiences and expertise than will be found among prepracticum students taking their first course as part of a master's program. Studies of the supervisee's level of experience (see Bernard & Goodyear, 1998, for an extensive review of this literature), the level of cognitive complexity (Birk & Mahalik, 1996; Borders & Fong, 1989; Holloway & Wampold, 1986; Rigazio-Digilio & Anderson, 1994), and the complexity of the client issues in relation to supervisee's theoretical sophistication (Bernard, 1992) have all enhanced our understanding of the relationship among selected variables of supervision, the supervisee, and the supervisor. Nonetheless, Bernard and Goodyear (1998) concluded, along with Russell, Crimmings, and Lent (1984) and Holloway (1987) before them, that supervision is but one of many events in the supervisee's personal and professional life and that the models to date have been too simplistic to predict the supervisee's behavior in any comprehensive and consistent way.

Clearly, a host of individual differences aside from members' skill levels or professional experiences are likely to influence the dynamic character of the group in supervision. Gender, racial, and cultural differences among members can complicate the introduction of potentially divisive topics depending upon how long the group has been together, the relative maturity of group members (especially related to these issues), and the general trust level that has already been established among group members. In his review of the literature, Merta (1995) found that the use of racially hetero-geneous groups increases interracial awareness and reduced racial preju-dice, while racially homogeneous groups provide greater support, have less conflict, and are more cohesive, especially for members of racial minority groups. Finding the right balance between these apparently conflicting group structures demands that the leader be aware of and respond to the diversity within as well as between subgroups in the larger supervision group and respond to potential miscommunications among members of different ra-cial subgroups. How one responds to these differences depends upon and is influenced reciprocally by the general goals of the supervisory group.

As noted above, these variables are known to some extent prior to the initial meeting of the group and are, therefore, more predictable and subject to greater control. Within academic settings, for example, the admissions process, combined with the structure of prerequisites within the curriculum, tend to control the selection and progression of supervisees on the basis of previous knowledge and level of mastery of relevant skills. In community agencies, hospitals, or clinics, however, staff members come and go more irregularly, and typically present a more heterogeneous mixture of profes-sionals. How the group is structured depends initially upon the supervisor's sensitivity to and knowledge of these dimensions of the group.

☐ Supervisory Goals

A review of the group supervision literature yields a general consensus on four components of group supervision and training that meet distinct but overlapping supervisory goals (Coche, 1977; Riva & Cornish, 1995; Shapiro, 1978; Tauber, 1978; Yalom, 1995). These goals may include the mastery of theoretical concepts, skill development, personal growth, or the integration of the supervisee's skills, knowledge, and attitudes as effective counseling tools.

The first of these goals is met most characteristically through some aca-demic component of the supervisee's training and is not a major goal of supervision. Nonetheless, the supervisor may require selected readings on general issues of concern to supervisees or may suggest readings relevant to the concerns of specific students.

The most frequent goal for supervision is skill development. The group format provides a forum for supervisees to develop their counseling skills through analysis and practice of the individual skills. Supervision should focus upon the identification and intervention in clinical situations that are common among supervisees or common in the clinical milieu. Yalom (1995) cautioned, however, that it is a mistake

to allow the group to move into a supervisory format where members de-scribe problems they encounter in their therapeutic work with patients: such discussion should be the province of the [individual] supervisory hour. Whenever a group is engaged in discourse that can be held equally well in another formal setting, I believe that it is failing to use its unique properties and full potential. (p. 524)

Moreover, when the supervisees are engaged in group work, skill development should be focused on issues that have a high relevance for the development of group as opposed to individual skills. When group supervision is used to address individual concerns one at a time, the unique characteristics of the group setting are not utilized (Wilbur, Roberts-Wilbur, Morris, Betz, & Hart, 1991).

In response to calls for more humanistic and experiential training practices (see Holloway & Johnston, 1985) to promote personal growth, counselor educators in the 1960s began to incorporate interpersonal process groups into their training programs. Despite methodological difficulties in proving the efficacy of such approaches in improving supervisees' functioning, "group supervision still retains, however, some of the early emphasis on the facilitator role in supervision" (Holloway & Johnston, p. 335). Although group supervision can be therapeutic, individual therapeutic change is a secondary consideration to the primary goals of training, which are "the intensive group experience, the expression and integration of affect, and the recognition of here-and-now process" (Yalom, 1995, p. 527).

Supervisors can help supervisees recognize the "here-and-now" through group process. For example, if the supervision group appears to be addressing only superficial issues, the supervisor could point this out to the supervisees and ask them what it is like for them to be spending group time on surface issues. By noting the process, supervisors provide an example of how to move groups into the here-and-now. The group supervisor should also consider ethical concerns that are raised when personal growth becomes a goal of group supervision, such as "captive therapy" issues (Prieto, 1996), and the complicated relationship that is created when the group leader acts as both therapist and evaluator.

Skill integration may be the most important goal of supervision. After supervisees begin to master the individual counseling skills such as reflective listening and reflection of feelings, supervision should focus on combining basic counseling skills. Group supervision, specifically, presents a unique training opportunity by providing a context for such integration. The experience within a group of situations illustrative of actual psychodynamic as well as group dynamic issues helps supervisees to make important connections between their academic knowledge and clinical practice. Supervisees learn "when to trust [their] intuition, how to use data from within, when to self-disclose and to what extent, when to push, and when to back off" (Coche, 1977, p. 237). Hillerbrand (1992) discussed the additional benefits the group model offers to promote novice skill development. Novices promote each others' learning by modeling, by offering explanations of information processing, and through increasing each others' motivation. This type of pacing is more difficult to achieve in individual supervision because the novice has a more difficult time understanding the expert supervisor's conceptualization strategies. The group setting, on the other hand, provides an ideal arena for novice counselors to develop these skills by providing recurrent examples from one's peers in process as part of the group process.

To the four goals of mastery, skill development, personal growth, and integration, evaluation may be added. Although inclusion in the group is based in part on previous performance, supervision often serves the purpose of ongoing evaluation. Beyond the ethical issues raised by the dual role of supervisor–evaluator (see Bernard & Goodyear, 1998; Reisman, 1985; Yalom, 1995) are the very real problems that arise when supervisees are asked to self-disclose personally and professionally relevant material to persons in a position to evaluate them. Despite the supervisor's best efforts to model openness, self-disclosure, and the professional limitations of assuring complete confidentiality, supervisees remain reluctant to self-disclose, especially in front of their peers and their supervisor at the same time.

Faced with the reality that administrators are often called upon to supervise, Yalom (1995) cautioned that "mere reassurance to the group that the leader will maintain strictest confidentiality or neutrality is insufficient to deal with this very real concern of members" (p. 521). Despite having personally used several approaches to overcome what he calls the "two-hat problem," Yalom (1995) concluded that the "group becomes a far more effective vehicle for personal growth and training if led by a leader outside the institution who will play no role in student evaluation" (p. 522). Those who find themselves in the dual role of administrator and supervisor are advised to make clear the extent to which self-disclosure will become part of any evaluation and what the penalties are likely to be, if any, for failing to participate (Merta & Sisson, 1991; Pierce & Baldwin, 1990; Reisman, 1985; Remley, 1992).

In summary, the important thing to note is that the characteristics that differentiate one group from another interact to create unique training conditions. Differences in the groups' characteristics require that adjustments be made to maximize the training opportunities to be found within each group. The interaction of member-related and goal-related characteristics creates the essential dynamic of the group and accounts for its success and uniqueness as a training medium. How the group supervisor can best exploit the learning opportunities presented by each group is a function of the group's dynamics, the second dimension of group supervision.

☐ Group Dynamics

Despite their characterization by the rather static dimensions of size, membership, duration, and the like, groups have a dynamic quality to them. As Knowles and Knowles (1959) noted, a group "is always moving, doing something, changing, becoming, interacting, and reacting" (p. 12). Just as the group's characteristics interact to place limits upon one another, so too the events that act themselves out in the group interact with one another and with the various dimensions of the group itself. The struggle by group members to balance the forces associated with accomplishing goal-related tasks and building a shared community creates the group's dynamics. As noted repeatedly, creating an effective group experience depends on the supervisor's ability to provide both high levels of positive interdependence for achieving a common goal and a superordinate group identity that unites the diverse members based on a pluralistic set of values (Johnson & Johnson, 1992).

According to Lakin (1976), eight core group processes occur in all types of experiential groups regardless of the quality of the members or the leader. These processes are described in what follows.

Cohesiveness

A unique characteristic of groups and one that contributes, perhaps more than any other, to the sense of "we-ness" members experience in more successful groups is cohesion. As noted above, the more homogeneous the group, the more likely the group is to become cohesive yet often at the risk of being more superficial, less creative, and less productive (Merta, 1995). The development of a shared frame of reference helps to bind members to common goals as well as to one another. The more stable structure that results helps members to tolerate greater diversity of opinion within the group and to withstand threats to group solidarity from without (Lakin, 1976; Merta, 1995). Whatever the goals of the group, therefore, the group supervisor should attempt to establish and maintain group cohesion, especially early in the group's history.

Supervisors may facilitate group cohesion through structured group activities, connecting members, or pointing out similarities among members. For example, if one supervisee brings up an issue with a depressed client the supervisor can facilitate cohesion by turning to another supervisee who has worked through the same issue with a client. At the same time supervisors can inhibit the development of group cohesion by remaining in the role of expert in the group. If the group revolves around each supervisee receiving individual guidance from the supervisor, cohesion will not develop.

Norms

Norms refer to behavior that is "expected" of others in the group. They act as guidelines for acceptable behavior in the group and are associated with certain rewards and punishments. Because norms may arise within the group as shared expectations, whether implicit or explicit, group members may not be consciously aware of the influence of group norms on their behavior in the group. These "parataxic distortions"—distorted perceptions or beliefs regarding interpersonal relationships (Yalom, 1995)—are more likely to arise early rather than later in heterogeneous groups. The task of the supervisor is to help group members to identify norms that may be operating within the group and to help members to examine their relevance for the group's activity. Because norms play such an important role in helping to socialize members into the group (Lakin & Carson, 1966), supervisors should take an active role in modeling appropriate behaviors, such as responding empathically, showing genuine concern and respect for others, or confronting out of caring. In addition, the supervisor should attend actively to culture building, acknowledging differences, challenging the passive acceptance of stereotypes, and acknowledging conflict. Such behaviors, especially early in the group's life, can be important in setting the tone for a productive supervisory group. Of course, the supervisor is cautioned not to be too directive in setting norms for the group. Supervisees are more likely to be committed to norms in which they have had a hand in their development (Hayes & Lunsford, 1994). Nonetheless, Merta (1995) noted that the optimal amount of group structure, especially early in the group, is related to one's cultural expectations. Potential positive outcomes are more likely when working with Asian American supervisees, for example, when the group is a highly structured, problem-solving group rather than a free-floating, process-oriented interactional group (Leong, 1992).

Diversity among group members provides many unique opportunities for growth. Supervisees in diverse groups will have the benefit of learning multicultural competencies through interaction with their diverse peer group. However, multicultural considerations also add another level to the development of norms. It is common for group members who are different from the majority of group members in terms of race, ethnicity, or sexual orientation to either isolate themselves from the group or to be isolated by other members (Gazda, 1989). Merta (1995), for example, cited research suggesting that groups be gender balanced to limit the scapegoating of males for an array of perceived grievances that may be held by some females, while also citing research that supports homogeneous grouping of African American women who are apt to be reticent in mixed-gender groups on issues related to gender equity. Ellis and Douce (1994) suggested that "supervisors need to ask how are race, gender, sexual orientation, religion, or other cultural based differences affecting the supervisor and the supervisory relationships?" (p. 523). Through the exploration of these questions in the group, norms can be established that promote the appreciation of diversity among its members while advancing the purposes of the larger group, as well.

Validation and Feedback

One of the important outcomes of participation in a group is the opportunity for members to test their perceptions and improve their communications with others. Group supervision provides supervisees the opportunity to receive validation for their own ideas in the company of their peers. As Jacobs (cited in Gazda, 1989, p. 73) and Stockton and Morran (1982) have cautioned, however, positive feedback, whether or not it is followed by negative feedback, is more effective than negative feedback in influencing members to change their behavior, especially in early sessions. Consequently, supervisors are advised to limit feedback in early sessions to behavior description and to emphasize that feedback represents only the giver's perceptions. This latter caution is especially relevant when leaders, as well as group members, are unfamiliar with their own and others' cultural assumptions about other group members. Corey (1995) believed that members can benefit from the collective feedback of a heterogeneous group as well as from the modeling of other group members (including the leader) as they challenge their biases and stereotypes.

Emotional Immediacy

The increased awareness of feelings, especially as generated within the here-and-now context of the group, is an important part of group work. Nonetheless, the expression of all feelings or even the full expression of some feelings is not necessarily in the best interests of either the group or its members (Rosenbaum & Snadowsky, 1976). Although full expression can and often does help an individual with her or his feelings, members react with feelings of their own, and if expressed, can generate feelings in yet other members in reaction. Further, the supervisor must be aware of cultural differences in communication styles and tolerances for confrontation. For example, Asian Americans are often more uncomfortable with confrontation than their Caucasian American counterparts, who in turn are more likely to be uncomfortable with confrontation than their African American counterparts (Merta, 1995). Sorting through the maze of feelings created in even the briefest exchange can lead to chaos. To reduce the potential for such breakdowns in communication, the supervisor is advised to limit such exchanges to either the full expression of feelings or to the clarification of ideas. Further, the supervisor should be active in acknowledging conflict while also pushing members to make explicit connections to the group's goals for supervision and to norms operating within the group.

Problem Solving

If one considers a problem as the difference between how things are and how one thinks they ought to be, then a group provides recurrent opportunities for problem solving as members test their own perceptions and ideals against those of other group members (Wasik & Fishbein, 1982). Not only does group supervision provide opportunities for problem solving, but it

should require the active participation of all members in assuming responsibility for the productivity of the group. Acting in the context of group-
effected problem-solving processes places responsibility upon supervisees
for their own conduct, both in and outside the group. Further, the full
exploration of alternatives by the group is likely to lead to a more effective
solution than one offered by single members or even the leader (see Johnson
& Johnson, 1992, 1997; Slavin, 1983). As Leong (1992) cautioned, however, members of certain racial or ethnic minority groups may be unfamiliar with group work or hold cultural values related to confrontation and
public self-disclosure that are in conflict with group work values of openness and direct expression of feelings (e.g., Asian Americans and Native
Americans). Taking a problem-solving approach to structuring the group
can reduce initial anxiety and unnecessary ambiguity.

Leadership

As used here, leadership refers to a dynamic function of the group wherein
members' activities are directed to the satisfaction of group goals. Therefore,
leadership is viewed as more a function of the group than it is a role occupied by a single member. As the needs of the group change, the demands
placed upon its members will change. Although the supervisor may begin
as the leader of the group, supervisees may be called upon periodically as
the group's needs demand. In Turquet's (1974) words, leadership requires
"appraisal" rather than "discharge." The supervisor acts not so much to
direct the group as to create a climate in which the group finds its own direction. The supervisees' efforts should be evaluated in relation to the group's
efforts rather than by comparison with the efforts of the supervisor.

  Reflecting upon the goals for group supervision, one can deduce that each
of the five goals can be expanded to include leadership development. Mastery of concepts relative to leadership theory should be included in the more
academic dimensions of group supervision. In addition, supervisees should
be given opportunities to develop skills in leading their supervisory group as
preparation for leading other, "less receptive" groups of their own. Practice
in leading their peers will provide supervisees with the opportunity to exert
their power and influence under somewhat controlled conditions.

  Given that a group presents a microcosm of society, replete with a wide
variety of personal and interpersonal problems, group supervision offers a
unique opportunity for integrating theoretical concepts with practical problems.
As a result, "the need for a wide variety of expertise will allow all group
members the opportunity to exercise their influence at one time or another.
Those who seek to dominate or to be dominated should emerge, and these
life-styles will then be grist for the group mill" (Gazda, 1989, p. 64). The
effective group supervisor must first and foremost be an effective group leader.
Beyond possessing the requisite group work knowledge and skills, however,

the multiculturally competent group supervisor will also understand the culture of the supervisee, his or her clients, and the potential advantages and disadvantages of using a group format with these supervisees. Moreover, the supervisor must be aware of his or her own cultural identity and be willing to take risks interpersonally to confront racial and ethnic conflict.

Finally, the possibility of evaluation gives rise to important considerations about the nature and extent of one's influence over the group process and the nature of the supervisor's authority. Just as the counselor's effectiveness is measured ultimately by the client's success in meeting his or her own goals, so too supervisees must learn that their success lies in meeting their own goals relative to standards previously agreed upon.

Self-Disclosure

The person who enters a group is faced with a dilemma: how to become a part of the group's collective identity and at the same time preserve one's individual identity. Self-disclosure needs come into conflict as members seek affirmation for the resolution of past struggles, on the one hand, while fearing the disapproval that can come with confessing one's weaknesses on the other (see Lakin & Carson, 1966). Many supervisees are unsure about how much self-disclosure is appropriate within the supervision group. This dilemma can lead to role ambiguity and confusion. Ladany and Friedlander (1995) found that the stronger the working alliance between supervisors and supervisees, the clearer roles became to supervisees. Although self-disclosure is the principal vehicle of group interaction, Corey (1995) cautioned that "self-disclosure is foreign to the values of some cultural groups. This premium that is placed on self-disclosure by most therapeutic approaches is often in conflict with the values of some European ethnic groups that stress that problems should be kept 'in the family'" (p. 117). Sensitivity to the cultural norms related to self-disclosure in groups will help to avoid passive acceptance of stereotyping of "strong, silent" males, "shy" women, "stoic" Native Americans, "boisterous" African Americans, and the like.

Group supervision poses the problem, as noted earlier, of subjecting oneself to the potential criticism of one's peers in an effort to gain the approval of one's supervisor, and vice versa. Complicating the situation for the supervisor is the realization that supervisees may have different levels of need satisfaction (see Stockton & Morran, 1982; Thibault & Kelley, 1959). Group supervision offers supervisees a vivid demonstration of the differential needs of persons to self-disclose and can serve as an important object lesson in the need to respect clients' rights to self-disclose in their own ways. The group also offers an arena for supervisees to try out perspective-taking skills. Through listening to and understanding the self-disclosure of other members, supervisees can begin to juxtapose several different perspectives and recognize the value in each.

The benefits of self-disclosure in groups notwithstanding, group counselors are not of one mind about the use of self-disclosure in groups whose members are also evaluated by the leader. Donigian (1993) considered dual relationships in training group counselors to be "the issue that won't go away." Although generally in agreement about the importance of attending to power differentials in leading groups of supervisees, researchers (Donigian, 1993; Forester-Miller & Duncan, 1990; Herlihy & Corey, 1992; Merta & Sisson, 1991; Pierce & Baldwin, 1990; Remley, 1992) disagree about how best to protect the rights of the individual group member to limit self-disclosure, while also creating the proper conditions for realizing the personal benefits to be realized from self-disclosure in a group.

Roles

One of the great benefits of participation in a group is the opportunity to try out different roles with different people. Indeed, the great benefit to group supervision is the possibility of testing a variety of roles in practice situations. For the supervisor, group work provides the opportunity to try on a variety of roles as well (see Stenack & Dye, 1982). In a study of group supervision behaviors, Savickas et al. (1986, p. 23) found that students judged the following role requirements to be most important for group supervisors: (a) modeling target behaviors; teaching skills, techniques, and strategies; (b) evaluating performance; and (c) facilitating exploration, critical thought, and experimentation. Clearly, the most important role of the supervisor may be in modeling the variety of behaviors necessary to respond to the demands posed by different supervisees experiencing different problems.

☐ Group Development

Research (Bonney, 1976; Gibbard, Hartman, & Mann, 1974; Mills, 1964; Tuckman & Jensen, 1977; Yalom, 1995) has suggested that, although each group is unique, effective small groups follow a generalizable pattern from initiation to termination. This pattern is formed by a sequence of overlapping stages that are characterized by a set of focal concerns that rise and fail in importance as the group moves toward maturity. Although the particular names and boundaries of these stages vary from description to description, a fair synopsis of this research would provide a sequence similar to the one that follows.

> *Forming*: A stage of testing and encounter during which members attempt to find out who the members are and how they will relate to one another. There is a concern for individual needs, where security and safety are important elements.

Storming: A stage of intragroup conflict, emotional expression, and role modeling. Primary concerns are focused on the nature of legitimate authority, the role of the leader, and the proper balance between task and process variables.

Norming: A stage of group cohesion through the development of social sanctions. Members are engaged in identifying and evaluating group norms, in establishing acceptable roles within the group, and in redefining group and individual goals.

Performing: A stage of role-relatedness and production during which members come to terms with the realities of this group, its work, and the members' roles relative to the tasks to be accomplished.

Mourning: A stage of separation, assessment, and evaluation during which members must deal with the termination of this group experience, the consolidation of any personal gains, and the transition to a life after the group.

The supervisor who is aware of these different stages recognizes that different tasks must be performed relative to the stage-related needs of the group. During the forming stage, for instance, the supervisor is advised to provide a greater degree of structure and direction in helping supervisees establish personal goals for supervision and in modeling group-appropriate behaviors. To move the group into the storming stage, supervisors need to challenge supervisees to examine their reasons for being in the group and to take greater responsibility for their behavior.

Movement into the norming stage is facilitated by helping the group to identify norms already operating within the group and to encourage an analysis of their effectiveness relative to accomplishing individual and group goals. Of course, the general goals for the supervisory group remain, and it is during the performing stage that supervisees are encouraged to get down to the actual work of the group. Finally, if the group has been at all effective, members will be reluctant to end the experience and/or will attempt to ascribe any success to some uniqueness in the group or its members. During this mourning stage, the supervisor should help members to confront this denial process directly and to facilitate the important work of "letting go" of the group experience, recognizing both the losses and opportunities to be gained from termination. The interested reader is encouraged to consult Bernard and Goodyear (1998), Corey (1995), Gladding (1995), and Keith et al. (1992) for more detailed descriptions of stage-related group leader behaviors.

☐ Ethical Issues

Although the ethical practice of supervision should be guided by the general standards of the profession, group supervision provides its own particular set of ethical issues, for which the Association for Specialists in Group Work has provided a set of relevant ethical guidelines (ASGW, 1989). Although space limitations preclude a presentation of the full range of ethical issues, several core issues should be noted. These issues include informed consent, confidentiality, dual relationships, and group counseling competencies.

Informed Consent

Group supervisors are expected to prepare supervisees for participation in the group by providing information about the group process and content before the group begins. As with any group, supervisors should explain the purpose and content of the group and, especially with groups of supervisees, the necessary evaluation procedures. Because supervisees often find themselves in new roles in the context of group supervision, it is critical to clarify any changes in role definitions. Similarly, it becomes important to clarify other dimensions of the group experience to avoid potential confusion that can arise when supervisees carry over expectations from their participation in other groups or in other settings with the supervisor into the group supervision experience. In particular, it is important to attend to the following standards:

1. Entrance procedures such as time parameters, participation expectations, and termination procedures should be explained.
2. Supervisors should communicate the role expectations, rights, and responsibilities of supervisees, especially as differentiated from other roles they may have occupied, particularly in relationship to the supervisor.
3. The group goals related to supervision should be stated concisely and defined in terms of who is responsible for what goals.
4. Supervisors should explain to supervisees the risks associated with participation, especially those related to self-disclosure, confidentiality, and evaluation.

Confidentiality

The group setting allows supervisees to learn more directly about difficulties in maintaining group confidentiality. Supervisors should discuss the complexity of confidentiality in the group. Unlike the individual setting, in the group, confidentiality cannot be assured by the supervisor. Instead, each member must make the decision for herself or himself to maintain confidentiality. It is also the supervisor's responsibility to explain the limits of confidentiality to the supervisee regarding such issues as unethical or illegal behavior on the part of the supervisee or similar disclosures by the supervisee's clients that may not be kept in confidence once revealed to the supervisor or other group members. In particular, group supervisors should take steps to protect members by defining confidentiality and its limits; they should also make members aware of the difficulties involved in enforcing and ensuring confidentiality in a group setting, noting that as supervisors they can only ensure confidentiality on their own parts, but that it is expected of the other members in their roles as professionals.

Supervisees that are required to participate in group supervision should be made aware of any reporting procedures that are required of the supervisor, and group supervisors are obligated to store or dispose of any records in ways that maintain confidentiality within the limits set by their contract as members of the group. This limitation is especially relevant for university faculty in their role as clinical supervisors who will be called upon to verify the supervisee's experience under supervision and perhaps to evaluate the supervisee's performance as part of degree requirements or for potential internship sites or employers. Setting such standards not only protects the welfare of the supervisees but models the relevant ethical behavior for supervisees leading their own groups.

Dual Relationships

The group setting places most supervisors in a dual relationship with supervisees. Often the supervisor serves as group leader, evaluator, advisor, and teacher at the same time. Although counselors typically avoid dual relationships with their clients, clear boundaries are usually not possible for the group supervisor. Because of their multiple relationships, it is important that group supervisors consistently monitor their own objectivity and professional judgment by adhering to the standards outlined above. As a hedge against the erosion of objectivity, the supervisor is advised to seek regular consultation with other colleagues. In addition to the customary admonitions to professional counselors not to misuse their professional role and power to advance personal or social contacts with clients, to engage in sexual intimacies, or to further their own interests either during the group or after the termination of the group, group supervisors are especially directed to discuss with supervisees the potential detrimental effects of group members engaging in intimate intermember relationships outside of the group. Because it is not uncommon for supervisees to have preexisting relationships as coworkers, colleagues, or friends, it is vital that the supervisor clarify these relationships publicly with the other supervisees and point out the potential difficulties that can arise within the group as sensitive interpersonal issues arise in the course of supervision.

In addition to these ethical standards, supervisors should consider the standards associated with referral, coercion and pressure, imposing counselor values, equitable treatment, voluntary/involuntary participation, leaving a group, and use of technique.

Group Counseling Competencies

A final standard for the ethical practice of supervision relates to the obligation of counseling professionals to "practice only within the boundaries of their competence, based on their education, training, supervised experience, state and national professional credentials, and appropriate professional experience" (American Counseling Association, 1995, p. 7). This obligation is especially relevant for group supervisors, given that training in this area is the least likely to be had of all forms of supervision. As with the ethical guidelines noted above, the Association for Specialists in Group Work (1990) has identified core competencies for group leaders (cognitive and applied) and set minimal standards for the preparation of group workers. Drawing upon an earlier version of these standards, Gazda (1989, pp. 477–480) has reproduced an extensive list of competencies and performance criteria for group counseling. Because space does not permit a detailed presentation of these competencies here, the interested reader is encouraged to consult the original sources. Certainly the supervisor interested in conducting group supervision should be familiar with and competent to at least these prescribed levels prior to initiating group supervision.

Additionally, in its *Core Group Work Standards*, ASGW (1998a) recommended the following types of supervised experience: (a) one course in basic group work knowledge and skills, and (b) observation and participation in a group experience (minimum of 10 hours and a recommendation of 20 clock hours for graduation from a master's level program).

These minimum requirements for training in group counseling are consistent with the standards currently in force for counselor education programs accredited by the Council for the Accreditation of Counseling and Related Educational Programs (CACREP). Nonetheless, they are considered to be minimal standards for beginning practitioners and do not constitute more advanced standards that might be appropriate for supervisors of group counseling supervisees. Certainly the aspiring group supervisor is encouraged to pursue the full range of training experiences. Recurrent immersion in multiple group formats with different leaders using different modalities promises to be the best course of action for enhancing the professional's skills in group supervision.

☐ Conclusion

Despite its shaky beginnings and the inflated claims of earlier proponents, group work continues to promise unique opportunities for training in counseling. Its wide acceptance in counselor supervision is tempered by the recognition that a systematic analysis of the process of group supervision has yet to be reported. Nonetheless, supervisors and counselor educators in search of ways to improve their supervision are faced with numerous excellent proposals. Until the necessary program of systematic research reveals the connections between group supervision and counselor effectiveness, supervisors are well advised to take heed of the suggestions for practice offered in the studies cited here. And above all, become involved in the systematic examination of your own and others' behavior both as a member and as a leader of supervised groups.

☐ References

Altfield, D., & Bernard, H. (1997). An experiential group for group psychotherapy supervision. In C. E. Watkins (Ed.), *Handbook of psychotherapy supervision* (pp. 381–399). New York: Wiley.

Amerel, M. (1989). Some observations on a model of professional training: The developmental teacher education program. *The Genetic Epistemologist, 17,* 31–38.

American Counseling Association. (1995). *Code of ethics and standards of practice.* Alexandria, VA: Author.

Association for Specialists in Group Work. (1989). *Ethical guidelines for group counselors.* Alexandria, VA: Author.

Association for Specialists in Group Work. (1990). *Professional standards for the training of group workers.* Alexandria, VA: Author.

Association for Specialists in Group Work. (1998a). *Core group work standards.* Alexandria, VA: Author.

Association for Specialists in Group Work. (1998b). *Principles for diversity-competent group workers.* Alexandria, VA: Author.

Bernard, J. M. (1992). The challenge of psychotherapy-based supervision: Making the pieces fit. *Counselor Education and Supervision, 31,* 232–237.

Bernard, J. M., & Goodyear, R. K. (1998). *Fundamentals of clinical supervision* (2nd ed.). Needham Heights, MA: Allyn & Bacon.

Birk, J. M., & Mahalik, J. R. (1996). The influence of trainee conceptual level, trainee anxiety, and supervision evaluation on counselor developmental level. *Clinical Supervisor,14,* 123–137.

Blocher, D. (1983). Toward a cognitive developmental approach to counseling supervision. *Counseling Psychologist, 11,* 9–18.

Bonney, W. C. (1976). Group counseling and developmental processes. In G. M. Gazda (Ed.), *Theories and methods of group counseling in the schools* (2nd ed., pp. 313–342). Springfield, IL: Charles C. Thomas.

Borders, L. D., & Fong, M. L. (1989). Ego development and counseling ability during training. *Counselor Education and Supervision, 29,* 71–83.

Burke, A. W. (1984). The outcome of the multi-racial small group experience. *International Journal of Social Psychiatry, 30,* 96–101.

Coche, E. (1977). Training of group therapists. In F. Kaslow (Ed.), *Supervision, consultation, and staff training in the helping professions* (pp. 235–253). San Francisco: Jossey-Bass.

Cohen, M., Gross, S., & Turner, M. (1976). A note on a developmental model for training family therapists through group supervision. *Journal of Marriage and Family Counseling, 2,* 48–56.

Cooper, L., & Gustafson, J. P. (1985). Supervision in a group: An application of group theory. *Clinical Supervisor, 3,* 7–25.

Corey, G. (1995). *Theory and practice of group counseling* (4th ed.). Pacific Grove, CA: Brooks/Cole.

D'Andrea, M. (1988). The counselor as pacer: A model for revitalization of the counseling profession. In R. L. Hayes & R. Aubrey (Eds.), *New directions for counseling and human development* (pp. 22–44). Denver, CO: Love Publishing.

Dagley, J., Gazda, G., & Pistone, C. (1986). Groups. In M. Lewis, R. Hayes, & J. Lewis (Eds.), *An introduction to the counseling profession* (pp. 130–166). Itasca, IL: F. E. Peacock.

Day, J. M. (1993). Moral development and small-group processes: Learning from research. *Journal for Specialists in Group Work, 18,* 55–66.

Dies, R. (1980). Group psychotherapy: Training and supervision. In A K. Hess (Ed.), *Psychotherapy supervision* (pp. 337–366). New York: Wiley.

Donigian, J. (1993). Duality: The issue that won't go away. *Journal for Specialists in Group Work, 18,* 137–140.

Ellis, M., & Douce, L. (1994). Group supervision of novice clinical supervisors: Eight recurring issues. *Journal of Counseling and Development, 72,* 520–525.

Forester-Miller, H., & Duncan, J. (1990). The ethics of dual relationships in the training of group counselors. *Journal for Specialists in Group Work, 15,* 88–93.

Gazda, G. (1989). *Group counseling: A developmental approach* (4th ed.). Boston: Allyn & Bacon.

Getzel, G. S., & Salmon, R. (1985). Group supervision: An organizational approach. *Clinical Supervisor, 3,* 27–43.

Gibbard, G., Hartman, J., & Mann, R. (Eds.). (1974). *Analysis of groups.* San Francisco: Jossey-Bass.

Gibbs, J. T. (1985). Can we continue to be color-blind and class bound? *The Counseling Psychologist, 13,* 426–435.

Gladding, S. T. (1995). *Group work: A counseling specialty* (2nd ed.). Englewood Cliffs, NJ: Prentice-Hall.

Greeley, A. T., Garcia, V. L., Kessler, B. L., & Gilchrest, G. (1992). Training effective multicultural group counselors: Issues for a group training course. *Journal for Specialists in Group Work, 17,* 197–209.

Hart, G. M. (1982). *The process of clinical supervision.* Baltimore: University Park Press.

Hayes, R. L. (1991). Group work and the teaching of ethics. *Journal for Specialists in Group Work, 16,* 24–31.

Hayes, R. L., & Lunsford, B. (1994). Elements of empowerment: Enhancing efforts for school renewal. *People and Education, 2*(1), pp. 83–100.

Herlihy, B., & Corey, G. (1992). *Dual relationships in counseling.* Alexandria, VA: American Association for Counseling and Development.

Hillerbrand, E. T. (1992). Cognitive differences between experts and novices: Implications for group supervision. *Journal of Counseling and Development, 68,* 684–691.

Holloway, E. L. (1987). Developmental models of supervision: Is it supervision? *Professional Psychology: Research and Practice, 18,* 209–216.

Holloway, E., & Johnston, R. (1985). Group supervision: Widely practiced but poorly understood. *Counselor Education and Supervision, 24,* 332–340.

Holloway, E. L., & Wampold, B. E. (1986). Relationship between conceptual level and counseling-related tasks: A meta-analysis. *Journal of Counseling Psychology, 33,* 310–319.

Johnson, D. W., & Johnson, R. T. (1992). *Positive interdependence: The heart of cooperative learning.* Edina, MN: Interaction Book Company.

Johnson, D. W., & Johnson, F. P. (1997). *Joining together: Group theory and group skills* (6th ed.). Boston: Allyn & Bacon.

Kaul, T., & Bednar, R. (1978). Conceptualizing group research: A preliminary analysis. *Small Group Behavior, 9,*173–191.

Keith, D. V., Connell, G., & Whitaker, C. A. (1992). Group supervision in symbolic experiential family therapy. *Journal of Family Psychology, 3,* 93–109.

Knowles, M., & Knowles, H. (1959). *Introduction to group dynamics.* New York: Association Press.

Ladany, N., & Friedlander, M. L. (1995). Trainees' experience of role conflict and role ambiguity in supervisory relationships. *Journal of Counseling Psychology, 39,* 389–397.

Lakin, M. (1976). The human relations training laboratory: A special case of the experiential group. In M. Rosenbaum & A. Snadowsky (Eds.), *The intensive group experience.* New York: The Free Press.

Lakin, M., & Carson, R. (1966). A therapeutic vehicle in search of a theory of therapy. *Journal of Applied Behavioral Science, 2,* 27–40.

Leach, M. M., Stoltenberg, C. D., McNeill, B. W., & Eichenfield, G. A. (1997). Self-efficacy and counselor development: Testing the integrated developmental model. *Counselor Education and Supervision, 37,* 115–124.

Leong, F. T. (1992). Guidelines for minimizing premature termination among Asian American clients in group counseling. *Journal for Specialists in Group Work, 17,* 218–288.

Merta, R. J. (1995). Group work: Multicultural perspectives. In J. G. Ponterotto, J. M. Casas, L. A. Suzuki, & C. M. Alexander (Eds.), *Handbook of multicultural counseling* (pp. 567–585). Thousand Oaks, CA: Sage.

Merta, R., & Sisson, J. A. (1991). The experiential group: An ethical and professional dilemma. *Journal for Specialists in Group Work, 16,* 236–245.

Mills, T. M. (1964). *Group transformation: An analysis of a learning group.* Englewood Cliffs, NJ: Prentice-Hall.

Paisley, P. O. (1990). Counselor involvement in promoting the development of beginning teachers. *Journal of Humanistic Education and Development, 29,* 20–31.

Pierce, K. A., & Baldwin, C. (1990). Participation versus privacy in the training of group counselors. *Journal for Specialists in Group Work, 15,* 149–158.

Power, C., Higgins, A., & Kohlberg, L. (1989). *Lawrence Kohlberg's approach to moral education.* New York: Columbia University Press.

Prieto, L. (1996). Group supervision: Still widely practiced but poorly understood. *Counselor Education and Supervision, 35,* 295–307.

Reisman, B. (1985). Conflict between teaching a group class and being an ethical counselor. *Michigan Personnel and Guidance Journal, 16*(2), 35–39.

Remley, T. (1992). A model for teaching a graduate course in group counseling. *Together: Association for Specialists in Group Work Newsletter, 20*(2), 10–11.

Rigazio-Digilio, S. A., & Anderson, S. A. (1994). A cognitive-developmental model for marital and family therapy supervision. *Clinical Supervisor, 12,* 93–118.

Riva, M. T., & Cornish, J. A. (1995). Group supervision practices at a psychology predoctoral internship program: A national survey. *Professional Psychology: Research and Practice, 26*(5), 523–525.

Rosenbaum, M., & Snadowsky, A. (1976). *The intensive group experience: A guide.* New York: Free Press.

Russell, R. K., Crimmings, A. M., & Lent, R. W. (1984). Counselor training and supervision: Theory and research. In S. D. Brown & R. W. Lent (Ed.), *Handbook of counseling psychology* (pp. 625–681). New York: Wiley.

Sansbury, D. (1982). Developmental supervision from a skills perspective. *The Counseling Psychologist, 10,* 53–58.

Savickas, M., Marquart, C., & Supinski, C. (1986). Effective supervision in groups. *Counselor Education and Supervision, 26,* 17–25.

Shapiro, J. (1978). *Methods of group psychotherapy and encounter.* Itasca, IL: F. E. Peacock.

Slavin, R. E. (1983). *Cooperative learning.* New York: Longman.

Sprinthall, N., Reiman, A., & Thies-Sprinthall, L. (1993). Role-taking and reflection: Promoting the conceptual and moral development of teachers. *Learning and Individual Differences, 5*(4), 283–299.

Stenack, R. J., & Dye, H. (1982). Behavioral descriptions of counseling supervision roles. *Counselor Education and Supervision, 21,* 295–304.

Stockton, R., & Morran, D. K. (1982). Review and perspective of critical dimensions of therapeutic small group research. In G. Gazda (Ed.), *Basic approaches to group psychotherapy and group counseling* (3rd ed.). Springfield, IL: Charles C. Thomas.

Swensen, C. (1980). Ego development and a general model for counseling and psychotherapy. *Personnel and Guidance Journal, 58,* 382–388.

Tauber, L. (1978). Choice point analysis-formulation, strategy, intervention, and result in group psychotherapy, and supervision. *International Journal of Group Psychotherapy, 28,* 163–184.

Tennyson, W. W., & Strom, S. M. (1986). Beyond professional standards: Developing responsibleness. *Journal of Counseling and Development, 64*, 298–302.

Thibault, J., & Kelley, H. (1959). *The social psychology of groups.* New York: Wiley.

Tuckman, B., & Jensen, M. (1977). Stages of small group development revisited. *Group and Organizational Studies, 2*, 419–427.

Turquet, P. (1974). Leadership: The individual and the group. In G. Gibbard, J. Hartman, & R. Mann (Eds.), *Analysis of groups* (pp. 349–371). San Francisco: Jossey-Bass.

Wasik, B. H., & Fishbein, J. E. (1982). Problem solving: A model for supervision in professional psychology. *Professional Psychology, 13*, 559–564.

Weinstein, G., & Alschuler, A. (1987). Educating and counseling for self-knowledge development. *Journal of Counseling and Development, 64*, 19–25.

Werstlein, P. O., & Borders, L. D. (1997). Group process variables in group supervision. *Journal for Specialists in Group Work, 22*, 120–136.

Wilbur, M. P., Roberts-Wilbur, J., Morris, J. R., Betz, R. L., & Hart, G. M. (1991). Structured group supervision: Theory into practice. *Journal for Specialists in Group Work, 16* (2), 91–100.

Yalom, I. (1995). *The theory and practice of group psychotherapy* (4th ed.). New York: Basic Books.

Yogev, S. (1982). An eclectic model of supervision: A developmental sequence for beginning psychotherapy students. *Professional Psychology, 13*, 236–243.

Young-Eisendrath, P. (1985, January). Making use of human development theories in counseling. *Counseling and Human Development, 17*, 1–12.

Sandy Magnuson
Ken Norem
Loretta J. Bradley

Supervising School Counselors

Kary was a first year, recently certified counselor in a small, rural K–12 school. Having graduated from a progressive counselor preparation program, Kary enthusiastically designed and planned implementation of a comprehensive developmental counseling program.

Kary's enthusiasm became a source of energy and flexibility during the first several weeks of school. Parents, students, faculty, and administration seemed receptive to several new ideas for developing a career resource center, conducting developmental guidance activities in collaboration with classroom teachers, and working with students in counseling groups.

Shortly after the first basketball game, Kary received a disturbing phone call from a parent. Mrs. Washington told Kary that her husband, the father of three children in the school, was dying of cancer. She said the children were having difficulties coping with their father's chronic illness and impending death. Mrs. Washington thought that Cassandra, the oldest child, was depressed. She had lost interest in many after-school activities she had previously enjoyed. Mrs. Washington was particularly concerned because Cassandra wanted to resign from her lead position on the debate team. Ten-year-old Shonteria had cried before going to school for the previous 2 weeks. She wanted to stay home to be sure her father was well cared for. Ivan, a typically rambunctious 5-year-old, had been awakened by nightmares during the past couple of weeks. Mrs. Washington requested family counseling to facilitate communication about the difficult challenges they encountered. She also asked Kary to schedule individual counseling for Cassandra.

Kary was in a quandary. The ethical codes prohibiting counselors from providing services for which they are not trained seemed to develop the capacity to speak . . . loudly. The fact that there was no other mental health professional in the rural community haunted Kary as well. Who could meet the critical needs of this family? To whom could Kary turn for help? The answer was uniform and clear: No one.

Kary's former classmate's experience as a beginning counselor was quite different. Upon graduation, Pat submitted an application to the state's board of examiners in counseling and began the process of selecting a supervisor. As soon as the board authorized a provisional license, Pat accepted a position in a community mental health center. Pat worked under the supervision of an approved clinical supervisor. In addition to weekly individual supervision and biweekly group seminars, the supervisor was available for consultation whenever Pat had questions or concerns.

The contrasts between Pat's and Kary's entries into the counseling profession are representative of the experiences their peers encounter in other communities, in other states.

In most states, counselor licensure requires supervised experience ranging from 2,000 to 3,000 hours beyond the master's degree. Typical regulations include specifications related to supervisors' experience and preparation as well as the frequency of supervision meetings. On the other hand, when school counselors, such as Kary, complete requirements for a master's degree they are expected to immediately provide proficient counseling services (Matthes, 1992; Van Zandt & Perry, 1992). This situation is exacerbated in isolated areas, where opportunities for continuing education and consultation with other counselors are limited (Sutton & Page, 1994). Indeed, these differences between postacademic supervision requirements for counselors who are certified to work in schools and counselors who wish to be licensed to work in community agencies warrant attention.

Competent school counselors are skilled clinicians who recognize and meet multiple and diverse needs of children. They respond to crises. They are astute in areas of curriculum planning and career development. They are skillful consultants. They plan and implement comprehensive counseling programs. They may be the only professional counselors who are available to provide mental health services. Indeed, school counselors often have a broader scope of responsibilities than their counterparts in community settings.

Having been school counselors who also had supervised experience in community settings, we recognize the value of clinical supervision. Like many school counselors, we relied on advanced clinical skills on a daily basis (Sutton & Page, 1994). We also appreciate the difficulties school counselors encounter in obtaining supervision. However, the challenges in securing supervision do not diminish its importance and value, particularly when we examine empirical evidence that has shown a correlation between supervised experience and counselors' professional growth. A commensurate correlation has not been shown between unsupervised experience and professional growth (Wiley & Ray, 1986).

Adequately addressing the complexity and depth of school counselors' roles requires comparable supervision, encompassing (a) administrative concerns, (b) clinical skills, (c) program development skills (Roberts & Borders, 1994; Schmidt, 1990), and (d) professional growth (Henderson & Gysbers, 1998). Principals typically provide administrative supervision as they oversee policies and procedures that govern the school community. Clinical supervision comprises conceptual understanding and skills related to counseling and consultation. Program supervision focuses on development, implementation, and coordination of comprehensive school counseling programs. Finally, developmental supervision contributes to supervisees' professional maturity and commitment.

Clearly, our intent is not to minimize the importance of principals' responsibilities. However, administrative supervision is readily available to most school counselors, whereas the clinical, program, and developmental elements of supervision often appear to be neglected. In fact, school counselors are typically supervised exclusively by building principals who are trained in administration; thus it is reasonable to expect that novice counselors will become more effective in areas related to administrative duties. This expertise may be at the expense of enhanced counselor effectiveness (Crutchfield & Borders, 1997). The foci of supervision advocated in this chapter will be on clinical, program, and developmental components.

☐ A Novel Idea, or One That Has Been Promoted Before?

The notion that school counselors need supervision is neither new nor novel. In fact, dialogue related to supervision of school counselors seems to parallel the profession's development. For example, in 1924, Brewer commended the work of vocational counselors in Boston schools; however, he expressed concern about the lack of coordination and supervision. A decade later, Fitch (1936) asserted that there was "no conceivable training which could be too broad for workers in this field of vocational guidance. . . . No one living is both intelligent enough and sufficiently well informed to deal with all the problems that may arise" (p. 760). Fitch further suggested that counselors' roles were subject to erosion when supervision was provided exclusively by building principals. Several years later, Boyd and Walter (1975) likened an unsupervised school counselor to a "cactus that does not receive needed sustenance" (p. 103). These authors asserted that the absence of supervision impeded the professional growth of counselors, rendering them "stunted specimens" (p. 103). In the 1980s, Barret and Schmidt (1986) emphasized the need for systematic supervision of school counselors and challenged the counseling profession to establish national standards for supervision of counselors in all settings. Contemporary journal literature reflects continued emphasis on the importance of clinical supervision for school counselors (e.g., Crutchfield & Borders, 1997; Sutton & Page, 1994). Within the broader field of postacademic supervision, Borders and Usher (1992) investigated exist-ing practices. School counselors represented the largest group of counselors to practice without supervision. Similarly, Ladany, Lehrman-Waterman, Mo-linaro, and Wolgast (1999) investigated ethical practices in supervision as perceived by counselors-in-training. Although the number of school coun-selors-in-training was limited, these participants reported a greater number of supervisory ethical violations than their colleagues in other settings.

The topic of supervision for school counselors was featured in two recent issues of *Counseling Today* (Crespi & Fischetti, 1998; Hayes, 1998). In a guest editorial Crespi and Fischetti emphasized its importance and called attention to the absence of clinical supervision for school counselors. They challenged school counselors and professional associations to assume leadership in ad-dressing the void in postacademic supervision. Crespi and Fischetti asserted that systematic clinical supervision is "one of the most important continu-ing education and professional development tools available for school coun-selors" that "could serve as a vehicle for emphasizing the unique and vital role counselors make in the schools" (p. 19).

A similar challenge was directed to individual counselors in a subsequent column (Hayes, 1998). The author quoted counselor educator Lori Crutchfield, who challenged school counselors to discuss the importance of clinical super-vision with their principals. School counselor Carl Bucciantini endorsed Crutchfield's statement, but added, "We are our own worst enemies. Once we have finished our training, many counselors figure we don't need super-vision anymore" (p. 19).

The need for school counselor supervision also attracted attention on CESNET, a listserv providing a forum of communication among profes-sional counselors interested in supervision and training. A recent series of entries affirmed the need to assure that counselors who work in schools receive clinical supervision. One subscriber suggested that children's needs warranted highly skilled school counselors who had the benefit of clinical supervision. Another subscriber spoke of the severity and diversity of chil-dren's problems as added support for postacademic supervision for school counselors. Another subscriber seemed to express the profession's frustra-tion related to postacademic supervision. Simply stated, she was tired of rhetoric and wanted to hear no more unless it was accompanied by action.

Several challenges have been encountered in the development of pro-grams designed to move beyond rhetoric and provide supervision opportu-nities for school counselors. Qualified supervisors are often unavailable (Bens-hoff & Paisley, 1996; Peace, 1995; Sutton & Page, 1994). In addition to the scarcity of school counselors who are trained as supervisors, financial re-sources are limited. Other potential obstacles relate to time restraints per-ceived by practicing counselors, potential supervisors, or building principals (Crutchfield et al., 1997; Schmidt, 1990). Counselors may also be reluctant to participate in supervision because they are anxious about recording counsel-ing activities and receiving feedback from others (Crutchfield et al., 1997).

☐ Moving Beyond the Rhetoric

Successful Initiatives

Despite the obstacles, many initiatives to provide supervision for school counselors have been quite successful. For example, school districts have employed counseling program coordinators who augment administrative leadership with clinical, program, and developmental supervision. In other districts colleagues meet informally for peer supervision. When cooperative relationships exist with counselor education programs, university faculty provide leadership and training in supervision for counselors.

Contemporary professional literature provides encouraging information about systematic efforts to provide supervision for school settings. Table 8.1 presents a summary of representative initiatives, and the following discussion highlights four of the projects.

A peer consultation approach was coordinated by Benshoff and Paisley (1996). Subsequent to a group orientation meeting, peer consultants met during eight sessions which were guided by a structured protocol. Session topics included discussions of professional issues, review of audiotapes, and presentations of case studies. Continuing education credits provided additional incentive for participating counselors.

Henderson and Lampe (1992) described a dyadic supervision model. Training sessions equipped experienced school counselors with fundamental supervision skills. Upon completion of the supervision training, they supervised counselors who conducted activities involving career or educational planning, individual counseling, consultation, and referrals. The supervision process involved (a) preobservation conferences, (b) observations, (c) observation data analyses, (d) postobservation conferences, and (e) analyses of the postobservation conference.

A counselor–mentor program also reflected a two-tier training and supervision model (Peace, 1995; Peace & Sprinthall, 1998). Experienced school counselors completed a 15-week sequence of training sessions. Subsequently the counselors participated in a supervised practicum during which they supervised novice school counselors, colleagues requesting supervision, or graduate student trainees. Group supervision-of-supervision was provided throughout the practicum. Research related to the professional development of both the supervisors and supervisees documented the efficacy of this program (Peace, 1995; Peace & Sprinthall, 1998).

Group formats have also been effective modalities for supervision of school counselors. For example, Crutchfield et al. (1997) participated in a series of weekly group supervision sessions. Group members played portions of recorded counseling sessions and invited feedback. Experiences were enhanced as group members assumed varying roles, perspectives, or tasks during the videotape segment and subsequently gave feedback from their assigned

TABLE 8.1. School counselor supervision models

Author(s)	Year	Modality	Key features
Boyd & Walter	1975	Group training, dyadic supervision	Head counselors trained as supervisors. Job descriptions modified to reflect supervisory responsibilities.
Henderson & Lampe	1992	Dyadic: Trained supervising counselor and new school counselor	Live observation followed by conference and conjoint evaluation of process.
Van Zandt & Perry	1992	Dyadic: Mentor/ protégé	Statewide project, training component for mentors.
Splete & Grisdale	1992	Large group	Monthly training sessions addressing topics determined via needs assessment.
Peace & Sprinthall	1995 1998	Group and dyadic	Extensive supervisor training. Clinical supervision provided during supervisors' practicum.
Benshoff & Paisley	1996	Dyadic: Peers	Nine-session structured format. Review of tapes. Presentations of case studies. Continuing education credits awarded for participation.
Crutchfield et al.	1997	Peer group	Structured weekly meetings. Taped counseling sessions reviewed. Roles assigned to group members.
Getz	In press	Peer group	A 3-year sequence including initial training in supervision, supervision-or-peer supervision, and autonomous peer supervision with consultation available.

perspectives. In this process, the supervisor (a counselor educator) served as a moderator and process observer.

Getz (in press) described a collaborative 3-year supervision project involving a counselor educator and elementary school counselors. During the first year, the counselor educator provided structure and training in various supervision methods. The next year counselors were divided into groups of four, which met four times for peer supervision. The counselor educator met one time with each group to provide supervision of the peer supervision process. Additionally, each peer group received feedback on the peer supervision processes after being observed by the other groups. During the third year the groups met autonomously, and the counselor educator remained available to provide consultation. Self-report data indicated that the processes contributed to counseling skills, supervision skills, and job satisfaction.

Recommended Initiatives for Individuals

Whether or not organized programs for supervision are available, individual counselor educators, school counselors, and school administrators can assume responsibilities for encouraging and creating supervision opportunities for school counselors. Collaboration among these stakeholders undoubtedly contributes to more efficient results. At the same time, counselors in schools where collaboration is not possible need not be deprived of the professional and personal benefits resulting from supervision. Counselor educators, practicum site supervisors, beginning school counselors, and building principals are encouraged to consider unique contributions they can offer to this endeavor as they peruse the following suggestions.

Counselor Educators

Counselor educators have many opportunities to promote supervision across the professional lifespan. For example, program faculty can emphasize the importance of clinical supervision, discuss alternatives for obtaining postgraduate supervision, and remain available to graduates of their programs, offering continuing education courses, consultation, and various forms of supervision. They can also collaborate with school administrators to provide consultation regarding comprehensive school counseling programs and appropriate strategies for effective administrative supervision of school counselors.

Skills required for effective supervision are distinctly different than those required to be effective as a counselor (Bernard & Goodyear, 1998; Magnuson & Wilcoxon, 1998a). Thus, counselor educators can engage other stakeholders by providing training and supervision-of-supervision to exemplary school counselors who, in turn, will become supervisors in schools. The

National Board for Certified Counselors (NBCC, 1998) Approved Clinical Supervisor designation may provide incentive for school counselors to acquire formal training in supervision. This certification, documenting supervisors' training and experience, was designed to be inclusive of counselor supervisors in school settings.

Counselor educators' most crucial contribution may be selecting practicum and internship sites where qualified supervisors are available and comprehensive school counseling programs are modeled. As program faculty design field experiences, they contribute to trainees' first impressions of nonacademic supervision. Indirectly, they support professionally adopted standards for school counseling. On the other hand, when counselor educators abdicate their responsibility for assuring that trainees receive scrupulous supervision addressing all elements of comprehensive school counseling programs, they risk indirectly perpetuating a cycle in which school counselors engage primarily in administrative and clerical activities while neglecting critical responsibilities such as individual counseling and prevention activities.

Practicum and Internship Site Supervisors

School counselors who supervise master's level trainees are in pivotal positions to simultaneously introduce counselors-in-training to quality supervision and cultivate sound school counseling practices. Conversely, when counselors without adequate preparation assume responsibility for supervising trainees, they may inadvertently portray supervision as a superficial requirement and miss opportunities to adequately prepare individual members of the next generation of school counselors.

As site supervisors participate with university personnel and trainees in structuring supervised experiences, they implicitly endorse the importance of supervision, and they indirectly teach counselors-in-training how to effectively participate in supervisory relationships. For example, investing time in becoming acquainted with trainees communicates, "Supervision is an interpersonal relationship." Defining goals, methods for attaining them, and procedures for assessment progress toward them conveys, "Supervision is an intentional relationship." Scheduling regular supervision meetings, observing developmental guidance lessons, reviewing tapes of individual counseling sessions, and giving feedback says, "As your supervisor, I am invested in this interpersonal, intentional relationship and in your professional growth."

Of course, site supervisors' primary mission is to support the growth and development of counselors-in-training through modeling, teaching, and mentoring. Initial reactions to practicum placements often include anxiety, confusion, and fluctuating levels of motivation (Stoltenberg, McNeill, & Delworth, 1998). Thus, beginning trainees rely on supervisors to facilitate a safe, encouraging, and structured environment, particularly until their anxiety dissipates and their confidence begins to grow.

Balancing support with the responsibility of fostering professional growth may constitute one of supervisors' greatest challenges. Site supervisors may be the first to recognize trainees' tendency to minimize the magnitude of school counselors' comprehensive responsibilities, their subtle efforts to avoid individual counseling, or their discomfort with classroom activities. As deficits in knowledge and skills manifest themselves, site supervisors are immediately available to address confusion, facilitate acquisition of clinical skills, and contribute to trainees' professional autonomy.

Practicing School Counselors

Practicing school counselors are probably the essential stakeholders for assuring that they receive supervision. Increased recognition of benefits derived from supervision as well as available opportunities for supervision can motivate school counselors to initiate supervisory relationships. As they understand the importance of postgraduate supervision, they will also be empowered to communicate the need for clinical supervision to their building principals. Ideally, principals will respond by (a) hiring or contracting with qualified counseling supervisors, (b) providing training in clinical supervision for experienced counselors in the district, (c) endorsing systematic supervision, or (d) negotiating a collaborative relationship with counselor education program faculty to provide supervision for school counselors. If clinical supervision is not provided by the school, counselors may acquire supervision by (a) enrolling in postgraduate courses, (b) engaging other counselors in peer group supervision, (c) requesting supervision from faculty in counselor education programs, or (d) individually contracting with a supervisor.

☐ Initiating a Supervisory Relationship With School Counselors: Considerations and Processes

Several entries in the professional literature propose models for coordinating programs to provide supervision for school counselors. Fewer models are available to guide individual supervisors who provide clinical supervision for school counselors. Thus, we recommend the broader literature related to clinical supervision of counselors for structuring supervisory relationships in schools. In that regard, many chapters within this book and the entries cited in this chapter's reference section are among the excellent resources available. Additionally, Kratochwill, Lepage, and McGivern (1997) provided guidelines specific to supervising counselors who work with children and adolescents.

Although many of the principles for effective supervision in community contexts generalize to school settings, unique elements of school counselors' responsibilities warrant discussion. For example, disagreements regarding appropriate and desired roles for school counselors often result in confusion, particularly for beginning school counselors. Novice counselors may ask, "How much time should I devote to individual counseling?" or "What is my role when working with families?" Beginning counselors often feel disempowered by discrepancies between administrative assignments and comprehensive counseling program models advocated by their professors. They may feel overwhelmed by the magnitude of students' diverse needs and cultural backgrounds. Because the nature of their work demands negotiation rather than avoidance of dual relationships, they may feel anxious about potential violations of ethical guidelines. School counselors also encounter dilemmas when administrative policies or laws contradict professional guidelines.

Thus seasoned school counselors who are skilled supervisors can become a powerful influence and a valuable resource for new counselors. The following recommendations for supervising new school counselors reflect an integration of fundamental guidelines related to clinical supervision and school counseling.

One of the most critical meetings between supervisors and supervisees occurs when they first meet to discuss the possibilities of engaging in a supervisory relationship (see Bordin, 1983). During this initial encounter, lasting impressions will develop that influence the decision to proceed with supervision, the quality of the interpersonal relationship, and the nature of supervisory processes. Well-advised supervisees and supervisors carefully prepare for inquiry sessions, which are often viewed as reciprocal interviews.

Counselors who provide supervision in school settings have the same ethical and legal responsibilities as their counterparts in community settings. Thus, it is important to continually review ethical guidelines, legislation, and court decisions governing both supervision and school counseling. Supervisors initially demonstrate ethical and legal competence by discussing (a) their professional credentials, experience, training, and areas of expertise; (b) their philosophies of school counseling and supervision; (c) their expectations and requirements; (d) parameters related to legal and ethical responsibilities; and (e) ethical codes to which they adhere. Financial arrangements, if appropriate, should also be predetermined. Disclosure statements required for NBCC Approved Clinical Supervisor certification (NBCC, 1998) may be used to communicate comprehensive information about supervisory approaches (see also Atkinson, 1997; McCarthy et al., 1995).

In preparation for the initial meeting, inquiring supervisees should identify their primary purposes for requesting supervision, their preferences for supervisory modalities, and the areas of professional growth they wish to emphasize during supervision. They should also prepare questions that will help appraise the potential for a productive supervisory relationship.

Supervisors may ask supervisees to authorize consultation with former supervisors. It would be equally appropriate for supervisees to request the supervisors' permission to contact former and current supervisees. In this context, both parties could take advantage of the opportunity to examine the potential for interpersonal and professional compatibility, as well as the correspondence between supervisors' areas of expertise and supervisees' primary professional needs and interests.

Contracting should be based on mutual confidence in the potential for a productive working relationship (Bordin, 1983). Written agreements are generally recommended to assure explicit understanding of the various facets of the supervisory relationship (Storm, 1997). Supervisors' requirements, supervisees' goals, schedules to be followed, projected duration, modalities and interventions to be employed, methods and purposes of evaluation, and procedures for responding to emergencies should be specified. Consideration should also be given to supervisors' roles vis-à-vis responsibilities attributed to school administration, as well as procedures for appropriately informing recipients of school counselors' services about supervisory relationships and related limits of confidentiality. Thus, building principals should be involved in defining the parameters of responsibility and liability. (Todd, 1997, provided additional guidelines that may be helpful.) When supervisees are working toward certification or licensure, contracts should also address those external requirements. (See also Osborn & Davis, 1996; Prest & Schindler Zimmerman,1997; Storm, 1997; Todd, 1997.) Needless to say, effective contracts include mechanisms for modification and renegotiation as the needs of supervisees and their clientele change (Storm, 1997).

The importance of counselor and client relationships is well documented. A collaborative relationship characterized by mutual respect, authenticity, and trust, is no less important for supervisory relationships (Bernard & Goodyear, 1998; Bordin, 1983; Kaiser, 1992). A working alliance can be enhanced through mutual identification of supervisees' professional strengths and limitations and reciprocal evaluation of the supervisory processes. Thus, initial contacts between supervisors and supervisees are often characterized by (a) endeavors to facilitate a collaborative relationship and (b) procedures to assess supervisees' level of skills.

The comprehensive nature of school counselors' responsibilities invites attention to a variety of skills to be considered in initial assessment and goal setting. In addition to individual and group counseling skills, supervisors should facilitate mutual examination of supervisees' competence for working with students representing diverse backgrounds, planning developmental guidance activities, consulting with teachers and parents, and implementing a comprehensive program that meets national and state standards. Supervisees' self-appraisal may be augmented with information provided by previous supervisors and impressions derived from direct observation. Supervisors may also refer to assessment instruments and professional state-ments of competencies (e.g., Association for Specialists in Group Work, 1991; Gladding & Pedersen, 1997; Sue, Arredondo, & McDavis, 1992). Henderson and Gysbers (1998) also provided useful instruments for assessing competencies.

Supervisory theories, modalities, and interventions employed in community settings (as described in this text: Bernard & Goodyear, 1998; Goodyear & Nelson, 1997) are equally appropriate for supervising school counselors. For example, supervisors of new school counselors may gain insight from theories that explicate professional development along a continuum from dependency to autonomy and maturity (Stoltenberg et al., 1998; Van Zandt & Perry, 1992). Astute supervisors respond to these dynamic needs of new school counselors as they engage in four general activities: (a) training and teaching, (b) consulting, (c) counseling, and (d) evaluating.

Co-leading groups with supervisees, observing developmental guidance lessons, and reviewing recordings of counseling sessions are examples of training and teaching activities. Supervisors appropriately adopt a consulting posture when supervisees request guidance related to working with a family, assisting a teacher in responding to a troubled child, or determining an appropriate resolution of an ethical dilemma. Consultation is often a collaborative and empowering process. For example, supervisors and supervisees may collaboratively plan ways to assure that time is invested in achieving counseling program goals or design instruments to evaluate the effectiveness of developmental guidance activities.

Within the boundaries of appropriate practice, supervisors adopt a counseling role when they recognize and address personal factors that may affect supervisees' performance. Quite appropriately, new school counselors become overwhelmed by multiple and unfamiliar responsibilities. They may be intimidated by veteran teachers or experience discomfort when working with a particular group of students. Supervisors' counseling activities are limited; thus, they must discern when a referral for personal counseling is warranted. (See chapter 14 of this volume, on "Ethical Issues in Counselor Supervision.")

Evaluation of supervisees' professional development is inherent in the supervisory process (Bernard & Goodyear, 1998; Borders, 1991; Fine & Turner, 1997). Based on initial supervisory agreements, assessment of supervisees' skills and professional development includes formative and summative components. Because skill development is a primary focus of clinical supervision, continuous feedback is an integral element of supervision (Borders, 1991). Ongoing, collaborative examination of supervisees' progress and professional development provides the basis for assessment at the conclusion of the supervisory relationship.

Whether the ending of a specific supervisory relationship is marked by the end of the school year, a time specified in the initial agreement, or the attainment of goals, certain tasks should be addressed. Supervisees and supervisors should assess supervisees' progress and identify continuing needs for professional development. They should also review the supervision processes. Finally supervisors should endorse supervisees' progress toward professional autonomy.

There are many avenues for assessing supervisees' progress and professional development. Initial goals provide important benchmarks (Bordin,

1983). Final reflection of supervisees' professional development throughout the supervisory relationships also facilitates identification of goals for additional supervision. In the process, the dyad can explore opportunities for continued professional development.

Culmination of supervision is also a time to evaluate the process of supervision. Ideally, supervisors and supervisees examine and discuss the effectiveness of supervision throughout the relationship. Formative evaluations include retrospective consideration of the activities that were helpful, as well as activities that were less effective (Bordin, 1983). This process can be valuable to both supervisors and supervisees in designing future supervision experiences.

☐ Closing Comments

We would be remiss if we did not return to Kary's dilemma described at the beginning of the chapter. Several resources for assistance in responding to the immediate need may have been available. For example, university professors often respond to requests for case consultation. Many school counselors contact colleagues in other schools for assistance with difficult situations; others engage in mentoring relationships with experienced counselors. Professional relationships with community counselors also offer possibilities for consultation. For the Washington family, Kary might have contacted a hospice counselor. Leaders of professional counseling associations may have also provided guidance and assistance.

Undoubtedly many counselors would have been willing to offer Kary support and direction in responding to the immediate need. However, formal arrangements for supervision would have offered significant advantages. Henderson and Gysbers (1998) asserted that "Supervision is most effective when it is ongoing, continuous and consistent, and the supervisor and the supervisee have mutual purpose: the enhancement of the professional performance of the supervisee to benefit the program clients" (p. 198). With continuous, structured supervision Kary would have experienced the advantages and opportunities for professional growth that Pat received in the community agency.

Supervision has been recognized as a critical factor in the professional development of counselors (Bernard & Goodyear, 1998; Magnuson & Wilcoxon, 1998b; Neufeldt, Iversen, & Juntunen, 1995; Usher & Borders, 1993; Watkins, 1997). Kary, and the many school counselors Kary represents, need not be deprived of this important resource for professional development.

☐ References

Association for Specialists in Group Work. (1991). *Ethical guidelines for group counselors and professional standards for training group workers.* Alexandria, VA: Author.

Atkinson, B. J. (1997). Informed consent form. In C. L. Storm & T. C. Todd (Eds.), *The reasonably complete systemic supervisor resource guide* (pp. 11–15). Boston, MA: Allyn & Bacon.

Barret, R. I., & Schmidt, J. J. (1986). School counselor certification and supervision: Overlooked professional issues. *Counselor Education and Supervision, 26,* 50–55.

Benshoff, J. M., & Paisley, P. O. (1996). The structured peer consultation model for school counselors. *Journal of Counseling and Development, 74,* 314–318.

Bernard, J. M., & Goodyear, R. K. (1998). *Fundamentals of clinical supervision* (2nd ed.). Needham Heights, MA: Allyn & Bacon.

Borders, L. D. (1991). Supervision ≠ evaluation. *The School Counselor, 38,* 253–255.

Borders, L. D., & Usher, C. H. (1992). Post-degree supervision: Existing and preferred practices. *Journal of Counseling and Development, 70,* 594–599.

Bordin, E. S. (1983). A working alliance based model of supervision. *The Counseling Psychologist, 11*(1), 35–41.

Boyd, J. D., & Walter, P. B. (1975). The school counselor, the cactus, and supervision. *The School Counselor, 23,* 103–107.

Brewer, J. M. (1924). *The vocational guidance movement: Its problems and possibilities.* New York: McMillan.

Crespi, T. D., & Fischetti, B. A. (1998, September). Clinical supervision in the schools: Forlorn, forgotten, or forsaken? *Counseling Today, 41,* 8, 19.

Crutchfield, L. B., & Borders, L. D. (1997). Impact of two clinical peer supervision models on practicing school counselors. *Journal of Counseling and Development, 75,* 219–230.

Crutchfield, L. B., Price, C. B., McGarity, D., Pennington, D., Richardson, J., & Tsolis, A. (1997). Challenge and support: Group supervision for school counselors. *Professional School Counseling, 1*(1), 43–46.

Fine, M., & Turner, J. (1997). Collaborative supervision: Minding the power. In T. C. Todd & C. L. Storm (Eds.), *The complete systemic supervisor: Context, philosophy, and pragmatics* (pp. 229–240). Boston, MA: Allyn & Bacon.

Fitch, J. A. (1936). Professional standards in guidance. *Occupations, 14,* 760–765.

Getz, G. G. (In press). Training in peer group clinical supervision: Professional development for elementary school counselors. *Virginia Counselors Journal.*

Gladding, S. T., & Pedersen, P. (1997, Winter). Cultural counseling competencies: A self examination. *ACES Spectrum, 58,* 4–5.

Goodyear, R. K., & Nelson, M. L. (1997). The major formats of psychotherapy supervision. In C. E. Watkins (Ed.), *Handbook of psychotherapy supervision* (pp. 328–346). New York: Wiley.

Hayes, L. L. (1998, December). Supervision of school counselors debated. *Counseling Today, 41,* 1, 19.

Henderson, P., & Gysbers, N. C. (1998). *Leading and managing your school guidance program staff.* Alexandria, VA: American Counseling Association.

Henderson, P., & Lampe, R. E. (1992). Clinical supervision of school counselors. *The School Counselor, 39,* 151–157.

Kaiser, T. L. (1992). The supervisory relationship: An identification of the primary elements in the relationship and an application of two theories of ethical relationships. *Journal of Marital and Family Therapy, 18,* 283–296.

Kratochwill, T. R., Lepage, K. M., & McGivern, J. (1997). Child and adolescent psychotherapy supervision. In C. E. Watkins (Ed.), *Handbook of psychotherapy supervision* (pp. 347–380). New York: Wiley.

Ladany, N., Lehrman-Waterman, D., Molinaro, M., & Wolgast, B. (1999). Psychotherapy supervisor ethical practices: Adherence to guidelines, the supervisory working alliance, and supervisee satisfaction. *The Counseling Psychologist, 27,* 443–475.

Magnuson, S., & Wilcoxon, S. A. (1998a). Clinical supervision of prelicensed counselors: A qualitative inquiry. *The Alabama Counseling Association Journal, 24*(1) 54–68.

Magnuson, S., & Wilcoxon, S. A. (1998b). Successful supervision of prelicensed counselors: How will we recognize it? *The Clinical Supervisor, 17*(1), 33–47.

Matthes, W. A. (1992). Induction of counselors to the profession. *The School Counselor, 39,* 245–250.

McCarthy, P., Sugden, S., Koker, M., Lamendola, F., Maurer, S., & Renninger, S. (1995). A practical guide to informed consent in clinical supervision. *Counselor Education and Supervision, 35,* 130–138.

National Board for Certified Counselors. (1998). *NBCC approved clinical supervisor* [Application form]. Greensboro, NC: Author.

Neufeldt, S. A., Iversen, J. N., & Juntunen, C. L. (1995). *Supervision strategies for the first practicum.* Alexandria, VA: American Counseling Association.

Osborn, C. J., & Davis, T. E. (1996). The supervision contract: Making it perfectly clear. *The Clinical Supervisor, 14*(2), 121–134.

Peace, S. D. (1995). Addressing school counselor induction issues: A developmental counselor mentor model. *Elementary School Guidance and Counseling, 29,* 177–190.

Peace, S. D., & Sprinthall, N. A. (1998). Training school counselors to supervise beginning counselors: Theory, research, and practice. *Professional School Counseling, 1*(5), 2–8.

Prest, L., & Schindler Zimmerman, T. (1997). The many styles of contracts: Formal to casual. In C. L. Storm & T. C. Todd (Eds.), *The reasonably complete systemic supervisor resource guide* (pp. 161–163). Boston, MA: Allyn & Bacon.

Roberts, E. B., & Borders, L. D. (1994). Supervision of school counselors: Administrative, program, and counseling. *The School Counselor, 41,* 149–157.

Schmidt, J. J. (1990). Critical issues for school counselor performance, appraisal and supervision. *The School Counselor, 38,* 86–94.

Splete, H. H., & Grisdale, G. A. (1992). The Oakland counselor academy: Professional development program for school counselors. *The School Counselor, 39,* 176–182.

Stoltenberg, C. D., McNeill, B., & Delworth, U. (1998). *IBM supervision: An integrated model for supervising counselors and therapists.* San Francisco: Jossey-Bass.

Storm, C. L. (1997). The blueprint for supervision relationships: Contracts. In T. C. Todd & C. L. Storm (Eds.), *The complete systemic supervisor: Context, philosophy, and pragmatics* (pp. 272–282). Boston, MA: Allyn & Bacon.

Sue, D. W., Arredondo, P., & McDavis, R. J. (1992). Cultural counseling competencies and standards: A call to the profession. *Journal of Counseling and Development, 70,* 477–486.

Sutton, J. M., & Page, B. J. (1994). Post-degree clinical supervision of school counselors. *The School Counselor, 42,* 32–39.

Todd, T. C. (1997). Privately contracted supervision. In T. C. Todd and C. L. Storm (Eds.), *The complete systemic supervisor: Context, philosophy, and pragmatics* (pp. 125–134.) Needham Heights, MA: Allyn & Bacon.

Usher, C. H., & Borders, L. D. (1993). Practicing counselors' preferences for supervisory style and supervisory emphasis. *Counselor Education and Supervision, 33,* 66–79.

Van Zandt, C. E., & Perry, N. S. (1992). Helping the rookie school counselor: A mentoring project. *The School Counselor, 39,* 158–163.

Watkins, C. E. (1997). Defining psychotherapy supervision and understanding supervisor functioning. In C. E. Watkins (Ed.), *Handbook of psychotherapy supervision* (pp. 3–10). New York: Wiley.

Wiley, M. O., & Ray, P. B. (1986). Counseling supervision by developmental level. *Journal of Counseling Psychology, 33,* 439–445.

CHAPTER

M. Kristine Bronson

Supervision of Career Counseling

You will come to a place where the streets are not marked. Some windows are lighted. But mostly they're darked. A place you could sprain both your elbow and chin! Do you dare to stay out? Do you dare to go in? How much can you lose? How much can you win?

—*Dr. Seuss*

The above quote, originally from a graduation speech (Seuss, 1990), describes the experience of choosing or changing a career. Clients in career counseling are trying to find their way, make sense of their options, and make good choices. They struggle with a lack of direction and with uncertainty and confusion. How can supervision prepare counselors to accompany clients on this journey?

This is a challenging question to answer. While the value of counselor supervision as well as the potential problems associated with supervision have been widely documented (Bernard & Goodyear, 1998; Watkins, 1997), the role of supervision in career counseling has been largely overlooked. In particular, career counseling supervision theory has not been identified or articulated, nor have the unique factors of career counseling supervision been described. Furthermore, few have investigated the role supervision plays in training career counselors (Heppner, O'Brien, Hinkelman, & Flores, 1996; Sumerel & Borders, 1995). The focus of this chapter is to delineate important issues in the supervision and training of counselors providing career counseling. First, a brief overview of effective supervision will be presented, followed by aspects of effective career counseling. Then, 10 components of effective career counseling supervision will be introduced and described.

☐ What Is Effective Supervision?

Supervision is an intervention that extends over time, with the multiple purposes of (a) enhancing the professional functioning of the supervisee, (b) monitoring the quality of professional services offered to clients seen by the supervisee, and (c) serving as a gatekeeper of those who enter the counseling profession. In addition, counselor supervision is the setting in which counselors learn to blend two general realms of clinical knowledge: the "science" of counseling and the "art" of counseling (Bernard & Goodyear, 1998). As has been described in preceding chapters, effective supervision consists of a number of features, including forming a positive supervisory working alliance (Bordin, 1983); flexibility in working from multiple roles (e.g., teacher, counselor, consultant; Bernard, 1997); considering the developmental needs of the supervisee (Stoltenberg & McNeill, 1997); clear communication about the expectancies, supervision goals, and evaluation criteria (Holloway, 1997); and the ability to facilitate learning about and improvements in human interaction (Kagan & Kagan, 1997). These qualities also describe effective career counseling supervision.

☐ What Is Effective Career Counseling?

To fully articulate the qualities of effective career counseling supervision, it is necessary to describe the qualities of effective career counseling. The National Career Development Association (NCDA) published a list of career counseling competencies in 1992 (NCDA Professional Standards Committee, 1992) and then updated them in 1997 (NCDA Professional Standards Committee, 1997). The list published in 1997 stated that a professional engaged in career counseling must demonstrate minimum competencies in 11 designated areas including a total of 84 specific competencies. The 11 designated competency areas are: (a) career development theory (i.e., theory and knowledge essential for providing career counseling and development); (b) individual and group counseling skills (i.e., individual and group counseling competencies essential for career counseling); (c) individual/group assessment (i.e., assessment skills essential for providing career counseling); (d) information/resources (i.e., basic information, resources, and knowledge essential for providing career counseling); (e) program promotion, management and implementation (i.e., skills needed to develop, plan, implement, and manage career development programs in various settings); (f) coaching, consultation, and performance improvement (i.e., essential knowledge and skills for assisting organizations and groups to promote individuals' career development); (g) diverse populations (i.e., knowledge and skills essential for providing career counseling and development with diverse client populations); (h) supervision (i.e., knowledge and skills essential for supervising, evaluating, and promoting the professional development of counselors providing career counseling); (i) ethical/legal issues (i.e., knowledge essential for the ethical and legal practice of career counseling); (j) research/evaluation (i.e., knowledge and skills essential for understanding and conducting career counseling research and evaluation); and (k) technology (i.e., knowledge and skills essential for using technology within career counseling). It is argued that these competencies comprise the basis of effective career counseling practice.

☐ Components of Effective Career Counseling Supervision

Given the scant research and theory on how to provide effective supervision of career counseling, the following recommendations extrapolate from the existing supervision and career counseling theory and research. The supervision and career counseling literature is integrated and extended to delineate essential components of career counseling supervision. These recommendations are deemed pantheoretical, that is, applicable across theories of supervision. Furthermore, this model applies to individual, one-on-one supervision of individual career counseling and is not intended to be generalizable to group supervision or to supervising career workshops, supervising psychoeducational career interventions, or supervising the creation and management of an entire school guidance program (Gysbers & Henderson, 2000; Henderson & Gysbers, 1998).

Effective career counseling supervision attends to 10 specific components. Briefly defined, these 10 components are: (a) the supervisory relationship (i.e., developing a relationship between the supervisor and supervisee that is characterized by a strong supervisory working alliance); (b) counseling skills (i.e., counseling competencies essential for effective career counseling); (c) case conceptualization (i.e., using career development theory to understand clients' career issues and devise a plan for intervening); (d) assessment skills (i.e., using testing to assess career-related factors such as interests, values, abilities, personality, self-concept, and other issues); (e) resources and information (i.e., possessing knowledge of and the ability to use basic career resources such as books, people, and technology which provide career-related information); (f) the interconnection between personal issues and career issues (i.e., an awareness that career development is impacted by personal characteristics, along with the ability to work with these factors in career counseling); (g) promoting supervisee interest in career counseling (i.e., motivating supervisees to provide quality career counseling by modeling that behavior and by addressing myths about career counseling); (h) addressing career issues in age-appropriate ways (i.e., acknowledgment that the development of a career occurs over an entire lifetime and that, as a result, counselors need to be able to intervene in ways that are age appropriate); (i) multicultural issues (i.e., the awareness, knowledge, and skills necessary to provide culturally competent career counseling); and (j) ethics (i.e., knowledge of and adherence to the ethical codes appropriate to career counseling). Each of these components will be discussed more thoroughly in subsequent sections.

Effective career counseling supervision is provided primarily via four models of supervision and utilizes a variety of supervision interventions. The four primary models used throughout this chapter are Kagan's interpersonal process recall model (Kagan & Kagan, 1997), the integrated developmental model (Stoltenberg & McNeill, 1997), the discrimination model (Bernard, 1997), and the systems approach to supervision (Holloway, 1997). Suggested supervision interventions include role plays, case conceptualizations, reading, audiotapes and videotapes of counseling sessions, and interpersonal process recall.

The Supervisory Relationship

The relationship component of effective career counseling supervision is listed first, emphasizing its importance as a foundation upon which effective career counseling supervision is built, grows, and develops. After all, it is within the supervisory relationship that all supervision and supervisory interventions take place (Watkins, 1997), and quite likely this relationship determines the effectiveness of supervision (Hunt, 1986). Attention to the supervisory relationship is recommended throughout the supervision process. Because the supervisory relationship is written about thoroughly in chapter 2 of this book, the current section will highlight only the salient factors in relation to supervising career counseling.

Bordin (1983) proposed that the supervisory working alliance is a collaboration for change comprising three aspects: mutual agreement and understanding of the goals of supervision, mutual agreement and understanding of the supervision tasks, and an emotional bond between the supervisor and supervisee. Each of these three aspects is exemplified below.

The goals in career counseling supervision are likely to be multiple and to vary in specificity. For example, the goals could include the supervisee's development of all 11 of the designated career counseling competency areas. Alternatively, a supervisor and supervisee might agree upon a very specific goal for supervision, such as developing proficiency and expertise in career counseling with women returning to work after raising children. The tasks of career counseling supervision should be related to the goals of supervision. For example, supervision tasks could include reviewing audiotapes of counseling sessions in supervision, discussing career development theory, applying theory to each client seen, and role-playing how to utilize assessment tools. A key feature related to the tasks is that the supervisor and supervisee have come to a mutual agreement regarding when and how these tasks will be utilized in supervision. It is also presumed that as the supervisor and supervisee negotiate a mutual understanding of the goals and tasks of career counseling supervision, a strong emotional bond will develop between them. This emotional connection involves a mutual caring, liking, and trust between the supervisor and supervisee. The development of a strong supervisory working alliance sets the stage for the implementation of supervisory interventions related to the remaining components.

Counseling Skills

Attention to the supervisee's development of counseling skills is the next component of effective career counseling supervision. Counseling skills include the actions and interventions used with clients, such as attending and listening, restatement, asking open questions, reflection of feeling, challenge, interpretation, self-disclosure, immediacy, information giving, and direct guidance (Hill & O'Brien, 1999). These are the counseling competencies essential for effective career counseling, and they provide the foundation upon which the interactions between counselor and client develop.

Hill and O'Brien (1999) propose that counseling skills integrating affect, cognition, and behavior are central to effective counseling and are what facilitate clients moving through a three-stage model of change, comprising first exploration, next insight, and then action. Likewise, it is herein proposed that effective career counseling involves these skills. Correspondingly, effective career counseling supervision helps the supervisee develop these counseling skills while also helping the supervisee employ this three-stage model of helping with clients. For example, supervision can facilitate the development of attending and listening skills through the use of role-playing. The supervisee, role-playing the counselor, practices repeating verbatim what the supervisor, role-playing the client, says. The goal of this type of role play is to practice listening carefully to and hearing exactly what the other is saying.

A variation of interpersonal process recall (Kagan & Kagan, 1997) is another way of facilitating supervisees' acquisition of counseling skills. The following example illustrates assisting a supervisee in learning the skill of challenge in counseling. The supervisor and supervisee listen to an audiotaped counseling session in which a client is conflicted or confused. They stop the tape after a period of time when the client has clearly disclosed the conflict or confusion. Together the supervisee and supervisor identify as many ways as possible that the supervisee could have challenged the client. Then, they evaluate the effectiveness of each possible challenge and explore the supervisee's reactions. The following example illustrates this process.

Steve, the client, says on audiotape: "I really love art. Ever since I was a child my favorite pastimes have been drawing and painting, music and dance. Art is who I am! But I can't make any money in art. I need to be practical. It's silly to want to spend all my time drawing and dancing. Art really isn't that important to me."

Questions for the supervisor and supervisee to think about are: Is there a discrepancy present? The discrepancy could be between two verbal statements, between words and actions, between two feelings, between values and behaviors, between strengths and weaknesses. Is this a defense? Is this an irrational belief?

Supervisor and supervisee brainstorm possible ways to challenge the client. Some sample challenging interventions include:

- "I noticed a discrepancy between two things you said, Steve. First you said 'I love art' and then you ended with 'Art really isn't that important to me'." (This notes a discrepancy between two verbal statements.)
- "Steve, you said that art really isn't important to you. Yet, I know that you spend a great deal of your free time involved in artistic activities." (This notes a discrepancy between words and actions.)
- "You seem to have some beliefs about careers in art that may or may not be true. You say that you can't make any money in art. You say that you need to be practical, implying that you are not practical if you pursue a career in art. I am not sure that these beliefs are accurate." (This notes irrational beliefs.)

Questions for the supervisor and supervisee to consider regarding the effectiveness of each possible challenge are:

- Is the client ready to hear the challenge?
- Could the challenge be phrased differently so that the client can hear the intervention?
- Is one challenge more important to the client's development at this time?
- Is the counseling relationship well developed enough for the challenge to be effective?

Questions the supervisor can utilize to explore the supervisee's reactions are:

- How do you feel about each of the challenges?
- Which, if any, of the challenges would be easiest for you to deliver? Why?
- Which, if any, of the challenges would be most difficult for you to deliver? Why?
- How do you imagine you would feel in a counseling session if you challenged this client?

Clearly, it would be an oversight to disregard the relevance of counseling skills within career counseling. Supervision needs to attend to the development of counseling skills as well as their use specifically with career-related issues, if the counselor is to provide true *counseling* and not serve merely as a technician. Attention must be paid to developing counseling skills throughout the supervision process.

Case Conceptualization

Case conceptualization is the use of career development theory (e.g., Holland, 1992; Mitchell & Krumboltz, 1990; Super, 1990) to understand clients' career issues and devise a plan for intervening and assisting the client in counseling. Conceptualizing cases allows one to use theory to guide both the counseling process and the supervisee's interventions, so that there is a sound rationale for the goals and tasks of the counseling.

Career counseling supervision can quite naturally facilitate a supervisee's case conceptualization skills. Regularly scheduled case reports can be a part of the supervision process, wherein the supervisee presents a written and verbal presentation of a client. The case report includes information such as client identifying data, presenting concerns, goals for counseling, theoretical understanding of the client and her or his presenting concerns, proposed course of counseling, assessment data, and current outcomes. The process of writing a case report allows the supervisee to thoroughly think through and write out the why, how, and what of the planned counseling interventions. Formally presenting and discussing the case allows the supervisee to rethink the case, while the supervisor helps the supervisee explore the validity of assertions made about the client, the strength and appropriateness of the theoretical understanding of the client, and the proposed course of counseling. For this process to be most effective, a collaborative approach between supervisor and supervisee is recommended; the mutual goal is the development of the supervisee's ability to conceptualize. If an antagonistic dynamic develops, then the process will likely feel punishing and belittling to the supervisee.

In the following example, the supervisee has written a case report and is discussing her client, Maria, who is a 30-year-old, married, Latina woman with two children ages 6 and 8. Maria has a B.A. degree in English and has worked part-time writing for a small public relations and marketing company since her first child was born. She has sought counseling because she is now interested in returning to work full-time and would like assistance in identifying her options, both within her current industry of public relations/marketing and in other industries and settings as well.

Supervisee: *According to Super's life-span theory of career development, Maria is recycling through the exploration stage, which is characterized by exploring occupational options, making an occupational choice, becoming more specific about the choice, and then ultimately implementing that choice by finding a job.*

Supervisor: *Tell me more about the occupational options Maria is exploring.*

Supervisee: *Well, she is working in PR and marketing now, which she enjoys. So, she is exploring opportunities within PR and marketing, like staying where she is part-time and finding another part-time position, or starting her own PR/marketing company, or working full-time at a company or organization in their PR/marketing department.*

Supervisor: *What interventions do you think would be helpful to Maria in exploring these options?*

Supervisee: *Super's theory suggests that knowledge about the world of work is necessary here. So, I think that interventions focused on Maria gathering information about these options would help. I have suggested that Maria read about marketing and PR in the* Occupational Outlook Handbook. *I also think that suggesting informational interviews would be a good intervention. I don't think that Maria knows about informational interviews.*

Supervisor: *Yes, those interventions seem timely and very consistent with Super's model. Do you anticipate any barriers to these interventions working with Maria?*

Supervisee: *Hmmm. I don't know. I really hadn't thought about that. Hmmm . . . what do you mean?*

Supervisor: *Well, sometimes a client could benefit from a particular intervention in counseling, and yet sometimes the intervention is not as successful as we had hoped. I wondered if that might be the case with Maria.*

Supervisee: *Well, I know that Maria is a bit shy. So the informational interviews might be intimidating for her. That hadn't occurred to me before. Hmmm. I still think they would be helpful to her, though. I wonder how to deal with that?*

Supervisor: *It seems that you are fine-tuning your conceptualization about Maria.*

Supervisee: *I guess I am.*

More informally, supervisors can assist counselors in developing conceptualizing skills by regularly attending to how the supervisee is conceptualizing each client. Examples of thought-provoking questions that get at the development of skills in conceptualizing clients include:

- How do you think the client's age (or gender, race, marital status) impacts the career development process?
- What led you to choose to use that particular assessment tool with this client? What are its advantages and disadvantages?
- What theory or theories are you using to understand this client's presenting concerns and developmental process? How does that theory relate to the interventions you are using with this client?

Utilizing case conceptualization in supervision also assists the counselor in developing her or his own theoretical orientation. Stoltenberg and McNeill (1997) posited that supervisees move through three levels of development in supervision. Level 1 is characterized by limited exposure to counseling, assessment, and conceptualizing. Level 2 is characterized by mastery of basic skills and some success experiences with clients, as well as feelings of conflict leading to vacillating between preferring dependency or autonomy within supervision. Level 3 is characterized by a calm focus on growth and often by rapid skill development. These three levels can be applied to the development of one's theoretical orientation and conceptualization skills.

Supervisees at level 1 have some idea of their theoretical orientation, but it is based on didactic learning and is largely untested by counseling experience. At level 2, supervisees' theoretical orientation has been challenged and tested some and is likely in flux and in revision. At level 3 and beyond, the theoretical orientation has survived many transformations as the result of both counseling experience and the evolution of the counselor as a person.

By always being mindful of its existence, the supervisor assists the supervisee in developing and fine tuning one's theoretical orientation. Asking the counselor to state her or his theoretical orientation at the beginning of the supervision relationship (and from time to time during the course of supervision) allows both to monitor its development. The supervisor may decide to intervene in a different manner depending on the developmental level of the supervisee. For a supervisee at level 1, assigning readings consistent with the supervisee's theoretical orientation and then discussing them in supervision may be facilitative. For a level 2 supervisee, it might be helpful to require the supervisee to conceptualize the same client case from various theoretical orientations, while for a supervisee at level 3, supervision could focus on helping the supervisee integrate counseling interventions with her or his theoretical orientation.

Assessment Skills

The term "assessment skills" refers to the use of testing (e.g., the Strong Interest Inventory, the Self-Directed Search, the Myers Briggs Type Indicator, SIGI PLUS) to assess career-related factors such as interests, values, abilities, achievement, personality, decision-making style, self-concept, career maturity, and other related developmental or lifestyle issues to promote clients' career development. Acquiring assessment skills is a complex process that includes developing a series of skills, such as: (a) the ability to evaluate and select valid and reliable instruments appropriate to the client (given the client's age, gender, sexual orientation, race, ethnicity, and physical and mental abilities); (b) the ability to administer, score and report assessment findings appropriately; (c) knowledge of and ability to utilize technology, including computer-delivered assessment measures such as SIGI PLUS and DISCOVER; (d) and the ability to interpret assessment data and present and utilize the data with clients (verbally as well as in written test reports) to facilitate their progress.

Given the complexity of this task, it is no wonder that the field has been critiqued for inattention to how to train counselors to master the array of interlocking skills (Watkins, 1993). While we cannot turn to empirical studies to guide us, some logical suggestions follow. First, within supervision it seems minimally necessary to acknowledge that developing assessment skills is a complex task. Acknowledging that assessment skills are really a set of skills may demystify the process and allow for the supervisor and supervisee to collaborate on how best to address assessment issues within supervision. This acknowledgment might also lead supervisors and supervisees to devote more time and attention to developing these skills. To this end, Fink, Allen, and Barak (1986) delineated an extensive, 5½-month internship experience designed to train counselors to administer, score, and interpret ability, interest, and personality tests with clients seeking career counseling. This internship entails two components: (a) seminar sessions focused on assessment issues, including the rationale for using a particular test, choosing the appropriate test for a particular client, as well as scoring and interpreting test results and the presentation and review of client cases; and (b) individual 1-hour supervision sessions with a total of three supervisors.

Elements of the internship described by Fink et al. (1986) can be used in any supervision context. Some supervision sessions could be didactic in nature, with the aim of training the supervisee in the elements of good assessment skills. The content of these sessions might include instruction on the validity and reliability of assessment tools, instruction in how to interpret the test data, and practice communicating results verbally and in writing. These didactic sessions could occur in individual supervision or could be provided in small group seminars with multiple supervisees present. Another alternative is for supervisors to simply require counselors to use assessment with clients when the test is appropriate and will yield useful information. This would result in counselors having the opportunity to choose, administer, score, interpret, and present the results to clients under close supervision.

Supervisees can also practice administering assessment tools and presenting the results by role-playing with the supervisor. This method can be quite helpful to supervisees in a number of ways. Role-playing allows the supervisee to become familiar with the test, make mistakes, and receive direct coaching from the supervisor, get stuck, struggle, ask questions and eventually get unstuck, without the added pressure of a real client relying upon the counselor for help. Over time, as the supervisee masters the use of assessment tools, the role plays can focus on using tests with more difficult or intimidating clients, such as a client who complains about taking a test, a client who is argumentative about the test results, or a client who views the test result not as a tool but rather as "the definitive answer." Each counselor likely has her or his own fears about using tests with particular types of clients or in certain situations, and supervisors are well advised to invite counselors to share their fears. Supervisors can also facilitate this type of discussion by disclosing some of the fears and struggles they themselves encountered with career clients when they were trainees (Ladany & Lehrman-Waterman, 1999).

Resources and Information

Resources and information are inherent aspects of quality career counseling. To make planful career decisions and pursue training, education, and employment, clients must know how to utilize resources and information such as books, Internet websites, job trends, job descriptions, computer systems and the like. Many clients are not familiar with such resources when they enter counseling; it is the career counselor who serves as a coach or educator, assisting the client to locate and use relevant resources. It is imperative, then, that counselors possess a demonstrable knowledge of and ability to use basic career resources (including books, people, and technology) which provide information about job tasks, functions, salaries, requirements, and future outlooks. They must also possess basic information about the world of work, such as trends in education, training, and employment; labor market information; and hiring practices. When counselors do not possess the knowledge needed to help a client, they need to be able to locate the information or resources, or refer the client to the information and resources.

Effective career counseling supervision attends to the supervisee's developing knowledge in these areas. A practical way to help a counselor become familiar with resources and information is to require the supervisee to come into contact with the materials. For example, a beginning counselor (i.e., a counselor at developmental level 1) may be required to locate and review the *Occupational Outlook Handbook* (U.S. Department of Labor, 1998/1999) and the *Dictionary of Occupational Titles* (U.S. Department of Labor, 1996), visit websites of recruiters and headhunters, and become familiar with current employment trends as compared to employment trends from the past. A more advanced counselor (i.e., a counselor at developmental level 2), already possessing basic knowledge of resources and the world of work, may be required to locate, identify, and evaluate career self-help books or identify local workers willing to engage in informational interviews with interested clients. Inevitably, as the supervisee counsels clients, the need for resources and information arises. As this happens, it is natural for the supervisor and supervisee to discuss what is available and also to brainstorm and investigate new options. Again, role-playing when, why, and how to introduce information and resources can be helpful to the supervisee, especially if the supervisee feels uncomfortable with these skills.

The Interconnection Between Personal Issues and Career Issues

Counselors and mental health professionals tend to dichotomize clients into those seeking career counseling and those seeking personal counseling, artificially separating the presenting problems as if a client's career life and personal life are not intertwined. Career development is impacted by clients' personal characteristics, such as social contextual factors, familial, cultural, and subcultural structures; decision-making style; developmental stage; identity formation and status; self-concept; psychological needs; psychopathology; and internal barriers (Blustein, 1987, 1992; Manuele-Adkins, 1992; NCDA Professional Standards Committee, 1997; Subich, 1993). Counselors who counsel the whole person assist clients in making psychologically congruent choices through a counseling process with richness and depth. To provide holistic career counseling, counselors must learn in supervision to address the overlap and interplay of personal and career concerns.

But how do we train counselors to treat the whole client and not just the career concern? Supervisors could start by never allowing themselves to dichotomize clients and client issues into "career" vs. "personal" domains. Supervisors begin by exemplifying a counselor who treats a *person* presenting with career concerns and by demonstrating how to take into consideration all the factors (personal, psychological, as well as career) that impact the person as well as the career concern. For example, when a supervisee talks about her or his client Kathy, a 20-year-old, depressed female college sophomore having difficulty choosing a major, the supervisor must attend not only to the discussion about choosing a major but also to the role that the client's depression plays in her life as well as in her college career.

If qualified, the counselor can provide counseling for the career issues as well as treatment for the psychological issues. Naturally, not all counselors possess the training and expertise to treat all of the psychological issues (including, but not limited to, depression) with which clients present. It is not necessary for the counselor who is addressing the career concerns to be able to treat all of these other concerns. It is, however, of utmost importance that the counselor be able to recognize, identify, and diagnose mental health concerns and be able to refer the client for proper treatment. The counselor can then continue to provide the career counseling while the client receives the mental health treatment with another professional. In the example of Kathy, a counselor would recognize the depression, talk with Kathy about the presence of depression, make a referral to a professional able to treat the depression (e.g., a counselor, psychologist, or psychiatrist), and continue to counsel Kathy on the process of choosing a major. Clearly, even after a referral is made, the counselor still needs to take into account how the psychological issues relate to the client's career development. In our example, the counselor working with Kathy would still need to address how the depression impacts her process of choosing a major. For example, Kathy's depression might artificially lower her scores on the Strong Interest Inventory or cause her to inaccurately evaluate her abilities.

Bernard's (1997) discrimination model of supervision suggests numerous ways the supervisor can promote a holistic approach to working with Kathy. When using this model the supervisor can intervene from the role of teacher, counselor, or consultant, yielding the following potential interventions.

Supervisor as Teacher

1. The supervisor identifies and informs the supervisee of referral options for treating the depression.
2. The supervisor teaches the supervisee how to arrange symptoms into the diagnosis of depression.
3. The supervisor models how to conceptualize the connections among Kathy's depression, her career concerns, and all of the other personal and psychological factors that Kathy brings to counseling.

Supervisor as Counselor

1. The supervisor explores with the supervisee her or his range of feelings about working with a depressed client.
2. The supervisor explores how the supervisee's feelings about Kathy impact the counseling process.
3. The supervisor works with the counselor to remember how feelings, events, and/or psychological distress impacted her or his own career development.

Supervisor as Consultant

1. The supervisor and counselor together brainstorm how Kathy's career concerns and depression are related and how they impact each other.
2. The supervisor engages in a conversation with the counselor about her or his strengths and weaknesses to help the counselor determine her or his expertise and limitations in regards to treating the career issues and the depression.
3. The supervisor encourages the supervisee to identify as many counseling interventions as possible that would facilitate Kathy to talk about the role of depression in her life and in her career.

Promoting Supervisee Interest in Career Counseling

Promoting supervisee interest in career counseling is an important and yet often overlooked function of career counseling supervision. This involves motivating supervisees to provide quality career counseling through modeling as well as through addressing myths about career counseling. This is an important component of effective career counseling supervision for a few reasons. First, promoting supervisee interest in career counseling helps to ensure that adequate services are provided to clients. Second, interested and motivated career counselors may be less likely to overlook career concerns or attend to mental health issues to the exclusion of career issues. Also, supervisors who successfully promote a supervisee's interest in career counseling assist that counselor in developing a broader repertoire of counseling skills.

Recent research suggests that counselors are not very interested in addressing career issues in counseling. In June 1999 the National Board of Certified Counselors voted to disband the National Certified Career Counselor specialization due to a lack of interest in the career speciality (Schmitt, 1999). It has been suggested that counselors and psychologists view career counseling as not being prestigious, lucrative, intellectually challenging, or psychological, and as focused primarily on preparing clients to enter the workforce (Blustein, 1992; Manuele-Adkins, 1992; Subich, 1993). For supervisees to provide quality counseling to their clients, supervisors must directly address these myths and this disinterest. This is one area where empirical support exists. Research shows that clients presenting with career issues express as much psychological distress as clients presenting with personal issues (Gold & Scanlon, 1993). This same study also found that in spite of the clients' significant psychological distress, clients presenting with career concerns received fewer sessions of counseling. Apparently, clients are very interested and concerned about the career issues for which they seek counseling. And yet, counselors may not always give these clients adequate services. Supervisors can expose their supervisees to literature that addresses the significance of career concerns to clients (Gold & Scanlon, 1993), as well as to literature that addresses the overlap and interplay of career and personal issues (Blustein, 1987, 1992; Manuele-Adkins, 1992; NCDA Professional Standards Committee, 1997; Subich, 1993) and challenges supervisees' myths in these areas.

Given that artificially dichotomizing "career counseling" and "personal counseling" impedes supervisee interest, supervisors need to be wary of dichotomizing. Research indicates that supervisors have a powerful effect on trainees' attitudes toward career counseling, such that supervisors can either increase or decrease supervisees' interest in career counseling (Heppner et al., 1996). Heppner et al.'s study suggested that supervisees' interest in career counseling was positively influenced by supervisors who clearly communicated that career and social-emotional counseling are integrated processes rather than two separate modalities, as well as supervisors and professors who shared their enthusiasm for and creativity within career counseling. Likewise, an article by Warnke et al. (1993) described the positive impact of a doctoral-level career counseling practicum on students' attitudes toward career services as well as their career interventions skills. Thus, it seems that supervisors foster their supervisee's interest in career counseling by respecting the seriousness of career concerns, modeling interest, sharing enthusiasm, and training supervisees that a client's career issues relate to that client's whole life and identity.

Addressing Career Issues in Age-Appropriate Ways

Given that the development of a person's career takes place over an entire lifetime, it is essential that counselors understand the developmental nature of career and intervene in ways that are age appropriate and developmentally appropriate. Ideally, supervisees would learn this directly by counseling a variety of clients who span a range of ages and developmental levels. When this is possible, so much the better. Then supervision can focus on each client's particular needs based on their age and their developmental status. For example, in a setting where counselors work with children between the ages of 6 and 18, the supervisor and supervisee can discuss the relative needs of students of different ages. They might note that elementary-age children need to develop their career awareness (i.e., awareness of various life roles, awareness of occupations) but do not need to make specific occupational choices (i.e., a college major or preferred occupation). Supervision can also address how to tailor intervention strategies for this age group, in particular given elementary children's abilities and needs. Then, as the supervisee works with clients of different ages and developmental stages, i.e., middle school students or high school students, supervision can serve as a forum for exploring the similarities and differences between the clients, as well as the similarities and differences between intervention strategies used. Utilizing the counselor role in supervision, the supervisor can help the supervisee reflect on how it feels to counsel clients at various ages and stages. Questions for discussion and reflection might include: How do you feel as you work with clients of each age group? What is especially difficult for you? What is especially easy? What were your career issues at that age?

Although it is ideal for trainees to counsel clients spanning a range of ages and developmental levels, this opportunity is probably more the exception than the rule. Most supervisors supervise counselors in a setting that tends to be more age-specific, such as an elementary, middle, or high school, a college campus or a community agency serving adult clients. When this is the case, supervision should at least acknowledge that career development needs to be delivered in age-appropriate ways, and supervisors should discuss what this means in that particular setting. For example, while it is age appropriate to help a high school senior explore several specific careers of interest, it would be premature to encourage an eighth grader to narrow her or his interests down to several specific careers. There are many possible supervision interventions that facilitate the supervisee's understanding of age-appropriate career counseling. The supervisee might think about and talk about what is age-appropriate in various settings. The supervisee might read the NCDA policy statement about career development with respect to various life stages (NCDA Board of Directors, 1993) and could read and discuss developmental approaches to career development such as Super (1990) and Gottfredson (1999). Supervisors should ensure that their supervisees use age-appropriate theory, assessment, and interventions in case conceptualizations. If the supervisee has had experience with clients of other ages, perhaps in another practicum or work setting, reflect with the supervisee about how the current population is similar to and different from that other population. Encourage the supervisee to alter interventions that were effective with other age groups to utilize those interventions with current clients.

Even within a fairly homogeneous setting there are discrepancies between individuals and subgroups. For example, while high school may seem somewhat homogeneous with regard to age and developmental stage, much diversity exists. The same interventions will not facilitate the developmental growth of all first year high school students. For example, both male and female first year students need assistance adjusting to high school and exploring the school, themselves, and prospective career interests. However, at this age females are at a greater risk for low self-esteem and low self-efficacy (Gilligan, 1982), ultimately putting them at greater risk for unnecessarily limiting their career goals. Thus, when counseling entry-level high school students, it is recommended that counselors look out for low self-esteem and low self-efficacy, especially in the girls.

Also, the needs of subgroups within high school can be quite distinct, although they are very close in age. Consider first year students vs. seniors. Typical career tasks for first year students include identifying and evaluating interests, participating in choosing courses, and exposure to jobs and career fields, while typical career tasks for high school seniors include experience working, planning for what to do after graduation, and preparing for a job search or choosing an institution of higher learning. Supervision should attend to the individual differences and mini-stages that occur even within a fairly homogeneous setting. Supervision should also assist the supervisee in noticing and working with these more subtle differences in age and development.

Multicultural Issues

Attention to multicultural issues in career counseling is the next component of effective career counseling supervision. For the purpose of this chapter, multicultural issues include but are not limited to issues of race and culture, gender, sexual orientation, socioeconomic status, age, and ability. This component focuses on the awareness, knowledge, and skills necessary to provide culturally competent career counseling. Developing cultural competence allows counselors to effectively counsel a wider range of clients and to ensure that all individuals have access to career development assistance.

To effectively train supervisees to acknowledge and work with diversity issues in career counseling, it is imperative that supervisors be culturally competent themselves. Supervisors must be able to acknowledge and work with diversity issues both in career counseling and within supervision. Supervisors need to possess the awareness, knowledge, and skills that are presented herein.

Multicultural counseling competencies have been written about, researched, and taught for some time, such that the salient attitudes, knowledge, and skills required to practice in a culturally competent manner have now been identified and described (Ponterotto, Casas, Suzuki, & Alexander, 1995; Sue, Arredondo, & McDavis, 1992). Briefly, culturally competent counselors possess attitudes and beliefs that allow them to counsel culturally diverse clients, without their own biases or values interfering with the counseling. A culturally competent career counselor would be willing and able to examine her or his prejudices about a client. Such a counselor might utilize supervision to sort through her or his prejudiced beliefs and how these beliefs could impact the counseling process. A culturally competent career counselor would be willing to learn more about how client characteristics (e.g., a client's religious beliefs) impact the client's career development as well as the career counseling process.

Culturally competent counselors possess knowledge about themselves, that is, about their own racial and cultural heritage and how it influences them as a person and as a counselor. For example, a culturally competent female career counselor knows how her gender has impacted her career development as well as the ways in which her gender impacts her professionally. Furthermore, culturally competent career counselors possess knowledge about the world, including knowledge of oppression, racism, discrimination, and stereotyping. In the career realm this specifically includes knowledge of discrimination and limited access to jobs and careers (Betz & Fitzgerald, 1987; Thomas & Alderfer, 1989); the damaging effects of the null-environment (Betz, 1989); limitations regarding applying career theory to diverse populations (Betz & Fitzgerald, 1987; Leung, 1995; Walsh & Osipow, 1994); the nature of women's career choices, women's career adjustment, and special issues in providing career counseling to women (Betz & Fitzgerald, 1987; Walsh & Osipow, 1994); and problems associated with using assessment tools with diverse populations (Betz, 1992; Hackett & Lonborg, 1994; Leung, 1995).

Culturally competent counselors have developed skills and interventions that enable them to work with culturally diverse populations. They are flexible in their counseling approach and can modify their interventions to accommodate differences. For example, a culturally competent career counselor would be able to modify typically individualistic career theories (possibly by using an integrative theoretical approach) to work with a client who utilizes a more collectivistic decision-making approach. Also, a culturally competent career counselor would utilize alternative assessment methods (i.e., vocational card sorts, values clarification exercises, work samples, observation) with clients for whom standardized tests and inventories are invalid or perpetuate bias (Goldman, 1990; Hackett & Lonborg, 1994).

A recent annual review of research and practice in career counseling and development noted two current trends related to diversity issues (Niles, 1997). These trends attend to making career theories useful to a more diverse population of clients and paying greater attention to the role of contextual factors in the career development process (Niles, 1997). Although this suggests that the field of career counseling is becoming more culturally competent there is still an absence of recommendations on how to address multicultural issues specifically in career counseling supervision. How is a supervisor to proceed?

At this point in time, it is presumed that academic courses such as career development, counseling theories, and the prepracticum address diversity issues in such a manner that the supervisee comes to supervision with an awareness of and openness to multicultural issues. When that is the case, effective supervision provides an environment in which the counselor can practice fine-tuning her or his cultural competencies. Sadly, however, it is often the case that supervisees lack the basic knowledge to begin providing culturally competent career counseling, while possessing fears, concerns, biases, and awkwardness about diversity. Given this state of affairs, it is the supervisor's responsibility to ensure that supervisees become aware of diversity issues in career development and develop requisite skills.

Holloway's (1997) systems approach to supervision suggested places where the supervisor can intervene to facilitate the supervisee's development of cultural competence. Holloway's model includes cultural characteristics as an important aspect of the supervision process and contends that "In SAS, cultural values are seen as salient to trainees' attitudes and actions toward their client and supervision—that is, in any interpersonal situation" (Holloway, 1995, p. 91). Thus, cross-cultural interactions may occur between the supervisor and supervisee, the supervisee and client, or both, making the supervision process ripe for multicultural learning and training regarding either of these cross-cultural relationships. For example, imagine a career counseling supervision situation involving a female supervisor, a male supervisee, and a female client. The topic of gender attitudes (i.e., Are certain professional roles more appropriate for men and less appropriate for women?) could be explored in relation to the interactions between the supervisee and supervisor as well as in relation to the supervisee and client.

For another example of how supervisors can teach supervisees to work with multicultural issues in career counseling, return to the case of Maria, the 30-year-old, married, Latina mother of two. Maria is working in counseling with Elizabeth, a 25-year-old, single, White woman with no children. In supervision, Elizabeth and her supervisor have just listened to a counseling session wherein Elizabeth and Maria discussed how Maria's shyness and lack of confidence in job search situations might impact Maria's career transition. The supervisor could utilize Bernard's (1997) discrimination model of supervision to explore the role of diversity issues in this case and to ultimately facilitate the supervisee's skills in this area. Example interventions from the role of teacher, counselor, and consultant follow.

Supervisor as Teacher

1. The supervisor assigns readings on the history of Latinas' occupational attainment to educate Elizabeth.

2. The supervisor models questions that Elizabeth might ask to more fully understand Maria's experience as a Latina woman conducting a job search.
3. The supervisor presents data and information on prejudice and racial discrimination in hiring practices.
4. The supervisor initiates discussions about multicultural counseling competencies, discrimination, limited access to jobs and careers, the null-environment, assessment validity, and alternative assessment tools to use with Latinas.

Supervisor as Counselor

1. The supervisor explores Elizabeth's comfort level with multicultural issues. With which populations is she most comfortable working? What contributes to her comfort? With which populations is she most uncomfortable working? What causes her discomfort?
2. The supervisor discusses with Elizabeth her feelings about working with Maria, a client who is different from Elizabeth in terms of age, race, marital status, and parental status.
3. The supervisor explores with Elizabeth how it would feel to process the cross-cultural counseling situation with Maria.
4. The supervisor helps Elizabeth examine how her socialized biases may influence her counseling.

Supervisor as Consultant

1. The supervisor asks Elizabeth how she would like to use supervision to help develop cultural competencies to provide effective career counseling to Maria.
2. In regard to working with a Latina woman, the supervisor and Elizabeth together discuss the supervisee's knowledge base. What does the supervisee already know? What knowledge is missing?
3. Together Elizabeth and her supervisor evaluate the relative strengths and weaknesses of various theories of career development when applied to Maria.
4. The supervisor asks Elizabeth to consider what types of supervision activities (i.e., brainstorming, case conceptualization, interpersonal process recall, role-playing) she prefers to use to develop multicultural career counseling skills.

Finally, developing culturally competent career counseling skills requires that supervisees see a diverse caseload of clients. Within whatever setting one is working, the supervisor can select clients to maximize the supervisees' exposure to diversity. Even on a predominantly white college campus it is possible for a supervisee to counsel clients from a range of ethnic, racial, and socioeconomic backgrounds, as well as women; gay, lesbian, or bisexual clients; and individuals with disabilities. These counseling experiences allow the supervisee to experience both their skills in regard to diversity issues as well as their discomfort and limitations. The supervisee's experience can then be explored in supervision to help the supervisee acknowledge, but not accept, limitations.

Ethics

Ethics refers to adherence to ethical codes related to the profession of counseling as well as to the profession of career counseling (e.g., American Counseling Association, 1995; NCDA Board of Directors, 1991) and supervision (Association for Counselor Education and Supervision, 1995). Ethical codes and counselors' adherence to them is essential for the protection of clients as well as to ensure clients' trust. Ethical issues in supervision are addressed more completely in chapter 14, so the focus here will be on ethical issues and dilemmas related to career development and career counseling.

Curiously, sometimes counselors believe that they do not need to adhere to ethical standards as strictly in career counseling as in other forms of counseling. Specifically, ethical standards are sometimes overlooked in regard to multiple relationship or confidentiality issues in career counseling. These are mistakes. Effective career counseling supervision ensures that the supervisee understands that ethical codes apply equally within career counseling as in any other counseling relationship.

Rules of confidentiality and rules requiring permission to disclose to a third party apply in counseling when the focus is on career issues just the same as when the focus is on other presenting problems. Conversely, the limitations to confidentiality are the same. If a client intends to harm herself or himself and discloses this to the counselor while discussing a career issue, the counselor is obligated to disclose this information in the service of protecting the client from harm just as if the client had been seeking counseling for depression. These issues need to be clearly acknowledged in supervision.

Also, given that some counselors are trained primarily to address career issues with clients and do not possess the expertise to address mental health concerns in counseling, these limitations need to be clearly addressed in supervision. If and when a counselor does not possess the ability to counsel both career and mental health issues, appropriate referrals need be available and supervision needs to attend to issues of how and when to refer. It is clearly unethical to practice outside of one's expertise.

Finally, multiple relationships between a client seeking career counseling and the counselor are unethical in the same way that multiple relationships between a client seeking psychotherapy and the psychotherapist are unethical. An example of a multiple relationship would be acting as a career counselor for a member of one's own family. It is ultimately the supervisor's responsibility to ensure that the supervisee does not engage in multiple relationships with clients. To this end, the supervisor can model ethical behavior by not engaging in dual relationships with the supervisee.

☐ Research Issues

The limited research in career counseling supervision allows for numerous interesting areas of further research. First, the 10 specific components of effective career counseling supervision and the proposed supervision approaches and techniques presented in this chapter need to be researched to determine their efficacy in relation to training career counselors. A second, related research area is to examine the impact that effective career counseling supervision has on clients and the outcomes of counseling. For example, does effective career counseling supervision promote clients' understanding of their interests, strengths, and weaknesses? If so, does that ultimately lead the client to make a career choice that is more satisfying for her or him? Research could also examine if career counseling supervision is most effective when matched to trainee developmental level. That is, when considering the 10 components presented earlier, is supervision most effective when certain components are the focus early in a supervisee's training and when other components are the focus later in a supervisee's training? And last, research could also examine the ways in which supervisors can be trained to conduct effective career counseling supervision. Such studies might examine the barriers to effective career counseling supervision (e.g., lack of interest, myths about career issues, or negative attitudes toward career counseling) as well as the qualities of effective career counseling supervisors.

☐ Concluding Comments

This chapter is a first step in providing direction for those supervising counselors engaged in career counseling. The primary goal of this chapter has been to guide current supervision practice. Hopefully, this chapter will also stimulate thought, discussion, and research that will lead to the development of clear guidelines for the supervision of career counseling. Ultimately it is hoped that the techniques and strategies presented for effective career counseling supervision will be used by supervisors to help counselors learn to provide holistic, effective career counseling.

☐ References

American Counseling Association. (1995). *Code of ethics and standards of practice*. Alexandria, VA: Author.

Association for Counselor Education and Supervision. (1995). Ethical guidelines for counseling supervisors. *Counselor Education and Supervision, 34,* 270–276.

Bernard, J. M. (1997). The discrimination model. In C. E. Watkins, Jr. (Ed.), *Handbook of psychotherapy supervision* (pp. 310–327). New York: Wiley.

Bernard, J. M., & Goodyear, R. K. (1998). *Fundamentals of clinical supervision* (2nd ed.). Boston: Allyn & Bacon.

Betz, N. E. (1989). Implications of the null environment hypothesis for women's career development and for counseling psychology. *The Counseling Psychologist, 17*(1), 136–144.

Betz, N. E. (1992). Career assessment: A review of critical issues. In S. D. Brown & R. W. Lent (Eds.), *Handbook of counseling psychology* (2nd ed., pp. 453–484). New York: Wiley.

Betz, N. E., & Fitzgerald, L. F. (1987). *The career psychology of women.* New York: Academic Press.

Blustein, D. L. (1987). Integrating career counseling and psychotherapy: A comprehensive treatment strategy. *Psychotherapy, 38,* 790–799.

Blustein, D. L. (1992). Toward the reinvigoration of the vocational realm of counseling psychology. *The Counseling Psychologist, 20*(4), 712–723.

Bordin, E. S. (1983). A working alliance based model of supervision. *The Counseling Psychologist, 11*(1), 35–41.

Educational Testing Service. (1999). *SIGI PLUS.* Princeton, NJ: Educational Testing Service.

Fink, R., Allen, R., & Barak, A. (1986). Teaching and supervising career assessment interns. *Michigan Journal of Counseling and Development, 17*(2), 27–30.

Gilligan, C. (1982). *In a different voice: Psychological theory and women's development.* Cambridge, MA: Harvard University Press.

Gold, J. M., & Scanlon, C. R. (1993). Psychological distress and counseling duration of career and noncareer clients. *Career Development Quarterly, 42*(2), 186–191.

Goldman, L. (1990). Qualitative assessment. *The Counseling Psychologist, 18,* 205–213.

Gottfredson, L. S. (1999). A theory of circumscription and compromise. In D. Brown & L. Brooks (Eds.), *Career choice and development: Applying contemporary theories to practice* (3rd ed., pp. 179–232). San Francisco: Jossey-Bass.

Gysbers, N. C., & Henderson, P. (2000). *Developing and managing your school guidance program* (3rd ed.). Alexandria, VA: American Counseling Association.

Hackett, G., & Lonborg, S. D. (1994). Career assessment and counseling for women. In W. B. Walsh & S. H. Osipow (Eds.), *Career counseling for women* (pp. 43–85). Hillsdale, NJ: Lawrence Erlbaum Associates.

Henderson, P., & Gysbers, N. C. (1998). *Leading and managing your school guidance program staff.* Alexandria, VA: American Counseling Association.

Heppner, M. J., O'Brien, K. M., Hinkelman, J. M., & Flores, L. Y. (1996). Training counseling psychologists in career development: Are we our own worst enemies? *The Counseling Psychologist, 24*(1), 105–125.

Hill, C. E., & O'Brien, K. M. (1999). *Helping skills: Facilitating exploration, insight, and action.* Washington, DC: American Psychological Association.

Holland, J. L. (1992). *Making vocational choices: A theory of vocational personalities and work environments.* Odessa, FL: Psychological Assessment Resources.

Holloway, E. L. (1995). *Clinical supervision: A systems approach.* Thousand Oaks, CA: Sage.

Holloway, E. L. (1997). Structures for the analysis and teaching of supervision. In C. E. Watkins, Jr. (Ed.), *Handbook of psychotherapy supervision* (pp. 249–276). New York: Wiley.

Hunt, P. (1986, Spring). Supervision. *Marriage Guidance,* 15–22.

Kagan, H. K., & Kagan, N. I. (1997). Interpersonal process recall: Influencing human interaction. In C. E. Watkins, Jr. (Ed.), *Handbook of psychotherapy supervision* (pp. 296–309). New York: Wiley.

Ladany, N., & Lehrman-Waterman, D. E. (1999). The content and frequency of supervisor self-disclosures and their relationship to supervisor style and the working alliance. *Counselor Education and Supervision, 38,* 143–160.

Leung, S. A. (1995). Career development and counseling: A multicultural perspective. In J. G.

Ponterotto, J. M. Casas, L. A. Suzuki, & C. M. Alexander (Eds.), *Handbook of multicultural counseling* (pp. 549–566). Thousand Oaks, CA: Sage.

Manuele-Adkins, C. (1992). Career counseling is personal counseling. *The Career Development Quarterly, 40,* 313–323.

Mitchell, L. K., & Krumboltz, J. D. (1990). Social learning approach to career decision-making: Krumboltz's theory. In D. Brown & L. Brooks (Eds.), *Career choice and development: Applying contemporary theories to practice* (2nd ed., pp. 145–196). San Francisco: Jossey-Bass.

National Career Development Association Board of Directors. (1991). *Career development: A policy statement of the National Career Development Association Board of Directors.* Alexandria, VA: National Career Development Association.

National Career Development Association Board of Directors. (1993). *National Career Development Association Ethical Standards.* Alexandria, VA: National Career Development Association.

National Career Development Association Professional Standards Committee. (1992). Career counseling competencies. *The Career Development Quarterly, 40,* 378–386.

National Career Development Association Professional Standards Committee. (1997). *Career counseling competencies, revised version.* Alexandria, VA: National Career Development Association.

Niles, S. G. (1997). Annual review: Practice and research in career counseling and development—1996. *The Career Development Quarterly, 46,* 115–141.

Ponterotto, J. G., Casas, J. M., Suzuki, L. A., & Alexander, C. M. (1995). *Handbook of multicultural counseling.* Thousand Oaks, CA: Sage.

Schmitt, S. M. (1999, August). NBCC drops career and gerontology counseling specialities. *Counseling Today, 1,* 19.

Seuss, Dr. (1990). *Oh, the places you'll go!* New York: Random House.

Stoltenberg, C. D., & McNeill, B. W. (1997). Clinical supervision from a developmental perspective: Research and practice. In C. E. Watkins, Jr. (Ed.), *Handbook of psychotherapy supervision* (pp. 184–202). New York: Wiley.

Subich, L. M. (1993). How personal is career counseling? [Special Section] *Career Development Quarterly, 42*(2), 129–192.

Sue, D. W., Arrendondo, P., & McDavis, R. J. (1992). Multicultural counseling competencies and standards. A call to the profession. *Journal of Counseling and Development, 70*(4), 477–486.

Sumerel, M. B., & Borders, L. D. (1995). Supervision of career counseling interns. *The Clinical Supervisor, 13*(1), 91–100.

Super, D. E. (1990). A life-span, life-space approach to career development. In D. Brown & L. Brooks (Eds.), *Career choice and development: Applying contemporary theories to practice* (2nd ed., pp. 197–261). San Francisco: Jossey-Bass.

Thomas, D. A., & Alderfer, C. P. (1989). The influence of race on career dynamics: Theory and research on minority career experiences. In M. A. Arthur, D. T. Hall, & B. S. Lawrence (Eds.), *Handbook of career theory* (pp. 133–158). New York: Cambridge University Press.

U.S. Department of Labor. (1998/1999). *Occupational outlook handbook.* Washington, DC: U.S. Government Printing Office.

U.S. Department of Labor. (1996). *Dictionary of occupational titles* (4th rev. ed.). Washington, DC: U.S. Government Printing Office.

Walsh, W. B., & Osipow, S. H. (1994). *Career counseling for women.* Hillsdale: Lawrence Erlbaum Associates.

Warnke, M. A., Jinsook, K., Koeltzow-Milster, D., Terrell, S., Dauser, P. J., Dial, S., Howie, J., & Thiel, M. J. (1993). Career counseling practicum: Transformations in conceptualizing career issues. *The Career Development Quarterly, 42,* 180–185.

Watkins, C. E., Jr. (1993). Career assessment supervision: Could what we don't know hurt us? *Counselling Psychology Quarterly, 6*(2), 151–153.

Watkins, C. E., Jr. (Ed.). (1997). *Handbook of psychotherapy supervision.* New York: John Wiley & Sons.

Marcia Kaufman
Keith J. Morgen
Nicholas Ladany

Family Counseling Supervision

Supervision is thought to be the primary component of counseling training and is the most frequently used method for teaching counseling procedures (Binder, 1993; Kaufman & Korner, 1997). Its importance in transmitting skills, knowledge, and attitudes of counseling to the next generation (Bernard & Goodyear, 1998; Steward, 1998) is not to be underestimated, and supervision in family counseling has itself become a subspecialty within the field (Goldenberg & Goldenberg, 1996; Liddle, 1991; Liddle, Becker, & Diamond, 1997). Despite the fact that the field of family counseling has grown enormously over the past two decades, due in part to an ever increasing public need for services (Everett, 1980), there continues to be a lack of consensus on best practices for preparing aspiring family counselors (Spruill, 1994; White & Russell, 1995). Preparation of the burgeoning family counselor includes teaching a set of therapeutic tools as well as a theoretical understanding of how, and under what circumstances, to use them (Goldenberg & Goldenberg, 1996). In addition, the family counseling trainee must be taught to attend to affective components and relational issues in the counseling hour in order to move the family along its maturational trajectory. To effect these goals, didactic methods coupled with the supervisor's use of the supervisory relationship tend to maximize learning for the family counseling trainee. How this teaching is accomplished can vary greatly, however, depending on the supervisor's school of thought and supervisory technique adherence.

The purpose of this chapter is to review the current "state of the art" in regard to family counseling supervision. To achieve this purpose we will discuss (a) a brief history of family counseling and family counseling supervision, (b) general characteristics of supervision, (c) if family counseling supervision differs from supervision of individual counseling, and if so, how, (d) strategies and techniques for conducting family counseling supervision, (e) attending to the affective component in supervision and supervisory relationship issues, (f) goals and outcomes of family counseling supervision, and (g) recommendations for the future. Issues relating to multiculturalism, ethics, and research will be integrated throughout the text.

☐ Brief History of Family Counseling and Family Counseling Supervision

Following World War II several pioneers contributed to the emergence of new theories and models within the family counseling field. Don Jackson, John Weakland, Jay Haley, and Virginia Satir developed "the communication model" at the Mental Research Institute (MRI). This model outlined a framework of communication theory and cybernetics applied to interpersonal behavior (M. P. Nichols & Schwartz, 1995). In the 1960s, Salvador Minuchin, Braulio Montalvo, and colleagues studied families in New York City, giving birth to the strategic and structural schools of thought (Broderick & Schrader, 1991), and following this, the Philadelphia Child Guidance Clinic was formed by Minuchin and Montalvo, with Haley subsequently joining them (Broderick & Schrader, 1991; Haley, 1976; Minuchin 1974, 1981; Montalvo, 1973; M. P. Nichols & Schwartz, 1995). Also in the 1960s, Nathan Ackerman, a child psychiatrist, began to practice psychodynamic family counseling, founding the Ackerman Institute in New York City, and cofounding the prestigious journal, *Family Process*, with Don Jackson (Broderick & Schrader, 1991).

Intergenerational theory, as discussed by Murray Bowen, began at the Menninger Clinic where Bowen worked as a psychoanalyst. He developed a radical intervention for the treatment of the schizophrenic child that involved mother and child living together on the clinic grounds during the course of treatment (Broderick & Schrader, 1991). By 1954 his family research projects moved to the National Institute of Mental Health, where he hospitalized both the schizophrenic individual and his or her family for observation. Eventually, Bowen relocated his program to Georgetown University, where he opened a family counseling training clinic. Ivan Boszormenyi-Nagy and his colleagues also focused upon the relationship between schizophrenia and the family, founding the Family Therapy Department at the Eastern Pennsylvania Psychiatric Institute. James Framo, who combined both intergenerational and object relations theory, emphasized an interactional and intrapsychic approach to family counseling (Framo, 1982, 1992; Nichols & Schwartz, 1995), and Virginia Satir and her collaborative work with Bowen and Gregory Bateson paved the way for the experiential approach to family counseling (Nichols & Schwartz). Carl Whitaker, also an experiential theorist, and perhaps the most irreverent and whimsical of the family counseling pioneers of the 1950s and 1960s, introduced the practice of co-therapy, where two counselors, rather than the traditional one, reside over a session (Broderick & Schrader, 1991; Napier & Whitaker, 1978; Nichols & Schwartz; Whitaker & Keith, 1981).

The family counseling supervisory process dates back to the mid-1950s, when Don Jackson met Charles Furweiler. At this time, Furweiler was utilizing a one-way mirror during supervision, entering a session when necessary to offer feedback. The supervisory and therapeutic nature of such actions were recognized, and this process eventually led to the development of the telephone technique (Liddle, 1991), applied at the Philadelphia Child Guidance Center (Montalvo, 1973). Also, during the early to mid-1970s, the American Association for Marriage and Family Therapy (AAMFT) produced the first professional supervisory standards (Everett, 1980) and Haley (1976), released *Problem Solving Therapy*, which outlined varying dimensions for counselor training and supervision. Liddle et al. (1997) underscored how Montalvo's (1973) and Haley's (1976) work produced the framework for much of present day family counseling training and supervision. Recently, new challenges have surfaced questioning epistemological issues in family counseling training, including constructivism, the feminist critique, recognition of diversity, and the need to assimilate research into training (R. Smith, 1993).

☐ General Characteristics of Supervision

Supervision is one component of the counselor training process, with reliance also being placed on course work and, in some cases, personal counseling of the trainee (Bernard & Goodyear, 1998; Kaufman & Korner, 1997; Strupp, 1986, 1992; Watkins, 1997). Research studies have suggested that counselor training may be as complicated as counseling itself (Henry, Schacht, Strupp, Butler, & Binder, 1993; Kaufman & Korner, 1997; also refer to relevant chapters in this text), and some in the field have theorized that the metamorphosis from fledgling to experienced counselor and/or supervisor occurs in developmental stages (Borders & Fong, 1994; Friedman & Kaslow, 1986; Hill, 1992; Leach, Stoltenberg, McNeill, & Eichenfield, 1997; Olsen & Stern, 1990; Rigazio-DiGilio & Anderson, 1994; Stoltenberg, McNeill, & Crethar, 1994; Stoltenberg, McNeill, & Delworth, 1998; Watkins, 1993). As this vital training component unfolds, characteristics of the trainee, the supervisor, and the supervisory dyad all interact to influence its development, and as indicated elsewhere in this text, effective supervision requires attention to the supervisory relationship, the supervisory role, trainee capacities and trainee development, and trainee and client outcomes.

Trainee and Supervisor Roles and Capacities

The trainee's capacities for openness to learning, curiosity, thoughtfulness, initiative, self-reflection, emotional and interpersonal self-monitoring, recognition of interpersonal patterns, flexibility, and motivation to change tend to promote a positive supervisory experience (Binder & Strupp, 1997; White & Russell, 1995). In addition, a trainee who possesses the ability to apply theory to clinical data, accepts the expertise of the supervisor, is psychologically minded and empathic, has the capacity to relate and a willingness to deal with uncomfortable feelings and insights, and is open to a discussion of personal issues, may be better able to assume the counselor, student, and, if desired, client roles (Binder & Strupp, 1997).

Although it has been said that the primary skills required to teach counseling are also those required to conduct counseling (Binder & Strupp, 1997; Ekstein & Wallerstein, 1972), the supervisor functions in a different capacity than the counselor trainee. Primary supervisory functions include monitoring and evaluating, instructing and advising, modeling, consulting, and supporting and sharing (Holloway, 1997), and supervisory tasks include teaching counseling and intervention skills, case conceptualization, professional role, emotional awareness, and self-evaluation (Bernard, 1997; Holloway). Characteristics of the effective supervisor include self-reflection and self-monitoring of the interpersonal process associated with the supervisor–trainee interactions, along with the ability to move between identifying with and observing the experiences of both the trainee and the clients (Binder & Strupp). Both supervisors and supervisees have been surveyed to obtain their views of the characteristics that determine an effective supervisor. These characteristics include expertise, trustworthiness, interpersonal attractiveness, tolerance of supervisee mistakes in an atmosphere of safety, openness to feedback about their own style of relating, and a significant investment of time (Binder & Strupp; Shanfield, Mohl, Matthews, & Hetherly, 1992; White & Russell, 1995).

Features of the Supervisory Relationship

Individual characteristics of the trainee and supervisor interact in the supervisory dyad, with the resulting supervisory alliance emerging as a potential vital determinant of supervisory outcome (Bordin, 1983; Efstation, Patton, & Kardash, 1990; Worthen & NcNeill, 1996). Bordin defined the supervisory alliance as the agreement on goals and tasks of supervision and an emotional bond between the supervisor and supervisee, and recent empirical data has supported that a strong supervisory working alliance is predictive of less trainee role conflict and ambiguity in supervision (Ladany & Friedlander, 1995). What occurs between the trainee and supervisor can also be used as a learning tool under the guise of "parallel process" or, as it has been described in the family counseling literature, "isomorphism" (which will be further elaborated upon later in this chapter). This concept has been used to describe the reciprocal relationship between the counselor–client interaction and the supervisor–counselor relationship, as relational processes between the counselor and client tend to replicate themselves in the supervisory relationship (Ekstein & Wallerstein, 1972; Liddle, 1991; Liddle et al., 1997; McNeill & Worthen, 1989; Raichelson, Herron, Primavera, & Ramirez, 1997). When relational processes are replicated in the supervisory relationship, the supervisor then has the opportunity to assess, model, and inform the trainee of these replications, thereby providing an extremely potent learning experience. In addition to relational elements per se, gender, race, and multicultural issues as well as concordance of professional discipline and counseling school of thought between the trainee and supervisor can also interact within the supervisory dyad to effect the teaching and learning process.

☐ Comparisons Between Family Counseling Supervision and Individual Counseling Supervision

Initially, family counselors who were largely self-taught graduated to become supervisors based on their seniority and experience (Liddle, 1991; Todd & Storm, 1997), and as the field progressed, supervisory methods tended to mirror the intervention strategies applied to a dysfunctional family in session. This has led to a situation in which there are both common and uncommon features between individual and family counseling supervision. This section will focus on the unique family counseling supervision aspects of client shift, ethics, and theoretical and clinical focus.

Client Shift

Family counseling, as opposed to individually oriented counseling, considers the couple or family unit as the client (W. Nichols & Everett, 1986; R. Smith, 1993). This "client shift" creates a new paradigm for the neophyte counselor who must now consider multiple personality dynamics and their interactions under the one auspice of a family unit. Individual dynamics are not given the same theoretical weight or emphasis of change as are interactions among family members, and these interactional processes become the focus of treatment. Changing the client focus from the individual to the family affects not only the conceptualization of the problem and treatment, but also practicalities such as potentially having to deal with more people in crises, ethical issues such as who holds the rights to waive privileged communication (R. Smith, 1993), and the possibility of increased coordination of community resources for various family members.

Counselors who work with families have historically differentiated their work from individual counseling by suggesting that the individual counselor must only deal with one other person in the counseling room, whereas the family counselor must deal with the family system that is present (Liddle et al., 1997; W. Nichols & Everett, 1986). With the advent of more relational therapies, however, many modern counselors might argue that even in individual counseling the family is "present." In other words, even the individual client brings her or his family-of-origin issues to the counseling session. What seems to differentiate family counseling from individually oriented counseling, then, may be the "actual presence" of the family system. The family's "actual presence" provides the family counselor with an opportunity to utilize a systemic approach which might encompass portions of structural, strategic, experiential, or behavioral theories (W. Nichols & Everett; R. Smith, 1993), with treatment focusing on such things as communication patterns in the family or on the reorganization of dysfunctional relationships and interaction (Cleghorn & Levin, 1973; W. Nichols & Everett). It is the job of the supervisor to ensure that these features unique to family counseling are taught to the trainee. This will be further elaborated upon in the section on theoretical and clinical focus.

Ethics

Inherent counseling differences between individual and family work invoke a variety of unique ethical cautions for the family counselor, and the AAMFT has drafted its own *Code of Ethics* (AAMFT, 1998) to address these ethical issues. Ethical considerations in family counseling include responsibility to clients (paying particular attention to the issue of who is the "client"), supervisees, and research participants; confidentiality; counselor competence, integrity, and professional development; as well as counselor social and legal responsibilities to clients (AAMFT; Doherty & Boss, 1991). It is the supervisor's responsibility to ensure trainee compliance with the ethical code. In addition, the supervisor must ensure the trainee's ethical execution of all family counseling techniques. For example, "deception," or paradoxical technique, is a recommended strategy in some schools of thought; therefore the family counseling supervisor should be particularly mindful of all ethical issues surrounding use of this technique (Doherty & Boss).

In addition to helping the supervisee remain ethical in the midst of the sometimes highly charged family session (Kaiser, 1992), the family counseling supervisor must also be aware of ethics within the supervisory relationship. Ethical concerns for supervising the impaired family counselor (Jordan & Quinn, 1996) and for dealing with sexual attraction both between counselor and client and between supervisor and trainee (Larrabee & Miller, 1993; Nickell, Hecker, Ray, & Bercik, 1995) should be attended to by the family counseling supervisor.

Theoretical and Clinical Focus

Cleghorn & Levin (1973), in their seminal paper on training family therapists, discuss perceptual, conceptual, and executive learning objectives for the beginning, advanced, and experienced family counselor. They describe the family counselor as a *catalyst* who influences interactions by taking in relationship messages, registering the effect upon herself or himself, labeling these messages verbally, and then demonstrating to family members what they are doing to each other. Becoming an effective catalyst requires intimate self-knowledge of the counselor, so that work is always done in the service of the family, and not in the service of the counselor. In order to attain this self-knowledge, many family counselor supervisors have encouraged discussions of family of origin as a part of counseling training (Buelow, Bass, & Ackerman, 1994; Costa, 1991; Getz & Protinsky, 1994; Kelly, 1990; Lawson, Gaushell, McCune, & McCune, 1995; R. Smith, 1993) and have assigned preparation of genograms to help identify the family patterns of both clients (Pistole, 1995) and trainees (Getz & Protinsky, 1994). Many responsible for training family counselors believe that as trainees explore both the functional and dysfunctional aspects of their own families of origin and analyze the roles they played in their families, they will be better able to understand how these roles may influence their relationships with clients (Buelow et al., 1994).

 Supervisors' use of family-of-origin work, however, is influenced by the school of thought ascribed to by the trainer. While Haley (1976) has opposed the inclusion of family-of-origin work as part of family training, other family therapists such as Bowen and Framo have advocated for this work, viewing it as the most significant aspect of training (R. Smith, 1993). Many trainers advocating for family-of-origin work have also recognized that these issues may influence the supervision process, in addition to the counseling process, through the persons of both the supervisor and the supervisee.

 In order to effect change in the family that is "actually present," the family counselor learns how to enter, join, or otherwise work with the system in order to recognize and manage dysfunction (W. Nichols & Everett, 1986), and it is the supervisor's role to teach the family counselor trainee how to accomplish these tasks and think in a more systematic, as opposed to a more linear fashion (Horne, Dagley, & Webster, 1993; R. Smith, 1993; Stevens-Smith, Hinkle, & Stahmann, 1993). W. Nichols, Nichols, & Hardy (1990) found in their survey of approved supervisors of the AAMFT that "there is a movement to the forefront of systems orientations as the theoretical underpinning for supervision" (p. 283), revealing a tendency of family supervisors to use theoretical orientations that developed specifically in connection with family counseling (Betchen, 1995; White & Russell, 1995), instead of borrowing and adapting individually based orientations or extrapolating from such approaches (Nichols et al., 1990).

 The intensity of having the family members actually present, coupled with having more people for whom one is accountable to at any one time, necessitate supervisory modifications not typically found in supervision of individual counseling. For example, live supervision and the use of videotape review of sessions is utilized much more in family than in individual counseling to enhance the supervisor's ability to accurately follow the sequence of events occurring with multiple people. Carlozzi, Romans, Boswell, Ferguson, & Whisenhunt (1997) surveyed directors of counseling and family counseling training programs and found a major supervisory difference related to the use of audiotape review. While directors of marriage and family therapy programs indicated low usage rates of audiotape review due to concerns over its effectiveness, counseling directors indicated that they still rely quite heavily upon audiotape review despite their acknowledgment of its weakness as a modality of supervision. An earlier national survey of AAMFT approved supervisors (McKenzie, Atkinson, Quinn, & Heath, 1986) revealed that although audiotape supervision was the most frequently utilized method, the most effective form of supervision according to the respondents was live supervision with immediate feedback.

☐ Family Counseling Supervision Strategies and Techniques

The following case example will be utilized in this section to enhance the reader's understanding of the various supervisory techniques: A 25-year-old White male counselor trainee is working with a lesbian couple composed of a 21-year-old African American woman and a 45-year-old White woman, and the 45-year-old woman's 17-year-old White son from a previous marriage. The trainee's supervisor is a 37-year-old African American woman.

Live Supervision

Live supervision is a generic term covering several techniques, such as co-therapy, bug-in-the-ear, telephone, and the team approach (Liddle, 1991). These techniques are similar in providing the supervisor with the ability to monitor the session as it occurs, but they are different in terms of the timing of supervisory feedback. As these techniques are discussed, it is important to note that different schools of family counseling support different types of supervisory techniques.

Co-Therapy

During co-therapy (or as it is sometimes called, direct observation) the supervisor is present in the room with the counselor, making interventions and comments when appropriate. As a supervisory tactic, co-therapy permits the supervisor to observe the supervisee and alleviates some supervisee anxiety regarding sole responsibility for the session (McGee & Burton, 1998; Whitaker & Keith, 1981). Although the supervisor is able to provide a model for the supervisee in session, most supervisory feedback is given following the session when utilizing this technique. Co-therapy appears to be a growing supervisory method of choice (Hoffman, 1993; Landau & Stanton, 1983) and provides the supervisor with an opportunity to truly gauge the emotionality of the session and make a direct intervention or supervisory comment (Carter 1982; West, Bubenzer, Pinsoneault, & Holeman, 1993). For instance, let us assume that in our case example the supervisor noticed that the trainee and the 17-year-old son both turned their heads away when the lesbian couple held hands. The supervisor could then make a supportive reflecting comment to the couple regarding their feelings toward one another and an empathic comment regarding her observation about the son. After session she could also gently discuss her observations and hypotheses (e.g., that perhaps the trainee was identifying with the son in regard to feelings about the couple's overt display of affection). Our case example also illustrates the opportunity of employing diversity in the co-therapy team to enhance the teaching and learning of diversity issues (Avis, 1986) because our trainee is a young White male and our supervisor is an older African American female. Disadvantages of this supervisory method include potential dependence upon the supervisor, conflicting strategies between supervisor and supervisee, a loss of supervisor objectivity, and ambiguity regarding case responsibility (Carter; Whitaker & Keith).

Co-therapy invokes variant reactions from the schools of family counseling. The experiential orientation emphasizes the benefit of dual counselors, whereas Minuchin (structural) and Haley (strategic) oppose the practice, noting that one counselor, rather than two, is likely more capable of decisively acting during the family counseling session. In addition, Bowenian (family systems) supervisors function within the ex post facto method and deemphasize the live supervisory style to such an extent that the Georgetown University Family Center (a Bowenian training facility) contains no observation rooms. Although some orientations take overt stances for or against the technique, other schools of family counseling do not openly debate the co-therapy counseling and supervisory strategy (M. P. Nichols & Schwartz, 1995).

Bug-in-the-Ear and Telephone Supervision

The bug-in-the-ear and telephone techniques are the two most popular forms of live supervision. The bug-in-the-ear method utilizes a hearing aid type of device to transmit communication from a supervisor watching behind a one-way mirror to the counselor trainee. Interventions are brief, and the supervisee is unable to clarify or discuss the supervisory message (Barker, 1998). This technique has been found to immediately improve counseling skills (Gallant, Thyer, & Bailey, 1991), but it has also been portrayed as an inhibitory supervisory strategy, with the intruding nature of the messages enhancing anxiety or confusion for novice supervisees (Barker, 1998). For instance, in our case example, if the supervisor transmitted her observation of the trainee's turning his head when the couple held hands, this might have increased his performance anxiety during the session, resulting in his being less emotionally aware throughout the rest of the session.

Telephone supervision, which evolved at the Philadelphia Child Guidance Clinic, provides a mechanism for monitoring counselor progress while also facilitating supervisor control over the session (Montalvo, 1973). This strategy incorporates two-way communication between supervisor and supervisee and provides a forum to clarify any supervisory comments. Unlike the covert bug-in-the-ear technique, the telephone overtly disrupts the session and acts as a supervisory intervention to stop inappropriate family interactions or ineffective counselor interventions (Liddle, 1991). Coopersmith (1980) developed several types of telephone supervisory techniques, including one that produces three-way supervisory and counseling communication, involving supervisor, counselor trainee, and family. Utilizing our case example, if the telephone technique were utilized, the supervisor could have called in her observation of the trainee and the son to the trainee, with some suggestive interventions. She could have suggested that the trainee make a reflecting comment regarding the couple's feelings toward one another and a supportive comment to the son noting his observation. The supervisor would need to weigh her choice to interrupt the session against the possibility of eroding the trainee's confidence (West, Bubenzer, & Zarski, 1989), however, and West et al. (1993) have suggested that the frequency of supervisor interruptions seems to be the most crucial consideration for trainers.

Liddle et al. (1997) underscored how live supervision allows for direct observation of the counseling process between supervisee and family, facilitating the identification of patterns, behaviors, or counseling content not noticeable to the supervisee engaged in the session. In addition, this direct observation might also prevent clinically important trainee nondisclosures (Ladany, Hill, Corbett, & Nutt, 1996). In our case example, the trainee might not have disclosed his reaction to the couple's hand holding on his own, thereby curtailing a possible valuable supervisory experience. Criticisms of these types of live supervision include dependency upon the supervisor, intrusion into the counseling session, and negative family reaction to such interruptions (Liddle et al., 1997). Though disruptive, some in the field believe that the benefits of supervisory interruptions seem to outweigh the awkwardness of the strategy (Breunlin & Cade, 1981; C. W. Smith, Smith, & Salts, 1991), and Frankel and Piercy (1990) found that effective use of the telephone by the supervisor produced positive supervisee behavior, resulting in a more cooperative family during counseling. The structural school is a proponent of the interruptive supervisory styles of the telephone or bug-in-the-ear methods, whereas family systems theory emphasizes little or no live supervision. Bowen argued that live supervision distracts the supervisee from his or her primary task of personal growth and differentiation from the supervisor (M. P. Nichols & Schwartz, 1995). Although counterarguments have been posed, the arguments appear to be largely theoretical rather than empirical at this time.

Team Supervision

Similar to the telephone or bug-in-the-ear methods, the team supervisory method entails a group of supervisors watching a session from behind a one-way mirror, but with team supervision, there is more of an emphasis on postsession commentary (Liddle, 1991). Heath (1983) listed several benefits of team supervision, including the facilitation of brainstorming regarding case material, an enhanced learning environment for both supervisee and supervisors, and the availability of a team that balances the strengths and weaknesses of individual members. Papp's (1980) "Greek chorus" exemplifies a type of team supervision. The "Greek chorus" is composed of both senior and peer supervisors who support, challenge, and provoke the family during session. Suggestions to both the supervisee and family continue throughout the session, and the counselor/supervisee may choose to side with or against the Greek chorus. This process tends to highlight any ambivalence within the family regarding motivation to change, and the counselor can capitalize on such resistance by moving against the Greek chorus and empowering the family to change. In our case example, if a Greek chorus were utilized, it could speak directly to the ambivalence the son might have regarding the couple's overt display of affection. The trainee could then side with the son, thereby provoking family movement.

Similar to the Greek chorus, Anderson (1987) developed the reflecting team approach to supervision, which utilizes a team seated behind a one-way mirror watching the family counseling session. Following the session, the counselor and family observe the supervisory team discussing the session, thus reversing the direction of the one-way mirror and producing an added potential for solutions to the dysfunctional patterns presented (Johnson, Waters, Webster, & Goldman, 1997; Landis & Young, 1994; Prest, Darden, & Keller, 1990; R. Smith, 1993). Utilizing a team composed of varying ethnicities and genders creates an opportunity for a wider and richer perspective on both family interactions and presenting problem (Grandesso, 1996; T. E. Smith, Yoshioka, & Winton, 1993). If, for example, our supervisor incorporated a diverse reflecting team, issues regarding race, gender, sexual orientation, and age might be better processed with our trainee.

Ackerman's theory (1966) and proponents of strategic theory support team approaches. Conversely, Framo has argued that any form of live supervision seems to benefit the family or supervisor more than the supervisee (Liddle, 1991). Haley emphasized the need for both live and ex post facto approaches, but stressed that live supervision should be completed without interruptions (M. P. Nichols & Schwartz, 1995). Regardless of live supervisory style, supervisees typically report feeling anxious about being watched

(Kaplan, 1987). To reduce this anxiety, Wetchler and Fisher (1991) have recommended preparing students by discussing the methods and goals of live supervision and utilizing role play. The family may also feel anxious about being watched and may have a desire to meet the supervisory team (Kaplan).

Ex Post Facto Supervision

Ex post facto supervisory strategies entail a review of the session following its conclusion through such methods as case presentation, case notes, and audiotape and videotape review. In contrast to the live supervisory strategies, ex post facto techniques typically do not provoke intense anxiety within trainees (McCollum & Wetchler, 1995); they also appear cost effective and promote trainee independence during the session. Limitations do exist regarding their efficacy, however (West et al., 1993).

Case Presentation and Case Notes

During a case presentation the supervisee orally reports case information to the supervisor, and this process helps to facilitate the trainee's developing capacity to concisely integrate session data with theory. When reviewing case notes, the supervisor reads the supervisee's notes of the session, requiring the supervisee to clearly outline all behaviors, hypotheses, goals, and interventions. This detailed report then serves as a catalyst for future supervisory dialogue (Fisher & Sprenkle, 1980). The potential for careful organization of session information is the primary advantage of case presentation and case notes (West et al., 1993). Supervisees also report a more relaxed learning environment resulting from both an emotional distance from the case and not being directly observed during the session (McCollum & Wetchler, 1995). Despite the advantage of experiencing a more relaxed supervisory session, there is the potential for the supervisor to receive an inaccurate and subjective portrayal of case material (West, et al., 1993) because the novice counselor might feel overwhelmed by the family counseling process (Weber, McKeever, & McDaniel, 1985). Utilizing our example, the 25-year-old trainee could have felt overwhelmed by the complexity of the presenting case and might have been unaware of the son's or his own reaction to the display of affection, thereby omitting this from case notes or a case presentation.

Audiotape Review

During an audiotape review, the supervisor listens to a component of the taped counseling session, in either the presence or the absence of the supervisee. Feedback from tape reviews facilitates the supervisee's development in recognizing family patterns and understanding the impact of counseling interventions. Typically, the supervisor encourages the supervisee to edit the tape into brief sequences that underscore areas where the supervisee requires assistance. Prior to reviewing the tape, the supervisor and supervisee may also decide upon specific skills or counseling elements to examine within the taped session. Throughout the process, the supervisor continually encourages the trainee's movement toward independence while facilitating an educational supervisory dialogue (West et al., 1993).

The primary advantage of audiotape review is that, unlike with the case presentation or case notes methods, the supervisor receives an accurate and objective perspective regarding the family counseling session. Though beneficial, some disadvantages include the ex post facto nature of audiotape review and the absence of crucial nonverbal communication. For instance, with audiotape review one loses important counseling data such as family member body language or seating arrangements (Carlozzi et al., 1997), as would be illustrated by our case example (e.g., an audiotape would not have picked up the turning of the son's and the trainee's heads). M. P. Nichols and Schwartz (1995) noted that audiotape, although very popular in the training of clinical and counseling psychologists, is typically ignored in family counseling, with the discipline favoring the use of videotape review. Videotape supervision affords a delayed but objective verbal and visual perspective on the session, with the supervisor acting as a commentator on counseling events and counselor efficacy (Everett, 1980; Liddle et al., 1997).

Videotape Review

The visual element makes videotape review the best of all ex post facto supervisory options (West et al., 1993). Spruill (1994) noted that videotape review allows for the freezing of time to study an important event, while providing the trainee with an opportunity to relive critical counseling moments from a more objective perspective. In our case example, the 25-year-old trainee would have an opportunity to actually observe his own reaction, as well as the son's reaction, to the couple's display of affection, which might provide a potent learning experience for him. For instance, he would have an opportunity to learn more about how his countertransference is related to family and individual dynamics, leading to a greater awareness of his own feelings and how they might be inadvertently communicated during a session. Avis (1986) underscored the importance of video analysis in increasing supervisee awareness of gender and diversity issues in counseling. Despite the advantageous nature of videotape review, limitations exist regarding its benefit to the supervisory process. For example, the ex post facto nature leaves the supervisor or supervisee helpless to intervene in order to protect the welfare of the family, and the ability to directly alter the executive skills of the supervisee is lost (West et al., 1993).

Videotape review has been embraced by many schools of family counseling, and a long-standing relationship has existed between family counseling training and videotape use, as evidenced by the classic video training tapes featuring Minuchin ("Taming Monsters"), Montalvo ("Family with a Little Fire"), and Haley ("Dog Phobia"; Liddle, 1991). Both the structural and strategic schools pioneered video use in training, and the Georgetown University Family Center practices video supervision for all trainees. Bowen has argued that video review is not about case conceptualization, but instead provides a means to investigate the counselor or trainee's functioning and growth, thereby enhancing the supervisory relationship (Liddle, 1991; M. P. Nichols & Schwartz, 1995).

☐ Attending to the Affective Component in Supervision and Supervisory Relationship Issues

In addition to utilizing supervisory methods and techniques, attending to the affective component in supervision and working with and through the supervisory relationship enhances the teaching and learning process of family counseling (H. Anderson & Rambo, 1988; Edwards & Keller, 1995; Kaiser, 1992; Liddle, 1986, 1988; Sand-Pringle, Zarski, & Wendling, 1995; White & Russell, 1997). Issues relating to the "real relationship" such as power, control, and hierarchy (Edwards & Keller; Kaiser; Liddle & Halpin, 1978; Mazza, 1988) and issues relating to "isomorphism" (Liddle, 1986, 1991; Liddle et al., 1997; White & Russell, 1997) contribute to the training process. The supervisory relationship, as compared to the counseling relationship, has limits that include an awareness of minimal professional standards and the supervisor's responsibility to monitor the supervisee's performance against these standards (Bernard, 1992). The components of instruction, evaluation, and involuntariness within the supervisory relationship therefore have the potential to interfere with its development. How these components are dealt with in the context of the supervisory relationship varies greatly depending on the supervisor's school of thought and individual personality.

Historically, the issue of the hierarchical nature of the family counseling supervisory relationship has been controversial, and, depending on both philosophy and model of counseling, it has been either emphasized or minimized (Kaiser, 1992; Liddle & Halpin, 1978). Just as supervisory method reflects a wide variety of opinions as to which approach is more effective, the definition and task of the supervisory relationship has similarly reflected heterogeneous thought. In fact, a continuum has emerged over the years, with some believing in an equal, personal, and more process-focused definition (H. Anderson & Rambo, 1988; McGoldrick et al., 1999), while others at the opposite pole feeling that supervision requires a more task-, skills-, and goal-oriented philosophy (Liddle & Halpin). Perhaps what is most important to note is that, despite the heterogeneity of the concept of the supervisory relationship, there is little disagreement about its importance in the training process. In addition, gender (Avis, 1986; Caust, Libow, & Raskin, 1981; Granello, Beamish, & Davis, 1997; Rigazio-DiGilio, Anderson, & Kunkler, 1995; R. Smith, 1993; Stevens-Smith et al., 1993), sexual orientation (Long, 1997), race (Betchen, 1995; Ladany, Brittan-Powell, & Pannu, 1997; McGoldrick et al., 1999), culture (Jordan, 1998; Kelly, 1990; Ladany et al., 1997; McGoldrick et al., 1999), and issues surrounding spirituality and religion (Prest, Russell, & D'Souza, 1999) have all been recently cited in the literature as influential family counseling and supervisory relationship variables which are universal to training.

The notion of isomorphism has been recommended as a concept to guide the practice of family counseling supervision (White & Russell, 1997), and yet there is probably no more misunderstood notion in the field (Liddle, 1991). The concept was borrowed from the field of mathematics and is a systematic reworking of the notion of parallel process, whereby material from the therapeutic relationship replicates itself in supervision. In addition to the notion of parallel process, however, it also conceptualizes the idea of the parallel between one's theory of supervision and one's theory of counseling, and it recognizes the similarities among patterns across systems (Liddle, 1991; Liddle et al., 1997; White & Russell). It is also conceptualized as a supervisory interventive stance, with isomorphic sequences providing opportunities for intervention in supervision, with the goal of altering the supervisee's in-session behavior (Liddle, 1991; Liddle et al., 1997; White & Russell). Utilizing our case example, if the trainee turned his head when the supervisor warmly discussed the lesbian couple's relationship, this would parallel the trainee's reaction during the actual therapy session. During this supervision session, then, the supervisor would have an opportunity to intervene by processing what had occurred. This intervention would then have the potential to alter the trainee's future in-session behavior.

When dealing with affective components and relationship issues in both counseling and supervision, as previously mentioned, family of origin may or may not be a training focus, depending on the supervisor's school of thought (Buelow et al., 1994; Costa, 1991; Getz & Protinsky, 1994; Kelly, 1990; Lawson et al., 1995; R. Smith 1993). Regardless of the supervisory school of thought utilized, however, attention to possible unresolved family-of-origin issues is not optional if these unresolved issues affect the trainee's competence (Jordan & Quinn, 1996). Working within a family context poses complex countertransference issues for many trainees (Caust et al., 1981), and it is incumbent upon the family counselor–supervisor not only to help the trainee deal with these complex issues, but also to recognize when a possible referral for personal counseling is warranted for the trainee. It is also important for the supervisor to be aware of his or her own unresolved family-of-origin issues and to seek personal counseling for herself or himself if supervisory competence is in jeopardy.

☐ Goals and Outcomes of Family Counseling Supervision

Although supervisors may vary philosophically with regard to their goal emphasis in training (Storm, 1997), the primary goal of family counseling supervision, as in other types of counseling supervision, is the trainee's acquisition of therapeutic skills (Binder & Strupp, 1997; Lambert & Ogles, 1997). Teaching clinical theory and techniques, applying theory to clinical data, applying techniques to particular clients, and helping the trainee acquire a professional role, an emotional awareness, and the capacity to self-evaluate (Bernard, 1997; Binder & Strupp, 1997; Holloway, 1997) are the foci of supervision. Because supervisory techniques are intended to enhance trainee competence, a need currently exists for controlled research inquiries into supervision, and reliable and valid instruments to measure trainee outcome and satisfaction with supervision need to be utilized (Avis & Sprenkle, 1990).

Several instruments have been developed to measure different aspects of family counseling supervisory outcome. One such instrument, the Allred Interaction Analysis (Allred & Kersey, 1977), provides family counseling supervisees with a strategy for obtaining objective and useful supervisory feedback. This instrument contains seven domains that measure counselor behaviors and three domains that measure client (family) behavioral patterns. Tucker and Pinsorf (1984) developed the Family Concept Assessment Task and Rating Scale, which measures counselor efficacy in conceptualizing session data using a family systems perspective, while the Family Therapist Rating Scale (Piercy, Laird, & Mohammed, 1983) assesses both in-session counseling skills and nonverbal behaviors. Landis and Young (1994) described the Family Therapist Trainee Rating Scale, adapted from the Family Therapist Rating Scale (Piercy et al., 1983), which measures domains of supervisee behaviors such as initiating counseling ground rules, establishing the counselor–family relationship, identifying and assessing familial interaction patterns, and record keeping or treatment plan construction. The Supervision Feedback Form (Williams, 1994) offers a quantitative assessment regarding the quality of supervision and has proven helpful to supervisors and supervisors-in-training who feel more comfortable eliciting and providing feedback about supervisory quality through a written assessment than a face-to-face discussion.

In general, there appears to be a dearth of psychometrically sound measures for supervision (Ellis, Ladany, Krengel, & Schult, 1996). Avis and Sprenkle (1990) have reviewed the psychometric properties of the aforementioned family counseling supervisory instruments, and the reader is referred to that review for more complete information regarding the instruments' usefulness. Overall, while some of the instruments appear to have adequate interrater reliability, validity studies for some have been inconclusive (Avis & Sprenkle), suggesting that the family counseling supervision measures may fare no better than individual counseling supervisory measures in regard to their psychometric properties.

☐ Conclusion and Recommendations for the Future

Although family counseling supervision has emerged as a distinct professional skill requiring formal training, there is a paucity of research on training in supervision (Caldwell, Becvar, Bertolino, & Diamond, 1997; White & Russell, 1995) and there is little consensus to support the variety of supervisory approaches and models employed (Liddle, Breunlin, & Schwartz, 1988; White & Russell, 1995). Because family counselor supervisors have tended to apply their model of counseling to their supervisory work (W. Nichols et al., 1990; White & Russell, 1995), numerous competing models of supervision are therefore currently apparent with little support for their efficacy. While a mystique surrounded the work of the early family counseling pioneers, this mystique has given way to a developing technology of family counseling, which should lead to a corresponding technology of its training (Liddle et al., 1988). An appreciation for the complexity of the training process (Henry et al., 1993; Kaufman & Korner, 1997; Liddle et al., 1988) and a recognition that training and its component, supervision, are the primary vehicles through which the family counseling field will evolve (Liddle et al., 1988) point to the necessity of ongoing research to help identify efficacious training procedures. Ultimately, the challenge is to provide empirical support for the following question: "What kind of supervision is effective when, from whom, for whom, under what conditions, and for what type of clinical situation?" (White & Russell, 1995, p. 43).

As supervisors of the 21st century work to prepare family counselors by teaching a set of therapeutic tools, an understanding of how and under what circumstances to use them (Goldenberg & Goldenberg, 1996), and an appreciation of relational patterns that keep families from moving along their maturational trajectories, trainee, supervisor, and client issues of family-of-origin (Buelow et al., 1994; Getz & Protinsky, 1994; Kelly, 1990; Lawson et al., 1995); gender (Avis, 1986; Caust et al., 1981; Granello et al., 1997; Rigazio-DiGilio et al., 1995; R. Smith, 1993; Stevens-Smith et al., 1993); sexual orientation (Long, 1997); race (Betchen, 1995; Ladany et al., 1997; McGoldrick et al., 1999); culture (Jordan, 1998; Kelly, 1990; Ladany et al., 1997; McGoldrick et al., 1999); and spirituality and religion (Prest et al., 1999) need to be considered and empirically investigated. In addition, although the importance of the supervisory relationship in the training process is fairly undisputed, the fact that it is by necessity instructional and evaluative (Bernard, 1992) creates potential hierarchical, power, and control issues that need to be better understood. There currently seems to be a push toward a more collaborative approach related to the supervisory relationship (H. Anderson & Rambo, 1988; Emerson, 1996; McGoldrick et al., 1999), but how best to teach family counseling and also nurture a successful working alliance between trainee and supervisor in order to effect a positive outcome for both client and student is not yet known.

What seems to be apparent is that the outcome of family counseling supervision depends on aspects of the supervisor, the supervisee, their relationship, what they do in supervision, and the setting in which supervision takes place (White & Russell, 1995). These interconnected variables should be examined empirically because successful family counseling supervision may be dependent upon their interactions and interrelationships (White & Russell, 1995). As family counseling and its supervision moves into the next millennium, this empirical investigation will help advance the family counseling field, and in so doing, will better serve the families who are increasingly seeking services.

☐ References

Ackerman, N. (1966). *Treating the troubled family*. New York: Basic Books.

Allred, G., & Kersey, F. (1977). The AIAC, a design of systemically analyzing marriage and family counseling: A progress report. *Journal of Marriage and Family Counseling, 3,* 17–26.

American Association for Marriage and Family Therapy. (1998). *Code of ethics.* Washington, DC: Author.

Anderson, H., & Rambo, A. (1988). An experiment in systemic family therapy training: A trainer and trainee perspective. *Journal of Strategic and Systemic Therapies,7,* 54–70.

Anderson, T. (1987). The reflecting team: Dialogue and metadialogue in clinical work. *Family Process, 26,* 415–428.

Avis, J. (1986). Feminist issues in family therapy. In F. Piercy (Ed.), *Family Therapy Sourcebook* (pp. 213–241). New York: Guilford Press.

Avis, J., & Sprenkle, D. H. (1990). A review on outcome research on family therapy training: A substantive and methodological review. *Journal of Marital and Family Therapy, 16,* 241–264.

Barker, P. (1998). *Basic family therapy* (4th ed.). London: Blackwell Science Limited.

Bernard, J. (1992). The challenge of psychotherapy-based supervision: Making the pieces fit. *Counselor Education and Supervision, 31,* 232–237.

Bernard, J. (1997). The discrimination model. In C. E. Watkins (Ed.), *Handbook of psychotherapy supervision* (pp. 310–327). New York: Wiley.

Bernard, J., & Goodyear, R. (1998). *Fundamentals of clinical supervision* (2nd ed.) Boston: Allyn & Bacon.

Betchen, S. (1995). An integrative, intersystemic approach to supervision of couple therapy. *The American Journal of Family Therapy, 23,* 48–58.

Binder, J. (1993). Observations on the training of therapists in time-limited dynamic psychotherapy. *Psychotherapy, 30,* 592–598.

Binder, J., & Strupp, H. (1997). Supervision of psychodynamic psychotherapies. In C. E. Watkins (Ed.), *Handbook of psychotherapy supervision* (pp. 44–62). New York: Wiley.

Borders, L. D., & Fong, M. (1994). Cognitions of supervisors in training: An exploratory study. *Counselor Education and Supervision, 33,* 280–293.

Bordin, E. S. (1983). A working alliance based model of supervision. *The Counseling Psychologist, 11,* 35–41.

Breunlin, D. C., & Cade, B. (1981). Intervening in family systems with observer messages. *Journal of Marital and Family Therapy, 7,* 453–460.

Broderick, C. B., & Schrader, S. S. (1991). The history of professional marriage and family therapy. In A. S. Gurman & D. P. Kniskern (Eds.), *Handbook of family therapy* (Vol. 2, pp. 3–40). New York: Brunner/Mazel.

Buelow, G., Bass, C., & Ackerman, C. (1994). Comparing family functioning of counselors in training with the family functioning of noncounselors. *Counselor Education and Supervision, 33,* 162–174.

Caldwell, K., Becvar, D., Bertolino, R., & Diamond, D. (1997). A postmodern analysis of a course on clinical supervision. *Contemporary Family Therapy, 19,* 269–287.

Carlozzi, A. F., Romans, J. S. C., Boswell, D. L., Ferguson, D. B., & Whisenhunt, B. J. (1997). Training and supervision practices in counseling and marriage and family therapy programs. *Clinical Supervisor, 15,* 51–60.

Carter, E. (1982). Supervisory discussion in the presence of the family. In R. Whiffen & J. Byng-Hall (Eds.), *Family therapy supervision: Recent developments in practice* (pp. 69–79). New York: Grune & Stratton.

Caust, B., Libow, J., & Raskin, P. (1981). Challenges and promises of training women as family systems therapists. *Family Process, 20,* 439–448.

Cleghorn, J., & Levin, S. (1973). Training family therapists by setting learning objectives. *American Journal of Orthopsychiatry, 43,* 439–446.

Coopersmith, E. I. (1980). Expanding uses of the telephone in family therapy. *Family Process, 19,* 411–417.

Costa, L. (1991). Family sculpting in the training of marriage and family counselors. *Counselor Education and Supervision, 31,* 121–131.

Doherty, W., & Boss, P. (1991). Values and ethics in family therapy. In A. Gurman & D. Kniskern (Eds.), *Handbook of family therapy* (Vol. 2, pp. 606–637). New York: Brunner/Mazel.

Edwards, T., & Keller, J. (1995). Partnership discourse in marriage and family therapy supervision: A heterarchical alternative. *The Clinical Supervisor, 13,* 141–153.

Efstation, J., Patton, M., & Kardash, C. (1990). Measuring the working alliance in counselor supervision. *Journal of Counseling Psychology, 37,* 322–329.

Ekstein, R., & Wallerstein, R. (1972). *The teaching and learning of psychotherapy* (2nd ed.). Madison, WI: International Universities Press.

Ellis, M., Ladany, N., Krengel, M., & Schult, D. (1996). Clinical supervision research from 1981 to 1993: A methodological critique. *Journal of Counseling Psychology, 43,* 35–50.

Emerson, S. (1996). Creating a safe place for growth in supervision. *Contemporary Family Therapy, 18,* 393–403.

Everett, C. (1980). Supervision of marriage and family therapy. In A. Hess (Ed.), *Psychotherapy supervision: Theory, research, and practice* (pp. 367–380). New York: Wiley.

Fisher, B. L., & Sprenkle, D. H. (1980). Family therapy conceptualization and use of "case notes." *Family Therapy, 2,* 177–184.

Framo, J. L. (1982). *Explorations of marital and family therapy: Selected papers of James L. Framo.* New York: Springer-Verlag.

Framo, J. L. (1992). *Family-of-origin therapy: An intergenerational approach.* New York: Brunner/Mazel

Frankel, B. R., & Piercy, F. P. (1990). The relationship among selected supervisor, therapist, and client behaviors. *Journal of Marital and Family Therapy, 5,* 15–22.

Friedman, D., & Kaslow, N. (1986). The development of professional identity in psychotherapists: Six stages in the supervision process. *The Clinical Supervisor, 4,* 29–49.

Gallant, J. P., Thyer, B. A., & Bailey, J. S. (1991). Using bug-in-the-ear feedback in clinical supervision: Preliminary evaluations. *Research on Social Work Practice, 1,* 175–187.

Getz, H., & Protinsky, H. (1994). Training marriage and family counselors: A family of origin approach. *Counselor Education and Supervision, 33,* 183–190.

Goldenberg, J., & Goldenberg, H. (1996). *Family therapy: An overview* (4th ed.). New York: Brooks/Cole.

Grandesso, M. A. (1996). The reflecting team: An analysis from the construction-of-meaning point of view. *Journal of Constructivist Psychology, 9,* 303–309.

Granello, D., Beamish, P., & Davis, T. (1997). Supervisee empowerment: Does gender make a difference? *Counselor Education and Supervision, 36,* 305–317.

Haley, J. (1976). *Problem-solving therapy.* New York: Harper Colophon.

Heath, T. (1983). The live supervision form: Structure and theory assessment in live supervision. In J. C. Hansen & B. P. Keeney (Eds.), *Diagnosis and assessment in family therapy* (pp. 143–154). Rockville, MD: Aspen Systems.

Henry, W., Schacht, T., Strupp, H., Butler, S., & Binder, J. (1993). Effects of training in time-limited dynamic psychotherapy: Mediators of therapists' responses to training. *Journal of Consulting and Clinical Psychology, 61,* 441–447.

Hill, W. (1992). Marital and family therapy supervision: A relational-attachment model. *Contemporary Family Therapy, 14,* 115–125.

Hoffman, L. (1993). *Exchanging voices.* London: Karnac Books.

Holloway, E. (1997). Structures for the analysis and teaching of supervision. In C. E. Watkins (Ed.), *Handbook of psychotherapy supervision* (pp. 249–276). New York: Wiley.

Horne, A., Dagley, J., & Webster, C. (1993). Strategies for implementing marriage and family counselor training in counselor education programs. *Counselor Education and Supervision, 33,* 102–115.

Johnson, C., Waters, M., Webster, D., & Goldman, J. (1997). What do you think about what the team said? The solution-focused reflecting team as a virtual therapeutic community. *Contemporary Family Therapy: An International Journal, 19,* 49–62.

Jordan, K. (1998). The cultural experiences and identified needs of the ethnic minority supervisee in the context of Caucasian supervision. *Family Therapy, 25,* 181–187.

Jordan, K., & Quinn, W. (1996). Ethical concerns for supervising the impaired marriage and family therapist. *Family Therapy, 23,* 51–57.

Kaiser, T. (1992). The supervisory relationship: An identification of the primary elements in the relationship and an application of two theories of ethical relationships. *Journal of Marital and Family Therapy, 18,* 283–296.

Kaplan, R. (1987). The current use of live supervision within marriage and family therapy training programs. *Clinical Supervisor, 5,* 43–52.

Kaufman, M., & Korner, S. (1997). Psychotherapists' perceptions of their trainers and training emphases. *The Clinical Supervisor, 16,* 97–115.

Kelly, G. (1990). The cultural family of origin: A description of a training strategy. *Counselor Education and Supervision, 30,* 77–84.

Ladany, N., Brittan-Powell, C., & Pannu, R. (1997). The influence of supervisory racial identity interaction and racial matching on the supervisory working alliance and supervisee multicultural competence. *Counselor Education and Supervision, 36,* 284–304.

Ladany, N., & Friedlander, M. (1995). The relationship between the supervisory working alliance and trainees' experience of role conflict and role ambiguity. *Counselor Education and Supervision, 34,* 220–231.

Ladany, N., Hill, C., Corbett, M., & Nutt, E. (1996). Nature, extent, and importance of what psychotherapy trainees do not disclose to their supervisors. *Journal of Counseling Psychology, 43,* 10–24.

Lambert, M., & Ogles, B. (1997). The effectiveness of psychotherapy supervision. In C. E. Watkins (Ed.), *Handbook of psychotherapy supervision* (pp. 421–446). New York: Wiley.

Landau, J., & Stanton, M. D. (1983). Aspects of supervision with the "Pick-A-Dali Circus" model. *Journal of Strategic and Systemic Therapies, 2,* 31–39.

Landis, L. L., & Young, M. E. (1994). The reflecting team in counselor education. *Counselor Education & Supervision, 33,* 210–218.

Larrabee, M., & Miller, G. (1993). An examination of sexual intimacy in supervision. *The Clinical Supervisor, 11,* 103–126.

Lawson, D., Gaushell, W. H., McCune, S., & McCune, E. D. (1995). Perception of counselor behavior and current intergenerational family relationships. *Counselor Education and Supervision, 34,* 356–368.

Leach, M., Stoltenberg, C., McNeill, B., & Eichenfield, G. (1997). Self-efficacy and counselor development: Testing the integrated developmental model. *Counselor Education and Supervision, 37,* 115–124.

Liddle, H. (1986). Redefining the mission of family therapy training: Can our differentness make a difference? *Journal of Psychotherapy and the Family, 1,* 109–124.

Liddle, H. (1988). Systematic supervision: Conceptual overlays and pragmatic guidelines. In H. Liddle, D. Breunlin, & R. Schwartz (Eds.), *Handbook of family therapy training and supervision* (pp. 153–171). New York: Guilford Press.

Liddle, H. (1991). Training and supervision in family therapy: A comprehensive and critical analysis. In A. Gurman & D. Kniskern (Eds.), *Handbook of family therapy* (Vol. 2, pp. 638–697). New York: Brunner/Mazel.

Liddle, H., Becker, D., & Diamond, G. (1997). Family therapy supervision. In C.E. Watkins, Jr. (Ed.), *Handbook of psychotherapy supervision* (pp. 400–418). New York: Wiley.

Liddle, H., Breunlin, D., & Schwartz, R. (1988). Family therapy training and supervision: An introduction. In H. Liddle, D. Breunlin, & R. Schwartz (Eds.), *Handbook of family therapy training and supervision* (pp. 3–9). New York: Guilford Press.

Liddle, H., & Halpin, R. (1978). Family therapy training and supervision literature: A comparative review. *Journal of Marriage and Family Counseling, 4,* 77–98.

Long, J. (1997). Sexual orientation: Implications for the supervisory process. In T. Todd & C. Storm (Eds.), *The complete systemic supervisor: Context, philosophy, and pragmatics* (pp. 59–71). Boston: Allyn & Bacon.

Mazza, J. (1988). Training strategic therapists: The use of indirect techniques. In H. Liddle, D. Breunlin, & R. Schwartz (Eds.), *Handbook of family therapy training and supervision* (pp. 93–109). New York: Guilford Press.

McCollum, E. E., & Wetchler, J. L. (1995). In defense of case consultation: Maybe "dead" supervision isn't dead after all. *Journal of Marital & Family Therapy, 21,* 155–166.

McGee, M., & Burton, R. (1998). The use of co-therapy with a reflecting mirror as a supervisory tool. *Journal of Family Psychotherapy, 9,* 45–60.

McGoldrick, M., Almeida, R., Preto, N., Bibb, A., Sutton, C., Hudak, J., & Hines, P. (1999). Efforts to incorporate social justice perspectives into a family training program. *Journal of Marital and Family Therapy, 25,* 191–209.

McKenzie, P., Atkinson, B., Quinn, W., & Heath, A. (1986). Training and supervision in marriage and family therapy: A national survey. *The American Journal of Family Therapy, 14,* 293–303.

McNeill, B., & Worthen, V. (1989). The parallel process in psychotherapy supervision. *Professional Psychology: Research and Practice, 20,* 329–333.

Minuchin, S. (1974). *Families & family therapy.* Cambridge, MA: Harvard University Press.

Minuchin, S. (1981). *Family therapy techniques.* Cambridge, MA: Harvard University Press.

Montalvo, B. (1973). Aspects of live supervision. *Family Process, 12,* 343–359.

Napier, A. Y., & Whitaker, C. (1978). *The family crucible: The intense experience of family therapy.* New York: Harper & Row.

Nichols, M. P., & Schwartz, R. C. (1995). *Family therapy: Concepts and methods* (3rd ed.). Boston: Allyn & Bacon.

Nichols, W., & Everett, C. (1986). *Systemic family therapy.* New York: Guilford Press.

Nichols, W., Nichols, D., & Hardy, K. (1990). Supervision in family therapy: A decade restudy. *Journal of Marital and Family Therapy, 16,* 275–285.

Nickell, N., Hecker, L., Ray, R., & Bercik, J. (1995). Marriage and family therapists' sexual attraction to clients: An exploratory study. *The American Journal of Family Therapy, 23,* 315–327.

Olsen, D., & Stern, S. (1990). Issues in the development of a family therapy supervision model. *The Clinical Supervisor, 8,* 49–65.

Papp, P. (1980). The Greek chorus and other techniques of paradoxical therapy. *Family Process, 19,* 45–57.

Piercy, F. P., Laird, R. A., & Mohammed, Z. (1983). A family therapist rating scale. *Journal of Marital and Family Therapy, 9,* 393–401.

Pistole, C. (1995). The genogram in group supervision of novice counselors: Draw them a picture. *The Clinical Supervisor, 13,* 133–143.

Prest, L. A., Darden, E. C., & Keller, J. F. (1990). "The fly on the wall" reflecting team supervision. *Journal of Marital and Family Therapy, 16,* 256–273.

Prest, L., Russel, R., & D'Souza, H. (1999). Spirituality and religion in training, practice and person development. *Journal of Family Therapy, 21,* 60–77.

Raichelson, S., Herron, W., Primavera, L., & Ramirez, S. (1997). Incidence and effects of parallel process in psychotherapy supervision. *The Clinical Supervisor, 15,* 37–48.

Rigazio-DiGilio, S., & Anderson, S. (1994). A cognitive-developmental model for marital and family therapy supervision. *The Clinical Supervisor, 12,* 93–118.

Rigazio-DiGilio, S., Anderson, S., & Kunkler, K. (1995). Gender-aware supervision in marriage and family counseling and therapy: How far have we actually come? *Counselor Education and Supervision, 34,* 344–355.

Sand-Pringle, C., Zarski, J., & Wendling, K. (1995). Swords into plowshares: Supervisory issues with violent families. *Journal of Systemic Therapies, 14,* 34–46.

Shanfield, S., Mohl, P., Matthews, K., & Hetherly, V. (1992). Quantitative assessment of the behavior of psychotherapy supervisors. *American Journal of Psychiatry, 149,* 352–357.

Smith, C. W., Smith, T. A., & Salts, C. J. (1991). The effects of supervisory interruptions on therapists and clients. *American Journal of Family Therapy, 19,* 250–256.

Smith, R. (1993). Training in marriage and family counseling and therapy: Current status and challenges. *Counselor Education and Supervision, 33,* 89–101.

Smith, T. E., Yoshioka, M., & Winton, M. (1993). A qualitative understanding of reflecting teams: I. Client perspectives. *Journal of Systemic Therapies, 12,* 28–43.

Spruill, D. (1994). Use of videotaped initial family interviews in training beginning family therapists. *Counselor Education and Supervision, 33,* 201–209.

Stevens-Smith, P., Hinkle, J. S., & Stahmann, R. (1993). Comparison of professional accreditation standards in marriage and family counseling and therapy. *Counselor Education and Supervision, 33,* 116–126.

Steward, R. (1998). Connecting counselor self-efficacy and supervisor self-efficacy: The continued search for counseling competence. *The Counseling Psychologist, 26,* 285–294.

Stoltenberg, C. D., McNeill, B. W., & Crethar, H. C. (1994). Changes in supervision as counselors and therapists gain experience: A review. *Professional Psychology: Research and Practice, 25,* 416–449.

Stoltenberg, C. D., McNeill, B., & Delworth, U. (1998). *IDM Supervision: An integrated model for supervising counselors and therapists.* San Francisco: Jossey-Bass.

Storm, C. (1997). The blueprint for supervision relationships: Contracts. In T. Todd & C. Storm (Eds.), *The complete systemic supervisor: Context, philosophy, and pragmatics* (pp. 272–282). Boston: Allyn & Bacon.

Strupp, H. (1986). Psychotherapy: Research, practice, and public policy (how to avoid dead ends). *American Psychologist, 41,* 120–130.

Strupp, H. (1992). The future of psychodynamic psychotherapy. *Psychotherapy, 20,* 21–27.

Todd, T., & Storm, C. (1997). Thoughts on the evolution of MFT supervision. In T. Todd & C. Storm (Eds.), *The complete systemic supervisor: Context, philosophy, and pragmatics* (pp. 1–16). Boston: Allyn & Bacon.

Tucker, S. J., & Pinsorf, W. M. (1984). The empirical evaluation of family therapy training. *Family Process, 23,* 437–456.

Watkins, C. E. (1993). Development of the psychotherapy supervisor: Concepts, assumptions, and hypotheses of the supervisor complexity model. *American Journal of Psychotherapy, 47,* 58–74.

Watkins, C. E., Jr. (Ed.). (1997). *Handbook of psychotherapy supervision.* New York: Wiley.

Weber, T., McKeever, J. E., & McDaniel, S. H. (1985). A beginner's guide to the problem-oriented first family interview. *Family Process, 24,* 357–364.

West, J. D., Bubenzer, D. L., Pinsoneault, T., & Holeman, V. (1993). Three supervision modalities for training marital and family counselors. *Counselor Education & Supervision, 33,* 127–138.

West, J. D., Bubenzer, D. L., & Zarski, J. J. (1989). Live supervision in family therapy: An interview with Barbara Okun and Fred Piercy. *Counselor Education & Supervision, 29,* 25–34.

Wetchler, J. L., & Fisher, B. L. (1991). A prepracticum course for beginning marriage and family therapy students. *Clinical Supervisor, 9,* 171–180.

Whitaker, C. A., & Keith, D. V. (1981). Symbolic-experiential family therapy. In A. S. Gurman & D. P. Kniskern (Eds.), *Handbook of family therapy* (Vol. 1, pp. 187–225). New York: Brunner/Mazel.

White, M., & Russell, C. (1995). The essential elements of supervisory systems: A modified Delphi study. *Journal of Marital and Family Therapy, 21,* 33–53.

White, M., & Russell, C. (1997). Examining the multifaceted notion of isomorphism in marriage and family therapy supervision: A quest for conceptual clarity. *Journal of Marital and Family Therapy, 23,* 315–333.

Williams, L. (1994). A tool for training supervisors: Using the Supervision Feedback Form (SFF). *Journal of Marital and Family Therapy, 20,* 311–315.

Worthen, V., & McNeill, B. (1996). A phenomenological investigation of "good" supervision events. *Journal of Counseling Psychology, 43,* 25–34.

IV

PROFESSIONAL ISSUES IN COUNSELOR SUPERVISION

11
CHAPTER

L. J. Gould
Loretta J. Bradley

Evaluation in Supervision

Evaluation in the supervision process is both widely recognized as an important component of supervision (Bernard & Goodyear, 1998; Halgin & Murphy, 1995; Hess, 1997; Holloway, 1997; Norcross & Halgin, 1997; Watkins, 1997) and specified as an aspect of supervision in the ethics codes and practice standards of professional organizations (American Association of Marriage and Family Therapy, 1993; American Counseling Association, 1995; Association for Counselor Education and Supervision, 1995; American Psychological Association Ethics Committee, 1992). In fact, evaluation has been called the main task of supervision (Pickvance, 1997), a core variable in counselor training (Halgin & Murphy, 1995), the "nucleus" of supervision (Bernard & Goodyear), and the main difference between counseling and supervision (Inskipp, 1996). Webster's Dictionary (Guralnick, 1970) defines evaluation as "to judge or determine the worth or quality of; appraise." While each of these statements underscores the importance of evaluation, neither gives any indication regarding the process or criteria involved. In fact, although the importance of evaluation cannot be denied, there is virtually no empirical research to determine what is essential for supervisees to learn and/or be evaluated on in the supervision process (Ellis & Ladany, 1997).

Evaluation is the conundrum of supervision. The confusion surrounding it leads us to ask, Exactly what is evaluation in counselor supervision? This question is difficult because no one has produced a definitive answer Thus, it is necessary to examine it in other ways. From the beginning of counseling as a profession, counselor supervisors have not only taught and encouraged their students but also monitored their progress towards professional status (Bernard & Goodyear, 1998). In the literature, evaluation has most often been described by its purpose, role, or responsibilities rather than by the actions involved in implementing it during the supervision process. Robiner, Fuhrman, Ristvedt, and Bobbitt (1994) stated that the purpose of evaluation in the supervision process is to enhance and evaluate supervisee competence, monitor her or his quality of professional performance, and assess the supervisee's readiness to practice independently. They also proposed that the role of the supervisor included facilitating the supervisee's development of clinical competence and evaluating her or his skills and professional judgment. Other authors stated that evaluation is critical in insuring skill refinement and quality of client care and that training programs provide effective counselor training (S. R. Friedlander & Dye, 1984; Newman, McGovern, Kopta, Howard, & McNeilly, 1988; Robiner, Fuhrman, & Ristvedt, 1993; Williams, 1995). Watkins (1997) agreed and added that it was the supervisor's responsibility to provide accurate feedback regarding the supervisee's progress and performance, to point out specific strengths and weaknesses to the supervisee, and to serve as gatekeeper for the profession by determining the supervisee's suitability for the profession. Stricker (1987) noted that training programs are responsible for evaluating supervisees with regard to the personal attributes, aptitudes, and values that best predict future competence; he further noted that unfortunately no systematic way of determining these personal characteristics currently exists. Borders and Leddick (1987) and Ladany, Lehrman-Waterman, Molinaro, and Wolgast (1999) stated that ethical guidelines for the mental health professions stress the importance of evaluation in the areas of performance and supervisee activities, professional roles, site standards, and expertise and competency issues.

To answer the overarching question of what evaluation is in counselor supervision, we must consider several other questions, and their answers, that are intimately related. These questions are:

- What are the criteria to be evaluated?
- Who is evaluated and who evaluates?
- When and where does evaluation take place?
- How is evaluation conducted in supervision?
- Why is evaluation problematic?

☐ What Are the Criteria to Be Evaluated?

The process of supervision is similar to the process of counseling, with a single important distinction: The progress or outcome of supervision cannot be used as definitive criteria for evaluating its success. The supervisor has a responsibility to both the profession and the supervisee's clients that demands external evaluative criteria that meet both professional standards of competence and institutional (university or training program) requirements (Robiner et al., 1994). Virtually all supervision approaches have an evaluation element regarding supervisee performance that is rated on a number of different variables (Lehrman-Waterman, 1999; Watkins, 1997). These variables generally include intervention, interpersonal, and assessment skills (Stoltenberg & Delworth, 1987); conceptualization (Borders & Leddick, 1987; Neufeldt, 1999); treatment goals and plans (Locke & Latham, 1990); professional and ethical behaviors (Ladany et al., 1999); multicultural counseling and assessment (Arredondo et al., 1996; Constantine, 1997); and behavior within supervision (Holloway, 1992).

The various accrediting bodies of the mental health professions have been pivotal in defining criteria for professional competency by setting educational requirements and standards for their disciplines (Bernard & Goodyear, 1998). These standards are then translated into criteria that address the evaluation of students in counseling programs and professionals seeking licensure or certification (counseling behaviors) or the performance of supervisors in training students to be competent practitioners (supervisory behaviors). Generally, however, professional standards are related to counseling behaviors and seldom include personal characteristics affecting counselor performance, with the exception of entrance and termination criteria. Hahn and Molnar (1991) noted that standards tend to increase over time, but whether this is because the field is becoming more complex or because it is human nature to add when criteria is involved is unknown. McLeod (1996) stated that competence is a complex issue with few satisfactory answers, which supports Magnuson's (1995) assertion that even when criteria are specified, expected competency levels often remain elusive.

Some studies have attempted to define competence areas, and by doing so, identify areas amenable to evaluation. Cross and Brown (1983) examined research on supervisory behaviors and found that half of the 44 variables they identified loaded on evaluation, including skill development, personal development, and monitoring and evaluating the supervisee's work. Similarly, Bent and Cannon (1987) defined six functional skill areas to be addressed in supervision: relationship, assessment, intervention, evaluation and research, consultation and teaching, and management of supervision. Overholser and Fine (1990) identified five areas of investigation in counselor competency: factual knowledge, generic clinical skills, orientation-specific technical skills, clinical judgment, and interpersonal attitude. In a similar study, Perlesz, Stolk, and Firestone (1990) identified four areas of investigation: perceptual skills, conceptual skills, executive-intervention skills, and demonstrated personal development. Neufeldt (1999) listed five areas to be evaluated at the end of practicum: clinical skills, relationship skills, professional presentation and behavior, knowledge, and agency behavior.

The previous studies were primarily concerned with behavioral and functional skills in counselor competency. However, in a different type of investigation, Frame and Stevens-Smith (1995) attempted to define the personal characteristics relevant to success as a counselor, including being open, flexible, positive and cooperative; willingness to accept and use feedback; awareness of her or his impact on others; ability to deal with conflict;

acceptance of personal responsibility; and the ability to express feelings effectively and appropriately. With the exception of Frame and Stevens-Smith, the studies described above have suggested that counselor competence primarily results from theoretical knowledge, skills in therapy-related behaviors, and often unnamed interpersonal skills. Few studies have attempted to define these competency areas explicitly. Finally, Arredondo et al. (1996), Larson et al. (1992), Pope-Davis and Dings (1995), and Sue (1996) have stressed the importance of training counselors to be competent in multicultural counseling. Research in multicultural competencies has identified a varying number of factors to be assessed, from the single factor of global assessment of cross-cultural competence (Laromboise, Coleman, & Hernandez, 1991) to the four factors of awareness, knowledge, skills, and relationship (Sodowsky, Taffee, Gutkin, & Wise, 1994).

McLeod (1996) compared the use of treatment manual approaches to taxonomies of counselor skills in defining areas of counseling competence and the skills required to achieve it. The treatment manual approach involves developing a manual that details types of interventions to be implemented in counseling according to a specific theory, and then training counselors in the use of the manual. Competence is determined by evaluating how precisely the manual is followed by the supervisee (Lambert & Ogles, 1988; Shaw & Dobson, 1988). McLeod noted that this approach is limited by measuring competence within the tenets of a single theory. This limits generalizability, and therefore, the skill competence acquired by the supervisee is unlikely to be relevant to the majority of counselors who describe themselves as eclectic or integrationist. A different approach to defining the skills necessary for competence involves the construction of taxonomies, or lists, and then developing methods to evaluate the counselor's level of competence in each of the skills listed in the taxonomy. Taxonomies of counseling skills have been produced by Ivey and Galvin (1984), Crouch (1992), and Larson et al. (1992).

Taxonomies are most often used in training courses, as they allow counseling performance to be assessed in a structured manner. Because taxonomies assess global performance, they are less precise measures of technical skills than manual training; however, they are more applicable in general and more economical to use. Taxonomies are limited as evaluation criteria primarily because the ability to perform a skill successfully in training does not assure the student's ability to use the skill successfully in actual practice with clients. Additionally, taxonomies tend to grow longer as more areas of importance are identified in the profession. McLeod (1996) stated that the danger inherent in this unrelenting growth is the problem of gathering enough pertinent information on each item to assure competence without turning the assessment process into a "stultifying, bureaucratic exercise" (p. 40). Finally, McLeod asserted that taxonomies have been derived from researchers' ideas about what counselors should know rather than from observations of what effective practicing counselors actually do know.

Other methods have attempted to define explicit criteria in various ways. One method involves the systematic investigation of behaviors and skills that supervisors tend to focus on in supervision; this eventually produces a list of criteria for evaluation (Carey & Lanning, 1993; Lanning & Freeman, 1994). A similar method involves a job analysis of the knowledge and skills used and believed important by counselors in practice (Fitzgerald & Osipow, 1986; National Board of Certified Counselors, 1993). Unlike taxonomies, the skills and behaviors derived from these methods are based in the practical knowledge of what counselors and supervisors do. In a related study, Mohl, Sadler, and Miller (1994) surveyed a psychiatric residency faculty to determine what they would be willing to evaluate and what they felt could be evaluated in both academic and clinical contexts. Bernard and Goodyear (1998) suggested that this type of evaluation could be applied to any training program.

Unfortunately, there is no simple answer to the question of criteria. At present, criteria are primarily derived from professional standards of practice and the few studies that have attempted to define areas of competence. This lack of generalized standards in the mental health field can lead to confusion for counselors in diverse settings. Additionally, professional standards of competence may be a case of finding the lowest common denominator rather than an attempt to ensure excellence in the field. Williams (1995) stated that evaluation criteria tend to be subjective and ambiguous, largely because counseling skills are complex, personal, and difficult to measure. We agree with his assessment of the problem with criteria and suggest that to be effective evaluators, supervisors must know and adhere to the professional standards of practice and ethics of counseling, stay current with regard to the research into criteria, support and/or conduct research into areas of job analysis and effective supervision, and monitor their own tendencies toward subjectivity and ambiguity in the performance of supervision.

☐ Who Is Evaluated and Who Evaluates?

The first part of this question—who is evaluated—appears to have a simple and obvious answer: the supervisee. Virtually all of the criteria discussed in the previous section are identified with the training of counseling practitioners. While the primary target of the evaluation process is the supervisee and her or his performance, in effective supervision the supervisor is also evaluated. Some researchers have suggested the importance of the supervisor inviting feedback on her or his supervision skills, style, and development (Borders & Leddick, 1987; Freeman, 1985; Stoltenberg, McNeill, & Delworth, 1998). However, it is from studies of supervisee satisfaction that the strongest implications for the need for ongoing supervisor evaluation emerge. Most, if not all, studies of supervisee satisfaction stress the importance of feedback (Allen, Szollos, & Williams, 1986; Hahn & Molnar, 1991; Heppner & Handley, 1982; Hutt, Scott, & King, 1983; Kadushin, 1992, 1993; Norcross & Stevenson, 1984), and many report the major area of dissatisfaction to be a lack of negative or corrective feedback from the supervisor. If supervisors follow the suggestions of Borders and Leddick, Freeman, and Stoltenberg et al. and periodically asked for feedback from supervisees on their performance, perhaps they will be more likely to give supervisees what they need in supervision. Most supervisors believe they are doing an adequate or better job as supervisors (Robiner et al., 1994), but without supervisee feedback, a supervisor cannot be sure.

The question of who does evaluation is somewhat easier to answer. Although the supervisor is most likely to have the sole responsibility for evaluating her or his supervisees (Borders & Leddick, 1987), there are performance evaluation scales available that may be completed by either the supervisor or supervisee (Borders & Fong, 1991; Fuqua, Newman, Scott, & Gade, 1986; Lambert & Ogles, 1997). Additionally, evaluation instruments are available that call for rating by a client, peer, or an independent outside rater. Lambert and Ogles (1997) reviewed 55 instruments concerned with supervisee performance and reported that 24 were designed for rating by an outside rater, 15 by the supervisor, 17 by the supervisee, 5 by the client, 1 by peers, and 3 were not classified. (Some of the instruments were designed for use by a combination of raters.)

In summary, evaluation is a two-way street, with supervisor and supervisee both evaluating and being evaluated. Of course, the primary subject of evaluation is the supervisee, but the supervisor who fails to encourage feedback on supervisory performance is depriving herself or himself of a valuable resource for improving and/or refining her or his skills as a supervisor. Additionally, failure to take advantage of the other sources of evaluation (peers, client-report instruments, outside evaluators) limits the impact of evaluation to the perceptions of the individuals in the supervisory dyad.

☐ When and Where Does Evaluation Take Place?

According to Stoltenberg et al. (1998), evaluation should be an ongoing aspect of the supervision process, providing the supervisee with timely feedback. In academic settings, the supervisor most likely meets with supervisees on a schedule that fulfills the university's demands for student–teacher contact. In a practicum course, this will probably be a weekly session that includes all students enrolled in the course with individual sessions set as needed; in an internship course, the faculty supervisor and intern will be more likely to meet only once or twice per semester, as the primary supervision will be provided by the site supervisor. Site supervisors, whether of practica students or interns, meet with supervisees on a schedule that is mandated by the site's standard operating procedures. At regularly scheduled meetings, the supervisor provides formative feedback for the supervisee; and at the midpoint and end of the term, the supervisor provides a formal evaluation of progress (Borders & Leddick, 1987). Walsh (1990) and Pickvance (1997) argued that it is the supervisor's responsibility to set both a specific time and number of meetings with the supervisee for review of her or his progress. The timing of supervision sessions is usually a matter of convenience or personal preference (Couchon & Bernard, 1984). Although there is little in the literature specifically regarding the timing of supervision, Disney and Stephens (1994) warned that setting supervision sessions for convenience alone may invite liability if provisions are not made for emergencies that may occur.

Couchon and Bernard (1984) studied the effects of timing on the supervisor–supervisee–client interaction. They discovered that supervision sessions conducted the day before a supervisee–client session appeared to be more content oriented, with the supervisor presenting and teaching conceptual material. Supervision sessions conducted immediately before a supervisee–client session were more focused and concerned planning strategies; supervisees in these sessions were more rewarded by expressions of supervisor approval of their strategies. Couchon and Bernard suggested that the timing of supervision sessions might be used to help supervisees of different developmental levels become more effective counselors. They suggested that those supervisees who were skilled in conceptualization but implemented strategies poorly would benefit from supervision sessions that provided them with strategies for use with the client immediately before a counseling session. On the other hand, supervisees who implemented strategies skillfully but were limited in their conceptualization skills would benefit from supervisory sessions the day before a counseling session, thus having time to process any material produced by the supervisor–supervisee interaction.

Little has been written about where supervision takes place, but generally, supervised practice occurs in an academic setting, an agency, or in a private practice setting. Supervisors in academic settings usually have participated in some aspect of the supervisee's previous coursework and training, and thus have some knowledge of the supervisee's developmental level as a counselor. They have direct control over the supervisee's caseload and can tailor counseling experiences to her or his abilities. Supervisors in academic settings usually have facilities available for observation of supervisees that may not be available in either private practice or agency settings. Additionally, they have the support of peers for consultation if difficulties occur in the supervision process (Cain & Markowski, 1989).

Supervisees in an agency setting are expected to adhere to the rules and regulations of the site with guidance from a site supervisor who is responsible for evaluating her or his progress on a day-to-day basis. The agreement between the site and the supervisee, and therefore the university, should specify the timing of supervision sessions (at least 1 hour per week), the clientele of the agency, and the process of evaluation used. Arrangements must also be made to provide the university supervisor with access to samples of the supervisee's work and periodic evaluations of the supervisee's progress (Boylan, 1995; Neufeldt, 1999; Scott, 1995).

Supervisors in private practice settings are individually responsible for organizing, monitoring, and evaluating the supervisee's counseling experience. They cannot control the supervisee's client caseload as closely as in the other settings because they are more often concerned with maintaining the caseload supporting their practice than assigning supervisees clients whose problems are appropriate for their developmental level. Private practice supervisors do not have the ready support of fellow supervisors, nor do they have the facilities available to them that university supervisors do (Cain & Markowski, 1989).

There is little doubt that the when and the where of evaluation is dependent on a number of factors, including program requirements, site placement, and the availability of a mutually convenient meeting time for supervisory sessions. We believe that student counselors should be supervised consistently, which requires a weekly session to provide timely feedback on counseling progress. Program supervisors should be certain that supervisees will be supervised on-site a minimum of 1 hour weekly. Further, the program supervisor should be advised of any problems on-site immediately. Additionally, because the program supervisor is responsible for the student's grade, he or she should periodically review samples of the supervisee's work and provide appropriate feedback rather than depend solely on reports from the on-site supervisor.

How Is Evaluation Conducted in Supervision?

The process of successful evaluation involves several elements: the supervisory relationship; a supervision-evaluation contract; goals of supervision; feedback, both formative and summative; and evaluation methods. Each of these elements will be discussed in this section.

The Supervisory Relationship

Supervision is an inherently unequal relationship in which power is primarily in the role of the supervisor (Holloway, 1997). Evaluation is the expression of the supervisor's power over the supervisee; its effects can be long-lasting and devastating to both the supervisee's personal and professional life if not conducted in a supportive and respectful atmosphere. If the relationship between supervisor and supervisee is not characterized by facilitative conditions (empathy, genuineness, positive regard, etc.) and support, evaluation may be ignored or perceived as a personal attack. Therefore, we suggest that the supervisor must attend to relationship-forming and alliance issues before attempting to evaluate the supervisee's counseling performance.

Evaluation from a supportive stance strengthens the therapeutic alliance (Lehrman-Waterman, 1999; Patton & Kivlighan, 1997), aids the supervisee in self-disclosure (Ladany & Lehrman-Waterman, 1999), and lessens supervisee role conflict and ambiguity (Ladany & Friedlander, 1995). Supervisee self-efficacy improves with experience and the ability to perform competently (Efstation, Patton, & Kardash, 1990; Johnson, Baker, Kopala, Kiselica, & Thompson, 1989; Larson et al., 1992; Melchert, Hays, Wiljanen, & Kolocek, 1996; Sipps, Sugden, & Favier, 1988). Evaluation plays the primary role in the learning process within supervision (Efstation et al., 1990; Holloway, 1992). Studies of supervisee satisfaction have not specifically addressed evaluation, but positive experiences suggest that evaluation, whether positive or negative, affects the supervisee's perceptions about supervision (Allen et al., 1986; Hutt et al., 1983).

Aspects of supervisory functioning also effect evaluation in the areas of supervisor style, role, focus, and techniques. The supervisor's style of relating to supervisees (task oriented, expert, confrontive and directive, facilitative) can affect both the supervisor's delivery and the supervisee's acceptance of evaluation (Shanfield, Mohl, Matthews, & Hetherly, 1992). It is unlikely that a supervisor whose style is facilitative will give feedback in the same manner as one whose style is confrontive and directive. The role of the supervisor (teacher, lecturer, monitor) also affects the delivery of feedback (Holloway, 1992). As a teacher, the supervisor may present feedback in a way that supports practice to remediate inadequate performance, whereas the supervisor as monitor may provide a report of inadequate behavior without providing for remediation. The supervisor's focus affects the type of feedback that is presented. Rodenhauser, Painter, and Rudisill (1985) suggested four foci of supervisors: professional and organizational factors; assessment and planning processes; implementation, intervention, and evaluation processes; and personal factors. Finally, the techniques used in evaluation, which are discussed later in this chapter, may be facilitative, confrontive, conceptual, prescriptive, or catalytic (Loganbill, Hardy, & Delworth, 1982).

The Supervision Contract

The supervision contract should always include specific information regarding the evaluation process, including methods and criteria to be used (Borders & Leddick, 1987; Norcross & Halgin, 1997; Osborn & Davis, 1996), performance goals (Walsh, 1990), procedures for formative and summative feedback (Neufeldt, 1999), and length and frequency of contacts (Bernard & Goodyear, 1998). Neufeldt stated that the evaluation process should be discussed with the supervisee at the first supervision meeting. At that time, the supervisor should provide the supervisee with written procedures for summative evaluation including explicit criteria and specific procedures to be used. The supervisor should also provide the supervisee with a copy of the final evaluation form; the form should include all areas to be evaluated and a written list of tasks to be successfully completed during the term of supervision. The supervisor should clearly respond to any questions or concerns that the supervisee has about the evaluation process.

Supervisory Tasks

Williams (1995) stated that the supervisor in her or his role as evaluator has eight specific tasks to perform. He or she should closely follow the supervisee's progress in goal attainment as specified in the supervision contract. The supervisor should closely follow client progress and determine if client interventions discussed in supervision sessions are implemented by the supervisee. The supervisee's knowledge of theory, therapy preferences, and personal qualities should be evaluated by the supervisor. He or she should help the supervisee discover her or his strengths and weaknesses. The supervisor should conduct regular progress reviews, confront supervisee counseling behaviors as appropriate, and monitor the supervisee's ethical standards and behavior. Williams (1995) also suggested five "precepts" for the supervisor as an evaluator. First, the supervisor should discover the supervisee's developmental level as a counselor so that her or his interventions will be appropriate. Second, the supervisor should encourage the supervisee's self-evaluation of her or his counseling skills. Third, he or she should observe and point out changes in the supervisee's counseling performance; when the supervisee is alert to changes in her or his abilities, clinical competence will improve. Fourth, the supervisor should use the supervisee's completed cases as teaching examples; discussion regarding the success or failure in counseling outcomes gives the supervisee practice in self-evaluation and professional coherence. Finally, the supervisor should confront the supervisee as required; supervisees want to know what they are doing right or wrong in counseling. However, the supervisor should be careful not to overconfront, or all of the supervision sessions will be devoted to performance practice and remediation.

Supervision Goals

Every method of supervision has procedures and processes for defining the goals to be accomplished during supervision. Supervision goals are specific tasks or proficiencies to be accomplished in a specified period of time (Calpin, Edelstein, & Redmon, 1988). Goals should be challenging but realistically attainable (Lehrman-Waterman, 1999). The supervisor and supervisee set supervision goals collaboratively, working through any disagreements or discrepancies (Mead, 1990; Talen & Schindler, 1993). The goals created in the initial stages of supervision are used in structuring formative and summative evaluation (Bernard and Goodyear, 1998; Freeman, 1985; Holloway, 1992; Locke & Latham, 1990; Newman et al., 1988; Talen & Schindler). In fact, some experts believe that the evaluation process consists of only two functions: goal setting and feedback (Freeman; Holloway, 1992; Osborn & Davis, 1996). Studies directly addressing goal setting as a component of evaluation are rare, but two studies (Levy, 1983; Norcross & Stevenson, 1984) found that the goals are generally global and vague. In a related study, Talen and Schindler investigated goal setting based on supervisee self-report of needs and objectives and found that significant positive change occurred over a 10-month period. Williams (1995) noted that everyone advocates the importance of goal setting, but few suggest how to evaluate the supervisee's progress in attaining those goals.

Feedback

One of the most important aspects of evaluation is providing feedback to the supervisee on her or his progress. Feedback is the supervisor's response to the supervisee's counseling performance. Brightman (1984/1985) stated that feedback is essential for the supervisee's growth as a counselor. Borders and Leddick (1987) argued that supervisees want criticism even though evaluation is anxiety provoking. Feedback should be timely and expected by the supervisee (Farnill, Gordon, & Sansom, 1997; Freeman, 1985). It should be delivered within a supportive and trusting relationship (Borders & Leddick; Farnill et al., 1997; Halgin & Murphy, 1995). Feedback should be concerned with behaviors that affect the counseling process (Borders & Leddick; M. L. Friedlander, Siegel, & Brenock, 1989; Harris, 1994; Lambert & Arnold, 1987; Munson, 1993). It should reflect the supervisee's progress as a counselor by addressing her or his strengths and weaknesses in a balanced manner (Farnill et al.; Halgin & Murphy; Stoltenberg et al., 1998). Feedback should be directly and clearly presented to the supervisee using explicit and specific examples of the supervisee's performance (Edelstein, 1985; Einhorn & Hogarth, 1981; Freeman, 1985; Newman et al., 1988; Poertner, 1986; Tyler & Weaver, 1981).

Freeman (1985) stated that feedback should be systematic, objective, accurate, consistent, and reliable without the influence of subjective variables. Supervisors should avoid global judgments and labeling that may be taken as personal rather than professional criticism (Borders & Leddick, 1987). Additionally, the supervisor should avoid accusatory comments or ultimatums that may result in defensive responses from the supervisee (Harris, 1994; Munson, 1993). Feedback may be oral, written, or a combination of both (Hoffman, 1990). Stoltenberg et al. (1998) stressed the importance of periodically asking the supervisee for feedback on her or his supervisory performance. This serves several purposes: It allows the supervisor to tailor supervision to the needs of the individual supervisee; it strengthens the supervisory relationship by emphasizing the importance of working collaboratively towards the achievement of supervision goals, and it allows the supervisor to modify any behaviors that are not effective in providing supervision. Lehrman-Waterman (1999) reported that the combination of appropriate feedback and realistic goal setting strengthened the supervisory working alliance and positively influenced both supervisee self-efficacy and satisfaction with supervision.

Two types of feedback are crucial to the evaluation process: formative feedback, which is ongoing, and summative feedback, which is presented at specific intervals. Formative feedback, presented at each supervision session, is usually informal and verbal and is used to stimulate discussion and behavioral change (Basarab & Root, 1992; Borders & Leddick, 1987; Neufeldt, 1999; Pickvance, 1997). In formative feedback, the supervisor should present specific examples of the supervisee's work that clearly demonstrate any criticism he or she is making. Formative feedback should stimulate discussion of alternative behaviors available in a given situation and practice of new counseling behaviors. Summative feedback is presented at specific intervals in supervision, usually at the midpoint and end, and is a more comprehensive, written report on supervisee progress that includes descriptions of behaviors that need to be changed (Borders & Leddick). The midpoint evaluation allows the participants to determine if the formative feedback to that point has been effective, and to then plan changes in the supervision process that are specific to the progress required to successfully reach the goals of supervision. Constructive criticism should be given at the midpoint evaluation so that the final summative feedback holds no surprises (Bernard & Goodyear, 1998). Summative feedback should always be delivered to the supervisee in a conference session so that the supervisee's concerns about the evaluation may be readily addressed (Belar et al., 1993; Compton, 1987).

Lehrman-Waterman (1999) noted that little attention has been paid to feedback in the supervision literature. From a survey of supervisee- and supervisor-perceived strengths and weaknesses, Kadushin (1992, 1993) stated that supervisees consider the lack of criticism, overly positive feedback, and constructive criticism delivered only at the end of the term to be the major weaknesses of clinical supervisors. Studies of supervisee satisfaction with supervision underscore the importance of feedback to successful supervisory experiences (Allen et al., 1986; Hahn & Molnar, 1991; Heppner & Handley, 1982; Hutt et al., 1983).

Evaluation Methods and Techniques

Evaluation methods and techniques should be used for the supervisee's advantage, that is, as tools to aid in refining counseling behaviors to achieve competence in performance. Borders et al. (1991) stated that supervision interventions had three general functions: assessing the learning needs of the supervisee; changing, shaping, or supporting supervisee behavior; and evaluating the supervisee's performance.

McCarthy, Kulakowski, and Kenfield (1994) reported that the most frequently used supervisory techniques involved offering support and encouragement, while the most rarely used was confrontation. Bernard and Goodyear (1998) stated that supervision methods are either structured or unstructured. Structured methods are an extension of training, usually directive, with high amounts of supervision activity, planning, and organized learning. For example, teaching a supervisee to use a specific technique, such as cognitive focusing, requires explaining the purpose of the technique, describing the performance of the technique, demonstrating or modeling the technique, and finally allowing the supervisee to attempt the technique. Novice supervisees are more likely to require structured methods (Tracey, Ellickson, & Sherry, 1989). Unstructured methods are almost consultative in nature, may be directed by either the supervisor or supervisee, and allow learning to occur without directing it. Discussing a problem and encouraging the supervisee to brainstorm possible solutions without resorting to solving the problem for the supervisee is an example of ustructured supervision. Unstructured methods are most effective with supervisees who are patient and tolerate ambiguity well.

Loganbill et al. (1982) defined five types of supervisor interventions: facilitative, confrontive, conceptual, prescriptive, and catalytic. Facilitative interventions are supervisee oriented and help promote her or his development as a counselor. They include encouraging, supportive, and positive responses to the supervisee's counseling behaviors, such as complementing a particularly well-performed intervention or insight. Confrontive interventions encourage the supervisee to examine discrepancies occurring in her or his behaviors or feelings during counseling or supervision or occurring between herself or himself and the client or supervisor. For example, while viewing a videotape of a session with the supervisee, the supervisor might point out an incident in which the supervisee's nonverbal and verbal behaviors are incongruent and ask the supervisee to examine her or his feelings at that moment. Conceptual interventions occur when the supervisor asks the supervisee to think either theoretically or analytically about a problem he or she is experiencing in counseling. This could involve asking the supervisee to conceptualize the problem from her or his own theoretical stance and then conceptualize from another theory base. For example, if the supervisee's theory base is cognitive, he or she might conceptualize the problem first from cognitive theory and then from a theory that is affectively based, such as psychodynamic theory. Prescriptive interventions involve coaching the supervisee in either performance or extinction of specific behaviors. For example, a supervisee who is overly reliant on questioning might be asked to conduct a practice session with the supervisor in which he or she counsels for 10 minutes without asking a question. Then, he or she is asked to videotape her or his next session with the client and repeat the exercise in the client session. Prescriptive interventions are the most directive interventions and can be damaging to the supervision process if used too often. Finally, catalytic interventions are movement strategies, usually used to encourage the supervisee in experimenting with new roles in counseling. Thus, a supervisee who primarily depends on talk therapy might be encouraged to use cognitive or behavioral interventions in counseling. Each of these interventions has an evaluative element that can be exploited by the supervisor for supervisee improvement.

The methods discussed in this section are amenable to evaluation. Each method will be described, and its evaluative properties discussed. Included are self-report, process notes, audio- or videotaping, and live observation (supervision).

Self-Report

Self-report often occurs spontaneously in the supervision process as supervisees talk about their clients and the problems they experience in counseling. Self-report involves discussing counseling progress without the support of case notes, audio- or videotaped records, or other forms of supporting data; the supervisee depends on her or his memory of significant events. At its best, the student is challenged both personally and conceptually to fine-tune her or his abilities and personal knowledge of the counselor–client relationship; at its worst, it is pro forma supervision (Bernard & Goodyear, 1998).

Self-report is not without problems. Muslin, Thurnblad, and Meschel (1981) and Wynne, Susman, Ries, Birringer, and Katz (1994) stated that self-report is subject to failure to report and distorted memories. Holloway (1988) argued that self-report is not appropriate for use with novice supervisees who are not experienced enough to report accurately. Although reports by supervisors revealed that self-report is a commonly used, if not the most used, method of supervision (Borders, Cashwell, & Rotter, 1995; Coll, 1995; Goodyear & Nelson, 1997; Magnuson, 1995; Romans, Boswell, Carlozzi, & Ferguson, 1995; Wetchler, Piercy, & Sprenkle, 1989), Campbell (1994) stated that it should not be the supervisor's total supervision strategy. Evaluation using self-report depends on the supervisor's trust in the supervisee's ability to report occurrences in counseling accurately and fully. Rogers and McDonald (1995) reported that in a comparison study of evaluation methods supervisors evaluating their students by more direct methods found them to be less prepared than when they were evaluated by self-report. We believe that self-report may be more effectively used as a method of gathering information about the supervisee's perceptions of counseling; however, as an evaluative method, it is of questionable value since it is solely dependent on the supervisee's memories.

Process Notes

Goldberg (1985) stated that controversy has long existed regarding the use of progress notes between those basing supervision on introspection and those basing supervision on direct access to examples of counseling. Goldberg asserted that progress notes give the supervisor information necessary to track the cognitive processes of the supervisee; Olsen and Stern (1990) supported Goldberg's contentions. However, Goldberg further reported that using process notes as the basis of supervision, and therefore for the purposes of evaluation, should be limited to advanced students to prevent compromising the accuracy of information presented. This supports the conclusions of Muslin et al. (1981), who found that when process notes were compared with actual session recordings, the notes were found to contain distortions and deletions. Bernard and Goodyear (1998) stated that process notes are valuable when used in conjunction with other methods to aid the supervisee in ordering her or his thinking. A simple worksheet can be used following each session (Schwartz, 1981); it should include diagnosis and hypotheses, assessment of past sessions' goals, strategies, and interventions; goals based on previous sessions; specific objectives for the next session; and strategies for obtaining those objectives. As with self-report, we find that the use of progress notes as an evaluation method is limited by the amount of trust the supervisor has in the supervisee's ability to report accurately and fully.

Videotapes and Audiotapes

Although some supervisors prefer one or the other, the methods involved in the use of audiotapes and videotapes are basically the same; therefore, the term *tape* will be used in discussing common elements. Tapes provide numerous areas of instruction for supervisees. Tapes can be used to aid the supervisee in refining specific therapy techniques (Goldberg, 1985), in learning perceptual-conceptual skills (West, Bubenzer, Pinsoneault, & Holeman., 1993), and, by replaying key moments, to analyze her or his counseling behaviors (Aveline, 1997).

When working with novice supervisees, the supervisor should view the entire tape; this allows her or him to get an overview of the supervisee's counseling skills and then select the portion of tape that will be used for the purpose of supervision (Bernard & Goodyear, 1998). Cashwell, Looby, & Housley (1997) proposed several reasons for selecting a segment of tape rather than attempting to use the entire tape in session: highlighting the most productive part of a session; highlighting the most important part of a session; highlighting the part where the supervisee struggles the most; underscoring content issues, such as metaphor or recurring themes; highlighting the most confusing part of a session; and focusing attention on interpersonal dynamics. Each of these areas can be used as the subject of feedback for the supervisee. As supervision progresses, the supervisor may ask the supervisee to select the part of the counseling session where he or she felt the most confused, overwhelmed, or frustrated; the supervisor and supervisee then view the tape together as the supervisee explains why he or she chose that segment, what happened up to that point, what he or she was trying to accomplish, and what specific help he or she wants from the supervisor (Bernard & Goodyear, 1998). Brandell (1992) suggested transcribing a 5- to 10-minute excerpt from a tape and then completing a checklist, about the client's focal conflict in the counseling session. A similar method involves using the transcript with a supervisee response checklist, which allows the supervisee to see how often he or she uses specific types of counselor responses.

Breunlin, Karrer, McGuire, and Cimmarusti (1988) suggested six guidelines for using tapes in supervision. First, focus supervision by setting realistic goals for the session; this serves to narrow the number of interactions to be considered to those specifically related to the session's goals. Second, the supervisee's internal process should be related in supervision; the supervisee's perceptions should be disclosed and validated by the supervisor before he or she expresses his or her opinions about the counseling process. (Interpersonal process recall is an example of this guideline.) Third, the segments of tape selected for review should be amenable to remediation; in other words, corrective feedback should focus on counseling behaviors that can be changed. Fourth, supervisor comments should create a moderate evaluation of performance; in other words, tape segments should be selected that are neither exemplary nor atypical of the stated goal, thus highlighting a moderate discrepancy between the target goal and actual performance for the purpose of optimal learning. Fifth, goals should be moderately refined; tapes offer a number of possibilities that may be beyond the scope of achievement for the supervisee's skill level. Sixth, the supervisee should be stimulated in his or her growth without becoming overly threatened.

There are advantages and disadvantages in the use of taped sessions for supervisory purposes. Aveline (1997) stated that the use of tape has the advantage of allowing the identification of supervisee and client behaviors that are disruptive to the counseling process. As a disadvantage, he noted that the equipment necessary for recording tapes always effects counseling, which requires that its meaning to both the supervisee and client be explored. Additionally, taping may be abusive to clients who are incapable of refusing its use. The supervisor must be prepared to address any issues arising from the use of taping in counseling sessions. Additionally, videotapes have the advantage of allowing the supervisor to see the client–supervisee interaction, which provides a wealth of data (Romans et al., 1995; Stoltenberg & Delworth, 1987); and paradoxically, this may be a problem for some students who experience an overload of information (Goldberg, 1985; Hart, 1982; Rubinstein & Hammond, 1982). Supervisees may also suffer from "performance anxiety" and the need to entertain observers

(Munson, 1993). However, videotapes allow the supervisee to become an observer of herself or himself in the role of counselor (Aveline, 1997; Sternitzke, Dixon, & Ponterotto, 1988). Rubinstein and Hammond (1982) argued that videotape presents a stark reality that may be disturbing to the supervisee. They suggested that videotape usage remain simple, without technological advances that detract from the lifelike experience of viewing the tape such as split screens, superimposed images, etc. However, Casey, Bloom, and Moan (1994) suggested that the supervisor needs to remain current with technological advances.

We advocate the use of tapes as a medium for evaluation. The supervisor can enter the counseling process to observe supervisee performance without disrupting the session by her or his presence. Taped sessions allow the supervisor to observe verbal and nonverbal behaviors and interactions in both supervisee and client and to evaluate the supervisee's knowledge and performance of counseling interventions and conceptualization abilities as demonstrated by comparison of self-report and direct observation of the counseling process.

Live Observation

Live observation (supervision) combines direct observation of a therapy session with a communication method that allows the supervisor to influence the supervisee's work. Thus, the supervisor is both training the supervisee and controlling the therapy session (Lewis, 1988). Various methods of communicating with the supervisee are used, including bug-in-the-ear, monitoring, in vivo, walk-in, and consultation breaks. There are many advantages to using live supervision. First, there is a greater likelihood that counseling will go well when a more experienced counselor is involved (Bubenzer, West, & Gold, 1991). Second, there is evidence that supervisees learn more efficiently from successful therapy sessions with an experienced counselor (Landis & Young, 1994; Storm, 1994). Third, clients are more directly protected by the supervisor being available (Bernard & Goodyear, 1998). Fourth, supervisees can work with more challenging clients (Cormier & Bernard, 1982). Fifth, supervisees tend to risk more in therapy because the supervisor is available to help with interventions (Berger & Dammann, 1982). Sixth, the supervisory relationship may be enhanced by the fact that, as a participant in the counseling process, the supervisor is more vulnerable (Bernard & Goodyear, 1998).

There are also disadvantages to using live supervision. It demands a great deal of the supervisor's time in scheduling clients (Bubenzer et al., 1991), and clients and supervisees may not be comfortable with the method (Bernard & Goodyear, 1998). There is some danger that supervisees may parrot the supervisor's suggestions; and the supervisee's lack of autonomy in the supervised counseling process can lead to counselors with little creativity or initiative (Adamek, 1994; Schwartz, Liddle, & Breunlin, 1988; Storm, 1994).

There is a chance that the supervisor will show off her or his expertise by suggesting inappropriate interventions (Goodman, 1985). Live supervision may not prepare supervisees for the isolated world of professional practice, and there is no evidence that the counseling skills learned in live supervision generalize to other situations (Gallant, Thyer, & Bailey, 1991; Kivlighan, Angelone, & Swafford, 1991).

Although live supervision shares the same advantages for evaluation as taped sessions, we believe it can be problematic because of the client's presence. Unless evaluation is handled very carefully, it can undermine the relationship between the supervisee and the client. We suggest that evaluation be conducted following the counseling session.

The Reflective Process

Schon (1983, 1987) described the reflective process as a continuous scientific inquiry allowing practitioners to frame problems and modify them appropriately in order to devise unique solutions to particular situations. Reflective practice encourages experimentation by recognizing that unexpected results can be used as valid information (Neufeldt & Forsyth, 1993). Reflectivity involves thinking about a problem; but more than that, it includes thinking about the actions that result from it (Copeland, Birmingham, de la Cruz, & Lewin, 1993). Skovholt and Rønnestad (1995) described professional reflection as a "central developmental process" consisting of three elements: ongoing personal and professional experiences; a process of searching within an open, supportive environment; and active reflection on one's experience. Neufeldt, Karno, and Nelson (1996) described a model of reflectivity based on interviews with experts in the field. Supervisees can be reflective only if they are cognitively complex, tolerate ambiguity, are open to ideas, and in a supervisory relationship providing a safe environment in which questioning is valued. Reflectivity starts with a problem that the supervisee feels confused about and is unsure of how to proceed. The process requires attention to the supervisee's own actions, thoughts, and emotions in the counseling session, and to interaction between the supervisee and client. The supervisee searches for understanding by being open to alternative solutions to the problem. Theory is used in conjunction with her or his own personal and professional experiences to understand the clinical experience. The supervisee also examines her or his own experience during the session as a source of understanding. Meaning and clarity are indicative of a reflection of depth. Thought processes must have consequences resulting in a reflective event, and the supervisee must show some change in the next counseling session. Reflection may also result in a different understanding of clients, the counseling process, or oneself. Recognizing the process of reflectivity, the supervisor should create an environment supporting the searching process and active reflection on counseling (Neufeldt & Forsyth, 1993; Rønnestad & Skovholt, 1993). Neufeldt (1999) stated that "examining one's clinical work on a regular basis is as important as practicing specific skills for therapist development" (p. 8).

The reflective process encourages supervisee self-evaluation in examining problems and her or his reaction to it. We consider this to be an asset to supervision, and as an evaluation method, it gives the supervisor an opportunity to determine if the supervisee has developed in her or his abilities to recognize, reflect on, and understand the counseling process.

Evaluation Instruments

Stoltenberg et al. (1998) stated that evaluative instruments include performance rating scales, self-report inventories, observations, and client reports. These instruments can provide valuable information related to counselor characteristics. Additionally, there is significant variation in evaluation instruments depending on who completes the scale (supervisor, supervisee, peer, client, outside observer), what is rated (in-session behavior, performance, progress), the purpose of the evaluation, theoretical orientation, supervisee development, and, in the case of outside evaluators, how the evaluator is trained (Borders & Fong, 1991; Borders & Leddick, 1987; Fuqua et al., 1986; Williams, 1995). Data from evaluation instruments are useful in formative or summative feedback (Galassi & Brooks, 1992; Hahn & Molnar, 1991).

Bernard and Goodyear (1998) stated that there are nearly as many evaluation instruments as there are training programs because supervisors tend to develop and use them for the purpose of evaluation feedback. However, Hess and Hess (1983) argued that there are few specific and direct evaluation instruments for assessing supervision quality, supervisee performance, and skill acquisition. Lambert and Ogles (1997), in their examination of 55 measures of supervisory performance, found that when context of counseling performance was considered, 14 instruments measured supervision, 20 measured counseling, and 4 measured both supervision and counseling (the others were analogue or not classified). Galassi and Trent (1987) and Vonk and Thyer (1997) suggested several instruments effective for counselor supervision in the areas of process measurement and outcome measurement: (1) process measurement instruments: the Supervisory Styles Inventory (SSI; Friedlander & Ward, 1984); the Supervision Questionnaire: Supervisor's Version (SQ:S; Shulman, 1982) and the Supervisory Questionnaire (SQ; Worthington & Roehlke, 1979); and (2) outcome measurements: the Supervision Perception Form (SPF; Heppner & Roehlke, 1984) and the Counseling Evaluation Inventory (CEI; Linden, Stone, & Shertzer, 1965). The Clinical Supervision Questionnaire (CSQ; Stebnicki, Allen, & Janikowski, 1997), which measures development as a counselor in personal, clinical, and conceptual areas as well as supervisor behaviors, is a new instrument developed for use in supervision of rehabilitation counseling that may be readily adapted to other areas. Several instruments designed specifically to measure multicultural competencies are the Multicultural Counseling Inventory (MCI; Sodowsky et al., 1994), the Multicultural Counseling Awareness Scale–Form B (MCAS-B; Ponterotto et al., 1996), and the Cross-Cultural Counseling Inventory, Revised (CCCI-R; LaFromboise, Coleman, & Hernandez, 1991). Galassi and Trent (1987) also recommend two observational scales that measure specific skills and behaviors: Blumberg's Interaction Analysis (BIA; Blumberg, 1970) and the Counselor Verbal Response Category System (Hill, 1978). Boylan, Malley, and Scott (1995) provided a number of evaluation forms for practicum and internship students.

Ellis and Ladany (1997) and Ladany (1997) argued that there is a lack of psychometrically sound evaluation measures for use in supervision. They suggested a framework for organizing and assessing evaluation measures that can be applied to existing instruments or used in the development of new instruments. The following components should be clearly identified: mode or therapy (individual, group, couples, family); domain of trainee behavior (therapy or supervision); competence area (techniques, theoretical conceptualization, professionalism, disorders, supervision behaviors, etc.); method (self-report, case notes, videotape, etc.); proportion of caseload (all clients, subgroup of clients, single client); segment of experience (total, part, specific session, or segment of session); time period (early, middle, late in client treatment or training experience); evaluator (supervisor, client, peer, objective rater); level of proficiency; reliability issues; validity issues; and format (quantitative/qualitative and structured/unstructured). Although it would be unreasonable to suggest that one evaluation instrument or approach could include all of the parameters mentioned above, the merit of a specific evaluation instrument can be assessed based on the extent to which the parameters are considered (Ladany, 1997).

Evaluation instruments vary greatly in their usefulness depending on what they are designed to measure. Because they are often psychometrically unsound, we think they should be limited to use in information gathering or as aids to stimulate discussion in supervision rather than solely for the purpose of evaluation.

In summary, evaluation is dependent on a supportive supervisory relationship and an explicit contract that defines both evaluative criteria and methods to be used and the specific goals that form the basis of supervision. It requires specific, timely feedback that allows the supervisee to achieve the goals of supervision as well as growth as a counseling professional. Each of the methods discussed in this section—self-report, process notes, audio- and videotaping, live supervision, reflective process, and evaluation instruments—are amenable to evaluation in some degree. Although we believe that taping allows the supervisor to most fairly evaluate the supervisee's counseling behaviors, we do not advocate relying on a single method of evaluation. Both self-report and process notes give the supervisor insight into the perceptions of the supervisee, as does reflective process. Evaluation instruments, although not without problems, also provide information that can stimulate discussion important to the supervisory process. We believe that a competent supervisor should use all the methods available to her or him in the process of evaluating her or his supervisees.

☐ Why Is Evaluation Problematic?

There is little doubt that problems exist within the process of evaluation. Although there is no doubt that other problem areas exist, we have selected the following for discussion: the supervisor's role, training, and perceptions; criteria and competency issues; feedback and evaluation methods; and supervisee' expectations.

Supervisors often have difficulty with their role as evaluator for a variety of reasons. Since the supervisor was a counselor first, he or she may find it difficult to partially abandon the role of accepting and supportive facilitator for the role of evaluator (Williams, 1995). He or she often suffers from anxiety caused by taking too much responsibility for the supervisee's skill development and learning process. Additionally, he or she may fear being seen as intrusive or dictatorial. Tarvydas (1995) stated that the supervisor's hesitancy to engage in evaluation may compromise the supervisee's ability to learn. Walsh (1990) reported that new supervisors are often only vaguely aware of the duties and responsibilities involved in supervision, and these unclear role expectations may be related to inadequate evaluation (Ladany et al., 1999). Robiner, Saltzman, Hoberman, and Schrivar (1997) advocated the need for specific training in supervision. Another problem is related to supervisor perceptions about supervisees that may influence evaluation, especially in the areas of similarity and familiarity (Blodgett, Schmidt, & Scudder, 1987; Carey, Williams, & Wells, 1988; Fried, Tiegs, & Bellamy, 1992; Turban & Jones, 1988; Turban, Jones, & Rozelle, 1990). Furthermore, each supervisor has an individualized set of priorities that effect her or his judgment when evaluating supervisee skills (Sternitzke et al., 1988). Bernard and Goodyear (1998) argued that evaluation is a blend of subjective judgment and objective criteria and cautioned against trying to eliminate the subjective element; however, they also cautioned that the supervisor's personal subjectivity can contaminate her or his professional subjectivity, which would cause evaluation to become biased. In spite of the problems inherent in evaluating supervisees, most supervisors believe they provide accurate evaluation and have reasonable confidence in their skills as evaluators (Robiner et al., 1997).

Rodenhauser (1997) reported that two major problems in supervision were related to competency issues: standards of competent performance are not uniform (Tasman, 1993) and competency standards are not sufficiently developed (Rodenhauser, 1996; Watkins, 1992). Sherry (1991) and Vasquez (1992) stated that issues of competence are central to client welfare and self-evaluative skills in supervisees. Robiner et al. (1994) and Williams (1995) argued that evaluative criteria is often subjective and ambiguous. The methods used in determining criteria are seldom based on the experiences of successful counselors (McLeod, 1996). Rinas and Clyne-Jackson (1988) and Rodenhauser (1992) stated that criteria placing too much emphasis on theory may leave the supervisee unprepared for the ethical and clinical complexities of actual practice. Herman (1993) argued that although accrediting bodies set skill standards and prescribe knowledge for competent performance of counseling, research continues to undermine the assertion that specific types of knowledge or levels of experience determine client outcome. The literature on client outcome has produced mixed results (Pinsof & Wynne, 1995; Shaw & Dobson, 1988) and indicates that nonspecific characteristics may be more predictive of success (Orlinsky, Grawe, & Parks, 1994).

Borders and Leddick (1987) stated that supervisors may be uncomfortable giving feedback because they have little or no training in evaluation skills. A common problem in evaluation is the supervisor's failure to give negative feedback and evaluations; several explanations for this reluctance have been offered: apprehension, legal concerns, feelings of responsibility for the supervisee's inadequate performance, lack of experience as a supervisor, and avoidance of conflict situations (Robiner et al., 1993). According to Robiner et al. (1993), rating idiosyncrasies can lead to bias (leniency, strictness, or central-tendency) in the rating of supervisees. Leniency bias is the most common bias in evaluation; it is a tendency to evaluate favorably and may be caused by lack of clear criteria, legal and administrative issues, interpersonal issues, or supervisory issues. Strictness bias is the rarest bias found in evaluation; it is the tendency to rate more severely than is actually warranted and usually results from supervisor issues such as unrealistic expectations and displaced personal frustration. Central-tendency bias occurs when the supervisor rates in a uniformly average manner; it can be damaging to supervisees who are unable to correct inadequate behavior because they are never informed of it. Kadushin (1993) reported that lack of criticism, overly positive feedback, and criticism given only at the end of the term are problems reported by both supervisees and supervisors.

Ladany (1997) reported that a review of the literature on evaluation revealed that evaluation was primarily qualitative (Norcross & Stevenson, 1984; Norcross, Stevenson, & Nash, 1986); 90% of supervisors used supervisee self-report as a method of assessing performance, while less than 60% used audiotapes and less than 40% used videotapes (Ladany & Lehrman-Waterman, 1997; Ladany & Melincoff, 1997); many supervisors may be failing to fulfill their evaluation responsibilities adequately or ethically (Cormier & Bernard, 1982; Keith-Speigel & Koocher, 1985; Ladany, Lehrman-Waterman, Molina, & Wolgast, 1999); and instruments used to assess trainee competence are largely outdated or psychometrically inadequate (Ellis & Ladany, 1997). Failure to provide adequate performance evaluations is the most common ethical failure attributed to supervisors, and this failure to effectively monitor and evaluate supervisee performance compromises client care (Ladany et al., 1999).

Supervisees are sensitive to evaluation across all supervisory settings and developmental levels (Stoltenberg et al., 1998). Evaluation has implications for the supervisee's grades, recommendations for internship, professional advancement, and licensure or certification. Additionally, evaluation accentuates the power differential in supervision which threatens the supervisee's personal and professional development and adds to the supervisee's anxiety. Hess (1997) argues that the supervisee's concerns about performance anxiety demand a response from the supervisor. Lehrman-Waterman (1999) stated that although it is repeatedly hypothesized that evaluation is difficult for both the supervisee and the supervisor, no studies have directly tested the impact of evaluation on the supervision process; therefore, more research is needed.

We believe that supervisors should be aware of and sensitive to the problems inherent in the process of evaluation. All of us who supervise students occasionally feel incompetent as evaluators; however, we suggest that feelings of incompetence can be lessened by specific training in supervision and evaluation. Additionally, we suggest that supervisors should be aware of any influences of similarity and familiarity on their perceptions of supervisees and of their own subjective attitudes about evaluation in order to minimize the effect of these influences on supervision. We believe that supervisors should be aware of any tendencies they have toward bias in evaluation and correct this bias by offering valid and realistic feedback on supervisee performance. Finally, we believe that it is imperative that competent supervisors be sensitive to the concerns and fears of their supervisees about evaluation, and that they address any supervisee concerns promptly and fully early in the supervision process.

☐ Conclusion

At the beginning of this chapter, we stated that evaluation was the conundrum of supervision. It is most often described by purpose, roles, and responsibilities rather than by the actions involved. In this chapter, we have attempted to solve the puzzle of evaluation by considering the following questions:

- What are the criteria to be evaluated?
- Who is evaluated and who evaluates?
- When and where does evaluation take place?
- How is evaluation conducted in supervision?
- Why is evaluation problematic?

The criteria evaluated in supervision is drawn from the competency standards set by the various accrediting bodies and from research into skill and behavior areas considered important in the counseling process. Criteria are generally considered to include: knowledge base, intervention skills and techniques, conceptual skills, and interpersonal skills. Unfortunately, with few exceptions, these competency areas are not explicitly defined. Therefore, we must agree with the contention of Robiner et al. (1994) and Williams (1995) who believed that evaluative criteria are often subjective and ambiguous. Until comprehensive competency standards and criteria are developed, this area will remain confusing, leading supervisors to depend on their own experience and subjective priorities.

There is little controversy regarding the questions of who is evaluated and who evaluates and of when and where evaluation takes place. Supervisees are the primary targets of the evaluative process. However, the supervisor should ask for feedback from supervisees in order to sharpen her or his skills as a supervisor and to give the supervisee the type of individualized supervision that he or she requires for a successful supervisory experience. Additionally, when using evaluation instruments, others outside of the supervisory dyad may offer valuable insights. Generally, the timing of supervision sessions is dependent on the policy of the university or training program; practica students usually meet weekly in a classroom session with faculty supervisors as well as individually with their site supervisors. Supervised practice takes place in various settings, including private practice sites, agencies, and academic counseling centers.

The supervisory relationship is crucial to effective evaluation. A supportive, collaborative learning alliance allows the supervisor to evaluate the supervisee's strengths and weaknesses and offer constructive feedback without unwarranted anxiety for the supervisee. The evaluation process should be included in the supervision contract, which should be specific concerning criteria, methods, goals, feedback procedures, and timing of supervisory sessions. Feedback on the supervisee's performance should be timely, direct, clearly presented, specific, and reflective of strengths and weaknesses. Formative feedback should be given at each supervisory session, and summative feedback should be formally presented at least twice during the term of supervision. The most objective evaluation method is audio- or videotape review, although valuable information can be gained from reflective self-report and process notes. Evaluation instruments are available; however, most are outdated and psychometrically inadequate. Most of the problems in the evaluation process are related to the supervisor. Supervisors may feel uncomfortable in the role of evaluator for a number of reasons: little or no training in evaluation skills; unclear role expectation; fear of harming the supervisee, either personally or professionally; and questions about what constitutes competency. Other problems are individualized priorities and subjective judgment.

Borders (1992) stated that the greatest challenge faced by supervisors was to think like a supervisor rather than a counselor. As an extension to this, we suggest that supervisors must also learn to think like evaluators. This requires putting aside our distaste for the evaluative process and doing what is necessary to insure that our students are competent practitioners.

We must search out evaluative criteria that allow us to evaluate competency objectively. We must use methods (process notes, audiotape, videotape) that allow us to monitor the progress of our supervisees. We must give them the feedback they require to achieve competence and ask them for feedback about our performance as supervisors so that we may grow more competent as well. There is no doubt that the evaluative process is anxiety provoking; no supervisor wants to cause her or his supervisees distress or negatively influence their academic or professional careers. However, we who supervise counselor trainees are ultimately responsible to potential clients and the profession, and this means that whether we like it or not, we must serve as gatekeepers for the profession.

☐ References

Adamek, M. S. (1994). Audio-cueing and immediate feedback to improve group leadership skills: A live supervision model. *Journal of Music Therapy, 31*, 135–164.

Allen, G. J., Szollos, S. J., & Williams B. E. (1986). Doctoral students' comparative evaluations of best and worst psychotherapy supervision. *Professional Psychology: Research and Practice, 17*, 91–99.

American Association for Marriage and Family Therapy. (1991). *Code of ethics* (rev. ed.). Washington, DC: Author.

American Counseling Association. (1995). *Code of ethics* (rev. ed.). Alexandria, VA: Author.

American Psychological Association Ethics Committee. (1992). Ethical principles of psychologists and code of conduct. *American Psychologist, 47*, 1597–1611.

Arredondo, P., Toperek, R., Brown, S., Jones, J., Locke, D. C., Sanchez, J., & Stadler, H. (1996). *Organization of the multicultural counseling competencies*. Alexandria, VA: American Counseling Association.

Association for Counselor Education and Supervision. (1995). Ethical guidelines for counseling supervisors. *Counselor Education and Supervision, 34*, 270–276.

Aveline, M. (1997). The use of audiotapes in supervision of psychotherapy. In G. Shipton (Ed.), *Supervision of psychotherapy and counselling* (pp. 80–92). Philadelphia: Open University Press.

Basarab, D. J., & Root, D. K. (1992). *The training evaluation process: A practical guide to evaluating corporate training programs*. Boston: Kluwer.

Belar, C. D., Bieliauskas, L. A., Klepac, R. K., Larsen, K. G., Stigall, T. T., & Zimet, C. N. (1993). National conference on postdoctoral training in professional psychology. *American Psychologist, 48*, 1284–1289.

Bent, R. J., & Cannon, W. G. (1987). Key functional skills of a professional psychologist. In E. F. Bourg, R. J. Bent, J. E. Callan, N. F. Jones, J. McHolland, & G. Stricker (Eds.), *Standards and evaluation in the education and training of professional psychologists: Knowledge, attitudes, and skills* (pp. 87–97). Norman, OK: Transcript Press.

Berger, M., & Dammann, C. (1982). Live supervision as context, treatment, and training. *Family Process, 21*, 337–344.

Bernard, J. M. (1982). *Laboratory training for clinical supervisors: An update*. Paper presented at the annual meeting of the American Psychological Association, Washington, DC.

Bernard, J. M., & Goodyear, R. K. (1998). *Fundamentals of clinical supervision* (2nd ed.). Boston: Allyn & Bacon.

Blodgett, E. G., Schmidt, J. F., & Scudder, R. R. (1987). Clinical session evaluation: The effect of familiarity with the supervisee. *Clinical Supervisor, 5*(1), 33–43.

Blumberg, A. (1970). A system for analyzing supervision-teacher interaction. In A. Simon &

G. Boyer (Eds.), *Mirrors for behavior* (Vol. 3, pp. 193–286). Philadelphia: Research for Better Schools.

Borders, L. D. (1992). Learning to think like a supervisor. *Clinical Supervisor, 10*(2), 135–148.

Borders, L. D., Bernard, J. M., Dye, H. A., Fong, M. L., Henderson, P., & Nance, D. W. (1991). Curriculum guide for training counseling supervisors: Rationale, development, and implementation. *Counselor Education and Supervision, 31*, 58–82.

Borders, L. D., Cashwell, C. S., & Rotter, J. C. (1995). Supervision of counselor licensure applicants: A comparative study. *Counselor Education and Supervision, 35*, 54–69.

Borders, L. D., & Fong, M. L. (1991). Evaluations of supervisees: Brief commentary and research report. *Clinical Supervisor, 9*(2), 43–51.

Borders, L. D., & Leddick, G. R. (1987). *Handbook of counseling supervision.* Alexandria, VA: American Association for Counseling and Development.

Boylan, J. C. (1995). Internship experience. In J. C. Boylan, P. B. Malley, & J. Scott (Eds.), *Practicum and internship: Textbook for counseling and psychotherapy* (2nd ed., pp. 57–69). Washington, DC: Accelerated Development.

Boylan, J. C., Malley, P. B., & Scott, J. (Eds.). (1995). *Practicum and internship: Textbook for counseling and psychotherapy* (2nd ed.). Washington, DC: Accelerated Development.

Brandell, J. R. (1992). Focal conflict analysis: A method of supervision in psychoanalytic psychotherapy. *Clinical Supervisor, 10*(1), 51–69.

Breunlin, D., Karrer, B., McGuire, D., & Cimmarusti, R. (1988). Cybernetics of videotape supervision. In H. Liddle, D. Breunlin, & R. Schwartz (Eds.), *Handbook of family therapy training and supervision* (pp. 194–206). New York: Guilford.

Brightman, B. K. (1984/1985). Narcissistic issues in the training experience of the psychotherapist. *International Journal of Psychoanalytic Psychotherapy, 10*, 293–317.

Bubenzer, D. L., West, J. D., & Gold, J. M. (1991). Use of live supervision in counselor preparation. *Counselor Education and Supervision, 30*, 301–308.

Cain, H. I., & Markowski, E. M. (1989). A private practice supervisory evaluation format. *Clinical Supervisor, 7*(4), 93–99.

Calpin, J. P., Edelstein, B., & Redmon, W. K. (1988). Performance feedback and goal setting to improve mental health center staff productivity. *Journal of Organizational Behavior Managment, 9*, 35–58.

Campbell, T. W. (1994). Psychotherapy and malpractice exposure. *American Journal of Forensic Psychology, 12*, 5–41.

Carey, J. C., & Lanning, W.L. (1993). Supervisors' emphases in the master's practicum. *Clinical Supervisor, 11*(1), 203–215.

Carey, J. C., Williams, K. S., & Wells, M. (1988). Relationships between dimensions of supervisors' influence and counselor trainees' performance. *Counselor Education and Supervision, 28*, 130–139.

Casey, J. A., Bloom, J. W., & Moan, E. R. (1994). Use of technology in counselor supervision. In L. D. Borders (Ed.), *Supervision: Exploring the effective components* (ERIC/CASS No. EDO-CG-94-25). Greensboro, NC: Educational Resources Information Center.

Cashwell, C. S., Looby, E. J., & Housley, W. F. (1997). Appreciating cultural diversity through clinical supervision. *Clinical Supervisor, 15*(1), 75–85.

Coll, K. M. (1995). Clinical supervision of community college counselors: Current and referred practices. *Counselor Education and Supervision, 35*, 111–117.

Compton, J. R. (1987). *The art of clinical supervision: A pastoral counseling perspective.* New York: Paulist Press.

Constantine, M. G. (1997). Facilitating multicultural competency in counseling supervision: Operationalizing a practical framework. In D. B. Pope-Davis & H. L. K. Coleman (Eds.), *Multicultural counseling competencies: Assessment, education and training, and supervision* (pp. 310–324). Newbury Park, CA: Sage.

Copeland, W. T., Birmingham, C., de la Cruz, E., & Lewin, B. (1993). The reflective practitioner in teaching: Toward a research agenda. *Teaching and Teacher Education, 9*, 349–359.

Cormier, L. S., & Bernard, J. M. (1982). Ethical and legal responsibilities of clinical supervisors. *Personnel and Guidance Journal, 60,* 486–491.

Couchon, W. D., & Bernard, J. M. (1984). Effects of timing of supervision on supervisor and counselor performance. *Clinical Supervisor, 2*(3), 3–20.

Cross, E. G., & Brown, D. (1983). Counselor supervision as a function of trainee experience: Analysis of specific behaviors. *Counselor Education and Supervision, 22,* 333–341.

Crouch, A. (1992). The competent counselor. *Self and Society, 20,* 22–25.

Disney, M. J., & Stephens, A. M. (1994). *Legal issues in clinical supervision.* Alexandria, VA: ACA Press.

Edelstein, B. A. (1985). Empirical evaluation of clinical training. *Behavior Therapist, 8,* 67–70.

Efstation, J. F., Patton, M. J., & Kardash, C. M. (1990). Measuring the working alliance in counselor supervision. *Journal of Counseling Psychology, 37,* 322–329.

Einhorn, H. J., & Hogarth, R. M. (1981). Behavioral decision theory: Processes of judgment and choice. *Annual Review of Psychology, 32,* 53–88.

Ellis, M. V., & Ladany, N. (1997). Inferences concerning supervisees and clients in clinical supervision: An integrative review. In C. E. Watkins, Jr. (Ed.), *Handbook of psychotherapy supervision* (pp. 467–507). New York: Wiley.

Farnill, D., Gordon, J., & Sansom, D. (1997). The role of effective feedback in clinical supervision. *Australian Journal of Clinical and Experimental Hypnosis, 25*(2), 155–161.

Fitzgerald, L. E., & Osipow, S. H. (1986). An occupational analysis of counseling psychology: How special is the specialty? *American Psychologist, 41,* 535–544.

Frame, M. W., & Stevens-Smith, P. (1995). Out of harm's way: Enhancing monitoring and dismissal processes in counselor education programs. *Counselor Education and Supervision, 35,* 118–129.

Freeman, E. M. (1985). The importance of feedback in clinical supervision: Implications for direct practice. *Clinical Supervisor, 3,* 5–26.

Fried, Y., Tiegs, R. B., & Bellamy, A. R. (1992). Personal and interpersonal predictors of supervisors' avoidance of evaluating subordinates. *Journal of Applied Psychology, 77,* 462–468.

Friedlander, M. L., Siegel, S. M., & Brenock, K. (1989). Parallel process in counseling and supervision: A case study. *Journal of Counseling Psychology, 36,* 149–157.

Friedlander, M. L., & Ward, L. G. (1984). Development and validation of the Supervisory Styles Inventory. *Journal of Counseling Psychology, 31,* 542–558.

Friedlander, S. R., & Dye, N. W. (1984). A developmental model for teaching and learning in psychotherapy supervision. *Psychotherapy, 21,* 189–196.

Fuqua, D., Newman, J., Scott, T., & Gade, E. (1986). Variability across sources of performance ratings: Further evidence. *Journal of Counseling Psychology, 33,* 353–356.

Galassi, J. P., & Brooks, L. (1992). Integrating scientist and practitioner training in counseling psychology: Practicum is the key. *Counselling Psychology Quarterly, 5,* 57–65.

Galassi, J. P., & Trent, P. A. (1987). A conceptual framework for evaluating supervision effectiveness. *Counselor Education and Supervision, 26,* 260–269.

Gallant, J. P., Thyer, B. A., & Bailey, J. S. (1991). Using bug-in-the-ear feedback in clinical supervision. *Research on Social Work Practice, 1,* 175–187.

Goldberg, D. A. (1985). Process notes, audio, and videotape: Modes of presentation in psychotherapy training. *Clinical Supervisor, 3,* 3–13.

Goodman, R. W. (1985). The live supervision model in clinical training. *Clinical Supervisor, 3*(2), 43–49

Goodyear, R. K., & Nelson, M. L. (1997). The major supervision formats. In C. E. Watkins, Jr. (Ed.), *Handbook of psychotherapy supervision.* New York: Wiley.

Guralnik, D. B. (Ed.). (1970). *Webster's new world dictionary* (2nd college ed.). New York: World Publishing.

Hahn, W. K., & Molnar, S. (1991). Intern evaluation in university counseling centers: Process, problems, and recommendations. *Counseling Psychologist, 19,* 414–430.

Halgin, R. P., & Murphy, R. A. (1995). Issues in the training of psychotherapists. In B. Bongar & L. E. Beutler (Eds.), *Comprehensive textbook of psychotherapy: Theory and practice* (pp. 434–455). New York: Oxford University Press.

Harris, M. B. C. (1994). Supervisory evaluation and feedback. In L. D. Borders (Ed.), *Supervision: Exploring the effective components*. Greensboro, NC: Educational Resources Information Center.

Hart, G. (1982). *The process of clinical supervision*. Baltimore, MD: University Park Press.

Heppner, P. P., & Handley, P. G. (1982). A study of the interpersonal influence process in supervision. *Journal of Counseling Psychologist, 28*, 437–444.

Heppner, P. P., & Roehlke, H. J. (1984). Difference among supervisees at different levels of training: Implications for a developmental model of supervision. *Journal of Counseling Psychology, 31*, 76–90.

Herman, K. C. (1993). Reassessing predictors of therapist competence. *Journal of Counseling and Development, 72*, 29–32.

Hess, A. K. (1997). The interpersonal approach to the supervision of psychotherapy. In C. E. Watkins, Jr. (Ed.), *Handbook of psychotherapy supervision* (pp. 447–507). New York: Wiley.

Hess, A. K., & Hess, K. A. (1983). Psychotherapy supervision: A survey of internship training practices. *Professional Psychology: Research and Practice, 14*, 504–513.

Hill, C. E. (1978). Development of a counselor verbal response category system. *Journal of Counseling Psychology, 25*, 461–468.

Hoffman, L. W. (1990). *Old scapes, new maps: A training program for psychotherapy supervisors*. Cambridge, MA: Milusik Press.

Holloway, E. L. (1988). Instruction beyond the facilitative conditions: A response to Biggs. *Counselor Education and Supervision, 27*, 252–258.

Holloway, E. L. (1992). Supervision: A way of teaching and learning. In S. D. Brown & R. W. Lent (Eds.), *Handbook of Counseling Psychology* (pp. 177–214). New York: Wiley.

Holloway, E. L. (1997). Structures for the analysis and teaching of psychotherapy. In C. E. Watkins, Jr. (Ed.), *Handbook of psychotherapy supervision* (pp. 249–276). New York: Wiley.

Hutt, C. H., Scott, J., & King, M. (1983). A phenomenological study of supervisee's positive and negative experiences in supervision. *Psychotherapy: Theory, Research, and Practice, 20*, 118–123.

Inskipp, F. (1996). New directions in supervision. In R. Bayne, I. Horton, & J. Bimrose (Eds.), *New directions in counselling* (pp. 268–280). London: Routledge.

Ivey, A. E., & Galvin, M. (1984). Microcounseling: a metamodel for counseling, therapy, business, and medical interviews. In D. Larson (Ed.), *Teaching psychological skills: Models for giving psychology away*. Monterey, CA: Brooks/Cole.

Johnson, E., Baker, S. B., Kopala, M., Kiselica, M. S., & Thompson, E. C. (1989). Counseling self-efficacy and counseling competence in prepracticum training. *Counselor Education and Supervision, 28*, 205–218.

Kadushin, A. (1992). *Supervision in social work* (3rd ed.). New York: Columbia University Press.

Kadushin, A. (1993). What's wrong, what's right, with social work supervision. *Clinical Supervisor, 10*, 3–19.

Keith-Speigel, P., & Koocher, G. P. (1985). *Ethics in psychology: Professional standards and cases*. New York: Random House.

Kivlighan, D. M., Angelone, E. O., & Swafford, K. G. (1991). Live supervision in individual psychotherapy: Effects on therapist's intention use and client's evaluation of session effect and working alliance. *Journal of Counseling Psychology, 22*, 489–495.

Ladany, N. (1997, August). *A descriptive model of assessing evaluation approaches for psychotherapy trainees*. Paper presented at the annual meeting of the American Psychological Association, Chicago.

Ladany, N., & Friedlander, M. L. (1995). The relationship between the supervisory working alliance and trainees' experience of role conflict and role ambiguity. *Counselor Education and Supervision, 34*, 220–231.

Ladany, N., & Lehrman-Waterman, D. (1997, June). *Psychotherapy trainee reactions to supervisor self-disclosures.* Paper presented at the annual meeting of the Society for Psychotherapy Research, Geilo, Norway.

Ladany, N., & Lehrman-Waterman, D. (1999). The content and frequency of supervisor self-disclosure and the relationship to supervisory working alliance and satisfaction with supervision. *Counselor Education and Supervision, 38,* 143–160.

Ladany, N., Lehrman-Waterman, D., Molina, M., & Wolgast, B. (1999). Psychotherapy supervisor ethical practices: Adherence to guidelines, the supervisory working alliance, and supervisee satisfaction. *Counseling Psychologist, 27,* 443–475.

Ladany, N., & Melincoff, D. S. (1997, June). *The nature and extent of what psychotherapy supervisors do not disclose to their trainees.* Poster session presented at the annual meeting of the Society for Psychotherapy Research, Geilo, Norway.

LaFromboise, T. D., Coleman, H. L. K., & Hernandez, A. (1991). Development and factor structure of the Cross-Cultural Counseling Inventory-Revised. *Professional Psychology: Research and Practice, 22,* 380–388.

Lambert, M. J., & Arnold, R. C. (1987). Research and the supervision process. *Professional Psychology: Research and Practice, 18*(3), 217–224.

Lambert, M. J., & Ogles, B. M. (1988). Treatment manuals: Problems and promise. *Journal of Integrative & Eclectic Psychotherapy, 7,* 187–220.

Lambert, M. J., & Ogles, B. M. (1997). The effectiveness of psychotherapy supervision. In C. E. Watkins, Jr. (Ed.), *Handbook of psychotherapy supervision* (pp. 421–446). New York: Wiley.

Landis, L. L., & Young, M. E. (1994). The reflecting team in counselor education. Special section: Marriage and family training methods. *Counselor Education and Supervision, 33,* 210–218.

Lanning, W., & Freeman, B. (1994). The Supervisor Emphasis Rating Form—Revised. *Counselor Education and Supervision, 33,* 294–304.

Larson, L. M., Suzuki, L. A., Gillespie, K. N., Potenza, M. T., Bechtel, M. A., & Toulouse, A. (1992). Development and validation of the Counseling Self-Estimate Inventory. *Journal of Counseling Psychology, 39,* 105–120.

Lehrman-Waterman, D. E. (1999). *Development and validation of the evaluation process within supervision index.* Unpublished doctoral dissertation, Lehigh University, Bethlehem, PA.

Levy, L. H. (1983). Evaluation of students in clinical psychology programs: A program evaluation perspective. *Professional Psychology: Research and Practice, 14,* 497–503.

Lewis, W. (1988). A supervision model for public agencies. *Clinical Supervisor, 6*(2), 85–91.

Linden, J. D., Stone, S. C., & Shertzer, B. (1965). Development and evaluation of an inventory for rating counseling. *Personnel and Guidance Journal, 44,* 267–276.

Locke, E. A., & Latham, G. P. (1990). *A theory of goal setting and task performance.* Englewood Cliffs, NJ: Prentice-Hall.

Loganbill, C., Hardy, E., & Delworth, U. (1982). Supervision: A conceptual model. *Counseling Psychologist, 10,* 3–42.

Magnuson, S. (1995). *Supervision of prelicensed counselors: A study of educators, supervisors, and supervisees.* Unpublished doctoral dissertation, University of Alabama, Birmingham, Alabama.

McCarthy, P., Kulakowski, D., & Kenfield, J. A. (1994). Clinical supervision practices of licensed psychologists. *Professional Psychology: Research and Practice, 25,* 177–181.

McLeod, J. (1996). Counsellor competence. In R. Bayne, I. Horton, & J. Bimrose (Eds.), *New directions in counselling* (pp. 37–49). London: Routledge.

Mead, D. E. (1990). *Effective supervision: A task-oriented model for the mental health professions.* New York: Brunner/Mazel.

Melchert, T. P., Hays, V. L., Wiljanen, L. M., & Kolocek, A. K. (1996). Testing models of counselor development with a measure of counseling self-efficacy. *Journal of Counseling and Development, 74,* 640–644.

Mohl, P. C., Sadler, J. Z., & Miller, D. A. (1994). What components should be evaluated in psychiatry residency? *Academic Psychiatry, 18,* 22–29.

Munson, C. E. (1993). *Clinical social work supervision* (2nd ed.). New York: Haworth Press.

Muslin, H. L., Thurnblad, R. J., & Meschel, G. (1981). The fate of the clinical interview: An observational study. *American Journal of Psychiatry, 138,* 823–825.

National Board for Certified Counselors. (1993). *A work behavior analysis of professional counselors.* Greensboro, NC: Author.

Neufeldt, S. A. (1999). *Supervision strategies for the first practicum* (2nd ed.). Alexandria, VA: American Counseling Association.

Neufeldt, S. A., & Forsyth, L. E. (1993, November). *Supervision for reflective practice: Facilitating clinical and scientific inquiry.* Paper presented at the annual meeting of the Western Association for Counselor Education and Supervision, Berkeley, CA.

Neufeldt, S. A., Karno, M. P., & Nelson, M. L. (1996). A qualitative analysis of experts' conceptualization of supervisee reflectivity. *Journal of Counseling Psychology, 43,* 3–9.

Newman, F. L., McGovern, M. P., Kopta, S. M., Howard, K. I., & McNeilly, C. L. (1988). Evaluating trainees relative to their supervisors during the psychology internship. *Journal of Consulting and Clinical Psychology, 56,* 659–665.

Norcross, J. C., & Halgin, R. P. (1997). Integrative approaches to psychotherapy supervision. In C. E. Watkins, Jr. (Ed.), *Handbook of psychotherapy supervision* (pp. 203–222). New York: Wiley.

Norcross, J. C., & Stevenson, J. F. (1984). How shall we judge ourselves? Training evaluation in clinical psychology programs. *Professional Psychology: Research and Practice, 15,* 497–508.

Norcross, J. C., Stevenson, J. F., & Nash, J. M. (1986). Evaluation of internship training: Practices, problems and prospects. *Professional Psychology: Research and Practice, 17,* 280–282.

Olsen, D. C., & Stern, S. B. (1990). Issues in the development of a family therapy supervision model. *Clinical Supervisor, 8*(2), 49–65.

Orlinsky, D. E., Grawe, K., & Parks, B. K. (1994). Process and outcome in psychotherapy—noch einmal. In A. E. Bergin & S. L. Garfield (Eds.), *Handbook of psychotherapy and behavior change* (3rd. ed., pp. 270–376). New York: Wiley.

Osborn, C. J., & Davis, T. E. (1996). The supervision contract: Making it perfectly clear. *Clinical Supervisor, 14*(2), 121–134.

Overholser, J. C., & Fine, M. A. (1990). Defining the boundaries of professional competence: Managing subtle cases of clinical incompetence. *Professional Psychology: Research and Practice, 21,* 462–469.

Patton, M. J., & Kivlighan, D. M. (1997). Relevance of the supervisory alliance to the counseling alliance and to treatment adherence in counselor training. *Journal of Counseling Psychology, 44,* 108–115.

Perlesz, A. J., Stolk, Y., & Firestone, A. F. (1990). Patterns of learning in family therapy training. *Family Process, 29,* 29–44.

Pickvance, D. (1997). Becoming a supervisor. In G. Shipton (Ed.), *Supervision of psychotherapy and counselling: Making a place to think* (pp. 131–142). Philadelphia: Open University Press.

Pinsof, W. M., & Wynne, L. C. (1995). The efficacy of marital and family therapy: An empirical overview, conclusions, and recommendations. *Journal of Marital and Family Therapy, 21,* 585–613.

Poertner, J. (1986). The use of client feedback to improve practice: Defining the supervisor's role. *Clinical Supervisor, 4*(4), 57–67.

Ponterotto, J. G., Rieger, B. P., Barrett, A., Sparks, R., Sanchez, C. M., & Magids, D. (1996). Development and initial validation of the Multicultural Counseling Awareness Scale. In G. R. Sodowsky & J. C. Impara (Eds.), *Multicultural assessment in counseling and clinical psychology* (pp. 247–282). Lincoln, NE: Buros Institute of Mental Measurements.

Pope-Davis, D. B., & Dings, J. G. (1995). The assessment of multicultural counseling competencies. In J. G. Ponterotto & J. M. Casas (Eds.), *Handbook of multicultural counseling* (pp. 287–311). Thousand Oaks, CA: Sage.

Rinas, J., & Clyne-Jackson, S. (1988). *Professional conduct and legal concerns in mental health practice.* Norwalk, CT: Appleton & Lange.

Robiner, W. N., Fuhrman, M. J., & Ristvedt, S. (1993). Evaluation difficulties in supervising psychology interns. *Clinical Psychologist, 46,* 3–13.

Robiner, W. N., Fuhrman, M. J., Ristvedt, S., & Bobbitt, B. L. (1994). The Minnesota Supervisory Inventory (MSI): Development, psychometric characteristics, and supervisory evaluation issues. *Clinical Psychologist, 47,* 4–47.

Robiner, W. N., Saltzman, S. R., Hoberman, H. M., & Schrivar, J. A. (1997). Psychology supervisors' training, experiences, supervisory evaluation and self-rated competence. *Clinical Supervisor, 16*(1), 117–144.

Rodenhauser, P. (1992). Psychiatry residency programs: Trends in psychotherapy supervision. *American Journal of Psychotherapy, 46,* 240–249.

Rodenhauser, P. (1996). On the future of psychotherapy supervision and psychiatry. *Academic Psychiatry, 20,* 82–91.

Rodenhauser, P. (1997). Psychotherapy supervision: Prerequisites and problems in the process. In C. E. Watkins, Jr. (Ed.), *Handbook of psychotherapy supervision* (pp. 203–221). New York: Wiley.

Rodenhauser, P., Painter, A. F., & Rudisill, J. R. (1985). Supervising supervisors: A series of workshops. *Journal of Psychiatric Education, 9,* 217–224.

Rogers, G., & McDonald, P. L. (1995). Expedience over education: Teaching methods used by field instructors. *Clinical Supervisor, 13*(2), 41–65.

Romans, J. S. C., Boswell, D. L., Carlozzi, A. F., & Ferguson, D. B. (1995). Training and supervision practices in clinical, counseling, and school psychology programs. *Professional Psychology: Research and Practice, 26,* 407–412.

Rønnestad, M. H., & Skovholt, T. M. (1993). Supervision of beginning and advanced graduate students of counseling and psychotherapy. *Journal of Counseling and Development, 71,* 396–405.

Rubinstein, M., & Hammond, D. (1982). The use of videotape in psychotherapy supervision. In M. Blumenfield (Ed.), *Applied supervision in psychotherapy* (pp. 143–164). New York: Grune & Stratton.

Schon, D. A. (1983). *The reflective practitioner: How professionals think in action.* New York: Basic Books.

Schon, D. A. (1987). *Educating the reflective practitioner.* San Francisco: Jossey-Bass.

Schwartz, R. (1981). The conceptual development of family therapy trainees. *American Journal of Family Therapy, 2,* 89–90.

Schwartz, R. C., Liddle, H. A., & Breunlin, D. C. (1988). Muddles in live supervision. In H. A. Liddle, D. C. Breunlin, & R. C. Schwartz (Eds.), *Handbook of family therapy training and supervision* (pp. 183–193). New York: Guilford.

Scott, J. (1995). Practicum experience. In J. C. Boylan, P. B. Malley, & J. Scott (Eds.), *Practicum and internship: Textbook for counseling and psychotherapy* (2nd ed., pp. 11–28). Washington, DC: Accelerated Development.

Shanfield, S. B., Mohl, P. C., Matthews, K. L., & Hetherly, V. (1992). Quantitative assessment of the behavior of psychotherapy supervisors. *American Journal of Psychiatry, 149,* 352–357.

Shaw, B. F., & Dobson, K. S. (1988). Competency judgments in the training and evaluation of psychotherapists. *Journal of Consulting and Clinical Psychology, 56,* 666–672.

Sherry, P. (1991). Ethical issues in the conduct of supervision. *Counseling Psychologist, 19,* 566–584.

Shulman, L. (1982). *Skills of supervision and staff management.* Itasca, IL: F.E. Peacock.

Sipps, G. J., Sugden, G. J., & Favier, C. M. (1988). Counselor training level and verbal response type: Their relationship to efficacy and outcome expectations. *Journal of Counseling Psychology, 35,* 397–401.

Skovholt, T. M., & Rønnestad, M. H. (1995). *The evolving professional self: Stages and themes in therapist and counselor development.* Chichester, England: Wiley.

Sodowsky, G. R., Taffe, R. C., Gutkin, T. W., & Wise, S. L. (1994). Development of the Multicultural Counseling Inventory: A self-report measure of multicultural competencies. *Journal of Counseling Psychology, 41*, 137–148.

Stebnicki, M. A., Allen, H. A., & Janikowski, T. P. (1997). Development of an instrument to assess perceived helpfulness of clinical supervisory behaviors. *Rehabilitation Education, 11*(4), 307–322.

Sternitzke, M. E., Dixon, D. N., & Ponterotto, J. G. (1988). An attributional approach to counselor supervision. *Counselor Education and Supervision, 28*, 5–14.

Stoltenberg, C. D., & Delworth, U. (1987). *Supervising counselors and therapists*. San Francisco: Jossey-Bass.

Stoltenberg, C. D., McNeill, B., & Delworth, U. (1998). *IDM supervision: An integrated developmental model for supervising counselors and therapists*. San Francisco: Jossey-Bass.

Storm, H. A. (1994). *Enhancing the acquisition of psychotherapy skills through live supervision*. Paper presented at the annual meeting of the American Psychological Association, Los Angeles.

Stricker, G. (1987). The evaluation of attitudes, aptitudes, and values. In E. F. Bourg, R. J. Bent, J. E. Callan, N. F. Jones, J. McHolland, & G. Stricker (Eds.), *Standards and evaluation in the education and training of professional psychologists: Knowledge, attitudes, and skills* (pp. 61–64). Norman, OK: Transcript Press.

Sue, D. W. (1996). Multicultural counseling: Models, methods, and actions. *The Counseling Psychologist, 24*, 279–284.

Talen, M. R., & Schindler, N. (1993). Goal-directed supervision plans: A model for trainee supervision and evaluation. *Clinical Supervisor, 11*(2), 77–88.

Tarvydas, V. M. (1995). Ethics and the practice of rehabilitation counselor supervision. *Rehabilitation Counseling Bulletin, 38*, 294–306.

Tasman, A. (1993). Setting standards for psychotherapy training: It's time to do our homework. *Journal of Psychotherapy Practice and Research, 2* (2), 93–96.

Tracey, T. J., Ellickson, J. L., & Sherry, P. (1989). Reactance in relation to different supervisory environments and counselor development. *Journal of Counseling Psychology, 36*, 336–344.

Turban, D. B., & Jones, A. P. (1988). Supervisor-subordinate similarity: Types, effects, and mechanisms. *Journal of Applied Psychology, 73*, 228–234.

Turban, D. B., Jones, A. P., & Rozelle, R. M. (1990). Influences of supervisor liking of a subordinate and the reward context on the treatment and evaluation of that subordinate. *Motivation and Emotion, 14*, 215–233.

Tyler, J. D., & Weaver, S. H. (1981). Evaluating the clinical supervisee: A survey of practices in graduate training programs. *Professional Psychology: Research and Practice, 12*, 434–437.

Vasquez, M. J. T. (1992). Psychologist as clinical supervisor: Promoting ethical practice. *Professional Psychology: Research and Practice, 23*, 196–202.

Vonk, M. E., & Thyer, B. A. (1997). Evaluating the quality of supervision: A review of instruments for use in field instruction. *Clinical Supervisor, 15*, 103–113.

Walsh, J. A. (1990). From clinician to supervisor: Essential ingredients for training. *Families in Society: The Journal of Contemporary Human Services, 71*(2), 82–87.

Watkins, C. E., Jr. (1992). Reflections on the preparation of psychotherapy supervisors. *Journal of Clinical Psychology, 47*, 1145–1147.

Watkins, C. E., Jr. (1997). Defining psychotherapy supervision and understanding supervisor functioning. In C.E. Watkins, Jr. (Ed.), *Handbook of psychotherapy supervision* (pp. 3–10). New York: Wiley.

West, J. D., Bubenzer, D. L., Pinsoneault, T., & Holeman, V. (1993). Three supervision modalities for training marital and family counselors. Special Section: Marriage and family counselor training. *Counselor Education and Supervision, 33*, 127–138.

Wetchler, J. L., Piercy, F. P., & Sprenkle, D. H. (1989). Supervisors' and supervisees' perceptions of the effectiveness of family therapy supervisory techniques. *American Journal of Family Therapy, 17,* 35–47.

Williams, A. (1995). *Visual and active supervision: Roles, focus, technique.* New York: W. W. Norton.

Worthington, E. L., & Roehlke, H. J. (1979). Effective supervision of beginning counselors-in-training. *Journal of Counseling Psychology, 26,* 64–73.

Wynne, M. E., Susman, M., Ries, S., Birringer, J., & Katz, L. (1994). A method for assessing therapists' recall of in-session events. *Journal of Counseling Psychology, 41,* 53–57.

CHAPTER

Nicholas Ladany
Janet L. Muse-Burke

Understanding and Conducting Supervision Research

The important thing is to not stop questioning.

—Albert Einstein

The two primary goals of supervision research are to (a) understand the process of supervision and its influence on counseling and (b) inform supervision practice. Although theoretical propositions regarding supervision can be traced back to Freud (1910/1957), empirical work in supervision did not begin until 1958 (Bernard & Goodyear, 1998; Harkness & Poertner, 1989). In part, researchers' ability to conceptualize and discover salient aspects of supervision is limited by knowledge about counseling (Lambert & Arnold, 1987). As a likely result, supervision research has lagged behind counseling research. This empirical state of affairs parallels the practicing supervisor's perpetual conundrum: "How can I teach my students things about which I myself have limited knowledge?" However, the picture may not be so bleak. Specifically, we know that counseling facilitates positive client change (Lipsey & Wilson, 1993). Moreover, it has been found that relationship variables common across most theoretical approaches account for 50% of the variance in treatment effects, while specific techniques and interventions account for 15% of the variance in treatment effects (Lambert, 1986). Further, we have additional evidence to suggest that graduate training leads to better counseling outcome (Stein & Lambert, 1995). Moreover, supervision researchers have recognized that supervision research includes much more than simply the effects on client outcome (Holloway, 1984). Thus, supervision researchers do seem to have an emerging foundation on which to venture forward.

In 1961, the journal *Counselor Education and Supervision* was founded and provided supervision researchers with a primary source devoted exclusively to supervision and training issues (Bernard & Goodyear, 1998). Since that time, over 200 empirical articles regarding supervision and training issues have been published in such journals as *Counselor Education and Supervision, Journal of Counseling & Development, Journal of Counseling Psychology, The Clinical Supervisor, The Counseling Psychologist, Journal of Consulting and Clinical Psychology, Professional Psychology: Research and Practice,* and *Psychotherapy.* To date, over 40 reviews of the supervision literature have been conducted, which, to varying degrees, summarize, critique, and integrate the empirical work in supervision (e.g., Bernard & Goodyear, 1998; Ellis & Ladany, 1997; Lambert, 1980; Lambert & Ogles, 1997; Neufeldt, Beutler, & Banchero, 1997; Russell, Crimmings, & Lent, 1984). It is from these reviews that much of this chapter is elicited.

Notably, the purpose of this chapter is fourfold. First, we will present a model identifying and categorizing the variables of supervision research. Second, we will provide an overview of the literature pertaining to supervision research. Third, we will offer a schema of the important elements of conducting supervision research. Fourth, we will apply our knowledge about research and methodology to offer a model for assessing the adequacy of trainee evaluation approaches. It is our hope that this chapter will prove useful for students who are interested in conducting supervision research as part of theses and dissertations, for professional supervision researchers, and for consumers of supervision research.

☐ Supervision Research Variables

The first step toward understanding supervision research is to conceptualize the primary, general research questions within which most supervision empirical work may be considered. These overarching research questions (Ladany et al., 1999) include: (a) How does supervision influence trainee outcome? (b) How does supervision influence client outcome? (c) How does counseling influence trainee learning? (d) How do counseling and supervision processes parallel one another? (e) How does counseling influence client outcome? and (f) How do external events outside of supervision influence supervision and counseling? As can be seen, much of supervision research involves examining relationships and events outside of the trainee–supervisor interactions (e.g., counseling, external events, etc.). Presently, the "outside supervision" variables have received the least attention in the supervision literature, and the "inside supervision" question (i.e., How does supervision influence trainee outcome?) has received the most attention.

Along with Wampold and Holloway (1997), we define supervision process as activities that occur within the supervision session as well as the perceptions of these activities by supervisors, trainees, and objective observers. Similarly, counseling process concerns the events that occur in counseling sessions and the perceptions of these events by counselor trainees, clients, supervisors, and objective observers. Furthermore, we define supervision and counseling outcome as variables that change as a result of supervision or counseling, and these changes endure beyond the session proper. Notably, in some instances, it may not be clear which variables concern supervision process or supervision outcome (e.g., trainee satisfaction can occur in session or postsession). However, we believe that the concepts of process and outcome are a useful means by which researchers can manage and conceptualize the whole supervision experience.

From these research questions, a framework for conceptualizing supervision variables can be proffered (see Figure 1). Similar to other models (e.g., Wampold & Holloway, 1997), it is important to recognize that there is likely to be a reciprocal relationship among most of the variables. For example, supervisor characteristics, such as supervisor style, may influence supervision process, like the development of the supervisory relationship. In turn, the supervisory relationship may influence supervisor style.

The second step toward understanding supervision research is to conceptualize the primary variables endemic to supervision that fit within the aforementioned primary research questions. Table 1 presents a sample of supervision variables that have been studied or that could be studied based on the theoretical propositions explicated and implied in the supervision literature. As can be seen, there are numerous variables to be considered

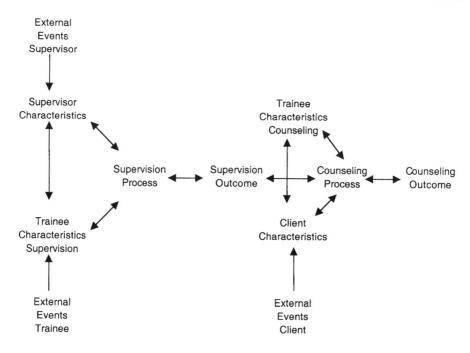

FIGURE 12.1. Interrelationships among supervision process and outcome and counseling process and outcome variables.

TABLE 12.1. Sample of supervision variables

Variables

Supervisor characteristics
  Sex
  Race
  Ethnicity
  Sexual orientation
  Age
  Socioeconomic status
  Religion
  Gender identity
  Racial identity
  Ethnic identity
  Sexual orientation identity
  Spiritual identity
  Personality (e.g., authoritativeness)
  Counseling experience
  Supervision experience
  Counselor developmental level
  Supervisor developmental level
  Experience as a client
  Experience as a therapist
  Experience as a trainee
  Supervisor self-efficacy
  Counseling theoretical orientation
  Supervision theoretical orientation
  Expectations for supervision
  Ability to tolerate ambiguity
  Supervisor didactic training
  Supervisor experiential training
  Supervisor style

Trainee characteristics
  Sex
  Race
  Ethnicity
  Sexual orientation
  Age
  Socialeconomic status
  Religion
  Gender identity
  Racial identity
  Ethnic identity
  Sexual orientation identity
  Spiritual identity
  Personality (e.g., openness)
  Experience as a client
  Counseling experience

Supervised counseling experience
  Trainee developmental level
  Experience as a trainee
  Experience as a supervisor
  Anxiety
  Counseling self-efficacy
  Counseling theoretical orientation
  Supervision theoretical orientation
  Supervision role induction
  Expectations for counseling
  Expectations for supervision
  Ability to tolerate ambiguity
  Reflectivity
  Counselor didactic training
  Counselor experiential training

Client characteristics
  Sex
  Race
  Ethnicity
  Sexual orientation
  Age
  Socioeconomic status
  Religion
  Gender identity
  Racial identity
  Ethnic identity
  Sexual orientation identity
  Spiritual identity
  Personality
  Previous counseling experience
  Expectations for counseling
  Presenting issues
  Psychopathology
  Social support
  Ability to tolerate ambiguity

Supervision process
  Supervisory relationship (e.g.,
    supervisory working alliance)
  Trainee disclosures
  Supervisor disclosures
  Trainee nondisclosures
  Supervisor nondisclosures
  Parallel process (as influenced by
    counseling process)

(Table continued on next page)

TABLE 12.1. Sample of supervision variables (*Continued*)

Variables	

Supervision process (*Continued*)
 Trainee role conflict and role
  ambiguity
 Trainee transference
 Supervisor countertransference
 Supervisor responsiveness
 Supervisor interventions
 Supervisor response modes
 Supervisor intentions
 Supervisor critical incidents
 Trainee critical incidents
	Counselor trainee nondisclosures
	 Client nondisclosures
	 Client transference
	 Counselor trainee
	  countertransference
	 Counselor trainee responsiveness
	 Counselor trainee interventions
	 Counselor trainee response modes
	 Counselor trainee intentions
	 Counselor trainee critical incidents
	 Client critical incidents

Supervision outcome
 Trainee self-efficacy (change)
 Trainee counseling skills (change)
 Trainee conceptualization skills
  (change)
 Trainee professional identity
  (change)
 Trainee satisfaction
 Trainee evaluation
 Supervisor self-efficacy (change)
 Supervisor supervision skills
  (change)
 Supervisor conceptualization skills
  (change)
 Supervisor professional identity
  (change)
 Trainee regrets
 Supervisor regrets
 Session impact
	Counseling outcome
	 Client level of distress (change)
	 Session impact
	 Client satisfaction
	 Client regrets
	 Counselor trainee regrets
	 Counselor trainee professional
	  identity (change)
	
	External events supervisor
	 Supervision of supervision
	 Environmental events (e.g.,
	  oppressive agency rules,
	  managed care)
	
	External events trainee
	 Peer feedback
	 Peer interactions
	 Environmental events (e.g.,
	  oppressive agency rules,
	  trainee evaluation policies)

Counseling process
 Counseling relationship (e.g.,
  counseling working alliance)
 Counselor trainee disclosures
 Client disclosure
	External events client
	 Environmental events (e.g.,
	  managed care, life experiences
	  that influence presenting issues)

when conducting supervision research. Hence, supervision should not be considered a unitary variable; rather, supervision should be recognized as a "heterogeneous set of conditions" (Lambert, 1980). To date, only a small percentage of these variables have been addressed in the supervision literature, and rarely have these variables been investigated in a systematic and programmatic fashion.

It is important to note that the interplay of these variables can be investigated either quantitatively (Kerlinger, 1986) or qualitatively (Creswell, 1998). Moreover, assessment of these variables can occur via self-report from the supervisor, trainee, and client, as well as through objective observer ratings. Each of these perspectives should provide unique and relevant information about supervision (Holloway, 1984). Also, our model is most relevant to individual supervision of individual counselor trainees. Modifications could be made to accommodate group supervision of individual counseling, group supervision of group counseling, and supervision of family counseling accordingly.

☐ What We Know From Supervision Research

As indicated previously, there have been numerous reviews of the supervision literature, which greatly vary in the extent to which they summarize and critique the research. Recently, the supervision research was examined systematically, comprehensively, and programmatically (Ellis & Ladany, 1997). Specifically, Ellis and Ladany reviewed every known empirical supervision article published from 1981 to 1995. From this review, a set of empirical themes or inferences that emerged from the literature were identified. Furthermore, a primary set of methodological issues was articulated.

From their review, Ellis and Ladany (1997) identified six themes or inferences regarding the state of supervision research. The first inference pertained to the supervisory relationship and contained studies related to the supervisory working alliance, client-centered conditions, Strong's social influence model, trainee role conflict and ambiguity, and the structure of the supervisory relationship. It was concluded from these studies that the supervisory relationship seems to be a key aspect of the supervision process, and it is likely to influence supervision process and outcome. However, it was also determined that the manner in which the supervisory relationship has been defined and studied has varied. These inconsistencies in definition and operationalization (i.e., measurement) have muddied the field's ability to understand how the supervisory relationship specifically influences process and outcome.

The second inference entailed trainee–supervisor matching. Specifically, this line of research examined the match between supervisor roles and supervision functions from Bernard's (1979) model, the match between supervisee needs and supervisor interventions, trainee–supervisor match in terms of individual difference (i.e., cognitive style, reactance, sex/gender, race, and theoretical orientation), and the match between trainee needs and the supervisory environment. The primary conclusion was that the inference that states that matching trainees and supervisors on a variety of characteristics leads to positive supervision process and outcome lacked empirical validation. For example, there is little evidence to suggest that trainee–supervisor matching by race will correspond with greater satisfaction with supervision. Moreover, the authors concluded that supervision researchers may be oversimplifying their assumptions about matching and should consider using more relevant psychological variables (e.g., investigate racial identity rather than race).

The third inference concerned developmental changes that purportedly occur in trainees over time. A variety of supervision models, including ego development (Loevinger, 1976); conceptual development (Holloway & Wampold, 1986); Littrell, Lee-Borden, and Lorenz's (1979) model; Hogan's (1964) model; Loganbill, Hardy, and Delworth's (1982) model; Sansbury's (1982) model; Stoltenberg's (1981) model; Stoltenberg and Delworth's (1987) model, and general developmental issues related to trainee experience level were identified and tested. The primary conclusions that emerged from this review were: (a) the investigations had numerous and pervasive methodological shortcomings (e.g., using cross-sectional research designs to make developmental inferences) that made their interpretability suspect at best and misleading at worse, and (b) the data indicate that the developmental models are probably overly simplistic and do not attend to trainee issues adequately.

The issue of using cross-sectional designs to make developmental or longitudinal inferences seems endemic to empirical articles assessing developmental notions in supervision. To illustrate this problem, consider a researcher who examines a group of 10 beginning trainees (5 men and 5 women) and a group of 10 advanced trainees (all of whom are women). If this researcher were to make a developmental or longitudinal inference based on the variable of trainee gender, then he or she might determine that male trainees are very likely to become female trainees as they go from beginning to advanced training levels. Although this inference is clearly nonsensical, it illustrates a common mistake that developmental researchers make in their investigations and interpretations of their data. As such, one cannot make developmental or longitudinal conclusions based on data derived from the cross-sectional investigation of different cohorts.

The fourth inference pertained to the evaluation of trainees. In general, it was concluded that (a) trainees are likely to be evaluated qualitatively; (b) general supervisor perceptions may influence evaluative estimations (e.g., if the supervisor likes the trainee, the supervisor is likely to evaluate the trainee positively); and (c) evaluative measures are largely psychometrically invalid.

The fifth inference regarded client outcome and, most typically, the issue of parallel process, to which only a few studies pertained. As defined elsewhere in this book, parallel process can be generally defined as similarities that exist between supervision process and outcome and counseling process and outcome. From the studies examining parallel process, it was concluded that there may be similarities between trainee–client interactions and supervisor–trainee interactions. However, the specific mechanisms operating between these dyads have yet to be identified.

Finally, the sixth inference regarded the development of new measures to assess supervision process and outcome. Of the seven measures reviewed, only two were recommended and considered psychometrically adequate. These tools were the Role Conflict and Role Ambiguity Inventory (Olk & Friedlander, 1992) and the Barrett-Lennard Relationship Inventory (Barrett-Lennard, 1962; Dalton, 1983; Wiebe & Pearce, 1973). The general consensus was that considerable work needs to be conducted to validate existing and new measures of supervision process and outcome.

The review by Ellis and Ladany (1997) not only offered insight into the knowledge gained through supervision research but also highlighted a number of methodological shortcomings of the supervision literature. Supervision researchers are advised to consider these research limitations when planning future studies. Ellis and Ladany evaluated the literature based on the 37 potential threats to each study's validity, derived from Cook and Campbell's (1979) validity threats; Wampold, Davis, and Good's (1990) hypothesis validity threats; and 8 supplemental threats described in the general methodological literature (Chen, 1990; Ellis, 1991; Kazdin, 1986; Kerlinger, 1986; Serlin, 1987; Wampold & Poulin, 1992). Across the 104 empirical studies reviewed, 14 threats emerged as the most salient methodological threats. These validity threats included: (a) inflated Type I error rate (i.e., multiple statistical comparisons without controlling for experimentwise error; 76%); (b) unreliability or invalidity of independent or dependent measures (64%); (c) inflated Type II error rate (low statistical power or not detecting a true effect; 51%); (d) nonrandom/nonrepresentative sample (39%); (e) nonrandom assignment (38%); (f) mismatch of purpose, hypotheses, design-methods, and analyses (29%); (g) violation of the assumptions of statistics (14%); (h) cohort effects such as making developmental inferences from cross-sectional data (11%); (i) confounded independent variables (e.g., single supervisor with multiple trainees; 10%); (j) uncontrolled variables (unknown third variables that moderate the effects; 8%); (k) differential attrition across groups (8%); (l) mono-method bias (7%); (m) di- or multichotomized continuously distributed independent variable or dependent variable (7%); and (n) participant heterogeneity (7%).

Clearly no one study could account for all of the potential threats to validity. Gelso (1979) referred to this inability to control for all potential threats as the "bubble hypothesis." Essentially, Gelso likened controlling for validity threats to placing a sticker on a car windshield. Inevitably, a bubble will emerge under the sticker and, when the bubble is pressed down, it creates another bubble elsewhere. In supervision research, for example, a researcher could account for the nonrandom assignment threat by randomly assigning participants to conditions in the study. However, this researcher will likely have limited generalizability, and thereby bring the external validity threat to the fore. Thus, researchers must select those validity threats that they are willing to accept for any given study with the intention of conducting future studies that will account for the threats left uncontrolled in the present study.

A closer look at the primary validity threats identified, however, reveals that most of these threats could have been easily remedied in their respective studies. For example, 76% of the studies demonstrated an inflated Type I error rate. As a result, it was likely that more than one of the findings determined to be significant were due to chance rather than actual effects in the data. A simple way to control for Type I error is to reduce the alpha rate (e.g., Bonferroni procedure) to account for the multiple statistical tests. Similar procedures could be implemented for many of the threats identified (see Ellis & Ladany, 1997, for a more thorough discussion).

☐ How to Create a Well-Designed Quantitative Supervision Research Study

With knowledge of the methodological shortcomings found in the empirical supervision literature, Ellis, Ladany, Krengel, and Schult (1996) explicated a series of issues relevant to creating a feasible and well-designed supervision study. Although these issues are most relevant to experimental, quantitative studies, they also have generalizability to other quantitative studies (e.g., ex post facto and survey research designs) and, to a lesser extent, qualitative research. In terms of writing the introduction, researchers should (a) explain the theoretical models on which they are relying and the theories' shortcomings, (b) create a logical argument and rationale linking the constructs of interest, (c) thoroughly define the constructs of interest, and (d) specify directional research hypotheses (i.e., make explicit what is implied). When composing the methods section, investigators are advised to (a) conduct an a priori power analysis based on the published research (Cohen, 1988; Haase, 1974; Haase, Ellis, & Ladany, 1989), (b) administer psychometrically sound instruments (i.e., valid and reliable measures used with a similar sample) and report the internal consistency for the sample studied, (c) employ random assignment whenever possible (e.g., randomly assign participants to conditions or the order of instruments), (d) collect and report comprehensive demographic information about the participants (e.g., gender, race, age, counseling experience, etc.), (e) use multiple methods (e.g., self-report and objective raters) when possible, (f) use multiple measures of the same construct when possible (e.g., trainee experience as months of counseling experience and total number of clients seen), (g) provide sufficient data regarding raters, (h) ensure that the constructs defined in the introduction are matched with the operationalizations of the constructs in the method, and (i) guarantee that hypotheses offered in the introduction are matched with the statistical analyses chosen.

Concerning the results, researchers should (a) control for Type I error; (b) control for Type II error; (c) use continuous variables when possible and not di- or multichotomize variables to avoid losing statistical power or explained variance (Cohen, 1983); (d) test for violations of the assumptions underlying the statistical procedures utilized (e.g., ceiling or floor effects, dispro-portional cell sizes, skewness), and make appropriate corrections to the data when assumptions are violated (e.g., data transformations); and (e) avoid violating the independence of observation assumption (e.g., each supervisor provides data for a single trainee and participants do not serve as both super-visor and trainee in a single study). In the discussion, investigators should (a) interpret the results in the context of theory, (b) stay close to the data and avoid overgeneralizing the results, (c) evaluate the study and provide relevant limitations as well as strengths, and (d) offer theoretical, empirical, and practical implications of the results.

Measuring Supervision Variables

As mentioned previously, psychometrically sound supervision measures are limited in number. However, new measures are being developed and older measures are being revised. Measures used for supervision research have varied from counseling measures revised to fit the supervision context to measures specifically designed for supervision (Bernard & Goodyear, 1998; Ellis & Ladany, 1997). In general, the most useful measures have been derived for the supervision context and have been validated (i.e., content-related, criterion-related, construct-related) and found to be reliable (e.g., internal consistency is greater than .80; Gall, Borg, & Gall, 1996). We have identified frequently used measures in the supervision literature in Table 12.2. The reader is encouraged to examine these measures and to evaluate the psychometric adequacy for her or his research purposes. Additionally, the reader may want to review the following references to determine the adequacy of these measures (Bernard & Goodyear, 1998; Ellis & Ladany, 1997; Lambert & Ogles, 1997).

Qualitative Designs and Supervision Research

As noted, the well-designed research study offers a framework for putting together and conducting a quantitative research investigation. Recently, a groundswell of interest has emerged related to conducting qualitative re-search investigations in supervision. Supervision researchers have begun to qualitatively investigate a variety of variables including parallel process (Doehr-man, 1976; Friedlander, Siegel, & Brenock, 1989), professional counselor development (Skovholt & Rønnestad, 1992), positive and negative experi-ences in supervision (Hutt, Scott, & King, 1983; Worthen & McNeill, 1996), trainee reflectivity (Neufeldt, Karno, & Nelson, 1996), supervisor counter-transference (Ladany, Constantine, Miller, Erickson, & Muse-Burke, 2000), trainee sexual attraction and use of supervision (Ladany, O'Brien, et al., 1997), experiences of novice counselors (Williams, Judge, Hill, & Hoffman,

TABLE 12.2. Frequently used measures to assess supervision processes and outcomes

Construct/variable	Subconstruct/subscale	Rater	Scale title	Reference
Trainee cognitive complexity	(1) Differentiation (2) Integration	O	Counselor Perception Questionnaire	Blocher et al. (1985)
Trainee counseling self-efficacy	(1) Employing microskills (2) Attending to process (3) Dealing with difficult client behaviors (4) Behaving in a multiculturally competent manner (5) Being aware of one's values	T	Counseling Self-Estimate Inventory	Larson et al. (1992)
Trainee counseling self-efficacy	Single score	T	Self-Efficacy Inventory	Friedlander & Synder (1983)
Trainee critical incidents in supervision	(1) Most important supervision issues (2) Most important supervision interventions	T	The Critical Incidents Questionnaire	Heppner & Roehike (1984); Rabinowitz, Heppner, & Roehike (1986)
Trainee developmental level	(1) Self- and other awareness (2) Motivation (3) Dependency/autonomy	T	Supervisee Levels Questionnaire—Revised	McNeill, Stoltenberg, & Romans (1992)
Trainee developmental level	(1) Trainee (2) Supervisory needs	T	Counselor Development Questionnaire	Reising & Daniels (1983)
Trainee multicultural counseling competence	Single score	T/S	Cross-Cultural Counseling Inventory-Revised	LaFromboise, Coleman, & Hernandez (1991)

Construct	Dimensions	Type	Measure	Source
Trainee multicultural counseling competence	(1) Multicultural awareness (2) Multicultural knowledge (3) Multicultural skills	T	Multicultural Awareness, Knowledge, Skills Survey	D'Andrea, Daniels, & Heck (1991)
Trainee multicultural counseling competence	(1) Multicultural awareness (2) Multicultural knowledge (3) Multicultural skills (4) Multicultural counseling relationship	T	Multicultural Counseling Inventory	Sodowsky, Taffe, Gutkin, & Wise (1994)
Trainee multicultural counseling competence	(1) Multicultural awareness (2) Multicultural knowledge	T	Multicultural Counseling Knowledge and Awareness Scale	Ponterotto, Rieger, Gretchen, Utsey, & Austin (1996)
Trainee multicultural case conceptualization ability	Etiology and treatment differentiation and integration	O	Multicultural Case Conceptualization Ability Measure	Ladany, Inman, Constantine, & Hofheinz (1997)
Trainee role conflict and ambiguity	(1) Role conflict (2) Role ambiguity	T	Role Conflict and Role Ambiguity Inventory	Olk & Friedlander (1992)
Trainee counseling and supervision behavior	(1) Counseling (2) Supervision	S	Counselor Evaluation Rating Scale	Myrick & Kelly (1971)
Trainee counseling and supervision behavior	(1) Purposeful counseling performance (2) Noncounseling behaviors (3) Supervision attitude (4) Counseling orientation	T	Counselor Evaluation Rating Scale	Benshoff & Thomas (1992)
Trainee satisfaction with supervision	Single score	T	Supervisee Satisfaction Questionnaire	Ladany, Hill, Corbett, & Nutt (1998)

(Table continued on next page)

TABLE 12.2. Frequently used measures to assess supervision processes and outcomes (*Continued*)

Construct/variable	Subconstruct/subscale	Rater	Scale title	Reference
Trainee and supervisor satisfaction with supervision	Trainee: (1) evaluation of supervisor (2) evaluation of self as trainee (3) level of comfort Supervisor: (1) evaluation of trainee (2) evaluation of self as supervisor (3) level of comfort	T/S	Trainee Personal Reaction Scale & Supervisor Personal Reaction Scale	Holloway & Wampold (1983)
Supervisor behaviors	Some subconstructs include: (1) degree of focus on therapist and client (2) dominance of the supervisor and the therapist (3) number of clarifying and interpretive comments (4) intensity of confrontation (5) empathy of the supervisor	O	Psychotherapy Supervisory Inventory	Shanfield, Mohl, Matthews, & Hetherly (1989)
Supervisor behaviors	1–12 Factors	T/S	Supervision Questionnaire–Revised	Worthington (1984); Worthington & Roehike (1979)
Supervisor behaviors	(1) Importance of different aspects of supervision (2) Frequency of behaviors (3) Time spent on supervisory functions (4) Supervisor roles and behaviors (5) Demographic variables	S	Level of Supervision Survey	Miars et al. (1983)

Construct	Type	Instrument	Dimensions	Reference
Supervisor developmental level	S	Psychotherapy Supervisor Development Scale	Single score	Watkins, Schneider, Haynes, & Nieberding (1995)
Supervisor ethical behavior	T/S	Supervisor Ethical Behavior Scale	Single score	Ladany, Lehrman-Waterman, Molinaro, & Wolgast (1999)
Supervisory expectations	T/S	Congruence of Supervisory Expectations Scale	(1) Role behaviors (2) Nature of relationship (3) Task focus and goals	Ellis et al. (1994)
Supervisor feedback	O	Supervisory Feedback Rating System	(1) Type (2) Specificity (3) Valence (4) Focus	Friedlander, Siegel, & Brenock (1989)
Supervisor focus	S	Supervisor Emphasis Rating Form—Revised	(1) Process (2) Professional behavior (3) Personalization skills (4) Client conceptualization	Lanning & Freeman (1994); Lanning, Whiston, & Carey (1994)
Supervisor focus	S	The Supervisory Focus and Style Questionnaire	(1) Personality (2) Supervisory focus (3) Supervisory style	Yager, Wilson, Brewer, & Kinnetz (1989)
Supervisor impact	T/S	The Supervision Perception Form	(1) Supervisory impact (2) Willingness to learn	Heppner & Roehlke (1984)
Supervisor self-disclosure	T/S	Supervisor Self-Disclosure Inventory	Single score	Lehrman-Waterman & Ladany (1999)

(Table continued on next page)

TABLE 12.2. Frequently used measures to assess supervision processes and outcomes (*Continued*)

Construct/variable	Subconstruct/subscale	Rater	Scale title	Reference
Supervisor style	(1) Attractive (2) Interpersonality sensitive (3) Task oriented	T/S	Supervisory Styles Inventory	Friedlander & Ward (1984)
Supervisory relationship	(1) Regard (2) Empathy (3) Unconditionality (4) Willingness to be known (5) Total score (i.e., overall of the relationship)	T	Relationship Inventory	Schact, Howe, & Berman (1988)
Supervisory working alliance	(1) Agreement on goals of supervision (2) Agreement on tasks of supervision (3) Emotional bond between the supervisor and trainee	T/S	Working Alliance Inventory	Bahrick (1990)
Supervisory working alliance	Trainee: (1) rapport (2) client focus Supervisor: (1) client focus (2) rapport (3) identification	T/S	Supervisory Working Alliance Inventory	Efstation, Patton, & Kardash (1990)

Note. The person doing the rating was classified as the trainee (T), the supervisor (S), the client (C), or a trained observer (O).

1997), multicultural supervision (Fukuyama, 1994), trainee nondisclosures (Hess & Hoffman, 1999; Ladany, Hill, Corbett, & Nutt, 1996), counterproductive events in supervision (Gray, Walker, Ladany, & Ancis, 1999), and harmful supervision (Nelson & Friedlander, 1999). These qualitative investigations seem to be filling important gaps in the supervision literature left untouched by quantitative researchers.

In general, qualitative research maintains several typical characteristics (Bergsjo, 1999; Bogdan & Biklen, 1992; Eisner, 1991; Lincoln & Guba, 1985; Merriam, 1988). First, qualitative research is field focused, emphasizing the natural setting as the source of the data. Second, the researcher is the primary instrument of data collection. A third characteristic is that data are collected using words or pictures to ascertain a rich, thorough description. Similarly, expressive language is used in qualitative research. Fourth, the outcome of qualitative research is perceived as a process rather than a product. Lastly, the data are analyzed using inductive reasoning (i.e., conclusions are drawn directly from the information provided in the data). (For more thorough descriptions of qualitative research the reader is directed to Creswell, 1998; Denzin & Lincoln, 1994; Flick, 1998; Lincoln & Guba, 1985; Maxwell, 1996; Miles & Huberman, 1994; Patton, 1990; Strauss & Corbin, 1990; Wolcott, 1994; Yin, 1994.)

The following features demonstrate ways in which qualitative research can be distinguished from quantitative research methodologies. Specifically, quantitative research frequently manipulates the research setting and utilizes instruments and measures to ascertain data. Further, quantitative data is collected and reported in the form of numbers (i.e., statistics), and these numbers are the product of the research. Rather than employ inductive reasoning, quantitative research entails deductive reasoning to make judgments. A common myth about qualitative research is that it lacks the rigor of quantitative methods. However, it is becoming better understood that qualitative research is, indeed, a rigorous methodological approach and that the previous disparaging beliefs were largely unfounded. Moreover, qualitative and quantitative methods maintain strengths and weaknesses that are complimentary in nature; thus, both add unique value to the supervision research enterprise.

As with quantitative research, a variety of qualitative research methodologies have been devised, many in recent years. One way to conceptualize and manage the disparate methods is to consider qualitative methods from the context of five general traditions (Creswell, 1998). These five primary traditions of qualitative research include: (a) phenomenology, (b) grounded theory, (c) biography, (d) ethnography, and (e) case study (Creswell). To date, the primary qualitative traditions used to study supervision have been phenomenology (e.g., Worthen & McNeill, 1996) and grounded theory (e.g., Neufeldt, Karno, & Nelson, 1996). Phenomenology research seeks to describe and understand the fundamental, underlying meaning of experiences for a few individuals with regard to a particular phenomenon. Researchers using this method collect data through in-depth interviews, typically with about 10 people. The interview questions are devised by the researcher and are directly linked to the phenomenon in question (e.g., good moments in supervision). In the end, a description of the "essence" of the experience is achieved.

Grounded theory, another tradition of qualitative research, aims to generate a theory which is based (or "grounded") in the data obtained from the field. Interviews are conducted with 20 to 30 individuals in order to saturate the categories (i.e., ascertain new information until no more can be found). The process of data analysis is systematic and follows a standard coding format. The purpose of a biography is to explore the life of a particular individual. Through interviews and historical documents, researchers gather individual stories of the person's life and group these stories according to themes of significant life moments. Next, the individual's life is placed in an historical context with consideration for the norms, issues, and ideologies of the day. In so doing, a detailed picture of one person's life is created.

An ethnography aspires to describe and interpret a cultural and social group. The researcher collects data through participant observation in which he or she is immersed in the daily lives of the people or person under investigation. Further, the researcher may engage in in-depth interviews with the individual or members of the group. Through this process, the researcher develops an understanding of the meanings of the behavior, language, interactions, and artifacts of the culture. Ultimately, a rich description of the cultural behavior of a group or individual is attained. The last major tradition of qualitative research is the case study. This method strives to develop an in-depth analysis of a single case or multiple cases over time. Case studies require thorough data collection using numerous sources of information, such as documents and reports, interviews, and observations. Moreover, the data are collected within the natural setting of the case. Through this process, a detailed description of a case or cases evolves.

Stemming from the grounded theory tradition, Hill, Thompson, and Williams (1997) have authored a promising qualitative methodology that has been used in counseling and supervision research entitled consensual qualitative research (CQR). There are nine general stages of the CQR method: (a) recruiting, (b) interviews, (c) data preparation, (d) coding into domains (e) abstracting core ideas, (f) auditing core ideas, (g) cross-analysis, (h) auditing cross-analysis, and (i) review by the entire team. The interested reader is directed to Hill et al. (1997) as well as to qualitative studies that have used the CQR format to study supervision (e.g., Hess & Hoffman, 1999; Ladany, O'Brien, et al., 1997; Ladany et al., 2000; Nelson & Friedlander, 1999; Williams et al., 1997).

☐ A Descriptive Model of Assessing Evaluation Approaches for Counselor Trainees

In the spirit of the scientist practitioner, our research skills can be used in the service of evaluating supervision practice. One supervision practice issue that seems well suited for the interface between supervision research and practice is in the context of evaluating counselor trainees. The ability to effectively evaluate counselor trainees is a primary task for supervisors of counselor trainees (Bernard & Goodyear, 1998). It is through the evaluation of trainees that supervisors are able to chart the progress of trainee growth as well as client change.

A review of the empirical literature examining the methods used to evaluate counselor trainees (Borders & Fong, 1991; Carey, Williams, & Wells, 1988; Dodenhoff, 1981; Fordham, May, Boyle, Bentall, & Slade, 1990; Lazar & Mosek, 1993; Mathews, 1986; Newman, Kopta, McGovern, Howard, & McNeilly, 1988; Newman, Kopta, McGovern, Meier & Davis, 1990; Norcross & Stevenson, 1984; Norcross, Stevenson, & Nash, 1986; Romans, Boswell, Carlozzi, & Ferguson, 1995; Snepp and Peterson, 1988) reveals the following: (a) trainees are evaluated primarily qualitatively (Norcross & Stevenson, 1984; Norcross et al., 1986); (b) most supervisors (90%) use trainee self-report as a method to assess trainee performance, while less than 60% rely on audiotapes and less than 40% rely on videotapes (Ladany & Lehrman-Waterman, 1999; Ladany & Melincoff, 1997); (c) general perceptions of the trainee by the supervisor may influence the evaluation (Carey et al., 1988; Dodenhoff, 1981); (d) many supervisors may not be fulfilling their evaluation responsibilities adequately or ethically (Cormier & Bernard, 1982; Keith-Spiegel & Koocher, 1985; Ladany, Lehrman-Waterman, Molinaro, & Wolgast, 1999), and (e) the measures used to assess trainee competence are largely outdated or psychometrically unsound (Ellis & Ladany, 1997). Hence, the literature concerning the trainee evaluation process seems to indicate several potential areas of concern. In particular, there is little evidence to verify that reliable, valid, and systematic methods of trainee evaluation exist. Instead, much of what is used appears to include either supervisors' subjective impressions of trainee performance or objective measures that have questionable psychometric properties.

Overall, it seems clear that the area of trainee evaluation is in need of new and innovative measures. However, along with the development of new measures, there is a need for a framework from which these methods of evaluation can be organized and assessed. The following is a summary of a model detailing how one may assess trainee evaluation approaches. This model is based in part on some previous propositions made by Ellis and Ladany (1997). It is anticipated that any given evaluation approach may be appraised based on its ability to attend to the salient components presently identified.

The fundamental components of this assessment model include: (a) mode of counseling (e.g., individual, group, family, or couples), (b) domain of trainee behaviors (e.g., counseling or supervision), (c) competence area (e.g., counseling techniques, theoretical conceptualization, professionalism, multicultural competence, clinical disorders, assessment, administration, countertransference, or supervision behaviors), (d) method (trainee self-report, case notes, audiotape, videotape, live supervision, co-therapy, role play, experiences in supervision), (e) proportion of caseload (all clients, subgroup of clients, one client), (f) segment of experience (e.g., entire training experience, part of the entire training experience, a specific session, or a segment of a session), (g) time period (early, middle, or late in client treatment as well as early, middle, or late in training experience), (h) evaluator (e.g., supervisor, clients, peers, objective raters), (i) level of proficiency (e.g., demonstrated skill, comparison to cohort group), (j) reliability issues (e.g., trustworthiness for qualitative assessments and statistical measurement error for quantitative assessments), (k) validity issues (e.g., construct validity), and (l) format (e.g., quantitative vs. qualitative and structured vs. unstructured). It would be unreasonable to suggest that one evaluation approach could take into account all the above parameters. Nonetheless, the merit of a given evaluation approach can be assessed based on the extent to which these components are considered.

To understand how to apply this assessment model, we may examine some example items from potential measures. Although it may be the case that there are as many evaluation measures as there are training sites (Bernard & Goodyear, 1998), there are probably common criteria that are used to evaluate all trainees (e.g., competence). For example, it is likely that an evaluation scale will ask for a supervisor's assessment of a trainee's competence on a number of items. This scale may ask the supervisor to rate her or his trainee's "counseling knowledge" on a 1 (very poor) to 5 (excellent) scale. Counseling knowledge might be defined for the supervisor as "demonstrated good understanding of theories and research in psychology, counseling/psychotherapy, and psychopathology." How might a scale with this item be evaluated? First, in the context of this scale, there is no mention of the mode of therapy, method, proportion of caseload, segment of experience, or time period the supervisor is to use to make this assessment. Furthermore, the area of competence seems to cover nearly the entirety of a full graduate training program (i.e., issue of overinclusiveness). It is difficult to imagine that a supervisor could make such an assessment adequately. Hence, this evaluation instrument (assuming there are similar items to the one listed above) seems to have multiple confounding features that may limit its use.

In another example, a common type of anchor used on evaluation scales asks the supervisor to evaluate a trainee's competence while taking into consideration his or her developmental level (e.g., beginning practicum, advanced practicum, internship). In this case, the supervisor must first assess the developmental level of the trainee, then consider the level of competence associated with that particular developmental level, and finally compare the trainee's expressed competence to the associated developmental level. Given the difficulty of defining and operationalizing trainee developmental level (Ellis & Ladany, 1997; Holloway, 1987), the ability of the supervisor to fulfill this requirement in a consistent and valid fashion appears doubtful. Furthermore, given the problems with this method, it seems likely that trainee evaluation may be influenced by the supervisor's general impressions of the trainee (e.g., how much the supervisor likes the trainee; Ellis & Ladany, 1997).

In general, it seems that supervisors' ability to adequately evaluate trainees may be compromised due to deficient instrumentation and approaches. The question then becomes: How do supervision practitioners and researchers address the inadequacy of trainee evaluation? First, it would seem important to consider the strengths of the current measures from which newer measures can be built. Working from that which we do know may provide us with the foundations to discover that which we do not know. Similarly, the continued identification and investigation of the numerous factors associated with supervision process and outcome beyond client outcome seems relevant (Holloway, 1992). Second, cross-discipline collaboration via multisite supervision research centers seems necessary to create and validate new approaches to trainee evaluation. As was previously noted, currently there may be as many trainee evaluation measures as there are training sites. These multisite cross-collaborative efforts would impart some standardization to the process of evaluating trainees. Finally, the continued promotion of counselor supervision as a field related to, but separate from, the field of counseling, must occur. Along with this continued promotion would come an increased recognition of the importance of defining and operationalizing trainee performance from which reliable and valid evaluation approaches can be derived.

☐ Conclusion

It has been proposed that the field of counseling and psychotherapy relies on a germ theory for the training of its students (Beutler, 1988). In essence, this theory suggests that if trainees are exposed to the theory and practice of counseling, they will "catch" the competence bug. Conversely, it has also been asserted that unless the systematic feedback and reflection provided by supervision accompanies counseling practice, trainees will only gain the illusion of professional competence (Bernard & Goodyear, 1998). As such, supervision is vital to the development of counselors in training. Despite this fact, much of the supervision realm has remained unexplored by researchers (Bernard & Goodyear) and warrants empirical investigation. In conducting it, the two primary goals of supervision research, to understand the process of supervision and its influence on counseling and to inform supervision practice, will be realized.

Consequently, the ultimate purpose of the preceding chapter was to inform the reader of the current state of supervision research as well as to incite the reader to engage in methodologically sound supervision research. More specifically, there were four key components of this chapter. First, we described a model that identified and categorized the variables of supervision research. In particular, some primary supervision research questions were delineated, the concepts of supervision and counseling process and outcome were defined, and a listing of relevant supervision variables was suggested. Second, we provided an overview of the literature pertaining to supervision research. Ellis and Ladany's (1997) six inferences of supervision research were considered, as were the most common threats to validity in supervision research. Third, we offered a schema that included the salient elements of conducting supervision research. Specific guidelines for writing the introduction, methods, results, and discussion were outlined. In addition, this section included an evaluation of quantitative instruments and a description of qualitative research methods. Fourth, we applied our knowledge about research and methodology and offered a model for assessing the adequacy of trainee evaluation approaches. In addition to providing a model, suggestions for future research regarding trainee evaluation were made. After reading this chapter, we hope that trainees and supervisors will feel compelled to engage in supervision research. It is also hoped that researchers will follow the guidelines presented in this chapter and employ appropriate research methods to extend the knowledge base of the field of supervision.

☐ References

Bahrick, A. S. (1990). Role induction for counselor trainees: Effects on the supervisory working alliance. *Dissertation Abstracts International, 51,* 1484B. (University Microfilms No. 90-14, 392).

Barrett-Lennard, G. T. (1962). Dimensions of therapist responses as a causal factor in therapeutic changes. *Psychological Monographs, 76*(43, Whole No. 562).

Benshoff, J. M., & Thomas, W. P. (1992). A new look at the Counselor Evaluation Rating Scale. *Counselor Education and Supervision, 32,* 12–22.

Bergsjo, P. (1999). Qualitative and quantitative research: Is there a gap, or only verbal disagreement? *Acta Obstetricia et Gynecologica Scandinavica, 78,* 559–562.

Bernard, J. M. (1979). Supervisory training: A discrimination model. *Counselor Education and Supervision, 19,* 60–68.

Bernard, J. M., & Goodyear, R. K. (1998). *Fundamentals of clinical supervision* (2nd ed.). Boston: Allyn & Bacon.

Beutler, L. E. (1988). Introduction to the special series. *Journal of Consulting and Clinical Psychology, 56,* 651.

Blocher, D., Christensen, E. W., Hale-Fiske, R., Neren, S. H., Spencer, T., & Fowlkes, S. (1985). Development and preliminary validation of an instrument to measure cognitive growth. *Counselor Education and Supervision, 25,* 21–30.

Bogdan, R. C., & Biklen, S. K. (1992). *Qualitative research for education: An introduction to theory and methods.* Boston: Allyn & Bacon.

Borders, L., & Fong, M. L. (1991). Evaluations of supervisees: Brief commentary and research report. *The Clinical Supervisor, 9,* 42–51.

Carey, J. C., Williams, K. S., & Wells, M. (1988). Relationships between dimensions of supervisors' influence and counselor trainees' performance. *Counselor Education and Supervision, 28,* 130–139.

Chen, H. T. (1990). *Theory driven evaluations.* Newbury Park, CA: Sage.

Cohen, J. (1983). The cost of dichotomization. *Applied Psychological Measurement, 7,* 249–253.

Cohen, J. (1988). *Statistical power analysis for the behavioral sciences* (3rd ed.). New York: Academic Press.

Cook, T. D., & Campbell, D. T. (1979). *Quasi-experimentation: Design and analysis for field settings.* Boston: Houghton Mifflin.

Cormier, L. S., & Bernard, J. M. (1982). Ethical and legal responsibilities of clinical supervisors. *The Personnel and Guidance Journal, 11,* 486–491.

Creswell, J. W. (1998). *Qualitative inquiry and research design: Choosing among five traditions.* Thousand Oaks, CA: Sage.

Dalton, J. E. (1983). Sex differences in communications skills as measured by a modified Relationship Inventory. *Sex Roles, 9,* 195–204.

D'Andrea, M., Daniels, J., & Heck, R. (1991). Evaluating the impact of multicultural counseling training. *Journal of Counseling and Development, 70,* 143–150.

Denzin, K., & Lincoln, Y. S. (1994). Introduction: Entering the field of qualitative research. In N. K. Denizen & Y. S. Lincoln (Eds.), *Handbook of qualitative research* (pp. 1–16). Thousand Oaks, CA: Sage.

Dodenhoff, J. T. (1981). Interpersonal attraction and direct-indirect supervisor influence as predictors of counselor trainee effectiveness. *Journal of Counseling Psychology, 28,* 47–52.

Doehrman, M. (1976). Parallel processes in supervision and psychotherapy. *Bulletin of the Menninger Clinic, 40,* 3–104.

Efstation, J. F., Patton, M. J., & Kardash, C. M. (1990). Measuring the working alliance in counselor supervision. *Journal of Counseling Psychology, 37,* 322–329.

Eisner, E. W. (1991). *The enlightened eye: Qualitative inquiry and the enhancement of educational practice.* New York: Macmillian.

Ellis, M. V. (1991). Research in clinical supervision: Revitalizing a scientific agenda. *Counselor Education and Supervision, 30,* 238–251.

Ellis, M. V., Anderson-Hanley, C. M., Dennin, M. K., Anderson, J. J., Chapin, J. L., & Polstri, S. M. (1994, August). *Congruence of expectation in clinical supervision: Scale development and validity data.* Paper presented at the American Psychological Association, Los Angeles.

Ellis, M. V., Ladany, N., Krengel, M., & Schult, D. (1996). Clinical supervision research from 1981 to 1993: A methodological critique. *Journal of Counseling Psychology, 43,* 35–50.

Ellis, M. V., & Ladany, N. (1997). Inferences concerning supervisees and clients in clinical supervision: An integrative review. In C. E. Watkins, Jr. (Ed.), *Handbook of psychotherapy supervision* (pp. 447–507). New York: Wiley.

Flick, U. (1998). *An introduction to qualitative research.* Thousand Oaks, CA: Sage.

Fordham, A. S., May, B., Boyle, M., Bentall, R. P., & Slade, P. D. (1990). Good and bad clinicians: Supervisors' judgments of trainees' competence. *British Journal of Clinical Psychology, 29,* 113–114.

Freud, S. (1910/1957). *The future prospects of psychoanalytic therapy* (Stand. ed., Vol. 11). London: Hogarth.

Friedlander, M. L., Siegel, S. M., & Brenock, K. (1989). Parallel process in counseling and supervision: A case study. *Journal of Counseling Psychology, 36,* 149–157.

Friedlander, M. L., & Snyder, J. (1983). Trainees' expectations for the supervisory process: Testing a developmental model. *Counselor Education and Supervision, 22,* 342–348.

Friedlander, M. L., & Ward, L. G. (1984). Development and validation of the Supervisory Styles Inventory. *Journal of Counseling Psychology, 31,* 541–557.

Fukuyama, M. A. (1994). Critical incidents in multicultural counseling supervision: A phenomenological approach to supervision. *Counselor Education and Supervision, 34,* 142–151.

Gall, M. D., Borg, W. R., & Gall, J. P. (1996). *Educational research: An introduction* (6th ed.). White Plains, NY: Longman Publishers USA.

Gelso, C. J. (1979). Research in counseling: Methodological and professional issues. *The Counseling Psychologist, 8,* 7–36.

Gray, L., Walker, J. A., Ladany, N., & Ancis, J. R. (1999, August). Counterproductive events in psychotherapy supervision. In M. L. Friedlander (Chair), *Psychotherapy supervision: For better or worse.* Symposium conducted at the annual meeting of the American Psychological Association, Boston.

Haase, R. F. (1974). Power analysis of research in counselor education. *Counselor Education and Supervision, 14,* 124–132.

Haase, R. F., Ellis, M. V., & Ladany, N. (1989). Multiple criteria for evaluating the magnitude of effects. *Journal of Counseling Psychology, 36,* 511–516.

Harkness, D., & Poertner, J. (1989). Research and social work supervision: A conceptual review. *Social Work, 34,* 115–119.

Heppner, P. P., & Roehlke, H. J. (1984). Differences among supervisees at different levels of training: Implications for a developmental model of supervision. *Journal of Counseling Psychology, 31,* 76–90.

Hess, S. A., & Hoffman, M. A. (1999, August). Supervisee's critical incidents of nondisclosure and disclosure in supervision. In M. A. Hoffman and N. Ladany (Chairs), *Things said and unsaid in supervision: Supervisee and supervisor perspectives.* Symposium conducted at the annual meeting of the American Psychological Association, Boston.

Hill, C. E., Thompson, B. J., & Williams, E. N. (1997). A guide to conducting consensual qualitative research. *The Counseling Psychologist, 25,* 517–572.

Hogan, R. A. (1964). Issues and approaches in supervision. *Psychotherapy: Theory, Research, and Practice, 1,* 139–141.

Holloway, E. L. (1984). Outcome evaluation in supervision research. *The Counseling Psychologist, 12,* 167–174.

Holloway, E. L. (1987). Developmental models of supervision: Is it development? *Professional Psychology: Research and Practice, 18,* 209–216.

Holloway, E. L. (1992). Supervision: A way of teaching and learning. In S. D. Brown & R. W. Lent (Eds.), *Handbook of counseling psychology* (pp. 177–214). New York: Wiley.

Holloway, E. L., & Wampold, B. E. (1983). Patterns of verbal behavior and judgments of satisfaction in the supervision interview. *Journal of Counseling Psychology, 30,* 227–234.

Holloway, E. L., & Wampold, B. E. (1986). Relation between conceptual level and counseling-related tasks: A meta-analysis. *Journal of Counseling Psychology, 33,* 310–319.

Hutt, C. H., Scott, J., & King, M. (1983). A phenomenological study of supervisee's positive and negative experiences in supervision. *Psychotherapy: Theory, Research, and Practice, 20,* 118–123.

Kazdin, A. E. (1986). Research designs and methodology. In S. L. Garfield & A. E. Bergin (Eds.), *Handbook of psychotherapy and behavior change* (3rd ed., pp. 23–68). New York: Wiley.

Keith-Spiegel, P., & Koocher, G. P. (1985). *Ethics in psychology.* New York: Random House.

Kerlinger, F. N. (1986). *Foundations of behavioral research* (3rd ed.). New York: Holt, Rinehart, & Winston.

Ladany, N., Constantine, M. G., Miller, K., Erickson, C., & Muse-Burke, J. (2000). Supervisor countertransference: A qualitative investigation into its identification and description. *Journal of Counseling Psychology, 47,* 102–115.

Ladany, N., Gray, L., Kaufman, M., Muse-Burke, J. L., Pate, L., Pradhan, M., Rarick, S., Silvestri, T., Spradlin, K., Tyson, A., & Walker, J. A. (1999, November). *Lehigh University Psychotherapy and Supervision Research Project: A preliminary look.* Poster presented at the meeting of the Mid-Atlantic Society for Psychotherapy Research, College Park, MD.

Ladany, N., Hill, C. E., Corbett, M. M., & Nutt, E. A. (1996). Nature, extent, and importance of what psychotherapy trainees do not disclose to their supervisors. *Journal of Counseling Psychology, 43,* 10–24.

Ladany, N., Inman, A. G., Constantine, M. G., & Hofheinz, E. W. (1997). Supervisee multicultural case conceptualization ability and self-reported multicultural competence as functions of supervisee racial identity and supervisor focus. *Journal of Counseling Psychology, 44,* 284–293.

Ladany, N., & Lehrman-Waterman, D. E. (1999). The content and frequency of supervisor self-disclosures and their relationship to supervisor style and the supervisory working alliance. *Counselor Education and Supervision, 38,* 143–160.

Ladany, N. Lehrman-Waterman, D. E., Molinaro, M., & Wolgast, B. (1996, August). *Supervisor ethical practices as perceived by the supervisees they train.* Poster session presented at the annual meeting of the American Psychological Association, Toronto, ON, Canada.

Ladany, N., & Melincoff, D. S. (1997, June). *The nature and extent of what psychotherapy supervisors do not disclose to their trainees.* Poster session presented at the annual meeting of the Society for Psychotherapy Research, Geilo, Norway.

Ladany, N., O'Brien, K., Hill, C. E., Melincoff, D. S., Knox, S., & Petersen, D. (1997). Sexual attraction toward clients, use of supervision, and prior training: A qualitative study of psychology predoctoral interns. *Journal of Counseling Psychology, 44,* 413–424.

LaFromboise, T. D., Coleman, H. L. K., & Hernandez, A. (1991). Development and factor structure of the Cross-Cultural Counseling Inventory-Revised. *Professional Psychology: Research and Practice, 22,* 380–388.

Lambert, M. J. (1980). Research and the supervisory process. In A. K. Hess (Ed.), *Psychotherapy supervision: Theory, research, and practice.* (pp. 423–450). New York: Wiley.

Lambert, M. J. (1986). Psychotherapy outcome: Implications for eclectic psychotherapy. In J. C. Norcross (Ed.), *Handbook of eclectic psychotherapy* (pp. 32–62). New York: Brunner/Mazel.

Lambert, M. J., & Arnold, R. C. (1987). Research and the supervision process. *Professional Psychology: Research and Practice, 18,* 217–224.

Lambert, M. J., & Ogles, B. M. (1997). The effectiveness of psychotherapy supervision. In C. E. Watkins, Jr. (Ed.), *Handbook of psychotherapy supervision* (pp. 421–446). New York: Wiley.

Lanning, W., & Freeman, B. (1994). The Supervisor Emphasis Rating Form. *Counselor Education & Supervision, 33,* 294–304.

Lanning, W. L., Whiston, S., & Carey, J. C. (1994). Factor structure of the Supervisor Emphasis Rating Form. *Counselor Education & Supervision, 34,* 41–51.

Larson, L. M., Suzuki, L. A., Gillespie, K. N., Potenza, M. T., Bechtel, M. A., & Toulouse, A. (1992). Development and validation of the Counseling Self-Estimate Inventory. *Journal of Counseling Psychology, 39,* 105–120.

Lazar, A., & Mosek, A. (1993). The influence of the field instructor-student relationship on evaluation of students' practice. *The Clinical Supervisor, 11,* 111–120.

Lincoln, Y. S., & Guba, E. G. (1985). *Naturalistic inquiry.* Newbury Park, CA: Sage.

Lipsey, M. W., & Wilson, D. B. (1993). The efficacy of psychological, educational, and behavioral treatment. *American Psychologist, 48,* 1181–1209.

Littrell, J. M., Lee-Borden, N., & Lorenz, J. (1979). A developmental framework for counseling supervision. *Counselor Education and Supervision, 19,* 129–136.

Loevinger, J. (1976). *Ego development.* San Francisco: Jossey-Bass.

Loganbill, C., Hardy, E., & Delworth, U. (1982). Supervision: A conceptual model. *The Counseling Psychologist, 10*(1), 3–42.

Mathews, G. (1986). Performance appraisal in the human services: A survey. *The Clinical Supervisor, 3,* 47–61.

Maxwell, J. A. (1996). *Qualitative research design: An interactive approach.* Thousand Oaks, CA: Sage.

McNeill, B. W., Stoltenberg, C. D., & Romans, J. S. (1992). The Integrated Developmental

Model of supervision: Scale development and validation procedures. *Professional Psychology: Research & Practice, 23,* 504–508.

Merriam, S. (1988). *Case study research in education: A qualitative approach.* San Francisco: Jossey-Bass.

Miars, R. D., Tracey, T. J., Ray, P. B., Cornfeld, J. L., O'Farrell, M., & Gelso, C. J. (1983). Variation in supervision process across trainee experience levels. *Journal of Counseling Psychology, 30,* 403–412.

Miles, M. B., & Huberman, A. M. (1994). *Qualitative data analysis: An expanded sourcebook* (2nd ed.). Thousand Oaks, CA: Sage.

Myrick, R. D., & Kelly, F. D., Jr. (1971). A scale for evaluating practicum students in counseling and supervision. *Counselor Education and Supervision, 10,* 330–336.

Nelson, M. L., & Friedlander, M. L. (1999, August). Nature of harmful supervision: A qualitative investigation. In M. L. Friedlander (Chair), *Psychotherapy supervision: For better or worse.* Symposium conducted at the annual meeting of the American Psychological Association, Boston.

Neufeldt, S. A., Beutler, L. E., & Banchero, R. (1997). Research on supervisor variables in psychotherapy supervision. In C. E. Watkins, Jr. (Ed.), *Handbook of psychotherapy supervision* (pp. 508–524). New York: Wiley.

Neufeldt, S. A., Karno, M. P., & Nelson, M. L. (1996). A qualitative study of experts' conceptualization of supervisee reflectivity. *Journal of Counseling Psychology, 43,* 3–9.

Newman, F. L., Kopta, S. M., McGovern, M. P., Howard, K. I., & McNeilly, C. L. (1988). Evaluating trainees relative to their supervisors during the psychology internship. *Journal of Consulting and Clinical Psychology, 56,* 659–665.

Norcross, J. C., & Stevenson, J. F. (1984). How shall we judge ourselves? Training evaluation in clinical psychology programs. *Professional Psychology: Research and Practice, 15,* 497–508.

Norcross, J. C., Stevenson, J. F., & Nash, J. M. (1986). Evaluation of internship training: Practices, problems and prospects. *Professional Psychology: Research and Practice, 17,* 280–282.

Olk, M. E., & Friedlander, M. L. (1992). Trainees' experience of role conflict and role ambiguity in supervisory relationships. *Journal of Counseling Psychology, 39,* 389–397.

Patton, M. Q. (1990). *Qualitative evaluation and research methods* (2nd ed.). Thousand Oaks, CA: Sage.

Ponterotto, J. G., Rieger, B. P., Barrett, A., Sparks, R., Sanchez, C. M., & Magids, D. (1996). Development and initial validation of the Multicultural Counseling Awareness Scale. In G. R. Sodowsky & J. C. Impara (Eds.), *Multicultural assessment in counseling and clinical psychology* (pp. 247–282). Lincoln, NE: Buros Institute of Mental Measurements.

Ponterotto, J. G., Rieger, B. P., Gretchen, D., Utsey, S. O., & Austin, R. (1999). *A construct validity study of the Multicultural Counseling Awareness Scale (MCAS) with suggested revisions.* Unpublished manuscript.

Rabinowitz, F. E., Heppner, P. P., & Roehlke, H. J. (1986). Descriptive study of process and outcome variables of supervision over time. *Journal of Counseling Psychology, 33,* 292–300.

Reising, G. N., & Daniels, M. H. (1983). A study of Hogan's model of counselor development and supervision. *Journal of Counseling Psychology, 30,* 235–244.

Romans, J. S. C., Boswell, D. L., Carlozzi, A. F., & Ferguson, D. B. (1995). Training and supervision practices in clinical, counseling, and school psychology programs. *Professional Psychology: Research and Practice, 26,* 407–412.

Russell, R. K., Crimmings, A. M., & Lent, R. W. (1984). Counselor training and supervision: Theory and research. In S. D. Brown & R. W. Lent (Eds.), *Handbook of counseling psychology* (pp. 625–681). New York: Wiley.

Sansbury, D. L. (1982). Developmental supervision from a skills perspective. *The Counseling Psychologist, 10,* 53–57.

Schact, A. J., Howe, H. E., & Berman, J. J. (1988). A short form of the Barrett-Lennard Inventory for supervisor relationships. *Psychological Reports, 63,* 699–703.

Serlin, R. C. (1987). Hypothesis testing, theory building, and the philosophy of science. *Journal of Counseling Psychology, 34,* 365–371.

Shanfield, W. B., Mohl, P. C., Matthews, K., & Hetherly, V. (1989). A reliability assessment of the Psychotherapy Supervisory Inventory. *American Journal of Psychiatry, 146,* 1447–1450.

Skovholt, T. M., & Rønnestad, M. H. (1992). *The evolving professional self: Stages and themes in therapist and counselor development.* Chichester, England: Wiley.

Snepp, F. P., & Peterson, D. R. (1988). Evaluative comparison of Psy.D. and Ph.D. students by clinical internship supervisors. *Professional Psychology: Research and Practice, 19,* 180–183.

Sodowsky, G. R., Taffe, R. C., Gutkin, T. B., & Wise, S. L. (1994). Development of the Multicultural Counseling Inventory: A self-report measure of multicultural competencies. *Journal of Counseling Psychology, 41,* 137–148.

Stein, D. M., & Lambert, M. J. (1995). Graduate training in psychotherapy: Are therapy outcomes enhanced? *Journal of Consulting and Clinical Psychology, 63,* 182–196.

Stoltenberg, C. (1981). Approaching supervision from a developmental perspective: The counselor complexity model. *Journal of Counseling Psychology, 28,* 59–65.

Stoltenberg, C. D., & Delworth, U. (1987). *Supervising counselors and therapists: A developmental perspective.* San Francisco: Jossey-Bass.

Strauss, A., & Corbin, J. (1990). *Basics of qualitative research: Grounded theory procedures and techniques.* Newbury Park, CA: Sage.

Wampold, B. E., Davis, B., & Good, R. H., III (1990). Hypothesis validity of clinical research. *Journal of Consulting and Clinical Psychology, 58,* 360–367.

Wampold, B. E., & Holloway, E. L. (1997). Methodology, design, and evaluation in psychotherapy supervision research. In C. E. Watkins, Jr. (Ed.), *Handbook of psychotherapy supervision* (pp. 11–27). New York: Wiley.

Wampold, B. E., & Poulin, K. L. (1992). Counseling research methods: Art and artifact. In S. D. Brown & R. D. Lent (Eds.), *Handbook of counseling psychology* (2nd ed., pp. 71–109). New York: Wiley.

Watkins, C. E., Schneider, L. J., Haynes, J., & Nieberding, R. (1995). Measuring psychotherapy supervisor development: An initial effort at scale development and validation. *Clinical Supervisor, 13,* 77–90.

Wiebe, B., & Pearce, W. B. (1973). An item analysis and revision of the Barrett-Lennard Relationship Inventory. *Journal of Clinical Psychology, 29,* 495–497.

William, E. N., Judge, A. B., Hill, C. E., & Hoffman, M. A. (1997). Experiences of novice therapists in prepracticum: Trainees', clients', and supervisors' perceptions of therapists' personal reactions and management strategies. *Journal of Counseling Psychology, 44,* 390–399.

Wolcott, H. F. (1994). *Transforming qualitative data: Description analysis and interpretation.* Thousand Oaks, CA: Sage.

Worthen, V., & McNeill, B. W. (1996). A phenomenological investigation of "good" supervision events. *Journal of Counseling Psychology, 43,* 25–34.

Worthington, E. L., Jr. (1984). Use of trait labels in counseling supervision by experienced and inexperienced supervisors. *Professional Psychology: Research and Practice, 15,* 457–461.

Worthington, E. L., Jr., & Roehlke, H. J. (1979). Effective supervision as perceived by beginning counselors-in-training. *Journal of Counseling Psychology, 26,* 64–73.

Yager, G. G., Wilson, F. R., Brewer, D., & Kinnetz, P. (1989). *The development and validation of an instrument to measure counseling supervisor focus and style.* Paper presented at the American Educational Research Association, San Francisco.

Yin, R. K. (1994). *Case study research: Design and methods* (2nd ed.). Thousand Oaks, CA: Sage.

Judith A. Lewis
James R. Cheek
C. Bret Hendricks

Advocacy in Supervision

The psychotherapist, social worker or social reformer, concerned only with his [sic] own clients and their grievance against society, perhaps takes a view comparable to the private citizen of Venice who concerns himself only with the safety of his own dwelling and his own ability to get about the city. But if the entire republic is slowly being submerged, individual citizens cannot afford to ignore their collective fate because, in the end, they all drown together if nothing is done; and again, as with Venice, what needs to be done is far beyond the powers of any one individual. In such circumstances . . . the therapist can no longer afford the luxury of ignoring everything that is going on outside the consulting room

—*C. R. Badcock*

According to the *Code of Ethics and Standards of Practice* of the American Counseling Association (1997), the primary responsibility of counselors is "to respect the dignity and promote the welfare of clients" (p. 2). Although all counselors may be committed to carrying out this charge, members of the profession vary significantly in their ideas about what it means. Some helpers remain convinced that they can "promote the welfare" of their clients solely through the provision of direct helping services. They continue to believe that they still have the luxury of ignoring everything that is going on outside the consulting room. Acting in sharp contrast to this mindset, increasing numbers of counselors have begun to realize that their responsibilities to their clients far exceed what they can accomplish within the four walls of their offices. They know that advocacy is an integral part of every counselor's role.

☐ The Counselor as Advocate

As advocates, counselors speak up on behalf of their clients and communities. When carrying out *client advocacy*, counselors work toward changes that make the environment more responsive to the needs of their own clients. They intervene actively in their clients' surroundings, helping to ensure that special needs are met. Counselors also participate in *social and political advocacy*, seeking ways to affect political, economic, and social systems so that these systems can be more effective in meeting the needs of total communities or populations.

Counselors take on both of these advocacy roles because they understand that their clients are deeply affected by their environments. They know that the degree to which they can be helpful to these clients is severely limited if they focus solely on those changes that are under the control of the individual. In order to be of assistance in the clinical setting, counselors must be willing to address the social issues that daily confront the clients with whom they work. They must also be ready to help the clients confront the entities and the institutions that are oppressive. If the client is unable to confront these on her or his own, then the counselor, as advocate, must confront these areas herself or himself (Sosin & Caulum, 1983).

The need to extend the boundaries of client practice becomes especially clear when we think about ways to meet the needs of individuals who are members of oppressed groups. In fact, Atkinson, Morten, and Sue (1993) suggest that advocacy may be the "service of choice" for people from ethnic-racial minority groups in the United States.

> The counselor speaks on behalf of the client, often confronting the institutional sources of oppression that are contributing to the client's problems. . . . In this role, the counselor represents a client or group of clients who have brought a particular form of discrimination to the counselor's attention. Being an empathic counselor who suggests alternative ways of coping with a particular problem is not enough; the counselor must be willing to pursue actively alternative courses with or for the client, including making a personal contact for the client who is overwhelmed with the bureaucracy of social service, legal, and/or employment agencies. (Atkinson et al., 1993, p. 301)

It is no coincidence that in the years since multiculturalism has been recognized as the "fourth force" in counseling (Pedersen, 1991) the profession has become increasingly aware of the importance of advocacy. Multiculturalism is built on the recognition that all of us are cultural beings and that culture deeply affects our lives.

> It is a short step from becoming aware of the impact of the cultural milieu to noticing the role of oppression in our clients' lives. Once we begin to notice

> systemic oppression, it is just one more short step to accepting our responsibility for social action. (Lewis & Arnold, 1998, p. 51)

Society is full of people who are denied the opportunity to act as full participants in establishing the rules, policies, expectations, and laws that have direct impact on their lives. They are the recipients of discrimination, prejudice, and various forms of negative stereotypes that serve to keep them separated and stigmatized by members of mainstream society. These populations include women, people of color, people who live in poverty, gay, lesbian, and transgendered persons, people living with chronic illness, and people with physical challenges and mental illnesses, as well as disenfranchised youth and older adults. Members of these groups deal with a variety of issues that have direct impact on their ability to function as creative members of society. They may feel a sense of helplessness and powerlessness that will not allow the maintenance of their dignity and sense of self-worth.

Counselors who believe that the welfare of the client is paramount know that they must address issues of oppression. They know that they cannot succeed if they think of their clients in terms of technical problems to be addressed by "neutral" professionals (Prilletensky, 1994). A counselor who wants to "become a pebble in oppression's shoe" (Sanders, 1999, p. 7) usually finds that both client advocacy and political advocacy are needed. When addressing violence against women, for example, counselors should help female clients understand their legal rights; train parents and teachers to be aware of the impact of stereotyping and discrimination; and work to ensure that victims of rape, harassment, or battery have access to sensitive, supportive help assistance from a network of helpers (Hansen, 1999). At a broader political level, counselors should also become involved in "working for social justice by organizing or participating in lobbying of state and federal legislators" (Aspy & Sandhu, 1999, p. 104); they should "ignite the criminal justice system to serve and protect women" (Arnold & Sobieraj, 1999, p. 4) and confront media to ensure that violence against women is portrayed as a societal problem that occurs across all strata of our society (Arnold & Sobieraj, p. 5). When counselors work with older adults, their advocacy strategies should include coaching their clients to ask for what they need from health care providers and bureaucracies, working with advocacy groups such as AARP and the Older Women's League, and monitoring legislation concerning Social Security, Medicare, and other issues that affect older people (Goodman & Waters, 1999). Counselors who work against racism make changes in their own institutions, agencies, and communities. At the same time, they recognize that "political advocacy has a proven history of success in fighting for civil liberties, lobbying for entitlements for the disenfranchised, demanding access to public facilities, or litigating against discrimination practices for African Americans" (Sanders, 1999, p. 6). Effective professionals welcome the advocacy role in both counselor–client and supervisor–supervisee relationships.

☐ The Advocacy Role: Barriers and Challenges

Despite the importance of environmental interventions, many counselors continue to put all of their efforts into the individual-remedial-intrapsychic mode of helping. Lewis, Lewis, Daniels, and D'Andrea (1998) suggested that there are several reasons why counselors may hesitate to use social action strategies. These reasons include (a) pressure from funding sources, (b) lack of emphasis on advocacy in graduate training programs, (c) lack of courage, (d) lack of analytical skills to think systemically, and (e) lack of knowledge of social change strategies.

Funding Issues

Funding sources tend to favor practitioners who provide direct, one-to-one clinical services. Unfortunately, dependence on this strategy lessens the ability of the counselor to serve a large and diverse population.

Graduate Training Issues

Graduate schools, like funding sources, still emphasize direct, remedial counseling services. Students and beginning counselors may take note of their clients' needs for advocacy services but avoid using this strategy because they believe that it is not considered professionally appropriate by their educators and mentors.

Issues Related to Courage

It is a daunting prospect to "take on City Hall" for the first time. Counselors may be as adverse to risk taking as anyone else. The result of this caution, however, may be an unconscious collusion with oppression, especially when it takes place within our own profession.

> It takes great courage to confront racism and other forms of oppression as they occur within our professional lives. Probably the most difficult—and most necessary—challenge is to become continuously involved in taking honest inventory of one's own life as a community member and as a counselor. (Lewis & Arnold, 1998, p. 58)

Thinking Systemically

It takes a high level of analysis to make a transition from thinking intrapsychically to thinking systemically. Counselors need to differentiate between those issues that can be addressed by individual change and those that require systemic change that is beyond the scope of the direct counseling process. It is especially relevant to understand that effective counselors emphasize both the intrapsychic and the systemic issues affecting their clients, recognizing the two processes as complementary. As Cebuhar (1998) points out, advocacy "serves as an effective manner in which to clear the board of solvable external problems so that effective counseling can begin."

Knowledge of Social Change Strategies

"Although many counselors possess the courage and motivation to promote social change for their clients, they often do not understand how to initiate practical strategies" (Lewis et. al., 1998, p. 219). Clearly, counselors who have been trained and supervised in traditional programs feel competent to provide direct services and *in*competent to carry out advocacy. It is this problem that supervision must now address.

☐ The Supervisory Challenge

Because counselors so often lack awareness of the ways that oppression occurs, a component of the supervision process must include the establishment of an educational model to facilitate the supervisee's recognition of societal and cultural inequities and the ethical and professional responsibilities for advocacy and empowerment of clients. How can the supervisor incorporate the concepts of multiculturalism, social justice, and advocacy into the supervisory process? We have acknowledged that counselors have traditionally tended to emphasize direct service at the expense of advocacy. Given this situation, we must face the fact that even the most experienced professionals, including supervisors, may lack competence in this important arena. Clearly, all people who act as supervisors will need to find ways to develop their own sense of self-efficacy around diversity issues and advocacy!

Before narrowing their focus to direct, one-to-one supervision, counselor educators should also pay attention to the climate within which training takes place. They need to ask themselves whether their programs provide an environment that engenders recognition of cultural, social, and political issues among educators and students. Herring (1999), for instance, pointed out that training programs for mental health professionals should emphasize the recruitment and training of Native American students as well as educating non-Native practitioners "to be aware of the stereotypes, historical genocide, within-group variances, levels of acculturation, value and belief systems, and other pertinent information regarding this population" (p. 2). Sanders (1999) suggested that "practicum and internship students need to have mandatory requirements to work with African Americans and other people of color built into the . . . curriculum" (p. 4). Chen-Hayes, Chen, and Athar (1999) stated that very few American counselor education programs make any accommodation at all for the needs of students from non-English-speaking backgrounds. Training programs also fail to prepare counselors for working with people who are nonnative English speakers. It is only within diverse, culturally competent organizations that effective advocacy-oriented supervision can take place.

☐ Implementation of Change in Supervision

For the purpose of examining the ways in which supervisors can help to engender successful advocacy, we must assume that the supervisor herself or himself values advocacy and has expertise in carrying it out. We can also assume that, given the lack of attention to advocacy in most training programs and practice settings, a sizable number of supervisees will initially be unfamiliar with these issues or unmotivated to address them. Given this circumstance, the supervisor must be ready to move supervisees along from a stage of unpreparedness to a readiness for action.

The implementation of change as part of the advocacy process must be addressed and directed by the supervisor as an integral component of supervision. One model of change that was originally proposed for addictive behaviors by Prochaska, DiClemente, and Norcross (1992) and Prochaska, Norcross, and DiClemente (1994) has potential application for the process of supervision. Prochaska and his colleagues identified five stages of change: precontemplation, contemplation, preparation, action, and maintenance. They suggested that helpers must adapt their helping strategies to the client's place in the cycle of change. As supervisors help their supervisees move from nonawareness of advocacy to competent action, they, too, must adapt their strategies to the cycle of change.

According to this model, *precontemplation* is a stage in which there is no awareness or intention for change to occur in the foreseeable future. If we apply the model to advocacy supervision, we place at this stage the student or counselor who has no indication that there is a need for advocacy to occur or who may actually be resistant to the possibility. If supervisees are encapsulated in their own cultural experiences, supervisors have to be prepared to educate and assist them toward contemplation of the possibility that advocacy might be useful. In order to facilitate development into the next stage, the supervisor tries to raise the supervisee's consciousness of advocacy while remaining supportive of the supervisee's initial attempts at self-exploration. A clear strength of this conceptualization lies in the fact that a student's resistance can be seen as explainable.

Attempts to prod supervisees toward practicing the skills of advocacy would be premature and unlikely to succeed at this point. As a part of the process, however, the expectations that the counseling supervisors have for their supervisees in terms of their advocacy role should be clearly stated. Supervisors have the responsibility of informing supervisees of the goals and the expectations of supervision (Bradley, 1989). This communication is imperative at the very beginning of supervision. The supervisor should also clearly communicate the ways that those expectations and goals can be successfully accomplished.

Case example: A supervisee at a local agency reports to her supervisor that she is having difficulty with a young girl who has just been diagnosed with juvenile diabetes. The 7-year-old girl is of African-American descent, living with both parents. The parents refuse to discuss the girl's medical condition, not wanting to "frighten" their daughter. Although the supervisee has attempted a variety of techniques, she does not feel effective in treating the depression that she believes is directly due to the diabetes. She believes the little girl may need medical intervention for depression.

The supervisee at this point is not able to view the entire environment of the child. She is only able to focus on the immediate issue of the child's disease. Realizing that the supervisee is in the precontemplation stage, the supervisor did not push the supervisee towards any definitive action. The supervisor raised questions for the supervisee, such as: "Is there possibly anyone else in the child's world that could have impact?"; "How are the parents responding?"; "What help are the medical professionals offering?"

At the next supervision session, the counselor still was not ready to advance into any action through confrontation, but was now prepared to lay the groundwork for future advocacy efforts. The supervisor broadened the supervisee's perspective on the outside issues facing the client, communicated expectations, and gave the supervisee permission to pursue further action-oriented steps.

Contemplation is the stage of change that occurs when there is an awareness of an issue, but there has not yet been a commitment to initiate any action towards a solution. Counselors at this stage have begun to see that there is a need for advocacy; however, they have not yet decided to implement action. Benjamin (1987) cited an example of the contemplation stage. He related an incident that occurred when he was walking home one evening and a stranger approached him and asked him the whereabouts of a certain street. Benjamin pointed out the location of the street and gave the stranger very specific instructions. After understanding the instructions, the stranger began to walk in the opposite direction. Benjamin told the stranger that he was walking in the wrong direction, and the stranger replied that he knew that he was going in the wrong direction, he just was not ready to go in the correct direction. This is the essence of the contemplation stage: the supervisee knows where to go and has some idea what to do but is just not ready to go there yet.

At this stage, the supervisee is still weighing the pros and the cons of change, assessing the amount of energy, effort, and loss that it will take to overcome the problem and go "in the right direction" (DiClemente et al., 1991). Counselors at this stage realize that there is a need for advocacy, but they are unsure of the steps needed to advocate and therefore may be unwilling to take any action at all.

Counselors' hesitancy toward active advocacy should not surprise us. Individual-level responses to injustice have been examined through a number of studies. Mikula (1986) found that the first possible individual response to injustice is to not react at all, even when in the face of recognition that a situation is unfair. Similarly, other studies have also found that the most common response to a witnessed act of oppression is to do nothing (Felstiner, Abel, & Sarat, 1980/1981). Encouraging a process of self-reevaluation is vital for helping the supervisee move beyond this stage of doing nothing toward a stage in which he or she begins to prepare to take even the most limited of actions. Supervisees may need to be guided gently through a process in which they feel free to make decisions about how to proceed.

Case study (continued): The supervisee now sees the case of the girl in a different light, but is not sure what needs to occur next. The supervisee is now starting to believe that some of the responsibility for actions could lie with the supervisee. She's starting to think about possible reactions and actions and how they could be implemented.

At this point of contemplation, the supervisor was supportive and encouraging as the supervisee tentatively explored various possibilities. The supervisor has now moved from broadening the supervisee's perspective on the client to broadening her perspective on her own role in the process.

Preparation is the stage that combines intention with behavior. In this stage, the intent to change is present, and behaviors that would predicate change may have been instituted. As a group, those in the preparation stage report that they have made some small behavioral changes, and although they have made some attempts at reducing problematic behaviors, they have not yet achieved effective behavioral change. They are, however, intending to make changes in the near future.

Supervisees at this stage have reached some awareness of the problems of oppression and the need for advocacy. They feel ready to take action. They may have attempted some advocacy work in the recent past and are intending to further this action in the future. Supervisees are ready to learn interventions that would help them attempt a change towards advocacy and are ready to have concrete learning experiences that would increase their knowledge in this area. They have begun to identify problematic behaviors in their own counseling and are ready to expand self-awareness and internalize these perceptions so that behavioral change can be achieved. At this point, supervisors can focus on the specific skills that underlie effective advocacy.

Behavioral modification is the desired outcome of the preparation stage, and supervisees may need to attempt new behaviors that exemplify their new awareness. Supervisees may now be enthusiastic about exposing themselves to new areas of awareness and learning. This stage might be typified by the supervisee experiencing increased exposure to other cultural groups or actuating advocacy for an oppressed group or client. Since a certain amount of fear or apprehension will often accompany these new behaviors, the supervisee will need encouragement and feedback from the supervisor to ensure that the beneficial behaviors are increased.

Case study (continued): Assisting the supervisee in gaining the necessary advocacy skills was now the focus of the supervisor. They discussed the possibility of talking to the parents on behalf of the child, or of setting up meetings between the child and parents together with medical personnel. The supervisor also had the supervisee role-play the conversations that were under consideration so that the supervisee could gain confidence. The supervisor has now given the supervisee more perspective on her own strengths and abilities.

The *action* stage is the stage at which individuals actually modify their behavior, environment, and experiences in order to create change. This stage requires the most direct action by the individual and requires the individual to begin to show behaviors that are visible and external in nature. These behaviors are concrete and behavioral, but they depend on the internalized awareness reached at earlier stages. Emotional feelings of frustration and resentment have an important influence on whether or not people take action, according to Wright, Taylor, and Moghaddam, 1990. Wright and his colleagues also found that emotion is the most important factor in determining whether action will occur, but not necessarily what form the actions will take. Supervisees at this stage are actually advocating for their clients (and themselves), even if they still find certain aspects uncomfortable. Again, the supervisor should be extremely supportive of these actions and provide frequent feedback.

The supervisor can utilize several processes to assist the movement from action to maintenance of these new behaviors. One of the first processes to be addressed should be reinforcement management. This can be achieved through contingency contracts, overt and covert reinforcement, and instructing supervisees to reward themselves for appropriate actions. Counter-conditioning through relaxation, positive self-statements, and assertion will also aid in maintaining the changes that have occurred.

Studies have found that one immediate reaction to possible injustice is to seek verification or social support from other people (Koss et al., 1994). When supervisees encounter situations that are ambiguous or about which they lack information, they may need to turn to the supervisor or peers for help. Helping relationships, including social supports and therapeutic alliances, will help support the changes that have been made.

Case study (continued): The counselor had taken action in carrying out her planned advocacy efforts. A conference was arranged and conducted with the parents regarding the girl's medical condition, and all parties were able to voice their fears and concerns. The girl is showing more improvement in her behavior. She is now openly talking about her diabetes and, with her parents' help, is planning on discussing it with her classmates.

The supervisor supported and praised the supervisee's efforts. As they discussed the process that the supervisee had worked through, the supervisor raised the question of advocacy efforts for a broader audience. The difficulties that the girl experienced could be common among others. The supervisee was given the assignment of looking at the larger scope of the problem the girl experienced.

Maintenance, when applied to addictive behaviors, is the stage at which people work to prevent relapse into detrimental behaviors and to continue to educate themselves in areas for growth. Maintenance is an active stage that is a continuation of the earlier stages of change. The person strives to remain free of earlier destructive behaviors and to incorporate new learned behaviors.

When we apply the model to advocacy supervision, we conceptualize that supervisees at this stage have achieved internal awareness of the issues of advocacy and oppression and see it as their moral and ethical duty to address these issues as part of their professional obligations. At this stage, they have achieved the change process of social liberation. They are now able to advocate for the rights of the oppressed, to empower their clients and themselves, and to intervene in policy-changing actions. They may find themselves in environments that fail to support their efforts, making it necessary for them to work at self-reinforcement and continued self-assessment.

Case study (continued): The supervisee reported to her supervisor that she had talked with the medical personnel at the girl's clinic and is planning to work conjunctively with the clinic to create a family group for juvenile diabetes. Furthermore, the parents of the girl will assist in implementing the educational efforts of the clinic as well. The supervisor discussed the broader social issues that impact the supervisee's other clients. The supervisor has now broadened the perspective of the supervisee to include the recognition of the need for and implementation of social change to positively impact her clients' lives.

Neither supervisors nor supervisees should expect change to occur in a linear progression through the stages. Research has shown that people actually move through the stages of change in a spiral pattern (Prochaska et al., 1992). As learning occurs or resistance by the outside world is encountered, supervisees may fall back on old attitudes and behaviors. Supervisors need to give feedback and support so that each time supervisees cycle through the stages, they can learn from their mistakes and can therefore try something different next time around (DiClemente et al., 1991).

Implementation of the Prochaska et al. (1992) model is one way to achieve the goals and expectations of supervision. The supervisor and supervisee should discuss their concepts of advocacy and the ways that the supervisee can implement these concepts in practice. It is vital that the supervisor also give regular feedback on the supervisee's progress and goal achievement.

Throughout this process, supervisors can help direct the progress of change by identifying the current stage of their supervisees and implementing appropriate activities to assist in movement through the processes and stages. The supervision process should be one of open communication, with the supervisor's observations helping the supervisee gain awareness of her or his own development toward competence. By modifying and applying this model of change into the supervisory relationship, supervisees are given a concrete format to become advocates for the dignity and welfare of their clients, regardless of the issues involved.

☐ Summary

In order to meet the needs of their clients most effectively, counselors should move beyond the boundaries of their offices to become involved in advocacy efforts. The fact that the counseling profession has accepted a framework of multiculturalism and contextualism has brought about an increased understanding of the importance of client advocacy and social and political activism. Even now, however, many counselors are hesitant to become involved, and the traditional focus on intrapsychic phenomena remains entrenched.

The strong efforts of supervisors are needed if advocacy is to become a central part of each counselor's professional life. This goal is highly challenging because both supervisors and supervisees vary significantly in terms of their readiness to participate in advocacy. A model delineating the stages of change can help to guide the efforts of supervisors as they encourage their supervisees to move from the stage of precontemplation through contemplation, preparation, action, and maintenance.

☐ References

American Counseling Association (1997). *Code of ethics and standards of practice*. Alexandria, VA: Author.

Arnold, M. S., & Sobieraj, K. (1999). Domestic violence: The case for social advocacy. American Counseling Association. Advocacy: A voice of our clients & communities [On-line serial]. Available: www.counseling.org/conference/advocacy10

Aspy, C. L., & Sandhu, D. S. (1999). *Empowering women for equity*. Alexandria, VA: American Counseling Association.

Atkinson, D. R., Morten, G., & Sue, D. W. (1993). *Counseling American minorities: A cross-cultural perspective* (4th ed.) Madison, WI: Brown & Benchmark.

Badcock, C. R. (1983). *Madness and modernity*. Oxford, England: Blackwell.

Benjamin, A. (1987). *The helping interview*. Boston: Houghton Mifflin.

Bradley, L. J. (1989). *Counselor supervision: Principles, process, and practice* (2nd ed.). Muncie, IN: Accelerated Development.

Cebuhar, J. (1998). Advocacy for people with HIV/AIDS. American Counseling Association. Advocacy: A voice for our clients and communities [On-line serial]. Available: www.counseling.org/conference/advocacy4

Chen-Hayes, S. F., Chen, M., & Athar, N. (1999). Challenging linguicism: Action strategies for counselors and client-colleagues. American Counseling Association. Advocacy: A voice of our clients & communities [On-line seriesl]. Available: www.counseling.org/conference/advocacy1

DiClemente, C. C., Prochaska, J. O., Fairhurst, S. K., Velicer, W. F., Velasquez, M. M., & Rossi, J. S. (1991). The process of smoking cessation: An analysis of precontemplation, contemplation, and preparation stages of change. *Journal of Consulting and Clinical Psychology*, 59, 295–304.

Felstiner, W. L. F., Abel, R. L., & Sarat, A. (1980/1981). The emergence and transformation of disputes: Naming, blaming, claiming. *Law and Society Review*, 15, 631–654.

Goodman, J., & Waters, E. (1999). Advocating on behalf of older adults. American Counseling Association. *Advocacy: A voice of our clients & communities* [On-line serial]. Available: www.counseling.org/conference/advocacy11

Hansen, S. (1999). Gender-based advocacy for equity and non-violence. American Counseling Association. *Advocacy: A voice of our clients & communities* [On-line serial]. Available: www.counseling.org/conference/advocacy15

Herring, R. (1999). Advocacy for Native American Indian and Alaska Native clients and counselees. American Counseling Association. *Advocacy: A voice of our clients & communities* [On-line serial]. Available: www.counseling.org/conference/advocacy7

Koss, M. P., Goodman, L. A., Browne, A., Fitzgerald, A. F., Keita, G. P., & Russo, N. F. (1994). *No safe haven: Male violence against women at home, at work, and in the community.* Washington, DC: American Psychological Association.

Lewis, J. A., & Arnold, M. S. (1998). From multiculturalism to social action. In C. Lee & G. Walz (Eds.), *Social action: A mandate for counselors.* Greensboro, NC: ERIC/CASS and American Counseling Association (ED417372).

Lewis, J. A., Lewis, M. D., Daniels, J., & D'Andrea, M. (1998). Community counseling: Empowerment strategies for a diverse society. Pacific Grove, CA: Brooks/Cole.

Mikula, G. (1986). The experience of injustice: Toward a better understanding of its phenomenology. In H. W. Bierhoff, R. L. Cohen, & J. Greenberg (Eds.), *Justice and social relations* (pp. 103–124). New York: Plenum.

Pedersen, P. A. (1991). Multiculturalism as a generic approach to counseling. *Journal of Counseling & Development, 70,* 6–12.

Prilleltensky, I. (1994). *The morals and politics of psychology: Psychological discourse and the status quo.* Albany: State University of New York Press.

Prochaska, J. O., DiClemente, C. C., & Norcross, J. C. (1992). In search of how people change: Applications to addictive behaviors. *American Psychologist, 47*(9), 1102–1114.

Prochaska, J. O., Norcross, J. C., & DiClemente, C. C. (1994). *Changing for good: A revolutionary six-stage program for overcoming bad habits and moving your life positively forward.* New York: Avon Books.

Sanders, J. L. (1999). Advocacy on behalf of African American clients. American Counseling Association. *Advocacy: A voice of our clients & communities* [On-line serial] Available: www.counseling.org/confernce/advocacy3

Sosin, M., & Caulum, S. (1983). Advocacy: A conceptualization for social work practice. *Social Work, 28*(1), 12–17.

Wright, S. C., Taylor, D. M., & Moghaddam, F. M. (1990). The relationship of perceptions and emotions to behavior in the face of collective inequality. *Social Justice Research, 4,* 229–250.

CHAPTER 14

Loretta J. Bradley
Jeffrey A. Kottler,
Deborah Lehrman-Waterman

Ethical Issues in Supervision

The supervisor sat very still in her chair, so motionless, in fact, that she might have been an inanimate object. Only if you looked closer would you notice that she was breathing, very slowly. Although her eyes were closed, she was hardly sleeping; far from it. She could feel the tension in her body so profoundly that she decided to freeze herself into this resting position until she calmed down.

A counselor she had been supervising just walked out of the office, oblivious to the turmoil he had begun with a simple question, a request actually. They had been working together for the better part of a year, a requirement of the state licensing board that mandated direct monitoring of cases during the apprentice years after graduation. Since the internship requirement was just about over, the counselor broached the subject of his supervisor writing a letter of endorsement that would be used for licensure, as well as future jobs.

This was certainly a reasonable request, even an expected event considering that one of the reasons the supervisor had been hired in the first place was to provide close monitoring and guidance. Over the course of the year, the counselor had worked hard in supervision, responding to feedback, doing everything in his power to put into practice what he was learning. The problem, unfortunately, is that in spite of all his effort and determination, he was still a marginal practitioner. Perhaps even that assessment was generous: The truth of the matter is that this counselor had neither the skills nor the temperament to grow very much as a counselor. He was still making mistakes more typical of a beginning student than an intern. He had lapses in judgment that led to some negative consequences for his clients. He just wasn't a very good counselor.

It seemed like a simple matter for the supervisor. Surely, she could not endorse a counselor who she knew might be a danger to others. She would also not be doing him much of a favor encouraging him to continue in a profession that appeared a poor match for his interpersonal style and personality. Furthermore, the supervisor was well aware of the ethical code of her profession, especially those principles that required her to protect the safety of clients, and the public-at-large, from a practitioner who was ill prepared if not incompetent.

Yet, the supervisor had developed quite a close alliance with the counselor, in spite of the poor progress. She genuinely cared for him and wanted him to succeed. She felt some responsibility for the unsatisfactory outcome. Maybe, she wondered, this was partially her fault; if she had done some things differently, perhaps been more direct and honest with him in the beginning, he might have done better in his development. Surely, she had some responsibility to this young man as well; after all, he was *her* client, a consumer who had paid for services.

The supervisor also felt some doubts because this student had managed to get through an accredited master's program. Although his grades in clinical courses were mediocre, at least several faculty felt that he had made sufficient progress to move him forward. Or perhaps they had been as hesitant as she now felt to take a firm stand and tell the guy he would be better off in another field. It just did not seem fair to her that after all his years of training and investment of time and money, it would fall on her to be the one to stop him from practicing his new profession.

The supervisor opened her eyes, pressed the palms of her hands to her head, and tried to rub the tension out. She felt a headache coming on. It struck her at that moment that as thorny as ethical issues in counseling could be, they were nothing compared to the challenges she felt as a supervisor. Dual relationships, for example, had long been worked out in her own practice. She was quite clear on boundaries to be enforced and, as a master practitioner, was quite skilled at dealing with most ethical issues that might come up. But now, however, she was faced with a dilemma for which she felt quite unprepared. It was hard enough as a practitioner to deal with the conflicting loyalties to clients, their families, and society as a whole; now, she had to reconcile the commitment she felt to her client, this supervisee, versus the responsibilities to her profession and prospective clients who might consult this new professional. She knew exactly what she was *supposed* to do, what the books would say, and what others would advise. But they didn't know this man. They had not worked with him, week after week, for a year. They didn't have to deal with his disappointment and anger when he was denied permission to practice his profession.

Deep breath, she reminded herself. Take a few steps back and apply what she already knew, what she already had used all her professional life in one context, to this new challenge she faced. She was confident she would work this through. She would talk things through with the counselor during the next session. She would consult with several other experienced counselors. She would collect more data from the counselor's previous supervisors and faculty. And then she would face her responsibilities, even though she sure didn't like it.

☐ Ethical Challenges for Supervisors

This very real and, unfortunately, not uncommon ethical dilemma is typical of what supervisors face as part of their jobs. Although there is sometimes an assumption that supervisor ethics is much the same as counselor ethics, that belief is about as accurate as the notion that supervision is just another form of counseling (Borders, 1997; Stoltenberg & Delworth, 1987). Yet, even though the ethical issues that confront supervisors may be slightly (or significantly) different from that of counselors, those distinctions are often confusing, if not ill defined (Whiston & Emerson, 1989). Throughout this book, quite a few authors have discussed in detail the unique facets of supervisory competence as distinct from counseling. The ethical conflict that gave the supervisor above such a splitting headache could have been reduced to some very clear ethical issues. First, in a ranking of priorities, the supervisor is ultimately responsible for the welfare of clients, even before that of the counselor under supervision (Pope & Vasquez, 1998). Second, she had been remiss in not providing more honest ongoing feedback to the counselor, which was considered part of her evaluation roles and functions (Bernard & Goodyear, 1998; Ladany, Lehrman-Waterman, Molinaro, & Wolgast, 1999). This failure to highlight weaknesses in a timely manner is, in fact, one of the most common sources of ethical complaints filed against supervisors (Koocher & Keith-Spiegel, 1998). Indeed, the supervisor featured in the case who began this chapter was not unreasonable in assuming that the counselor would be very upset once he learned that she would not endorse him for licensure.

The whole issue of dual relationships in supervision and the unique boundary issues that arise as a result of the complexity involved are inherent in this professional activity (Herlihy & Corey, 1997). That is one reason why specific ethical standards have been developed for supervisors (Association for Counselor Education and Supervision [ACES], 1995) and why a separate chapter on the subject is needed in this book. In light of the example that began this chapter, and many others that have been raised throughout this book, it is clear that supervisors need to be intimately familiar with those ethical principles that are unique to the practice of this professional activity.

☐ The Development of Ethical Codes

Over the last decade, ethical issues in counseling have received increased attention, resulting in guidelines developed in a number of different specialty areas. As the concept of client as consumer has evolved, the number of books and manuscripts on ethical issues have multiplied as well. This proliferation of codes to guide behavior is so critical that such guidelines have become the foundation of one's professional identity (Allen, 1986).

One of the earliest codes, the Hippocratic Oath, was established for the medical profession. In more recent times, various professions have established codes of ethics that guide their professional behaviors. Some of the organizations establishing codes for counselors and psychological practitioners are the American Counseling Association, the American Association for Marriage and Family Therapy, the American Psychological Association (APA), the National Academy of Certified Clinical Mental Health Counselors, and the National Association for Social Workers. Additionally, specialty guidelines have been prepared for specific types of practitioners, including the National Association of Social Workers for the private practice of clinical social work; the APA for clinical psychology, counseling psychology, industrial and organizational psychology, and school psychology; the American Psychiatric Association; and a half dozen different divisions of the American Counseling Association related to group work, family counseling, rehabilitation counseling, and assessment. In addition, the ACES has also developed guidelines for its members.

Besides their obvious functions to protect the public from harm, ethical codes exist for three reasons (Van Hoose and Kottler, 1978): They allow professions to govern and regulate themselves rather than to risk governmental oversight; they are designed to protect the profession from internal struggles and establish consensual standards of care; and they protect the practitioner from malpractice suits providing that the practitioner has behaved in accordance with standards judged acceptable by the profession.

☐ Ethical Guidelines for Supervisors

In their review and study of the supervisor ethics, Ladany et al. (1999) referred to the ACES (1995) guidelines as the building blocks of ethical practice for supervisors. However, they noted that these guidelines failed to address three key issues within supervision: multicultural sensitivity toward clients, multicultural sensitivity toward trainees, and client termination and follow-up issues. Therefore, they recommended adding these components and developed a list of 18 ethical guidelines for supervisors. These guidelines will be reviewed in subsequent sections in the order in which they are anticipated to arise in the course of supervision and can be seen in Table 14.1.

Preliminary Considerations

Most supervisors are employed in settings where they provide direct services to supervisees. A typical situation may involve a college or university

TABLE 14.1. Supervisor ethical guidelines

Ethical guidelines	Definition	Examples from data
Supervisor competency as a supervisor	The supervisor should have training in supervision before he or she agrees to train a developing counselor.	Not available.
Able to work with alternative perspectives	Information about theory or practice presented by the supervisor is informed by current knowledge and includes alternative points of view, such as the supervisee's. The supervisor clearly presents her or his theoretical orientation.	Supervisor had never learned any theory other than psychoanalytic theory. I had to explain to her what cognitive therapy was and she was pretty shocked at the concept. Didn't really explain her theoretical approach. She is staunchly psychoanalytic and generally unwilling to consider alternative perspectives.
Financial issues related to counseling	The supervisor ensures that the supervisee handles financial issues with clients in an appropriate manner.	Not available.
Financial issues related to supervision	The supervisor clearly communicates his or her fee structure to the supervisee when the supervisee is paying for services.	Not available.
Confidentiality issues in supervision	Confidentiality issues are handled appropriately by supervisor (e.g., agency policy toward supervision disclosure is explained, limits of supervisory confidentiality).	Was not informed about the agency's policy toward supervision disclosure. Supervisor did not explain agency policy toward supervision confidentiality.
Session boundaries and respectful treatment	Adequate protection of supervision session conditions and respect for supervisee (e.g., privacy, scheduling, avoiding demeaning supervisee) are ensured by the supervisor.	Supervisor constantly missed supervision sessions and allowed them to be interrupted by others. Supervisor did not always keep door closed during supervision sessions.

Orientation to professional roles and monitoring of site standards	Supervisor and supervisee roles and responsibilities are clearly defined. The supervisor ensures that the supervisee is engaged in appropriate and relevant counseling activities.	Supervisor did little to explain my role. I had to learn by doing; she never thoroughly explained my responsibilities.
Disclosure to clients	The supervisor ensures adequate disclosure to client (e.g., conditions of counseling, supervisee's status, research participation, limits of confidentiality).	It was never addressed! Said to refer to self as staff, not student.
Crisis coverage and intervention	Adequate communication between supervisor and supervisee in the event of crisis as well as the provision of appropriate supervisory backup is ensured by supervisor. Supervisor handles situations appropriately where someone involved with the client is threatened by client's behavior or when a client is at risk for hurting herself or himself.	Was never informed about what to do in the event of a crisis. I had a very volatile, suicidal client and was never quite sure what would happen in a crisis/emergency. We never discussed crises.
Multiple roles	The supervisor handles role-related conflicts appropriately (e.g., supervisor and supervisee have personal relationship, advisor/advisee, or administrative work relationship).	Our supervisor is the director of the agency as well as a prominent member of the academic faculty; this is somewhat uncomfortable but never addressed.
Performance evaluation and monitoring of supervisee activities	Adequate communication between supervisor and supervisee concerning supervisee evaluations occurs. The supervisor provides ongoing feedback, verbal and written, and works with the supervisee on the establishment of goals. The supervisor reviews actual counseling sessions via video- and audiotapes and reads the supervisee's case notes periodically.	This just didn't happen. No review of tapes even though they were handed in. No reference to supervisee performance has been made at all. It will not be done, presumably, until the end of internship.

(Table continued on next page)

TABLE 14.1. Supervisor ethical guidelines (*Continued*)

Ethical guidelines	Definition	Examples from data
Expertise and competency issues	The supervisor makes appropriate disclosure to supervisee when the supervisee or supervisor is not competent to treat a particular client or condition. The supervisor ensures adequate coordination of all professionals involved in client treatment.	I had a mentally retarded client, whom the supervisor did not know exactly how to work with. The issue was never directly addressed.
Modeling ethical behavior and responding to ethical concerns	The supervisor discusses and models ethical behavior. The supervisor adequately responds to ethical violations.	My supervisor played a practical joke on me my second day at the site, which I felt was inappropriate. Has clients do yardwork.
Multicultural sensitivity toward clients	Racial, ethnic, cultural, sexual orientation, and gender issues (e.g., stereotyping, lack of sensitivity) toward clients are handled appropriately by supervisor.	Supervisor is quick to counter a racial/cultural focus for a more superficial explanation of client behavior. In some cases, some of her perceptions of African American clients, I believe, were misinformed or distorted. Comments about women taking care of men in traditional ways; seemed to be inflexible in his thinking about roles.
Multicultural sensitivity toward supervisee	Racial, ethnic, cultural, sexual orientation, and gender issues are discussed appropriately and sensitively by the supervisor toward the supervisee.	This supervisor would on occasion speak about women in very stereotypical fashion (e.g., wanting a commitment from a man). She explicitly stated several times that racial and cultural differences were easier to deal with if ignored. She stated that men very rarely make good counselors due to their inflated sense of self or lack of self-esteem.

Differentiating supervision from psychotherapy and counseling	The supervisee's personal issues in supervision are treated appropriately (i.e., delineating therapy and supervision adequately, making appropriate referral of supervisee to counseling or therapy).	In most supervision meetings the supervisor took a lot of time dealing with gossiping and advice giving on how we should handle our personal lives.
Sexual issues	The supervisor treats sexual and romantic issues appropriately.	She instructed me to avoid or sidestep this issue and deal with what was appropriate at the time. This possibility demands attention.
Termination and follow-up issues	Termination and follow-up issues are handled appropriately (e.g., supervisor assures continuity of care, prevents "abandonment" of client).	Never talked about it even when I asked her how to handle termination. She referred me back to my professor at school for information.

Note. Supervisor ethical guidelines and examples are from "Psychotherapy Supervisor Ethical Practice," by Ladany et al., 1999, *The Counseling Psychologist, 27,* pp. 443–475.

faculty member supervising students enrolled in practicum or internship classes or a doctoral level counseling student supervising a master's level counseling student enrolled in clinical coursework. In the administrative arena, supervisors who work in schools, mental health and community agencies, and private practice are often assigned (or hired) to provide evaluation, endorsement, and close monitoring of counselor progress during apprenticeship years. Regardless of setting, before a counselor begins the process of supervising another, he or she must engage in a self-assessment process to determine whether or not he or she is competent to supervise. Did he or she receive training (formally or informally) regarding how to supervise a developing counselor? Only those professionals who have been appropriately exposed to supervision theory and practice should consider becoming supervisors themselves (Guideline 1).

The second ethical issue a potential supervisor must consider is whether or not he or she is able to work with diverse counseling-theoretical orientations. Ladany et al. (1999) pointed out that given the diversity of effective theoretical approaches to counseling, it is imperative that supervisors be knowledgeable about an array of orientations, including the one that their supervisee prefers. While the supervisor can communicate his or her orientation, he or she must be flexible in helping the supervisee find the approach that feels the most natural to the supervisee (Guideline 2). If the potential supervisor decides he or she "passes" these initial issues, he or she can attend to the final preliminary consideration of fee schedules regarding both what the client will be paying the counselor in training (Guideline 3) and what, if anything, the supervisee will be paying the supervisor (Guideline 4).

☐ Initial Supervisory Ethical Concerns

Once a supervisory relationship has commenced, the supervisor must attend to an array of ethical concerns. Perhaps one of the most important is conveying to the supervisee the limits of confidentiality within the supervisory relationship (Guideline 5). The supervisee should be informed of what will be held in confidence by his or her supervisor and what may be shared with other professionals within the agency or his or her academic institution. For example, if the supervisee decides to disclose that he or she suffers from a current drug addiction, he or she should have a clear sense before disclosing this information whether self-disclosure of this type will be revealed to his or her academic program. Second, the supervisor sets very clear session boundaries with his or her supervisee (Guideline 6). This entails the supervisor treating supervision sessions with the same degree of respect and care that he or she treats counseling sessions. Privacy is assured and interruptions (such as phone calls) are avoided. Third, the supervisor orients the supervisee to his or her professional roles within the agency and assures that the supervisee is engaged in appropriate activities while on-site (Guideline 7). This orientation entails explaining what activities the supervisee will (and won't) be doing and what he or she can expect from his or her supervisor. Initial research in this area suggests that this kind of orientation may be particularly important for beginning trainees, who appear to experience more role ambiguity than do advanced trainees (Olk & Friedlander, 1992). This kind of monitoring also assures that the trainee will be engaged in counseling activities, rather than filing, answering the phone, running copies, and so forth, that might occur if office staff (or other clinicians) attempt to take advantage of a trainee. Fourth, supervisors need to ensure that their supervisees have made appropriate disclosures regarding the counseling relationship (Guideline 8). For example, supervisors must verify that supervisees have described to clients the limits of confidentiality within the counseling relationship and told clients that the counselor is receiving supervision (i.e., informed consent). Again, this may be particularly important with beginning trainees who may experience awkwardness in admitting both that the counseling relationship has confidentiality limits and that they are in training. Fifth, supervisors need to explicitly discuss crisis issues with their supervisee and ensure he or she knows what to do and whom to contact in the event of a client emergency (Guideline 9). Supervisors may want to engage in role-playing with their trainees to ensure that the trainee not only has the knowledge to act appropriately in a crisis, but feels reasonably comfortable handling his or her own emotions during these times. The sixth initial ethical consideration is that of multiple roles. Ethical supervisors are aware of the inherent difficulties of multiple roles (such as being the supervisee's advisor as well as supervisor) and seek to both address these dual roles when they occur and minimize or avoid them as much as possible (Guideline 10). Certainly, if potential supervisors and supervisees have a preexisting relationship, they should not commence a supervisory one. One kind of multiple role that could develop easily in counseling supervision is when the supervisor and supervisee enjoy each others company to the extent that a friendship develops. While it is very understandable that supervisors and supervisees may want to become friends given the possibility of shared values and interests, friendships should be avoided for the duration of the supervisory relationship. This includes not inviting supervisees for after-work get-togethers or social events, since these kinds of informal interactions foster friendships and would likely cloud the supervisory relationship. One reason that friendship is seen as inappropriate is that it tends to make objective assessment difficult or impossible. As the case example illustrates, evaluation can be a tricky enough task when we merely like our trainees, but when we add genuine friendship to the mix, the task can become overwhelming for both parties. However, there are times when multiple roles exist based on reasonable circumstances (e.g., faculty professor and supervisor). In these instances, supervisors are encouraged to discuss these multiple roles with their supervisees and work through relationship issues that could confound the development of an effective supervisory working relationship.

Ongoing Ethical Concerns

As the supervisory relationship develops, supervisors have additional ethical concerns to consider. The supervisor is responsible for helping the supervisee create learning goals for his or her experience, which should take place at the beginning of supervision and be refined as needed throughout supervision. The supervisor provides timely and ongoing oral and written feedback to the supervisee regarding his or her progress (Guideline 11). To ensure that his or her feedback is accurate, the supervisor should monitor the supervisee's counseling skills by reviewing audio- or videotapes of sessions and reading case notes from time to time. Initial research in supervisory ethics indicates that of all ethical guidelines, inadequate evaluation is the most frequent violation (Ladany et al., 1999). This may be because supervisors, like the one cited in the beginning of the chapter, dislike and/ or are uncomfortable providing negative feedback to supervisees. Rather than disappoint or upset their supervisee, supervisors may try to rationalize by saying that their trainees have come this far and question their own judgment.

In light of the apparently widespread problem of supervisee evaluation, several procedures are recommended. While some feedback may be oral, it is important that the supervisor also provide formal, written feedback to the supervisee, which can be referred back to in the future. In the case of negative feedback, even if given orally, it is essential that the supervisor record what, when, how, and why events occurred in supervision, with the information maintained in a record known to both the supervisee and the supervisor. For example, if a supervisee was struggling with her ability to move clients beyond a superficial level of exploration, the supervisor could coauthor a letter with her, signed by both, that says:

> I have trouble using skills other than active listening in my sessions because of a fear of pressing people too hard. I realize that this gets in the way for me, and for my clients. We have talked about how this is related to my fear of rejection and weak training I received in more action-oriented strategies. I understand that I must improve my competence by attending several workshops in brief counseling methods, doing supplemental reading that we have identified, and including more varied interventions in my sessions. I propose to begin this plan by bringing a tape next week in which I demonstrate the use of confrontation, as well as other skills we have reviewed. I agree with this assessment and understand that I must improve in these identified areas if I am to reach satisfactory competence levels as a counselor.

In situations where the supervisee is deemed to be lacking in important skill areas and runs the risk of not passing his or her practica, it can be

useful to bring in a third party. Given the inherent power differential between the supervisor and supervisee, the supervisee may feel obligated to
sign a letter such as the one detailed above, whether he or she believes it to
be accurate or not. If an impartial but trained third party (such as a professor from the student's graduate program) sits in on a supervision session
and listens to or watches some of the supervisee's work (via audio- or
videotape), he or she can offer a second opinion on the supervisee's skills.
This second opinion can either validate the supervisor's view or, conversely,
maintain that the supervisee is progressing at a reasonable pace.

A second ethical concern that arises as supervision proceeds is that of
supervisor expertise. The supervisor should only supervise trainees on those
clients he or she is qualified to treat himself or herself and also insure that
supervisees only work with clients who are within their range of competency (Guideline 12). Sometimes it isn't immediately clear that the supervisee has taken on a client that is beyond both the counselor's and supervisor's
competency because the client reveals this information (or exhibits troubling behaviors or symptoms) after the counseling relationship has already
begun. An example might be a beginning practicum student working with
an apparently depressed and homesick freshman in college who exhibits
psychotic symptoms at the fifth session. At this point, the supervisor should
help his or her supervisee transfer the client to a competent clinician. In
those situations where the supervisee inadvertently begins a counseling
relationship with a client and has concerns that are beyond the expertise of
the supervisor, the supervisor should communicate his or her lack of competency in this area to the supervisee. At this point, the supervisor and
supervisee must decide together if the client should be transferred to another counselor or whether an outside consultant can be brought in to
discuss this particular case with the supervisee.

A third ethical concern of which supervisors should remain aware is that
of modeling ethical behavior and responding to the ethical concerns of
their supervisees (Guideline 13). Modeling ethical behavior entails being
mindful of the various ethical codes of counselors and demonstrating one's
commitment to them. For example, supervisors should strive to demonstrate that they respect client confidentiality, right to autonomy, respectful
treatment, and so forth. This guideline also includes responding to trainees'
ethical concerns in a timely manner. For example, if one's supervisee men-
tions in supervision that the support staff has been leaving client files in
nonsecure locations, the supervisor should promptly inform the appropriate personnel and let his or her supervisee know that this problem has
been addressed.

A fourth ongoing ethical concern is that of maintaining multicultural
sensitivity toward clients (Guideline 14) and supervisees (Guideline 15). It
is essential that supervisors be able to work effectively with clients and
supervisees from a variety of cultures. Multicultural sensitivity toward
clients entails educating supervisees about how race, culture, gender, sexual

orientation, language, and possible discrimination experiences may factor into the client's world view, current problems, or view of himself or herself. Relatedly, multicultural sensitivity toward supervisees involves recognizing how the above factors may play a role in the supervisory relationship. Ethical supervisors address any real or potential differences between themselves and their trainees and seek to create an environment where supervisees feel comfortable discussing diversity issues. Conversations like these can begin with the supervisor noting the differences between them: "As we sit here, I cannot help but notice that I am a 40-year-old White woman and you are a 21-year-old Asian male. I wonder how the diversity between us may affect our relationship or how we view clients?" and invite the supervisee to initiate a dialogue regarding how diversity plays a role in the relationship. This kind of discussion also helps the supervisee consider differences between himself or herself and his or her clients.

A fifth thorny ethical issue that may arise during the supervisory relationship is that of differentiating between supervision and counseling (Guideline 16). As supervision unfolds, it is expected that the supervisee will disclose a fair amount of personal information. This information will likely include some of the supervisee's personal issues. The supervisor must then determine where supervision ends and counseling starts. Various authors (Green & Hansen, 1989; Kitchener, 1988) have suggested that supervisors mention at the beginning of supervision that personal issues may arise during the course of supervision. When a supervisee's personal issue arises, the supervisor can point out what seems to be occurring and recommend that the supervisee consider counseling elsewhere. The supervisor should not attempt to help the supervisee resolve the issue within supervision, since this may be the point at which supervision becomes counseling. An example of this would be when a supervisor notices her supervisee making extra appointments with a recently widowed client. Upon inquiry, the supervisee reveals she was widowed a year before and feels so lonely that she imagines her client feels equally lonely and desires more sessions. The supervisor can explore this decision with her supervisee, and if she senses that the extra appointments have more to do with the supervisee than the client, she can point this out and encourage her supervisee to consider counseling as a way to address her own feelings of loss and loneliness.

A sixth ethical consideration that may arise during the course of a supervisory relationship is that of sexual attraction and sexual contact. One recent study (Rodolfa et al., 1994) found that one in four interns in postdoctoral internship sites experienced sexual attraction toward their clinical supervisors, indicating that sexual attraction toward one's supervisor is not an unusual occurrence. Although currently there are no studies evaluating how often supervisors experience sexual attraction toward their supervisees, given the close relationship and sharing of personal information that occurs in supervision, we can assume that supervisors and supervisees sometimes experience attraction toward one another. Sexual attraction, therefore, in and of itself, is a normal dynamic that may arise in supervision. If it occurs, the supervisor should seek consultation to ensure that the sexual issues are handled appropriately. Sexual contact, on the other hand, is an ethical violation and must be avoided (Guideline 17). Several studies demonstrate how important this guideline is to uphold: Pope, Schover, & Levenson (1979) found that 10% of psychologists admitted to having sexual relationships as students with their instructors or supervisors, and 13% reported having had sexual contact with students when they became instructors or supervisors themselves. In their review of this study, Bartell and Rubin (1990) reported that respondents who indicated they had had a sexual relationship as a student reported a higher incidence of sexual relationships with their students, suggesting that poor modeling when one is a trainee may lead to continuation of unethical practices when one becomes a professional. An earlier study by Glaser and Thorpe (1986) found that those professionals who as students engaged in sexual contact with their educators looked back on the relationship as unethical and coerced. Therefore, even if the sexual attraction is mutual and the desire for sexual contact appears mutual, supervisors should be aware of how the power differential confounds this process and makes any sexual relationship unwise and unethical for the duration of the supervisory relationship.

A final ethical guideline is that of appropriately managing termination and follow-up issues. The supervisor must ensure that supervisees are knowledgeable about termination issues and prepare clients appropriately for termination (Guideline 18). Furthermore, supervisors ensure that clients are not abandoned if a supervisee needs to terminate prematurely (such as at the end of a semester) and are referred as needed. Exploring termination with a supervisee should occur on two levels. The first level involves talking to supervisees about how they will terminate with their clients and help clients summarize and integrate their experience. The second level is the supervisor engaging in a similar process with the supervisee: terminating and helping the supervisee integrate his or her learning over the course of the supervisory relationship.

Ethical Decision Making

Despite their many assets, ethical codes and guidelines all have their weaknesses. Sometimes they conflict with one another, and often circumstances will arise that are not addressed by the codes or guidelines (Talbutt, 1981). In some instances the needs of the client and the institution or agency conflict, and thus counselors or supervisors must decide where their primary responsibility lies. A decision may be in conflict with one of two powerful forces: the client whose rights need to be protected and the institution or agency for which the counselor works.

For supervisors, the situation is made infinitely more complex by the third loyalty to the counselor being supervised. In one study of how counselors resolve ethical dilemmas, Hayman and Covert (1986) reported that 93% of the counselors surveyed relied on common sense. Fewer than one-third used published professional guidelines. Such a decision-making process works well only if the so-called "common sense" is consistent with established professional and societal standards of conduct.

Kitchener (1984) and Welfel (1998) suggested a more scientific approach. Building upon Kitchener's model, Welfel detailed a nine-step model to ethical decision making. The steps are as follows:

1. Develop ethical sensitivity.
2. Define dilemma and options.
3. Refer to professional standards.
4. Search out ethics scholarship.
5. Apply ethical principles to situation.
6. Consult with supervisor and respected colleagues.
7. Deliberate and decide.
8. Inform supervisor; implement and document actions.
9. Reflect on the experience.

Let us consider our example at the beginning of the chapter and how the troubled supervisor might proceed with this model in mind. Regarding developing ethical sensitivity, this supervisor seems to have gotten off on a poor footing. Although she is aware that she needs to protect the public at large, she has clearly overlooked the ethical guideline of providing ongoing feedback to supervisees. In regard to step 2, defining the dilemma and her options, she seems to have done a reasonable job of defining the dilemma; that is, this supervisee is a poor counselor at the end of his training, who needs to be informed that he does not appear to be cut out for the field after many years of training. At that point, she may want to more clearly define her options. These might include (a) saying nothing and writing him a positive and inaccurate evaluation, (b) finding a middle ground and reporting what his strengths are as a counselor (presuming he has any), as well as defining his many deficits and making recommendations about how he may remediate these deficits (if she thinks this is possible) or (c) telling him he does not possess the skills to be successful in the field and discussing other options with him. To address the third step of referring to professional standards, the supervisor should review the guidelines we have described above, which detail how she should have been providing him feedback throughout his supervision experience, so that his poor performance is not a surprise to him at the end. Moreover, she still has a responsibility to provide him with accurate feedback about his current functioning. The fourth step of searching out ethics scholarship may involve her reviewing relevant articles discussing the ethics of handling poorly performing trainees (e.g., Bernard & Goodyear, 1998; Lamb, Cochran, &

Jackson, 1991). These authors speak of the importance of due process, which refers to the supervisee's rights to be knowledgeable about training objectives, assessment procedures, and evaluation criteria. Due process is violated when supervisees are dismissed or told they are incompetent at the end of their supervisory experience without having any prior warning that their performance has been substandard. Given that the supervisee seems to be unaware of his poor performance, the supervisor would be violating the practice of due process if she tells him now that he has failed the training experience. For step 5, the supervisor must apply the ethical principles to the situation. The ethical principles include (a) respect autonomy, (b) do no harm, (c) seek beneficence, or do good, (d) pursue justice, and (e) be faithful (Welfel, 1998). The relevant principles in this case involve doing no harm and being faithful. The supervisor is ultimately seeking to ensure that the supervisee does not harm any future clients with whom he may work. Yet, she is also struggling with the principle of being faithful to an individual who she has been trying to assist and who has been working hard to become successful. Unfortunately, these principles are obviously in conflict. Beauchamp and Childress (1989) recommended that when principles conflict, "do no harm" is the guiding principle to follow. Therefore, following the model, the supervisor needs to act and not let this counselor simply pass the training experience. Step 6 recommends consulting with supervisors and colleagues. This step may be particularly important because several minds working together may produce some novel and creative approaches the supervisor would not have considered by herself. Perhaps others may recommend a second year of training with her (or with someone else), this time with his deficits clearly delineated and specific goals created. Step 7 calls for the supervisor to deliberate and decide upon her course of action. Certainly, at the very least, she needs to say something to him regarding his inadequate performance. Yet, due to her own negligent behavior of not providing him with ongoing feedback about his progress, she cannot ethically "fail" him and dismiss him entirely. Once she has made her decision, she should inform her supervisor, if she has one (step 8). Last, this supervisor would be wise to reflect upon her experience (step 9) and consider how she might do things differently next time. Clearly, she needs to implement regular feedback, both oral and written, in the future with all her supervisees so as to head off the due process concern in the future. Perhaps she will decide to consult more regularly with colleagues about supervision dilemmas as they arise, rather than let them fester as the relationship develops.

☐ Legal Considerations

In addition to attending to ethical concerns within the supervisory relationship, supervisorsmust also be mindful of some important legal considerations of supervision. Perhaps the most significant legal concern is that of liability. There are two kinds of liability supervisors must accept for their supervisees. The first is direct liability. Supervisors can be found directly liable when their own actions are the cause of harm to the client (Bernard & Goodyear, 1998). For example, a supervisor who instructs a supervisee to disregard and ignore a client's statement of suicidal intent as a lame cry for help would be directly liable if the client completes a suicidal act. The second kind of liability is referred to as vicarious liability (Bernard & Goodyear, 1998). This occurs when the supervisor is held liable for the behavior of the supervisee that the supervisor neither knew about nor proposed. The supervisor is held responsible because he or she has accepted the responsibility of training the counselor and is ultimately responsible for all the clients on the supervisee's caseload. While it is certainly a frightening notion for supervisors to become aware that they are responsible for all the behaviors of their supervisees, one way to manage this responsibility is to maintain an open, noncritical relationship in which supervisees feel comfortable disclosing their concerns, questions, and errors, rather than hiding them from the supervisor and allowing potential problems to escalate.

A second legal concern is the issue of malpractice. Malpractice, which is a kind of negligence, is defined as negligence in the performance of professional duties (Bednar, Bednar, Lambert, & Waite, 1991). Given this broad definition, malpractice could apply to supervision. The courts and case law have restricted interpretations of malpractice such that, for a malpractice claim to succeed, it must include four essential components: (a) a "professional relationship" must be present, thus creating a "legal duty of care"; (b) there must be a "demonstrable standard of care" that has been neglected; (c) the client must have been injured or harmed; and (d) the "practitioner's breach of duty" must be the primary factor in the client's injury (Bennett, Bryant, Vanderbos, & Greenwood, 1990). In their review of issues in supervisory malpractice, Guest and Dooley (1999) argued that supervision is a professional relationship and that supervisors do have a legal duty of care to their supervisees. If supervisees are able to point to a specific guideline that has not been met (e.g., they were not provided with feedback until the end of their training experience), the second component of a malpractice action would be met. Regarding the issue of "harm," psychological distress has been found to be a legitimate claim (Guest & Dooley, 1999) and one that the supervisee in the initial example could certainly claim if he failed his final training experience without any prior warning. Supervisees could also plead harm if they, for example, were treated with a lack of respect (e.g., told their sexual orientation was an aberration), or if their supervisor insisted upon conducting therapy with them against their wishes. The last component of a malpractice claim, that of establishing whether the supervisor's behavior caused the harm, may be difficult to prove. However, Guest and Dooley pointed out that whether the actions of the supervisor were the predominant cause of harm, a plaintiff may successfully argue contributory negligence of the supervisor. Although no suits to date have been brought against supervisors by supervisees for inadequate supervision (Bernard & Goodyear, 1998), supervisors should be aware of the risks involved in practice and protect themselves by recognizing the legal implications of supervision.

☐ Conclusions

The more supervisors consider the ramifications of ethical and legal issues raised in this chapter, the more confusing such conflicts can become. Yet one mark of professionalism is to be able to simultaneously weigh these considerations and to make sound judgments that are in the best interest of both the client and others (Herlihy & Sheeley, 1987).

Given the potential for ethical issues to arise, what is the role of the administrative or clinical supervisor in training for ethics? We believe that supervisees must be given as much information as possible to help them make informed decisions when ethical dilemmas arise. This information can be presented in writing, at staff meetings, through an audiotape or videotape, or during supervision sessions. Welfel's (1998) model can be discussed and case examples reviewed in conjunction with this model. While a number of ways exist to disseminate the information, supervisors have the responsibility to try to prevent ethical violations whenever possible. Beyond our work in providing skills training, conceptual development, constructive work habits, case management skills, and attitudes consistent with professional conduct, we teach people to behave with the highest moral and ethical standards. During these formative years of apprenticeship, we guide supervisees to reason through ethical dilemmas, sort through ethical codes, and make sound decisions that are consistent with the profession, the cultural norms of the client, and one's own value system.

☐ References

Allen, U. B. (1986). A historical perspective of the AACD Ethics Committee. *Journal of Counseling & Development, 64,* 293.

Association for Counselor Education and Supervision. (1995). Ethical guidelines for counseling supervisors. *Counselor Education and Supervision, 34,* 270–276.

Bartell, P. A., & Rubin, L. J. (1990). Dangerous liaisons: Sexual intimacies in supervision. *Professional Psychology: Research and Practice, 21,* 442–450.

Beauchamp, T. L., & Childress, J. F. (1989). *Principles of biomedical ethics* (3rd ed.). Oxford, England: Oxford University Press.

Bednar, R. L., Bednar, S. C., Lambert, M. J., & Waite, D. R. (1991). *Psychotherapy with high-risk clients.* Pacific Grove, CA: Brooks-Cole.

Bennett, B. E., Bryant, B. K., Vanderbos, G. R., & Greenwood, A. (1990). *Professional liability and risk-management.* Washington, DC: American Psychological Association.

Bernard, J., & Goodyear, R. (1998). *Fundamentals of counseling supervision.* Boston: Allyn & Bacon.

Borders, L. D. (1997). Subtle boundary issues in supervision. In B. Herlihy & G. Corey (Eds.), *Boundary issues in counseling: Multiple roles and responsibilities.* Alexandria, VA: American Counseling Association.

Glaser, R. D., & Thorpe, J. S. (1986). Unethical intimacy: A survey of sexual contact and advances between psychology educators and female graduate students. *American Psychologist, 41,* 42–51.

Green, S. L., & Hansen, J. C. (1989). Ethical dilemmas in family therapy. *Journal of Marital and Family Therapy, 12,* 149–158.

Guest, C. L., & Dooley, K. (1999). Supervisor malpractice: Liability to the supervisee in clinical supervision. *Counselor Education and Supervision, 38,* 269–279.

Hayman, P. M., & Covert, J. A. (1986). Ethical dilemmas in college counseling centers. *Journal of Counseling and Development, 64,* 318–320.

Herlihy, B., & Corey, G. (1997). *Boundary issues in counseling: Multiple roles and responsibilities.* Alexandria, VA: American Counseling Association.

Herlihy, B., & Sheeley, V. (1987). Privileged communication in selected helping professions: A comparison among statutes. *Journal of Counseling and Development, 65,* 479–483.

Kitchener, K. S. (1984). Intuition, critical evaluation, and ethical principles: The foundation for ethical decisions in counseling psychology. *The Counseling Psychologist, 12,* 43–55.

Kitchener, K. S. (1988). Dual role relationships: What makes them so problematic? *Journal of Counseling and Development, 67,* 217–221.

Koocher, G. P., & Keith-Spiegel, P. (1998). *Ethics in psychology: Professional standards and cases* (2nd ed.). New York: Oxford University Press.

Ladany, N., Lehrman-Waterman, D., Molinaro, M., & Wolgast, B. (1999). Psychotherapy supervisor ethical practice: Adherence to guidelines, the supervisory working alliance, and supervisee satisfaction. *The Counseling Psychologist, 27,* 443–475.

Lamb, D. H., Cochran, D. J., & Jackson, V. R. (1991). Training and organizational issues associated with identifying and responding to intern impairment. *Professional Psychology: Research and Practice, 22,* 291–296.

Olk, M. E., & Friedlander, M. L. (1992). Trainees' experiences of role conflict and role ambiguity in supervisory relationships. *Journal of Counseling Psychology, 39,* 389–397.

Pope, K. S., Schover, L. R., & Levenson, H. (1979). Sexual intimacy in psychology training: Results and implications of a national survey. *American Psychologist, 34,* 682–689.

Pope, K. S., & Vasquez, M. J. T. (1998). *Ethics in psychotherapy and counseling* (2nd ed.). San Francisco: Jossey-Bass.

Rodolfa, E., Hall, T., Holms, V., Devena, A., Komatz, D., Antunez, M., & Hall, A. (1994). Training interns respond to sexual dilemmas. *Professional Psychology: Research and Practice, 21,* 313–315.

Stoltenberg, C., & Delworth, U. (1987). *Supervising counselors and therapists: A developmental approach.* San Francisco: Jossey-Bass.

Talbutt, L. C. (1981). Ethical standards: Assets and limitations. *Personnel and Guidance Journal, 60,* 110–112.

Welfel, E. R. (1998). *Ethics in counseling and psychotherapy: Standards, research, and emerging issues.* Pacific Grove, CA: Brooks/Cole.

Whiston, S., & Emerson, S. (1989). Ethical implications for supervisors in counseling of trainees. *Counselor Education and Supervision, 28,* 318–325.

15
CHAPTER

Loretta J. Bradley
Peggy P. Whiting

Supervision Training: A Model

Recent books (Bernard & Goodyear, 1998; Borders & Leddick, 1987; Falvey, 1987; Holloway, 1995; Kaslow, 1987; Neufeldt, Iverson & Juntunen, 1995; Stoltenberg, McNeill, & Delworth, 1998; Watkins, 1997) and articles (Borders et al., 1991; Bradley & Ricardson, 1987; O'Byrne & Rosenberg, 1998; Porter, 1994; Powell, 1996; Rich, 1993; Rigazio-DiGilio, 1998; Stoltenberg, 1997; Talen & Schindler, 1993; Ward & House, 1998; Watkins, 1994) have described models of supervision training. After examining the models, it becomes apparent that supervision is a complex process, yet an important experience for both administrative and clinical supervisors.

A model for training supervisors is presented in this chapter. The model has three major components originally suggested by Loganbill, Hardy, and Delworth (1982): conceptual, experiential, and integrative. The model separates the supervision process into stage components and thereby provides a viable method for isolating and teaching techniques germane to each specific stage. This model provides, especially for inexperienced supervisors, the discovery that supervision can be learned in smaller, logical segments. Additionally, training in logical segments allows time for the supervisor to identify and understand the segments prior to their implementation in actual supervision settings.

It was an alarming fact in the late 1980s that although supervision training was advocated, only a few counselor education programs and agencies provided supervisory training (Borders & Leddick, 1988; Hart & Falvey, 1987; Holloway, 1982; Richardson & Bradley, 1986). Borders and Leddick (1988) reported that only one-third of the counselor preparation programs provided training in supervision. Similar results were obtained in earlier studies by Hess and Hess (1983) and Richardson and Bradley (1986). During the decade of the 1990s, more attention was given to the models and methods of supervision. Additionally, the movement toward credentialing through accreditation and licensure has supported and required supervision training and delivery (Freeman & McHenry, 1996). Most recently, the National Board for Certified Counselors has established a new credential, approved clinical supervisor (ACS). This chapter reinforces the need for systematic training by providing a supervision training model. The model demonstrates how didactic and experiential components may be integrated to provide effective supervision training.

☐ Supervision Training

What Is Supervisory Training?

Although most of the literature on supervision training discusses the needs of the student-in-training, a need also exists for training for the supervisor in the field so as to increase and improve supervisory competency areas. In addition, many agency directors, in filling vacancies, request experienced supervisors. Whether in an administrative or a clinical setting, supervisory training is needed. Experience alone cannot qualify one for supervision.

Borders et al. (1991) described supervisory training as the development of a curriculum guide that utilizes three emphases of current professional standards: self-awareness, theoretical and conceptual knowledge, and skills and techniques. They also outlined seven core curriculum areas that compose effective supervisory education. These areas are: models of supervision; counselor development; methods and techniques; the supervisory relationship; ethical, legal, and professional regulatory issues; evaluation; and executive and administrative skills. The model of supervisory training described in this chapter incorporates conceptual, integrative, and experiential elements as outlined by Borders et al.

Initial Planning

Prior to the initial supervisory training session, a meeting is needed with the supervisor to provide an overview of the supervisory training session(s). During this initial meeting, background information should be obtained to ensure that the supervisor has the requisite background and interest to participate in the training sessions. The supervisor should be informed of the anticipated structure and format of the training session(s). Additionally, the supervisor should understand the expectations and requirements for successful completion of the supervision training. The following topics should be discussed: amount of time anticipated for completing the supervisory training, information about who is responsible for the training session, responsibilities for the supervisor in training, overview of evaluation procedures, clarification of how satisfactory and unsatisfactory performance will be determined, and a discussion of confidentiality issues. The preceding list of topics is intended to be exemplary, not comprehensive, as topics will vary depending on the individual needs of the supervisor in training. The important emphasis is that an initial meeting should be planned before the actual supervision training is begun so as to lay the cornerstone for future training.

Goals

Four major goals guide the planning of the supervision training:

1. to provide a theory or knowledge base relevant to supervisory functioning;
2. to develop and refine supervisory skills;
3. to integrate the theory and skills into a working supervisory style; and
4. to develop and enhance the professional identity of the supervisor.

Table 15.1 presents an overview of supervision training. As illustrated in Table 15.1, the four supervisory goals can be achieved through a combination of didactic and experiential learning modes. In providing a synthesis of conceptual and experiential exposure, the overview presents an integrative training component. The training is similar to that described by Loganbill, Hardy, and Delworth (1982), who stated that "integration allows conceptual material to become more than mere intellectual data, [it becomes] meaningful input which can organize and make sense of the experiential" (p. 38). Borders et al. (1991) described one of the assumptions underlying their curriculum guide as being the need to "involve a sequence of didactic and experiential instruction" (p. 61). The instructional events listed in Table 15.1 offer opportunities for theoretical solidification, clarification of personal supervisory style, internalization of supervisory identity, and peer feedback.

Training

A study on supervision training was conducted by Borders and Leddick in 1988. The researchers mailed a survey to the 450 counseling programs listed in *Counselor Preparation* (Hollis & Wantz, 1983). A total of 60 counselor education program administrators responded to the study. From the 60 respondents, 47 indicated that their program offered a supervision course. The authors received 35 course syllabi with 23 syllabi containing a course outline. The authors reviewed the course syllabi and classified them into class topics. Table 15.2 presents the topics specified in the supervision course syllabi. The authors concluded that supervision models were taught more frequently than supervision techniques. Additionally, evaluation, ethical and legal issues, and the supervisory relationship were frequently discussed. Other

TABLE 15.1. Overview of supervision training

Goals	Instructional mode	Instructional outcome
Theory	Didactic	Listens and understands lectures on supervision model. Demonstrates knowledge about supervision models. Acquires information about supervisory roles. Obtains information about effective and ineffective supervision.
Skills	Didactic and experiential	Knows and understands supervisory techniques. Exhibits knowledge about supervisory skills. Develops skill-mastery appropriate to direct supervisee.
Integration	Experiential	Integrates skills into supervisory style. Demonstrates the integration of theory and skills training via live supervision, videotape, audiotape, and role-play. Organizes, understands, and translates knowledge into actual practices. Effectively assumes supervisory role with supervisee.
Identity	Didactic and experiential	Advocates and uses effective principles endorsed by the profession. Implements professional supervisory terminology. Develops professional supervisory maturity. Internalizes the identity of the profession. Exhibits professional and emotional maturity.

popular topics included the history and definition of supervision, research on supervision, group versus individual supervision, and administrative supervision (p. 276). These topics are analogous to the core content areas outlined by Borders et al. (1991). Additionally, courses providing information on supervision should offer instruction regarding multiculturally responsive models and techniques of supervision, professional credentialing for supervisors, and specific developmentally appropriate supervision techniques.

Overview

After incorporating the information obtained from the Borders and Leddick (1988) study and from the curriculum guide proposed by Borders et al. (1991),

TABLE 15.2. Class topics specified in supervision course syllabi

Topics	Frequency
Supervision models and theoretical approaches	
Instructional or behavioral	12
Developmental	11
Client-centered or personal growth	10
Psychoanalytic	10
Skill training and development	9
Integrative-integration	9
Microcounseling	4
Cognitive-behavioral	3
Eclectic	3
Adlerian	2
Co-therapy	2
Social learning	2
Systems	2
Existential	1
Multimodel	1
Triadic	1
Vertical	1
Supervision techniques	
PR	7
Live supervision	1
Evaluation of supervisee (general)	10
Preparing for and giving feedback	2
Evaluation instruments or rating scales	2
Initial assessment of counseling skills	1
Characteristics of effective counselors	1
Quality control issues	1
Ethical or legal issues	10
Relationship issues (general)	1
Parallel process	4
Counselor–supervisor relationship	3
Client–counselor supervisor relationship	1
Supervision versus therapy	2
Supervisee resistance, games	3
Supervisee "problems with learning"	1
Concerns of beginning supervisees	1
Supervisee anxiety	2
Supervisee expectations	1
Expectations of on-site staff	1
Sex role, racial, ethnic, and social class issues	3
Supervision in particular settings	
Schools (elementary through college)	4
Community agencies	4
On-campus counselor training programs	2

(Table continued on next page)

TABLE 15.2. Class topics specified in supervision course syllabi (*Continued*)

Topics	Frequency
Supervision in particular settings (*Continued*)	
Private practice	1
Rehabilitation agencies	1
State Department of Education	1
Supervision of specialized counseling	
Marriage and family counseling	6
Group counseling	2
Counseling adolescents	1
History of supervision	6
Definition of supervision	
Roles or role conflict of supervisors	5
Responsibilities of supervisors	2
Purposes of supervision	3
Transition from counselor to supervisor	1
Research on supervision (general)	
Components of effective supervision based on research	2
Group versus individual supervision	5
Administrative supervision (e.g., staff development, organizational goals, policies, procedures)	5
Consultation	2
Training for supervisors	2
Case conceptualization skills	1
Emergency procedures	1
Intake responsibilities	1
Paraprofessions	1
Standards for counselor education programs	1

Note. From "A National Survey of Supervision Training" by L. D. Borders and G. R. Leddick, 1988, *Counselor Education and Supervision, 27,* 271–283. Copyright 1988 by the American Association for Counseling and Development. Reprinted by permission.

a model of supervisory training components includes conceptual, integrative, and experiential components. The model is based on the premise that the goal of supervision training is development and supervision training is a process that evolves over time. Similar to the definition provided by Williams (1987), supervision is depicted as "a process of incremental learning, adjusted to the differential, developmental needs of trainees" (p. 253). Since the training is planned in incremental stages, it can be implemented as a seminar or practicum for students enrolled in clinical supervisory training or as an in-service workshop for administrative supervisors. Therefore, the model addresses training needs for both administrative and clinical supervisors.

A model of supervision training is presented in Table 15.3. The model contains the four goals identified earlier in this chapter. The training components incorporate conceptual, experiential, and integrative learnings with the teaching modalities using didactic presentations, modeling, simulation exercises, and supervised practice. Five major content areas are: (a) conceptualizing the supervisory function, (b) orchestrating a supervisory relationship, (c) focusing supervision goals toward mastery and maturity, (d) facilitating a supervisory learning environment, and (e) developing a theory base, supervisory technology, and personal style. Evaluation consists of knowledge, practice, and personal components and is conducted throughout the training process. According to Freeman & McHenry (1996), the most important supervision functions are teaching professionalism and ethics, teaching the supervisee to conceptualize client themes, personalization issues, and instruction in specific skills. These functions are included in the five content areas.

☐ Supervision Training Modules

Conceptualizing the Supervisory Function

Supervisors-in-training need to have a clear understanding of what supervision is and how it differs from counseling. Perpetuation of the belief that supervision is the mere application of sophisticated counseling techniques must be avoided. To avoid this error, a working definition of supervision needs to be provided. A good beginning is to simply ask: What is supervision? As supervisors respond to the question, three distinctions might be considered and outlined in columns. The columns should read as follows: effective supervision, ineffective supervision, and counseling. Columns 1 and 2 can be contrasted. This information should provide the impetus for Column 3. Supervisors should be challenged to identify differences between supervision and counseling. Supervisors-in-training should also realize that one can be a good counselor and know nothing about supervision. Distinctions between supervision and counseling are important and must be understood in order for supervision training to be successful.

This portion of the training session should conclude with an agreed-upon working definition of supervision. A definition similar to that provided by Hess (1986) is suggested:

> A supervisor is a lecturer who conveys global schemes and techniques, a teacher of specified content and skills, a case reviewer to explore ways of thinking and conceptualizing cases, a monitor to ensure at least minimal levels of competence, a therapist to nurture growth and a colleague to give support and provide a different view. (p.58)

Supervision must also be conceptualized from a culturally responsive model (Porter, 1994). Porter recommended introducing a cross-cultural view that

TABLE 15.3. A model of supervision training

I. Goals
   A. To provide a theory knowledge base relevant to supervisory functioning
   B. To develop and refine supervisory skills
   C. To integrate the theory and skills into a working supervisory style
   D. To develop and enhance the professional identity of the supervisor

II. Training components
   A. Conceptual
   B. Experiential
   C. Integrative

III. Teaching modalities
   A. Didactic presentations
   B. Modeling
   C. Simulation exercises
   D. Supervised practice

IV. Content modules
   A. Conceptualizing the supervisory function
      1. Supervision defined
      2. Supervision differentiated from other counseling roles
      3. Portrait of an ideal clinical or administrative supervisor
      4. Supervision as pacing leadership
      5. Ethical and legal considerations of supervision
   B. Orchestrating a supervisory relationship
      1. Relational dimensions between supervisor and supervisee
      2. Supervision as a working alliance
      3. The establishment of goals and means
      4. Progression of the supervisory relationship by stages
      5. Group supervision
      6. Environmental/agency context for supervision
   C. Focusing supervision goals toward mastery and maturity
      1. Developmental issues of supervisees
      2. Roles of supervisors which promote development
      3. Supervision aimed toward processes of professional identity solidification
         and autonomy
   D. Facilitating a supervisory learning environment
      1. The interaction of a learner and a learning environment in supervision
      2. Blocher's developmental learning environment; the seven basic dynamics
      3. Supervisee's development
      4. Supervisors stimulate maturity
   E. Developing a theory base, supervision technology, and personal style
      1. Theoretical approaches to supervision: psychotherapeutic, behavioral,
         experiential, developmental, systems
      2. Multitechniques for supervisors
      3. Supervisory interventions based on developmental level
      4. The development of a justifiable personal style of supervision
      5. Integration of theory, skill, and style

V. Evaluation
   A. Evaluation of knowledge component
   B. Evaluation of practice component
   C. Evaluation of personal component

includes a sociocultural framework, an exploration of personal bias, and a social-action perspective. Borders and Fong (1994) discussed the exploration of changes in cognitive understandings of beginning and more seasoned supervisors in order to identify catalysts for prompting cognitive shifts in the conceptualizations of the supervisory function.

After supervisors-in-training have a clear conception of what supervision is and is not, the training can focus on a portrait of an ideal supervisor, clinical or administrative. Carifio & Hess (1987) synthesized the research and stated that "high-functioning supervisors perform with high levels of empathy, respect, genuineness, flexibility, concern, investment and openness" (p. 244). Herein lies the thesis that regardless of role differences between administrative and clinical supervisors, these personal characteristics are primary to any supervisory function. These authors continued to describe ideal supervisors as "knowledgeable, experienced and concrete in their presentation . . . [using] appropriate teaching, goal-setting and feedback techniques during their supervisory interactions" (Carifio & Hess, 1987, p. 244).

Loganbill et al. (1982) described the ideal supervisor as being at a higher competence, maturity, and experience level than the supervisee. These qualities impact on the authoritative nature of supervision. The authoritative role of supervision with its evaluative component is more likely to be accepted if the supervisor is perceived (by the supervisee) as having achieved a higher level of competence. While the ideal supervisor may effect and help produce several changes in the supervisee, the primary goal is the development of professional competence, even to the exclusion of other considerations (Sansbury, 1982).

Another function of the supervisor is the pacing of the supervisee. As the term implied, the supervision and related activities are to be paced so as to occur at the appropriate time. It is important that supervisory methods not be presented too quickly or too slowly to the supervisee. Another concept involving pacing was proposed by D'Andrea (1984), in which counselors are viewed as pacers in the development of their clients. This idea is applicable to supervisors in that master supervisors should provide provocative, stimulating, and psychologically challenging leadership for promoting the development of their supervisees. The opportunity for pacing occurs in both administrative and clinical supervision. The need to influence the development of effective supervision occurs in both settings. Stoltenberg's (1997) concept of the integrated developmental model of supervision speaks to the issue of choosing supervisory interventions that relate to the supervisee's developmental level. Shaughnessy & Carey (1996) also discuss linking supervision with adult developmental understanding. All of these authors speak to the timing and intentionality of supervision intervention choices.

The final component of this module is the ethical consideration involved in supervision. Supervisors must attain the knowledge necessary for good ethical practice. Upchurch (1985) stressed that "ethical standards for the supervisory process are necessary for the protection of the client, the supervisor, and the supervisee, all of whom are vulnerable in different ways" (p. 17). These same principles apply for administrative supervision, with the added component of promoting sound ethical behavior congruent with organizational accountability. The content of ethical training in either administrative or clinical settings cannot be complete without attending to the legal implications with statutory trends and implications for practice (Herlihy & Sheeley, 1988).

In this module, both ethical and legal issues relating to supervision should be provided to present an integrated understanding of responsibilities within the supervision process. Such concepts as confidentiality, duty to warn, due process, dual relationship, and informed consent should be stressed. Other information about ethics is provided by the Association for Counselor Education and Supervision (1995); Bernard & Goodyear (1998); Corey, Corey, Callanan, and O'Phelan (1998); Davenport (1992); Dye & Borders (1990), who outlined the standards for counseling supervisors; a special issue of the *Journal of Counseling and Development* (Sadler, 1986); Knapp & VandeCreek (1997); Ladany, Lehrman-Waterman, Molinaro, and Wolgast (1999); Powell (1992); and Rubin (1997).

Ethical training should be presented during the first training module to allow the trainee to understand and incorporate sound ethical practice into the supervisory role. It is important to teach a method for collaborating about ethical issues and concerns. One method involves a demonstration of ethical dilemmas via videotapes. Supervisors-in-training describe the ethical dilemmas and, by referring to ethical principles and codes of ethics, supervisors discuss the most appropriate ethical behavior. This training approach incorporates a demonstration-discussion-feedback training format. The resolution of the ethical dilemma comes from open and collaborative dialogue with others as a way of expanding our own level of moral and ethical reasoning. Chapter 14 of this volume elaborates upon ethical considerations in supervision.

The model for conceptualizing the supervisory function is one of five proposed in the supervision training model. It is important, for it provides the foundation for the remaining aspects of the supervision process. In summary, the content for this model includes the following:

1. a clear definition of supervision and delineation of the supervisory functions to facilitate professional growth and to assure quality service delivery;
2. a portrayal of an ideal clinical or administrative supervisor;
3. a clear differentiation between supervision and counseling;
4. a perspective of supervisory leadership whereby the supervisor serves as pacer; and
5. a conceptualization of supervision as an ethical responsibility with legal ramifications for practice.

Instructional approaches in this module include reading from books and journals, viewing audio- and videotapes depicting supervisory functions, conducting role-playing with other supervisors-in-training to illustrate different supervisory roles, reviewing case studies, and viewing vignettes of actual and potential ethical dilemmas.

Orchestrating a Supervisory Relationship

Holloway (1987) stated that the "supervisory relationship itself creates a trainee's initial vulnerability and final independence" (p. 215). Holloway further stated that "the trainee's feelings are not intrinsic to becoming a counselor or establishing a professional identity but are the result of being in an intensive, evaluative, ongoing and demanding relationship" (p. 215). Throughout supervision literature, attention is devoted to the supervisor's ability to form a working relationship with the supervisee (Kaiser, 1997; Ladany & Friedlander, 1995). Clearly, knowledge about the activities of supervision cannot substitute for understanding the feelings that emerge within the supervisory relationship.

The second training module is focused upon the relational dimension between supervisor and supervisee. Because Chapter 2 of this book is devoted to the supervisory relationship, this discussion will focus on the training techniques involved in the supervisory relationship, for it becomes the vehicle by which learning is facilitated or hampered. Bordin (1983) presented a model of the relationship he called the "supervisory working alliance." He described the supervisory working alliance as a relationship targeted toward supervisee goals, including mastery of specific skills, enlargement of the understanding of client concerns and of process issues, awareness of the impact of self on the therapeutic process, and initial translation of theory into practice. An important procedure to establish is a working understanding of the nature and purpose of the supervisory relationship (Bordin; Loganbill, Hardy, & Delworth, 1982). The supervisor must realize that the relationship develops over time and in stages (Kaiser, 1997).

The most logical place to begin is to have the supervisor and supervisee describe their expectations about the relationship with the understanding that new expectations will develop with time. After expectations are understood, means for completing expectations should be discussed. Within this module, attention should be devoted to anxiety. The mere fact that the relationship is uneven suggests that anxiety may be present, especially since the supervisor at some time will be in an evaluative role. Resistance and conflict also should be discussed. Table 15.4 provides a listing of some of the fundamental tasks necessary for an effective supervisory relationship.

In training supervisors for clinical and administrative settings, the relationship should not be envisioned as only one-to-one between supervisor and supervisee (Bernard & Goodyear, 1998). Supervisors must be educated

TABLE 15.4. A checklist of fundamental tasks involved in the formation of a supervisory relationship

Achieved	Fundamental tasks
_____	1. The supervisor and the supervisee address their respective expectations.
_____	2. The supervisory function is clearly articulated in terms of content, context, boundaries, and opportunities.
_____	3. The supervisor and supervisee establish mutual goals, respective tasks, a timeline for their alliance, and a statement of confidentiality.
_____	4. The evaluative means are clearly specified, and the supervisor addresses with the supervisee the anxiety associated with performance and assessment.
_____	5. The supervisor and the supervisee engage in a trust-building phase of their alliance, which is facilitated by affirmation and structure.
_____	6. The supervisor attends to supervisee resistance, which may stifle the working alliance.
_____	7. As the alliance solidifies, the working phase emerges wherein mastery of skills, understanding of issues, and focus on goal attainment are targeted.
_____	8. The supervisor delivers feedback in a sensitive yet challenging fashion.
_____	9. Supervisee feelings are explored and addressed within the supervisory alliance.
_____	10. The supervisor addresses the impact of the environmental context within which the supervisee operates.
_____	11. The supervisor evaluates the supervisee through the means that have been previously established.
_____	12. The supervisee has the opportunity to deliver feedback to the supervisor about any aspect of the supervision experience.

to conduct group supervision. This is particularly important in administrative supervision, where, realistically, supervisors may be unable to supervise every subordinate. Educators must also attend to the need for exposure to group supervision when those in training supervise several people.

The impact of the environmental or agency context within which the supervisor operates must be considered. Environmental issues such as time, policy, agency procedures, client population, facilities, and organizational stresses can and often do impact the quality and nature of the relationship offered by the administrative supervisor. Similarly, clinical supervisors must attend to the influence of environmental factors on their supervisees.

In the relationship module, the imparting of knowledge can occur through didactic and experiential learning. Readings and group discussions should be an integral part of training. Students can progressively move from cognitive information about the supervisory relationship to (a) case studies illustrating the working relationship; (b) observations of other supervisors via live supervision, videotape, and role-play modeling; and (c) actual monitored supervisory practice. In summary, this training module includes the following:

1. Primary attention is focused on the relational dimension between supervisor and supervisee and factors that facilitate or inhibit the development of the relationship.
2. The supervisory relationship is illustrated as a "working alliance" that produces developmental progression within the supervisee toward professional competence and independence.
3. The supervisory relationship begins by addressing the expectations brought into the relationship by both persons, expectations which continue to be articulated as the relationship progresses.
4. The supervisory relationship is characterized as developing in predictable, identifiable phases.
5. Supervisee resistance is managed sensitively as a manifestation of performance and evaluation anxiety.
6. The working relationship is orchestrated using both individual and group supervision modalities.

Focusing Supervision Goals
Toward Mastery and Maturity

Explicit in the formation of a supervisory relationship is the mutual agreement on goals for the supervisory experience. Although specific goals of supervision will be tailored to the needs of the individual supervisee, the global aims of supervision can be viewed as the development of supervision mastery and of professional identity (maturity and autonomy). These aims are consistent with those proposed by Stoltenberg, McNeill, & Delworth (1998), who discuss three stages of developmental functioning of supervisees: self- and other awareness, motivation, and autonomy. This third training module focuses on the developmental issues of supervisees and the roles of supervisors in promoting developmental issues and progression of supervisees. A more complete perspective on developmental supervision is provided in Chapter 5 of this book.

Hess (1986) described four processes of professional development that seem common to various stage theories of supervision. First, a time of "inception" exists involving the induction of the professional into her or his roles and tasks. The move is from the unfamiliar to the more familiar. This perspective could find application to transitions from theoretical learnings to performance applications that occur with novice practitioners as they become supervisees, and later as they assume supervisory positions. Fear, often felt as crisis, is characteristic of this process. Both professional identity and autonomy are unrealistic in this introduction period. Second, a process of "skill development" follows wherein the supervisor-in-training, understanding more clearly her or his expected roles and tasks, begins to accumulate some tools of practice. Professional identity and autonomy begin as the supervisor risks assuming the roles and performing the tasks. Third, a "consolidation" period occurs as the professional emerges in self-definition, refines skills, and develops competence. Finally, a process of "mutuality" is developed whereby the individual can function as an independent, autonomous professional with an integrated sense of identity. Supervisors-in-training are transformed into supervisors with leadership capacity. Professional development has matured, although it is never completed.

Stoltenberg and Delworth (1987) described supervision development by stages. The beginning supervisor is described as one lacking in professional identity and skills. The beginning supervisor needs training that is structured with opportunity to practice the new learnings. Beginning supervisors, especially those with little experience, need concrete information about how you supervise. At this stage, global anxiety and power-playing are often present. Often the power-playing centers around expertise and evaluation elements. At this stage, a discussion of feelings of anxiety and issues related to the mechanics of supervision and evaluation is important. Direct instructional supervisory roles are less effective as the supervisor moves to the second stage. At this stage, the supervisor is beginning to develop competence and a belief in her or his ability as a supervisor.

As the supervisor becomes more experienced and mature, the supervisor becomes more committed to the growth of the supervisee. Maturity and competence emerge within the supervisory style. At the last stage, the supervisor has an integrated identity and is perceived as more secure and competent. The supervisor permits the supervisee's agenda to dominate the sessions. Assuming the supervisee has the competence, the supervisor will employ a more collaborative and consultative role, one that is in keeping within the developmental needs of the supervisee.

In Module 3, the broad goals are mastery and maturity. The training module entitled "Focusing Supervision Goals Toward Mastery and Maturity" includes the assignment of reading materials to illustrate developmental supervision. Simulations are presented to illustrate different supervisory roles. Using case studies, supervisors-in-training are asked to conceptualize and defend their supervisory role. Effective supervisors are often asked to demonstrate and explain their rationale for supervision with a supervisee.

In summary, Module 3 incorporates the following content emphases:

1. The global aims of supervision are viewed as mastery and maturity, processes involving professional identity and autonomy.
2. Supervisors develop by stages moving from dependence, confusion, and ambiguity to independence, self-direction, and competence.
3. Maturation progresses and increases in conceptual complexity, emotional expression, and professional awareness and judgment.
4. The choice of supervisory role is aimed at promoting mastery, and maturity is based on the developmental level of the supervisee.

☐ Facilitating a Supervisory Learning Environment

Lambert and Arnold (1987) concluded that both skills and attitudes are affected during supervision and that "the most efficient way of maximizing learning [of these] . . . is to systematically structure their acquisition" (p. 222). In this training module, the successful supervisor creates learning conditions that are optimal for the supervisee. The supervisee's development is the central issue, and supervision tasks are sequenced to provide for that development.

Blocher (1983) proposed a learning environment that is composed of seven dynamics: (a) challenge, (b) involvement, (c) support, (d) structure, (e) feedback, (f) innovation, and (g) integration. The dynamics of Blocher's learning environment address interaction between the supervisor and supervisee. In either administrative or clinical supervision, the supervisory experience is the environment and the person in supervision training (student at university, supervisor at agency) is the learner. Regardless of setting, the supervisory experience is directed by a master practitioner who attends to the needs of the supervisee.

The training module in this section of the chapter incorporates Blocher's seven principles for providing a learning environment. Similar to the components described by Loganbill et al. (1982), the module creates conceptual, experiential, and integrative opportunities. Although readings are assigned, the main feature of this module is the modeling of a learning environment. Adequate conditions of structure and support are built with the intent that the supervisor will carefully monitor the learning environment and will increase and decrease the structure and support in accordance with the needs of the supervisee. The intent of this module is to provide the impetus and opportunity for the development of the effective supervisor in either an administrative or a clinical setting. Table 15.5 provides questions that may be used in assessing the presence of an optimal learning environment. An optimal experience will yield a "yes" response to each question.

TABLE 15.5. An evaluation of the dynamics of a supervisory learning environment

Achieved	Components of optimal learning environment
_____	1. Is the level of challenge great enough to sufficiently motivate the supervisee?
_____	2. Is the dissonance realistically resolvable for the supervisee?
_____	3. Does the supervisee possess the skill and/or maturity to meet the demands of the task?
_____	4. Is the supervisee invested in the learning process and tasks?
_____	5. Does the supervisee have a sense of worth and esteem that is separate from his/her perceived professional success or failure?
_____	6. Does the supervisee have a felt sense of warmth, empathy, and support within the supervisory relationship?
_____	7. Is the amount of support proportional to the amount of challenge?
_____	8. Is the experience structured so as to specify the supervision goals and means?
_____	9. Are the evaluative means objective, accurate, relevant, and interpretable?
_____	10. Is the supervisee able to process feedback?
_____	11. Does the supervision experience allow the safety necessary for practice attempts at new skills and behaviors?
_____	12. Does the supervisor assist the supervisee in integrating mastery with the development of professional identity, autonomy, and maturity?
_____	13. Is the termination of the alliance managed purposefully so as to identify progress, delineate further concerns, and address the interpersonal experience of the supervisory relationship? Are issues of professional identity, autonomy, and competence emphasized?

In summary, the training module includes and incorporates the following content:

1. The supervisory experience provides a model learning environment.
2. Within the supervisory learning environment, the supervisee's development is the core issue.
3. The seven basic dynamics described by Blocher (1983) provide the foundation for stimulating the supervisory learning environment in both clinical and administrative settings.
4. Within the learning environment, supervisors will learn to facilitate levels of challenge, involvement, support, structure, feedback, innovation, and integration which collectively stimulate professional maturation.

☐ Developing a Theory Base, Supervisory Technology, and Personal Supervisory Style

The last training module emphasizes the development of a theory base, supervision technology, and personal style. The process of professional maturation, autonomy, and identity requires a synthesis of science (theory) and art (practice), which translates into an identifiable and justifiable personal style of supervision. The goal is to help the supervisor mature to the extent that he or she can transfer cognitive and experiential learning into future situations and take ownership of the knowledge and skill. The knowledge base presented in the previous modules is fundamental and provides the foundation for this module.

While the knowledge base presented in this module is considered basic for both clinical and administrative supervisors, the content might be focused differently to accommodate the needs of clinical and administrative settings. Additionally, theoretical approaches and case illustrations might be focused toward specific supervisor roles. For the administrative supervisor, the systems model might focus on organized objectives, demonstrated effectiveness, program efficiency, and problem-solving potential. In contrast, the clinical supervisor, while needing to know about systems theory, might benefit more specifically from case illustrations adapted from various theoretical approaches often applied in clinical settings.

Supervisors must be exposed to a variety of theoretical approaches and supervisory techniques in order to provide effective supervision. Secondly, supervisors must be aware of a wide range of supervisory technology which will allow them to select and decide from among the various approaches. In the end, this knowledge base and selection process will allow them to own a particular supervisory style. Integrative approaches which combine understandings and techniques of supervision delivery are important bases of knowledge for expanding the supervisee's personal style. Prochaska and Norcross (1999) presented examples of approaches across various theories of supervision, and Bradley, Gould, and Parr discussed integrative techniques in Chapter 4 of this text.

This module advocates a "macroscopic" or "multimodal" approach to supervision. The skill repertoire needed for the multimodal (multitechniqued) approach includes skills related to developmental assessment (of both the individual and the learning environment), relationship building (with both individuals and groups), confrontation (the compassionate presentation of discrepancy), and case conceptualization (the selective attention given to themes and patterns which collectively form a prescription for action). Holloway (1995) presented a systems approach to supervision which includes the use of multiple theories and varied methodologies in actual supervision practice. This model is akin to the macroscopic and multimodal idea of this module.

In summary, this module includes the following content emphases:

1. Supervisory maturation requires a synthesis of theory and application which can be translated into an accountable personal style of supervision.
2. A supervisory knowledge base is identified and taught, and this base must provide exposure to a variety of approaches.
3. Supervisors must be armed with an encompassing supervisory technology to insure that choice of intervention is in accordance with the needs of the supervisees and with the dynamics necessary to promote an effective learning environment.
4. Supervisors in training must be able to integrate training and practice and translate this into a personal supervisory style with evidence of personal identity and demonstrated competence.

☐ Evaluation

The evaluation portion of the supervisory training model contains three components: the knowledge component, the practice component, and the personal characteristics component. Whether in an administrative or clinical setting, the three should be evaluated.

While evaluation can present an anxiety-producing situation for the supervisor-in-training, evaluation does not have to be an uncomfortable process. Careful planning prior to the beginning of supervisory training can help to reduce the anxiety associated with evaluation. Prior to the first training session, it is recommended that means for evaluation be described. Evaluation should be explained as directly and accurately as possible. If forms are going to be used in the evaluation process, supervisors-in-training should know the content and, if possible, be given a copy of the evaluation form(s). If written materials or direct observations by site supervisors are a part of the procedure, the supervisor-in-training should be provided with as much concrete information as is available. Issues related to confidentiality and its impact on evaluation should also be provided. Basically, the supervisor should be given as much information as possible for the evaluation procedures. Anxiety usually decreases in direct proportion to the amount of information provided. Discussion should be directed to insure that the supervisor-in-training understands that the aim of evaluation is to enhance the learning experience, and in no way is it intended to criticize or be perceived as condescending.

Knowledge Component

In this component, the intent is to assess whether a knowledge base of the supervisory process has been acquired. Examples of competence areas include supervision models, supervision techniques, knowledge of ethical and legal issues and standards related to supervision, supervisory intervention strategies, supervision research, supervisory organizational structure, individual and group supervision strategies, and requirements associated with credentialing. Methods for assessing competence might include: testing (including cognitive and experiential components), writing or verbally presenting one's supervision theory, preparing a paper that compares and contrasts administrative and clinical supervisory roles, developing an in-service workshop on the basics of supervision, creating ethical supervision dilemmas for class discussion, and demonstrating (written, verbal) knowledge of the rationale for the appropriate supervisory methodology to implement with supervisees at different stages of development. The curriculum guide proposed by Borders et al. (1991) is an excellent resource concerning the knowledge base we hope is acquired.

Practice Component

The practice component encompasses an evaluation of how supervisors-in-training deliver supervision. The practice component involves the actual demonstration of the total realm of supervisory learning. Audiotapes, videotapes, and direct observation represent three frequently used methods for evaluating the implementation of supervision skills. A combination of verbal and written feedback is needed in evaluating the practice component. In instances where negative feedback is given, a written summary should be provided. The summary should include suggestions for improvement and should be signed and dated by both the supervisor and supervisee. The signature of the supervisee indicates that he or she has received and read the evaluation. Table 15.6 presents an example of an evaluation form that may be used in assessing supervisory skills. Before the written evaluation is given to the supervisee, a verbal summary should be presented. A highly recommended procedure is for the two to occur in the same session. The written evaluation should never be given without an accompanying verbal evaluation with ample opportunity for questions.

Many supervisors-in-training are supervised by an on-site person. Consultation should occur with the on-site supervisor to obtain that individual's input and evaluation about the performance of the supervisor-in-training. Table 15.7 presents an example of an evaluation form that may be completed by the on-site supervisor. The on-site supervisor should both discuss the evaluation with and give a copy of the evaluation to the supervisor-in-training. Both the on-site supervisor and the supervisor-in-training should sign and date the form. A copy of all evaluation forms and other information related to evaluation should be kept in the supervisee's training file. Additionally, an evaluation by the supervisee(s) can provide insight into the supervisor's service delivery.

TABLE 15.6. Form for evaluation of supervisor-in-training

Supervisor-in-training's name _____

Evaluator's name _____

Date _____

Directions: Rate the following supervisory functions using a scale ranging from 1 (low) to 5 (high). A score of 1 (one) indicates poor with 5 (five) indicating excellent skills. A rating below 3 indicates supervisory standards were not met. (Ratings may be made in quartile increments.)

Rating Scale	1	2	3	4	5
	Poor		Acceptable		Excellent

_____ 1. Supervisor-in-training greets supervisee in warm, friendly manner and opens supervisory session with appropriate amount of structure.

_____ 2. Supervisor-in-training provides overview of supervisory process (goals, roles, expectations, length of session meetings, time & place for meetings, ethics, confidentiality, evaluation, etc.).

_____ 3. Supervisor-in-training is accepting, understanding, and exhibits interest in supervisee.

_____ 4. Supervisor-in-training listens to and encourages supervisee to discuss counseling issues.

_____ 5. Supervisor-in-training attends to both verbal and nonverbal behaviors of supervisee.

_____ 6. Supervisor-in-training tracks supervisee accurately, does not lead or lag behind.

_____ 7. Supervisor-in-training responses accurately reflect both the content and affect of supervisee's message.

_____ 8. Supervisor-in-training accurately employs supervisory roles (teacher, counselor, consultant, etc.).

_____ 9. Supervisor-in-training understands supervisory functions and does not overly control the direction of the supervisory session.

_____ 10. Supervisor-in-training exhibits good knowledge of supervision theory.

_____ 11. Supervisor-in-training understands supervisory techniques.

_____ 12. Supervisor-in-training effectively integrates supervisory theory and techniques and implements these in actual supervisory practice.

_____ 13. Supervisor-in-training effectively promotes the development of the superviseee.

_____ 14. Supervisor-in-training exhibits a personal supervisory style.

_____ 15. Supervisor-in-training develops professional maturity and identity.

TABLE 15.6. Form for evaluation of supervisor-in-training (*Continued*)

Comments: _____

_____

_____

_____

Evaluator's signature _____

      Date _____

Supervisor-in-training's signature _____

      Date _____

_____

      Date _____

In evaluating the practice component, it is advisable to obtain information from a variety of supervisory activities. For example, evaluative information should be obtained about the supervisor's delivery in both group and individual supervisory sessions. Direct observation of the supervisor can provide information on several supervisory practice elements.

The evaluation of the practice component usually centers on *what* supervisory function is to be implemented and *how* that function is being implemented. The "what" in supervision refers to the behaviors in which the supervisor-in-training engages, and the "how" describes the way in which the supervisory behaviors occur. Supervision evaluation of tasks should include a rationale and theoretical basis for supervision, methods for how supervision occurs, and information on the planning and achievement of supervisory goals.

Personal Component

In the personal component, the intent is to evaluate characteristics that indicate whether the supervisor has developed competency. Information

Table 15.7. Form for on-site supervisor to evaluate supervisor-in-training

Supervisor-in-training's name
_____

Evaluator's (on-site supervisor) name _____

1. Please rate (using an "x") the following supervisory functions using a scale
   ranging from poor to excellent. If you have not observed the supervisor
   performing a function, please indicate by marking N/A (not appropriate).

	N/A	Poor	Good	Excellent	Comments
Individual supervision	___	___	___	___	_____
Group supervisions	___	___	___	___	_____
Consultation	___	___	___	___	_____
Relationships with colleagues	___	___	___	___	_____
Participation in supervisory training	___	___	___	___	_____
Interest in supervision	___	___	___	___	_____
Acceptance of supervisee	___	___	___	___	_____
Understanding of supervision theory	___	___	___	___	_____
Understanding of supervision techniques	___	___	___	___	_____
Implementation of good supervisory skills	___	___	___	___	_____
Overall performance	___	___	___	___	_____
Potential as future supervisor	___	___	___	___	_____

2. If you were in a position to employ this person, would you employ him/or as
   supervisor?   Yes _____   No _____

   Comments _____

   _____

   _____

Evaluator (on-site supervisor) _____
                                          (Signature)
       Date _____

Supervisor-in-training _____
                                          (Signature)
       Date _____

should be obtained about the quality and nature of the supervisor's personal characteristics. Evaluation about the supervisor-in-training's professional maturity and identity and ability to promote the development of the supervisee(s) should be assessed. Additionally, assessment about such personal tolerance traits as being flexible, accepting, empathic, fair, sensitive, objective, and honest should be made. Further assessment should be made about the supervisor-in-training's ethical beliefs and behavior and about the appropriateness of their interventions from a diversity viewpoint.

The personal component can be difficult to assess because of its qualitative nature. Many supervisory training programs conduct a cursory, if any, evaluation of this area. This component is important and should not be overlooked. Supervisors-in-training should understand from the onset that a knowledge base of supervision and skills can never substitute for the personal component.

Effective personal characteristics must be modeled and demonstrated throughout the supervisory process. The supervision provides a direct means for assessing the personal component. Information about the supervisor-in-training's personal characteristics can also be obtained during in-service training in agency settings; classroom training in supervision courses; and feedback from supervisees, on-site supervisors, and other colleagues.

The explicit goal of evaluation is the assessment of information about the supervisor-in-training's mastery of supervisory knowledge, implementation of supervisory skills, and demonstration of effective personal characteristics throughout the supervision process. Evaluation should include both quantitative and qualitative data, direct and indirect observations, and formal and informal methods of assessment. The overall intent of the evaluation is to determine whether the supervisor-in-training has reached professional competency. In delivering evaluative feedback to those in training, it is important to make available explicit due process procedures in the event the supervisor trainee does not agree with the content of the evaluation.

☐ Summary

In summary, this chapter presented a model for supervision training. Administrative and clinical supervisors were characterized as catalysts for helping supervisors-in-training develop greater counseling competence. The model proposed a means for equipping the supervisor-in-training with a knowledge base and skill repertoire for implementation in actual supervisory practice.

Five training modules and an evaluation component were presented. The five training modules were (a) conceptualizing the supervisory function, (b) orchestrating a supervisory relationship, (c) focusing supervision goals toward mastery and maturity, (d) facilitating a supervisory learning environment, and (e) developing a theory base, supervisory technology, and a personal supervisory style. The evaluation components included knowledge, practice, and personal aspects.

In summary, the training of supervisors must consider three essential components (see Table 15.8): *model, setting,* and *modality.* From exposure to several models, supervisors can be motivated to sort through and integrate the knowledge into a workable supervisory style.

The second component addresses the need for supervisory training in either an administrative or a clinical setting. Clearly, many supervisory skills and techniques are shared by administrative and a clinical supervisors, and yet administrative and clinical supervision differ. The focus of administrative supervision is on the tasks that directly affect the organization. In clinical supervision, the focus is on the supervisee's clinical interventions that directly affect the client.

Modality, the third component, is composed of interaction and means. Interaction refers to mutual or reciprocal action or influence. While individual supervision is usually the modal type, interaction may be achieved by cosupervision or group or peer supervision. At least four means (methods) are available: academic, observation, experiential, and supervisory training.

Depending upon experience, expertise, and work setting, supervisory training may vary its focus on the three essential components. The omission of one component can have a serious impact on the other components and on the overall success of counselor supervision. The supervisory training model proposed in this chapter and throughout the book is based on the premise that supervision is a process that can be enhanced by training if its essential components are understood and incorporated into the overall supervision training process.

TABLE 15.8. Modal, setting, and modality: three essential components of counselor supervision

Model	Setting	Modality
Cognitive-behavioral	Administrative	Interaction
Developmental (person-process)	Clinical	Individual
Eclectic		Cosupervisor
Gestalt		Group
Humanistic-existential		Peer
Integrative		
Personal growth		
Person-process		Means
Psychoanalytic		Academic
Psychotherapeutic		Observational
Social learning		Experiential
Systems		Supervisory
Transactional analysis		

☐ References

Association for Counselor Education and Supervision. (1995). Ethical guidelines for counseling supervisors. *Counselor Education & Supervision, 34*, 270–276.

Bernard, J. M., & Goodyear, R. G. (1998). *Fundamentals of clinical supervision* (2nd ed.). Needham Heights, MA: Allyn & Bacon.

Blocher, D. H. (1983). Toward a cognitive developmental approach to counselor supervision. *The Counseling Psychologist, II*, 27–34.

Borders, L. D., Bernard, J. M., Dye H. A., Fong, M. L., Henderson, P., & Nance, D. W. (1991). Curriculum guide for training counseling supervisors: Rationale, development, and implementation. *Counselor Education and Supervision, 31*, 58–80.

Borders, L. D., & Fong, M. L. (1994). Cognitions of supervisors-in-training: An exploratory study. *Counselor Education & Supervision, 33*(4), 280–293.

Borders, L. D., & Leddick, G. R. (1987). *Handbook of clinical supervision.* Alexandria, VA: American Association for Counseling and Development.

Borders, L. D., & Leddick, G. R. (1988). A national survey of supervision training. *Counselor Education and Supervision, 27*, 271–283.

Bordin, E. S. (1983). A working alliance based model of supervision. *The Counseling Psychologist, II*, 35–42.

Bradley, L. J., & Richardson, B. (1987). Trends in practicum and internship requirements: A national study. *The Clinical Supervisor, 5*, 97–105.

Carifio, M. S., & Hess, A. K. (1987). Who is the ideal supervisor? *Professional Psychology: Research and Practice, 18*, 44–250.

Corey, G. M., Callanan, P., & O'Phelan, M. (1998). *Issues and ethics in the helping profession* (5th ed.). Pacific Grove, CA: Brooks/Cole.

D'Andrea, M. (1984). The counselor as pacer: A model for revitalization of the counseling profession. *Counseling and Human Development, 16*, 1–15.

Davenport, D. S. (1992). Ethical and legal problems with client-centered supervision. *Counselor Education and Supervision, 31*(4), 227–231.

Dye, H. A., & Borders, L. D. (1990). Counseling supervisors: Standards for preparation and practice. *Journal of Counseling & Development, 69*, 27–32.

Falvey, J. E. (1987). *Handbook of administrative supervision.* Alexandria, VA: American Association for Counseling and Development.

Freeman, B., & McHenry, S. (1996). Clinical supervision of counselors-in-training: A nationwide survey of ideal delivery, goals, and theoretical influences. *Counselor Education and Supervision, 36*, 144–158.

Hart, G., & Falvey, E. (1987). Field supervision of counselor trainees: A survey of the North Atlantic Region. *Counselor Education and Supervision, 26*, 204–212.

Herlihy, B., & Sheeley, V. (1988). Counselor liability and the duty to warn: Selected cases, statutory trends and implications for practice. *Counselor Education and Supervision, 27*, 203–216.

Hess, A. K. (1986). Growth in supervision: Stages of supervisee and supervisor development. *The Clinical Supervisor, 4*, 51–67.

Hess, A. K., & Hess, K. A. (1983). Psychotherapy supervision: A survey of internship training practice. *Professional Psychology, 14*, 504–513.

Hollis, J., & Wantz, R. (1983). *Counselor preparation 1983–86.* Munice, IN: Accelerated Development.

Holloway, E. L. (1982). Characteristics of the field practicum: A national survey. *Counselor Education and Supervision, 22*, 75–80.

Holloway, E. L. (1987). Developmental models of supervision: Is it development? *Professional Psychology: Research and Practice. 18*, 209–216.

Holloway, E. L. (1995). *Clinical supervision: A system approach.* Thousand Oaks, CA: Sage.

Kaiser, T. L. (1997). *Supervisory relationships: Exploring the human element.* Pacific Grove, CA: Brooks/Cole.

Kaslow, F. W. (Ed.). (1987). *Supervision and training: Models, dilemmas and challenges.* New York: Haworth.

Knapp, S., & Vande Creek, L. (1977). Ethical and legal aspects of clinical supervision. In C. E. Watkins, Jr. (Ed.), *Handbook of psychotherapy supervision* (pp. 589–602). New York: Wiley.

Ladany, N., & Friedlander, M. L. (1995). The relationship between the supervisory working alliance and trainees' experience of role conflict and role ambiguity. *Counselor Education and Supervision, 34,* 356–368.

Ladany, N., Lehrman-Waterman, D. E., Molinaro, M., & Wolgast, B. (1999). Psychotherapy supervisor ethical practices: Adherence to guidelines, the supervisory working alliance, and supervisee satisfaction. *The Counseling Psychologist, 27,* 443–475.

Lambert, M. J., & Arnold, R. C., (1987). Research and the supervisory process. *Professional Psychology: Research and Practice, 18,* 217–224.

Loganbill, C., Hardy, E., & Delworth, U. (1982). Supervision: A conceptual model. *The Counseling Psychologist, 10,* 3–42.

Neufeldt, S. A., Iverson, J. N., & Juntunen, C. L. (1995). *Supervision strategies for the first practicum.* Alexandria, VA: American Counseling Association.

O'Byrne, K., & Rosenburg, J. (1998). The practice of supervision: A sociocultural approach. *Counselor Education and Supervision, 38,* 34–42.

Porter, N. (1994). Empowering supervisees to empower others: A culturally responsive supervision model. *Hispanic Journal of Behavioral Sciences, 16(1),* 43–56.

Powell, D. (1996). A peer consultation model for clinical supervision. *Clinical Supervisor, 14,* 163–169.

Powell, D. J. (1992). Ethical and legal concerns in supervision. *The Counselor, 10(6),* 24–27.

Prochaska, J. O., & Norcross, J. C. (1999). *Systems of psychotherapy: A transtheoretical approach* (4th ed.). Pacific Grove, CA: Brooks/Cole.

Rich, P. (1993). The form, function, and content of clinical supervision: An integrated model. *Clinical Supervisor, 11(1),* 137–178.

Richardson, B., & Bradley, L. (1986). *Community agency counseling: An emerging specialty in counselor preparation programs.* Washington, DC: American Association for Counseling and Development.

Rigazio-DiGilio, S. A. (1998). Toward a reconstructed view of counselor supervision. *Counselor Education and Supervision, 38,* 43–51.

Rubin, S. S. (1997). Balancing duty to client and therapist in supervision: Clinical, ethical and training issues. *Clinical Supervisor, 16(1),* 1–23.

Sadler, H. (Ed.). (1986). Professional ethics [Special issue]. *Journal of Counseling & Development,* 65.

Sansbury, D. L. (1982). Developmental supervision from a skills perspective. *The Counseling Psychologist, 10,* 53–57.

Shaughnessy, E. A., & Carey, J. C. (1996). Validation of a cognitive-developmental model of clinical supervision. In M. L. Commons & J. Demick (Eds.), *Clinical approaches to adult development* (pp. 223–238). Norwood, NJ: Ablex.

Stoltenberg, C. D. (1997). The integrated developmental model of supervision: Supervision across levels. *Psychotherapy in Private Practice, 16,* 59–69.

Stoltenberg, C., & Delworth, U. (1987). *Supervising counselors and therapists: A developmental approach.* San Francisco: Jossey-Bass.

Stoltenberg, C. D., McNeill, B., & Delworth, U. (1998). *IDM supervision: An integrated developmental model for supervising counselors and therapists.* San Francisco: Jossey-Bass.

Talen, M. R., & Schindler, N. (1993). Goal-directed supervision plans: A model for trainee supervision and evaluation. *Clinical Supervisor, 11(2),* 77–88

Upchurch, D. W. (1985). Ethical standards and the supervisory process. *Counselor Education and Supervision, 25,* 90–98.

Ward, C., & House, R. (1998). Counseling supervision: A reflective model. *Counselor Education and Supervision, 38,* 23–33.

Watkins, C. E. (1994). Developmental models, psychotherapy supervisors, and clinical supervision research. *Journal of Psychotherapy, Practice, and Research, 3*(3), 274–275.

Watkins, C. E., Jr. (1997). *Handbook of psychotherapy supervision*. New York: Wiley.

Williams, A. (1987). Parallel process in a course on counseling supervision. *Counselor Education and Supervision, 26*, 245–254.

INDEX

Assn. for Specialists in Group Work, 188, 200, 202, 217
Assn. of Multicultural Counseling and Development, 77, 81
Athar, N., 335
Atkinson, B. J., 216, 252
Atkinson, D. R., 77, 331
Attending, 171
Audiotape review, 256–257
  in evaluation, 285–287
Ault-Riche, M., 47, 66
Austin, M., 5
Austin, R., 315
Authier, J., 161
Aveline, M., 100, 285–287
Avis, J., 257, 259–261

Badcock, C. R., 330
Bahrick, A. S., 36, 318
Bailey, J. S., 253, 288
Baird, B., 39–40, 116, 160
Baker, E., 41
Baker, S. B., 18, 279
Baldwin, C., 192, 198
Banchero, R., 305
Bandura, A., 161, 171
Barak, A., 231
Barker, P., 253
Barmann, B., 152
Barret, R. I., 209
Barrett-Lennard Relationship Inventory, 311
Barrett-Lennard, G. T., 311
Bartell, P. A., 355
Basarab, D. J., 282
Basile, S. K., 134
Bass, C., 251
Bateson, G., 246
Batten, C., 156
Beamish, P., 259
Beauchamp, T. L., 357
Beck, A. C., 19
Beck, A. T., 165–166
Beck, J. S., 162, 166–167
Beck, T. D., 20, 40
Becker, D., 245
Becker, H. S., 9
Becvar, D., 261
Bednar, R. L., 186, 358
Bednar, S. C., 358
Behavioral model, 156–164
  assumptions, 156–157
  case example, 163

generalization of learning, 163
goals, 157–158
microtraining, 161–162
modeling, 160–161
peer supervision, 160
reinforcement, 160–161
role playing, 161
self-appraisal, 160
self-instructional modules, 159–160
self-management techniques, 162
skills analysis, 158
strengths, 164
supervisory relationship, 157
techniques, 158–163
weaknesses, 164
Behling, J., 47
Belar, C. D., 282
Bellamy, A. R., 291
Benjamin, A., 336
Benjamin, D., 152
Bennett, B. E., 358
Benshoff, J. M., 5, 210–212, 315
Bent, R. J., 273
Bentall, R. P., 321
Bercik, J., 250
Berg, I. K., 119
Berger, M., 287
Berger, S. S., 149, 151
Bergsjo, P., 319
Berman, J. J., 318
Bernard, H., 185–186
Bernard, J. M., 4–5, 7, 10, 14–19, 29, 32, 36, 38–41, 43, 48, 55, 64, 94–99, 104, 128, 131, 134, 147, 174, 184, 186–189, 192, 199, 213, 217–219, 222–223, 225, 233, 239, 245, 247–248, 258, 260–261, 271, 273, 275, 277, 279, 281–286, 287, 289, 291–292, 304–305, 309, 313, 321, 322–323, 344, 356, 358–359, 361, 370–371
Bertolino, R., 261
Betchen, S., 251, 259, 261
Betz, N. E., 238
Betz, R. L., 185, 191
Beutler, L. E., 113, 117, 156, 305, 323
Biklen, S. K., 319
Binder, J. L., 148–149, 151–152, 154, 245, 247–248, 260
Biography, 319–320
Birk, J. M., 189
Birmingham, C., 288
Birringer, J., 284
Black, J., 5